# MANAGEMENT FOR SUSTAINABLE DEVELOPMENT

*Integrating Social, Economic, and Environmental Goals*

# MANAGEMENT FOR SUSTAINABLE DEVELOPMENT

*Integrating Social, Economic, and Environmental Goals*

*Edited by*

**Vishal Jain, PhD**

**Amit Mittal, PhD**

APPLE ACADEMIC PRESS

First edition published 2025

**Apple Academic Press Inc.**
1265 Goldenrod Circle, NE,
Palm Bay, FL 32905 USA

760 Laurentian Drive, Unit 19,
Burlington, ON L7N 0A4, CANADA

**CRC Press**
2385 NW Executive Center Drive,
Suite 320, Boca Raton FL 33431

4 Park Square, Milton Park,
Abingdon, Oxon, OX14 4RN UK



**Library and Archives Canada Cataloguing in Publication**

CIP data on file with Canada Library and Archives

**Library of Congress Cataloging-in-Publication Data**

CIP data on file with US Library of Congress

ISBN: 978-1-77491-670-4 (hbk)
ISBN: 978-1-77491-671-1 (pbk)
ISBN: 978-1-00350-575-4 (ebk)

# About the Editors

**Vishal Jain, PhD**
*Associate Professor, Department of Computer Science and Engineering, School of Engineering and Technology, Sharda University, Greater Noida, U.P., India*

Vishal Jain, PhD, is Associate Professor in the Department of Computer Science and Engineering, School of Engineering and Technology, Sharda University, Greater Noida, U.P., India. Before that, he worked for several years as Associate Professor at Bharati Vidyapeeth's Institute of Computer Applications and Management (BVICAM), New Delhi, India. He has more than 14 years of experience in the academics. He has more than 400 research citation indices with Google Scholar (h-index score 10 and i-10 index 11). He has authored more than 90 research papers in reputed conferences and journals, including the Web of Science and Scopus. He has authored and edited more than 30 books with various reputed publishers. His research areas include information retrieval, semantic web, ontology engineering, data mining, ad hoc networks, and sensor networks. He received a Young Active Member Award for the year 2012–13 from the Computer Society of India and a Best Faculty Award for the year 2017 and Best Researcher Award for the year 2019 from Bharati Vidyapeeth's Institute of Computer Applications and Management, New Delhi. He holds the degrees of PhD (CSE), MTech (CSE), MBA (HR), MCA, MCP, and CCNA.

**Amit Mittal, PhD**
*Professor and Pro Vice Chancellor (Research Programs) at Chitkara University, Punjab, India*

Amit Mittal, PhD, is a Professor and Pro Vice Chancellor (Research Programs) at Chitkara University, Punjab, India. Dr. Mittal has over two decades of domestic and international experience in academic leadership, teaching, research, consulting, training, and mentorship. His current mandate is to manage the PhD programs offered at Chitkara University. Sixteen scholars have been awarded PhD degrees under his guidance. He has published over 60 Scopus/SSCI indexed papers with a number of accredited and well-regarded journals. He was the recipient of the Chitkara University Excellence Award 2021 for being the highest cited author and for publications with the highest H-index (business school category). His areas of research and consulting expertise are international marketing and emerging market studies, consumer behavior, brand management, shopping behavior, and business research methods. He is an active resource person for faculty development programs, management development programs, and corporate training programs. He is a member of the thesis review boards of a number of universities. He presently reviews for reputable journals such as *Technological Forecasting and Social Change* (Elsevier), *Public Health* (Elsevier) *Benchmarking* (Emerald), *Technology Analysis and Strategic Management* (Taylor and Francis), *International Journal of Consumer Studies* (Wiley), *Journal of Public Affairs* (Wiley), *Routledge Studies in Global Student Mobility, International Journal of Emerging Markets* (Emerald), *Sustainability* (MDPI), *Management Decision* (Emerald), *IIM Kozhikode Society & Management Review* (Sage), and others.

# Contents

# Contributors

**Temitayo Adedeji Adedoyin**
Department of International Relations, Obafemi Awolowo University, Ile-Ife, Osun State, Nigeria

**Ayodeji Anthony Aduloju**
Department of History and International Studies, Edo State University Uzairue, Edo State, Nigeria

**Muhammad Makarfi Ahmad**
Department of Agricultural Economics and Extension, BUK, Kano, Nigeria

**Muhammed Assif**
Department of EEE, Amal Jyothi College of Engineering, Koovappally, Kerala, India

**Vijay Anant Athavale**
Walchand Institute of Technology, Solapur, Maharashtra, India

**C. V. Suresh Babu**
Department of Information Technology, Hindustan Institute of Technology and Science, Bay Range Campus, Padur, Chennai, India

**Abhiram Baiju**
Department of EEE, Amal Jyothi College of Engineering, Koovappally, Kerala, India

**Bhawya Bansal**
Chandigarh Business School of Administration, Landran, India

**Tripti Barthwal**
Lal Bahadur Shastri Institute of Management & Development Studies, Lucknow, India

**Bhupal Bhattacharya**
Department of Law, Raiganj University, Raiganj, West Bengal, India

**Sarmistha Bhattacharya**
Department of Social Work& Cyber Law, Amex College, Burdwan, West Bengal, India

**Dhruv Kishore Bole**
State Institute of Hotel Management, Siddhpur, Gujarat, India

**Aju Mathew George**
Department of Civil Engineering, Amal Jyothi College of Engineering, Koovappally, Kerala, India

**Prasenjit Ghosh**
Department of Economics, Jadavpur University, Kolkata, India

**Asutosh Goswami**
Department of Earth Sciences and Remote Sensing, JIS University, Agarpara, West Bengal, India

**Ashok Sen Gupta**
School of Management Sciences, Lucknow, India

**Goonjan Jain**
Delhi Technological University, Delhi, India

**Himanshu Jain**
Panipat Institute of Engineering & Technology, Panipat, Haryana, India

**Elias John**
Orma Ecobricks, Thiruvananthapuram, Kerala, India

**Shivinder Kaur**
Chitkara Business School, Chitkara University, Punjab, India

**S. N. Kumar**
Department of EEE, Amal Jyothi College of Engineering, Koovappally, Kerala, India

**Sari Luthfiyah**
Department of Medical Electronics Technology, Health Polytechnic Ministry of Health Surabaya, Surabaya, Indonesia

**Priyanka Majumder**
Department of Earth Sciences and Remote Sensing, JIS University, Agarpara, West Bengal, India

**Manoj Mehrotra**
School of Management Sciences, Lucknow, India

**Shishir Kumar Munshi**
Bangladesh Academy for Rural Development, Cumilla, Bangladesh

**Diana Musara**
Earthly Touch Foundation, Johannesburg, Gauteng, South Africa

**Stanley Oliver**
Management Learning and Management Practice, Doctoral College, United Kingdom

**Neha Punetha**
Department of Applied Mathematics, Delhi Technological University, Delhi, India

**Ruby Rani**
Department of Computer Science, University of Warwick, England

**Mayurika Roy**
Department of Law, Raiganj University, Raiganj, West Bengal, India

**Sanusi Mohammed Sadiq**
Department of Agricultural Economics and Extension, FUD, Dutse, Nigeria

**Ramandeep Saini**
Chandigarh Business School of Administration, Landran, India

**Abdesselam Salmi**
Ajman University, Ajman, United Arab Emirates

**Suhel Sen**
Department of Geography, Lovely Professional University, Phagwara, Punjab, India

**Mohit Kumar Sharma**
Vellore Institute of Technology, Bhopal, Madhya Pradesh, India

**Pankaj Kumar Shrivastava**
Mechanical Engineering Department, AKS University, Satna, Madhya Pradesh, India

**Abhijeet Singh**
Department of Applied Science & Humanities (Electronics), Rajkiya Engineering College, Banda, Uttar Pradesh, India

**Invinder Paul Singh**
Department of Agricultural Economics, SKRAU, Bikaner, India

**Pushpendra Singh**
Department of Electrical Engineering, Rajkiya Engineering College, Banda, Uttar Pradesh, India

**Devendra Kumar Somwanshi**
Department of ECE, Poornima College of Engineering, Jaipur, Rajasthan, India

**D. Raj Srikar**
Department of Information Technology, Hindustan Institute of Technology and Science, Bay Range Campus, Padur, Chennai, India

**Akanksha Srivastava**
Babu Banarasi Das University, Lucknow, India

**Ajay Tripathi**
Mechanical Engineering Department, AKS University, Satna, Madhya Pradesh, India

**Triwiyanto**
Department of Medical Electronics Technology, Health Polytechnic Ministry of Health Surabaya, Surabaya, Indonesia

**Asad Kareem Usmani**
School of Management Sciences, Lucknow, India

**Amrutha Mary Varkey**
Faculty of Economic Sciences, University of Warsaw, Warsaw, Poland; Coventry University, UK

**Parminder Varma**
Chitkara Business School, Chitkara University, Punjab, India

**Suchita Vishwakarma**
IILM Academy of Higher Learning, Lucknow, India

# Preface

Sustainable development provides an approach to making better decisions on issues that affect all our lives. By incorporating health plans while planning new communities, for instance, we can ensure that residents have easy access to healthcare and leisure facilities. Management for a sustainable development appears as a process from which organizations try to use all its resources, as well as improve its organizational and technological development in order to answer not only to the present but also to future human and social needs. This book, *Management for Sustainable Development: Integrating Social, Economic, and Environmental Goals*, integrates social, economic, and environmental objectives, taking into account their implications. Through studies and research on sustainable development, we will help readers understand the concept in its various manifestations, its challenges, and its advantages.

Chapter 1 evaluates the impact of India's CSR Policy 2013 using the firm-level panel data from 2013 to 2021 and analyzes the innovation activity of the country's manufacturing firms and the relation between sustainable innovation and corporate social responsibility.

Chapter 2 concludes that it is important to recall, realize, and start re-practice of lost customs and values by taking a U-turn toward cultural sustainability as an endeavor toward overall sustainability.

Chapter 3 summarizes the interconnections of microplastic particles with marine resources and, ultimately, the environment.

Chapter 4 proposes the design and making of eco-bricks from plastic waste and its utilization in the real world.

Chapter 5 gives insight into the general public's opinions regarding ethical issues with AI in healthcare.

Chapter 6 concludes that while economic growth and its sustainability for development are important to the SSA region, the reality has had a major negative impact on the region.

Chapter 7 discusses the ability to utilize ICT critically and confidently. Study and communication are all made possible by having a strong understanding of digital media literacy.

Chapter 8 shows the trend of digital marketing in the direction of education. This study discusses marketing strategies with special reference to digitization.

Chapter 9 builds on previous studies by delving deeper into the business value of sustainability and its implementation challenges, causes, and potential solutions.

Chapter 10 assesses how the disruption caused by fintech and smart banks impacts sustainability of retail banks in India.

Chapter 11 discusses the findings and recommendations for stakeholders to work on integration for the development of sustainable smart cities.

Chapter 12 gauges the benefit–cost proportion, business pay, return-over-factor cost and family work pay of marigold production based on standard costs or expenses of those parameters.

Chapter 13 discusses the environmental risk and green economy for sustainable development.

Chapter 14 focuses on a government organization Uttar Pradesh Public Works Department and conceptualizes a Centralized Mechanical Resource System (CMRS).

Chapter 15 shows the study of sustainability in Indian businesses, sustainability reporting, India's performance on sustainable development goals, and customers' perception toward sustainable products and the various challenges.

Chapter 16 conducts an analysis of the outcomes of previous attempts to implement sustainable innovations.

Chapter 17 provides a description of how mathematical optimization tools can be applied to the method of analyzing the sentiment of news headlines in order to forecast stock market trends.

# CHAPTER 1

# Sustainable Innovation and Corporate Social Responsibility: Firm-Level Evidences from Developing Economies

AMRUTHA MARY VARKEY[1,2]

[1]*Faculty of Economic Sciences, University of Warsaw, Warsaw, Poland*

[2]*Coventry University, UK*

## ABSTRACT

This chapter evaluates the impact of India's CSR Policy 2013 using the firm-level panel data from 2013 to 2021 and analyzes the innovation activity of the country's manufacturing firms and the relation between sustainable innovation and corporate social responsibility. By introducing Section 135 in the Companies Act, 2013, India turned out to be the first nation to have statutorily mandated CSR for specific companies. This paper analyzed the patterns of CSR spending of Indian firms after the CSR policy of India was mandated in 2013. The trend shows that there is an increase in the CSR spending of the polluting firms in India after the implementation of the policy. This study covers the impact of CSR policy and investigate how the changes in firm's innovation activity are impacted by the policy shift. This policy shift has spurred innovation, especially in polluting firms, since the implementation of the policy in 2014.

## 1.1 INTRODUCTION

Innovation has been referred to as the engine of economic development through the process of creative destruction.[49] In the last century, economic growth was

Management for Sustainable Development: Integrating Social, Economic, and Environmental Goals.
Vishal Jain & Amit Mittal (Eds.)

largely driven by an increase in productivity, efficiency, and technological change.[52] However, many of the innovations which have enhanced productivity and efficiency are largely destroying the environment; in other words, innovation also has its dark side.[14] One of these dark sides is the increased pollution and unsustainable production practices. Sustainable development involves countries and firms moving toward more environmentally friendly products and sectors. This transformation requires sustainable innovation strategies and capability accumulation at different levels. Firms play a central role in this process. Firms are assumed to be the key players behind this process. Firms can use energy-efficient technologies through sustainable innovation strategies to curtail pollution and to make production more efficient. Despite various policy adoptions of emission reduction, India's total GHG emission was 3571 million metric tons in 2018, which is close to 7% of global emission. Statistics show that around half of the GHG emissions come from the industrial sector in India.[1] Relative to India's GDP, the emissions are twice as high as the world's average. India has a wide range of environmental regulations, but it has relatively weak institutions.[26] Recognizing this, this paper intends to look at the impact of the recent CSR act (2013) in India on sustainable innovation and answer the following question:

> *What is the empirical evidence regarding the impact of CSR policy 2013 on innovation in firms belonging to polluting and nonpolluting industries?*

Sustainable innovation plays a major role in the sustainable growth of a firm. It is a best practice that gives socially relevant and environmentally friendly outcomes.[54] It is intertwining the socioeconomic goals of customers and stakeholders, and firms are increasingly demonstrating interest in sustainable brands. Sustainable innovation is the result of a firm's long-term effort and planning to guarantee sustainable production and processes. Sustainable innovation is not just a capability of a firm,[31] but it is also an inevitable part of a growing firm's performance with socially responsible behavior. Recent policies to ensure sustainable development practices in India also involve the CSR Act (2013), which mandates spending of at least 2 percent of profits on CSR activities including environmental sustainability and pollution control. However, the impact of this policy on innovation firms is less clear from empirical evidence. Bearing these things in mind, I address the effect of the new CSR policy on the innovation of firms belonging to polluting and nonpolluting industries. In this paper, I use data from the Center for Monitoring Indian Economy Pvt. Ltd. (CMIE) Prowess database for firms from 2013 to 2022. This paper contributes to the developing literature on

---

[1]https://www.climatelinks.org/sites [2]https://sdgs.un.org/goals/goal9

CSR and the role of CSR spending in fostering sustainable innovation by (1) offering a trend in the current trends in the CSR expenses of the postmandate period, (2) analyzing the CSR spending of polluting and nonpolluting firms, (3) assessing the financial performance of CSR firms, and (4) innovation–CSR relation of the firms.

### 1.1.1 CURRENT TRENDS IN CSR EXPENDITURE IN INDIA

Countries such as India, Indonesia, and the Philippines have made deliberate efforts to mandate CSR expenditures by corporations.[25] By law, the Indian government issued voluntary guidelines proposing that corporations should allocate 2% of their net profits to CSR activities. In August 2012, this legislation came into effect, requiring large Indian companies to mandatorily spend 2% of their net profits on CSR activities. Figure 1.1 shows the current trends in the CSR expenses of the top firms operating in India for the year 2021. Mukesh Ambani's Reliance Industries limited indicates the highest spending for the corporate social responsibility spending in India with 922 crores, topping the other companies. The other leading spending firms are Tata Consultancy Services Limited with 674 crores and Tata Sons Private Limited with 545.83 crores spending, respectively. The Tata group together spent more than 1000 crores on CSR in the year. The other highest spending is by HDFC Bank, ONGC, IOC, etc. The CSR expenditures of the leading companies are given below.

The CSR spending of the firms in the postmandate period shows visible changes from 2014 to 2021. In India, 80% of the top 100 companies aim for sustainability. CSR efforts in 2021 will integrate the sustainable development goals (SDGs) in their reliable business actions. It is observed that the top 25 companies map their company goals with SDGs. The global pandemic showed a decreasing trend in the CSR expenditure, albeit dominated by listed companies. The expenditure will certainly see a leap after normalizing, although inefficiencies may persist. Research shows that strict, stringent implementation makes CSR similar to tax policy, based on the notion of benevolence and look at the spending of the selected few companies as per their sustainability and CSR relations (Futurescape Report).

Godrej Consumer Products Ltd. (GCPL) spent Rs. 304 million on CSR activities in the year 2020–2021. The company's CSR initiatives focus on vulnerable communities; they have significant sustainability considerations. Its climate disclosure project scored an 'A' rating in climate disclosure. Wipro is a leading company that has supported significant projects with its

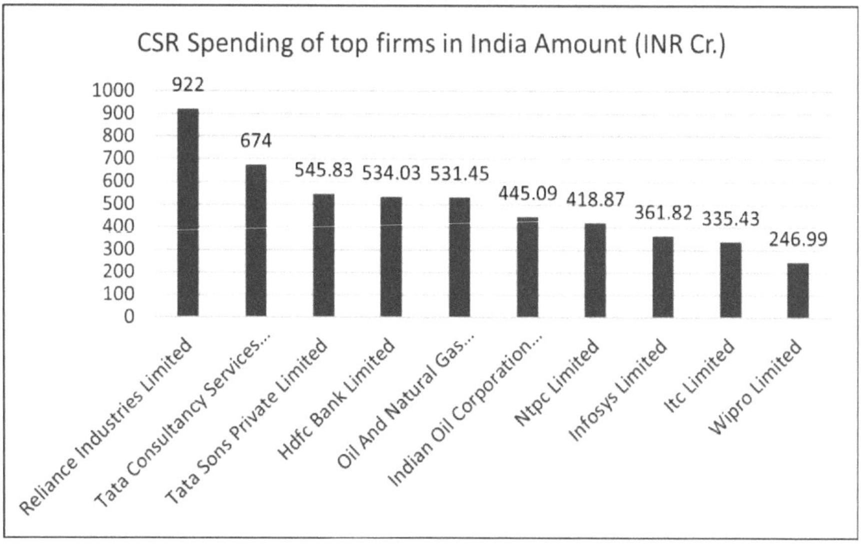


**FIGURE 1.1** CSR spending of the top ten companies in India.

*Source:* Compilation by the author using data from the Ministry of Corporate Affairs 2021, India.

**TABLE 1.1** CSR Spending of Top Companies.

| S. no | Company name(s) | Amount (INR Cr.) |
|---|---|---|
| 1 | Reliance Industries Limited | 922 |
| 2 | Tata Consultancy Services Limited | 674 |
| 3 | Tata Sons Private Limited | 545.83 |
| 4 | HDFC Bank Limited | 534.03 |
| 5 | Oil and Natural Gas Corporation Limited | 531.45 |
| 6 | Indian Oil Corporation Limited | 445.09 |
| 7 | NTPC Limited | 418.87 |
| 8 | Infosys Limited | 361.82 |
| 9 | ITC Limited | 335.43 |
| 10 | Wipro Limited | 246.99 |

*Source:* Ministry of Corporate Affairs, 2021.

philanthropic outlook and sustainability practices, cumulatively reaching over 10 million. Another leading sustainability champion over the past few years is Tata Chemicals. It launched multiple initiatives and projects to conserve the environment for sustainable development via various sustainability initiatives. Jubilant Life Sciences Limited has positioned itself in the top 10 companies.

Its focus is on health, education, livelihood, and social entrepreneurship. Grasim influences above 31.6 lakh people through CSR interventions, with a focus on sustainability and social welfare aspects. Vedanta Limited primarily focuses on agriculture and the development of rural areas. The firm-specific aspects of CSR are adequately discussed in the theories related to CSR.

**TABLE 1.2** CSR Spending of Sample Companies in the Postmandate Period

| Company | 2014 | 2015 | 2016 | 2017 | 2018 | 2019 | 2020 | 2021 |
|---|---|---|---|---|---|---|---|---|
| Godrej Consumer Products Ltd. | 160.8 | 145.7 | 165.2 | 188.8 | 219 | 194.9 | 340.9 | 304.6 |
| Grasim Industries Ltd. | 167.1 | 150.5 | 180.6 | 298.4 | 471.4 | 589.8 | 846.6 | 424.7 |
| I T C Ltd. | 2140.6 | 2475 | 2759.6 | 2909.8 | 3069.5 | 3264.9 | 3534.6 | 3511.3 |
| Infosys Ltd. | 2395.4 | 2023 | 2894.4 | 3126 | 3420.4 | 3599.4 | 3253.2 | 3449.1 |
| Jubilant Pharmova Ltd. | 15.6 | 17.8 | 10.3 | 10.9 | 38.2 | 44.4 | 56.7 | 50.4 |
| Reliance Industries Ltd. | 7605.8 | 6515.7 | 6592 | 7450.4 | 8493.2 | 9087.1 | 9220 | 8130 |
| Tata Chemicals Ltd. | 102 | 116.1 | 150 | 142.8 | 256.8 | 378.1 | 209.2 | 158.8 |
| Vedanta Ltd. | 255 | 661.7 | 484.8 | 451.9 | 517.2 | 526.6 | 388.6 | 1381.2 |
| Wipro Ltd. | 1327 | 1598.2 | 1863 | 1866 | 1853 | 1818 | 1656 | 2216 |

*Source:* CMIE Prowess

## 1.2 THEORIZATION

Theoretical foundations of CSR depict firm-specific internal resources and capabilities. The interlink between CSR and innovation is supported by both resource-based view (RBV)[47] and knowledge-based view (KBV). Scholars point out that firms with more internal resources are able to invest in CSR activities. The resource-based view states that the firms with adequate resources should opt to engage in CSR in order to create firm-specific resources, which are rare and inimitable. According to Ref. [6], the resources of the firm consist of capabilities and fostering firm performance, and it recognizes the significance of internal resources. Due to the limitations of the RBV, it is important to integrate the knowledge-based view, implying the firms distributing and integrating knowledge. Firms are oriented by certain factors to take part in various CSR activities voluntarily. According to Ref. [22], it is important for a firm to go beyond maximization of shareholders' interests to balance the interests of various stakeholders for better performance. Institutional aspects talk about CSR as a tool adopted by organizations to attain fairness within the country through formal and informal regulations.

However, there is less discussion about the sustainability dimensions in the theories related to CSR. I discuss the relation between sustainable innovation aspect of corporate social responsibility (CSR).

## 1.3 SUSTAINABLE INNOVATION ASPECT OF CORPORATE SOCIAL RESPONSIBILITY (CSR)

Sustainable innovation is of great significance in maintaining sustainable development because companies focus on environmental issues and regulations. Husted and Allen[32] argue that CSR is an opportunity for innovation and reconfiguration of the sustainable landscape. Sustainable innovation is associated with corporate social responsibility (CSR), integrating the economic, social, and environmental dimensions.

According to McElroy,[39] "sustainability of innovation artifacts is relative to meeting financial or business goals, social and environmental goals, and moreover, sustainability of innovation processes is relative to the validity of their outcomes and their internal authenticity. Sustainable innovation refers to innovation activities that contribute to the triple bottom line of sustainable development such as economic, ecological, and social benefits.[9,62] Sustainable innovation is deliberately associated with corporate social responsibility (CSR), incorporating these three dimensions of the economic, social, and environmental aspects in an inclusive manner. The integration of CSR with these three dimensions is a critical issue. Economic, social, and environmental aspects imply three types of responsibilities that are interrelated in a nonhierarchical circular way, each containing its own intrinsic values.[20] Continuous growth in CSR, in the context of the three dimensions of sustainability, drives sustainable innovations.[5] Sustainability issues offer significant possibilities for innovation and opportunities for competitive advantage.[29]

Sustainability is a major issue as the firm's production processes contribute to pollution. Indian firms contribute to CSR via donations, social and community expenses, and environmental spending. However, the extent of environmental spending by Indian firms is considerably low. Hall and Vredenburg[28] argue about the need for integrating innovation and the objectives of sustainable development, in which sustainable innovation must be marketed in an environmentally friendly way. To a great extent, sustainable innovation is linked with corporate social responsibility. The company's activities add value and create a competitive advantage as they reduce costs, create product differentiation, or drive customers through their acquisitions. Sustainable innovation is accountable for the firm's financial, social, and environmental performance; furthermore, it is useful in solving environmental issues.

### 1.3.1 IMPACT OF CSR POLICY ON FIRMS IN POLLUTING AND NONPOLLUTING INDUSTRIES

Environmental sustainability is considered as a pillar of CSR. Firms' decisions to invest in sustainable strategies change the performance of the firms. Studies on environmental management by organizations suggest that firms are progressively paying attention to sustainable environment and adopting measures to lower their negative impact on the environment.[3] A firm's investment in sustainability is decided by its stakeholder environment; therefore, differences in CSR spending on sustainability by firms imply differences in firm-specific characteristics. The variables such as age, firm size, and sales are analyzed in relation to the firm's CSR spending and are checked to see if they are positively related. Corporate sustainability spending can enhance the reputation of the firm, encourage regulatory action, and make the firm a more appealing investment to the socially responsible investors.

CSR is more than a cost or a charitable deed; it is a source of opportunity, innovation, and competitive advantage.[44] There is a shift to sustainable production with a rise in ecologically sustainable organizational and environmental relations by the businesses, and the evidence is more clear in the context of advanced economies.[18] Various studies focus on sustainable practices under the umbrella of corporate social responsibility (CSR) and explore the drivers of environmental behavior.[3] What is more important here is that polluting companies perform more environmental responsibilities in the long run than nonpolluting companies. In the coming years, research on CSR and environmental sustainability will continue to increase as it is a priority for most of the firms. CSR performance enables nonpolluting companies to obtain more short-term financing. Polluting companies are obliged to perform their environmental responsibilities in the postmandate period.

Although there is a large volume of literature suggesting CSR and sustainability issues in general, there is a limited discourse on CSR and green innovativeness with respect to the polluting and nonpolluting firms. Some of the firms choose to include energy and carbon reduction initiatives as a part of CSR policy or as a standalone policy as per UNIDO[2] guidelines on climate change and CSR in 2011. Both sustainability and innovativeness must be considered as elements positively associated with CSR activities. Efficiency principles are used as a CSR tool to achieve the sustainable development goals in the 2030 Agenda. Against this backdrop, I analyze the impact of CSR policy on polluting firms and nonpolluting firms with respect to India's CSR regime.

Figure 1.2 illustrates the amount of CSR spending by the polluting and the nonpolluting firms. It is observed that there is an increasing trend in the CSR expenditure, from Rs. 21,118.9 (in million) in 2014– 2015 to Rs. 67,837.5 (in million) in 2019–2020, i.e., a 20.77 percentage increase in the CSR spending in the polluting firms, whereas the CSR spending was zero for the nonpolluting firms for the year 2014–2015.

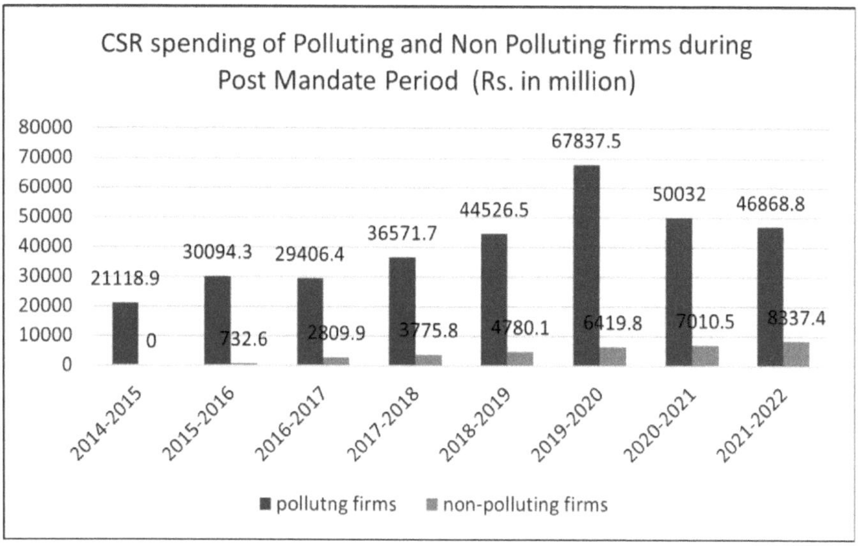


**FIGURE 1.2** CSR expenditure of polluting and nonpolluting firms in the postmandate period.

*Source:* Compilation by the author using CMIE data of 2738 polluting firms and 2840 nonpolluting firms.

However, a spike has been observed since 2015–2016, and it is highest at Rs. 8337.4 for the year 2021–2022. It was found that the polluting firms in India had the highest spending on CSR in the postmandate period compared

[2]4UNIDO. (2011). Guidelines on climate change and corporate social responsibility.

to the nonpolluting firms. The classification of the polluting firms is as per the categorization[3] of the Central Pollution Control Board of India.

Figure 1.3 shows that polluting firms witnessed an increase in expenditure from 6.46% in 2014–2015 to 20.77% in 2019–2020. A visible increase was observed in the enhancement of CSR expenditure in polluting firms in the mandatory period. Polluting firms contribute to the sustainable and innovative practices via the production of green or environmentally friendly products or by increasing their spending on environmental CSR.

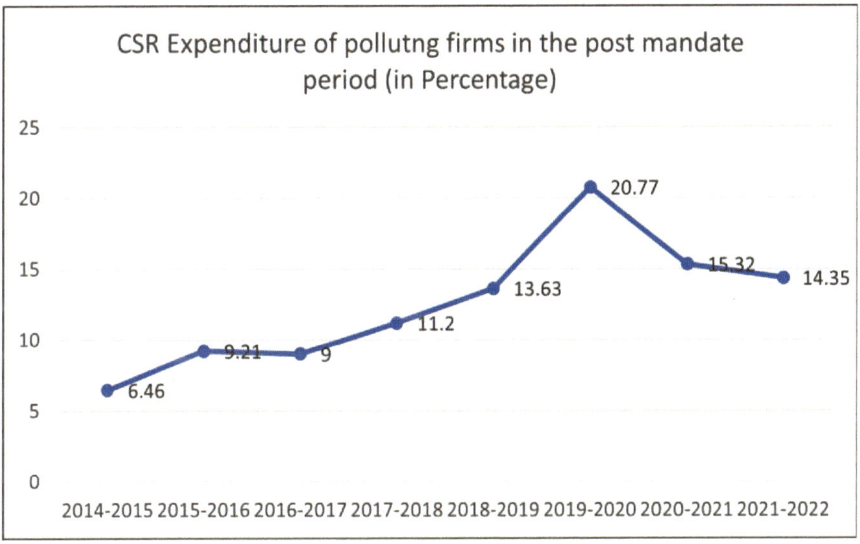


**FIGURE 1.3** CSR expenditure of polluting firms in the postmandate period.

*Source:* Compilation by the author using CMIE Prowess Data.

## 1.4 DATA AND METHODOLOGY

This paper uses firm-level data from the Centre for Monitoring Indian Economy Pvt Ltd. (CMIE) Prowess data from 2013 to 2021. The database is made up of company annual reports, financial statements, stock exchange feeds, etc. Our dataset is a panel of both polluting and nonpolluting firms over 10 years (from 2013 to 2021). This paper intends to contribute to the mounting literature on CSR with a focus on polluting and nonpolluting industries and

[3]As per Central Pollution Control Board (CPCB) classification, companies in India are of two categories-polluting industries and nonpolluting industries. There are 17 polluting industries.

the role of CSR spending in fostering sustainable innovation by offering a trend in the current trend in the CSR expenses of the postmandate period and by understanding two aspects: (1) the firm's financial performance—CSR performance and (2) the relation between innovation and CSR.

**TABLE 1.3** List of Industries.

| A list of pollution-intensive industries in India | |
|---|---|
| Aluminum smelter | Integrated iron and steel |
| Caustic soda | Tanneries |
| Cement | Pesticides |
| Copper smelter | Petrochemicals |
| Distilleries | Drugs and pharmaceuticals |
| Dyes and dye intermediates | Pulp and paper, oil refineries |
| Fertilizer | Sugar |
| Zinc smelter | Thermal power plants |

*Note:* Listing as per the Department of Pollution Control in India

For the purpose of the analysis, the list of industries in the polluting segment is taken from the category of 17 highly polluting industries. These polluting industries are classified by the Central Pollution Control Board of India (CPCBI) as given in Table 1.3; the same is used for the purpose of the analysis. The latest classification provided by CPCBI distinguishes the sectors into red, orange, green, and white categories, where the red category is the most polluting and the white is the least polluting. In this study, I use the above category of polluting industries, and the nonpolluting industries category includes food products, floriculture, other agricultural products, agricultural machinery, glass and glassware, leather and related products, and air conditioners.

### 1.4.1 *ECONOMETRIC MODEL*

This paper follow a panel data analysis to control firm heterogeneity and lower collinearity among the variables that are used in the model. For the purpose of analysis, 605 manufacturing firms are selected, including 335 polluting firms and 270 nonpolluting firms. CSR–profitability relation, innovation–CSR relation is analyzed using the panel data model. The estimated regression equations models are provided as follows:

$$ROA = \alpha 0 + \beta 1\ (RND\_intensity) + \beta 2\ (lagged\_CSR) + \beta 3\ (total\_assets) + \beta 4\ (growth) + \beta 5\ (advertising\_intensity) + \varepsilon it \quad (1.1)$$

The innovation–CSR relation is given below.

$$Ln\ RND\_intensity = \alpha 0 + \beta 1\ (CSR\_intensity) + \beta 2\ (total\_assets) + \beta 3\ (\ln sales) + \beta 4\ (\ln employees) + \beta 5\ (advertising\_intesnity) + \varepsilon it \quad (1.2)$$

**TABLE 1.4** Variable Definition.

| Variables | Symbol | Description |
|---|---|---|
| Profitability | Ln ROA | Ln (Net Profit/Total Assets) |
| Research and Development | Ln RND_intensity | Ln (Research and Development Expenses/ Sales) |
| Size | Total_Assets | Total assets of the firm/sales |
| Advertising intensity | Advertising_intsensity | Advertising expenditure/sales |
| Growth | Growth | Percentage change in sales |
| Employees | Ln employees | Logarithm of the employees |
| CSRt-1 | Lagged CSR | Annual spending on CSR/sales lagged for one period |

Profitability is captured by ln ROA, in which ROA is net profit divided by the total assets. RND_intensity refers to the research and development expenses of the firms divided by their sales. The size of the firm is denoted by the total assets. Advertising intensity refers to the ratio of advertising expenses and sales. A firm's growth is denoted by a percentage change in sales. For the purpose of analysis, the lagged value of CSR for one period is used.

**TABLE 1.5** Descriptive Statistics of the CSR Firms Used in the Model.

| Variable | Mean | Std. dev. | Min | Max |
|---|---|---|---|---|
| Ln ROA | .1453651 | .9563552 | 6.827626 | 14.3525 |
| Ln RND_intensity | .0323325 | .0740232 | .2406441 | .469995 |
| Lagged CSR | .0018556 | .0015221 | .0000283 | .005677 |
| total_assets | 1.940238 | 6.562371 | .2634902 | 74.7791 |
| Growth | 9.175052 | 1.605469 | 4.683981 | 13.3436 |
| Advertising_intensity | .0109532 | .0362122 | 9.001207 | .299323 |

Table 1.5 shows the descriptive statistics of the total sample of manufacturing firms for the period of 2013–2021. Ln ROA is the dependent variable in the model 1, and Ln RND_intensity is the dependent variable in the model 2.

## 1.5 RESULTS AND DISCUSSION

### *1.5.1 CSR AND FIRM PERFORMANCE*

Corporate social responsibility is considered a determining factor of financial performance both in developed and developing economies.[15] Mishra and Suar[41] found that firms listed in the stock market have more responsible business practices and better financial performance than nonlisted firms. In the existing stream of literature, CSR and firm performance are checked mostly in stock-listed firms; most of them use firm-specific variables such as size, return on assets (ROA), return on equity, asset age, and return on sales, which are the frequently used FP measures. The relation between corporate social responsibility (CSR) and firm performance has conjured more enthusiasm among researchers in the fields of sustainability and CSR. Studies by McGuire et al.[40] reveal a positive relation between CSR and firm performance, but some other scholars point out a negative relation. Yannan et al.[59] examine the impact of corporate social responsibilities, innovation, and sustainability on the sales growth of manufacturing industries in China and Saudi Arabia. Studies examine the influence of individual as well as aggregate CSR dimensions on firm performance.

CSR efforts are actions taken to benefit stakeholders, i.e., CSR is significant to the firm's performance. Companies participating in the CSR enhance their competitiveness, their reputation, brand, and trust.[6,44] Such deliberate efforts draw attention from new customers focusing on sustainability and growth, the social consciousness, and the effort to bring sustainability, which results in directly increasing companies' profitability.[21,,46,48] The contribution of Garcia–Castro et al.[24] reveals that CSR is a determined firm characteristic, and the link between CSR and performance is albeit subject to various endogeneity problems. I use the lagged CSR expenditure as a variable as it helps to comprehend the longterm impact of CSR on firm performance, as the findings of some of the studies suggest. Callan and Thomas[11] found that the direct effect of lagged CSP on current CFP is positive. This finding[47,57] refers to a positive relationship.

Studies that analyze the relation between CSR and firm performance include[35] findings that point out both positive and negative relations in the case of CSR and firm performance. In the existing strand of literature, there are less recent empirical analysis, which explored the impact of CSR in the context of India.[1,2,19,51] In order to identify the relation between CSR and firm performance, various firm performance measures are used. They include firm size, return on assets (ROA), return on equity, asset age, and return on sales. In this paper, I use ROA as a measure of determinant of firm performance. According to 55, Indian firms have genuinely integrated environmental considerations into their business strategies and reduced the extent of pollution and waste in the environment. The decision of a firm to engage in CSR activities positively influences whether the firm is a polluting or nonpolluting entity. I use a panel data model to explain the determinants of profitability for the CSR firms.

**TABLE 1.6** Dependent Variable ln ROA Showing the Profitability of the Firms.

| Regressor | Beta | S.D. | Z | P value |
|---|---|---|---|---|
| RND_intensity | .678461 | .036908 | 1.84 | $0.066^{*}$ |
| Lagged CSR | 085697 | .011717 | 7.31 | $0.000^{***}$ |
| total_assets | .007042 | .002247 | 3.13 | $0.002^{***}$ |
| growth | .576482 | .040725 | 14.16 | $0.000^{***}$ |
| advertising_intensity | .003091 | .000695 | 4.45 | $0.000^{***}$ |
| Constant | 5.29346 | .310523 | 17.05 | $0.000^{***}$ |
| R Squared | 0.477 | | | |
| No. of Observations | 7865 | | | |

$^{***}p < .01$, $^{*}p < .1$.

*Source:* Author's calculation.

The determinants of the profitability of the firm include research and development expenses, the firm's inclination for CSR, firm size, sales growth, number of employees, and advertisement intensity. It is examined that innovation has a significant positive impact toward the financial performance of Indian manufacturing firms as observed through ROA, a profitability measure of the firm. Innovation activities are a good signal for the manufacturing firms while encouraging their financial performance. The profitability of the firm is significantly related to innovation via new products, services, or processes that help manufacturing firms to perform better in the market compared to their rivals in a similar industry. Similarly, the financial performance of the firm depends on the sales growth of the firm.[63,64] The profitability of the firm is determined by firm size as denoted by the total assets of the firm. The extent of employees in the firm and the advertisement intensity are the important factors related to firm performance. These two factors are significant and positive. More significantly, the lagged value of the CSR spending shows that the financial performance of the firm is significant and positive. (i.e., beta = 0.085, standard deviation = 0.011, t-value = 7.31, and p-value = 0.000.) Working for the social responsibilities creates a good influence while directly providing a boost to a firm's financial performance.

### 1.5.2 INNOVATION–CSR RELATION IN POLLUTING FIRMS

Studies reveal the effect of CSR activities on innovation.[33,38,65] Mbanyele et al. state that treatment firms in countries that imposed mandatory CSR produce more environmental patents relative to their counterparts in other countries that did not implement CSR mandates. Globalization, the dissemination of new technologies, and the diversification of ecosystems across industries have also contributed to the corporate adoption of sustainable business practices. This paper complement mandatory CSR and the innovation relation of the firm in the postmandate period in India.

**TABLE 1.7** Innovation (ln RND_intensity) and CSR Relation of the Polluting Firms.

| Regressor | Beta | SD | t | P value |
|---|---|---|---|---|
| CSR intensity | .8512 | .42269 | 1.82 | 0.068* |
| Total_assets | .1687 | .04140 | 4.08 | 0.000*** |
| Ln sales | .6331 | .15242 | 4.15 | 0.000*** |
| Ln employees | .1866 | .17932 | 1.04 | 0.298 |
| Advertising_intensity | -.5490 | .32518 | 1.69 | 0.091* |
| Constant | 1.828 | .11737 | 1.64 | 0.010*** |
| R Squared | 0.4001 | | | |
| No. of Observations | 3510 | | | |

$^{***}p < .01$, $^{*}p < .1$.

*Source:* Author's calculation.

The RND intensity and firm's CSR relation show a direct and positive relation. The significant relation between innovation and CSR is indicated (i.e., beta = 0.85, standard deviation = 0.422, t-value = 1.82, p-value = 0.068). Furthermore, the findings show a positive and significant association between innovation and firm size as denoted by total assets. There is also a positive relation between innovation and sales growth, but the number of employees does not show a significant relation. It is found in the polluting firms that they have a greater inclination to spend on socially responsible activities with a focus on the creation of innovative products. Higher spending on innovative activities of the firm has a positive indication of its sales growth and the firm's size. However, advertisements show a significantly negative trend in the innovativeness of the firms. It has been found that polluting firms focus on the production of innovative products by adequately focusing on the socially responsible activities. Empirical analysis shows that polluting firms focus on innovative production practices to promote sustainability and innovation. As the trend shows, the implementation of CSR policy 2013 in India led to significant changes in the Indian manufacturing sector. Companies increased their environmental spending and focused on the sustainable and innovative production practices.

## 1.6 SUSTAINABILITY AND CORPORTAE SOCIAL RESPONSIBILITY (CSR)

CSR and environmental sustainability-related innovation research has examined the adoption of environmental management practices by organizations, indicating that companies are increasingly paying attention to their impact on the environment and adopting management practices to reduce their negative impact on the environment[56,58] and they find innovative means of production to reduce pollution and environmental damage. Literature on CSR and environmental sustainability integrates environmental, economic, and social concerns.[42] Firms' businesses focus on ecologically sustainable organization–environment relations thereby fostering the sustainable development goals.

According to Husted and Allen,[32] CSR paves the way for innovation and reconfiguration of the competitive landscape. Sustainable innovation is deliberately associated with corporate social responsibility (CSR), incorporating three dimensions of the economic, social, and environmental aspects in an inclusive manner. The integration of CSR with these three dimensions forms a critical issue.

Strategic growth in CSR, combining the three dimensions of sustainability, drives sustainable innovations (Barbieri et al.).[5] Sustainability is a major issue as the firm's production processes contribute to pollution. Indian firms contribute to CSR via donations, social and community expenses, and environmental spending. But the extent of environmental spending by Indian firms is considerably low. Hall and Vredenburg[28] argue about the need for a strategy that integrates innovation and sustainable development objectives, in which sustainable innovation must be marketed. Sustainability challenges offer significant potential for innovation and the competitive advantage of the firm.[29] To a great extent, sustainable innovation is related to corporate social responsibility as a company's activities can add value and generate competitive advantage.

### *1.6.1 ENVIRONMENTAL CSR POLICY IMPLICATIONS AND SUSTAINABLE INNOVATION*

This paper examined the practical implications of sustainability practices in India and implications for CSR in relation to the goals of sustainable development. CSR policy is likely to have an effect on the environmental considerations of the firms as they reduce their pollution and produce environmentally friendly products. Environmental consideration is an important part of the CSR policy and the sustainable development goals of the United Nations. Polluting firms have taken a deliberate interest to curtail the pollution and to move toward innovative environmentally friendly production practices. Indian firms have set a practice of adopting environmentally friendly CSR practices in the postmandate period.

Sustainable development incorporates three aspects of CSR such as economic, environmental, and social dimensions, which refer to a policy perspective.[30] The economic, ethical, and philanthropical responsibilities of CSR are found to have a positive impact on society. CSR is a driver of companies' innovation practices.[23] The drive for sustainable innovation is driven by environmental considerations. There is a dire need for sustainable practices at the firm level, albeit with a smaller number of studies on corporate social responsibility and innovation.[61] Environmental CSR practices focus on optimal usage of natural resources and the minimization of ecological externalities in production; moreover, they promote the production of ecofriendly products.[13] In terms of the sustainability and environmental CSR aspect on innovation, creating environmentally friendly processes and products requires firms to be more innovative.[7] In the developing world, alternative innovative production techniques are required to produce energy-efficient products, reducing emissions. It is important to reduce the pollution by adopting sustainable production practices via innovative techniques. There is a dire need for sustainable innovation strategies.

Growth in CSR, incorporating three dimensions of sustainability, drives sustainable innovations (Barbieri et al.).[5] Organizational growth necessitates that products, services, processes, and business models be accompanied by sustainable innovations[34] and responsibility for sustainable development. In this context, we draw the conclusion that the relationship between innovation and CSR is bidirectional.[23,66] As stated by Branco and Rodrigues,[10] corporate performance is associated with CSR to attain economic viability by minimizing the detrimental effects on the environment. The need for a strategy that integrates innovation and sustainable development objectives is known as sustainable innovation.[28] Strategies related to innovation with a focus on sustainability lead to the creation of economic, ecological, and social value.[8,28] The key to progress is the sustainability-related innovation, developing superior skills, and providing a source of competitive advantage for firms.

With the implementation of the CSR policy, the necessity to relate economic objectives to social and environmental demands has led organizations to develop strategies to make the best use of available resources and capacities. These strategies find ways to innovations in sustainable practices with corporate social responsibility (CSR).[23] Processes of sustainable innovation necessitate a competitive landscape, pushing businesses toward innovative products, better technologies, and better business models.[43]

Environmental CSR practices encourage firms to pay close attention to government policies and public interests.[36] This information flowing from outside a firm fosters innovative product development.[50] Sustainability-focused firms adopt both product and process innovation in order to increase energy efficiency and to reduce pollution[4] and with a less impact of the use of products or services on the environment, as well as $CO_2$ emissions, among others.

Key drivers of CSR include internal drivers and external drivers. Internal drivers refer to inspiring employees to participate in sustainable business practices and the firm-specific factors, and external drivers refer to increasing competitive advantage and threats within industries.[44] CSR practices integrate environmental responsibility into the theory.[44,67] CSR theory is accepted worldwide at present, and its relevance with respect to sustainability management varies from country to country. Research analyzing corporate social responsibility (CSR) focuses on the developed countries largely based on environmental regulation. Corporate social responsibility is considered as an extension of the sustainable development concept and shares the responsibilities of the environmental sustainability aspect (Delbard).[16] Corporations commit to sustainable innovation,[53] increase societal demand for environmentally friendly products, and green technologies encourage firms to engage in sustainable production practices.

## 1.7 CONCLUSIONS

Sustainable innovation is an important goal of the SDGs of the UN. Firms move toward the path of the sustainable innovation via the creation of green products, focusing more on sustainability in their production practices. This paper finds that firms belonging to polluting industries spend on research and development. These firms make deliberate efforts to invest in CSR activities after the implementation of the mandatory CSR policy in 2013 in India. Polluting firms engage in more socially committed activities and try to curtail pollution and unsustainable production practices. Developing countries move toward the path of sustainable development by making constant efforts. Often innovation enhances output and reduces costs, but technology can have a detrimental impact on the environment. Therefore, an alternative sustainable pathway is needed with a focus on people, society, and sustainability by reducing the cost of production and energy consumption, thereby reducing environmental problems and emissions. Sustainable innovation is achieved through internal factors such as R&D capabilities and external factors such as the environment as it adds more value to society by reducing pollution.

Sustainable innovation plays an inevitable part in a growing firm's performance. Developing countries do not have the capacity to reduce the environmental damages, but moving toward sustainable innovation practices with cost reduction and reduction of emission can control environmental damages. Fostering technological innovation is considered an important element of the policies toward sustainable development.

Sustainable innovation is understood as a continuous and systematic endeavor that governs the enterprises. The managers of the firms can focus on philanthropic initiatives and measures to foster sustainable innovation and curtail unsustainable production practices.


## KEYWORDS

- **firm capabilities**
- **sustainable innovation**
- **corporate social responsibility**
- **sustainability**

- **panel data**
- **polluting industries**
- **firm performance**
- **Indian firms**
- **prowess data**

## REFERENCES


1. Aggarwal, V. S.; Jha, A. Pressures of CSR in India: An Institutional Perspective. *J. Strat. Manag.* **2019** *12* (2), 227–242.
2. Anser, M. K.; Zhang, Z.; Kanwal, L. Moderating Effect of Innovation on Corporate Social Responsibility and Firm Performance in Realm of Sustainable Development. *Corp. Soc. Responsib. Environ. Manag.* **2018,** *25* (5) 799–806.
3. Babiak, K.; Trendafilova, S. CSR and Environmental Responsibility: Motives and Pressures to Adopt Green Management Practices. *Corp. Soc. Responsib. Environ. Manag.* **2011,** *18* (1) 11–24.
4. Bansal, P.; Roth, K. Why Companies Go Green: A Model of Ecological Responsiveness. *Acad. Manag. J.* **2000,** *43* (4) 717–736.
5. Barbieri, J. C.; Gouveia de Vasconcelos, I. F.; Andreassi, T.; Carvalho de Vasconcelos, F. Innovation and Sustainability: New Models and Propositions. *Revista De Administração De Empresas* **2010,** *50,* 146–154.
6. Barney, J. Firm Resources and Sustained Competitive Advantage. *J. Manag.* **1991,** *17* (1), 99–120.
7. Bocquet, R.; Le Bas, C.; Mothe, C.; Poussing, N. Are Firms with Different CSR Profiles Equally Innovative? Empirical Analysis with Survey Data. *Eur. Manag. J.* **2013,** *31* (6) 642–654.
8. Boons, F.; Montalvo, C.; Quist, J.; Wagner, M. Sustainable Innovation, Business Models and Economic Performance: An Overview. *J. Clean. Prod.* **2013,** *45,* 1–8.
9. Boersema, J. J.; Bertels, J. Sustainable Development in the Developed Countries: Will Theory and Practice Meet? *Global Sustainable Development in The 21st Century*; 2000; pp 31–96.
10. Branco, M. C.; Rodrigues, L. L. Corporate Social Responsibility and Resource-based Perspectives. *J. Bus. Ethics.* **2006,** *69,* 111–132.
11. Callan, S J.; Thomas, J. M. Corporate Financial Performance and Corporate Social Performance: An Update and Reinvestigation. *Corp. Soc. Responsib. Environ. Manag.* **2009,** *16* (2) 61–78.
12. Pan, X.; Sinha, P.; Chen, X. Corporate Social Responsibility and Eco-Innovation: The Triple Bottom Line Perspective. *Corp. Soc. Responsib. Environ. Manag.* **2021,** *28* (1) 214–228.
13. Choi, S.; Ng, A. Environmental and Economic Dimensions of Sustainability and Price Effects on Consumer Responses. *J. Bus. Ethics* **2011,** *104,* 269–282.

14. Coad, A.; Nightingale, P.; Stilgoe, J.; Vezzani, A. The Dark Side of Innovation. *Indus. Innov.* **2021,** *28* (1) 102–112.
15. Cheng, S.; Lin, K. Z.; Wong, W. Corporate Social Responsibility Reporting and Firm Performance: Evidence from China. *J. Manag. Gov.* **2016,** *20,* 503–523.
16. Delbard, O. CSR Legislation in France and the European Regulatory Paradox: An Analysis of EU CSR Policy and Sustainability Reporting Practice. *Corporate Governance: Int. J. Bus. Soc.* **2008.**
17. Demirel, P.; Kesidou, E. Stimulating Different Types of Eco-Innovation in the UK: Government Policies and Firm Motivations. *Ecol. Econ.* **2011,** *70* (8) 1546–1557.
18. Desjardins, J. R. *Business, Ethics, and the Environment: Imagining a Sustainable Future*; Pearson/Prentice Hall, 2007.
19. Khanna, V. S.; Dharmapala, D. The Impact of Mandated Corporate Social Responsibility: Evidence from India's Companies Act of 2013. *Available At SSRN 2808366;* 2018.
20. Enderle, G. Global Competition and Corporate Responsibilities of Small and Medium-Sized Enterprises. *Available at SSRN 528347*; 2004.
21. Flammer, C. Does Corporate Social Responsibility Lead to Superior Financial Performance? A Regression Discontinuity Approach. *Manag. Sci.* **2015,** *61* (11) 2549–2568.
22. Freeman, R. E, Harrison, J. S.; Wicks, A. C.; Parmar, B. L.; De Colle, S. Stakeholder Theory: The State of the Art; 2010.
23. Gallego-Álvarez, I.; Prado-Lorenzo, J. M.; García-Sánchez, I.-M. Corporate Social Responsibility and Innovation: A Resource-Based Theory. *Manag. Decision* **2011,** *49* (10) 1709–1727.
24. Garcia-Castro, R.; Ariño, M. A.; Canela, M. A. Does Social Performance Really Lead to Financial Performance? Accounting for Endogeneity. *J. Bus. Ethics* **2010,** *92,* 107–126.
25. Gowda, H. The Evolution of Corporate Social Responsibility (CSR) in India. *Indian Streams Res. J.* **2013,** *3* (5), 1–10.
26. Greenstone, M.; Hanna, R. Environmental Regulations, Air and Water Pollution, and Infant Mortality in India. *Am. Econ. Rev.* **2014,** *104* (10), 3038–3072.
27. Gujarati, D. N. *Basic Econometrics*; Prentice Hall, 2022.
28. Hall, J.; Vredenburg, H. The Challenges of Innovating for Sustainable Development. *MIT Sloan Manag. Rev.* 2003.
29. Hansen, E. G.; Grosse-Dunker, F.; Reichwald, R. Sustainability Innovation Cube—A Framework To Evaluate Sustainability-Oriented Innovations. *Int. J. Innov. Manag.* **2009,** *13* (04), 683–713.
30. Salvador, H.; Ortiz-Martínez, E.; Santos-Jaén, J.-M. Sustainability, Corporate Social Responsibility, Non-Financial Reporting and Company Performance: Relationships and Mediating Effects in Spanish Small and Medium Sized Enterprises. *Sustain. Prod. Consump.* 2022.
31. Horbach, J.; Rammer, C.; Rennings, K. Determinants of Eco-Innovations by Type of Environmental Impact—The Role of Regulatory Push/Pull, Technology Push and Market Pull. *Ecol. Econ.* **2012,** *78,* 112–122.
32. Husted, B. W.; Allen, D. B. Strategic Corporate Social Responsibility and Value Creation among Large Firms: Lessons from the Spanish Experience. *Long Range Plann.* **2007,** *40* (6), 594–610.
33. Khatami, F.; Scuotto, V.; Krueger, N.; Cantino, V. The Influence of the Entrepreneurial Ecosystem Model on Sustainable Innovation from a Macro-Level Lens. *Int. Entrep. Manag. J.* **2021,** 1–33.

34. Kneipp, J. M.; Gomes, C. M.; Bichueti, R. S.; Frizzo, K.; Perlin, A. P. Sustainable Innovation Practices and Their Relationship with the Performance of Industrial Companies. *Revista De Gestão* **2019,** *26* (2) 94–111.
35. Luo, X.; Bhattacharya, C. B. Corporate Social Responsibility, Customer Satisfaction, and Market Value. *J. Mark.* **2006,** *70* (4) 1–18.
36. Luo, X.; Du, S. Exploring The Relationship Between Corporate Social Responsibility and Firm Innovation. *Mark. Lett.* **2015,** *26,* 703–714.
37. Macgregor, S. P.; Fontrodona, J. Exploring the Fit Between CSR and Innovation. 2008.
38. Mbanyele, W.; Wang, F. Environmental Regulation and Technological Innovation: Evidence from China. *Environ. Sci. Pollut. Res.* **2022,** *29* (9) 12890–12910.
39. Mcelroy, M. W.; Jorna, R. J.; van Engelen, J. Sustainability Quotients and the Social Footprint. *Corp. Soc. Responsib. Environ. Manag.* **2008,** *15* (4), 223–234.
40. Mcguire, J. B.; Sundgren, A.; Schneeweis, T. Corporate Social Responsibility and Firm Financial Performance. *Acad. Manag. J.* **1988,** *31* (4), 854–872.
41. Mishra, S.; Suar, D. Does Corporate Social Responsibility Influence Firm Performance of Indian Companies? *J. Bus. Ethics* **2010,** *95,* 571–601.
42. Montiel, I. Corporate Social Responsibility and Corporate Sustainability: Separate Pasts, Common Futures. *Organ. Environ.* **2008,** *21* (3), 245–269.
43. Nidumolu, R.; Prahalad, C. K.; Rangaswami, M. R. Why Sustainability is Now the Key Driver of Innovation. *IEEE Eng. Manag. Rev.* **2013,** *2* (41).
44. Porter, M. E.; Kramer, M. R. The Link between Competitive Advantage and Corporate Social Responsibility. *Harv. Bus. Rev.* **2006,** *84* (12), 78–92.
45. Porter, M. E.; van der Linde, C. Toward a New Conception of the Environment-Competitiveness Relationship. *J. Econ. Perspect.* **1995,** *9* (4), 97–118.
46. Rodgers, W.; Choy, H. L.; Guiral, A. Do Investors Value a Company's Commitment to Social Activities? *J. Bus. Ethics*, 2013
47. Russo, M. V.; Fouts, P. A. A Resource-based Perspective on Corporate Environmental Performance and Profitability. *Acad. Manag. J.* **1997,** *40* (3), 534–559.
48. Saleh, M.; Zulkifli, N.; Muhamad, R. Looking for Evidence of the Relationship between Corporate Social Responsibility and Corporate Financial Performance in an Emerging Market. *Asia-Pacific J. Bus. Admin.* **2011,** *3* (2) 165–190.
49. Schumpeter, J. A. 49. Capitalism, Socialism and Democracy. In *Democracy*; Columbia University Press, 2016; pp 259–264.
50. Shu, C.; Zhou, K. Z.; Xiao, Y.; Gao, S. How Green Management Influences Product Innovation in China: The Role of Institutional Benefits. *J. Bus. Ethics* **2016,** *133,* 471–485.
51. Sekhon, A. K.; Kathuria, L. M. Analyzing the Impact of Corporate Social Responsibility on Corporate Financial Performance: Evidence from Top Indian Firms. *Corporate Governance: Int. J. Bus. Soc.* **2020,** *20* (1), 143–157.
52. Solow, R. M. Technical Change and the Aggregate Production Function. *Rev. Econ. Stat.* **1957,** 312–320.
53. Tello, S F.; Yoon, E. Examining Drivers of Sustainable Innovation. *Int. J. Bus. Strat.* **2008,** *8* (3), 164–169.
54. Verloop, J. The Shell Way to Innovate. *Int. J. Technol. Manag.* **2006,** *34* (3–4), 243–259.
55. Walley, N.; Whitehead, B. It's Not Easy Being Green. In *Reader in Business and the Environment*; 1994, vol. 36, no. 81, p 4.
56. Wahba, H. Does the Market Value Corporate Environmental Responsibility? An Empirical Examination. *Corp. Soc. Responsib. Environ. Manag.* **2008,** *15* (2), 89–99.

57. Waddock, S. A.; Graves, S. B. The Corporate Social Performance–Financial Performance Link. *Strateg. Manag. J.* **1997,** *18* (4), 303–319.
58. Williamson, D.; Lynch-Wood, G.; Ramsay, J. Drivers of Environmental Behaviour in Manufacturing Smes and the Implications for CSR. *J. Bus. Ethics* **2006,** *67,* 317–330.
59. Yannan, D.; Al Ayub Ahmed, A.; Kuo, T.-H.; Malik, H. A.; Nassani, A. A.; Haffar, M.; Suksatan, W.; Iramofu, D. P. F. Impact of CSR, Innovation, and Green Investment on Sales Growth: New Evidence From Manufacturing Industries of China and Saudi Arabia. *Econ. Res.-Ekonomska Istraživanja* **2022,** *35* (1), 4537–4556.
60. Yu, Y.; Choi, Y. Corporate Social Responsibility and Firm Performance Through the Mediating Effect of Organizational Trust in Chinese Firms. *Chinese Manag. Stud.* 2014.
61. Zhou, G.; Zhang, L.; Zhang, L. Corporate Social Responsibility, the Atmospheric Environment, and Technological Innovation Investment. *Sustainability* **2019,** *11* (2), 481.

# CHAPTER 2

# "U-Turn" in Achieving Cultural Sustainability

SUCHITA VISHWAKARMA[1], MANOJ MEHROTRA[2], ASHOK SEN GUPTA[2], and ASAD KAREEM USMANI[2]

[1]*IILM Academy of Higher Learning, Lucknow, Uttar Pradesh, India*

[2]*School of Management Sciences, Lucknow, Uttar Pradesh, India*

## ABSTRACT

The achievement and expansion of humans is an unmatched example of cultural adaptations and sustainability. In this dynamic era, sustainability or utilization of earthly resources to the optimal level for the benefit of all life has gained the utmost importance. It has been observed that the pursuit of sustainability is being possible only through the sustainability of the cultural heritage. The early civilizations had their own unique ways to handle the challenges and simultaneously evolving. These practices still can be seen as pathways to achieving sustainability goals or SDGs. The paper draws on the historical and contemporary issues of cultural studies to offer a variety of solutions to the present world's challenges. In this paper, an attempt has been taken to consider the cultural practices from across the world. The methodology used for submission in the paper is indicative rather than observational or data interpretation. The focus has been on critically highlighting those practices that can be exemplary approaches to the attainment of the overall well-being of the society. Thus, the chapter concludes that it is important to recall, realize, and start re-practice of lost customs and values by taking a U-turn toward cultural sustainability as an endeavor toward overall sustainability.

Management for Sustainable Development: Integrating Social, Economic, and Environmental Goals. Vishal Jain & Amit Mittal (Eds.)

## 2.1 INTRODUCTION

The achievement and expansion of humans around the world is a story of our unmatched abilities for cultural adaptation. Since the beginning of Homo sapiens on earth, which dates to around 250,000 years ago, people have lived together in the form of small groups or communities to survive and have expressed themselves uniquely. From the era of the hunter gatherer to the most civilized societies in today's world, humans have evolved with each passing day. The journey of human evolution includes the story of their physical and ideological adaptation.

Ancient history reveals that thousands of civilizations and cultures existed in the past. Each culture had its own distinct identity and its own way of expressing themselves, their ideologies, beliefs, values, and artifacts. Among the thousands of cultures that existed, a few evolved, expanded, and spread to various parts of the world. However, there were some cultures that could not sustain the external pressures of change and got lost, and about them even history does not have sufficient evidence. Ancient and mediaeval history explains that one of the major reasons for such cultural decline could be the disinterest of such tribes and groups in socializing with the world. On the other hand, there are certain indigenous, ancient cultures that are still thriving and surviving. These societies have been able to preserve and sustain their heritage of knowledge, wisdom, and beliefs and have gained a reputation for their ingenuity and innovation.

Taking a look into the past through historical manuscripts and the literary contributions in multi-disciplinary studies helps us understand that Darwin's contribution to the study of evolution does not restrict itself only to the evolution of mankind but can also be beneficial for understanding how cultures have evolved. His concept of the "effect of use and disuse" stands true, even in the case of cultural inheritance and existence.

The sketch of social evolution clearly states that the present cultures are historical continuations of past civilizations, with considerable levels of growth, specialization, and differentiation. Though most cultures originated in isolation and were originally conservative and repelled change, a few more than others were, they fought, implementing laws to preserve and protect their traditional cultural patterns and erecting barriers to alienate their identity, ideas, and belongings. Such aloofness, at times, has also been seen as the reason for decline. But for some, the detachment from the outer world has been the essence of existence too. One such tribe that has remained isolated from the world even after approx. 55,000 years of their existence is the Sentinelese, the native people who live on North Sentinel Island in the Bay of Bengal. This tribe remains so isolated that no one has been able to reach them or enter their island until today. It is considered illegal to approach them, and their lives and cultures have remained mysteries to the outside world. The Government of India has forbidden people from traveling within 3 nautical miles of this island. The Sentinelese are not the only ones. Even the Mayan culture, which existed in parts of Mexico and Central America, has now a prominent existence in Guatemala and other parts of the world too.[1,2]

**FIGURE 2.1** Sentinelese culture.

## 2.2 UNDERSTANDING CULTURE

The word "culture" seems to have its roots in many literatures. According to the Latin lexicon, it originates from the word "cultura," which refers to a particular thought, cult, or the supporter of a particular philosophy. While in French literature, world culture is symbolic of "being associated with the mother earth and growth." The Indian literature, which is considered one of the most ancient and historical manuscripts, describes culture as being associated with development, continuous advancement, and the attainment of excellence that can be achieved by a community or an individual.

**FIGURE 2.2** The corngod (left) and the rain god, Chac, a representation from the Madrid Codex Mayan sacred book.

*Image Courtesy*: Museo de America, Madrid. https://www.britannica.com/topic/Madrid-Codex#/media/1/356145/3171

In today's world, people perceive culture as predominantly comprising the symbolic, ideational, and intangible aspects of human society. On the contrary, the spirit of a culture is embedded in the thoughts and actions of people, and cannot be merely restricted to its symbols, idols, artifacts, or additional tangible cultural elements. It pertains to how an individual or group interprets life and the environment. It includes the thoughts, values, and the way these are conveyed to the next generation that distinguish one from another. "The Center for Advanced Research on Language Acquisition" defines "culture as collective patterns of behaviors and communications, reasoning paradigms, and wisdom that are learned by socialization."

Culture can be understood as one of the seven genres or theme of life which includes structure or design, purpose, process, result, refinement, authority or philosophy, or group membership. Various thinkers in the past have attempted to relate the concept of culture with different disciplines from their own perspective, such as political philosophers classifying culture into postmodernism and post-colonialism based on the power system prevailing in society.[3] While aesthetes of the Victorian period have related the understanding of culture to the material facts that a civilization inherits over time, which can be more popularly explained as "cultural heritage."

In a broader sense, culture can be understood as the way in which people express their gestures, behaviors, attitude, and social interaction with the outside world, which are indicators of what individuals are within their inner selves. Thus, the culture of a people or nation is the cumulative product of the cultures of the individuals constituting the nation. The culture or way of expression thus acts as an identity for the community or nation. With time, the means of expression have evolved. The thoughts, beliefs, and expressions are communicated in the form of rituals and stories to future generations. Each community has its own set of stories, which help people configure what, why, and how of their lives. Culture also guides the community toward progress and helps understand what our priorities are as human beings. It helps us lead a happy and fulfilling life in the present as well as in years to come.

## 2.3 WHAT IS CULTURAL SUSTAINABILITY?

Sustainability is an important aspect of human life, which advocates that the utilization of earthly resources should be done only to the extent that they remain in good shape for future generations too. In today's world of fast technological advancement and virtual global connectivity, the linkage between culture and sustainability becomes extremely imperative. Culture facilitates building bridges between people of different interests and encourages a sense of acknowledgement, empathy, and inclusion among them. It helps us visualize the future through the eyes of the past and present.

In the last few years, cultural sustainability has suddenly gained a lot of importance. It has recently been highlighted as the fourth pillar of sustainability by the members of the United Cities and Local Governments and UNESCO on November 17, 2010 and has become an important aspect of the Sustainable Development Goals (SDG). Cultural sustainability can be understood as the ability to preserve cultural uniqueness while simultaneously allowing changes that are consistent with the values of a people. By preserving the diversity, uniqueness, and wisdom of the distinct societies, we can create a sense of mutual respect, creativity, critical thinking, trust, and a willingness to take risks among all. Thus, we can say that cultural sustainability is the remedy for societal, economic, and ecological sustainability.

It is believed that each culture that existed on this earth had its own unique and intellectual saga of magnificent styles of art, technological innovation, and elaborate networks of kin relationships. Thus, the decline of one culture or community is a loss to all of humanity because the inhabitants' abilities perish. This can be better understood by understanding the excellent capabilities of the Polynesians, who existed almost ten centuries before Christ. At the time, European sailors were struggling to calculate longitudes to navigate the oceans. However, Polynesians were successfully sailing across the Pacific to all islands, from Hawaii to Rapa Nui and the Marquesas to New Zealand, with no written descriptions. The secret to their success was their magical ability to sense every shift of wind, change of current, speed, and interpret geophysical signals like impressions from the sea, stars in the sky, clouds, etc. They remembered the names of more than 250 stars in the night sky. Their unrivalled navigation sense was driven by the sight of distance from the horizon, which they observed by perceiving the echo of waves across their boats' hulls and its reflection.[4]

Polynesians were not the only community to exhibit such an extraordinary skill. There are several other examples of such cultures with bizarre capabilities. Barasanas, who lived in Colombia's northwest Amazon, had an inseparable relationship with the Amazon's plants and animals. They taught the world a highly effective method of land management that is considered a supreme model for how humans can live in harmony without destroying the surrounding ecosystem while also benefiting it in the long run.

The incomparable power of introspection and self-discipline is also a lesson, which can be learned from the Buddhists of Tibet, who spend their entire lives preparing for the end of life. Many such untold stories and sagas exist among the Haida of Native America, Montana of America, nomadic Penan living in Borneo's rain forests, Yanomam of the Amazon, Ogoni people of the Niger Delta, and many other civilizations. These tales explain how humanity can live in harmony with nature and yet have the technical know-how to face all the challenges of life, unlike us today. Despite having such extraordinary and exemplary skills, many of these cultures died. The story of several such cultures' decline validates Darwin's theory of survival of the fittest. Few of these cultures got eroded, due to the external influences and dominance of others, while others could not sustain the challenges and changes of the dynamic world.

In today's era, we refer to the world as culturally diverse. Each country has a population consisting of most of its own native people and a few people from other countries who have migrated and lived as well as evolved in that piece of land. This kind of migration has led to the rise of a relatively new cultural community, which arises from the blend of their own set of beliefs carried from their own native land and the set of beliefs that have been adopted from the province of their residence. This cultural mixing sometimes further enriches the diversity, but at times it may result in cultural convergence, cultural divergence, or, at an extreme level, cultural bereavement. No matter what, the existence and merger of a few cultures set an example of their cultural sustainability. Taking a close look into such communities helps us understand how the rich practices of any culture help them grow and prosper despite challenges. One such example of cultural mixing and sustenance is the Parsi community living in the western coastal areas of peninsular India.

## 2.4 CHALLENGES IN CULTURAL SUSTAINABILITY

In the modern era, globalization is not restricted to trade and financial flows only but also pertains to the flow of culture. Various factors, including migration of communities, lead to cultural mixing, which in turn is the source of cultural convergence and dilution. Cultural convergence happens when people from diverse communities become alike and come together on a common platform of beliefs and value systems.[5] Cultural divergence takes place when followers of a particular ideology get separated or go in diverse directions. The bereavement of Aryans living in India is a typical example of cultural divergence. Under the influence of Islamic invasion, the unified race of Aryans, who were originally Hindu, became divided into Hindu and Muslim communities.[6]

Language is an important aspect of any community. It is the means of communication among people who exist at a particular time and the mode of dissemination of its richness from one generation to another. Loss of language has also been observed to be one of the reasons for the decline of culture. This simply means that if a culture and its practices are to survive, we must also work to preserve the language. Many languages across the world are getting lost every day because of the growing trend in the practice of "English" as an internationally accepted language. The widespread popularity of the English language is also an outcome of cultural mixing. UNESCO states that there are approx. 7,000 languages spoken in the world, but more than half of them will go extinct by the end of this century. UNESCO has provided a classification to display the level of vulnerability of languages in terms of vulnerable, endangered, extremely endangered, and extinct.[7] The dominance of a few languages across the world will result in the death of the pool of knowledge and culture known in other languages.

For example, Rosa Andrade, the last speaker of the Amazonian language, was murdered in Peru in 2016. The culture of the Ocaina and Resgaro tribes died with her. Another old-age language, Dunser, is now used only at religious occasions like marriages in a village in Indonesia and has only three speakers left, as was reported in 2011. Even in India, 42 languages are reported to be on the verge of extinction, which includes 11 from the Andaman and

Nicobar Islands, 21 tribal languages, 74 dialects, and many other languages from various states of the country that add up to the linguistic diversity. This simply means that preserving and translating the stories and sagas of these communities is important for preserving the essence of any culture.

**FIGURE 2.3** Vulnerable languages across the world.

*Source:* Git Hub https://github.com/mc2637/INFO5100Project1.git

Communities living in African and Asian countries have also faced a substantial amount of pressure and influence from the western world. This is referred to as "cultural invasion," which, when it happens continuously for many years, gives rise to hybrid cultures. These hybrid cultures can be understood as cultures of convenience, where people are accepting, adopting, and following the practises according to their own choice without understanding the relevance of the belief or essence or its impact on themselves and their surroundings. Even the vast acceptance of social media by populations across nations has led to cultural dilution. The reflection of cultural dilution can be seen in everyday actions, behaviors, and consumption habits too. For example, the popularity of western culture-influenced food (McDonalds, KFC, Instant Foods), the watching of entertainment programs, listening to music, or the consumption of global brands, etc. The influence extends beyond the education system, traditions, and lifestyle, resulting in both temporary and long-term changes.[8] Though change is a continuous process, being a part of change for good or for bad has to be chosen rationally.

It has been observed in the past that a certain amount of dominant western influence has led to the abandonment of a few local cultural ethnicities and customs, diluting, and at times eradicating their distinctiveness. However, there have been a few indigenous practises that were originally possessed or followed by one or a few tribes or a small community that later became popular with time, such as dances of different tribes and religions (Garbha in Gujarat, Katak in Uttar Pradesh, Bamboo Dance in the North East of India, Greeting/Namaskar (India), Bowing Down (Japan), eating on a banana leaf with hands, and environmental protection practices. This clearly indicates that to sustain the beliefs, values, richness, and practises of a culture, we must spread its goodness and uniqueness by exploring and practising them.[9]

## 2.5 PRACTICING CULTURAL PHILOSOPHY FOR ATTAINING CULTURAL SUSTAINABILITY

In today's VUCA era, the world is on the cusp of pandemonium in all spheres of society. Every aspect of societal systems, be it food, energy, resources, humanity, empathy, or ecological balance, is suffering under a state of continued oppression. The essence of life and peace has taken a back seat to the illusion of development. Governmentalcataclysms and corruption, widespread poverty and wealth disparities, human rights atrocities, and mental health issues are at an all-time high, as an increasing number of people feel alienated and deprived of a feeling of community and connection. The thought of independence and self-reliance has conquered all other viewpoints.

Seeing this discordant and unrest situation, UNESCO devised sustainable development goals to ensure global peace and prosperity. In 2015, UNESCO felt the importance of including the concept of culture and cultural sustainability in its SDG framework, and thus cultural sustainability became an intricate part of SDG 10. Besides this, the role of culture was also recognized to impact other sustainability development goals directly or indirectly, and thus culture became integral to UNESCO's sustainability development goals.

In this chapter, we would look back at the various cultural practises that are unique to it and give people advice on how they should live their lives. Understanding such deeply rooted cultural philosophies also helps us solve major issues in the world in a more humanitarian way and simultaneously help sustain cultures.

### 2.5.1 PHILOSOPHY OF "NO POVERTY"

Although different nations define poverty differently, the UN has stated that poverty can be defined as having a daily income of less than $2 US. The percentage of people living in poverty around the world decreased sharply in the first two decades of the twenty-first century, going from 35% to 9%. However, as a result of the epidemic, climate change, and local wars that impacted many millions of people in 2020, poverty grew all over the world.

Although the definition of poverty is not limited to financial issues, economists are now more interested in defining it as a lack of resources to meet specific requirements. However, contemporary economists like Amartya Sen[11] refine the definition to include capability deprivation in addition to financial consideration.

Taking a glance at ancient cultural history, a relationship can be found between "no poverty" and cultural beliefs. Buddhists are one such community that considers poverty bad because it involves dukkha. Buddhist philosophy advocates a non-materialistic way of life, which means avoiding attachment to physical goods, and endorsing the virtue of having lesser wants, Buddha states, "for an individual who relishes sense and worldly delights, he endures poverty, because it leads to borrowing and growing debts, and thus ever-increasing pain." This assumption was later supported by Gallup surveys[13] conducted in 114 countries during 2009. The study concludes that the most religious countries are relatively poor, with a per-capita GDP below $5000, while most of the high-income countries like Denmark, France, the UK, and Hong Kong are toward the bottom of the religiosity continuum. This reflects a strong association between a country's socioeconomic status and the religious sentiments of its citizens.

Buddhist scripture, "The Sabbasava Sutta," emphasizes the importance of having clothing, food, housing, and medicine as the four requisites for life.[12]

The Anaa Sutta, written by Shakyamuni Buddha over 2600 years ago, described four types of bliss that an individual can experience:

- The happiness of making a living through moral means.
- The happiness of freely donating money and acts of kindness to family and friends.
- The happiness of being debt-free.
- The happiness of blamelessness, the ability to live without doing wrong in word, deed, or thought.

According to Buddhist practices, poverty has its own descending spiral path, which is explained by the hymn in the Digha Nikaya:[12]

Poverty grows because of not being generous to the needy; as poverty grows, the tendency to steal, use weapons, and engage in illegal activities grows, leading to an undesirable life, and eventually, death.

According to Buddhist beliefs, tangible possessions like silver and gold can be taken away by the uncertainties of life and people, leading to financial poverty, but cultivating the riches in terms of moral virtues, such as faith, virtuous behavior, learning, generosity, knowledge, and moral.

Shame and dread will always exist and can never be eradicated, thereby reducing poverty around the world.

The Jewish community places a strong focus on "TZEDAKAH," or charitable giving. Preventing someone from falling into poverty by giving them a loan, a gift, or a job so that they may sustain themselves adequately is the ultimate type of tzedakah.[14]

Understanding of Islam may be had from the Quran, which contains the message of Allah for mankind that was revealed to Prophet Mohammad, and Hadith, which are the sayings and practises of the Prophet. The Quran and Hadith both provide insights into Muslim culture. The third tenet of Islam or pillar of Islam is zakat, or almsgiving. Muslims who fall into the category of "Saahib-e-Nisab" are obliged to donate part of their wealth to the underprivileged and poor people in the community so as to ensure that these marginalized people are brought out of the pangs of poverty and that they too are able to live a decent life.

### *2.5.2 PHILOSOPHY OF "NO HUNGER"*

According to a United Nations report, there were 828 million people who were hungry worldwide in 2021, up from roughly 46 million in 2020 and 150 million after the COVID-19 epidemic broke out. The Sikh community's "Langar" rituals, which give meals to everyone gratis regardless of faith, caste, gender, economic status, or ethnicity, can help to some extent with the rise in malnutrition. The Sikhism-based beliefs that emphasize the value of work, prayer, and sharing your possessions and income with others are the foundation of the langar institution. This selfless service is demonstrated not only in Gurudwaras, but also in places of crisis and distress throughout the world. The Sikh community came forward to serve free food to Ukrainians during the Ukraine War.

Hindus too since ages have believed on the ideology of "शतहस्त समाहर सहस्रहस्त संकरि" that means—Earn with 100 hands and donate with 1000 hands. The Hindu manuscript Bhavishya Purana narrates the importance of

"Anna-dan" through a story where the Lord, Shri Krishna, tells Yudhishthir that the wealth accumulated during life would not follow you on your journey after death, but the food that one has donated during his life will ensure that the individual will not starve during his journey after death. And so, Hindus believe in feeding the poor at various important events and distributing a portion of holy food (Prasad) after the worship. Not only this verse, but other scriptures also highlight the importance of feeding animals and birds as a means of maintaining ecological balance. According to observations, the langar kitchen of the Sri Harmandir Sahib (Golden Temple) in Amritsar alone provides food for more than a lakh people every day, while the Bangla Sahib gurdwara kitchen in New Delhi provides food for 45,000–50,000 people.

The Muslim community's daily activities and practises are guided by the tenets of Islam, also known as the "five pillars of Islam." The fourth pillar is that of "sawm," which is commonly referred to as "fasting." The month-long fasting during the month of Ramadan, apart from being a way of worship, is also seen as a way of understanding the plight and suffering of individuals who are unable to arrange for food for them. It reminds the blessed and fortunate of the suffering and hunger of the underprivileged and poor, causing the wealthy to take actions such as arranging food for the poor. Thus, it can be inferred that the solution to bigger problems does lie in community practices, but the need is to make such practises more sustainable.

### *2.5.3 PHILOSOPHY OF IMPARTING "QUALITY EDUCATION"*

Culture is characterized by both material and immaterial characteristics of a civilization, like social organizations, oral and written literature, religion, mythology, and values and conventions. Cooking, shelter, and clothing are examples of social behaviors and technology use. Expressive forms of art like music, dance, rituals, and education are a few other characteristics that symbolize any culture.

Every country and its government work hard to provide a suitable platform and facilities for its citizens to receive a high-quality education. The idea of quality is at the epicenter when it comes to matters related to education. There are various elements of quality that are now included in education for sustainable development (ESD). ESD supports high-quality education in a variety of ways. Countries around the world gathered in Senegal in 2000 for the World Education Forum, where they reaffirmed their commitment to Education for All (EFA) and adopted the Dakar Framework for Action.

Since ancient times, the Indian education system has been known for the diverse, in-depth knowledge and wisdom that the sages had accumulated and disseminated. The richness of Indian education has been quite evident in the ancient literature, manuscripts, and townships, as well as in the field of medicine. Various old-age construction and physical artifacts like town planning, rainwater collection systems, and irrigation canals are examples of the vast knowledge and in-depth understanding of technical aspects. Knowledge of Indian medicine is just another example of the expertise that people had in terms of how to use different herbs and methods for balancing nutrition, medication, emollients, and mind-body healing. The ancient Indian medical system had proficiency in medical diagnosis, skin grafting, surgery, and many other things. These were the results of rigorous study and experience.[16]

The history of the Indian education system India is quite fascinating. The Gurukula education system was used in ancient times. everything that the pupil desired to learn and was capable of learning or required by the virtue of his position in society, including Sanskrit, sacred texts, mathematics, and metaphysics, was taught by the guru. The Gurukul system was thus an advanced version of current education in which learning was tailored to the individual student. The importance of education was well recognized and can also be depicted in the Sanskrit shloka: "svarajyepujyate raja vidvansarvatrapujyate," which means that a king is respected only by his own people, but a learned individual is respected throughout the world. Scholars from India, including "Charaka and Susruta, Aryabhata, Bhaskaracharya, Chanakya, Patanjali, and Vatsayayna, among many others," contributed significantly to the advancement of knowledge in a wide range of disciplines, including mathematics, astronomy, physics, chemistry, medical science and surgery, fine arts, mechanical and industrial technology, civil engineering and architecture, shipbuilding and navigation, sports, and games.

The Indian educational system before the invasion of English in India was meant to preserve the historical culture, support intercultural harmony, and instill social ideals and a sense of responsibility. All modern educational systems, especially those in Asia and Europe, have drawn inspiration from the old Indian educational system.[20] Many changes have occurred over the course of the ancient Indian education system's history, which spans several million years. This change makes sense, given how closely the curriculum is related to an individual's objectives and achievements. When people's views of the world change, or when numerous new domains of knowledge are created, the curriculum taught at universities and schools changes inevitably.[15]

**FIGURE 2.4** Gurukul system.

*Source:* National Digital Library, Developed by ASAl tekar.

*Image credit*: Neesha Thunga K. https://creativecommons.org/licenses/by-sa/4.0/

India has experienced a variety of educational systems, including Takshashila, which was a renowned center of study for Buddhist religious teachings for many years. Until its demise in the fifth century CE, it kept luring students from all over the world. The curriculum included classes in ancient scriptures, law, medicine, astronomy, military science, and the eighteen silpas, or arts. It was renowned for its higher education. The choice of pupils, the creation of the curriculum based on personal preferences, and the timing of the course's conclusion were all entirely up to the teachers. Philosophy, law, statecraft, defence, warfare tactics, grammar (multiple languages), the 18 arts (music, dance, fine arts, etc.), mathematics, astronomy, astrology, plants and herbs, medicine (Ayurveda, Ayurvedic acupuncture, etc.), and surgery were among the 68 elective courses that made up the curriculum. A few other very famous educational hubs of India included Nalanda University where much of the knowledge comes from the writings of pilgrim monks, educational activities in Benares, the education system during Muslim reign, and many more.[17]

**FIGURE 2.5** Nalanda university.

*Source:* Odantapuribs. https://creativecommons.org/licenses/by-sa/4.0/

Education is an intricate part of human life, and an education system that supports students' holistic development and progress is a crucial component of a student's life. It is important to understand that education requirements differ from individual to individual, so a standard set of educational offerings as practiced by many countries today is not relevant. Moreover, education is required not only for generating a source of income but also to be a better person and help the society grow in totality, which shall also include peace, harmony, and a spirit of sustainability among all. Modern education has influenced Indian society and culture to a great extent. It has given access to the treasures of contemporary science and democratic thinking, but has alienated individuals from their cultural heritage, resulting in the waning of Indian ideologies and richness.[18] Thus, there is a need to develop a model of education influenced by Indian and Asian ancestral educational models.

### 2.5.4 PHILOSOPHY OF MAINTAINING "GOOD HEALTH AND WELL BEING"

The COVID-19 epidemic has recalled an old but still relevant adage: "Health is Wealth." Physical, mental, emotional, and spiritual health are all components of one's overall well-being. Total health is "a complete state of physical, mental, and social well-being and not only the absence of disease or infirmity," according to the World Health Organization in 1948.

Religion, medicine, and healthcare have long coexisted in harmony. These healing mechanisms have just recently been split, and this has mostly happened in highly industrialized countries. According to mediaeval history, the first types of hospitals were the centers of religion in society, where illnesses were treated not only with drugs but also with the comforting sounds of hymns and worship.

One such tradition that dates to the very beginning of Indian civilization is yoga. The Vedas, Upanishads, Smritis, teachings of Buddhism, Jainism, Panini, Hindu Epics, and Puranas all contain information about the history and specifics of yoga practices. Yoga represents the integration of mind and body, thought and action, restraint and satisfaction, equilibrium between man and nature, and the belief that no illness can be cured. Yoga discusses:

- Proper body alignment exercises (Asans) and routine metabolic cleaning techniques (Shat kriyas) that enhance physical wellness.
- Strengthening the mind through meditation and focus (Dhyana and Dharana).
- Moral and social well-being is ensured by discipline and observance (Yama and Niyama).
- Breath control techniques (pranayama) and self-management of the senses (pratyahara) for improved emotional well-being. Yoga also stresses the significance of "Ishvarapranidhana," or total surrender to the Almighty. This promotes a person's growth of spiritual wellness. Thus, yoga helps in maintaining harmonious state of the mind and body.

The COVID-19 epidemic also compelled us to follow an age-old practice among Jain monks. Jain monks cover their nose and mouth with a cloth called a "Muhapatti" to stop airborne microbes from entering and being killed. Many sects in India also practice the tradition of washing their hands and feet before entering the house or place of worship, which is symbolic of regular sanitization. As a result, we can see that age-old practices are still relevant today and help us face larger challenges in life.

**FIGURE 2.6** Jain Monk covering mouth (File: Jain Sthanakvasimonk.jpg|thumb|Jain Sthanakvasimonk).

*Image credit*: Shree Diwakar Prakashan © public domain

### 2.5.5 PHILOSOPHY OF USING "AFFORDABLE ENERGY AND WATER MANAGEMENT SYSTEMS"

Scientists today are trying to design various solar-powered machines to harness the energy of the sun in our daily lives. But using the sun and other natural renewable sources of energy is not new. Instances can be seen in many ancient Greeks, Romans, Native Americans, and Chinese cultures regarding the importance and utilization of the sun as the most powerful source of energy. Ancient Egyptians were known to use solar energy on a large scale to heat their homes. Their house designs were intended to store the sun's heat in the building walls during the day, which would then be released after the sun set, regulating the temperature of the home. Similar concepts are also seen in Anasazi Culture in the American Southwest, where people used passive solar principles to warm their cliff dwellings in the winter and shade them in the summer.

**FIGURE 2.7** A step well.

**FIGURE 2.8** Courtyard used for rain water harvesting.

The Jharokas, Roshandans, Baori (Stepwells), sloping roofs, Chajjas, and high ceilings were all meant to cool interiors and allow sufficient light inside. These architectural features were found in the ancient Indian and Mughal monuments, which are architectural marvels and benchmarks to be adopted and followed by the modern world. The various tanks, linked networks of reservoirs, cisterns, drainage canals, public and private wells, baths, dams, and piers (in Lothal) seen in various locations such as Dholavira, Banawali, Kalibangan, and others demonstrate the brilliance of the water management system of the period.[19]

Stone walls were traditionally built using internal plastering and lime mortar. In the winter, solid stone walls prefer to absorb and hold heat by radiating it internally, whereas in the summer, the heat is projected outward. As a result of a lack of traditional scientific method and experience, high-rise buildings frequently face energy-related issues, leading to an increase in energy demand and, ultimately, contributing to global climate change.

### 2.5.6 PHILOSOPHY OF "ENVIRON MENTAL PROTECTION"

Due to the negative effects of climate change, deforestation, global warming, and other factors that are readily apparent today, there has been an increase in global attention paid to environmental protection. To speed up the work toward environmental protection, a few strategic decisions and agreements have been made. However, few civilizations have long been ingrained with a sense of the need to conserve the environment. The Vedas and Upanishads, which date from between 2500 and 1500 BC and represent the Aryan period, make multiple references to behaviors linked to the conservation and protection of flora and animals. The Rigveda has also spoken about many ecological components and methodical tree planting. The Rigveda forbids cutting down trees that are standing on the beaches and uprooting trees that provide food for wildlife in paragraph 5.54.6. The necessity of air, water, and greenery for human existence is intimate, according to the Alhravaveda (para 8.7.10). The Yajurveda also discusses the energy flow and equilibrium that the universe maintains, and how the destruction of "vanaspati" (vegetation) may alter how the seasons, such as unexpected rain, heavy rain, drought, and flood, warm winter, and cool summer, function (para 13.49). In Hindu mythology, a variety of wild animals were worshipped as the "vahanas," or vehicles, of gods and goddesses. This identification highlights not just a respect for these animals but also a justification for their protection.[21]

An individual's relationship with the environment has been discussed, even within the Islamic faith. According to Islam, mankind is tasked with the care of Earth and her biodiversity because they serve as God's khalifa, or trustee. Islam views biodiversity as a manifestation of God's omniscience and wisdom and as a force for human progress. Moreover, the Buddha instructed his followers to transmit their desires for peace and happiness to animals, but they could only do this if they refrained from eating the animals' flesh and did not harbor any animosity toward them. Jainism is founded on the idea of ahimsa (nonviolence) toward people and all of nature, much like Buddhism. The Jains also hold that every living thing possesses an immaterial soul that is just as pure and eternal as the soul of a human being.[22] The Jains are vying for leadership in environmental ethics on a global scale. Their minimal consumption and low position in the food chain are praised as examples of an ecologically sound way of life.[23]

### *2.5.7 PHILOSOPHY OF "PEACE AND JUSTICE"*

Most of the debate between universalists and relativists about cultural differences relates to psychological processes. Universalists claim that, except for the obvious, humans are essentially the same wherever they go, while relativists are of the opinion that humans differ drastically on psychological aspects that cannot and should not be judged and compared.

Psychological dispositions vary greatly, sometimes incomparably. Scholars of cross-cultural issues see justice as an important element of study and are of the opinion that perception of justice typically falls somewhere between two extremes. Cross-cultural research is on the rise, and there have been attempts to pinpoint minor cultural distinctions within more general cross-cultural patterns of resemblance among fields of psychology. From Aristotle to Rawls, philosophers have long pondered the impartial rules of justice. In other words, they have tried to pinpoint social norms that are reasonable by the criteria of outside reasoning. Social psychologists have just recently begun to research subjective notions of fairness. In other words, psychologists have addressed the issue of what criteria people use to judge whether a social situation is right or unfair. This research has created sophisticated models of the psychological processes that influence how one perceives fairness in a particular allocation of limited resources or in the making of a significant social choice.[24]

There are several different ways to understand "cultural justice." It may allude to ideas of what is just that—particular to a culture. Alternately, it might mean determining what constitutes justice among people from various cultural backgrounds. A more focused issue has recently dominated scholarly discussion, specifically how the state should treat minority cultures fairly in multicultural countries when the state's institutions reflect the culture of the majority. Another line that may be drawn is in situations where culture serves as a distinguishing factor for certain groups that experience discrimination or unfair access to resources. They could also come across instances where culture itself is the target of injustice, such as when its members repress their practices, values, or beliefs.[25] Distributive, procedural, and retributive justice are often distinguished in models of justice and fairness (e.g.[26,27]). Distributive justice deals with the issue of perceived fairness in resource distribution. Models of procedural justice include both the decision-making process and how decisions are carried out. The apparent impartiality of punishment and penalties results in the acceptance of retributive justice. While this idea is strongly related to procedural and legal issues, it is often explored independently. Revenge-based justice.

All the world's main faiths have long encouraged serenity and urged people to embrace all people as brothers. The Semitic religions, such as Judaism, Christianity, and Islam, which share the fundamental ideas of monotheism, prophets, and life after death, describe peace and reconciliation among intra- and interreligious groups as carrying great rewards in the hereafter, whereas Ahimsa, or non-violence, forms a cardinal principle of almost all Aryan religions, such as Hinduism, Buddhism, and Jainism. Men do not always uphold the ideals they espouse, even though religions often include an ethical code that addresses personal conduct. The oldest active religion in the world today is Hinduism. No prophet established it. The Vedas, Upnishads, Bhagvad-Gita, and six Darshanas are the key scriptures and major repositories of Hindu philosophy, even though Hinduism maintains an extensive number of sacred texts. The Mahabharata, a religious scripture found in the Bhagavad Gita, uses Arjuna's awful predicament to illustrate how Hindus view conflict and peace. Arjuna had to face fighting his relatives, family, and teachers, and he was horrified by the prospect of the carnage that would ensue. Krishna advised him that to defeat bad forces, it is occasionally necessary to wage a good battle. Arjuna is reminded by Krishna that battling for justice, truth, and peace is to fulfil the law made by God. The Bhagavad Gita (2:31) says: "Think also of your duty and do not waver. There is no greater good for a warrior than to fight in a righteous war."[28]

In India, Jainism is an active religion that professes to have universally applicable teachings. Ahimsa is understood and practiced in Jainism in a more extreme and all-encompassing manner than in any other religion. "To harm" is the term for the act of killing a living being out of passion. Ahimsa is the term for refraining from such an act (no injury). The first of the "five vows of Jainism" is thought to be the vow of ahimsa. Buddhism is fundamentally a religion of peace, much like all the great world faiths. Buddhism, one of the Aryan religions, is characterized as a Godless religion (agnostic, not atheistic) since, unlike other faiths, it does not accept belief in God as a basic idea. Buddhism was founded by Gautama Buddha (b. 567 BC) and is one of the Aryan religions. Buddhism is fundamentally based on a moral philosophy or an ethical style of living that aims to effect personal change. It is obvious in one of the principles that the Buddha established.[29]

Sikhism is one of the newest faiths, founded by Guru Nanak (1469–1539), who had mystical experiences. The sacred text of Sikhism, the Guru Granth Sahib, comprises wise sayings and noble poetry from numerous supernatural poets and seers. The most acquisitive Indian religion is Sikhism, which considers the factual world to be potentially beneficial for the advancement of humanity. It has a separate ethical code that mandates selfless service to one's fellow humans. In addition to their superb hospitality, langar, almsgiving, and humanitarian assistance, their sacred writings also offer explicit guidelines and a code of behaviors that apply in every circumstance.[30]

The idea of peace is essential to Judaism. It is one of the three fundamental Jewish principles, along with truth and justice. Shalom, which means "full" or "whole" and is derived from one of God's names, is the Hebrew word for peace. Judaism dates back over three thousand years. The Jewish legend holds that God handed the Israelites the foundational Ten Commandments, which were to guide their social existence, after they fled Egypt and arrived in the Sinai wilderness. These laws and commandments are intended to operate as principles for developing positive relationships with both God and other people.[31] The Bible uses the term "peace" in a broad sense. Along with the lack of violence, it considers the happiness and health of the populace. The New Testament contains the teachings of Jesus Christ. The well-known "Sermon on the Mount" of Jesus is as follows: "To him who strikes you on the one cheek, offer the other also." And do not withhold your tunic from him who takes away your cloak. Give to anyone who requests it. And do not demand your goods back from the person who takes them away.(6:29-30).[31]

The world's newest revealed religion is Islam. It is not a new religion, but rather an expanded and renovated version of the eternal Divine religion based on the concept of the afterlife, God's unity (Tauheed), and the medium of the Prophets (Risalah) (Akhirah). Islam and the other two remaining Abrahamic religions, Judaism and Christianity, both adhere to these three foundations. The wording of the Quran itself makes this clear: "The same religion has He established for you as that which He enjoined on Noah—that which we have sent by inspiration to thee—and that which we enjoined on Abraham, Moses, and Jesus." (Al-Quran 42:13).[32]

## 2.6 RESULT AND CONCLUSION

It is evident that cultures across the world include elements, customs, beliefs, and traditions that are in some way, or another related to sustainable development goals. Adhering to one's culture can lead to the attainment of growth and development in a sustainable manner. However, in the race for development and wealth creation, humans have ignored sustainable practices in their culture and adopted methods that have resulted in resource overexploitation, social and environmental imbalance, and the gradual decay and extinction of cultures.

Pursuing cultural practices is crucial for the existence of culture; practices that are not followed get lost, and over a period, the culture itself faces a threat of extinction. Cultural practices are the essence of any society and civilization and are passed on from one generation to another. The change in the demographic structure of society, particularly the shift from a joint family pattern to a nuclear family, has limited the adoption of cultural practices by new generations. Cultures face the threat of extinction primarily for two reasons: firstly, due to being too self-centric and remaining cut-off from other cultures and not evolving with time, and secondly, due to letting go of the practices of their own culture or letting the impact of other cultures dominate their own culture.

Maintaining a balance between one's own culture and the cultures of others is therefore critical, especially at a time when multiculturalism is becoming more common. Sustainable practices across cultures need to be cherished and taken forward, along with being open to adopting such practices from other cultures within the permissible boundaries of one's own culture.

Concerns about adopting sustainable practices have arisen primarily because of the human race's tendency, under the pressure of technological advancement and occupational engagements, to ignore such practices that have helped societies and civilizations prosper and flourish.

It is thus of utmost importance that a conscious and deliberate effort is made to make people aware of their culture and sustainable cultural practices. These cultural practices aided in the progress and advancement of humans; if such practices could lead to advancement when humans lacked access to cutting-edge technology, imagine the wonders they could create with the technological advancements available today. It is important that we take a U-turn toward our culture and explore the ways in which our cultural practices can make our activities, transactions, and businesses sustainable. This is applicable to all cultures across the world. It is time to let go of the feeling of superiority and dominance of one culture over another and work in collaboration to take advantage of the good and sustainable practices of all. Survival and resurgence amid the numerous massive threats that humans have faced in recent times in the form of wars, natural disasters, diseases, and pandemics like COVID, monkey pox, the economic crisis, floods, droughts, volcanic eruptions, earthquakes, etc. is possible only if we, as a unified force, move toward long forgotten cultural values and practices.

## 2.7 CONTRIBUTION OF STUDY TO SOCIETAL DEVELOPMENT

From the above study, it is understood that human beings have been associated with culture since evolution. With the change in time, we accept, modify, and reject cultures according to our beliefs and sustainability, but the basic thing remains the same. Human beings are different from other living things on Earth because of culture and its solicitations for a better life. Yet, humans are part of society; therefore, we adopt culture according to society. In the current scenario, humans are suffering from stress, anxiety, and mental and physical pressure due to various factors in the environment, this directly diminishes our culture and values.

This paper will help to understand the basic evaluation of culture and how it will help to be a better human being. Today, we are busy in our routinised task and created our own culture of living which only makes us feel that we are happy, but it is not true, it may be superficial or self-generated thing. Original happiness is driven when we sustain our basic culture by various methods followed by regions in all parts of the world. It helps society to transform from a caustic attitude to an ingenious attitude.

## KEYWORDS

- **culture**
- **sustainability**
- **SDG**
- **cultural adaptation**
- **cultural convergence**
- **ancient literature**
- **cultural heritage**


## REFERENCES


1. Chan, C. S.-C. No Title2011 Divorcing Localization from the Divergence Paradigm: Localization of Chinese Life Insurance Practice and Its Implications. *Int. Social.* **2011,** *26* (3), 346–363, doi: 10.1177/0268580910392261.
2. Prasad, A.; Prasad, P. No TitleMix, Flux and Flows: The Globalization of Culture and Its Implications for Management and Organizations. *J. Glob. Bus. Issues Burbank* **2007,** *1* (2), 11–20.
3. John, S. L. L.; Baldwin, R.; Faulkner, S. L.; Hecht, M. L. *Redefining Culture Perspectives Across the Disciplines*; Routledge, 2006.
4. Davis, W. Last of Their Kind: What Is Lost When Cultures Die? *Support Sci. Journalism,* 2010.
5. Kelly, D.; De Block, A. Culture and Cognitive Science. In *The Stanford Encyclopedia of Philosophy*; Zalta, E. N., Ed.; Metaphysics Research Lab, Stanford University, 2022.
6. Hammersley, M. *The Concept of Culture A History and Reappraisal*, 1st ed.; Palgrave Pivot. Cham., 2019.
7. Gemignani, M.; Peña, E. Postmodern Conceptualizations of Culture in Social Constructionism and Cultural Studies. *J. Theor. Philos. Psychol.* **2007,** *27–28* (2–1), 276–300, doi: 10.1037/h0091297.
8. Banks, E.; James, A., ed. Banks, Cherry A. McGee, —Multicultural Education: Issues and Perspectives. *ERIC* **1989,** *0* (0), 337.
9. Bartolone, D. L. Culture as Sustainability: *The Case Study of Go e as Sustainability: The Case Study of Govardhan Ecovillage Village and Vedic Culture in India*; CUNY Hunter College, 2019.
10. Held, D.; McGrew, A. G. The Global Transformations Reader: An Introduction to the Globalization Debate.
11. Wolff, J.; Lamb; Zur-Szpiro, E. A Philosophical Review of Poverty; 2015. [Online]. https://www.jrf.org.uk/report/philosophical-review-poverty
12. Senauke, H. A. No Poverty: The Sustainable Development Goals and Buddhism No Title. *Budhistdoor Global* 2021. https://www.buddhistdoor.net/features/no-poverty-the-sustainable-development-goals-and-buddhism/ (accessed Aug 24, 2022).

13. Crabtree, S. Religiosity Highest in World's Poorest Nations. *Gallup*, 2010. https://news.gallup.com/poll/142727/religiosity-highest-world-poorest-nations.aspx (accessed Aug 24, 2022).
14. Schwartz, R. Issues in Jewish Ethics: The Jewish Response to Hunger No Title. *Jewish Virtual Liabrary*. https://www.jewishvirtuallibrary.org/the-jewish-response-to-hunger (accessed Aug 24, 2022).
15. Lynn Payne, O. J. K. Cultural Sustainability in Higher Education. In *Encyclopedia of Sustainability in Higher Education*; Springer, 2019; pp 1–7.
16. Singh, S. He Educational Heritage of Ancient India: How an Ecosystem of Learning was Laid to Waste.
17. Altekar, A. *Education in Ancient India*, Second; Banaras Hindu University, 1944.
18. Sarkar, S. Role of Indian Culture in Manifestation of Integrated Development in Modern Day Education, 2022. https://ezyschooling.com/parenting/expert/role-of-indian-culture-in-manifestation-of-integrated-development-in-modern-day-education(accessedAug26,2022).
19. Sivaraman, S. P. *Concepts from Traditional Indian Architecture to Reduce Energy Consumption in Modern Indian Architecture*; Harvard University, 2017.
20. Kumar, P. M. *Indian Culture and Indian Education*; The Vedanta Kesri, no. Special, 2016; pp 61–65.
21. Mandalia Hiren, P. C.; Yogesh, R. Bio-Cultural Importance of Indian Traditional Plants and Animal's For Environment Protection. *Rev. Res.* **2012,** *1* (VI), 1–4, [Online]. https://www.researchgate.net/profile/Dr-Hiren-Mandalia/publication/221657820_Bio-cultural_Importance_of_Indian_Traditional_Plants_and _Animal's_For_Environment_Protection/links/0d1c84f54eb50a8641000000/Bio-cultural-Importance-of-Indian-Traditional-Plants-a
22. Negi, C. S. Religion and Biodiversity Conservation: Not a Mere Analogy. *Int. J. Biodivers Sci. Manag.* **2005,** *1* (2), 85–96, doi: 10.1080/17451590509618083.
23. Chapple, C. K. Contemporary Jaina and Hindu Responses to the Ecological Crisis. *Ecol. Spirit Relig. Reflect. Environ. Conscious.* **1994,** 209–220.
24. Leung, M.; Kwok; Morris, W. Justice Through the Lens of Culture and Ethnicity. In *Handbook of Justice Research in Law, Sanders and Hamilton*; Ed. Plenum, 2020.
25. Maddox, M. Cultural Justice. In *Institutional Issues Involving Ethics And Justice, Encyclopedia of Life Support Systems*; 2020.
26. Deutsch, M. Cooperation, Conflict, and Justice. In *Distributive Justice: A Social Psychological Perspective*; Springer, 1986; pp 3–18.
27. Folger, R.; Konovsky, M. A. Effects of Procedural and Distributive Justice on Reactions to Pay Raise Decisions. *Acad. Manag. J.* **1989,** *32* (1), 115–130, doi: 10.5465/256422.
28. Anjum, M. R. Concept of Peace in World's Major Religions: An Analysis. *Int. J. Sci. Res. Publ.* **2017,** *7* (4), 248.
29. Anjum, M. R. Concept of Peace in World's Major Religions: An Analysis. *Int. J. Sci. Res. Publ.* **2017,** *7* (4), 251, doi: 10.13140/RG.2.2.14003.66088.
30. Anjum, M. R. Concept of Peace in World's Major Religions: An Analysis. *Int. J. Sci. Res. Publ.* **2017,** *7* (4), 252.
31. Anjum, M. R. Concept of Peace in World's Major Religions: An Analysis. *Int. J. Sci. Res. Publ.* **2017,** *7* (4), 253.
32. Anjum, M. R. Concept of Peace in World's Major Religions: An Analysis. *Int. J. Sci. Res. Publ.* **2017,** *7* (4), 254.

## CHAPTER 3

# Plastic Debris and the Marine Environment: Integrating Transformational Strategies in Achieving a Sustainable Environment

BHUPAL BHATTACHARYA[1], ABDESSELAM SALMI[2], SARMISTHA BHATTACHARYA[3], and MAYURIKA ROY[1]

[1]*Department of Law, Raiganj University, West Bengal, India*

[2]*Ajman University, Ajman, United Arab Emirates*

[3]*Department of Social Work & Cyber Law, Amex College, Burdwan, West Bengal, India*

## ABSTRACT

A significant quantity of plastic enters the world's oceans as a result of human activity, which has serious impacts on aquatic ecosystems. Plastic is convenient for industrial production because it is relatively inexpensive, has chemically stable characteristics, and is decently water-resistant. The manufacturing of plastic is continuously increasing every year. The components which are frequently used in plastics include polystyrene, nylon, polyurethane, and polypropylene, among others, which are very harmful to the survival of organisms, human beings, and the environment. These plastic materials slowly, over time, disintegrate in the environment because of their physical, chemical, and biotechnological influences. Plastics are conveniently scattered under the impact of natural forces and end up in our day-to-day lives by entirely breaking down. This issue has the potential to jeopardize the health and structure of marine habitats. There are numerous

Management for Sustainable Development: Integrating Social, Economic, and Environmental Goals.
Vishal Jain & Amit Mittal (Eds.)

risks to maritime life as a result of microplastic pollution, which has already sparked increasing concerns.

This study looked through the scientific literature on the impacts of marine nanoplastics as well as their capability to affect the well-being of the living community. This article summarizes the interconnections of microplastic particles with marine resources and ultimately the environment.

## 3.1 INTRODUCTION

Plastic is composed of artificial organic polymers, which are extensively used in various applications such as garments, beverages, food containers, pharmaceuticals, electrical products, industrial equipment, etc. Plastics in e-waste have emerged as a major global public health issue and environmental concern as a result of their high volume of output and the inadequate management regulations in many nations, including India.

Plastics have become an imperative and durable creation within a large variety of products targeting the various needs of daily consumers. Plastic materials made of petroleum-based polymers are abundant in human surroundings and domestic environments. Whenever these plastics reach the end of their useful lives, they are typically dumped in landfills alongside municipal solid trash without following the proper environmental regulations. Even though plastic has been initially believed to be safe, the many decades of plastic waste in the surroundings have resulted in a wide range of inherent risks affecting largely the environmental conditions.

Plastic garbage is now considered a major environmental threat, particularly in the water habitats, where there has been a prolonged physical and biological meltdown resulting in causing harmful impacts on wildlife, human being, living organisms, and ecological resources. A significant quantity of plastic enters the world's oceans as a result of human activity, which has serious impacts on aquatic ecosystems. Plastic has convenient industrial production which is relatively inexpensive, has chemically stable characteristics, and has decent water resistance. The manufacturing of plastic is continuously increasing every year. Frequently used plastics that largely degrade the environment, including polystyrene, nylon, polyurethane, and polypropylene, among others, are on the rise. These plastic materials slowly, over time, disintegrate because of external physical, chemical, and biotechnological influences. There are numerous risks to environmental life and biology as a result of microplastic pollution, which has already sparked increasing concerns. The investigation into checking and enhancing the use of plastic waste is still in its early stages; however, the statistics of their impacts so far are concerning.

Plastic production companies and businesses use large quantities of plastic in their distribution networks. Plastics are conveniently scattered under the impact of natural forces and end up in our day-to-day lives by entirely breaking down. This issue has the potential to jeopardize the health and structure of the food chain and the entire environmental system. This study looked through the scientific literature on the impacts of nanoplastics on the environment as well as their capability to affect the well-being of living communities. It is a sign of development that rapidly increasing public understanding, with resulting shifts in demand from customers, is impacting the business sector and ultimately the consumer base.

## 3.2 SIGNIFICANCE OF THE STUDY

From 1950 to 2021, approximately 7 billion tons of plastic were generated globally, with 9 and 12% reprocessed and combusted, respectively. The growing human population and steady desire for plastic products are to blame for the constant rise in production, increase in trash, and ultimately damage to the environment.

Harmful chemicals are present in a variety of plastic materials utilized in the manufacture of several consumer items. An estimated 8 million tons of plastic are released into the body of water each year, causing aquatic habitat depletion and directly affecting aquatic life.

As of 1964, polycarbonate manufacturing has grown twentyfold. Until the year 2014, 311 million tons of plastics had been manufactured worldwide, and that production is expected to double within another 20 years and potentially expected to quadruple by 2050.[19] According to the World Energy Outlook 2015, plastic wrapping (26% of total volume) is predicted to continue to expand over the next 15 years, with a potential fourfold rise by 2050.[10]

The steadily increasing consumer use and manufacturing of plastic in emerging market economies are deeply concerning. The complexity of their infrastructure for waste management could not be designed at a sufficient pace to cope with their increased amounts of plastic trash, and thus it requires effective policy measures for maintaining sustainability.

## 3.3 REVIEW OF LITERATURE

(Katyal, 2020) Plastic is a synthetic material that, due to its mutability and durability, has steadily been embedded into almost all facets of human existence. It is widely used in everyday textiles and apparel, personal care products, and food containers. The widespread use of plastic-based products in the societal structures poses dangers to both human health and the environment.

(Du, 2021) Plastic particles have started to receive greater public interest in recent years due to their dissemination in the atmosphere, posing a possible danger to organisms and ecosystems. This article was reviewed and analyzed through the methodological approaches, which included physiochemical classification. Throughout this article, the character traits, application spectrum, and positives and negatives of each analytical technique have been evaluated and compared.

(Machado, 2018) Soils are crucial parts of ecological processes, which are presently under worsening pressure. Fouling of soil and environmental resources by plastic particles is becoming more common, with possible resultant negative consequences for wildlife habitats and all forms of life, deteriorating the health condition. Ironically, information on the impacts of such pollutants on soil resources is mainly lacking. This study investigated the potential of plastic litter to disrupt crucially important soil–water interactions and the effects on topsoil and microorganisms' function.

(Wright, 2013) Plastic waste on the microparticles and, conceivably, nanoscales is widespread in the environment. In current history, plastic particles have piled up in seawater and soil particles around the world, with the highest concentration approaching 100,000 particulate $m^3$. Microbeads, owing to their compact size, could get consumed by lowering down the unforeseeable effects on the organism's physical well-being. The aim of the analysis of this research was to examine echinoderms and their vulnerability to the physiological symptoms of microplastic absorption.

(Cole, 2011) Plastic particle pollutants in the marine ecosystem have become a massive issue ever since the 1940s, when mass plastic manufacturing emerged. Nanoplastic consumption has now been observed in a variety of aquatic creatures, which might allow the transmission of artificial ingredients or water-insoluble pollutants to living organisms. The article concludes by pointing out research directions for policymakers and researchers like microplastics' ability to get adsorbed into living organisms, including human beings, to be further researched. The outcome of nanoplastics in aquatic ecosystems is unknown, and they are gradually entering the food chain system.

## 3.4 RESEARCH GAP

The idea of a sustainable environment has failed to define and develop the policy for guiding manufacturing and rampant uses of plastics in the human environment. Whenever a new environmental policy initiative is tried to be adopted, there is an evolution of community pressure in restricting the initiative.

From the various previous types of research and analysis of the existing literature, it can be observed that most of the existing literature mainly focused on the effect of plastic pollution on the aquatic environment. This proposed research through critical analysis is intended to include current data and study observations on the causes, dissemination, and environmental effects of microplastics in the land, surroundings, and waterbody, which have not been previously addressed through research properly.

## 3.5 RESEARCH OBJECTIVES

1) to explore the attributes of microplastics in the food system through oceanic sources;
2) to assess dynamical trends in microplastic abundance in the environment;
3) to analyze the impact of microplastics on the environment and aquatic living organisms; and
4) to suggest effective measures addressing the research gaps for future research on the conclusion of this research.

## 3.6 RESEARCH METHODOLOGY AND DESIGN

In this paper, an attempt has been made to evaluate the most appropriate literature on the use of varieties of plastics addressing different kinds of consumer utilities, emphasizing the public health and ecological consequences of prolonged use of plastic products. This paper also analyzes the application of various toxic substances in the manufacturing process, the prevalent treatment and disposal mechanisms, and the negative impacts of these constituent elements on living organisms and human health. This document also contains suggestions for worldwide waste plastic regulation and its avoidance.

## 3.7 SOURCES AND TYPES

Over the past 65 years, there has been a substantial growth in both the usage and manufacture of plastic. Plastic is commonly used in numerous commonplace items for raising the worldwide standards of living.[4] About 50% of the plastic items are found in throwaway items that generate a sizable amount of trash.[31] Plastic waste from improperly disposed of plastic products is a serious worldwide problem. Most plastics are chemically inert and challenging for marine life to get decomposed, and they finally end up as debris in the oceans.[17] Maritime organisms that consume or become enmeshed in such litter are directly impacted by the presence of litter in the marine environment, which may suddenly become vulnerable to the possible threats associated with plastic environmental damage.

## 3.8 DYNAMICAL TRENDS IN MICROPLASTIC ABUNDANCE

The abundance of microplastics in the environment has increased dramatically in recent years due to the proliferation of single-use plastic products and poor waste management practices. Some of the key trends in the dynamics of microplastic abundance include the following:

1. Rapid Increase: The amount of microplastics in the environment has increased rapidly in recent decades, particularly in oceans and other aquatic systems.
2. Regional Variations: The abundance of microplastics varies between regions, with higher concentrations in areas with high population densities and poor waste management practices.
3. Depth Distribution: Microplastics have been found at all depths in the ocean, from surface waters to the deep sea, and their distribution is influenced by ocean currents and other environmental factors.
4. Impact on Marine Life: Microplastics are having a significant impact on marine life, including the ingestion of microplastics by a variety of species, and the entanglement of wildlife in plastic debris.
5. Human Health Concerns: The potential health risks of microplastics to humans are a growing concern as microplastics can enter the food chain and potentially harm human health.

The original sources of nanoplastics in the open sea include plastic bags, foam, and fibers, which are drained causing marine plastic pollution.[23]

Microplastics are primarily sourced from land flow in surroundings in the sea. Because of coastal tourism, plastic bags, mineral plastic bottles, and other scrap materials are often thrown away carelessly by visitors and gradually break down into microplastics in the marine environment.[14]

Ocean waters are contaminated by plastic trash; it can be commonly found in the open ocean, on the seashores of some of the most isolated islands, and in the deep sea. Largescale convergence zones of plastic trash have been found at the world scale in various studies because of the main longshore drift, which has become a serious concern to look into for a possible and immediate solution.

## 3.9 PLASTICS AND ENVIRONMENTAL HAZARDS

Considering all of the benefits of plastics, toxic plastic debris can cause a severe environmental hazard. About 50% of the plastic made is used in lowend single-use items.[5] Plastic is extremely resilient due to its chemical inertness, a quality that is frequently desired by the consumers. Nevertheless, whenever plastic items are not properly disposed of or recycled, they create a problem for the nature.[3] Since there has not been enough research to fully assess plastic's persistence, it is difficult to say with certainty how long it can persist in the environment.

Additive chemicals while manufacturing plastics are added to enhance the item's desirable characteristics.[9] Numerous of these compounds are believed to be harmful and can drain off the surface. Plastics also could acquire known persistent organic pollutants after being exposed to the environment.

The majority of plastics are believed to endure in the environment for at least a few decades, while it has been calculated that somewhere between 60 and 80% of the globe's garbage is made of plastic.[1] Various studies around the world depicting different samples have concluded that the plastic trash ultimately ends up in the open ocean surface, which is more or less 88% of the total plastic waste.[30]

A considerable portion of the Earth's new biomass and even half of all photosynthetic rate have been ascribed to phytoplankton, which converts solar radiation's energy into the chemical energy that drives ecological networks.[13] Due to their significance, there is fear-mongering regarding the possible harm that micro and nanoplastics may bring to organisms.

## 3.10 NANOPLASTICS AND MARINE ENVIRONMENT

Microplastics and plastic debris are produced as a result of improper land disposal, wastewater treatment, paint failure, and the cleaning of textiles, resulting in ocean water damage.[12] Plastic waste has economic consequences on fishermen, which include impairment to ships and fishing equipment induced by marine debris, losing revenues because of decreased fishing induced by ghost fishing, infected catches, and time wasted due to diversions used to prevent aquatic waste experiences. Marine microplastics damage several parts of the aquatic fish and other marine food chains.[33] The plastic particles can have a toxic effect on fish and other aquatic organisms, lowering calorie consumption and overall economic growth, inducing cell stress, and causing undesirable behaviors.[15] Additionally, microplastic particles get across from the physiological barrier and build up in cells, affecting the lipid metabolism and molecular effects.[18]

Nanoplastics are known to be ingested by living things. There are numerous ways through which marine species are exposed to microplastics, which enter through their mouths and subsequently pass from their digestive systems or through their gills.[28] It is a widely proven fact that microplastics can be ingested, and the digestive system of microorganisms is frequently affected by the presence of such microplastics.

Another reason for the availability of microplastics in the ocean is because vessels most often dump a lot of plastic garbage there.[8] A significant number of plastic products may potentially enter the water as a result of sea transport mishaps. Due to friction and entanglement, catching fish ropes and nets used in combing becomes worn, and that gradually increases the amount of microplastics present in marine environments.

Additionally, a significant amount of plastic fishing equipment is discarded in the sea each year due to inadequate long-term usage and management of these tools; microplastic particle contamination in the environment is intricately intertwined with regional marine economic activity.[32] Furthermore, as the consumer becomes aware that seafood can contain plastic particles, their confidence in seafood may be reduced.

## 3.11 ENTRY CHANNEL OF PLASTIC AND OCEANIC ECOSYSTEM

Plastic enters the ecosystems and food chains through the oceanic system from two primary routes, one is through the land-based channels such as rivers, rainwater runoff, sewage, and landlocked litter carried to the ocean, leaving behind coastlines and the other is through the marine industries, which include fishing activities and improper disposal of waste. Most of the plastic that ends up in the ocean is primarily from densely populated areas.[16] Once plastic enters into the atmosphere, especially the environmental ecosystems, it becomes challenging to remove it.[27] Due to its small size, it gets passed through the sewage treatment and ends up in the rivers and eventually the oceans.[22] It is practically impossible to remove microplastics from the ocean using various existing purifying methods and that heavily impairs the ecological integrity. Roughly 10% of the total of the plastic waste, which makes up between 60% and 80% of waste disposal and as much as 90%–95% in some regions, is ultimately discharged into the body of water through numerous mediums.[22]

The majority of plastics produce tiny plastic particles; microplastics are defined as plastic particles with a diameter of less than 5 mm.[21] Numerous research studies are regularly published on the harmful consequences of plastic particles in the marine environment. These studies are very relevant from the health perspective of ecosystems and the cycles of nutrients, with the goal of evaluating the potential effects of plastics on environmental level. Plastics and microplastics pose an increasing hazard to the environment and marine biota as the global human population increases along with the frequency of industrial processing. Additionally, the quantity of products dumped into the body of water has greatly increased along with the expansion of the overall population and the growing preference for plastic goods. Approximately, 8 million tonnes of plastic enter the ocean annually.[20] The majority of the microplastics in the ocean comes from inland river flows, the fishing industry, oil, and other sources.[11] The movement of plastic from the river to the ocean eventually includes all types of nanoplastics added to everyday items.

## 3.12 ATTRIBUTES OF MICROPLASTICS IN THE FOOD SYSTEM

Microplastics in the food system from oceanic sources can have the following attributes:

1. Small size: Microplastics are defined as particles less than 5 mm in size. This small size makes it easy for them to enter the food chain.
2. Persistence: Microplastics are not biodegradable and can persist in the environment for a long time. This means that they can accumulate in the oceans and be ingested by marine life.

3. Toxicity: Some microplastics can contain toxic additives, such as heavy metals and harmful chemicals, which can be harmful to the environment and wildlife, including those that are consumed by humans.
4. Abundance: The abundance of microplastics in the ocean is a growing concern as they can be found in all parts of the world's oceans, from surface waters to the deep sea.
5. Adhesion: Microplastics can adhere to other substances, such as plastic litter and pollutants, making them even more dangerous to marine life and potentially to humans.

## 3.13 IMPACT OF MICROPLASTICS ON THE ENVIRONMENT

Microplastics have significant negative impacts on the environment, including the following:

1. Marine Life: Microplastics can harm marine life in a variety of ways, including the ingestion of microplastics by a range of species, leading to physical harm, chemical toxicity, and decreased feeding and reproductive success.
2. Ocean Ecosystems: Microplastics can cause imbalances in ocean ecosystems by changing the abundance and distribution of marine species. This can have a cascading effect throughout the food chain.
3. Biodiversity: The proliferation of microplastics in the ocean can harm biodiversity by reducing the population sizes of certain species and altering the structure of marine communities.
4. Physical Debris: Microplastics contribute to the overall problem of marine debris and plastic pollution, which has a range of negative impacts on the physical, chemical, and biological characteristics of the ocean.
5. Chemical Contamination: Some microplastics can absorb and concentrate pollutants from the surrounding water, making them even more harmful to marine life and potentially to humans.
6. Human Health: The potential human health risks associated with microplastics are not fully understood, but there are concerns about the potential for microplastics to enter the food chain and harm human health through the ingestion of contaminated seafood.

## 3.14 PLASTICS AND THEIR IMPACT ON MARINE LIVING ORGANISMS

All endangered species, particularly marine turtles, are vulnerable to a variety of human stresses. Various life forms come into contact with the microplastic which is present in the water bodies. Plastic intake and entanglement pose a major threat to the living organisms of the marine environment. Passive ingestion can happen when infected prey, including molluscs and crustaceans, which have consumed and absorbed microplastics in their tissues, are devoured.[6] Sometimes nanoplastics are not consumed directly but are ingested in a passive manner, which includes inadvertent absorption, and that can happen when plastic debris is combined with regular food or for a case of misidentification. Ingestion of plastic by sea turtles can lead to severe gastrointestinal system injury, clogging the intestinal tract, lowering down the eating stimulation, and diminishing stomach size, which over time may cause food dispersion and malnutrition and ultimately result in the death of the living species.[19]

According to published data, about 30% of the fishes are tested for microplastic debris in them.[26] Various research studies have confirmed that there are no organisms which have never ingested tiny particles of plastic,[29] which is a very serious concern to be looked into immediately.

The impacts of fish species ingesting microplastics have also been amply demonstrated by numerous scholars. In this sense, a variety of fish species caught in the oceans, seas, and rivers have been found to have ingested microplastics.[25] Additionally, a number of scientists have investigated, under controlled circumstances, the effects of ingesting microplastics alone or in combination with other harmful substances on living beings.

The large quantities of afloat plastics that have built up in their intestinal fortitude may change how they swim and regulate their propulsion, which could adversely impact their capacity to avoid predators and sustain human risks. Additionally, detrimental effects like a decrease in productivity, growth, reproductive success, and procreation have been noted, which suggests that plastic particles pose a threat to the safety and supportability of endangered marine societies.[7]

The impact of microplastics on the aquatic environment is significant and can be seen in the following ways:

1. Marine Life: Microplastics can harm marine life in a variety of ways, including ingestion, entanglement, and physical damage to the digestive system and other internal organs.

2. Biodiversity: The accumulation of microplastics in the ocean can negatively impact biodiversity by altering the abundance and distribution of marine species and reducing the populations of certain species.
3. Food Chains: Microplastics can enter the food chain and potentially harm a variety of species, from tiny planktons to large predatory fishes. This can have a cascading effect on the entire food chain.
4. Chemical Contamination: Some microplastics can absorb and concentrate toxic pollutants, including heavy metals and persistent organic pollutants, making them more harmful to marine life and potentially to humans.
5. Physical Impacts: Microplastics contribute to the overall problem of marine debris, which can cause physical damage to marine habitats, interfere with the movement of marine animals, and alter the physical and chemical characteristics of the ocean.
6. Water Quality: Microplastics can alter water quality by changing the balance of nutrients and dissolved organic matter in the water, potentially affecting the survival and growth of aquatic plants and animals.

The impact of microplastic particles on microalgal species is another issue that is becoming more and more of a priority. Since they provide food for a variety of creatures, from tiny zooplankton to molluscs and crabs, microalgae serve as a major energy resource for the majority of aquatic habitats. These creatures are the primary source of energy and nutrition for the food chain and are eventually intruded upon.

## 3.15 PLASTICS AND THE POTENTIAL CONSEQUENCES TO HUMAN AND LIVING ORGANISM'S HEALTH

To determine if the amount of microplastics in the water is rising or falling, observations throughout the different times are crucial in this aspect. An increase in plastic particles is almost certainly the result of more plastic waste being dumped into the surroundings. However, a variety of other factors, such as asymmetrical decomposition owing to climatic change, enhanced turbidity on the ocean floor, etc., might also influence the creation of microplastics.

It is well-established that extended exposure to microplastic particles can have negative impacts on a variety of organisms. Marine creatures are important to the fish industry and are at a stage of vulnerability because they swallow microplastics. It seems sensible to speculate about potential consequences to human health. The possible impacts of microplastics, either alone or in combination with other environmental pollutants, consumed by adult mammals, at the subcellular, cellular, and tissular levels, have been the subject of numerous investigations.[24]

In the coastal ecosystems, along with some maritime and lowland species, microplastics can cause oxidative, reproductive, and pathological stress; impair immunological functioning; and even cause cancer.[2] A decline in metabolic reserves, feeding activity, fecundity, longevity, and growth can be seen in these situations.

The alterations that have been seen at the inter- and intracellular and tissular levels in several investigations potentially influence both ecosystem functions and individual survival within the ecological conditions. The typical molecular structure of the polymer is significantly reduced as a result of a chemical change occurring in seawater. Any large amount of deterioration necessarily degrades the substance because the physical durability of plastics depends upon their substantial molecular weight. Plastics undergo extensive degradation and finally get broken into various dust pieces. Even these pieces, which are frequently invisible to the naked eye, can degrade further due to the polymer's carbon being transformed into $CO^2$.

## 3.16 CONCLUSIONS

Plastic waste is pervasive in the aquatic domain, where it is primarily brought in by anthropogenic activities. Small plastic particles are known to be present in large quantities in the ecological system. They can be discovered all over the globe in sediment samples and in aquatic environments. Microbeads can be found by a number of creatures in the marine ecosystem due to their microscopic size. Microplastics pose dangers to species not just because of the substance itself but also because of their capacity to collect and accumulate marine contaminants in the atmosphere and then pass those pollutants via food chains.

Since the start of largescale production in about 1950, the general public is now more dependent on plastics. Global consumption has been stoked by their adaptability, consistency, low weight, and affordable manufacturing costs. The majority of plastics are used and discarded on land at first. However, it is anticipated that by 2030, the quantity of microplastic particles in some ocean water portions will get doubled and is on a rising trend.

Chemicals are typically applied to plastic at a range of levels that are high enough to guarantee the presence of a gradient of concentration and the transmission of the chemical to the environment. Toxic chemical levels released from the debris of polyethylene or polypropylene particles in the saltwater may reflect in the environmental concentrations. Alternately, measurements of trace levels may allow for the calculation of contaminant concentrations in microparticles for further evaluation of the risk posed by these concentrations. The impact of microplastics on the aquatic environment is extensive and can have far-reaching consequences for marine ecosystems and the species that depend on them.

Plastic particles can harm the immune response, induce cancer, and develop oxidative, reproductive, and neurological distress in several maritime and lowland species that live in marine areas. Within those conditions, a drop in metabolic capacity, feeding activity, fecundity, longevity, and growth can be observed. In order to assess their possible implications not just on an individual level but also on an ecological level, a large number of additional research on the adverse effects of the ingestion of microplastics by aquatic organisms are essential for the protection of the health of the ecosystems and the cycles of nutrients. As the entire human population expands and the processing industry occurs more often, plastics and microplastics constitute an enormous hazard to the environment and marine lifeforms. Overall, the impact of microplastics on the environment is significant and far-reaching, and significant action is required to reduce their production and mitigate their environmental impacts.

## 3.17 SUGGESTION

Overall, the dynamics of microplastic abundance in the environment indicate a growing problem that requires significant action to mitigate its impacts on the environment and human health. The endeavor to strike a balance between the proportions of plastics released and those assessed is a crucial factor to take into account when assessing the impact of any sort of contamination. To do this, it is important to evaluate the measured and projected plastic particle levels. Finding exact, reliable techniques to measure environmental plastic contamination has long been a problem, and doing so is still very difficult.

1. Despite there being significant growth in microplastic pollution research, it is a primary concern to conduct investigations of microplastic pollution in regions that have received little attention, such as Antarctica, the Arctic, and the Indian Ocean.

2. It is necessary to develop a standardized technique for the investigation of the availability of large-scale microplastics in the marine environment. In this regard, this research proposes that all investigations of microplastics are to be built utilizing cutting-edge modern scientific procedures.
3. Sea organisms, particularly craniate species like turtles, are significantly impacted by microplastics, according to the IUCN Red List, and need to be given special attention.

The level of concern polymers cause for marine environments depends significantly on their chemical and structural properties. The plastic's percentage of elastic modulus and its breakdown characteristics are crucial. It is imperative that every study should involve the objective of improving the characterization of the plastic, which broadly influences the behavior of the polymer. Understanding plastic composition, physical forms, uses, transportation, and fragmentation into microplastics is necessary to address this global issue.

## KEYWORDS

- **microplastics**
- **marine environments**
- **waste management**
- **sustainable development**
- **plastic-free initiative**
- **ocean conservation**
- **environmental impact**

## REFERENCES

1. Abbing, M. R. *Plastic Soup: An Atlas of Ocean Pollution*; Island Press, 2019.
2. Aldridge, D. C.; Ollard, I. S.; Bespalaya, Y. V.; Bolotov, I. N.; Douda, K.; Geist, J.; Haag, W. R.; et al. Freshwater Mussel Conservation: A Global Horizon Scan of Emerging Threats and Opportunities. *Glob. Change Biol.* **2023,** *29* (3), 575–589.
3. Bano, N.; Younas, T.; Shoaib, F.; Rashid, D.; Jaffri, N. Plastic: Reduce, Recycle, and Environment. In *Environmentally-benign Energy Solutions*; Springer International Publishing, 2020; pp 191–208.

4. Barnes, D. K.A.; Galgani, F.; Thompson, R. C.; Barlaz, M. Accumulation and Fragmentation of Plastic Debris in Global Environments. *Philos. Trans. R Soc. Lond. B Biol. Sci.* **2009,** *364* (1526), 1985–1998.
5. Bhattacharya, R. R. N.; Chandrasekhar, K.; Roy, P.; Khan, A. *Challenges and Opportunities: Plastic Waste Management in India*; 2018.
6. Md Bhuyan, S.; Md Nabi, R.-U.; Md Wahidul, A.; Md Nazrul, I.; Lenin, C.-F.; Levent, B.; Mohamed Saiyad, M.; Sang, Y. C.; Venkatramanan, S.; Alonzo, A.-N. Impacts of Microplastics on Marine Organisms and in Human Health. 2021.
7. Dobbs, K. *Marine Turtles in the Great Barrier Reef World Heritage Area: A Compendium of Information and Basis for the Development of Policies and Strategies for the Conservation of Marine Turtles*; Great Barrier Reef Marine Park Authority, 2001.
8. Galgani, F.; Hanke, G.; Maes, T. Global Distribution, Composition and Abundance of Marine Litter. In *Marine Anthropogenic Litter;* 2015; pp 29–56.
9. Galloway, T. S. Micro-and Nano-plastics and Human Health. In *Marine Anthropogenic Litter*; 2015; pp 343–366.
10. Geyer, R.; Jambeck, J. R.; Law, K. L. Production, Use, and Fate of All Plastics Ever Made. *Sci. Adv.* **2017,** *3* (7), e1700782.
11. Gomiero, A.; Strafella, P.; Fabi, G. From Macroplastic to Microplastic Litter: Occurrence, Composition, Source Identification and Interaction with Aquatic Organisms. Experiences from the Adriatic Sea. In *Plastics in the Environment*; IntechOpen, 2018.
12. Hale, R. C.; Seeley, M. E.; La Guardia, M. J.; Mai, L.; Zeng, E Y. A Global Perspective on Microplastics. *J. Geophys. Res. Oceans* **2020,** *125* (1), e2018JC014719.
13. Hutchins, D A.; Fu, F. Microorganisms and Ocean Global Change. *Nat. Microbiol.* **2017,** *2* (6), 1–11.
14. Jayasiri, H. B. Marine debris. In *Marine Pollution and Climate Change*; CRC Press, 2017; pp 136–162.
15. Kumar, R.; Manna, C.; Padha, S.; Verma, A.; Sharma, P.; Dhar, A.; Ghosh, A.; Bhattacharya, P. Micro (nano) Plastics Pollution and Human Health: How Plastics can Induce Carcinogenesis to Humans? *Chemosphere* **2022,** *298,* 134267.
16. Kurtela, A.; Antolović, N. The Problem of Plastic Waste and Microplastics in the Seas and Oceans: Impact on Marine Organisms. *Croat. J. Fish.* **2019,** *77* (1), 51–56.
17. LI, W. C.; Tse, H. F.; Fok, L. Plastic Waste in the Marine Environment: A Review of Sources, Occurrence and Effects. *Sci. Total Environ.* **2016,** *566,* 333–349.
18. López de las Hazas, M.-C.; Boughanem, H.; Dávalos, A. Untoward Effects of Micro-and Nanoplastics: An Expert Review of their Biological Impact and Epigenetic Effects. *Adv. Nutr.* **2022,** *13* (4), 1310–1323.
19. Lusher, A.; Hollman, P.; Mendoza-Hill, J. *Microplastics in Fisheries and Aquaculture: Status of Knowledge on Their Occurrence and Implications for Aquatic Organisms and Food Safety*; FAO, 2017.
20. Mishra, S.; Rath, C.; Das, A. P. Marine Microfiber Pollution: A Review on Present Status and Future Challenges. *Marine Pollut. Bull.* **2019,** *140,* 188–197.
21. Mistri, M.; Infantini, V.; Scoponi, M.; Granata, T.; Moruzzi, L.; Massara, F.; De Donati, M.; Munari, C. Small Plastic Debris in Sediments from the Central Adriatic Sea: Types, Occurrence and Distribution. *Marine Pollut. Bull.* **2017,** *124* (1), 435–440.
22. Moore, C. J. Synthetic Polymers in the Marine Environment: A Rapidly Increasing, Long-Term Threat. *Environ. Res.* **2008,** *108* (2), 131–139.

23. Napper, I. E.; Thompson, R. C. Plastic Debris in the Marine Environment: History and Future Challenges. *Glob. Chall.* **2020,** *4* (6), 1900081.
24. O'Hara, T. M.; Hart, L. Environmental Toxicology. In *CRC Handbook of Marine Mammal Medicine*; CRC Press, 2018; pp 297–318.
25. Pawar, P. R.; Shirgaonkar, S. S.; Patil, R. B. Plastic Marine Debris: Sources, Distribution and Impacts on Coastal and Ocean Biodiversity. *PENCIL Public. Biol. Sci.* **2016,** *3* (1), 40–54.
26. Pellini, G.; Gomiero, A.; Fortibuoni, T.; Ferrà, C.; Grati, F.; Tassetti, A. N.; Polidori, P.; Fabi, G.; Scarcella, G. Characterization of Microplastic Litter in the Gastrointestinal Tract of Solea Solea from the Adriatic Sea. *Environ. Pollut.* **2018,** *234*, 943–952.
27. Qi, R.; Jones, D. L.; Li, Z.; Liu, Q.; Yan, C. Behavior of Microplastics and Plastic Film Residues in the Soil Environment: A Critical Review. *Sci. Total Environ.* **2020,** *703*, 134722.
28. Ribeiro, F.; O'Brien, J. W.; Galloway, T.; Thomas, K. V. Accumulation and Fate of Nano-and Micro-Plastics and Associated Contaminants in Organisms. *TrAC Trends Anal. Chem.* **2019,** *111,* 139–147.
29. Ryan, P. G. Ingestion of Plastics by Marine Organisms. In *Hazardous Chemicals Associated with Plastics in the Marine Environment*; 2019, pp 235–266.
30. Schmidt, C.; Krauth, T.; Wagner, S. Export of Plastic Debris by Rivers into the Sea. *Environ. Sci. Technol.* **2017,** *51* (21), 12246–12253.
31. Thompson, R. C. Plastic Debris in the Marine Environment: Consequences and Solutions. *Marine Nat. Conserv. Eur.* **2006,** *193,* 107–115.
32. Wootton, N. K. Occurrence of Microplastic in Fish: Presence, Knowledge and Solutions. Ph.D. Thesis, 2021.
33. Zhang, F.; Wang, X.; Xu, J.; Zhu, L.; Peng, G.; Xu, P.; Li, D. Food-web Transfer of Microplastics Between Wild Caught Fish and Crustaceans in East China Sea. *Mar. Pollut. Bull.* **2019,** *146,* 173–182.

# CHAPTER 4

# Eco-Bricks from Plastic Waste: Toward Ensuring a Sustainable Circular Green Economy

S. N. KUMAR[1], AJU MATHEW GEORGE[2], MUHAMMED ASSIF[1], ABHIRAM BAIJU[1], ELIAS JOHN[3], and DIANA MUSARA[4]

[1]*Department of EEE, Amal Jyothi College of Engineering, Kerala, India*

[2]*Department of Civil Engineering, Amal Jyothi College of Engineering, Kerala, India*

[3]*Orma Eco bricks, Kerala, India*

[4]*Earthly Touch Foundation, Johannesburg, Gauteng, South Africa*

## ABSTRACT

Plastic waste is crucial in today's scenario, and the disposal of plastic waste is necessary to ensure healthy living for future generations. This research work proposes the design and making of ecobricks from plastic waste and their utilization in the real world. The ecobrick is essentially a plastic bottle that has been densely stacked with things that are made up of used or discarded plastic. Ecobricks are an efficient method of waste management at a low cost. In the construction of ecobricks, the net surface area of the packed plastic is drastically reduced to prevent it from degrading into toxins and microplastics. Ecobricks are used for making furniture, garden walls, and other structures. Ecobricks focus on the waste plastics that are being simply thrown away into the environment. The waste plastic, when thrown into the environment, will not get decay,

Management for Sustainable Development: Integrating Social, Economic, and Environmental Goals.
Vishal Jain & Amit Mittal (Eds.)

and it is a source of pollutants. PET bottles are used for packaging waste plastics since they have good reliability and resistance against ultraviolet rays. This research work also focuses on indoor and outdoor structures made with ecobricks.

## 4.1 INTRODUCTION

Universally, the generation of solid waste surges with economic growth, urbanization, and development and will keep on increasing at rapid rates. With worldwide solid waste generation rates increasing more rapidly than ever, urban development experts caution that the growth will maximize in this century and will not start to drop without transformational changes in how we use and reuse materials. Over the last 20 years, apprehension of overall environmental problems has resulted in the United States and the European Union (EU) announcing new legislation to endorse waste reduction.[1] The global production of plastic has been pointedly augmented from 60 MT in 2011 to 8.3 MT in 2017. The majority of nations face problems in controlling the environmental issues associated with plastic waste, which has become a global concern.[2–4] Most of the existing practices used for the management of plastic waste do not aid a sustainable green circular economy.

The main methods for managing plastic trash are recycling, landfilling/disposal, and incineration. The incineration unquestionably contributes to $CO_2$ gas emissions, while landfills' methane gas emissions contribute to global warming. About 5% of plastic garbage is dumped in the ocean, 43% in landfills, and 52% is shipped to nations with lax environmental regulations.[5,6] High-income countries in the group of eight also export 70% of their plastic waste to developing countries in Asia and the Pacific. Waste plastics are occasionally dumped into the environment in large quantities in some places. This pollutes the environment, endangers aquatic life, clogs waterways, and causes flooding. Recycling of plastic waste promotes a circular green economy. Nevertheless, the current volume of waste plastic produced each day overwhelms the recycling facilities that already exist and the point at which plastic can no longer be retained. Therefore, finding a long-term solution to the management of plastic trash is essential. Scientists are investigating the possibility of using plastic trash in the manufacture of building construction materials.

## 4.2 DIFFERENT STRATEGIES INVOLVED IN THE PROFICIENT UTILIZATION OF PLASTIC WASTE

Plastic waste is extensively used in the construction sector as an ingredient in concrete and mortar as well as in asphalt. Crushed waste plastic into particles was found to be used in concrete.[7] The use of plastic trash in the creation of mortar and concrete was further studied in some subsequent studies, including.[8–10] In Ref. [11], researchers looked into the usage of plastic waste in the manufacture of paver blocks and bricks. Only a few studies have looked into using recycled plastic bottles (PET) as an ingredient in the production of bricks. Since extensive screening is not needed in the manufacturing process, the manufacturing of ecobricks using PET as an encapsulation benefits developing and low-tech countries greatly. Sand or plastic trash was filled into used plastic bottles before they are filled to make ecobricks using recycled PET bottles. In Ref. [12], the authors created ecobricks using 500 cc of used PET bottles as infill constituents instead of discarded plastic bags. Compressive strengths between 2.55 and 2.90 N/mm$^2$ were attained in the study. Ecobricks made from recycled PET bottles that ranged in size from 250 mL to 2 L were suggested in Ref. [13] and a compressive strength of 8–17.44 N/mm$^2$ was mentioned in the work. In a comparable investigation, using sand as the filler in recycled 250–1.5 L PET bottles increased the compressive strengths.[14] In Ref. [17], authors filled 600 mL PET bottles with soil, which was used as a building material with a compression strength of 8.99 N/mm$^2$. In Ref. [15], the authors investigated the properties of sand-filled plastic bottle clay panels for sustainable housing. In Ref. [16], ecobricks were created from used PET bottles, with one set of samples being filled with water and the other with sand. The study explained how adding water to particular bottles could provide significant advantages, such as thermal comfort, but at the risk of strength.

Significant variations in results were found in the work published by Refs. [12,14] as a result of the usage of various filler materials in the research work. Therefore, more research on various infill materials is required to assess ecobricks and determine their feasibility for use in construction. Most importantly, bottle bricks are used in construction to minimize capital costs. However, the qualities of the soils from various sites may vary, which could affect how well the resulting ecobricks perform. Similar to how the nature of soil material is affected, the moisture content may affect the qualities of ecobricks. Regular and extensive disposal of plastic debris into the environment, and occasionally into the sea, causes environmental annoyance and disturbs marine life. These extortions have sparked research for the advancement of the circular economy in the management of plastic trash. The current research study examines ecobricks as a prospective construction material that can reduce plastic waste.

The features of the flash-based geopolymer ecobricks and their durability were thoroughly studied in Ref. [18]. Fly ash serves as the base material for geopolymer bricks, and the polymerization procedure was accelerated using an alkaline activator. The processes utilized to create plastic bricks are economical and environmentally friendly, according to Ref. [19], which also states that using plastic trash to create construction bricks is a cost-efficient and effective technique for reducing the risks associated with improper disposal of plastic waste. The replacement of conventional bricks with ecobricks also reduces $CO_2$ emissions since manufacturing conventional bricks involves $CO_2$ emissions. By replacing bricks in buildings with recycled plastic bottles, embodied energy is reduced, and cement pollution is reduced. At the moment, used plastic garbage is successfully transformed into valuable building materials, including bricks, interlocks, roof tiles, railway sleepers, etc.[20] The ecobricks promote proficient utilization of plastic waste; without deformation, they can withstand a density range between 0.33 g/mL and 0.7 g/mL.[21] Since plastic is nonbiodegradable and poses risks to soil, it can pollute land, waterways, and oceans, as evidenced by the large number of marine and terrestrial organisms that have perished as a result of plastic pollution.[22] Plastic waste can also be used to make plastic bricks.

The utilization of plastic was discussed in Ref. [23]. Plastic extrusion is a process in which the plastic is melted and molded into a continuous profile and used as a construction material. Biosolids from wastewater treatment plants gain importance in the manufacturing of ecobricks, which are found to be good since they can cause pollution, and using biosolids as one of the raw materials also minimizes clay consumption.[24] A great substitute for conventional earthy bricks is plastic brick. Plastic bricks are appropriate for external and partition walls but not for load-bearing walls. Plastic bricks can be used in underwater buildings since they are water-resistant. Recycling plastic garbage reduces environmental pollution.[25] In Ref. [26], ecobricks were found to be a good option in plastic waste management and utilized for construction purposes. An ecobrick is a recyclable construction block that is made from a plastic bottle that has been filled with spent plastic to a specific density. Numerous products, such as furniture, garden walls, and other buildings, can be made using ecobricks.[27] One of the biggest environmental problems of the twenty-first century is, without a doubt, the plastic threat.

Tiny plastic particles are swirling around the oceans, ending up in landfills, and are accountable for detrimental impacts on the environment and perhaps humans, animals, and plants. In Ref. [28,29], the ecobricks are highlighted as a good alternative to reusing plastic waste. The eco-BLAC bricks are both an economically and environmentally sustainable solution for turning industrial waste into masonry construction materials. In addition to reducing the manufacture of these energy-intensive building materials, this research intends to reduce trash disposal by recycling some industrial byproducts into more environmentally friendly bricks.

In Ref. [30] ecobricks were considered a solution to environmental problems, thereby improving the creativity of the children. The case study focussed on Baruga District, Kendari City. Glue was not used for making ecobricks since plastic bottles are made of PET. Plastic waste management plays a crucial role. Different types of plastic waste were analyzed in this work, and its role in civil engineering applications was also discussed.[31] In Ref. [32] a detailed study was conducted that gave the characteristics of ecobricks and estimated the strength of an ecobrick with varying density ratios. Various tests like the compressive test, drop test, and failure test were investigated on ecobricks. Due to increased awareness about plastic pollution, people have now begun to collect plastic bottles and use them as an infill material in the construction of small-scale structures. Research has been done on the fire safety of these ecobrick structures. A sample made from the cob plaster mixture along with the ecobrick combination achieved a one-hour fire rating test.[33]

The ecofriendly and sustainable nature of ecobricks makes them a good construction material in the field of civil engineering. Studies have been made to improve the optimum setting time of plastic bottles for their application in building ecological buildings.[34] The soil characteristics are different in each place, and it affects the performance of the ecobricks.[35] Recycling of waste materials promotes material ecology and methods to tackle the problems caused by the production of high-end carbon emissions and the scarcity of natural resources. In the modern world, industrial waste is used in the development of building components, i.e., ecobricks.[36] A geopolymer ecobrick was constructed using fly ash, and its properties and durability were studied. The brick dimension is 20 cm × 20 cm × 40 cm. A proper ratio of different components is made into a waste plastic bottle to create an efficient and strong ecobrick.[37]

The COVID-19 pandemic created a huge increase in the amount of plastic waste, i.e., plastic-packed food stuff, bottles, protection shields, etc. The huge pile of plastic waste made its disposal nearly impossible. The likelihood of environmental pollution could be decreased by recycling plastic garbage and reusing it as an environmentally acceptable building material. Numerous studies demonstrate that polymer-based plastic wastes can be successfully employed as recycled materials, reducing the need for conventional resources and, consequently, construction costs.[39] The increased production and disposal of plastic waste are degrading the environment. According to studies, four different brick development processes use plastic and stubble debris. Applying stubble with a cement-to-sand ratio of 1:5 created the first brick. The second method used PET bottles with a cement-to-sand ratio of 1:3. Waste plastic polybags were utilized to create the third and fourth bricks.[40] After usage, PET (polyethylene terephthalate) bottles make up a significant portion of solid trash. PET bottles are frequently utilized in construction, mostly as filler in adobe or concrete walls, in many underdeveloped nations. India is among developing nations that struggle with issues related to environmental degradation brought on by the production of solid waste. Reusing plastic bottles as construction materials can reduce pollution in cement production by lowering the amount of cement used, as well as embodied energy by replacing bricks in the walls with them instead of plastic bottles.[41] Indiscriminate disposal of plastic on land and water and the release of toxic gases into the air by burning induce numerous health problems, killing hundreds of marine species from ingesting these toxic wastes. By using the ecobrick method, plastic waste could be effectively managed at the individual or household level.[42] The most common construction material used in building construction is brick. It also has side effects on the environment and human health. An ecobrick is a polyethylene terephthalate (PET) bottle filled with a mixture of plastics, foams, packaging, and cellophane. Numerous studies investigated the characteristics and properties of an ecobrick and proved that it's an ecofriendly replacement for a building block.[43] Numerous studies have shown that utilizing recyclable and reusable building materials, such as plastic bottles, can lower the overall cost of a construction project. Plastic bottles, which are the second most common plastic garbage to be produced, can be used in construction as a sustainable building material to cut down on the amount of plastic waste produced annually.[44]

## 4.3 EFFICIENT UTILIZATION OF ECOBRICKS FOR MAKING VALUE-ADDED PRODUCTS OR MODELS

Plastic waste is the input for the making of ecobricks; in our domestic scenario itself, plastic waste is generated daily. The wrappers, cover, and outer lining material for the products are made up of plastic. Rather than being simply dumped into the environment, the plastic waste generated in our day-to-day lives should be collected and stored. The wet plastic waste should be cleaned and dried in sunlight to eliminate the moisture content. For efficient packing of plastic waste, the cutting of plastic waste can be done so that maximum quantity of waste can be packed in a bottle. Figure 4.1 shows the different steps involved in the making of ecobricks.

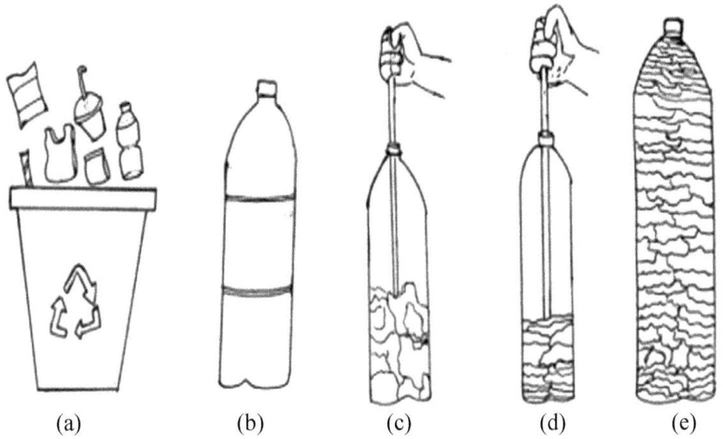

**FIGURE 4.1** Steps involved in making ecobricks.

The steps in the making of ecobricks are as follows:

- A 1.5–2 L bottle is appropriate for making ecobricks; it is filled with all kinds of plastic waste.
- A stick is used to pack the waste in the bottle as tight as possible and avoid air gaps by arranging the waste plastic inside the bottle as close as possible
- The bottle is sealed with its original lid and you have made an ecobrick.
- To make it sturdy and robust, you must pack your ecobrick as tightly as possible.

Excessively soft bricks cannot be used for building ecobricks because they could be crushed by large loads. Additionally, the less plastic enters the environment, the more you can fit in your plastic bottle. Depending on the size of your bottle, the weight of your brick will vary, but a full 500 mL bottle should weigh about 175 g, and a full 1.5 L bottle should weigh about 500 g. The indoor application of efficient utilization of ecobricks is depicted in Figures 4.2 and 4.3.

**FIGURE 4.2** Steps involved in the processing of plastic waste for indoor applications.

Nine 1.5 L bottles packed with plastic waste are used in the making of this product. Similarly, ecobricks can be used for making indoor structures for domestic and office purposes.

**FIGURE 4.3** Finished product made up of ecobricks (sitting stool).

The materials required for the making of the ecobrick products depicted in the figure are represented in Table 4.1. The details in Table 4.1 reveal that, at an optimum cost, waste plastics can be utilized for making indoor structures.

**TABLE 4.1** Details of Materials Used for Making Sitting Stools from Plastic Waste.

| Sl no | Materials | Details | Quantity |
|---|---|---|---|
| 1 | Plastic bottle | 1.5 L | 9 |
| 2 | Plastic waste | 3.2 kg | - |
| 3 | Packaging tape | 2 inch | 1 |
| 4 | Thread | 10 m | 1 |
| 5 | Cloth | 0.5 $m^2$ | 1 |

The ecobricks had many applications outdoors too. Figures 4.4–4.7 depict the different configurations of ecobricks. Figure 4.4 depicts the hexagon module and the triangular module arrangement of ecobricks.

(a) (b)

**FIGURE 4.4** (a) Hexagonal module arrangement and (b) triangular module arrangement.

Figure 4.5 depicts the arrangement of ecobricks comprising 19 bottles and 12 bottles. In this manner, a bigger structure comprising ecobricks is framed; Figure 4.7 depicts the bigger structure.

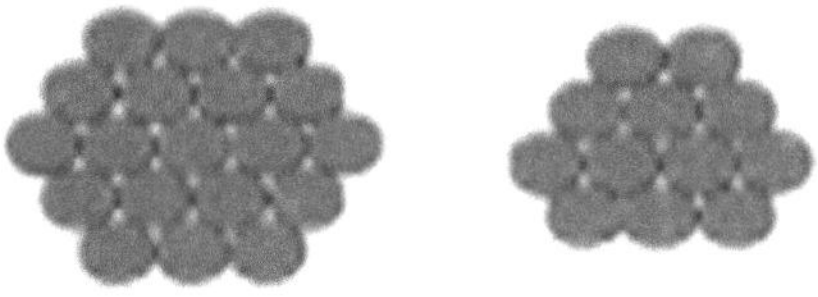

(a) (b)

**FIGURE 4.5** (a) 19 bottles and (b) 12 bottles.

Figure 4.6 depicts the typical arrangement of ecobricks; bottles are placed in such a manner that in the top layer, the bottle is placed down, while in the bottom layer, bottles are placed up. Any type of plastic waste that is flexible, like wrappers or plastic covers made of polystyrene, is used for making ecobricks, subjected to the condition that waste is washed and dried in the sunlight. Some of the plastics that cannot be recycled are dumped into the environment, which thereby causes a serious health hazard. In Ref. [45], the authors reported a timber-framed ecobrick building where they tightly bound bottles in a row-wise manner using chicken wires and attached them to a metal frame. The cement is applied on both sides of the walls made up of ecobricks, and the bottles are arranged to face the upward direction in one row and face the downward direction in the second row.

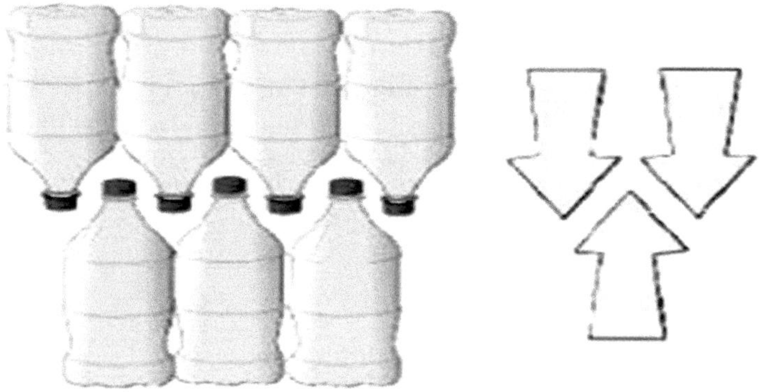

**FIGURE 4.6** A typical arrangement of ecobricks.

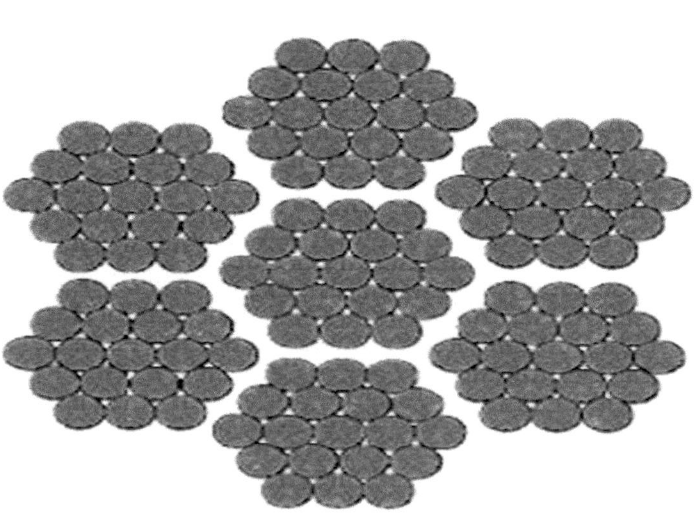

**FIGURE 4.7** A bigger ecobrick module made by combining smaller modules.

Figures 4.8–4.12 depict different structures made from ecobricks utilizing plastic waste. The description of each structure is also provided here. Five different structures (E1–E5) are represented here.

**FIGURE 4.8** Efficient utilization of ecobricks for outdoor applications.

**FIGURE 4.9** Bench surrounding a tree made up of ecobricks (E1).

**FIGURE 4.10** Sitting bench surrounding a tree made up of ecobricks (E2).

**FIGURE 4.11** Bench made up of ecobricks for placing pots in the garden (E3).

ORMA is a nongovernment organization in Kerala focusing on the efficient utilization of plastic waste for making ecobricks. The volunteers of this organization conduct several awareness programs and training programs for public, school, and college students on plastic waste management and the making of ecobricks. The organization follows the basic principles involved in the making of ecobricks from trash plastic.[44]

The current working plan of ORMA NGO is to make a community shelter in Sri Chitra Tirunal Institute for Medical Science and Technology, Trivandrum, Kerala, by using ecobricks. It was a joint initiative with the help of the Rotary Club, and it was planned to design the shelter with 2500 ecobricks.

**FIGURE 4.12** (a) Fish pond made up of ecobricks (E4), (b) Sitting bench made up of ecobricks (E5).

Figure 4.13 depicts the community shelter layout using ecobricks. The shelter will be a resting place for the public, and it will be a model demonstrating to the public the proficient utilization of plastic waste. This is an approved project from the host institute, and the Orma ecobrick organization in Trivandrum is leading the project. This project aims to utilize 2500 ecobricks.

The ecobricks were used extensively for building construction as well. Figures 4.14 and 4.15 represent the real-time building structures made in South Africa. The classrooms are constructed at 42 sqm utilizing ecobricks for the construction of walls.

**FIGURE 4.13** Community shelter layout using ecobricks.

**FIGURE 4.14** Classroom constructed using ecobricks in South Africa (front view).

## 4.4 CONCLUSIONS

Plastic waste is a threat to the ecosystem, and it is a major source of pollutants. This research work addresses the proficient utilization of plastic waste that is being generated in our day-to-day life activities. The plastic waste generated in domestic usage of products is being simply thrown away into this environment.

Ecobricks are made from this plastic waste and thus provide a simple remedy for waste management. The real-time uses of ecobricks are also highlighted in this chapter with real-time case studies in India and abroad. The ecobricks can be used for making products for indoor use as well as they can be deployed for construction in the outdoor environment. Many successful stories are there in the utilization of ecobricks. The outcome of this research work paves the way toward the simple and cost-effective management of plastic waste, thereby saving the environment and marching toward a sustainable circular green economy.

**FIGURE 4.15** Classroom constructed using ecobricks in South Africa (side view).

## KEYWORDS


- **plastic waste**
- **ecobricks**
- **environment**
- **PET bottle**
- **sustainable engineering**
- **fly ash**
- **geopolymer**
- **solid waste**

## REFERENCES


1. Subramanian, P. M. Plastics Recycling and Waste Management in the U.S. In *Resources, Conservation and Recycling*; 2000, vol 28; pp 253–263.
2. Petersen, M. In *Restoring Waste Management Following Disasters*, 2004 International Conference and Student Competition on Post-Disaster Reconstruction "Planing for Reconstruction," 2004; pp 22–23. http://citeseerx.ist.psu.edu/viewdoc/download?doi=10.1.1.523.3210 &rep=rep1&type=pdf
3. Bjerregaard, M.; Meekings, H. *Domestic and Refugee Camp Waste Management Collection & Disposal*. Oxfam GB, Oxfam Tech. Brief. notes; 2008**,** vol 15, 1–8. https://oxfamilibrary.openrepository.com/bitstream/handle/10546/126686/?sequence=5
4. Wang, T.; Kim, J.; Whelton, A. J. Management of Plastic Bottle and Filter Waste During the Large-Scale Flint Michigan Lead Contaminated Drinking Water Incident. In *Resources, Conservation & Recycling*, 2019, vol. 140; pp 115–124.
5. Worldwatch. Just One Word: Plastic; 2018 [Online]. http://www.worldwatch.org/just-one-word-plastics
6. Brooks, A. L.; Wang, S.; Jambeck, J. R. The Chinese Import Ban and Its Impact on Global Plastic Waste Trade. *Sci. Adv.* **2018,** *4,* 6. DOI: 10.1126/sciadv.aat0131
7. Akinyele, J. O.; Ajede, A. The Use of Granulated Plastic Waste in Structural Concrete. *Afr. J. Sci. Technol. Innov. Dev.* **2018,** *10* (2), 169–175. DOI: 10.1080/20421338.2017.1414111
8. Thorneycroft, J.; Orr, J.; Savoikar, P.; Ball, R. J. Performance of Structural Concrete with Recycled Plastic Waste as a Partial Replacement for Sand. *Constr. Build. Mater.* **2018,** *161,* 63–69.
9. Ge, Z.; Sun, R.; Zhang, K.; Gao, Z.; Li, P. Physical and Mechanical Properties of Mortar Using Waste Polyethylene Terephthalate Bottles. *Constr. Build. Mater.*, **2013,** *44,* 81–86.
10. Wang, R.; Meyer, C. Performance of Cement Mortar Made with Recycled High Impact Polystyrene. *Cem. Concr. Compos.* **2012,** *34,* 975–981.
11. Dinesh, S.; Dinesh, A.; Kirubakaran, K. Utilization of Waste Plastic in Manufacture of Bricks and Paver Blocks. *Int. J. Appl. Eng. Res.* **2016,** *11* (3), 364–368.
12. Taaffe, J.; O'Sullivan, S.; Rahman, M. E.; Pakrashi, V. Experimental Characterisation of Polyethylene Terephthalate (PET) Bottle Eco bricks. *Mater. Des.* **2014,** *60,* 50–56.
13. Muyen, Z.; Barna, T.; Hoque, M. Strength Properties of Plastic Bottle Bricks and Their Suitability as Construction Materials in Bangladesh. *Progress. Agric.* **2016,** *27* (3), 362–368.
14. Mokhtar, M.; Sahat, S.; Hamid, B.; Kaamin, M.; Kesot, M. J.; Wen, L. C.; Xin, L. Y.; Ling, N. P.; Lei, V. S. J. Application of Plastic Bottle as a Wall Structure for Green House. *ARPN J. Eng. Appl. Sci.* **2016,** *11* (12), 7617–7621.
15. Kim, B.; Wisniewski, J.; Baker, T.; Oyinlola, M. Behaviour of Sand-Filled Plastic Bottled Clay Panels for Sustainable Homes. *J. Build. Eng.* **2019**. DOI: https://doi.org/10.1016/j.jobe.2019.100895
16. Oyinlola, M.; Whitehead, T.; Abuzeinab, A.; Adefila, A.; Akinola, Y.; Anafi, F.; Mosugu, E. Bottle House: A Case Study of Transdisciplinary Research for Tackling Global Challenges. *Habitat Int.* **2018,** *79,* 18–29.
17. Rawat, A.S.; Kansal, R. PET Bottles as Sustainable Building Material: A Step Towards Green Building Construction. *J. Civil Eng. Environ. Technol.* **2014,** *1* (6), 1–3.
18. Kumar, S. A Study on Geopolymer Eco Bricks. *Open J. Civil Eng.* **2015,** *5,* 139–148.

19. Ahmed, H. A Study on Interlocking Brick Innovation Using Recycled Plastic Waste to Support the Acoustic and Thermal Performance of a Building. *ARTEKS: Jurnal Teknik Arsitektur*, **2021,** *6* (3), 335–348.
20. Raut. A.; Patel, M. S.; Jadhwar, N. B.; Khan, U.; Dhengare, S. W. Investigating the Application of Waste Plastic Bottle as a Construction Material: A Review. *J. Adv. Res. Mech. Civil Eng.* **2015,** *2* (3), 73–83.
21. Ariyani, D.; Warastuti, N.; Arini, R. N. Ecobrick Method to Reduce Plastic Waste in Tanjung Mekar Village, Karawang Regency. *Civil Environ. Sci. J.* **2020,** *4* (1), 22–29.
22. Kognole, R.; Shipkule, K.; Patil, M.; Patil, L.; Survase, U. Utilization of Plastic Waste for Making Plastic Bricks. *Int. J. Trend Sci. Res. Develop.* **2019,** *3,* 878–880.
23. Suresh Kumar, R.; Kumar, H.; Karthick, R.; Karthik, B. Experimental Investigation and Comparision of Plastic Bricks with Existing Brick Materials. *Int. J. Eng. Appl. Sci. Technol.* **2020,** *4* (12), 2455–2143, 576–588.
24. Ascencio, J. G.; Fuentes, N.; Britto, T. S. Eco Bricks: A Strategy for the Use of Wastewater Biosolids. *Contemp. Eng. Sci.* **2018,** *11* (87), 4321–4328.
25. Bhushaiah, R.; Mohammad, S.; Rao, D. S. Study of Plastic Bricks Made from Waste Plastic. *J. Eng. Technol.* **2019,** *6* (4), 6.
26. Sharma, H. Innovative and Sustainable Application of PET Bottle a Green Construction Overview. *Indian J. Sci. Technol.* **2017,** *10* (16), 1–6.
27. Wardani, F.; Khotimah, N. Making Eco bricks as a Solution to Environmental Problems through Empowering Creative Children: A Case Study in Baruga District, Kendari City. *Int. J. Sci. Soc.* **2021,** *3* (2), 214–221.
28. Jani, M.; Thakur, A. S. Plastic: A Menace to the Environment. *Agric. Environ. E News Lett.* **2021,** *2* (2).
29. Aravindhan, B.; Arniha, J.; Ganeshkumar, S.; Gayathri, C.; Mohanasundari, S. Experimental Study On Eco-Blac Bricks. *Synthesis* **2019,** *6* (03).
30. Wardani, F.; Khotimah, N. Making Eco bricks as a Solution to Environmental Problems through Empowering Creative Children: A Case Study in Baruga District, Kendari City. *Int. J. Sci. Soc.* **2021,** *3* (2), 214–221.
31. Ogundairo, T. O.; Olukanni, D. O.; Akinwumi, I. I.; Adegoke, D. D. In A Review on Plastic Waste as Sustainable Resource in Civil Engineering Applications, *IOP Conference Series: Materials Science and Engineering 2021 Mar 1*; IOP Publishing, Vol. 1036 (1), p 012019.
32. Ali, R.; Marsi, N.; Kamal, N. F.; Muhamad, M. S.; Sunar, N. M.; Harun, H.; Hamid, N. H.; Hamidon, N. A Study on the Characteristic of an eco-Brick as a Replacement to the Conventional Brick. *Prog. Eng. Appl. Technol.* **2020,** *1* (1), 22–29.
33. Sander, Z. R. *Fire Behaviour of Plastic Bottle Eco Bricks as an Infill Building Material.* Doctoral Dissertation, Stellenbosch: Stellenbosch University.
34. Maldonado, A.; Corvalan, A.; Cohenca, D.; Monteiro, M. Setting Time of Ecological Bricks with Different Percentage PET. *KnE Eng.* **2018,** 354–362.
35. Edike, U. E.; Ameh, O. J.; Dada, M. O. Production and Optimization of Eco Bricks. *J. Clean. Prod.* **2020,** *266,* 121640.
36. Saleh, A. M.; Rahmat, M. N.; Ismail, N. In *SWPS ECO Bricks: Development of Sustainable Brick Utilising Solid Waste Fly Ash and Paint Sludge*, IOP Conference Series: Earth and Environmental Science 2021 Feb 1, IOP Publishing, Vol. 641 (1), p 012025.
37. Hardeniya, K.; Mudgal, B. P.; Kumar, P. Study and Properties of Geopolymer Eco Bricks. *United Int. J. Eng. Sci.* **2022,** 3 (2).

38. Adiyanto, O.; Mohamad, E.; Abd Razak, J. Systematic Review of Plastic Waste as Eco-Friendly Aggregate for Sustainable Construction. *Int. J. Sustain. Constr. Eng. Technol.* **2022,** *13* (2):243–257.
39. Puri, V.; Kumar, S.; Grover, K.; Sharma, M. In *Development of Eco-Friendly Bricks for Sustainable Construction,* IOP Conference Series: Materials Science and Engineering 2022 Jul 1, IOP Publishing, Vol. 1248 (1), p 012109.
40. Pradeep, L.; Dash, S. P.; Pati, D. J.; Boby, N. M. Determining the Feasibility of Using PET Bottles as Construction Material in Urban Context. *Mater. Today: Proc.* **2022,** *60,* 384–393.
41. Singh, E. J.; Singh, N. R. Eco Bricks—An Effective Technique to Manage Plastic Waste at Home. *Indian J. Environ. Sci.* **2022,** *26* (2):61–64.
42. Lim, M. C.; Ali, R.; Marsi, N. A Comparison of Properties between Eco-Brick and Lightweight Brick by Using SolidWorks Software. *Progress Eng. Appl. Technol.* **2022,** *3* (1), 104–111.
43. Yen, C. L.; Kamarazaly, M. A.; Tatt, S. L.; Hashim, N.; Ling, S. C.; Yaakob, A. M. In *The Potential of Plastic Waste as Building Material*, Proceedings of the 5th International Conference on Sustainable Civil Engineering Structures and Construction Materials; 2022. Springer, Singapore, pp 1441–1464.
44. https://www.ecobricks.org
45. https://bottleschools.org

# CHAPTER 5

# Attitudes and Opinions on Ethics Position for AI in Healthcare

VIJAY ANANT ATHAVALE[1], HIMANSHU JAIN[2], TRIWIYANTO[3], and SARI LUTHFIYAH[4]

[1]*Walchand Institute of Technology, Solapur, Maharashtra, India*

[2]*Panipat Institute of Engineering & Technology, Panipat, Haryana, India*

[3]*Department of Medical Electronics Technology, Health Polytechnic Ministry of Health Surabaya, Indonesia*

[4]*Department of Medical Electronics Technology, Health Polytechnic Ministry of Health Surabaya, Indonesia*

## ABSTRACT

Artificial intelligence (AI) in healthcare is a vibrant topic that many people and experts have different opinions about. Due to different norms and cultures, the usage and opinions about AI in healthcare differ around the world. Consequently, ethical questions regarding AI in healthcare are complex. AI in healthcare is a sensitive subject because of the delicate nature of healthcare. In this chapter, we address two research questions. The first research question is: How does the public think that decision-making on ethical issues within AI in healthcare should be handled? The second research question is: Is the public prepared to hand over decision-making in different scenarios in healthcare to artificial intelligence? Through these questions, we aim to understand more about public opinion rather than the experts and organizations working in this area. This chapter was motivated by the lack of research on the general public in this matter. Therefore, a survey was created

Management for Sustainable Development: Integrating Social, Economic, and Environmental Goals. Vishal Jain & Amit Mittal (Eds.)

to collect data about this subject. The data collected through the survey led to a result. Some of the findings were that the general public wants the government to decide on ethical issues within AI in healthcare. Furthermore, respondents were skeptical about giving all the decision-making to AI in most of the given scenarios in the survey. This chapter answers these questions and gives insight into the general public's opinions regarding ethical issues with AI in healthcare.

## 5.1 INTRODUCTION

Developments in artificial intelligence (AI) and digitalization continue to be extensive in society. This means that AI is making many changes in many fundamental parts of society one of them is healthcare. With the development that society's digitalization entails, it is natural to explore the possibilities that today and the AI of the future can offer to the healthcare system. Public opinion about this is therefore becoming increasingly important to investigate because AI is something that is developing very fast. Throughout the ages, different types of perspectives and approaches have been used to describe the concept of AI. Today, many people think of different things, and therefore, it is natural that this study needs to define what we mean when we talk about AI. Here, the meaning will be something that is autonomous, adaptable and that can interact with others—whether it is another AI or humans. This can involve algorithms, machine learning, robots, and various forms of systems.

Healthcare itself, and changes that take place in this area affect the population. Therefore, it is worth examining what the public thinks about changes that are taking place and that may take place in the future in this area. Thus, this study mainly relates to what the public thinks about certain types of ethical issues concerning AI and its introduction into Indian healthcare. By examining this, the opinions of the Indian public are shown, where there has previously been a lack of research. Sociocultural groups have different values and norms and therefore, it is interesting to examine India in particular to see the public's different opinions rather than just opinions from experts in the field. Since the sociological aspect of the study focuses on the public and its opinions, it is natural that the work is based on the sociological perspective when describing what AI means. In this work, the starting point for what AI is, will also be based on the assumption that what concerns our position of AI is autonomous, adaptable and can interact.[1–3]

## 5.2 PURPOSE AND ISSUES

This study aims to investigate how the public thinks about how ethical/moral issues should be taken into account regarding AI in healthcare. This study thus wants to contribute with an increased understanding of how the public's attitude relates to ethical issues linked to AI in healthcare. This study may contribute for the improvement in the existing knowledge about the public's perception and attitude toward the subject concerned. This is considered important because in a democratic country, it is important what the public thinks about public positions. The insight is also relevant when it comes to understanding the extent of the acceptance of AI and which parts of resistance can occur during an introduction.

This purpose has resulted in two issues:

- How does the public think that decision-making on ethical issues within AI in healthcare should be handled?
- Is the public prepared to hand over decision-making in healthcare scenarios to AI?

## 5.3 RELATED RESEARCH/SURVEY OF LITERATURE

This section presents previous as well as related research to the study. The related research concerns different definitions of AI and how AI is used in healthcare in the USA, China, and India. It also touches upon the public's ethical view of AI based on sociocultural differences and ethical approaches.

### *5.3.1 WHAT IS AI?*

Through the ages, different perspectives have been used to describe what AI is. When people today hear the words AI, everyone thinks of different things. Many different definitions are used to describe different types of AI, but there are also different views on what it actually consists of. This leads to a need to define what is meant by AI in this work. Some of the approaches that can be used in the description of AI are the starting point of Computer Science.[1,4] This approach sees AI as a way to build smart systems in a way that exhibits qualities that we humans associate with intelligence. By building these systems, this perspective believes that we can more easily solve problems in the world. The inclusion of the perspective of computer science makes one interested not only in how the systems should be built but also in what kind of computational mechanisms are required to imitate intelligent behavior.

Another perspective that Dignum[1,5,6] describes is the philosophical perspective. Here, the focus shifts from how this type of system can be built to why and how these systems are built. This perspective is used, for example, to answer questions such as what it means for a machine to act intelligently and how this is distinguished from human intelligence. Another perspective that can imply a starting point is a sociological perspective. Here, issues dealing with human behavior were examined. To start, two ways of understanding human behavior, and two concepts are used. These concepts are agent and structure. In this context, the term agent means to describe someone/something who has the ability to act independently and be able to make free decisions. The concept of structure is referred to as a way of seeing how choices are limited and made possible due to surrounding arrangements and environment.[7,8] To explain the concept of AI, one can start by seeing AI as an agent and from there try to explain what the concept means. An agent becomes an agent when it is autonomous and has adaptability and an opportunity to interact with other agents —whether they are artificial or human.[9–11] Autonomy creates opportunities for the agent to act on its own in its decided environment to solve the problem it is created to do. There are different levels of autonomy that AI can have. The core of an agent's adaptability is that it is aware of its surroundings and can make decisions based on this. By making appropriate decisions based on their surroundings, future occurrences can change into something better. This includes machine learning and algorithms that learn from large amounts of data. An agent can interact with other AI or people is a big part of how AI is developed and used. By combining intelligence, meaningful decisions can be made; this type of combination also provides the opportunity to utilize the best in both humans and AI. This interaction also leads to both parties being unintentionally affected on some level. This in turn leads to both parties modifying their actions because of their partner. All of these elements are cornerstones of what defines AI.[1,12]

### 5.3.2 HOW IS AI USED IN HEALTHCARE IN DIFFERENT COUNTRIES?

In China, the healthcare sector is one the sector which has invested the most in new technology. Here, AI is used in many ways and is seen as a major potential improvement in healthcare. AI is used to take medical records, design treatment plans and perform repetitive work.[3,13–15] A clear example of the type of AI that is integrated is a system called IBM Watson. This system is used to answer questions from people seeking care and to construct treatment plans based on relevant medical literature. An example of this is people who need treatments for various forms of cancer. The system assists doctors in decisions regarding various care matters with a huge knowledge bank of medical literature, treatment guidelines, clinical trials, previous medical records data and treatment history of similar patients. The database is updated weekly and the more the system is used, the more it learns to be more accurate and improved for each patient it treats. Patients can choose whether they think the doctor should use Watson in their own treatment. In 2017, Watson was used in 42 public hospitals in China.[13,16,17] Something that has been experienced when using IBM Watson in China is that there is a certain problem with how the system has been trained before when it was created. IBM Watson was created in the USA and was therefore trained according to American patient files. This creates difficulties in use.

In the US, robots are also used in different ways. There are robots that perform surgery. However, these are always observed by a human doctor and almost never operate on themselves. In gynecological and head and neck surgeries, there are self-propelled robotic surgeons. AI is also used in most other areas of the United States, such as performing administrative tasks. The phasing out of human intervention in healthcare, and how many jobs are disappearing due to AI are the biggest issues being discussed in the United States. Ethical issues are also something that many see as a test regarding AI in healthcare.[18,19]

In Sweden's healthcare, there is a lot of research on AI. Large resources are used to see what opportunities there are for the use of AI in healthcare in different ways and in different departments[20] shows that some of the research and development projects that are taking place now will lead to increased use of AI support in healthcare in the near future. Right now, AI is mainly used in areas, such as radiology, cardiology, dermatology, digital pathology, and laboratory analyzes. AI is used here to be able to diagnose and act as decision support for staff in healthcare.-During the COVID-19 AI was used in India and in several other counties for a variety of tasks, including early COVID-19 identification, patient assistance, and drug repurposing.[21–23]

The research and use of AI that takes place have several different things that it should relate to. Financial aspects, quality of care, information security and ethical issues are areas that must be taken into account in order for the use and research on AI to go right here according to the requirements that exist. What it is about when it comes to financial aspects is, among other things, that the demonstrated AI should make healthcare more efficient, which in turn creates positive economic effects through more efficient work. The quality of care and how it is affected by the use of AI is something that should be considered. The quality of care increases if one takes advantage of the individual benefits of people and machines, then people are better at seeing the big picture and machines are generally better at performing specific tasks. Here, some researchers also describe how the quality of care increases due to the subjectivity of assessments in healthcare being given less space when AI is used. Information security is about AI being able to be used to protect healthcare and patient information from being disseminated to other actors, by, among other things, identifying cyber-attacks.

The ethical aspects are important to identify in order to be able to implement AI in healthcare. Here, the work is very much about the large amounts of data that AI develops through must not be discriminatory or non-representative of the designated target group. Another thing that is important ethically is how transparent algorithms are around decision-making. This is due to the ethical difficulties that arise if healthcare professionals do not understand how an algorithm has arrived at a decision and what grounds on which that decision is based. Many players in healthcare are working toward a more integrated digital and physical care where AI has an important place. This integration is important for healthcare to be able to function as a whole.

### *5.3.3 THE PUBLIC'S ETHICAL VIEW OF AI—SOCIOCULTURAL DIFFERENCES*

Attitudes toward AI look different depending on which groups and countries one chooses to consider. This is because values around ethics and morality often appear different in different sociocultural groups. Here is how different sociocultural differences can be expressed regarding AI in healthcare and how this affects what people think about this area. However, there is no related research in this area for India. In a study from the United States[24] regarding public attitudes and confidence in the use of AI in healthcare during COVID-19, the study focused on four groups. These groups are African Americans, Hispanics, Southeast Asians, and Native Americans. Common to the four study groups was that skepticism, and concerns were expressed about the possible negative effects of AI. The concern that was expressed is based on not knowing who is responsible for this technology and whether the companies' interest and motivation over this technology are really in line with society's interest. There are further concerns that racial differences would be created during how the technology would be designed and distributed. Other concerns expressed were that AI would widen the digital divide. The study also showed a mutual reflection between the groups where they felt that there is an increased need for inclusion of different voices from society in the development and distribution of AI in healthcare. Furthermore, concerns were expressed that AI in healthcare could lead to an increase in the digital divide. Where the term digital divide aims to describe the distance between those who adopt new technology compared with those who do not have access to or sufficient knowledge to use digital technology.[25] Because it can put more pressure on the public to have access to the right understanding and knowledge to feel safe with AI in healthcare.[24] Not having enough knowledge about something or that something feels foreign can make human's experience full of with fear and anxiety. For example, this is because when people do not have enough knowledge in a certain subject that can arouse negative emotions—then fear arises when the negative aspects associated with this subject become stronger. For example, it can be a fear that it will affect one's body negatively.[26,27]

Finally, the study showed that the participants also have some positive attitudes toward technology and AI. Among other things, a positive attitude was expressed toward the speed and how safely AI can be used to establish diagnoses and treatments. Also that there were negative attitudes toward AI regarding the risk of racial differences may enter the design. But the study also showed that some of the participants believed that AI gives hope that discrimination against patients in care can be reduced. Furthermore, a positive attitude was expressed toward implementing AI in healthcare regarding the possibility of being able to eliminate language barriers.[24]

The Swedish public has a very high level of confidence in the government and the public sector compared with many other countries. This is relevant as Sweden has a good public health service. This can be compared with the United States, where only 25.1% considered themselves to have quite a lot of confidence in the US government. The survey also showed that the public in China has a lot of confidence in the government, where 47% considered themselves to have quite a lot of confidence. In India, only 10.42% showed confidence in the government and public sector health service system.

This study shows that the trust and confidence of the public in the government can vary greatly in different countries. The reasons for this are several, and it also affects the public's view of the work and decisions that governments carry out in each country.

### 5.3.4 ETHICAL APPROACHES

When it comes to ethical dilemmas or difficult ethical decisions, the person's norms are reflected, which means that the decisions in question can be very different from each other even though it is about the same situation.[1] The discussions about what AI's ethical approaches should look like are thus very extensive. This is because the technology in AI is constantly increasing its intelligence, which means that it puts pressure on its competence and responsibility and that it increases expectations of what the technology should perform for more complex tasks. AI must therefore understand and act according to moral and ethical approaches.

Organizations like WHO and the EU are involved in the debate about which guidelines AI should follow. These organizations thus also affect the development and implementation of AI in any country. According to the European Commission's expert group on AI (HLEG), the development of AI in healthcare should reflect the four principles of medical ethics as much as possible. The specific principles developed for AI consist of respect for human autonomy, prevention of harm, justice and being explicable. In contrast, there are also some existing initiatives for how AI should relate to ethics in healthcare that have encountered some difficulties.[28] This is because many initiatives are sponsored by companies. These initiatives are characterized as signaling goodness, where the ethical initiatives for AI have been intended to strengthen their own position rather than to create a more abstract debate. In this way, the regulation of AI has been delayed. This has led to discussions about principles in AI ethics that from some quarters can be considered vague, and that there is usually a lack of focus on different areas of tension such as integrity and justice.[9,28]

WHO states that AI in healthcare can contribute to both increased accuracy and improve the speed of diagnosis and treatment. The WHO is also in favor of AI to the extent that it can be used to bridge gaps in access to health services and care in resource-poor countries and in rural communities. Furthermore, the WHO warns of the risk of overestimating the benefits of AI in healthcare, especially as they believe that there may be a risk that the development of AI may take place at the expense of the investments that are otherwise used to achieve universal health coverage of healthcare in the world. The concerns expressed by the WHO in the report are also based on the challenges and risks posed by AI in healthcare entails. This includes, among other things, the risk of lack of cyber security, algorithms with encoded prejudices, unethical collection and use of health data. There is therefore a fear that unregulated use of AI in healthcare may subordinate patients' and society's rights under the strong commercial interests of technology companies. In addition to this, the unregulated use of AI also creates a risk of performing surveillance and social control. To avoid this, the WHO therefore believes that governments, together with designers and suppliers, must work based on more principles and laws to ensure that ethics and human rights are in focus in both the development and implementation of AI in healthcare. Furthermore, the WHO has presented six principles as a basis for regulating AI and its governance, which are respect for human autonomy, promoting human security and well-being and following the public interest, ensuring transparency, comprehensibility and explainability, that it should be based on responsibility to ensure participation and justice and that AI should be promoted as responsive and sustainable. Based on these principles, there is hope that both the development and implementation of AI in healthcare will be transparent and regulated in such a way as to be able to maximize its benefits. In this way, the WHO believes that the principles that can guide future work with AI will be used for the benefit of the public.

Thus, there is extensive work within and between large organizations with guidelines for the use and development of AI in healthcare. Common to the WHO's and EU's guidelines and principles that have been developed is to ensure that AI in healthcare is used in both a transparent and regulated manner to ensure use.

## 5.4 METHOD

This chapter describes the method used to gather the empirical data in this study. The survey has been the primary source of empirical data. To present the questionnaire, we took the help of two preparatory interviews and related research. The questionnaire was completed and when an adequate amount of answers had been collected, data analyzes were performed using the tests shown in the figure below. The data analysis then forms the basis for the Results chapter. This chapter describes each part that is part of our method.

### *5.4.1 PREPARATORY INTERVIEWS*

In this study, part of the data collection consisted of two semi-structured interviews. The choice to conduct the interviews in a semi-structured form was based on the desire to gain a deeper understanding of the work and handling of ethical issues in the development and implementation of AI in healthcare in India. Together with the interview and the previous research, it provided the basis for the creation of the study's questionnaire and further analysis. The second interview also provided relevant background information that we took with us in this study. The interview guide was therefore formulated with neutral and open questions. In addition to contributing to a clearer picture of the respondent's perspective, open-ended questions prevent the interview from leading in any specific direction. On the other hand, this most likely results in different respondents being able to perceive and interpret the questions in different ways. However, this does not have to be considered as something negative, as it can lead to new interesting topics and perspectives.[29] This was done when the interviewees were experts in the subject, and we therefore wanted them to be able to speak freely. The selection for the two interviews that took place to gather information for this completed study was based on a snowball selection. This has been done through contacts that have guided us to relevant people to interview who are researching and working with AI linked to healthcare. The opportunity to use a snowball selection has contributed with significant benefit as we have received a lot of information and facts. To analyze the data collected from the interviews, they were transcribed. This has helped us in designing our survey and has given us a broader understanding of the subject.

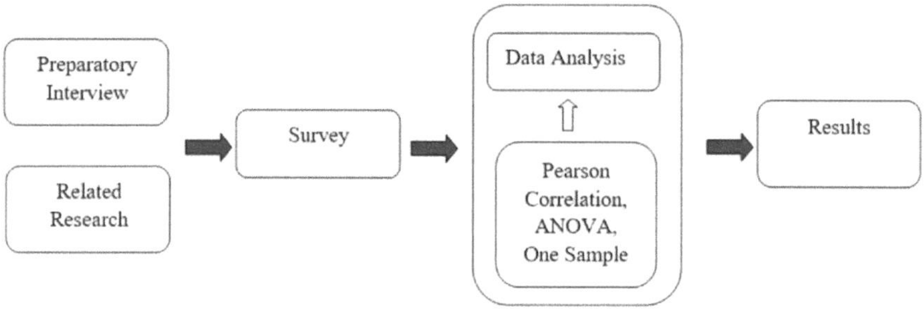


**FIGURE 5.1** Descriptive figure of the method used.

### *5.4.2 SURVEY*

The main part of collecting data for the study consisted of a survey. This decision was based on the desire to reach as many people as possible in order to create a broader perception and understanding. The material we collected from the previous interviews determined the type of questions that should be asked and what they should be about.

The survey was created in Microsoft Forms. Compared with the semi-structured interviews conducted, this form of data collection is completely standardized. This means that the questions have been asked to all respondents in exactly the same way. Because the survey consisted of a number of multi-answer alternatives and scales to be based on, the answers are to some extent predefined. The survey that was conducted therefore has a high level of structured character. In addition to this, the survey also consisted of a number of free text questions in order to give the respondents the opportunity to express thoughts linked to the questions. In this way, the opportunity is also created to capture interesting answers and reflections that would otherwise have been missed.[30]

The questions were first about the age and gender of the respondents. Thereafter, the respondents were asked to answer how much knowledge they think they have about AI. Then they answered questions about how comprehensive AI should be in Indian healthcare. After this, they had to answer various questions about who should decide on AI in healthcare and indicate which scenarios where they believe that AI can be used/not used in healthcare. Surveys generally cover a very wide range of factors and causes, as opposed to, for example, interviews and experiments.[31] This is rewarding as we want to answer two questions from the public's perspective in this study.

#### *5.4.2.1 SELECTION OF RESPONDENTS*

The selection of respondents who answered the survey was based on the desire to reach as wide an audience as possible, as we want many respondents of all possible ages. To do this, the survey has been published on various social media platforms (Instagram and Facebook), and distributed via e-mail. This was done when the expectation was to reach many younger people through social media, and many older people via e-mail. The selection of respondents via the survey can be seen as a convenient selection, as we have chosen to try to reach many people in different age groups, via social media that we already have and contacts that have already been created.[32] The questionnaire was available to answer for 2 weeks. About 84 people responded to the survey. In this study, the respondents from the survey are referred to as "Respondents 1–84."

#### *5.4.2.2 DATA ANALYSIS*

Initially, in the data analysis of the questionnaire study, data were presented in an excel document. At this stage of the analysis, the data were cleaned and converted to an analyzable format. In order to continue to analyze and visualize the data, the tool SPSS was used. With the help of the tool SPSS functions, the data were transformed and concretized in order to make different values visible. In this way, statistical analyses of the data were performed.

The data analyses we chose to perform were above the study's mean value, significance, and correlations. This was performed using two different mean value tests, ANOVA, and one sample t-test. We used ANOVA to compare the groups that responded to the survey. Here, two mean values have been compared for gender distribution and how to answer the scale questions. One sample t-test was used to see if the mean was significant. Mean value analysis was performed on the scale questions included in the survey to see what the respondents answered on average to each question. Here, the significance of the mean values was also analyzed. Then Pearson's Correlation was used to see correlations between the respondents' knowledge of AI and how they answered the questionnaires. For the free text questions, the answers are categorized and then we developed key concepts. Using the key concepts, we calculated the number of answers per concept.

### *5.4.3 ETHICS*

At the beginning of the questionnaire and at the start of the interviews, the respondents were informed about the research principles that this study follows. A study must follow different research principles in order to be able to collect data from different individuals. These principles are based on four main requirements that exist to protect individuals. These requirements consist of consent, information, confidentiality, and use requirements. The consent requirement is based on individuals participating in the data collection giving consent on, how and under what conditions they want to participate. They must also be informed that their participation or non-participation will not have consequences for the participant. The information requirement means that those who contribute to the study must be informed about the study, why they are participating, that their participation is voluntary and that participation can be terminated whenever they want. The confidentiality requirement is based on those who are responsible for data collection and the study having a duty of confidentiality and responsibility for the material from the data collection being stored confidentially. The use requirement means that information about the participants may under no circumstances be used for any purpose other than scientific and it must not affect those who participated.

Sohlberg and Sohlberg[31] describe how it is relevant to relate to good research practice. This is done by being transparent about methods and results, truthful and by striving to conduct research without harming other people, animals, or the environment. In the survey, the respondents have been informed about this, as it appears that they are completely anonymous in their answers to the survey. They have also been informed that the answers from the survey are only used in this study, and that their participation is voluntary and that it can be terminated at any time. The respondent interviewed was also informed of this orally, before the interview began. These respondents have also received a form explaining about what information will be stored, how long it will be stored and their anonymity and what the collected data will be used for.

### *5.4.4 METHOD DISCUSSION*

Based on the purpose of the study, the method has been mainly characterized by a quantitative approach. This method was chosen because it seemed appropriate to use a quantitative method to be able to collect attitudes from a large number of individuals. Therefore, a study in the form of survey appeared to be an obvious choice. In this way, we easily received comparable answers from many different individuals, unlike if we conducted interviews. Through the quantitative analysis, we have been able to calculate a result. But, the questions in the quantitative analysis are fixed and very specific, which to some extent limits the respondents' information in terms of content.[30]

In order to still be able to take part in the respondents' feelings and reasoning, the questionnaire study was provided with a number of free text questions. In order to be able to access even more data, and above all, qualitative ones, interviews would have been an appropriate approach. In the end, this is no longer possible due to the current time limit. The alternative with interviews was therefore chosen in order to be able to focus entirely on the survey study. Continuing to be able to create an even more interesting picture of the respondents, a question about the profession would have been a good way. In this way, a more in-depth comparison and understanding could possibly have been created by the respondents' answers. Despite this, we believe that the study has a high validity as it answers the purpose and the questions. The reliability can also be considered high as no random measurement errors have occurred. At the same time, reliability can be discussed because the questions in the survey are of a subjective nature, which means that the respondents' answers are linked strongly to their own thoughts and feelings.

Furthermore, in order to gain access to more information on the subject, an interview was conducted with an experienced researcher on this subject. The information was then used as a basis for the preparation of the questionnaire questions. During our data handling, we lost a total of three answers from two different questions. This was a small loss that made us choose to keep the questions. This is because we felt that the result was not overly affected by the lost data. Due to the current time limit, the collection of evidence was chosen to be limited to a questionnaire study.

Due to the opportunity that has existed to distribute the survey, there is a relatively large chance that the people who responded to the survey belong to approximately the same sociocultural group. This is because the methods used to disseminate the survey reach people who are in a relative proximity to us or the contacts we have. This may have led to the following difficulties in reaching a broad and large target group that includes more sociocultural groups. The majority of the respondents who answered the survey belong to the age group 20 to 29 years. This can lead to a somewhat misleading image of the public as those in the other age groups do not receive as much representation. Since we discovered during the course of the work that this topic is very much about how much trust and confidence individuals have in authorities and organizations, it would have been appropriate to include more questions about the respondents' trust in institutions/the state. This is something we should also have discussed together with the experts we interviewed. This could have contributed to a better analysis.

Finally, there was a clearer and more specific demarcation within AI in order to be able to more clearly present the public's opinions and attitudes about this in Indian healthcare. Due to the broad name of AI in the study, it creates the risk that it becomes more difficult to perceive the type of AI that it is actually about. This makes it possible to question whether this study deals with AI as such or whether it is also about expert systems in healthcare that are rule-based.

## 5.5 RESULTS AND ANALYSIS

The following chapters report and analyze the results of the survey. To facilitate the compilation of the results, subheadings have been made where more questions that are designed in the same way are summarized under each heading. Then the analysis made in SPSS is shown under a heading and after this comes an in-depth analysis of the survey results.

### 5.5.1 PARTICIPANTS

**TABLE 5.1** Age Distribution Among Respondents.

| Age group | No. of respondents |
|---|---|
| 16–19 years | 2 |
| 20–29 years | 42 |
| 30–39 years | 8 |
| 40–49 years | 15 |
| 50–59 years | 15 |
| 60–69 years | 2 |
| 70–79 years | 0 |

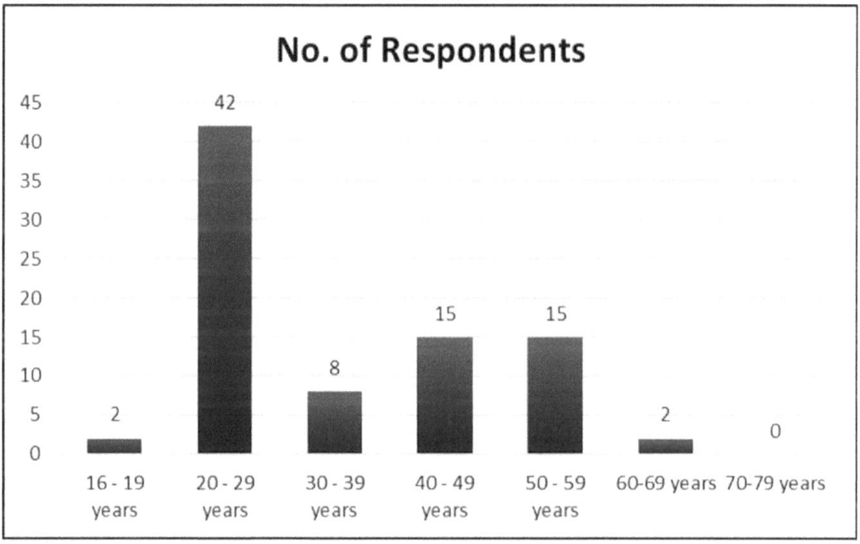


**FIGURE 5.2** Age distribution among respondents.

The questionnaire was answered by 84 unique respondents (52 women, 32 men). The respondents were then asked to indicate the age group to which they belong between 16 and 19 to 70 and 79 years. There, two respondents stated that they were part of the age group 16 to 19 years. The largest age group consisted of respondents between 20 and 29 years. The second largest age groups consisted of respondents in the age range 40–49 and 50–59 years. See the remaining age groups in the table above. More women than men responded to the survey.

**TABLE 5.2** Distribution of Knowledge about AI Among Respondents in Percentage Form.

| How much knowledge do you think you have about AI? | Respondents (Percent) |
|---|---|
| 1- No Knowledge | 23.80% |
| 2- Little Knowledge | 56.00% |
| 3- Moderate Knowledge | 17.90% |
| 4- Great Knowledge | 2.40% |

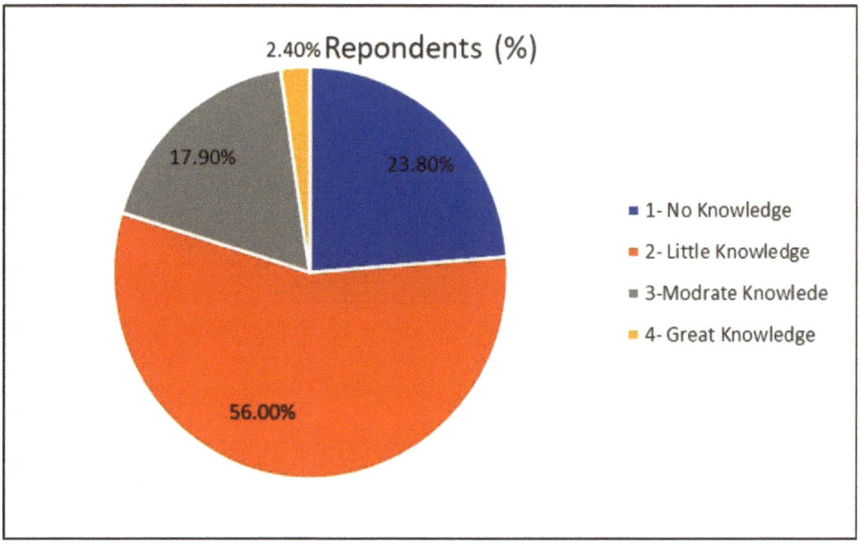


**FIGURE 5.3** Distribution of knowledge about AI among respondents in percentage form.

After this, the respondents had to answer a question regarding their own knowledge of AI. This question was answered on a scale from 1 to 4. The rating 1 was considered no knowledge and 4 was considered a great knowledge. About 23.8% of the respondents answered that they do not possess any previous knowledge of AI. And 56% of the respondents thought they had some knowledge of AI. About 17.9% of the respondents claimed that they had quite a lot of knowledge about AI. And 2.4% of the respondents considered that they had extensive knowledge of AI. No differences in the level of knowledge could be found (ANOVA). Most of the participants were between 20 and 29 years old and the majority had low or very low knowledge of AI. Most respondents chose option 2 on a scale of 1–4 regarding how much knowledge they thought they had about AI.

### *5.5.2 HOW COMPREHENSIVE SHOULD AI BE IN INDIAN HEALTHCARE?*

To present the result, the mean value will be presented from the questions that have scales. The scale that has been used is 1–4, where 1 means that you think it is not ethically correct and 4 means that you think it is ethically correct. To see the survey in its entirety.

**TABLE 5.3** Mean Values of the Respondents' Answers to the Questions.

| S. no. | Question | Mean |
|---|---|---|
| 1. | How integrated do you think AI should be in Indian healthcare? | 2.53 |
| 2. | How much independence and opportunity do you make your own decisions that artificial intelligence should have in Indian healthcare? | 2.51 |
| 3. | Do you think it is ethically correct for a system to be able to independently decide whether a patient should have access to treatment or not? | 1.82 |
| 4. | Do you think it is ethically correct to have a surgical robot perform an operation independently? | 2.38 |
| 5. | Do you think it is possible to decide what artificial intelligence should be considered ethically correct, for example in the case of very serious complications during an operation? | 2.01 |

Here we see the different averages that are calculated from what the respondents have answered for each question. Overall, these averages are more negative than positive, some of which are more in a neutral direction. Most positivity from the respondents was directed at how integrated AI should be in Indian healthcare (m = 2.53). The participants were also positive that it is ethically correct to let a surgical robot carry out an operation independently (m = 2.38). The respondents generally considered that it is not ethically correct for an AI system to be able to independently decide whether a patient should have access to treatment or not (m = 1.82). The respondents also generally believe that it is difficult to decide what AI should consider be ethically correct (m = 2.01). They also considered that AI should not have such a great deal of independence and the opportunity to make its own decisions in healthcare (m = 2.1). Further, on the question "If you had to undergo surgery yourself, would you be willing to hand over the operation and decision-making to a surgical robot without human intervention other than observation?" About 55% of the respondents answered no and 45% of the respondents answered yes.

Based on these responses from the respondents, it is possible to deduce certain negativity toward AI rather than positivity. The different averages are relatively even. The average value was highest in the question of how integrated AI should be in Indian healthcare. Thereafter, the mean value was the third highest in that it is ethically correct to have a surgical robot independently perform an operation. This means that the respondents are most accepting of this in comparison with, for example, that a system should be able to independently decide whether a patient should have access to treatment or not.

In the survey, the respondents were given the opportunity to submit other views and opinions. Here, they mainly expressed opinions on the extent to which it is acceptable to hand over responsibility to AI and in which areas this is appropriate.

> *"AI can work as a complement to doctors, etc., but does not believe that you alone can rely on AI"*—Respondent 2

> *"I think AI in healthcare is the right way to go. The most important thing is how to programs and instruct AI to act."*—Respondent 17

Some respondents were generally skeptical about the implementation of AI in Indian healthcare.

> *"I myself who have undergone most operations with various complications could never imagine anything worse than if it had been performed by a robot."*—Respondent 11

> *"That you have to watch with the utmost care so that AI does not get a too big area of responsibility"*—Respondent 5

The mean value was lowest in the question of whether it is ethically correct for a system to be able to independently decide whether a patient should receive treatment or not. This means that the respondents were most negative about handing over this responsibility to AI. Respondent 11 expresses strong opposition to surgical robots due to her previous experience in healthcare. Tushar is the only one of the respondents who describes his previous experience and links it to what it could have looked like if AI was involved.

#### *5.5.2.1 CORRELATION BETWEEN BACKGROUND KNOWLEDGE AND ATTITUDES*

There was also a correlation here between the respondents' knowledge of AI and the question "Do you think it is ethically correct to have a surgical robot perform an operation independently?" However, this correlation was lower and not as significant as the previously mentioned one. The questions correlated with each other in two cases, which is to be expected as they concern the same subject. There are no significant differences between the answers of the different sex among the scale questions (ANOVA). What is shown here is that the respondents who considered that they had higher knowledge of AI were those who thought that AI should be more integrated into Indian healthcare. This was at the same time as those who considered themselves to have lower knowledge of AI felt that AI would be less integrated into healthcare. Through this correlation, you can then see that the more you know about AI, the more you want it to have a greater integration.

**TABLE 5.4** Correlation between Background Knowledge and Attitudes.

| | **How much knowledge about AI?** | | |
|---|---|---|---|
| | **Pearson correlation** | **Sig. (2-tailed)** | **N** |
| How much knowledge about AI? | 1 | | 84 |
| Do you think it is ethically correct for a system to be able to independently decide whether a patient should have access to treatment or not? | .183 | .097 | 84 |
| Do you think it is ethically correct to let a surgical robot independently perform an operation? | .259 | .017 | 84 |
| Do you think that it is possible to decide what artificial intelligence should consider ethically correct, for example in case of serious complications during an operation? | .043 | .698 | 84 |
| How much independence and ability to make own decisions do you think artificial intelligence should have in the Indian healthcare system? | .169 | .125 | 84 |
| How integrated do you think AI should be in Indian healthcare. | .410 | <00 | 84 |

(Answer on a scale of 1–4 where 1 is that you don't think and 4 is that you think.)

### *5.5.3 WHO SHOULD DECIDE ON AI IN HEALTHCARE?*

The questionnaire contained free text questions where the respondents themselves had to write down what they thought about different things. This has been summarized in various ways as described below.

**TABLE 5.5** Key Concepts from Free Text Question.

| S. no. | Right entity to decide about AI in healthcare | Number of respondents |
|---|---|---|
| 1. | Healthcare/Medical Professionals | 46 |
| 2. | Experts/Researchers | 17 |
| 3. | State/Parliament/Authority | 16 |
| 4. | Patients/Relatives | 12 |
| 5. | Public | 7 |
| 6. | AI | 2 |
| 7. | Region | 2 |
| 8. | Do not know | 7 |

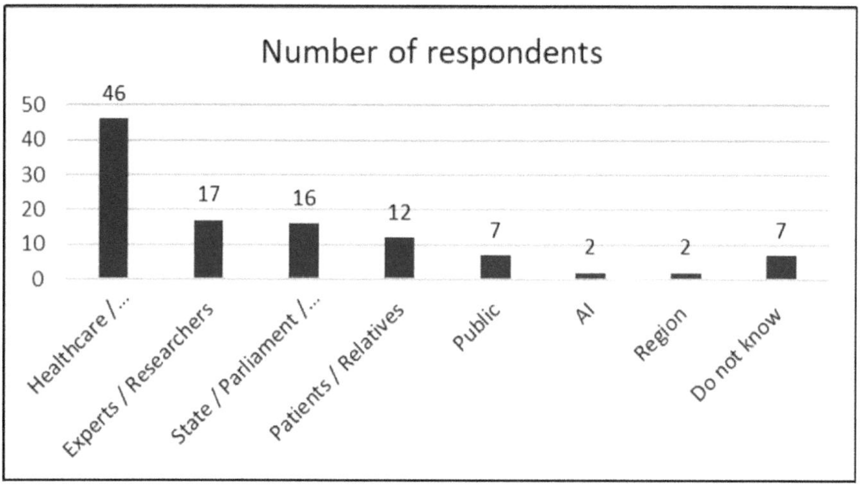


**FIGURE 5.4** Key concepts from free text question.

For the free text question "What do you think who has the right to decide what is an ethically correct decision for AI in the Indian healthcare system?" The answers were coded based on eight key concepts. These key concepts emerged by categorizing all answers to the question. The concepts that emerged were healthcare/medical professionals, experts/researchers, State/Parliament/authority, patients/relatives, the general public, AI, region, and do not know. The concept that was most recurring among the respondents' answers was health care/medical professionals. This occurs in more than half of the respondents' answers. Experts/researchers and the state/parliament/authority were the two second largest groups where there was a similar view among the respondents' answers. These were considered good alternatives for deciding what is an ethically correct decision for AI in healthcare. The third largest group was patients/relatives. This was followed by two groups of exactly the same size the public and the Do not know. This was followed by Region and the last came AI.

Based on this, it can be interpreted that the respondents have a certain caution against the implementation and use of AI in Indian healthcare. They believe that healthcare and the medical professionals themselves are most suitable to determine what are ethically correct decisions. Thereafter, the respondents have the highest confidence in experts and researchers as well as the state, the Parliament and authorities and their ability to decide what are ethically correct decisions. It is also noteworthy that the group Healthcare/Medical professionals and Experts/Researchers are two groups whose legitimacy rests on having expert knowledge in the field. While the groups Patients/Relatives, the public and State/Parliament/Authority are democratic groupings.

### 5.5.4 HOW AI SHOULD BE USED IN HEALTHCARE

In the survey, there were two multiple-choice questions. Below, the results from these two multiple-choice questions will be presented. The data have been analyzed and presented in exact numbers based on the tool SPSS. The number in the tables corresponds to the total number of respondents who have chosen each individual alternative.

**TABLE 5.6** The Departments that Respondents Believe Should Not Use AI in Percentage Form.

| S. no. | Right entity to decide about AI in healthcare | Respondents (Percent) |
|---|---|---|
| 1. | Which of these departments in healthcare do you think should not use AI? | 45.24% |
| 2. | Psychiatry | 42.86% |
| 3. | Childbirth | 39.29% |
| 4. | Palliative care | 23.81% |
| 5. | Emergency care | 19.05% |
| 6. | Gynecology/Urology | 13.10% |
| 7. | OPD | 26.19% |
| 8. | I think you can use AI in all departments | 5.95% |

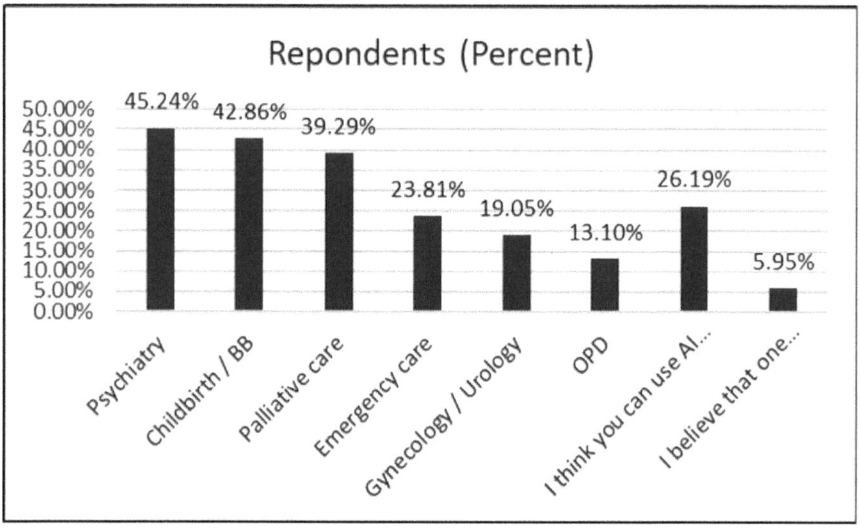


**FIGURE 5.5** The departments that respondents believe should not use AI in percentage form.

When asked "Which of these departments in healthcare do you think should not use AI if any?" the respondents had to start from different possible departments as alternatives. The options that respondents could choose from included the following: I think you can use AI in all departments, Psychiatry, Palliative care, Childbirth, Gynecology/Urology, Emergency care, and Health center, and I believe that one should not use AI in any department. Psychiatry was the department that most respondents felt should not use any AI in. Then came childbirth as the department where the second most respondents thought that one should not use AI in.

OPD was the department in which most respondents were least opposed to using AI. This shows that often a relatively large majority of respondents believe that there are acceptable reasons to use AI in most of the departments mentioned. For example, there were positive majorities for the use of AI in departments, such as OPD, Emergency care, Palliative care and Gynecology/Urology. The two departments—Psychiatry and Childbirth/BB where most of the respondents considered that AI should not be used. These wards are the ones that can be considered the most sensitive and intimate. More respondents considered that Emergency care department should use AI, and this is because it is the department that is very demanding and stressful for healthcare staff. Because AI is not affected by emotions and stress, the respondents may consider that it is therefore appropriate to use this in emergency care. When asked "In which scenario (s) is it conceivable to hand over the work entirely to artificial intelligence?" the respondents had to start from different possible departments as alternatives. The options that respondents could choose from included the following: Administrative tasks, such as medical records and reception, Printing of medicine, Patient care, Provisions regarding care queues, Diagnosis, Operation, Creation, and selection of treatment plan. The results show that the respondents had relatively different opinions about which scenarios are acceptable to hand over the work entirely to AI. There was a relatively large positive majority of 77.38% of the respondents to surrender in the scenario "Administrative tasks such as journal work and reception." This was the scenario in which the respondents were most amenable to handing over the entire work to AI. Many scenarios had a relatively even distribution. Including scenarios "Printing of medicine," "Patient care" and "Provisions regarding care queue." "Operation" And "Creation of treatment plan" were the scenarios that the respondents considered the least acceptable to hand over the work entirely to AI. Finally, it is interesting that the respondents consider themselves positive that AI should be able to take care of prescribing medicine and patient care, but not in the creation and choice of a treatment plan. Because these three scenarios can otherwise be perceived as similar.

### *5.5.5 SUMMARY*

The results from the survey make it clear that there are several contexts where there is a relatively negative majority among the respondents. Among other things, reluctance shows up against a total transfer of responsibility to AI in various areas of Indian healthcare. The relatively negative attitude can be interpreted in several different ways. The group of respondents represented in the survey also turned out to have no major prior knowledge of AI, which may have affected the negative outcome as; however, a clear correlation was shown between the respondents who answered that they have a higher prior knowledge of AI and how integrated it was considered that AI should be in Indian healthcare. There, the desire for high integration of AI increased in connection with how much knowledge the respondents had. At the same time, the results of the multiple-choice questions show that there is instead a positivity to using AI in certain departments within healthcare. This can be interpreted as meaning that the respondents are willing to let AI have a place in most departments, but possibly to varying degrees. In the question of which departments in healthcare should not use AI so was Psychiatry and Childbirth largest. This may be due to the public see these areas as highly sensitive. These departments handle sensitive matters and therefore this can show that the respondents believe that it is important to maintain safe human contact when it comes to sensitive departments like these. This shows a greater belief in human factors.

## 5.6 DISCUSSION

In the following section, a discussion will be conducted regarding the results and previous analysis linked to the related research.

### *5.6.1 HOW DOES THE PUBLIC THINK THAT DECISION-MAKING ON ETHICAL ISSUES WITHIN AI IN HEALTHCARE SHOULD BE HANDLED?*

Based on the results and analysis that have been carried out, we see that the public believes that decision-making within AI in healthcare should primarily be handled by the healthcare itself and the medical professionals. The respondents also had a high level of confidence that experts, researchers and the state could handle and make good decisions on ethical issues within AI in healthcare. This may be because we have captured a sociocultural group that has a high level of trust in healthcare and other significant institutions in society in this regard. This can be shown in contrast to the previous research[24] where some of the concerns expressed are taken in the form of whether the real interest in technology is in line with society. This indicates that the respondents in our survey do not have a similar distrust of those who have influence over the processes and development of AI in healthcare. This is something that is also reinforced by previous research where trust is compared between the USA, China and India.[33]

Furthermore, it can be assumed that the study has captured a certain type of sociocultural group since the questionnaire was sent out through our social media emails. Based on the previous research that has been presented, attitudes toward AI and how its technology affects society can be distinguished depending on which sociocultural group one belongs to. This makes it all the more reasonable that the study captured a sociocultural group as the attitudes were relatively similar between the respondents, where the amount of concern for AI in healthcare expressed by the respondents in our study was relatively small. What also differs between the studies is that only seven respondents from our study considered that the public has the right to decide what an ethically correct decision for AI is. At the same time, the previous study showed a mutual reflection between the different sociocultural groups where they felt that there is a need to increase inclusion with different voices from society in the development and distribution of AI in healthcare. This can again be linked to the fact that there is greater confidence in healthcare and the medical professionals in India. Another questionnaire that deals with the perception of decisions about ethics were "Do you think that you can decide what AI should consider being ethically correct, for example, in the case of very serious complications during an operation?" As previously described, this was a scale question with a mean value of 2.01. This means that the respondents mostly lean toward the fact that it is relatively difficult to decide what is ethically correct. However, the respondents were fairly in agreement that the health care/medical professionals were the ones best suited to be able to decide what is fairly ethical in such cases. This also clearly shows the strong trust that the respondents have in medical professionals.[34]

Furthermore, based on the results of our study, it can be deduced that only two respondents have explicitly answered that the regions should have the right to decide what is an ethically correct decision for AI in Indian healthcare. This can be seen as problematic as it is actually the regions that are responsible for healthcare. The fact that so few respondents have explicitly answered "region" may be due to several reasons. One possible reflection is that respondents did not choose to answer "region" because they can be interpreted as meaning that the decision on what AI should consider ethically correct in healthcare in such cases can be differentiated in different regions. And that this meant that more respondents chose to answer "the state" or similar for the decisions to be the same in Indian healthcare. However, this is something we can only speculate about.

### *5.6.2 IS THE PUBLIC PREPARED TO HAND OVER DECISION-MAKING IN SCENARIOS IN HEALTHCARE TO AI?*

This question can be answered in several different ways. What is clear throughout this study is that there is a general skepticism toward handing over decision-making entirely to AI in relatively many scenarios in Indian healthcare. In the questionnaire question "In which scenario or scenarios is it conceivable to hand over the work entirely to AI?" The largest positive majority was to hand over decision-making and work entirely in the alternative administrative work such as journal work and reception. This may reflect the current debate about how much administrative work doctors and nurses need to perform. This can therefore be thought of as a way to use

AI to maximum utilization of the time of healthcare professionals. Another thing that was interesting about this question was that the respondents were positive that AI could prescribe medicine and handle patient care. However, they were negative about AI being able to create and choose a treatment plan. This is interesting as all these three scenarios are equally important in that they are well executed. One possible reflection is that the prescription of medicine is considered more determined and thus a more appropriate task for AI than when choosing a treatment plan. Because the choice of a treatment plan is very individual and differs a lot from patient to patient, compared with prescribed medication that has clear variables to start from in each patient. In patient care, the respondents may have considered that AI is appropriate because it may be perceived as less diminishing to get help with certain sensitive tasks compared with getting help from a human being.

Most were negative about handing over decision-making to the scenario operation. This was also shown in the free text questions when respondents expressed doubts about this possibility that may manifest itself in the increasingly near future. Respondent 5 believes that one should monitor with the utmost care so that AI does not have too large an area of responsibility. This can also be linked to what respondent 11 expresses his strong feelings about that it would feel worse to have complications from an operation performed by a surgical robot than by a human one. This may be because it feels more difficult to accept that AI can make mistakes in an operation than that a human can. On the question of scale "How much independence and opportunity do you think AI should have in Indian healthcare?" the mean value of the respondents' answers was 2.1. This means that they believe that AI should have a relatively small opportunity to be independent and make its own decisions. This relatively critical view of how much decision-making AI should be able to take is understandable. This can also be linked to the negative attitude toward handing over decision-making to AI in the scenario of operation. This critical view of decision-making as well as surgery performed by AI may be due to a fear of the unknown that one does not understand.[26]

The respondents were more positive about daring to be operated on by a surgical robot themselves, compared with operation as a scenario. Respondents may have separated these two alternatives due to the possibility that everything related to operations and their area would be decided by AI in the scenario operation. This is in contrast to the option of undergoing a single operation yourself with the help of AI, which is still monitored by a human. This shows, just as previously mentioned, the great confidence that the respondents have for the medical professionals and the state to be able to make this possible in a way that does not risk negative consequences. This is also consistent with how they reason in the US about surgical robots, as they use this type of robot to a greater extent than what is done in India today, but it is never carried out without humans' supervision and they operate almost never yourself.[18]

This may indicate a coherent opinion in both India and the United States that independent surgical robots are something that should be approached with caution. Something that is shown here is that they may have come further in the USA with, for example, independent surgical robots due to the extensive privatization of healthcare there and the opportunities this creates for certain hospitals. The skepticism shown in the respondents' answers can be seen in the report. This is because they have many major criteria and considerations in different areas that must be taken into account in AI in healthcare. Emergency care continued to be one of the departments that the respondents considered more appropriate to hand over decision-making to AI in. This may be due to the fact that it is a department that the respondents perceive as demanding and stressful for the healthcare staff and that AI therefore becomes extra suitable to use. At the same time, there was a much larger proportion of respondents who considered that psychiatry and childbirth is a department that should not use AI. Which are also two departments that involve a lot of stress and are demanding for the staff. However, the use of AI in childbirth/BB can be seen as more complicated as it is also about an extra life. The respondents can therefore consider childbirth department as a more sensitive department and therefore it should not use AI because it is not perceived as equally safe. This reasoning can also be linked to the fact that there were much fewer proportions of the respondents who thought that gynecology/urology department should not use AI. It is also possible that the use of AI in psychiatry is considered too sensitive and is thus in great need of human healthcare personnel.

The result would naturally have looked different if the general public surveyed had consisted only of researchers and people working with AI. But, it is very important to take into account the caution and skepticism expressed, as India's population consists of people with varying degrees of knowledge about AI. It is important that this type of change in healthcare takes place in the right way and that those affected by it are informed about it. The respondents clearly see some difficulties regarding the transfer of decision-making to AI in healthcare, but they also have confidence that it will work and that it will be rewarding. The scenarios in which the respondents are most willing to hand over decision-making are administrative tasks. Also prescribing medicine, patient care and emergency care were three scenarios in which the respondents were positive about using AI. However, there was a more negative attitude toward scenario surgery, psychiatry and childbirth/BB. This shows that the respondents are more prepared to hand over decision-making to AI within the scenarios and departments that have monotonous tasks and where it can make it easier for the healthcare staff.

### *5.6.3 SETTING TO AI*

The results showed that there is a relatively negative attitude. This attitude mainly refers to the extent to which AI should have in Indian healthcare. Where several respondents expressed that a combination of AI and traditional care in the form of doctors and nurses feel like a good way to develop Indian care. This is also in line with the WHO report (2021).[35]

Continuing through the previous research and the preventive interview we conducted, a positive spirit was created toward AI in healthcare, which otherwise may not be shown in the same detailed way in the study results. This can be relatively linked to the respondents' own assessed low knowledge of AI. In addition to this, it can also be understood that some of the issues have been perceived as uncomfortable to address.[36] On the other hand, this reinforces the image of how this group trusts the Indian healthcare system and the teaching staff in distributing AI in healthcare. Confidence in healthcare can also be shown in how the respondents have chosen the questionnaire question "Which of these departments in healthcare do you think should not use AI if any?" Here, a larger negative number of respondents were of the opinion that AI should not be used in certain more sensitive departments. These were, for example, Childbirth-and Psychiatry. This shows that it is important for people to preserve human contact even more precisely when it comes to a more sensitive area in which care is needed. The great confidence in the people who work in the Indian healthcare system makes it possibly more difficult to feel that you want to renounce that contact, which is understandable. There may be a greater need for human contact within these departments. Another factor that may have influenced this is the fact that it is more difficult to deal with ethical issues in sensitive areas, such as Childbirth/B B and Psychiatry

There may be more difficult ethical dilemmas to deal with here compared with within the Health center for example, which had a very high positive majority of respondents who considered it possible to use AI in that area. The group that answered the survey has a majority of people who think they have relatively little knowledge about AI. This was also seen in the correlation that was discovered between how people with high or low knowledge of AI had answered the question "How integrated do you think AI should be in Indian healthcare?" Through this correlation, it is possible to understand that people with greater knowledge showed greater acceptance for the integration of AI in, for example, healthcare. This may indicate that if this study had been conducted with a focus on a general audience of experts in the field, another result would have been shown with high probability. This is compared with the general population now surveyed who have a relatively low level of knowledge about AI.

## 5.7 CONCLUSION AND FURTHER RESEARCH

Ethical questions become more complex to answer when it comes to healthcare due to the sensitive nature of healthcare. The answers to ethical questions in this area, therefore, become very individual and are influenced by the individual's individual norms and feelings. Sociocultural and trust in authorities also play a role in how the individual wishes ethical issues to be handled.

Based on the results of the study, we can conclude that the surveyed public believes that decision-making on ethical issues in healthcare should primarily be made by healthcare and medical professionals. Thereafter, the public has the second highest confidence that the state, experts, and researchers will be able to make decisions on these issues. Based on this conclusion, it is clarified that the surveyed public has a high level of trust in the previously mentioned public circles. Another conclusion that has been drawn is that the public is not prepared to hand over decision-making in healthcare entirely to AI. However, it depends on the area in question. Above all, administrative work is the most accepted to hand over AI to. The surveyed public was prepared to hand over decision-making entirely within administrative tasks within healthcare, but not within more complex areas such as surgery. One of the interpretations made of this is that it may be due to the relatively low knowledge of AI that the respondents expressed themselves to have. This in itself can contribute to increased skepticism as people are naturally afraid of what they do not understand.[37,38]

A proposal for further research on this subject is to continue trying to capture different sociocultural groups and their views in order to get a broader picture of the public's views. This can be done by trying to reach people in a different way so that the survey becomes more accessible to more people in society. This would thus contribute to a fairer picture of the public. Furthermore, this could also contribute to a more even distribution between age groups, which would thus create a better representation of society.

## KEYWORDS


- **artificial intelligence**
- **digitization**
- **healthcare sector**
- **ethics**
- **decision-making by AI**


## REFERENCES


1. Dignum, V. *Responsible Artificial Intelligence: How to Develop and use AI in a Responsible Way*; Springer Nature, 2019. https://link.springer.com/book/10.1007/978-3-030-30371-6
2. Lysaght, T.; Hannah, H. Y.; Xafis, V.; Ngiam. K. Y. AI-Assisted Decision-Making in Healthcare. *Asian Bioeth. Rev.* **2019,** *11* (3), 299–314. https://link.springer.com/article/10.1007/s41649-019-00096-0
3. Athavale, V. A.; Bansal, A.; Nalajala, S.; Aurelia, S. In *Integration of Blockchain and IoT for Data Storage and Management*, Materials Today: Proceedings, 2020. https://www.sciencedirect.com/science/article/pii/S2214785320373685
4. Kumar, S.; Jain, H.; Arora, S.; Singh, A. Soft Computing Based Two Novel Machine Learning Approaches. *Test Eng. Manag.* **2020,** *83,* 14073–14079. http://www.testmagzine.biz/index.php/testmagzine/article/view/6185
5. Sharma, R.; Athavale, V. A. A Survey on Security Aspects of Wireless Sensor Network, *Int. J. Manag. Tech. Eng.* **2018,** *8,* 2829–2843. http://ijamtes.org/gallery/362.%20oct%20ijmte%20-%20as.pdf
6. Arora, S.; Verma, D. C.; Athavale, V. A. In *A Secured Automated Attendance Management System implemented with Secret Sharing Algorithm*, 2020 Sixth International Conference on Parallel, Distributed and Grid Computing (PDGC); IEEE, 2020; pp 141–145. https://ieeexplore.ieee.org/abstract/document/9315854
7. Russel, S.; Norvig, P. Artificial Intelligence: A Modern Approach Pearson Education, 2009. https://zoo.cs.yale.edu/classes/cs470/materials/aima2010.pdf
8. Rani, S.; Acharjee, P. B.; Kaswan, S.; Athavale, V. A.; Udhayamoorthi, M.; Pant, K. In *A Face Spoof Detection in Artificial Neural Networks Using Concepts of Machine Learning*, 2022 2nd International Conference on Advance Computing and Innovative Technologies in Engineering (ICACITE); IEEE, 2022, pp 1604–1607. https://ieeexplore.ieee.org/abstract/document/9823587
9. Morley, J.; Machado, C.; Burr, C.; Cowls, J.; Joshi, I.; Taddeo, M.; Floridi, L. The Ethics of AI in Health Care: A Mapping Review. *Soc. Sci. Med.* **2020,** *260,* 113172. https://www.sciencedirect.com/science/article/abs/pii/S0277953620303919
10. Arora, S.; Athavale, V. A.; Maggu, H.; Agarwal, A. Artificial Intelligence and Virtual Assistant-Working Model. In *Mobile Radio Communications and 5G Networks*; Springer, Singapore, 2021; pp 163–171. https://link.springer.com/chapter/10.1007/978-981-15-7130-5_12

11. Wihantara, A.; Hariwisana, I. D. G.; Pudji, A.; Luthfiyah, S.; Athavale, V. A. QRS Complex Detection on Heart Rate Variability Reading Using Discrete Wavelet Transform. *Indonesian J. Electronic. Electromed. Eng. Med. Inform.* **2022,** *4* (4), 153–159. http://ijeeemi.poltekkesdepkes-sby.ac.id/index.php/ijeeemi/article/view/236
12. Chauhan, D.; Kumar, A.; Bedi, P.; Athavale, V. A.; Veereaiah, D.; Pratap, B. R. An Effective Face Recognition System based on Cloud based IoT with a Deep Learning Model. *Microprocess. Microsyst.* **2021,** *81,* 103726. https://www.sciencedirect.com/science/article/abs/pii/S0141933120308711
13. Sun, T. Q.; Medaglia, R. Mapping the Challenges of Artificial Intelligence in the Public Sector: Evidence from Public Healthcare. *Gov. Inf. Q.* **2019,** *36* (2), 368–383. https://www.scirp.org/reference/referencespapers?referenceid=3487372
14. Rani, S.; Singh, B. K.; Koundal, D.; Athavale, V. A. Localization of Stroke Lesion in MRI Images Using Object Detection Techniques: A Comprehensive Review. *Neurosci. Inform.* **2022,** 100070.
15. Kumar, S.; Nassa, V. K.; Uike, D.; Sahu, A. K.; Athavale, V. A.; Saravanan, V. A Comparative Analysis of Blockchain in Enhancing the Drug Traceability in Edible Foods Using Multiple Regression Analysis. *J. Food Qual.* 2022. https://www.hindawi.com/journals/jfq/2022/1689913/
16. Panch, T.; Mattie, H.; Celi, L. A. The "Inconvenient Truth" about AI in Healthcare. *NPJ Digit. Med.* **2019,** *2* (1), 1–3. https://www.nature.com/articles/s41746-019-0155-4
17. Arora, S.; Jain. H.; Singh, A. Google Reads Mind-The Magic. *J. Emerg. Technol. Innov. Res.* **2018,** *5* (11), 179–183. https://www.jetir.org/view?paper=JETIRDS06026
18. Davenport, T.; Kalakota, R. The Potential for Artificial Intelligence in Healthcare. *Future Healthc. J.* **2019** *6* (2), 94. https://www.ncbi.nlm.nih.gov/pmc/articles/PMC6616181/
19. Jiang, F.; Jiang, Y.; Zhi, H.; Dong, Y.; Li, H.; Ma, S.; Wang, Y.; Dong, Q.; Shen, H.; Wang, Y. Artificial Intelligence in Healthcare: Past, Present and Future. *Stroke Vasc. Neurol.* **2017,** *2* (4). https://svn.bmj.com/content/svnbmj/2/4/230.full.pdf
20. The National Board of Health and Welfare, Digital Healthcare Services and Artificial Intelligence in Health and Healthcare; 2019. https://www.socialstyrelsen.se/globalassets/sharepoint- document / article catalog / other / 2019-10-6431.pdf
21. Shaheen. M. Y. *Applications of Artificial Intelligence (AI) in healthcare: A review.* ScienceOpen Preprints, 2021. https://www.scienceopen.com/document_file/a8536285-4c3c-47c2-8d5c-78cf38231c76/ScienceOpenPreprint/Applications%20of%20Artificial%20Intelligence%20%28AI%29%20in%20healthcare%20A%20review.pdf
22. Nagpal, S.; Athavale, V. A.; Saini, A. K.; Sharma, R. In *Indian Health Care System is Ready to Fight Against Covid-19 a Machine Learning Tool for Forecast the Number of Beds*, 2020 Sixth International Conference on Parallel, Distributed and Grid Computing (PDGC), IEEE, 2020, pp 61–65. https://web.archive.org/web/20210429110252id_/https://ieeexplore.ieee.org/ielx7/9315294/9315319/09315825.pdf
23. Arora, S.; Athavale, V. A.; Singh, T. Machine Learning: A Tool to Combat COVID-19. *Enabling Healthcare 4.0 for Pandemics: A Roadmap Using AI, Machine Learning, IoT and Cognitive Technologies* 2021; pp 299–316. https://onlinelibrary.wiley.com/doi/abs/10.1002/9781119769088.ch15
24. Zimmer, M.; Franco, Z.; Madiraju, P.; Echeveste, C.; Heindel, K.; Ogle, J. *Public Opinion Research on Artificial Intelligence in Public Health Responses: Results of Focus Groups with Four Communities*;AAAS Center for Public Engagement with Science and Technology, Washington, DC 2021; pp 2–28. https://www.aaas.org/sites/

default/files/2021-09/AI%20in%20Public%20Health%20Focus%20Groups%20-%20Final%20Report%20with%20Appendix.pdf. https://www.tandfonline.com/doi/full/10.1080/1369118X.2020.1781916
25. Van Dijk, J. *The Digital Divide*; John Wiley & Sons 2020. https://doi.org/10.1080/1369118X.2020.1781916
26. Carleton, R. N. Fear of the Unknown: One Fear to Rule Them all?, *J. Anxiety Disord.* **2016,** *41,* 5–21.
27. Bartoletti, I. In *AI in Healthcare: Ethical and Privacy Challenges*, Conference on Artificial Intelligence in Medicine in Europe; Springer, Cham, 2019; pp 7–10. https://link.springer.com/chapter/10.1007/978-3-030-21642-9_2
28. Mittelstadt, B. Principles Alone Cannot Guarantee Ethical AI. *Nat. Mach. Intell.* **2019,** *1* (11), 501–507. https://www.nature.com/articles/s42256-019-0114-4
29. Kvale, S.; Brinkmann, S. *The Qualitative Research Interview*, 2nd ed.; Sage, 2009. https://www.scirp.org/(S(i43dyn45teexjx455qlt3d2q))/reference/ReferencesPapers.aspx?ReferenceID=1977777
30. Barmark, M.; Djurfeldt, G. *Statistical Toolbox: Understanding and Changing the World with Numbers*; 2015.
31. Sohlberg, P.; Sohlberg, B. Knowledge Forms—Theory of Science, Research Method and Research Ethics. *Liber* 2019. https://www.aau.in/sites/default/files/Unit%203%20RESEARCH%20AND%20RESEARCH%20ETHICS%20(Repaired).pdf
32. Thornberg, R.; Fejes, A. *Handbook of Qualitative Analysis. Liber*. 2015.
33. Haerpfer, C.; Inglehart, R.; Moreno, A.; Welzel, C.; Kizilova, K.; Diez-Medrano, J.; Lagos, M.; Norris, P.; Ponarin, E.; Puranen, B.; et al. Eds., *World Values Survey: Round Seven—Country-Pooled Datafile*; JD Systems Institute & WVSA Secretariat, Madrid, Spain & Vienna, Austria, 2020. https://www.worldvaluessurvey.org/WVSDocumentationWV7.jsp
34. Lehmann, L. S. Ethical Challenges of Integrating AI into Healthcare. In *Artificial Intelligence in Medicine;* Springer International Publishing, Cham, 2021; pp 1–6. https://link.springer.com/referenceworkentry/10.1007/978-3-030-58080-3_337-2
35. W. H. O. Guidance, Ethics and Governance of Artificial Intelligence for Health, *World Health Organization*; 2021. https://hash.theacademy.co.ug/wp-content/uploads/2022/05/WHO-guidance-Ethics-and-Governance-of-AI-for-Health.pdf
36. G. Karimian, G.; Petelos, E.; Evers, S. M. *The Ethical Issues of the Application of Artificial Intelligence in Healthcare: A Systematic Scoping Review*; AI and Ethics **2022,** 1–13. https://link.springer.com/article/10.1007/s43681-021-00131-7
37. Kumar, S.; Athavale, V. A.; Kartikey, D. AI-assisted Decision-Making in Healthcare. *Asian Bioethics Review* **2021,** *6,* 18–29. https://www.researchgate.net/profile/Vijay-Athavale/publication/354313006_Security_Issues_in_Cloud_Computing_A_holistic_view/links/6130a94f2b40ec7d8bdcf450/Security-Issues-in-Cloud-Computing-A-holistic-view.pdf
38. Athavale, V. A. Application of Artificial Intelligence in Magnetic Resonance Imaging to Reduce Gadolinium Accumulation in Patients with Multiple Sclerosis: A Review. *Sci. Prog. Res.* **2022,** *2* (1). https://www.researchgate.net/publication/356381317

# CHAPTER 6

# Economic Crisis in Sub-Sahara Africa and Its (Un)Sustainable Development Implications

AYODEJI ANTHONY ADULOJU[1] and TEMITAYO ADEDEJI ADEDOYIN[2]

[1]*Department of History and International Studies, Edo State University Uzairue, Edo State, Nigeria*

[2]*Department of International Relations, Obafemi Awolowo University, Ile-Ife, Osun State, Nigeria*

## ABSTRACT

Sub-Saharan Africa (SSA) is not only one of the richest regions in the world with a high concentration of natural resources but also one of the poorest (if not the poorest). The region has been ravaged over the years by intrastate and interstate wars, poverty, underdevelopment, famine, food insecurity, economic crisis, political instability, disease outbreaks, and terrorism, among others. Although previous studies have found the failure of states in SSA to be self-sustaining and less dependent on the West by using their natural resources for development, the problems of the high rate of underdevelopment and the above challenges facing the region have aggravated. This study then examines the problem of the economic crisis in terms of sustainable development in SSA. It examines the region's economic growth and development patterns to determine whether the region's level of economic growth and development is sustainable or otherwise unsustainable for its development. This is done through an explanatory study and a review of the concept of economic crisis and sustainable development in the region's milieu. It also determines whether economic growth and sustainable development, or vice versa, are

Management for Sustainable Development: Integrating Social, Economic, and Environmental Goals.
Vishal Jain & Amit Mittal (Eds.)

perceptible in the SSA region. The study finds that SSA has not experienced any real growth and development historically, and the prospects for this are uncertain. It also shows that states in SSA suffer from persistently low GDP, loss of household income, a high unemployment rate, continued capital spending, poor capacity utilization, declining business incomes, and a high inflation rate due to intensifying domestic security challenges and are heavily dependent on foreign aid and assistance from the West. This has hampered development and increased conflict, political instability, famine, civil war, disease outbreaks, and terrorism. The study concludes that while economic growth and its sustainability for development are important to the SSA region, the reality has had a major negative impact on the region.

## 6.1 INTRODUCTION

The frequent development problems in the sub-Saharan Africa (SSA) region have undoubtedly made development impossible. Since the wave of independence in 1960, states in the region have doggedly struggled with breathtaking economic growth, food crises and security, political instability, unemployment, poverty, health, and poor governance (Heidhues,[18] 1). This has placed countries in the SSA region on a pedestal of unrealistic development aspirations and upgrades. Despite the vast supply of socioeconomic propellers such as agriculture, oil and gas, culture and tourism, and other commodities and natural resources that could have propelled the region into the realm of development, they have, without exaggeration, been plagued with poverty in the region.

The problems of development and the striving to achieve and sustain them have been at the heart of states, although they have not been doggedly pursued. Similarly, previous studies (see Refes.[2,17,24,43]) indicate that the failure of countries in the regions that sustain themselves by using their natural resources to increase their gross domestic product (GDP) has led to poverty and underdevelopment. This also brings to bear the SSA countries' high reliance on the West for economic growth and development to address their underdevelopment deficits. The West has attempted to address this by periodically increasing its development frugality in the form of foreign aid and assistance.

Consequently, for dependency theorists, the problems of underdevelopment, poverty, and the economic crisis in sub-Saharan Africa are the result of the incorporation of poor states into the capitalist world system dominated by the West and North America.[31] It is undeniable that most of the countries in the region are the poorest in the world, and the solution to this problem provided by the West is stifling the region and making economic growth and development unrealistic. According to the Global Finance Magazine survey,[16] out of the 23 poorest countries in the world, 19 are SSA countries.

Countries like Nigeria and South Africa, which are said to be the engine rooms of Africa's regional economy, are both threatened by slow economic growth and underdevelopment. In the fourth quarter of 2019, some of the region's economies plunged into dismal economic growth that has held back anticipated development. Although the economic policies of various governments in the region have been slandered, the argument has focused on their lack of good governance. Based on this premise, the study asks whether the different economies of the SSA countries grew at any given point in time. And have growth and lack of it translated into sustainable development and underdevelopment? As a result of these questions, this study examines the progression and regression patterns of the economies of the countries in the SSA. It examines the impact of failed economic growth in the region on sustainable development.

## 6.2 SUB-SAHARAN AFRICA: A HISTORY IN SUCCINCT GLANCE

The term sub-Saharan Africa is used to define a portion of the African continent that lies south of the Sahara.[33] It consists of 48 countries including Benin Republic, Botswana, Burkina Faso, Cameroon, Congo (Brazzaville), Congo (DRC-Kinshasa), Ethiopia, Ghana, Guinea, Ivory Coast, Kenya, Lesotho, Madagascar, Malawi, Mauritius, Mozambique, Namibia, Niger, Nigeria, Rwanda, Senegal, Sierra Leone, South Africa, Swaziland, Tanzania, Togo, Uganda, and Zambia. However, Algeria, the Western Sahara, Egypt, Sudan, and Morocco are geographically separated from the sub-Saharan region.

Sub-Saharan Africa is also referred to as Black Africa and is quite different from Arabian North Africa as shown in the map above. Before 1880, a small part of the territory was directly under the control of the European colonizers. Until 1884, during the Berlin Conference or, in other words, the Scramble for Africa, the European powers were as follows: Germany, Spain, Portugal, Italy, Great Britain, France, Belgium, the Scramble for Territories to Control in Africa, and as such.[39] From 1913, the entire continent, with the exception of Ethiopia, Liberia, and South Africa, was under European colonial control (ibid.). Arbitrary demarcations by the colonial powers separated some tribes and cultures that had been graphically related until then. While this was done out of selfish efforts by the colonial powers to control areas in Africa, it had some negative consequences for African states immediately after the decolonization process that took place from 1957 to the 1960s.

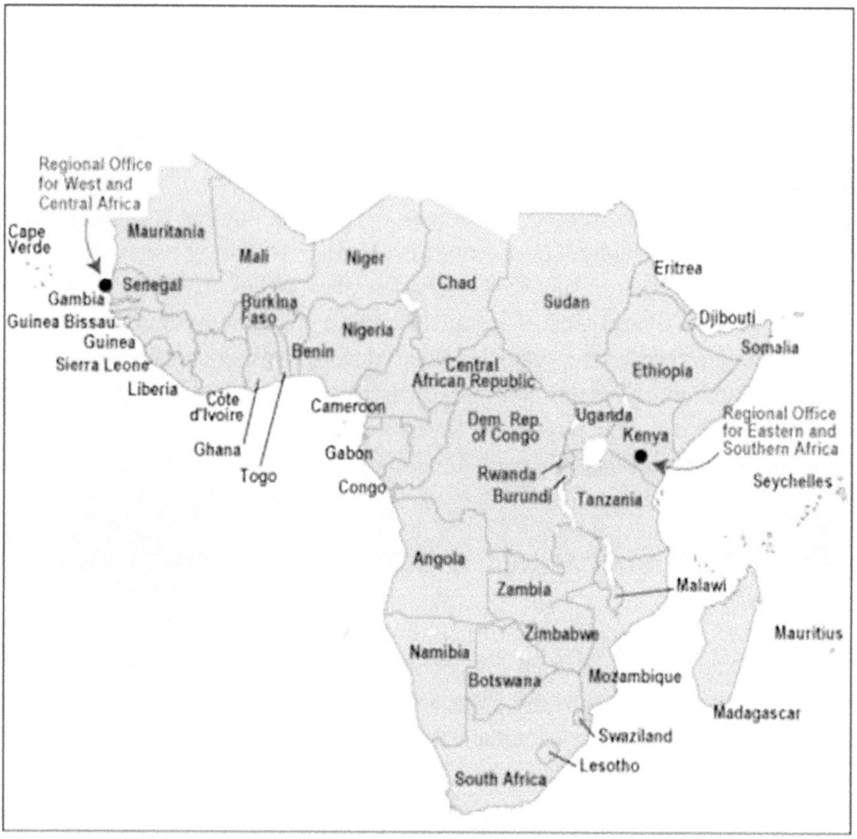


**FIGURE 6.1** Map of Sub-Saharan Africa.

*Source:* EOI.http://www.eoi.es/blogs/lauraambros/2012/01/17/millenium-development-goalsfor-sub-saharan-africa/

Traditionally, the SSA states have been predominantly agricultural and pastoral due to the vast amount of arable land. But then, after the wave of independence from their former colonial powers, the states of the region began to explore their natural resources. Today, the region has relatively shifted from agriculture to mining for gold, iron, manganese, diamonds, and copper, as well as for oil and natural gas production. This is reflected in the fact that the political economy of several African states and the entire region grows out of the raw material industry and its importance. According to IMF,[21] a larger proportion of the oil-producing states in sub-Saharan Africa generate only about 70 to 80% of their national revenues from oil exports and rely on oil for about 35 to 60% of the region's gross domestic product (GDP). Other states with large GDPs from mining also accounted for about 43% of the region's exports.[43] Globally, sub-Saharan Africa's growing importance is increasing day by day, and the world now relies on the region for global energy supply.

With the above explanations of the increasing importance of SSA for the survival of the world, one would like to assume that countries in the region are among the developed countries of the world. Conversely, the region is rather a hotbed of conflict, political instability, famine, civil war, outbreaks of disease, terrorism, and sea piracy. While the region is important to the world's energy supply, it also depends on the rest of the world to resolve its internal crisis, which has resulted in little or no economic growth. This has made the region vulnerable to economic crises. If the region is prone to economic crises, has the region at any point experienced growth, and has this led to development? How are the countries in the region coping with their ongoing economic crisis while working on development and preservation?

All of these questions are a guide to the unfolding arguments that drive this study.

## 6.3 DISCOURSING ECONOMIC CRISIS AND SUSTAINABLE DEVELOPMENT WITHIN THE AMBIENT OF SSA

Striving for economic growth and development is vital for all regions and countries of the world. To achieve this, policies are being enacted by national leaders that are ending the economic crisis while affecting GDP. If state economic and development policy fails, then the economic crisis and underdevelopment are unstoppable. In order to start a discourse on economic crisis or growth and how it unbundles development in SSA, it is necessary to understand the conceptual interpretations of the themes of economic crisis, growth, and development. In this section, this study organizes the subheading as follows for a well-learned analysis: (1) conceptualization of the economic crisis in the context of SSA; (2) conceptualization of sustainable development in the context of SSA; and (3) economic crisis and sustainable development around SSA.

## 6.4 CONCEPTUALIZING THE ECONOMIC CRISIS WITHIN THE AMBIENT OF SSA

An economic crisis is a sudden downturn resulting from a financial crisis. Perera[29] views the economic crisis as a downturn that has persistently detrimental effects on the people involved in the performance of an economy. Falling GDP and rising commodity prices are the short- and long-term effects of the economic crisis. Jickling[25] is more precise in his definition of the economic crisis. He argues that it relates to the real economy, unemployment, low wages, and lack of economic growth. This position undoubtedly explains Perera's[29] submission. He pointed to the impact of the economic crisis on people who depend on the economy for their survival. This powerful effect could perhaps be what Jickling[25] called unemployment, low wages, and lack of economic growth.

In other arguments related to the conceptual clarification of the economic crisis, Jickling[25] anticipated a confusion in the operationalization of the notion of the economic crisis. For him, the economic crisis is not the same as a financial crisis. He says that a financial crisis is when the apparatus, i.e., the currency, is in crisis, leading to inflation, devaluation, and a stock market collapse. Aziz, Caramazza, and Salgado[9] explain that financial crises can possibly be understood if they are grouped into three broad categories: currency crises, banking crises, and external debt crises. In other words, they say that financial crises mostly occur when the value of financial assets falls and the financial and stock markets in an economy are affected.[29] However, Pettinger[30] brushes aside the gray areas, arguing that there is no clear distinction as both the economic crisis and the financial crisis are closely related. For him, the financial crisis refers to the problems in the financial sector and includes precisely the defaults on mortgages and the increase in bank losses, which lead to a decrease in bank credit (ibid.). Due to the lending inability of financial institutions in a given economy, investment suffers, and this leads to an economic recession (ibid.).

At the point where a conclusion is drawn about the confusion surrounding the concept of an economic crisis and why it is not the same as a financial crisis, the concept of an economic recession emerges. It's important not to abuse these concepts without understanding how best to apply them, if only for analytical reasons. According to the Central Bank of Nigeria (CBN),[36] an economic recession refers to an overall slowdown in economic activity for two consecutive quarters (p. 1). The recession leads to a decline in some macroeconomic indicators such as GDP, household income, employment, capital expenditure, capacity utilization, corporate income, and inflation, with a consequent increase in the percentage of unemployment (ibid.). The CBN definition of an economic recession is no different from the Jickling[25] definition of what an economic crisis is. On the other hand, one should not point out that the CBN definition emphasizes periodization (i.e., where it says for two consecutive quarters (CBN,[36]: 1). In practice, economists believe that an economic recession lasts no more than a few months or may plunge into a crisis before it sets in. Just for the record, the economic crisis is then the final stage of economic hardship that can have an overwhelming impact on a nation's overall economic activity.

In order for this study to not lose its focus, it is necessary at this time to narrow all of these above conceptual clarifications of the economic crisis and its relatives (financial crisis and economic recession) to confirm that the economic problem in SSA is an economic crisis. In other words, if the financial crisis affects only the financial sector and the economic recession affects both the financial sector and other economic activities as mentioned above and occurs or lasts for a specific period of time, then the SSA economy cannot be said to be in recession or crisis. It is evident today that states in the SSA suffer from persistently low GDP, loss of household income, high unemployment, low investment, underutilization of capacity, declining business income, and high inflation.

According to the International Monetary Fund (IMF),[24] various countries in sub-Saharan Africa are affected by falling commodity prices, tighter financing conditions, and severe famine in southern and eastern Africa (Ref.[22]: 2). IMF statistics indicate that growth fell to the lowest level in 2015 and is likely to slow further to lower percentages in 2016 compared to the current decline (ibid.: 2). Record growth is expected for oil-exporting countries, but the drop in global oil prices has led to significant shortfalls in oil-related tax revenues, leading to cuts in public spending (ibid.). Currently, one of the economic powerhouses of sub-Saharan Nigeria is struggling due to the oil revenue shortfalls mentioned above. The economic recession hit Nigeria hard in the second quarter of 2016. According to Focus Economies,[15] all of the major oil exporters in the region and South Africa are recording most of the regional slump. The economies of Angola and Nigeria, the region's largest oil and gas exporters, are expected to have contracted by 0.2% and 1.8%, respectively, in 2016 as these countries faced severe financial and economic strains.[15]

Akanonu and Onyekwena[6] claim that the recent slowdown in sub-Saharan growth is caused by factors such as falling commodity prices, tightening global financial conditions, weak export demand, and political uncertainty, among others.[6] It is argued that the economy of sub-Saharan Africa is in recession, with huge implications for development in the region.

### *6.4.1 CONCEPTUALIZING SUSTAINABLE DEVELOPMENT WITHIN THE AMBIENT OF SSA*

If there is noticeable improvement and development in the aspects of a state's economy and other social conditions, it could be agreed that such a state is undergoing development. More importantly, development must demonstrate that all aspects of human and societal endeavor are positively impacted. According to Myint,[27] there are two general approaches to development. The first approach is what he called poverty reduction, which explains and emphasizes the problems of widespread hunger, poverty, and depression, especially in the developing world. This approach also raises the question of possible solutions to perhaps make progress in the short term.[34]

Myint's second development approach speaks of the analysis of long-term economic and social development. In it, he argues that in order to understand the factors that have long-term effects on socioeconomic development, one must start by comparing developments in different countries, regions, and historical periods.[34] These above approaches better explain the development challenges that have plagued the sub-Saharan Africa region as all Myint's approaches are meticulously linked to development policies and plans at the national, regional, and international levels. Taking this argument further, it is worth accepting that development is mostly generally measured in terms of economic growth, which undoubtedly increases a nation's wealth.

Taking all of this for granted, the understanding of development in the SSA should be socioeconomically tailored and growth-oriented. Now an argument can be built around development in the SSA that development is not the bone of contention in the SSA but its sustenance. This is according to the IMF's annual economic growth report. If you look at a 10-year report on economic growth in SSA, you will find that growth in the region has typically been on a downward trend. From this, it becomes clear that the problem in the SSA is the preservation of development. So how do we conceive of sustainable development around the SSA?

Turner[38] defines sustainable development as optimal policies (sustainable growth) aimed at maintaining an acceptable growth rate in real income per capita without depleting the national capital stock or the stock of natural environmental assets. Turner's understanding of sustainable development captures and explains a nation's economic growth and the well-being of its citizens. He makes a point of maintaining that growth and curbing the decline.

Literally, sustainable development refers to sustaining development over time. By the early 1990s, it was thought that more than 70 definitions of sustainable development were in circulation, relating specifically to improvements in the management of an area's natural and human resources to create wealth and improve people's lives.

## 6.5 SUSTAINING THE UNSUSTAINABLE: DEVELOPMENT IMPLICATIONS OF ECONOMIC CRISIS IN SSA

Since the birth of the 21st century, there has been a significant increase in Africa's assimilation into the global economic landscape, particularly in the SSA region. The increased involvement of the SSA countries is a consequence of the growing demand for their main exports, which can be attributed to the fair political stability that prevailed in many countries in the region at the time. Although the EU remained the region's largest trading partner, China and India were the main emerging economies driving the region's growth process in the early 2000s.[12]

The absorption of the long-neglected SSA into the global economy has made virtually all countries in the region more vulnerable to the spillover effects of the Great Recession, with extreme repercussions for development structures that are heavily built on the defunct MDGs or the SDGs in their current form—for the countries of the subregion. Therefore, this section examines the developmental impact of the economic crisis in SSA. The economic crisis has affected many SSA countries in different ways. But before presenting that analysis, this section begins by summarizing the premise that, apart from the global trade slowdown, dwindling investment and cuts in foreign aid to SSA countries are an appendage of how the economic crisis has affected the region's development dynamics.

In 2009, world trade was forecast to fall by 11%, the first of its kind since 1982. This does not depend on the fact that the US, EU, and China account for about 71% of Africa's raw materials, causing African exporters to suffer a huge drop in demand from different parts of the world. For example, in early 2009, there was a 63% decline in overall exports of commodities from countries under the AGOA to the US, while virtually all countries in sub-Saharan Africa depend on the monetization of their primary commodities. But with the sharp drop in market prices and allegedly due to the economic crisis, the overall African economy has grown by a deplorable figure, accounting for about 1.8% of the total world trade. Even after the internal crisis and conflicts in some African states, regardless of the global economic crisis, tourism has become the core business in many SSA countries, such as the tourism industry, which largely deterred investors from the region.[45]

However, the market and trade situation for most SSAs appeared bleak after the economic crisis, but the lack of fiscal contraction and trade restraint policies by some African governments preserved some optimism that buoyed future growth. For example, Liberia has seen a revival in its timber, palm oil, and mineral production coupled with increased exports of cocoa and coffee. The Malawian economy has also been boosted by the expansion of the Kayelekeran uranium mine. Along with the rapid recovery of Burkina Faso's cotton industry, Burkina Faso's gold exports also saw an increase as four newly established mines went into full production. In recognition of these internal reactions to the global trade deficit, the IMF commended many African governments in its 2009 Regional Economic Reports.[19]

This introduction will be insufficient without adding the Chinese spices. Before and especially after the economic crisis, African countries became more vulnerable to fluctuations in China's economic growth. While about 10% of goods imported into Africa come from China, almost 14% of African goods exports were destined for China. Despite the global impact of the economic crisis, Sino-African trade grew from $74 billion in 2008 to $107 billion in 2009, an increase of 62%, and to date, the geometric economic growth metrics between Africa and China have not changed.[32] The immediate impact of this interaction is that it has helped to ease the constraints on economic competitiveness for countries in the SSA.

Undoubtedly, the economic crisis has affected the SSA in many ways. In a region populated by many low- and middle-income countries, with increasing numbers of poor and starving people and with various domestic challenges remaining, the economic crisis appears to be a distraction from SSA countries' tentative progress toward levels of development that might have been sustainable. Not only did the growth rate of SSA's GDP decline from 6.2% in 2007 to 4.9% in 2008, but the figure continued to decline to 1.6% in 2009.[41] As an explanatory limitation applies, a rising GDP is the forerunner of the development; however, an increase in GDP without a positive change in people's living standards cannot be interpreted as development.

However, in 2014, the World Bank reported a slowdown in the SSA economy, with the growth rate declining from 4.6% to 3.7% between 2014 and 2015.[21] Although growth was expected to pick up marginally in 2016 and rise steadily in 2017, the forms of conflicts and risks (such as crime, sea piracy, drought, terrorism, violent extremism, drug trafficking, the outbreak of Ebola disease in some parts, insecurity, etc. are changing) in various SSA countries have turned wild expectations into huge wails. To put it another way, using the development indices produced by the MDG/SDG auditorium, the impact of the economic crisis has degenerated sub-Saharan Africa's efforts to achieve real development in real terms.

In separating politics and economics, a superficial review of China's remarkable economic development might lead one to believe that authoritarian regimes drive economic development and its sustainability more impressively, which also corresponds to the achievements of authoritarian regimes in Ethiopia and Rwanda. However, some studies have also shown that the liberal regimes in SSA perform better in sustaining human and economic development, while the apparent growth under an undemocratic regime may not be sustainable. This view is also reflected, inter alia, in the situations in Malawi and Botswana. Having established that most SSA countries have an unshakable propensity for both economic development and nonauthoritarian regimes, the immediate aftermath of the economic crisis and its lasting legacies manifested themselves in the development of several hostile policies not usually recognized by the young and slow-moving improving democracies in the subregion.[26] As a result, certain policies that supplant majority interests but enhance minority interests reappeared in the styles of government of many SSA governments; the long-term effects are of course reflected in the growing gap between rich and poor in each of the countries of the SSA.[46]

More specifically, however, the economic crisis triggered—like a seesaw—a significant increase in the official level of external development assistance, financial flows, remittances, and private money flowing into the region. For example, comparing figures between 1990 and 2012, financial flows increased from $20 billion in the first to $120 billion in the second. The immediate consequence of this development is the strategic placement of SSA as an attractive hub for investors, both in government bonds and in other private sectors.[13] The second best FDI destinations in 2014, for example, regional economies such as Mozambique, Ghana, Zambia, Uganda, Tanzania, South Africa, Nigeria, and Kenya, attracted increased FDI numbers, representing a 4.7% growth in financial flows into the region in 2014 (ibid.).

Although China has been an active player in reviving the African economy through its numerous investments in the commodity sector and its lavish spending on infrastructure projects in several SSA countries, the staccato improvement in China's economy since 2014, due to changing global economic trends and partnerships, has led to a 40% drop in Chinese investment in Africa, the impact of which became more apparent toward the end of 2015.[42]

Another important developmental impact of the economic crisis is that it exposed SSA economies to external shockwaves of natural resource exploitation. African exports are home to durable goods and commodities such as unrefined agricultural products, minerals, and fuels. For example, the top five exports from SSA in 2013 were natural resources, which are nonrenewable and also accounted for about 61% of all total exports in 2013. Resources include petroleum, bituminous minerals, iron ore, natural gas, and gold.[46] A recent World Bank report also listed seventeen SSA countries as being rich in natural resources, while Equatorial Guinea, Angola, Chad, DR Congo, Gabon, South Sudan, Nigeria, and Sudan are all oil exporters, as are Botswana, Guinea, Sierra Leone, Liberia, Mauritania, Namibia, Niger, and Zambia. In addition, Liberia has the potential to explore offshore oil, while Uganda, Sao Tome and Principe, and Mozambique have vast oil and gas reserves.[20]

In all of these cases, however, the availability of abundant natural resources does not automatically mean prosperity for SSA as extractive industries do not provide more jobs and opportunities for other sectors within the economy. Thus, the succession of monolithic economies or dependency on a single export commodity continues to expose many SSA states to external flows or the exponential impact of the economic crisis on developed countries. To put it bluntly, the economic crisis has not worsened the development status of many SSA states but has pushed many states further away from real-time development.

Obviously, in a positive sense, the economic crisis has prompted many SSA countries to take charge of their own development agenda and diversify their income base for wealth expansion. Contrary to the decade-long debate over Nigeria's resource curse, since 2014, Nigeria appears to be reaping tremendous benefits from its oil wealth and diversification. Not only has Nigeria risen to become the largest economy in the subregion, but its robust stature of political instability and weak economic performance has been slimming. While the deficits in good governance persist in virtually all African countries, we can currently talk about the rapid gains made with diamonds from Botswana, cobalt from Congo, gold from Ghana, copper from Zambia, uranium from Niger and Namibia, bauxite from Guinea, and coffee from Ethiopia, Sierra Leone's iron ore, and the relative economic transformation reported by a few other countries.[5]

Likewise, one of the positive effects of the economic crisis in SSA is to ignite infrastructure investment, without which development will be limited to only its face value.

Undeniably, several perspectives confirm that investments in infrastructure are crucial for economic development. Likewise, over time, the key factor thwarting poverty alleviation, economic growth, trade integration, and the overall development of SSA is weak infrastructure. Therefore, the needs of the regions that became more widespread during and after the economic distress included ports, railways, roads, pipelines, energy, ICT infrastructure, airports, and further development of manufacturing capacities. The poor and unfortunate infrastructure situation in sub-Saharan Africa has reportedly reduced productivity by at least 40% and also pierced economic growth expectations by 2% annually between 2008 and 2010.[14]

After observing the gaps left by infrastructure decay, many SSA countries adjusted to China's economic growth model, and by 2012, the number of infrastructure projects actively geared toward development totaled over 800 (ibid.). Additionally, SSA appears to have been plagued by a thirst for infrastructure as the region spends approximately $7 billion a year on road construction.[37] For example, in 2016, paved roads connecting Cape Town to Cairo were completed, while the Trans-Saharan route from Lagos to Algiers is in the completion phase. In addition, rehabilitation and construction of major railway lines are ongoing with China as an arbiter.[11] In 2015, the newly built electric railway linking Djibouti with Addis Ababa opened for easy transportation, while the railway linking Zambia, Congo, and Angola was renovated for commercial purposes.

## 6.6 THE HIPPOCRATIC ECONOMIC GROWTH AND DEVELOPMENT INDEX IN SSA

The development challenges in sub-Saharan Africa are fundamental and extremely worrying. While many scholars have linked their low development status to long years of civil wars and authoritarian rule, some scholars have endlessly traced underlying economic progress to problems of insecurity, population explosion, and leadership factors in many SSA states. The placement of many SSA states based on Western values is arguably a likely source of the region's unsustainable development. But then, without fully expelling the Western imprints, the alternative roles of development, particularly from Asia and other parts of the world, seemed to have spurred SSA into a growth model that is also managed through to the end of development. However, what remains a mystery is that GDP or economic growth numbers are increasing on average without a corresponding increase in the region's economic development. Furthermore, it is safer to say that the nature of SSA development is unsustainable.[1]

While SSA countries continue to suppress alleged external constraints on their development, this section argues, with a different tone, that Hippocratic economic growth requires a reassessment of the region's leadership accent or quality of leadership, viewed as a key converter of economic growth feedback into national or regional development and thus in their sustainability. That is, without the right leadership and inquisitive attitude toward development, exhausting the entire treasuries of the IMF, World Bank, and Asian banks will not succeed in translating SSA's economic growth into development. Therefore, the results of economic growth remain with little or no impact on the development of the region.

However, the disproportionate economic position of individual SSA countries, despite the relative improvement in their average GDP over the past decade, not only highlights the probably inadequate responses of some states to the economic crisis but also reflects the acute internal resistance to development in sub-Saharan Africa. As predicted by some economic institutions such as the World Bank and the IMF, health, safety, and education systems in sub-Saharan Africa deteriorated while child mortality, unemployment, and poverty increased—all of which are a recipe for discord and conflict throughout the region.[20] In 2015, the daunting progress of sub-Saharan Africa's economy became legendary as nearly all countries in the region have populations living on less than a dollar a day, while a larger percentage equally wallow in hunger—a standard that falls short of the United Nations MDG 2015 assessment.[40]

Although the improvement in the SSA economy has been erratic throughout since 1990, GDP per capita remains historically low in almost all countries. As security and political conditions continue to improve, democratic governance and macroeconomic apparatuses have also improved in a parallel direction. For example, the SSA region, which accounts for a staggering 12% and 1.5% of the world's total population and nominal world GDP, respectively, has experienced minimal levels of conflict during its brief resurgence in economic growth. For example, a region that was largely among the Heavily Indebted Poor Countries (HIPCs) in the late 1990s, and sadly, with the 2005 Multilateral Debt Relief Initiative (MDRI), has reduced debt by about $100 billion in over 25 SSA issuers of bonds on the global financial market radars at moderately low interest rates.[48]

As previously mentioned, the Lighthouse of Directions for SSA's economy as an entity has not been adequately managed. Thus, warnings of deindustrialization and instability replaced signaling investors' growing confidence in the region's economy. For example, Ghana's main exports fell due to falling gold, oil, and cocoa prices, while its national debt likewise matured to over 70% of its GDP. By 2014, 31% of Ghana's currency had depreciated, while the budget deficit widened to around 11%.[21] Although the Ghanaian experience cannot be separated from its overwhelming recurring spending, a situation is available in virtually every other country in sub-Saharan Africa.

Awareness of unsustainable improvement in their economies invariably forced some of the countries to enter into a stabilization agreement with the IMF in 2015, but the risk of noncompliance with the agreed terms remains.[10] For example, Zambia, which relied for 70% on copper export earnings, was hit by a shocking thaw in copper prices and a 45% devaluation of its currency, owing to the ineptitude of Zambian leaders and the accompanying macroeconomic imbalances.[10]

Without wasting counts, the 2015 African Pulse reports revealed that other sub-Saharan countries, such as Angola, South Africa, Uganda, Nigeria and a few others, have weakened their currencies and economies; however, this is of greater importance for countries that rely on single or dual exports of commodities for their revenue base and foreign earnings.[47]

What has been critically discussed in the most recent subsection is the flow of SSA countries from the era of economic collapse to the era of economic renaissance and the ongoing transition to what is perceived as challenging time ahead for the SSA region. But in this order, it is important that the period of economic boom or growth is without real economic development, in part because these countries' populations are affluent, thus reigniting competition for dwindling infrastructure facilities—an index of a country's or region's level of development in general.

However, one should not be too hasty in blaming SSA's depressing level of development for not reaping the dividends of the economic upswing. While it is reasonable to characterize the short duration of economic growth as a setback, the thrust of this paper has objectively established that these countries' development is inherently unsustainable. Using different semantics, the legacy of the economic crisis is still imprinted on the countries of the SSA region. As Mandela affirmed in his Unparalleled Development Principles, sustainable development requires a strategic vision from a leader willing to blur the lines between morality and politics to guide the required transformation and development, with the support and partnership of existing development centers around the world.[1]

## 6.7 CONCLUSIONS

In conclusion, this paper has critically argued that the economic crisis has affected many SSA countries in various ways. As revealed in the insightful analysis, the hat-trick of falling global trade, dwindling investment, and cuts in foreign aid to SSA countries are byproducts of the economic crisis and its impact on the region's development dynamics. Although many African leaders seem to be outspoken like them, while impeding the development of countries under their oversight, some have nonetheless acknowledged that handing over the largest operations of their development agenda to outside agencies is merely an invitation to exploitation and vulnerability to universal economic emergencies. Despite the impact of the global economic crisis around the world, the sub-Saharan Africa region experienced challenges mainly related to its monetary value and exchange rate, among other impacts. Being a subregion with mostly monolithic economies, the recovery was faster as commodities reached significant price levels.

But unfortunately, the breadth of economic growth between 2012 and 2015, as reported by the African Pulse, did not improve development indicators for most countries in SSA. The times before, during, and after the economic crisis only justify the discovery of hidden development potential that is not sustainable in itself. But for now, we can insist that there has been no real development, and the following recommendations are deemed central to unleashing the masks that are hiding the real development of the sub-Saharan region. First, it is evident that there is a tenuous link between the sub-Saharan economy and the world economy as the relativity of global economic conditions has watermarked the economy of sub-Saharan Africa for better or for worse. Therefore, regimes within the SSA should further scale back their protectionist policies and develop broader policies that guarantee additional employment opportunities for the growing population.[1] The perception of leadership must also change from its linear monolog of governance to a broader dialog with the people. This will restore altruism in service and consequently shorten the growing database of poor people in all countries, not just within sub-Saharan Africa but also across the African continent.

Equally, the elites have to deal with it; the development apparatus rests on the collective shoulders of their intellect and the elected leaders. Therefore, collaborative policies for a positive transformation of society must not remain in the hands of a few bureaucrats as key decision-makers but must involve the professionals and academicians, who are by default key stakeholders in development and sustainability policies. In addition, governments across the SSA must seek to diversify their economies and broaden their income bases. In a rapidly evolving world, the policy menu should pay particular attention to sectors that are seen as crucial catalysts for each country's sustainable development. To name a few, the science, technology, research, and agriculture sectors must be synchronized with the single-track economies of SSA countries. The incorporation of technical value will disproportionately help overcome the daunting socioeconomic trials (such as drought, famine, disease, crime, etc.) and similarly help meet the related development challenges that continue to plague the SSA region pop up. For example, advances in technology offer limitless opportunities for willing nations to advance on their development scale. Recently, Kenya launched the world's leading low-level subscription mobile application. Retailers use the Bond app to save, with just a 10% approval fee on $30, and this has opened up another revenue stream for the Kenyan government as the technology system has enabled them to seal leaks, streamline tax collection, and increase revenue.[7]

Therefore, and perhaps eventually, although the economic crisis affected some important pulleys of economic development in SSA, the relative recovery and brief economic pickup decoupled the long-term effects of the economic crisis in SSA. However, the twin deficits in the successive fiscal and managerial accounts of most countries in the SSA appear to have redefined their development needs rather than perpetuating the unsustainable development configurations of countries in the region.

## KEYWORDS

- **development**
- **sustainable development**
- **unsustainable development**
- **Africa**
- **Sub-Saharan Africa**
- **economic crisis**

## REFERENCES

1. Acheoah, O. A. Local Government: The Underutilized Governance Structure in Nigeria. *Arts Soc. Sci. J.* **2018,** *9* (412).
2. Addae-Korankye, A. Causes and Control of Loan Default/Delinquency in Microfinance Institutions in Ghana. *Am. Int. J. Cont. Res.* **2014,** *4* (12), 36–45.
3. Aduloju, A. A.; Adedoyin, T. A. The Tech-Novation Pathway from Pandemic to Prosperity: A Post Covid-19 Roadmap for African Economy. *Econ. Consultant* **2020,** *30* (3).
4. Aduloju, A. A.; Pratt, O. O. Human Security and Developmental Crisis in the Contemporary West Africa. *J. Hum. Secur.* **2014,** *10* (2), 46–58.
5. African Centre for Economic Transformation (ACET). *African Transformation Report* [Online] 2014. https://www.cgdev.org/sites/default/files/ACET%20ATR%20presentation%20to%20CGD%20042914.pdf (Accessed August 25, 2022).
6. Akanonu, P.; Onyekwena, C. A Note on the Economic Downturn in Sub-Saharan Africa: The Nigeria-South Africa Comparison. *Centre for the Study of the Economies of Africa Policy Brief*; 2016, Issue 1/16.
7. Ali, M.; Shifa, A. B.; Shimeles, A.; Woldeyes, F. Building Fiscal Capacity: The Role of ICT. Working Paper Series N° 290, African Development Bank, Abidjan, Côte d'Ivoire; 2017.
8. Azeng, T. F.; Yogo, T. U. Youth Unemployment and Political Instability in Selected Developing Countries. African Development Bank, Working Paper Series, No. 171, [Online] 2016. https://www.afdb.org/fileadmin/uploads/afdb/Documents/Publications/Working_Paper17Youth_Unemployment_and_Political_Instability_in_Selected_Developing_Countries.pdf (Accessed July 15, 2022).
9. Aziz, J.; Caramazza, F.; Salgado, R. Currency Crises. In *Search of Common Elements*; IMF Working Paper No. 67. International Monetary Fund: Washington, DC, 2000.
10. Bloomberg. Bloomberg Intelligence 2015 [Online] 2015. Outlookhttps://data.bloomberglp.com/professional/sites/4/2015/03/Bloomberg-Intelligence-2015-Outlook.pdf (Accessed August 22, 2022).
11. Brookings Institution. Picking Up Steam: The Expansion of Chinese Railways in Africa, 2014. https://www.brookings.edu/blog/africa-in-focus/2014/09/26/picking-up-steam-the-expansion-of-chinese-railways-in-africa/ (Accessed August 25, 2022).
12. Chauvin, S.; Geis A. Who has been Affected, how and why? The Spillover of the Global Financial Crisis to sub-Saharan Africa and Ways to Recovery, Occasional Paper Series, No. 124, Frankfurt, 2011.
13. EY. Africa Attractiveness Survey: Africa 2014 Executing Growth, 2014. http://mb.cision.com/Public/1179/9588229/b0664e1207a65aa4.pdf (Accessed August 25, 2022)
14. EY Africa Attractiveness Survey [Online], 2013. https://saiia.org.za/wp-content/uploads/2013/12/ EY-Africa-presentation-FY14-3.pdf (Accessed August 25, 2022).
15. Focus Economies. Sub-Saharan Africa's 2016 & 2017 Growth Rates [Online], 2017. https://www.focus-economics.com/blog/posts/sub-saharan-africas-2016-2017-growth-rates (Accessed August 25, 2022).
16. Global Finance Magazine. Central Banker Report Cards 2013 [Online], 2013. https://www.gfmag.com/magazine/october-2013-1/central-banker-report-cards-2013 (Accessed May 21, 2022).
17. Handley, G.; Higgins, K.; Sharma, B.; Bird, K.; Cammack, D. Poverty and Poverty Reduction in SubSaharan Africa: An Overview of Key Issues, Overseas Development Institute,

Working Paper 299 [Online], 2009. http://www.africaneconomicoutlook.org/fileadmin/uploads/aeo/PDF /Nigeria%20Full%20PDF%20 Country%20Note.pdf (Accessed August 25, 2022).
18. Heidhues, P.; Kőszegi, B. Futile Attempts at Self-Control. *J. Eur. Econ. Assoc.* **2009,** *7* (2–3), 423–434.
19. IMF. *IMF Annual Report 2009—Fighting the Global Crisis* [Online], 2009. https://www.imf.org/-/media/Websites/IMF/imported-flagshipissues/external/pubs/ft/ar/2009/eng/pdf/_ar09engpdf. ashx (Accessed August 25, 2022).
20. IMF. *International Monetary Fund Annual Report 2013: Promoting a More Secure and Stable Global Economy* [Online], 2013. https://www.imf.org/en/Publications/AREB/Issues/2016/12/31/International-Monetary-Fund-Annual-Report-2013-Promoting-a-More-Secure-and-Stable-Global-40629 (Accessed August 25, 2022).
21. IMF. Regional Economic Outlook (Sub-Saharan Africa Navigating Headwinds) [Online], 2015. https://www.worldbank.org/content/dam/Worldbank/document/Africa/Report/Africas-Pulse-brochure_Vol7.pdf (Accessed August 25, 2022).
22. IMF. *IMF Annual Report 2016* [Online], 2016. https://www.imf.org/external/pubs/ft/ar/2016/eng/pdf/ ar16_eng.pdf (Accessed August 25, 2022).
23. IMF. Regional Economic Outlook. Sub-Saharan Africa. Dealing with Gathering Clouds [Online], 2015. https://www.imf.org/-/media/Websites/IMF/imported-flagshipissues/external/pubs/ft/ reo/2015/afr/eng/pdf/_sreo1015pdf.ashx (Accessed August 25, 2022).
24. International Monetry Fund. *IMF Annual Report 2016* [Online], 2016. https://www.imf.org/external/ pubs/ft/ar/2016/eng/pdf/ar16_eng.pdf (Accessed September 2, 2022).
25. Jickling, M. *Causes of the Financial Crisis (R40173)*. Congressional Research Service: Washington, DC [Online], 2009. https://core.ac.uk/download/pdf/5125888.pdf (Accessed August 25, 2022).
26. Munganga, D. The Effectiveness of U.S. Development Assistance in Fostering Sustainable Development in Sub-Saharan Africa [Online], 2018. https://commons.emich.edu/cgi/viewcontent. cgi?article=1593&context=honors (Accessed August 25, 2022).
27. Myint, H. *The Economics of the Developing Countries*; Fred erick A. Praeger: New York, 1980.
28. Okwechime, I.; Yange, J. T.; Aduloju, A. A. Africa and the Global Economic and Financial Crisis. *World Rev. Political Econ.* **2016,** *7* (4), 208–225.
29. Perera, M. Migration in the Global Recession and in its Recovery in Sri Lanka. In *South Asia Migration Report 2017 (Recruitment, Remittances and Reintegration)*, Rajan, S. Irudaya, ed.; Routledge, London, 2016.
30. Pettinger, R. Standards: A Behavioural Approach to Management. In *The True Value of CSR*; Fryzel, B., ed.; Palgrave Macmillan, London, 2015. https://doi.org/10.1057/9781137433206_16.
31. Randall, V.; Theobald, R. Dependency Theory and the Study of Politics. In *Political Change and Underdevelopment*; Palgrave, London, 1998. https://doi.org/10.1007/978-1-349-26856-6_5.
32. Reuters. TIMELINE—Financial Crisis Gathers Pace in 2009 [Online], 2009. https://www.reuters.com/article/uk-financial-timeline-sb-idUKTRE53049J20090401 (Accessed August 25, 2022).
33. Berglee, R. World Regional Geography: People, Places, and Globalization [Online], 2013. https://catalog.flatworldknowledge.com/catalog/editions/berglee-10997-world-regional-geography-people-places-and-globalization-1-0-1 (Accessed August 25, 2022).

34. Szirmai, A. Developing Countries and the Concept of Development. In *The Dynamics of Socio-Economic Development: An Introduction*; Szirmai, A., ed.; Cambridge University Press, 2005. https://doi.org/10.1017/CBO9780511817342.
35. Abebe, T.; Quaicoe, N. Causes of Poverty in Sub-Saharan Africa: A Layered Theory Approach to Understanding Significant Factors. *J. Econ. Int. Finance* **2014,** *6* (6), 112–124.
36. The Central Bank of Nigeria (CBN). Quarterly Economic Report 2012 [Online], 2012. https://www.cbn.gov.ng/out/2013/ccd/cbn%20economic%20report%20for%20the%20fourth%20quarter%20of%202012.pdf
37. The Economist. African Roads and Rails [Online], 2015. All aboard https://www.economist.com/middle-east-and-africa/2015/02/26/all-aboard (Accessed August 25, 2022).
38. Turner, R. K. Pluralism in Environmental Economics: A Survey of the Sustainable Economic Development Debate. *J. Agric. Econ.* **1988,** *39* (3), 352–359.
39. Tyler, Z. C.; Gopal, S. Sub-Saharan Africa at Cross-Roads: A Quantitative Analysis of Regional Development. *The Pardee Papers*, No. 10/MAY 2010, 2010.
40. UN. The Millennium Development Goals Report—the United Nations [Online], 2010. https://www.un.org/millenniumgoals/pdf/MDG%20Report%202010%20En%20r15%20-low%20res%2020100615%20-.pdf (Accessed August 25, 2022).
41. United Nations (UN). Economic Commission for Africa; African Union Commission (2010-03). Economic Report on Africa 2010: Promoting High-level Sustainable Growth to Reduce Unemployment in Africa Overview [Online], 2010. https://hdl.handle.net/10855/3230" (Accessed August 25, 2022).
42. Voice of America (VOA). Chinese Investment in Africa, China's Ministry of Commerce. Also Reported in Financial Times, 21st October 2015 [Online], 2015. https://elibrary.worldbank.org/doi/10.1596/978-1-4648-0615-5 (Accessed August 25, 2022).
43. World Bank. Exports of Goods and Services (% of GDP), 2016. https://data.worldbank.org/indicator/NE.EXP.GNFS.ZS (Accessed August 25, 2022).
44. World Bank. World Bank Annual Report 2016 [Online], 2016. http://pubdocs.worldbank.org/en/596391540568499043/worldbankannualreport2016.pdf (Accessed August 25, 2022).
45. WTO. World Trade Report 2009 [Online], 2009. https://www.wto.org/english/res_e/booksp_e/anrep_e/world_trade_report09_e.pdf (Accessed August 25, 2022).
46. Zamfir, I. *Africa's Economic Growth: Taking off or Slowing Down?* Members' Research Service. Directorate-General for Parliamentary Research Services, European Parliament, 2016.

# CHAPTER 7

# Evincible Digital Gender Divide in Post-Covid-19 Pandemic Era: Vincible or Invincible?

SANUSI MOHAMMED SADIQ,[1] INVINDER PAUL SINGH,[2] and MUHAMMAD MAKARFI AHMAD[3]

[1]*Department of Agricultural Economics and Extension, FUD, Dutse, Nigeria*

[2]*Department of Agricultural Economics, SKRAU, Bikaner, India*

[3]*Department of Agricultural Economics and Extension, BUK, Kano, Nigeria*

## ABSTRACT

As e-learning and telecommuting became the new standard as a result of the Covid-19 problem, the adoption of IT-based solutions increased dramatically. However, access to and use of technology are not gender-neutral. In emerging markets and developing economies, women are less likely than men to only have access to the internet and other modern conveniences (EMDEs). The lack of access to technology may limit women's opportunities for fiscal advancement. The digital vacuum, a socioeconomic problem, prevents people from using the net and perhaps other ICT routes to receive public services. According to Intel research, when there are an additional 600 million women online, the global Gross Domestic Income (GDI) will rise by USD 13–18 million. The McKinsey Global Initiative (MGI) reports that 2.2 billion nonmen (52%) remain offline. This is based on data on digital and financial inclusion. Therefore, having digital equality for women in this age of internet expansion would significantly affect workplace gender equality. The heads of state acknowledged the truth of gender variance in digital access in their concluding comments at the world conference of the

Management for Sustainable Development: Integrating Social, Economic, and Environmental Goals.
Vishal Jain & Amit Mittal (Eds.)

United Nations on society's information and reaffirmed their commitment to advancing gender equality. There is a critical need to increase women's digital media literacy, as well as to build their ability to contribute to society, particularly in ICT-related professions. The ability to utilize ICT critically and confidently, study, and communicate is all made possible by having a strong understanding of digital media literacy.

## 7.1 INTRODUCTION

Estimates indicate that women are "less likely to be web-based, are more likely to face lesser or no digital skills, and are at increased danger of being both socially and economically ostracized by the prevalent digital disruption,"[1] regardless of where in the world they reside. Of the four billion people who are not part of the digital economy, the majority are women. In the least developed nations of the globe, women have a 31% lower likelihood of having internet access than men do[2] because of social, cultural, and economic barriers. The digital economic system has the potential to alter the nature of labor and claim policy narratives. 30 more jobs are anticipated to be created by the digital economy in India alone by 2024–2025.[3] The chances of women utilizing these opportunities provided by the new information society are estimated to be one-third lower than those of men. According to studies, the gender disparity in developing nations will widen further, and by 2020, more than 75% of all women worldwide will still be without a connection.

Since then, the "digital disparity," which was once only comprehended in terms of reach to state-of-the-art ICT and the division between have individuals versus have not people, has changed.[3]

Because "access" and "use" are frequently used interchangeably, there is not enough emphasis placed on the knowledge, time, and resources needed to use ICT effectively. Therefore, it is more accurate to think of the digital divide as the product of the interplay between a skill gap and even a true availability denial to ICT, with the two (2) hurdles feeding off of one another. The alienation of female from the internet age is further exacerbated by the fact that utilization is dependent on the availability of time, opportunities, autonomy in use, and social support.[4] Therefore, simply granting physical access is insufficient. The phrase "digital inclusion" describes people who are able to use ICTs to actively participate in, mobilize, and interact in public life. It is crucial to keep this in mind when discussing digital equality. The primary focus of policy narratives is on the enabling potential of ICTs, but there are worries that even in the absence of access equity and skill arrangements, they will compound already-existing imbalances and support traditional gender hierarchies.

## 7.2 WOMEN AND SOCIAL INEQUALITIES

Nearly four out of five women reside in underdeveloped countries, where they frequently encounter even more discrimination based on gender than their colleagues in developed countries.[3] Nearly 60% of them end up working as unpaid family careers, and they have a higher likelihood of being unemployed as well as have fewer career and educational options. These women are restricted by traditional family responsibilities and do not possess the core computer literacy skills necessary to realize their full potential. Roles have a strong influence on how and why women utilize technology, which contributes to many of these limitations. Southern Indian women are defined as being a source of inspiration for their families as well as the wellness of the whole family.[5] Even in households with educated women, they are often discouraged from taking care of their own requirements or pursuing personal growth because cultural, the media, and society define what women are expected to do. In Ghana, there are analogous connections between a person's place of employment and the availability of digital resources. Although on the surface, this access would seem to be gender-neutral, a disproportion number of women are drawn to the informal sector, where access opportunities are limited, due to conventional gender roles, institutional structures, and economic realities.[5]

Across all age groups, the proportion of people of the other sex who use the internet is lower in less developed nations than the proportion of males. The fact that highly literate women use the internet equally to men is a notable exception, though. The implication is that women will utilize the internet just as often as men if given the chance and resources to do so, refuting the notion that women's capacity prohibits them from doing so. Researchers that attempted to quantify the gender inequity in six French-speaking West African countries (Senegal, Cameroon, Benin, Mali, Burkina Faso, and Mauritania) found no distinction in access or usage between young women with elementary school education and postgraduates.[6] This would seem to demonstrate that education can be a powerful tool in the struggle against the gender gap in internet utilization and access. However, it is well-known that women, irrespective of their age, find it challenging to pursue their educational goals because they are short on time, are burdened with caring for their families and homes, and are susceptible to sociocultural practices that place low importance on education.[7] The spread and application of ICTs, as well as the advantages they provide, tend to fit within the boundaries of already-existing economic and income disparities, thereby alienating or isolating the poor. In light of this, it is likely that, in the absence of meticulous planning, ICTs will make gender disparities worse.

## 7.3 WOMEN'S EMPOWERMENT

The literature contains numerous definitions of empowerment. Powerless individuals can take charge of their own lives, develop skills, and solve problems by being aware of their condition, organizing collaboratively to improve it, and accessing possibilities. Expanding people's capacity for strategic life decision-making, particularly in situations when this capacity had previously been denied to them, is what Mądra-Sawicka et al.[8] define as empowerment. In order to effectively promote their well-being, women must confront the culture and conventions that already exist. This process is known as female empowerment. It is a process that encourages individuals to take control of their lives in their communities and societies. Many studies[7] contend that empowerment is a hard concept to define and that it is best understood by its absence than by its presence. Improving women's economic and social standing is essential, especially in emerging and underdeveloped countries, because there is a strong association between these factors and economic growth and development.[9] Sequel to the advocacy of women's rights and freedom in diverse fields—politics, healthcare, employment, and education—women will play a greater role in growth and development by increasing their economic contribution. Mądra-Sawicka et al.[8] noted that while female empowerment may be viewed differently in different societies, it is generally agreed that it is stronger when women are more educated and have greater employment possibilities. The discourse on digital technology and women's empowerment has several recurring topics, including the use of digital media, remote female's connections to services and companies, e-governance, and statistics. Three essential components for empowerment were listed by Mądra-Sawicka et al.,[8] referencing Herawati. The first facet of meaningful access is the capacity for each individual to employ technology to enhance social living. Second, rather than simply being able to use technology, motivation is linked to what is accomplished through its usage. The capacity for individuals to use digital platforms in a confident, socially responsible manner is the third facet of empowerment.[10] Women's empowerment, according to Suwana and Lily,[11] aims to improve women's authority and strengths to fully engage, negotiate career paths, negotiate small, medium, or large enterprises, and create employment opportunities. Also, it modifies the duties and roles of domestic women's organizations so that women can actually engage in remote programs through the media. ICT has the ability to significantly improve women's economic, political, and social empowerment as well as gender equality.

## 7.4 DIGITAL MEDIA

Digital media now includes social media as a crucial component. This phrase has numerous definitions. According to Acilar and Saeb,[12] a social media plan is an example of an online tool that facilitates social interaction. Social media are "a compilation of internet-rooted apps that expand upon the conceptual and technological foundations of Web 2.0 and enable the production and transfer of user-generated content," according to Acilar and Saeb.[12] It is described by Cheshmehzangi et al.[13] as a platform that encourages and supports engagement from media users in the creation and distribution of content. Communities of people come together online to exchange knowledge via conversational media, which makes it possible to easily create and transmit information in the form of text, images, videos, and audios. On social media, you can find user-generated material that is created by user interactions. Information and entertainment may be easily created and shared thanks to social media. Social networking websites, media-sharing websites, and microblogs are just a few examples of the many varied forms that social media can take. Social structures, such as those found on social networking sites like Facebook, LinkedIn, and Google+, are made up of a group of people and organizations who interact to form interlinks. A variety of multimedia material can be hosted, published, managed, and shared by users through media exchange platforms (like YouTube). The broadcast channel of microblogging allows for the dissemination of mini—a brief piece of information—in the style of a condensed message, images, or video links. Twitter is the widely known platform. Social media platforms foster interaction and the exchange of information or materials among members of virtual communities, notwithstanding privacy concerns.[14] Social media platforms also have many benefits in a variety of other industries.

### *7.4.1 DIGITAL MEDIA LITERACY*

The term "media literacy" refers to a wide range of digital production abilities, including "the aptitude to develop, to be critical, and to offer as well as to accept" digital data.[11] The study of media literacy involves more than just learning to interpret. The development of social and cultural competencies through networking that are founded on traditional literacy (writing and reading), research skills, and media-critical analytical competencies is what is referred to as new media literacy, also known as digital media literacy. In order to effectively solve problems and communicate, the society needs to have these five (5) digital media competencies:

1. **Access:** locating and effectively utilizing media and technological tools, as well as disseminating pertinent information;
2. **Analyze and critique:** understand messages while applying critical thinking to assess the truthfulness and viewpoints of messages while taking important effects or ramifications into account;
3. **Create:** one creates content using original ideas and expression, keeping their audience and technique in mind;
4. **Reflect:** Integrate morality and societal responsibility into one's identity, experiences, communication, and activities; and
5. **Act:** Participate in communities at all levels—local, regional, national, and international—as a member of a community and work both independently and collaboratively to exchange knowledge and address problems in the office, the home, and the community.

Digital literacy courses must provide the framework of how, where, and when to implement newly learned expertise, skills, and information in addition to coaching or capacity building in the fundamental ICT skills. In order to work properly in a digital environment, the participant must have the necessary confidence. Additionally, ICT training increases self-confidence, which in turn improves the lives of women.

## 7.5 DIGITAL DIVISION: THE CAUSES, REACTIONS, AND MAINTENANCE OF DIGITAL INEQUALITY

The term "digital gap" was first used to call attention to the unequal access to computers among students from different racial backgrounds in the 1990s.[15] It was less about the straightforward "haves" vs "have-nots" of digital technology and infrastructure and more about systematic imbalances that produce both winners and losers in the connected world.[3,16] The digital divide is a timely topic that has emerged in the academic and policy communities as a result of ICT advancements. The "digital gap," as it is commonly understood, refers to uneven technology access, which may have broad-reaching effects. Alternatively, the phrase "digital divide" refers to the unequal access that people have to ICT as well as to the knowledge and skills necessary to effectively utilize this technology. The gap between those who have access to and comprehend technology well and those who do not is frequently referred to as the "digital divide," which can compound socioeconomic and other problems for already underprivileged groups. The argument has been made that the inequity actually reflects a multilayered and nonstatic social mismatch that mirrors the prior advantages or disadvantages of people of various races and geographic locations.[17] The digital gap is a result of socioeconomic disadvantages experienced by certain individuals or communities, including poverty, a lack of educational possibilities, and gender inequality.[18,19] These communities or groups have limited access to ICT infrastructure and products, and many of them cannot afford them. It is essential to look more closely at the sources of the disparity using a context-specific, multilevel approach in order to more accurately depict the difficulties and realities of everyday life.[16] Two separate levels of the digital divide have been proposed by academics to better comprehend this issue.[20] At the "reach to technology" stage of the digital fractionate, the "haves" and "have-nots" are distinguished based on one's capacity to use or finance the advantages of digital technology. More specifically, the cost of mobile gadgets with internet connection packs may be a problem in developing nations for several people with little resources. The second component of the disparity is the "skill gaps," which relate to a broad range of operational skills needed to access, read, and evaluate internet information as well as exchange materials using desktop or smartphone devices.[20] Although making digital technology accessible assumes that end users have the necessary abilities, there are notable distinctions between privileged and disadvantaged groups in terms of who uses technology more effectively once they have access. Determining whether or not the gap between the different categories can be closed depends in large part on the skill or knowledge disparities.

### 7.5.1 WOMEN AND THE DIGITAL DIVIDE

Millions of young females are compelled to do so in the area of the digital gap due to pressure to drop out of school or pursue higher education.[3] Numerous young girls and women found the digital era to be unsatisfactory, despite the fact that it provided a means of knowledge dissemination and ensured that they could learn unhindered at home. The least number of women from indigenous tribes have access to education and the internet. For instance, India's Ministries of Social Justice and Empowerment, Information Technology and Electronics, and Women and Child Development have begun to support indigenous women and adolescent girls with development initiatives.[21] The Kishori Shakti Yojana (KSY), for instance, aims to enhance health, hygiene, and the chance for juvenile women between the ages of 11 and 18 to acquire life skills.

Along with offering actual or vocational education for making a living, it also sought to close both the skill and knowledge gaps. Self-paced learning is available through a number of online platforms, including NPTEL, e-Pathshala, Swayam-Prabha DTH, and SWAYAM channels. The goal is to make integrated learning possible and give everyone free access to excellent instructional resources. It has made it possible to access digital and online education in a variety of ways, including through listening to podcasts that contain e-content for the blind. However, such digital learning platforms were not easily accessible, were not inexpensive, and were little known in rural regions, particularly among young indigenous women. The Centre for Catalyzing Change[22] in Jharkhand reported that adolescent tribal girls living in remote areas faced significant obstacles to using the internet due to their fear of technology and lack of expertise. They do not have a supportive environment for online learning nor do they comprehend the notion. However, little research has been done on how household, community, and governmental connections affect rural tribal women's access to digital technology, either maintaining it or making it worse.

## 7.6 THE DIGITAL DIVIDE'S ORIGINAL IDEA

Recently, the idea of "digital disparity" has drawn a lot of attention due to the need to coordinate worldwide technological advancement and examine its effects on society. Because there is such a great need to control the development of technology, politicians have also tried to close the digital gap among their constituents by using the best tools.[23,24] The term "digital divide" refers to the disparity between citizens' access to ICT and their level of proficiency and expertise using it. The gender, geography, skills, and financial dimensions of the digital gap can all be used to explain it. The availability of the internet and computers, their usability, and the socioeconomic divide between developed and poor countries are other issues that are relevant. The digital divide and e-government are both highlighted by social changes, and the government is now responsible for closing the gap.[14]

The "digital divide" is the gap between those who can utilize ICT technologies and those who cannot in terms of access to hardware and software. It necessitates having sufficient access to or ownership of ICT, including hardware like computers and mobile devices, software like user-friendly webpages and apps, and the necessary skills to use ICT tools. According to several studies, there are two components of the digital gap: availability and use. Not everyone will use something in the same way. Use, on the other hand, pertains to having the necessary skills to run ICT equipment. Access refers to having physical resources, such as being able to access computers and phones. The disparity in digital use is mostly caused by a lack of available bandwidth and expensive technology and software that must be purchased or rented. Additional problems include physical infirmity and a dearth of ICT support and expertise. Numerous variants of the digital literacy divide, such as the digital gender imbalance (DGI), the digital difference based on race, the digital divide based on disability, and the digital gap based on age, education, and wealth, have been the subject of substantial research.[25] Some studies use the e-readiness index as a measure to evaluate the digital divide. This metric consists of a wide range of parts, including the legislative framework, talents, and telecommunication infrastructure.

### *7.6.1 THE DIGITAL GENDER DIVIDE (DGD)*

Prior to industrialization, women's roles were confined to the home and the hearth. However, modern civilizations' most recent technological advances have made it feasible for women to compete with men on a level playing field. Gender biases, however, still prevent certain women from using and accessing ICT, even in industrialized nations like Sweden and Japan. DGD is a result of how traditional gender biases function in this technological age. In terms of social, political, economic, and cultural spheres, DGD is an unequal chance for men and women to use ICT. Gender inequality and gender division are terms that some scholars swap. The underrepresentation of women in the ICT industry is another definition of DGD.

The digital divide, or the difference between those with access to ICT and those without it, is caused by a combination of factors, including disproportionate accessibility to technology, a lack of actual engagement and use of it, concerns about such use, and a lack of actual engagement and use. According to Rivera,[26] any disparity within the digital society, such as accessibility between males and women, the wealthy and the poor, developed and developing countries, and so forth, is known as the "digital gap." The two varieties of the digital barrier are those caused by access and ability gaps or by differences in ICT usage amongst those who currently have access. The imbalance in digital media usage and access between various groups or powers is referred to as the "digital gap." The gender gap (digital gender divide), which results in women having less access to digital media and fewer chances to participate in ICT environments than men, is one factor contributing to the uneven use of computer tools or digital media all over the globe. This is supported by a number of stereotypes that contend that women are tech-averse, uninterested in technology, and technologically incompetent. However, women use and have less access to digital media than men due to their poorer levels of employment, education, and income.[27]

Mohieldin and Ramadan[28] assert that gender stereotypes and the association of technology with men are at the root of DGD. Men tend to adopt new ICT first and use it more often than women, according to a Spanish study. Additionally, males use ICT more frequently than women do. The Aragonese Observation of the Community of Information (AOCI) for the year 2008 and data from international websites were used by the writers to reach this conclusion. The DGD is ignored while governments support more and more ICT-based initiatives for women in remote areas. Despite evidence that suggests that ICT may be used to promote women and give them access to healthcare, food, and education, women are becoming more and more marginalized in e-government initiatives. According to research, the majority of e-government applications have not taken into account the needs or problems that women experience.[25,29]

### *7.6.2 DIGITAL EXCLUSIONS AND INCLUSIONS: AN ANALYSIS*

New digital technologies have the potential to make it easier for women to participate in the labor market and pursue self-employment, according to the 2016 World Development Report by the World Bank. Additionally, more and more government functions are being carried out digitally. Examples include online government form submissions and online grievance redress using social media platforms. Consequently, women's disproportionate digital exclusion keeps them out of the workforce, out of public life, and out of politics. Although there are different degrees of digital divide within the G20, poorer groups and rural women tend to be the least digitally integrated.

The G20 needs to address the insufficient use of digital technologies as a result of rising costs and a lack of ICT-based infrastructure, which includes erratic electricity delivery. It is also necessary to handle the lack of access to opportunities that influence digital skilling and potentials that permit the uninhibited use of access and skills, both of which are influenced by socio-cultural perceptions. Infrastructure provision has frequently been the focus of policy narratives within the G20, and it is undoubtedly an important step. The digital skill gap and its sociocultural factors, however, have not received enough attention. To fully realize the transformative potential of ICTs, it is imperative to eliminate obstacles that both subtly and overtly discriminate against women and girls' access to the same academic achievement and digital training.

### *7.6.3 THE EFFECTS OF DIGITALIZATION ON EMPLOYMENT ON DIFFERENT GENDERS*

Women now have new chances to expand their participation in the economy thanks to recent advancements in big analytics, cloud computing, autonomous robotics, and artificial intelligence.[30] They have a lot of options for enhancing their degree of social and economic freedom. Women may not be able to benefit from the vast opportunity that is associated with the digital-internet era, though, because of the persistent gender gaps in these areas as well as in the labor market integration and financial inclusion. It's also uncertain whether and how the digital labor market revolution, which incorporates the automation of numerous tasks, will alter the employment that men and women already hold, and, if so, who will profit from it the most.

There are at least two potential effects of the digital revolution on gender equality. First of all, it alters the variety of occupations available and the skills needed to fill them. The automation–digitization of work procedures, made possible by digital advancement, may affect the involvement of women in the labor market by altering the need for employment for men and women in various ways. Numerous employees will undoubtedly be replaced by robots and algorithms in industries like administrative support, accounting, assembly-line manufacturing, and machine operation. On the other hand, they will support vocations in management, investigation, engineering, legal assistance, and healthcare. Second, recent developments in digital services, such as digital payments, data fintech services, and numerous digital platforms that connect employees and employers' start-ups and funders of new firms, may assist women in overcoming long-standing obstacles to their full integration into the economy, the arts, or finance.

With the aid of these innovative digital services, women may be able to expand their horizons in terms of markets they can access, work remotely and flexibly, communicate with clients, obtain training and mentorship, increase their financial independence, and get funding for their initiatives. Not to mention, the use of digital technologies could lessen discrimination against women.

What effects will future digitization have on both men's and women's jobs? While the relative need for tasks and competencies that technology may replace will decline, the proportionate requirement for occupations and skills that it can enhance will increase. In the past, computerization and robotics of workplaces have not only typically complemented nonroutine abstract occupations that are routinely handled by highly skilled individuals, such as administrators and experts, but have also replaced conventional activities that are typically carried out by partially skilled individuals, such as clerical and factory line workers. It has also raised requests for "nonroutine manual" and "interactive" jobs, which are typically held by low-skilled workers like telcos in the domestic help, security, and healthcare industries. The authors of a new study by Frey and Osborne,[31] as reported by Krieger-Boden and Sorgner,[32] estimated the anticipated vulnerability of professions in the United States to digital technology. By working with robotics and machine learning experts using ONet, a sizable dataset on the precise task contents of occupations, and speaking with experts in the field, they forecast the likelihood of digitization for 702 professions. According to their findings, 47% of the US workforce will likely experience job digitization in the foreseeable future. Numerous administrative and machine-operating and maintenance vocations are among those with a high risk of automation. STEM (Science, Technology, Engineering, and Mathematics), healthcare, teaching careers, as well as creative fields in the arts and design, are the vocations with the lowest likelihood of being digitized.

### 7.6.4 THE ROOTS OF THE INTERNET GENDER GAP

The digital divide and gender parity are linked concepts because the former affects the latter. Women's access to ICT is still hampered by ingrained cultural prejudices that see them as less valuable than men, even in developed nations like South Korea. The fact that South Korea is considered to be among the most developed countries has significance for its technological development and readiness for e-government. One of many facets of the gender split issue is how men and women were socialized. Males often have higher levels of schooling than females, and this has an effect on DGD.[33] Men and women also have different levels of employment. Nahar[33] reached this result by researching the IT trends in five different countries, notably Japan, South Korea, Singapore, and the US. On the basis of sex, age, education, and income, they concentrated on inequalities in IT access and utilization among countries. In a survey of Finnish schoolteachers and students, Norman et al.[27] found a correlation between ICT skills and generational and gender inequalities. Although male students and teachers believed that their skills were in a greater position than those of female teachers and students, they pointed out that men are typically given more latitude to learn and use ICT. Instructors and students were familiar with various traditional apps as well as innovative applications.

According to Nayak and Alam,[3] environmental factors, including social direction during childhood and how boys and girls are treated in schools and the media, have an impact on the DGD. When girls are given housekeeping responsibilities in school, gender inequalities begin to emerge. Girls live with this notion their entire lives, which plants the roots of the gender pay gap.[27] Another aspect in the GDD is the creation of media and educational resources that reinforce prejudices. Men are frequently portrayed in the media as being stronger and more skilled than women in TV shows, movies, and video games. ICT tools are used differently by men and women, as per Faulkner et al.[34] According to their research, men are drawn to the technical aspects of ICT (maintenance, programing, etc.), which have an impact on job decisions and pay. ICT features that are related to communication are more popular with women. Such gendered disparities in ICT tool preferences ultimately have the result of expanding the gender digital gap. Educational institutions may move to better encourage women to use ICT as a result of these findings.

## 7.7 EFFECTS OF THE COVID-19 EPIDEMIC'S GENDER DIGITAL SPLIT ON YOUTH/JUVENILE EDUCATION IN OUTLYING AREAS

Because of its technical advancement and readiness for e-government, South Korea's status as one of the most developed nations is significant. Since Covid-19 spread quickly and widely and had an impact on almost every part of life, the state's apparatus began concentrating on reducing mortality rates and preventing community transmission.[35] The growth of communication and information technology (ICT) has allowed academic institutions to exchange ideas and deliver instruction via online channels.[36] The issues with uneven distribution and substandard ICT use cannot be ignored, even when technology is being promoted as a provider of alternatives.[37,38] The Covid-19 epidemic enhanced awareness of the importance of bridging various digital divides between wealthy and developing nations. The digital divide and access to ICTs are long-standing problems.[39] The pandemic has elevated concerns about gender inequity, exclusion, and accessibility in conversations about educational policy.[40] For instance, it has been asserted that the goal of digitization cannot be achieved until all citizens have equitable access to digital inventions.[40] Additionally, socioeconomic and demographic realities have divided society at the family and individual levels, making it difficult for some members to access high-quality digital infrastructure. It was found that young women in rural areas had restricted access to digital technology.[41] E-learning during the pandemic confinement forced the educational institutes and instructors to make hasty attempts to adopt online delivery because it was uncharted territory for many.[42] Despite the availability of numerous and more advanced digital platforms, it was found that many teachers primarily used WhatsApp to instruct their students.[42] Teachers attributed their choice for WhatsApp to it being simpler to use compared to other online platforms because they were more adapted to it in their daily lives. Due to a dearth of internet infrastructure, it was also difficult for instructors and students to fully benefit from online learning (such as a lack of desktops or laptops, blackouts, slow internet access, and expensive internet data packages). If the basic issues relating to accessibility, skill levels, and the cost-effectiveness of digital infrastructure are not addressed, the digital divide could widen and the educational value could be substantially hindered.[43]

Particularly, Covid-19 disturbed the traditional method of receiving educational services in person, which significantly worsened people's lives all over the world.[3,44] The Covid-19-induced lockdown forced numerous international educational institutions to close their campuses and switch to predominantly online instruction.[45] The transition from a physical to a virtual classroom was seamless for wealthy students and educational institutions in urban areas, but it caused chaos in access to or delivery of educational services in rural areas where stable internet connections are hard to come by and digital devices are expensive.[46] The differences in affordability and accessibility of e-education, where there is a widening gap among those who have access/ingress to digital infrastructure and those who do not, are referred to as the "digital gap."[21] Moreover, media reports have stressed how difficult it was for students in remote locations to participate in online classes because they lacked access to laptops, mobile devices, and internet connectivity.[42] There is little thought given to how the digital barrier might manifest itself as a result of additional cultural and social variables that vary across different geographic areas, aside from the cost and internet problems.[47] More specifically, more research has to be done on the difficulties faced by female students from less affluent neighborhoods in terms of the digital gender difference.[3,22] Understanding the gendered digital divide is crucial because it can show how boys and girls may have received different treatment when it comes to using online resources to access education. In-depth studies that are focused on a particular environment are also needed to determine how Covid-19 has affected females' educational opportunities.[3,22,48]

### *7.7.1 THE NUMEROUS AND ACCUMULATIVE NEGATIVE EFFECTS OF THE DIGITAL DIVIDE DURING COVID-19*

The education sectors of emerging and underdeveloped countries were significantly impacted by Covid-19's exposure out of the myriad causes of digital inequality in these nations.[49] For instance, studies on digital segregation and education in India found that many metropolitan and rural households missed internet access, digital devices, and educational resources. The inability of parents, students, and instructors to use digital media effectively was yet another issue that was raised. Numerous cases of mistreating kids whose parents could not afford to pay the fee because of financial difficulty were recorded, including excluding them from an online learning group. For children from low-income households, where some students claimed that pandemic contingencies prohibited them from completing their education, these school activities widened the digital divide.[48] Men and women share domestic responsibilities unequally in every nation and society, and the "invisible labor" that women do at home is economically devalued.[49] The typical gendered division of work in the home was also exacerbated during the Covid-19 confinement episode, with the female students being assigned to care for household members.[50] Gender-specific norms made the problem significantly worse, and girls or women from socially marginalized communities who lived in remote places experienced special challenges utilizing the digital infrastructure.[22]

## 7.8 GENDERING THE G20

The G20 economies, which make up 85% of the world economy, 80% of global commerce, and 2/3 of the world's population, can serve as a strong platform for fostering sustainable and gender-equal economic ties and policymaking.[51] The majority of G20 initiatives, however, have a tendency to be gender-neutral, which has an adverse effect on gender equality. The movement to mainstream gender in all policies has gotten stronger during the past few years. Contrary to common assumptions, rates of female involvement in the labor force have stagnated or even declined globally in recent years. In the World Economic Forum's Global Gender Gap Index, which ranks countries' levels of gender equality from highest to lowest, five G20 economies—India (87), Turkey (130), Saudi Arabia (114), and Indonesia (88)—were rated 80 or higher out of 144.[52]

It is widely accepted that gender equity is a prerequisite for long-term economic success. The advancement of women is predicted to boost the global GDP by $12 trillion by 2025 and result in more environmentally friendly communities. This is in line with the G20's main goal, which is to promote GDP growth on a worldwide scale. The G20 and the rest of the international community acknowledge in their written comments the necessity and significance of giving gender equality top priority. The Sustainable Development Goals' fifth standalone goal, "empower all women and girls," was adopted by the international community in September 2015. Additionally, the G20 members committed to "ensure that women engage fully in the economy and society," "bridge the gender participation variance by approximately 25% by 2025," and "boost the population of women in the workforce by far more than 100 million."[53] The platform has, however, previously come under fire for tokenism rather than offering practical policy answers because there are not many women's perspectives and little room for in-depth discussion on gender equality. The Women Twenty, or W20, outreach group was established in 2015 as a reaction to this and to ensure strict implementation.

One of the Goals for Sustainable Development's (SDG) four objectives is to expand scholarships for engineering, science, and ICT-related vocational training. Goal 4 of the SDGs calls for "providing all-inclusive and equal quality education and encouraging chances for life-long learning for all." Other developed and emerging nations are included in this objective. The specific gender objective (Goal 5) promises to use enabling technology, especially ICT, more frequently in order to support women's empowerment. By aiming to considerably increase ICT links by 2020 as well as to offer universal and relatively inexpensive internet access in low-income nations, Goal 9 also aims to "build robust systems, foster equitable and sustainable industrialization, and drive innovation." The G20 member states are obligated by the "agreed suggestions," viz., Status and Rights of Women 2016 and the New Urban Agenda by the UN, which were made public at the

UN Biodiversity III convention in December 2016, to make ICTs accessible to women and girls and to consider gender equality when instructing technology literacy. The G20 places a high priority on macroeconomic stability, but the UN procedures purport to be rights-based. The G20's focus should attempt to build upon the current agenda with broad, growth-oriented, and genuine economic solutions rather than starting from scratch. This is because the UN's Sustainable Development Goals (SDGs) already provide a list of specific goals and standards for attaining global prosperity. For the G20 to merely raise awareness of the gender gap in invention at this time without taking steps to close it is insufficient. In addition to communiqués, W20, L20, and T20 have provided "implementation plans." A monitoring dashboard is also part of the W20 concept to make evaluation easier. It will be interesting to see how different countries react to these plans and how they combine domestic initiatives with international obligations.

The G20 organization has vowed to eliminate the gender gap in technology. Technology is neither inherently disenfranchising nor exclusive. The digital era will also affect men and women differently due to the current gender disparities. In the future, closing the digital gender gap will depend on egalitarian and cheap access to ICTs and a strong ICT infrastructure. But meaningful engagement requires more than just physical access to the internet. It also requires education, digital literacy, and challenging patriarchal value structures. In the absence of these, gender hierarchies will only get worse as a result of the digital revolution. Additionally, as a result of digitization, "online" and "offline" are becoming more and more entwined. As a result, the G20's policies promoting technical innovation and women's empowerment cannot be pursued in isolation.

As evidence grows that the G20's previous gender-neutral policies have resulted in gender-unequal consequences, efforts to concentrate the G20 framework on gender parity have been getting ground. The G20 will need to develop strategies to combine country-specific paths with more generalized common aims in the future due to its heterogeneity. Because countries with different sociocultural characteristics will not respond to too general, Eurocentric policy narratives, solutions must strike a balance between the local and the global. In industrialized economies, for instance, technology serves as a source of skills and is frequently incorporated into classroom instruction. Since this is taken for granted in many G20 discussions about digital inclusion, the need for alternative approaches to lifelong learning for women and girls must be equally prioritized, and this gap cannot be disregarded. The majority of research studies on women's empowerment and digital inclusion within the G20 framework have also stayed anecdotal.

There are currently limited qualitative studies on the attitudes and beliefs that contribute to unconscious prejudice, as well as statistics on women's reach to and usage of ICT that are broken down by gender. The Digital Change Index (DCI) or Digital Opportunity Index (DOI) was established in 2005 to track digital inclusion. However, gender-specific data were not gathered by the DOI. It is possible to do empirical research to identify potential future policy directions. Finally, the effectiveness of the G20 platform needs to be reassessed. It has been successful for the group to draw attention to significant concerns with international implications. The formation now recognizes the interdependence of social and economic stability, and engagement organizations like the W20 have gained influence, broadening the formation's agenda significantly. The UN Sustainable Development Goals (SDGs) already tie the entire community together with a comprehensive list of objectives for global development, so the G20 should abstain from doing so. By leveraging its influence to develop practical, inclusive, growth-oriented solutions, the platform must contribute value to the current agenda. The G20 must now attempt to define a specific plan of action to address the "digital gender difference" rather than simply mentioning it in its discussions. The platform must strive to enable stronger cooperation, monitoring, evaluation, and incentive-driven execution given the current substantive and procedural constraints.

## 7.9 DIFFICULTIES IN GENDER DIGITAL DIVIDE

Given the rising liberation of women, it is remarkable that barriers like restricted access to the internet and computers impede more women from pursuing careers in science and technology.[54] In a study on women's enrollment in undergraduate computer science programs, it was discovered that there are differences in both the abilities displayed by male and female students in addition to a steady decline in the proportion of female students. One of the main issues facing female students is the absence of the internet and computers at home.[55] Research that labeled the gender gap as a societal problem noted that several developing nations (such as Somalia and Kenya) lacked government statistics on the DGD. Cultural issues like gender discrimination, low income, poverty, geographical obstacles, and economic factors are blamed for this negligence. Within developing countries as well as across developed and developing nations, the study discovered variation in the DGD. While many other developing nations have opted to ignore this split, some have undertaken attempts to research the DGD in order to bridge this gap.

1. The digital revolution has given the G20 more chances than ever to pursue its aim of gender equality. The digital transformation, which is highlighted by big data, artificial intelligence, cloud computing, and mobile robotics, has the potential to expand female participation in the workforce and their social and economic autonomy in at least three ways. First off, because of mobile and digital technology, especially in developing and emerging countries, women have the chance to overcome some of the traditional mobility and cultural barriers. With the aid of digital technologies, women may be able to reach new markets, work remotely and flexibly, engage with clients, obtain training and mentorship, increase their financial independence, and find funding for their projects. Second, women frequently have stronger social skills than men do, and in the digital era, these talents will be valued more and more in the workforce. Positions held predominantly by women usually exhibit these social skills, which include, for instance, a greater sense of responsibility toward the broader community, higher empathy, better communication, and a higher propensity to adapt to changing conditions. The significant lost jobs driven on by automated processes, which are predicted to represent up to 60% of all jobs in advanced nations over the next twenty years, should be helped by them by helping women. The fact that very little is understood about how digitization is altering labor markets in developing and emerging economies is notable. Third, women have an advantage in social skills that could be increased even more if they also possess the greater computer literacy and cognitive (or abstract) skills necessary in the digital age. It is projected that these skill complementarities will increase, and they could open up management and leadership jobs with higher salaries for women.
2. Women may not be able to fully take advantage of the potential provided by digitalization due to current gender imbalances. Current gender inequalities make it difficult for women to advance, which keeps them in a vicious cycle. So, in many emerging and developing economies, there are still legal and cultural barriers to women's autonomy, which often hinder women from having access to digital gadgets that could assist them overcome some of these barriers. Due to poorer female enrollment numbers in higher education, notably in STEM areas, women are unable to fully take advantage of the opportunities given by digitalization, even in the most advanced G20 countries. In the digital age, women run the risk of missing out on

the best possibilities. There will probably be a huge variety of new business prospects brought about by digitalization. Women may be prevented from recognizing and advancing these entrepreneurial opportunities due to current gender inequities, such as discrepancies in entrepreneurship skills, a lack of social networks designed for female business proprietors, a lack of female mentors, and a plethora of financial constraints. If women are to succeed in the digital age to their full potential, the G20 nations must address these gender disparities. Many of these gender inequalities can be effectively eliminated by the application of new digital technology.

## 7.10 FUTURE INSIGHT ON THE DIGITAL GENDER DIVIDE

Policy is required in order to help women successfully seize the new opportunities offered by the digital era. The G20 leaders must act because the gender gap has the potential to damage any future benefits that women may derive from digitization. The G20 leaders appear committed to taking the following actions: They have frequently vowed to remove obstacles prohibiting women from participating fully in society and the economy since the historic 2012 Los Cabos summit.[52] From a multitude of earlier studies evaluating the issue of digital for gender parity, corrective policy approaches have already been suggested.[56] With the aid of cutting-edge e-government and digital finance technologies, these policies promote female financial empowerment, higher education, STEM vocations, web-based female entrepreneurship, and female digital literacy. Additionally, they offer open, affordable, universal, and secure broadband internet access. Governments from many different countries have already started to implement these plans. Even so, the pace of development is modest. The most recent study by Sorgner and Krieger-Boden[51] endorses the conclusions of the earlier studies and recommends that the G20 act in the five areas listed below.

1. Create a method for early detection of potential harm from digitization to gender equality. The G20 has to keep track of how improvements in digitalization are affecting women's employment opportunities. An early-warning system can then trigger policy actions with the help of such a national effort. The G20 should focus on more than just how digitization affects women's labor outside of developed nations. As emerging and underdeveloped nations may especially be vulnerable to digitalization, the G20 should instead take into account starting

high-profile studies for these regions. Current predictions indicate that women's employment will be less vulnerable to digitization than men's employment, particularly for low-skilled positions. This is because low-skilled males have a higher probability of holding regular jobs, including those in factories, where industrial robots have long ago supplanted such jobs. Due to the difficulty of digitizing nonroutine physical labor, low-skilled women are more likely to operate in industries like the healthcare industry. However, more technical advancement may be able to spread digitalization into areas that were once believed to be beyond the capability of computers, as demonstrated by the most recent advancements in artificial intelligence. In light of this, many occupations that were previously thought to be immune to automation may, in the future, also become obsolete. The next wave of digitalization may consequently have a disproportionately negative impact on female employment. The G20 should be able to identify new dangers to female employment with the use of the early warning system, which will also make it easier to respond to these concerns quickly. Further study is imperative to comprehend how prone female labor engagement is in these locations given that developing and emerging economies frequently rely on low-skilled labor.

2. Redesign existing government initiatives to promote women's involvement in the business and technology sectors. In order to further female emancipation, the G20 should launch a program to capitalize on present government efforts, notably in emerging and developing economies. Existing government initiatives, including programs for social assistance, can be modified to focus on women's economic and online engagement in addition to accomplishing their primary objectives. These programs may help to increase women's economic inclusion by designating them as the receivers of monetary transfers to their households or communities. Therefore, these adjustments will not only promote women's economic involvement but also increase the effectiveness of the program by actively exploiting women's capabilities in regards to their social and family responsibilities for the sake of the program's primary aims. The initiatives may raise the digital involvement of women and reduce the cost of program conveyance by embracing digital technology more extensively for billing, management, or monitoring. Programs that use conditional cash transfers (CCTs), such as the "Prospera" in Mexico and the

"Bolsa Familia" in Brazil, are excellent examples of how these two factors work in tandem to achieve program success. Some of these initiatives already leverage mobile money technologies for money transfers, such as Colombia's "Más Familias en Acción." In order to capitalize on the same kind of synergy between program performance and female economic and digital inclusion, it is still viable to apply these gains to CTT initiatives in other countries where they are implemented and to create programs that are analogous to those.

3. In all G20 nations, assist women in enhancing their social abilities with sophisticated digital education. The G20 needs to take a more active role in encouraging women to pursue graduate degrees, participate in cutting-edge research, and develop cutting-edge digital skills. Jobs that strongly rely on the interactions between abstract (or cognitive) skills that can be learned through postsecondary learning, like logical thinking and creativity, are predicted to be encouraged by digitalization. In the digital age, it will also be essential to have high levels of competence in digital skills. Women could profit from utilizing these complementarities because many of them have superior social skills to those of their male counterparts. Women may not have access to these opportunities due to the current gender gaps in postsecondary education and computer literacy, which are particularly noticeable in emerging economies. They may also be prevented from furthering those high-profile positions in management, STEM fields, or businesses that are predicted to thrive the most in the internet age. For instance, a number of G20 countries have launched numerous initiatives, such as coaching programs, hackathons, and coding workshops, to encourage interactive web-based literacy and to pique young women's interest in STEM fields. To ensure that women are fully prepared for the needs of the current job market, the G20 must support these programs more regularly. These initiatives constitute a critical step in the direction of gender equality.
4. Encourage women to use top-tier digital platforms to hone their entrepreneurship skills. The G20 should support excellent online resources that educate aspiring female entrepreneurs and allow them to network with more established female businesses. New prospects for entrepreneurship will probably be produced by digitalization. Women frequently lack the requisite entrepreneurial abilities and role models, which prevents them from spotting and exploring more lucrative company prospects in the digital age, in contrast to

their male counterparts. Higher education, employment experience, particularly in STEM professions, and regular connections with entrepreneurial peers are all ways to gain human capital that is important to entrepreneurship. Many women who are now excluded from the job market still have no access to this opportunity. The internet is a hopeful new tool for providing business training to women and connecting them with mentors and role models. Women who reside in areas with a dearth of female entrepreneurs or who encounter barriers in accessing these role models may benefit particularly from high-quality internet training and mentoring programs for female entrepreneurs.

5. Promote cutting-edge web-based tools that make it easier for female entrepreneurs to acquire funding. The G20 should support cutting-edge web-based tools that help women-owned enterprises access finance for their endeavors. It needs to spread awareness of top-notch online marketplaces that connect female investors and female businesses, such as equity crowd-funding, angel investing, and venture capital. It ought to additionally support cutting-edge methods of risk assessment that depend less on traditional securities and more on deal histories and other Big Data. It can be challenging for female company owners to get the funding they need to launch and expand their enterprises. Many women do not have the requisite collateral that traditional financial institutions require, which is one explanation for these issues. Another factor is that man-led enterprises are frequently preferred for funding by the networks of angel investors and venture capitalists, which are still overwhelmingly male. There is a need for new online platforms that offer mentoring from more seasoned peers to rookie female investors, similar to the Next Wave Ventures program in the US. By using the internet trade and behavior histories to draw conclusions about the client's reliability, groundbreaking risk evaluation techniques, like those used by Sachs' Goldman 10,000 women project, allow us to get around the lack of security available to borrowers from women.

## 7.11 CONCLUSIONS

Numerous opportunities for female emancipation and more equitable female involvement in the labor, financial, and entrepreneurial sectors are presented by digitalization. Today's digitization appears to benefit the female workforce because they are generally less likely than men to have their jobs replaced by machines. Compared to men, women typically have stronger social skills, which, when combined with better digital proficiency and greater education, can give them an advantage in the digital age. However, the same restrictions and barriers that keep women from furthering themselves in many countries today might also keep them from benefiting from a number of advantageous resources in the digital age, such as new business opportunities. To remove these obstacles, policymakers must make significant efforts. To achieve gender equality, more decisive use of new digital technologies is required.

## KEYWORDS

- **digital divide**
- **gender**
- **empowerment**
- **digital era**
- **post-Covid-19**
- **ICT**
- **social**
- **education**

## REFERENCES


1. Kerras, H.; Sánchez-Navarro, J. L.; López-Becerra, E. I.; de-Miguel Gomez, M. D. The Impact of the Gender Digital Divide on Sustainable Development: Comparative Analysis Between the European Union and the Maghreb. *Sustainability* **2020,** *12* (8), 3347.
2. Van Thanh, D. The Role of Digital Education in Narrowing the Gender Digital Divide in Vietnam. *VNU J. Soc. Sciand. Humanit.* **2022,** *8* (2), 192–220.
3. Nayak, K. V.; Alam, S. The Digital Divide, Gender and Education: Challenges for Tribal Youth in Rural Jharkhand During Covid-19. *Decision* **2022,** 1–15.
4. Liu, C.; Wang, K.; Goay, M.; Yoon, S. In *Note: Examining the Gender Digital Divide in ICT: A Closer Look At Ghana, South Africa, and India,* ACM SIGCAS/SIGCHI Conference on Computing and Sustainable Societies (COMPASS); 2022; pp 623–627)
5. Joshi, A.; Malhotra, B.; Amadi, C.; Loomba, M.; Misra, A.; Sharma, S.; ... Amatya, J. Gender and the Digital Divide Across Urban Slums of New Delhi, India: Cross-Sectional Study. *J. Med. Internet Res.* **2020,** *22* (6), E14714.

6. Adeleke, R. Digital Divide in Nigeria: the Role of Regional Differentials. *Afr. J. Sci. Technol. Innov. Dev.* **2021,** *13* (3), 333–346.
7. Ogbo, E.; Brown, T.; Gant, J.; Sicker, D. When Being Connected is Not Enough: An Analysis of the Second and Third Levels of the Digital Divide in A Developing Country. *J. Inform. Policy* **2021,** *11* (1), 104–146.
8. Mądra-Sawicka, M.; Nord, J. H.; Paliszkiewicz, J.; Lee, T. R. Digital Media: Empowerment and Equality. *Information* **2020,** *11* (4), 225.
9. Acilar, A. Age and Digital Divide: the Case of a Developing Country, Turkey. *Int. J. Innov. Digit. Econ.* **2021,** *12* (3), 17–29.
10. Lopez-Sintas, J.; Lamberti, G.; Sukphan, J. The Social Structuring of the Digital Gap in a Developing Country. The Impact of Computer and Internet Access Opportunities on Internet Use in Thailand. *Technol. Soc.* **2020,** *63*, 101433.
11. Suwana, F.; Lily Empowering Indonesian Women through Building Digital Media Literacy. *Kasetsart J. Soc. Sci.* **2017,** *38* (3), 212–217.
12. Acilar, A.; Sæbø, Ø. Towards Understanding the Gender Digital Divide: A Systematic Literature Review. In *Global Knowledge, Memory and Communication*; 2021.
13. Cheshmehzangi, A.; Zou, T.; Su, Z. The Digital Divide Impacts on Mental Health during the COVID-19 Pandemic. *Brain, Behav. Immun.* **2022,** *101*, 211–213.
14. Acilar, A. Exploring the Gender Digital Divide in E-Government Use in A Developing Country. *Int. J. Public Admin. Digital Age* **2020,** *7* (4), 1–15.
15. Straubhaar, J.; Tufekci, Z.; Spence, J.; Rojas, V. Digital Inequity in the Austin Technopolis: An Introduction. In *Inequity in the Technopolis*; University of Texas Press, 2021; pp 1–32.
16. Hargittai, E. *The Digital Reproduction of Inequality*. In Routledge, Milton Park, 2018; pp 660–670
17. Goedhart, N. S.; Broerse, J. E.; Kattouw, R.; Dedding, C. Just Having A Computer Doesn't Make Sense: the Digital Divide From the Perspective of Mothers with a Low Socio-Economic Position. *New Media Soc.* **2019,** *21* (11–12), 2347–2365.
18. Mubarak, F.; Suomi, R.; Kantola, S. P. Confirming the Links between Socio-Economic Variables and Digitalization Worldwide: The Unsettled Debate on Digital Divide. *J. Inf. Commun. Ethics Soc.* **2020,** *18* (3), 415–430.
19. Serrano-Cinca, C.; Muñoz-Soro, J. F.; Brusca, I. A Multivariate Study of Internet Use and the Digital Divide. *Soc. Sci. Q.* **2018,** *99* (4), 1409–1425.
20. Van Deursen, A. J.; Van Dijk, J. A. The First-Level Digital Divide Shifts from Inequalities in Physical Access to Inequalities in Material Access. *New Media Soc.* **2019,** *21* (2), 354–375.
21. Rajam, V.; Reddy, A. B.; Banerjee, S. Explaining Caste-Based Digital Divide In India. *Telemat. Inform.* **2021,** *65*, 101719.
22. Centre For Catalyzing Change (2021) Bridging the Digital Divide For Girls In India [Online]. https://www.c3india.org/ uploads/news/bridging_the_digital_divide-policy_brief_2021_(website)1.pdf (Accessed 6/9/2022).
23. Jane, E. Gendered Cyberhate: A New Digital Divide?. In *Theorizing Digital Divides*; Routledge, 2017; pp 186–198.
24. Hidalgo, A.; Gabaly, S.; Morales-Alonso, G.; Urueña, A. The Digital Divide in Light of Sustainable Development: An Approach through Advanced Machine Learning Techniques. *Technol. Forecast. Soc. Change* **2020,** *150*, 119754.
25. Choi, E. Y.; Kim, Y.; Chipalo, E.; Lee, H. Y. Does Perceived Ageism Widen the Digital Divide? and Does it Vary By Gender?. *Gerontologist* **2020,** *60* (7), 1213–1223.

26. Rivera, B. The Digital Divide: Identifying and Reducing the Gap. In *Edmedia+ Innovate Learning*; Association for the Advancement of Computing in Education (AACE), 2022; pp 954–959.
27. Norman, H.; Adnan, N. H.; Nordin, N.; Ally, M.; Tsinakos, A. The Educational Digital Divide for Vulnerable Students in the Pandemic: Towards the New Agenda 2030. *Sustainability* **2022,** *14* (16), 10332.
28. Mohieldin, M.; Ramadan, R. Would Closing the Gender Digital Divide Close the Economic Gender Gap in Emerging Markets and Developing Economies? An Empirical Assessment. In *Economic Research Forum Working Papers* (no. 1548), 2022.
29. Macaya, J. F.; Ribeiro, M. M.; Jereissati, T.; Dos Reis Lima, C.; Cunha, M. A. Gendering the Digital Divide: the Use of Electronic Government Services and Implications for the Digital Gender Gap. *Inform. Polity* **2021,** *26* (2), 131–146.
30. Frederick, D. E. The New Feminine Face of the Digital Divide. *Library Hi Tech News*; (Ahead-Of-Print), 2022.
31. Frey, C. B.; Osborne, M. A. The Future of Employment: How Susceptible are Jobs to Computerisation? *Technol. Forecast. Soc. Change* **2017,** *114*, 254–280.
32. Krieger-Boden, C.; Sorgner, A. Labor Market Opportunities for Women in the Digital Age. *Economics* **2018,** *12* (1).
33. Nahar, S. Exploring the Characteristics of Gender Digital Divide Among Secondary School Teachers in Bangladesh. *Bangladesh J. Public Admin.* **2022,** *30* (1), 49–66.
34. Faulkner, P. E.; Cobb, R. Jr.; Kipkurgat, T. K.; Alinat-Abed, S. O. How Closing the Digital Divide Can Improve Women's Employability. In: *Gender Perspectives on Industry 4.0 and the Impact of Technology on Mainstreaming Female Employment*; IGI Global, 2022; pp 1–30.
35. Thadikaran, G. B.; Chellaswamy, K. P. Bridging Digital Divide in India: Positive Outlook Amid COVID-19. *Prabandhan: Indian J. Manag.* **2022,** *15* (6), 46–56.
36. Chandwani, J.; Shah, D.; Shaikh, A. A Study on Role of Digital Technologies and Employee Experience. In *Innovations in Information and Communication Technologies (IICT-2020)*, Springer, Cham, 2021, pp 15–25.
37. Mathrani, A.; Han, B.; Mathrani, S.; Jha, M.; Scogings, C. Interpreting Academic Integrity Transgressions among Learning Communities. *Int. J. Educ. Integ.* **2021a,** *17* (1), 1–16.
38. Mathrani, A.; Sarvesh, T.; Umer, R. Digital Divide Framework: Online Learning in Developing Countries During the COVID-19 Lockdown. *Glob. Soc. Educ.* **2021b,** 1–16.
39. Yildirim, S.; Demirtas, I.; Yildirim, D. C. A Review of Alternative Economic Approaches to Achieve Sustainable Development: the Rising Digitalization and Degrowth Post COVID-19. In *Handbook of Research on Sustainable Development Goals, Climate Change, and Digitalization*; 2022; pp 288–307.
40. Harb, B.; Sidani, D. Smart Technologies Challenges and Issues in Social Inclusion–Case of Disabled Youth in a Developing Country. *J. Asia Bus. Stud.*
41. Bozkurt, A.; Jung, I.; Xiao, J.; Vladimirschi, V.; Schuwer, R.; Egorov, G.; ... Paskevicius, M. A Global Outlook to the Interruption of Education due to COVID-19 Pandemic: Navigating in a Time of Uncertainty and Crisis. *Asian J. Dist. Educ.* **2020,** *15* (1), 1–126.
42. Mishra, L.; Gupta, T.; Shree, A. Online Teaching-Learning in Higher Education during Lockdown Period of COVID-19 Pandemic. *Int. J. Educ. Res. Open* **2020,** *1*, 100012.
43. Biswal, B.; Rath, N. Digital Divide and Risked Communities: A Case Study of the Vulnerabilities of Women in India during the Pandemic. *Int. J. Instruc. Technol. Educ. Stud.* **2022,** *3* (4), 19–25.

44. García-Morales, V.J.; Garrido-Moreno, A.; Martín-Rojas, R. The Transformation of Higher Education after the COVID Disruption: Emerging Challenges in an Online Learning Scenario. *Front. Psychol.* **2021,** 12:196.
45. Maity, S.; Sahu, T. N.; Sen, N. Panoramic View of Digital Education in COVID-19: A New Explored Avenue. *Rev. Educ.* **2021,** *9* (2), 405–423.
46. Ticona, J. *Left to Our Own Devices: Coping with Insecure Work In A Digital Age*; Oxford University Press, 2022.
47. Reddick, C. G.; Enriquez, R.; Harris, R. J.; Sharma, B. Determinants of Broadband Access and Affordability: An Analysis of a Community Survey on the Digital Divide. *Cities*, **2022,** *106*, 102904.
48. Jain, S. *Gender Dimensions of School Closures in India During Covid-19: Lessons From Ebola*; Observer Research Foundation, 2020.
49. Iivari, N.; Sharma, S.; Ventä-Olkkonen, L. Digital Transformation of Everyday Life-How COVID-19 Pandemic Transformed the Basic Education of the Young Generation and Why Information Management Research Should Care? *Int. J. Inform. Manag.* **2020,** *55*, 102183.
50. Mclaren, H. J.; Wong, K. R.; Nguyen, K. N.; Mahamadachchi, K. N. D. Covid-19 and Women's Triple Burden: Vignettes from Sri Lanka, Malaysia, Vietnam and Australia. *Soc. Sci.* **2020,** *9* (5), 87.
51. Sorgner, A.; Krieger-Boden, C. Empowering Women in the Digital Age. *G20 Insights*; 2017.
52. Mishra, V. Gendering the G20: Empowering Women in the Digital Age. *ORF Issue Brief [Online]*. New Delhi: Observer Research Foundation. Recuperado A Partir de. http://cf. orfonline.org/wp-content/uploads/2017/06/orf_issuebrief_186_g20women.pdf.
53. Mishra, V.; Aneja, U.; Mishra, V. Empowering Women in a Digital Age in South Africa [Online]; New York City: OECD. https://www. orfonline. org/research/digital-age-south-africa-empowerment-women/ (Accessed on 6/9/2022).
54. Krishnaswami, M.; Iyer, L. S.; John, C.; Devanathan, M. Countering Educational Disruptions Through an Inclusive Approach: Bridging the Digital Divide in Distance Education. In *Socioeconomic Inclusion during an Era of Online Education*; IGI Global, 2022; pp 204–224.
55. Wenham, C.; Smith, J.; Morgan, R. COVID-19: The Gendered Impacts of the Outbreak. *Lancet* **2020,** *395* (10227), 846–848.
56. Vaidehi, R.; Reddy, A. B.; Banerjee, S. (Explaining Caste-based Digital Divide in India. 2021, Arxiv:2106.15917.

## CHAPTER 8

# Digitization and Sustainability: Transitions in Indian Education

DEVENDRA KUMAR SOMWANSHI[1] and MOHIT KUMAR SHARMA[2]

[1]*Department of ECE, Poornima College of Engineering, Jaipur, Rajasthan, India*

[2]*Vellore Institute of Technology, Bhopal, Madhya Pradesh, India*

## ABSTRACT

In this digital era, every industry is witnessing changes to sustain itself; the Indian education industry is no different. Due to changes at the global level in the educational industry, its implications and effects are affecting the sustainability of Indian education. For economic and social developments, digitization is one reliable solution. Social transformations and engagement are possible only through education. The knowledge acquisition would help people to acquire intellectual maturity and wisdom over a period of time.

To sustain itself in this digitization era, the Indian Government has taken many significant initiatives. Due to this, the Indian education system is undergoing a transition phase, which benefits the society at large in terms of sustainability, survival, and growth. More than 300 million students are studying in more than 1.5 million schools in various parts of the country. The literacy level has significantly grown by more than 10% from the year 2001 to 2011 in India. This progress is without a doubt extremely certain, and further formative exercises must be finished to teach them all.

For guaranteed financial commitments to our general public, the public authority and confidential instructive establishments have added to the scholarly advancement of individuals in this country. These dynamic

Management for Sustainable Development: Integrating Social, Economic, and Environmental Goals.
Vishal Jain & Amit Mittal (Eds.)

commitments and moderate estimates should proceed to sustain the developments. On the basis of different reports, there are several issues which are standing up to this framework. These intellectual activity engagements also lead to economic activity engagement and contributions, which benefit families, groups, communities, and our society at large.

By 2030, India would turn into the most youthful country of the world with 1,000,000 school-going gatherings. So to address the number of developing youth who are presently advancing through instructive drives and measures, persistent help is especially required.

The public authority and confidential foundations are fulfilling their commitments to the degree and level conceivable here. Anyway, we likewise observe that there is an adjustment of the instructive necessities and prerequisites of more youthful ages, which is particularly obvious at advanced education levels. Their discernment, approach, and mentality toward training overall and advanced education in unambiguous ways have changed a great deal.

These more youthful people are innovation-oriented, and they effectively participate in virtual entertainment networks for at least 4–5 hours per day. This clearly demonstrates that coordinated advertising efforts must be changed by higher educational institutions of India.

This chapter is an attempt to interpret and discover the role of digitization, its strategies, and its impacts in identifying the choice of educational institutions in India. This chapter explores and examines the aspect of digital marketing on the choices of the students and tries to quantify the value and need identification habits of the students. In this chapter, the trend of digital marketing in the direction of education is analyzed. This study concludes the marketing strategies with special reference to digitization.

## 8.1 LITERATURE REVIEW—APPROACH

In this review, the ideas—advanced promoting procedures, inbound showcasing, SEO advertising, SMO advertising, computerized commitment, computerized enchantment, brand worth, and brand value—would be examined exhaustively. As these ideas are given in a reasonable system, this survey would be exceptionally purposive and centered in nature.

The writing audit would be furnished with twin viewpoints:

- Verifiable point of view
- Contemporary viewpoint

Concerning legitimate beginning stages of thoughts and their ideas, an unquestionable perspective would be used. This suggests that the review would recognize articles and disseminations beginning from the very outset of the thought; its new developments, issues, perspectives, open entryways, impediments, and convincing procedures to manage these challenges would be investigated, evaluated, and inspected comprehensively.

Contemporary perspectives would in like manner be acknowledged in thought as this review would in like manner give the most critical, latest, and the most recent disseminations which are available. In the latest ten years of coordinated review regarding the matter, appropriate, free, and subordinate variables picked in this review would be evaluated, broken down, and analyzed, and fundamental speculations would be given. An alternate discussion would in like manner be obliged to get an unquestionable and genuine perspective.

In this study, we would be likewise giving a table to this survey, which would give a point-by-point synopsis of the examinations directed, example size, spots of the review, research techniques, and discoveries of the review.

We would also be providing research gaps which are available in the field of study and would suggest suitable areas of research for research scholars and professionals in the field.

## 8.2 HISTORICAL PERSPECTIVE: DIGITAL MARKETING TOOLS

To showcase the business commitment of a client across the world, digitization is a stage in which complex instruments like SEO, web journals, surveys, viral promotion, show promotions, and online entertainment message popups, which can be computerized, are utilized. It can likewise increment transformations and rehash traffic to guarantee that imminent understudies are changed over completely to understudies in instructive foundations.

Social media became a prominent tool for usage, differentiation, and exclusive reach both in B2B and B2C segments by 2002. Facebook came in to public access as a tool developed for American college students by 2006. This large number of advancements has impacted the manner in which we carry on with our existences, impart and showcase our items and administrations. This prompted the improvement and formation of shrewd apparatuses and applications, which can completely change us and which can upgrade and draw in computerized support for advanced purchasing of items and administrations, famously called computerized promotion.

Urban obviously expresses that associations are currently involving digital showcasing as a device for upper hand, which joins web and data innovation. This apparatus is more viable in applications and reach of clients than conventional advertising draws near.

Hudson et al.[9] give a rundown of computerized showcasing instruments like versatile promotion, web journals, search advertisements, and online networks. These are specific apparatuses as they vary from conventional types of notice and limited-time devices as they offer simple access and moderation.

Wertime and Fenwick[25] suggest the rundown of different advanced advertising devices like web, email, viral promotion, portable stage, gaming, client-produced content, computerized signage, and IPTV.

## 8.3 SEO MARKETING AND ITS IMPLICATIONS

Moran and Hunt have completely said that it is the most generally and famously involved technique for client fascination and the board in the internet.

There is a wide assortment of web-based web indexes, and a couple of them have stayed reliable and stood the test of time.

These well-known web indexes, utilized by millions from one side of the planet to the other, empower clients to track down their particular record or content by looking through a couple of words or barely any watchwords. Google, Yahoo, Bing, and MSN are continuously overwhelming in this search area, and Google topped the search field with more than 1.6 billion clients each month.

The search engines are programed with thousands of words to provide the search results to clients. So, when a person types a word, we can find thousands of pages of information which appear. To influence clients and customers to visit, enhance awareness, and get profits, companies use digital marketing tools. Different outcomes can be given, and these outcomes are sorted into two fundamental sorts called natural and inorganic (given in a reasonable system). Natural could mean the progressions made in the site by organizations by adjusting calculations and it can show rankings and positions, which could require 3 to a half year. Moment results on positioning, mindfulness, and leads are conceivable with paid administrations called natural. Instructive foundations should focus on search questions and utilized words.

Google Inside Ad Words (2015)[29] report determines the circumstances to find actual success for organizations to expand their traffic. Instructive organizations should zero in more on custom and executed SEO to increase the number of individuals visiting the sites, increase mindfulness, and change the leads into business. Pictures are utilized to a greater degree to make an impact on the crowd. So client tastes and inclinations are likewise considered while settling on a computerized showcasing effort.

## 8.4 SOCIAL MEDIA—EVOLUTION, REACH, AND IMPLICATIONS

### *8.4.1 FACEBOOK*

Stokes (2011) followed the verifiable development of online entertainment and said that this media advanced during 2002, which changed the authoritative, individual, and social correspondences of the planet altogether. It led to a complete transformation in the management of communication and information, which led people to become passionately addicted to staying in touch and communicating all over the world. This eradicated geological and social limits, and it became more straightforward and easy to get messages across. FB was authoritatively accessible for correspondence to a worldwide audience in 2006. It has now become an irreplaceable apparatus for data trade, updates, gatherings, and business advancement. Content management and distribution have become much easier without physical touch; communications have become easier; and personal growth and development have been assured. So, instructive establishments should have the option to combine these web-based entertainment applications with objectives and reason.

They can frame effective, suitable strategies to win students and increase their engagement and participation in colleges. This would enable them to develop a college-of-choice approach.

### *8.4.2 YOUTUBE*

Dickey[6] depicts that Youtube engages in electronic continuous downloading and moving of accounts from one side of the planet to the next. This is an internet-based diversion stage in which it shows their account and restricts time materials; this is called information establishment. Viral, exhibiting the most well-known gadget for electronic advancement, would be truly administered and controlled for informational establishments as well. In 2005, the mechanical assembly was made, and it achieved such remarkable unerring quality with the most significant existence that we cannot imagine the existence of a more energetic age group without this. It creates informational establishments on the basis of likes, extending care, and communications.

### 8.4.3 TWITTER

Kingston[13] mentioned that Jack Dorsey worked on a pilot project as an inside help for odeo delegates, but after successful work in 2006, it was introduced for public use. It was spread out considering frameworks, organization, and microblogging. On the basis of hashtags, clients can talk with people from one side of the planet to the other. Initially, it was limited to 140 characters, but now the limit is extended to 280 characters. This virtual diversion stage is less generally elaborated by informational starting points for publicizing and progressions. The time has come for this overall unquestionable and well-known mechanical assembly to be involved in informational foundations for making market care, client care, and reach.

### 8.4.4 INSTAGRAM

Miles (2014) fundamentally assesses the benefits of Instagram. In this virtual entertainment application, it is exceptionally simple to make a profile as it requires extremely less data. It is exceptionally simple and easy to utilize. Like Twitter, it utilizes hashtags in which photographs of viewers are given, which would match the point. This empowers perspectives and likes to get expanded.

The depictions must be given, which are simple, straightforward, and clear. At the point when clients recall photographs, it empowers brand-recognizable proof, mindfulness, and maintenance of clients. It also provides marketing solutions like other social media applications. A specific target-oriented material would provide content visibility and attraction.

This large number of social media applications was planned and made with an expectation of data trade and simple correspondence with individuals across the world. The trading of perspectives and conclusions makes sound sympathetic collaboration of individuals. This correspondence-based online entertainment apparatus, as it came to successfully reaching billions of individuals across the world, has additionally been stretched out in utilization for business-based applications and arrangements. This has led to new, successful, and creative approaches to contacting individuals. It also facilitated business transactions, customer relationships, and retention of customers. It helped to increase brand visibility, brand loyalty, and brand equity.

The social media developments and their origins, changes, and advancements are presented in a table below for clear understanding.

Digital marketing is empowered by social media tools. These tools are used extensively to make organizations successful. The social media tools could be comprehended as verifiable available resources for improvement.

## 8.5 CONTEMPORARY PERSPECTIVE

In this section, after the internet revolution, what are the modern technological changes initiated and how these affect the B2B and B2C marketing strategies are evaluated and discussed. Further, the next revolution, social media revolution, and the changes would be discussed. The third major developmental change, called the digital revolution, which encompasses the internet, social media, business, products and services, its tools, and applications in business, would be analyzed. These media and communication tools and how effective they are in reaching the younger generation would be assessed.

A proper digital marketing methodology, structure, approach, and strategies would be accommodated when arriving at a more youthful age. An essential viewpoint for advanced educational organizations to arrive at the planned understudies, careful commitment, and computerized enchantment techniques and their effects would be given. By following this key computerized showcasing model, Indian higher instructional establishments would be benefitted as they would have the option to arrive at the forthcoming understudies successfully and effectively.

## 8.6 INTERNET REVOLUTION AND ITS IMPACT

Miniwatts Marketing Group (2011) reported about the web and added how it has become most important for the worldwide population and businesses everywhere. According to the report, the worldwide reach increased exponentially to 3.5 billion in 2015 from 1 billion clients in 2005.

Court (2009) worked on web insurgency. He initially recognized the issue and then investigated the progressions and reported the changes which occurred due to the web insurgency. He admitted that the web initiated a new

**TABLE 8.1** Historical Perspective.

| Author | Year | Contributions | Comments |
|---|---|---|---|
| **Digital marketing** | | | |
| Urban | 2004 | Digital marketing is a tool for gaining an upper hand by consolidating web and data innovation. | Very effective in reach<br>Anytime reach<br>Reaches customers and clients across the globe |
| Wertime and Fenwick[25] | 2008 | Web, internet, email, viral marketing, portable stage, gaming, client-produced content, advanced signage, and IPTV. | The other forms of digital marketing tools enable marketers to understand, evaluate, and use various tools as per the nature and requirements of users. |
| Simon Hudson, Martin S. Roth, and Rupert Madden[9] | 2012 | Digital marketing tools were listed and explained such as blogs, online communities, mobile marketing, search ads, etc. | Way, nature, approach, functioning, and reach are very different in nature and very purposeful and significant as a modern tool for companies. |
| **SEO marketing** | | | |
| Moran and Hunt | 2011 | The most popular and widely used tool on the internet. | It still continues to dominate its influence as the most reliable tool for marketers for customer engagement and delight.<br>Organic and inorganic ways of reaching customers are very powerful ways to reach them effectively. |
| Google Inside AdWords. | 2015 | Conditions for the successful reach of customers are ensured by following simple, easy steps. | Content, pictures, user-based contents, and attractive features must be provided in the website. |
| **Facebook** | | | |
| Stokes | 2011 | It was available for public use by 2006, and it has reached almost every living soul in the planet. | Marketers cannot imagine reaching targeted, specific customers without FB. |

**TABLE 8.1** *(Continued)*

| Author | Year | Contributions | Comments |
|---|---|---|---|
| **YouTube** | | | |
| Dickey[6] | 2013 | Webpages, which have reached millions in the planet, have also facilitated viral marketing as the most powerful marketing tool. | Viral marketing is enabled by reaching groups and communities, and brand building, retention, and customer delight are ensured with this tool. |
| **Twitter** | | | |
| Kingston[13] | 2013 | It has provided innovative, novel solutions for business applications. | Celebrity branding, celebrity following, and their brand endorsements are the most popular methods here. |
| **Instagram** | | | |
| Miles | 2014 | Easy to create and use | Brand identification, brand evaluation, brand awareness, and brand promotions are easier with this social media tool. |

dimension to promotions across the world and changed the thought process of all in higher than ever. The result of this was that it is the intrinsic requirement of every organization to show their organization sites across these web indexes so that they can be searched by relative clients, and it became the guarantee for business advancement.

Curran[5] has said that search engine enhancement is an instrument which empowers organizations to further develop their organization's site position and positioning on the web search page, and it guarantees a superior perception of the organization's brand and its maintenance. The search engines evaluate the websites based on certain criteria and information. On the basis of these criteria, information ranking is decided on web search pages. Points are as follows to decide the ranking:

- Website establishment year
- Update regularity for website content, quality, and management
- Keyword ratio with availability on the website
- Incoming link quality to the website

Jerkovic (2010) added that the external links are crucial points to check the connectivity to the webpage and, especially, the ranking of the web page.

However, the process of ranking the website is that the algorithm provision in the website is scrutinized and evaluated by SEO, on the basis of which the ranking of the website is finalized. The ranking improvement takes a minimum of six months. Due to the quickness and robustness of the process, companies get benefitted in a minimum time period.

Miller (2011) said that pay per click and site design improvement appear to be twin crease methodologies that are embraced by organizations for expanding their image esteem and for client maintenance systems. Pay per click appears to be more compelling; because of it, inquiries and extra awareness increase.

## 8.7 THE CONTEMPORARY EDUCATIONAL SYSTEM—CHALLENGES

Sharanabasappa et al. marked the issues regarding higher education. They stated that public involvement in higher education is just 20%, which should improve to a larger number. In India, schooling admittance is a major issue till date. In India, many things affect the higher education challenges such as the rustic metropolitan ratio and male–female contrast. There are many revolutionary gadgets and novel techniques which are not used to teach understudies so that the advancements in higher studies could take place. Portable promotion with viral advertising strategies must be used to get the right direction in the educational system. In the New Educational Policy of 2019, Dr. Kasturi Rangan suggested and proposed that an audit must take place on instructive approaches in the previous fifty years. They further suggested that to prepare the assets, understudy-driven training and novel techniques must be carried out thoroughly to prepare the framework.

Lekha and Thomas[14] proposed the advanced education framework, for which there is a need of radical changes in the whole framework. They included financing as a significant issue by which the whole framework can be converted into a robust foundation.

Sanklecha[20] provided the inputs about strengths, challenges, and weaknesses in HEI, India. He asserts that India continues to be way away from universal literacy, and it is yet to achieve it even after 70 years of independence.

The higher education institutions, with the aid of nature, now do not have proper adequate infrastructure, which is the basic assignment.

The esteemed educational institution is confronted with a twofold challenge: achieving excellence in both quality and quantity, necessitating immediate attention to both aspects. The issue lies in the fact that the youth do not approach research-based colleges in the country. Just 10% of the total youth accessible in the nation take part in advanced education. The circumstance in modern nations is that half of the adolescent population takes part in advanced education and this proportion is 15% in China. We could observe that there is a lack of talented labor supply in this country too. The academic research and its quality have to improve a lot. This is a challenge as these higher education institutions have an inflexible academic structure. The initiatives by private sector enterprises in higher education are laudable; however, they do not suffice. We could find that the regulatory system provided by the government has failed to a greater extent on many critical issues in higher education. We could find that in the entire country, there is a very small base of quality institutions offering higher education, and these conditions must improve. The standard and quality of higher education must improve, and they must not be compromised for anything. The teaching and learning process must change and adapt to the latest global changes which happen. The institutions must be capable and adaptive in nature and respond to those changes by bringing in changes and reforms in the entire higher education system.

Still, we find that the growth in higher education remains at 7% only in this country. Supply–demand gaps are wider and more prevalent in this sector as we still witness that the gross enrollment ratio is very low. If we are able to achieve 30% of GRE in higher education by 2030, we will have 100 million potential students looking for higher education careers in this country, but we do not have proper adequate infrastructure, which is pathetic to know. We could find that uneven growth opportunities prevail in this country, which is due to lack of opportunities and access to higher education. The higher educational institutions, by nature, must concentrate on research and R&D to instill creativity, innovation, and novelty in these institutions.

Kapur and Mehta[12] have given a ton of monetary viewpoints and conversations with respect to its execution and its utility in India. He completely expresses that advanced education is not more common in engineering and medication. The all-out venture on a per capita basis has been declining generally somewhat recently.

He describes the minimum signaling effect, which means the higher educational institutions concentrate and focus less on pedagogy and resources as they incur huge expenses to manage and maintain.

He further elaborates that the vicious circle of ideological commitment by the government in establishing these higher education institutions has not been achieved nor is it moving in that direction. The ideological commitment on starting and providing higher education in India by the government is to provide a quality, uniform education throughout the country, which is not executed.

We could find that educational institutions differ, and these differences are the basic criteria on which choices and decisions are made. So in order to avoid these types of issues, a common education program under one single organization must evolve from the government. The government is yet to take a decision in this regard.

The UGC report on higher education in the country clearly states that there are 43 central universities, 312 state universities, 183 private universities, and 115 deemed universities in the country. The UGC report also states that there are 9195 affiliated colleges in the country.

Bhargava (2006) states that there is a requirement for 3000 more colleges in the nation, and the base limit is that it should have the option to oblige basically another 10,000 understudies each year.

Nayar (2011) has stated that the number of private higher education institutions increased from 43% in 2000–01 to 2005–06.[18] The gross enrollment has also increased from 33% to 52% during this period of time.

Dhanuraj and Rahul Verma (2015) identify six major challenges which prevail with special reference to higher education systems and processes in India. They are as follows:

- Regulatory challenges
- Ambiguous legislations at the state level
- Ambiguous guidelines
- The UGC does not allow private universities to start affiliated colleges
- Fee decision-making
- Course design and lesser autonomy on curriculum and pedagogy

Kumari and Sharma[19] assessed the role of advanced education in the monetary turn of events and the flourishing of the country. Efficient interest in human resources is finished on an ordinary, methodical, and periodical premise, which gave the basis for the improvement and development of India. The review stresses on efficient and periodical changes, which are expected to change the scene of advanced education in India.

Hiremath and Albal[8] analyzed the entire system and gave a point of view on higher education system. The system enables scope for development, but there seems to be less seriousness regarding higher education from a total perspective. Quality, affordability, and ethics are the three major challenges which affect the entire process. Huge opportunities for growth and excelling are found in higher education in the upcoming years. In terms of the workforce, this estimate is expected to reach around 250 million by 2030.

Jonaki and Prasenjit[10] stated that India has developed greatly today from 20 universities and 500 affiliated colleges all over the country for 0.1 million people during Indian independence. The three major indicators of higher education are as follows:

- Gross enrollment ratio 13.2%
- Net enrollment ratio 13.2%
- Eligible enrollment ratio 52%

Both the gross enrollment extent and net selection extent are far below the overall average, which needs to move along. The concentrate in like manner communicates that organization practices in the country ought to change and progress to oblige overall students and examples.

Rohan Mukherjee (2008) analyzes the crisis, contemporary difficulties, and issues which win in the high-level training structures of India. This concentrate, in like manner, communicates that there are 18,000 foundations in India, which manage to show 11 million students. The concentrate further communicates that there is a hard-and-fast reduction in the public hypotheses for high-level training. There is a package of issues concerning the authoritative framework, and it has influenced without a doubt the informational cycle. The high-level training structure in India ought to ensure an incentive for all disturbing chances.

Chahal and Dar[3] have communicated that there are acceptability challenges in high-level training and its organization in India. They concentrated further on the prerequisites for creating a legitimate model which can enable India to attract worldwide students.

Singh[24] assessed the nature and ordinariness of high-level training structures in India. In this paper, different permit frameworks are comprehensively analyzed to determine which wins in the country. At any rate, the large number of strategies which exist ought to provoke student affirmations for high-level training in this country.

UGC (Ministry of Higher Education) reports state that Indians spend Rs. 25,000 crore every year to study various courses of interest in other countries of their choice. 1.5 lakh students leave for abroad studies every year. 4–5 lakh students are in abroad at any particular point of time. Rs. 3000 crores are spent by approximately 6 lakh students every year to study for entry into dream aspirations—IIT and IIM.

Sen Gupta and Vikram Parekh[22] talk about the different difficulties which are pervasive in the whole framework, which are quality, administration, and content administration in the higher instructive foundations of India.

## 8.8 DIGITAL DELIGHT AND DIGITAL ENGAGEMENT

All companies and organizations aspire to engage and delight the customer, which leads to consumer awareness, brand engagement, brand management, customer involvement and orientation, and customer retention. It is an advanced technology-enabled strategy which can provide a competitive advantage and bring in new customers and maintain brand loyalty for products and services.

Ball and Barnes[1] say that client brain research and needs can be consolidated actually to give clients amusement and viable client commitment rehearses. This paper gives a calculated conversation on whether client amusement is conceivable, and it says that advanced showcasing systems empower such awesome commitment with organizations.

McNeilly and Barr[16] express that there is no method for pleasing and connecting with the client as there are various potential outcomes which exist.

Schouten et al.[21] viewed that as novel, associating with a new combination of experiences which make shocks in client mind and attract them forever, and they will for the most part hold this pleasurable experience for a longer period of time, which achieves brand responsibility and support.

## 8.9 ONLINE INFORMATION USAGE BY STUDENTS—VARIETIES AND VARIED IMPLICATIONS

Madden et al.[15] clearly communicate that electronic information expects to be a basic critical part in individual, family, prosperity, preparation, finance, and in all designs and circles of life.

Bruno and Dąbrowski[2] took apart and said that informational associations give content and information of which the student neighborhood is extraordinarily mindful. Client-made content is seen as more dependable than informational establishment-delivered content, which should be carefully considered before taking a decision.

Brodie et al. (2013) say that these responsibilities create pleasurable experiences for clients, and they get appreciation and feel delighted to be connected with the association, and they become brand ambassadors for the association.

Chitturi and Mahajan[4] say these lively relationships with the association loosen up in their own day-to-day schedules additionally, and it makes delighted encounters and bright organizations in the public field.

Carlson et al. (2008) say that these enjoyments of searching for clients, once they become bright, will commonly spread the message of fulfillment and responsibility practices for their connected circles intentionally. These practices by associations achieve stiff-necked responsibility and brand progression by clients.

## 8.10 DISCUSSION

It is very clear from the literature review that:

- A lot of reforms and changes need to be done in the higher education system.
- There is a need for a global perspective.
- There is a need to have a global focus by the higher education institutions in India.
- Attracting global students to campus must be a priority.
- Students perceptions and needs have to be evaluated, and necessary inputs have to be provided.
- A change in the entire curriculum methodology of higher education is needed.
- Strategic digital marketing strategies have to be utilized by educational institutions to provide consumer delight and happiness.

**TABLE 8.2** Contemporary Practices.

| Author and year | Contributions |
|---|---|
| Miniwatts Marketing Group (2011) | Growth and reach of the internet |
| | The development of the internet revolution |
| Plaza (2009) | Transition and development of internet-based marketing |
| | Implications for products and services |
| Curran (2004)[5] | Role and importance of SEO |
| | Customer traffic is increased on the website |
| Jerkovic (2010) | External links to website, which are crucial in SEO and its management by companies |
| Miller (2011) | Pay per click |
| | SEO |
| | Twin strategies for student engagement and delight |
| Sharanabasappa, Basavaraj Nagesh Kadamudimatha (2017) | Provided the educational system challenges and the need for drastic changes in the higher education system of India |
| Lekha and Thomas (2017)[14] | Emphasize and focus on the importance to bring in drastic changes in the higher education system and practices |
| Sanklecha (2017)[20] | Focused on strengths, issues, and challenges in higher education systems and practices |
| Kapur and Mehta (2004)[12] | An economic perspective on higher education systems and practices in India has been highlighted |
| UGC report on higher education | Highlights the present scenario of higher education in the country |
| Bhargava (2006) | Future need of 3000 more universities in the country is emphasized |
| Nayar (2011)[18] | Discusses about enrollments in higher education |
| Dhanuraj and Rahul Verma (2015) | Identified six major challenges in higher education |
| Hiremath and Albal (2016)[8] | Provides a diagnostic view of the entire higher education system |
| Jonaki and Prasenjit (2016)[10] | Evaluates the higher education systems and practices with 3 major indicators |

**TABLE 8.2** *(Continued)*

| **Author and year** | **Contributions** |
|---|---|
| Chahal and Dar (2015)[3] | Sustainability challenges in the higher education system of India are discussed |
| Singh (2016)[24] | Assessment of the nature and prevalence of higher education in India is discussed and evaluated |
| UGC (Ministry of Higher Education) | Abroad education studies and student spending are discussed |
| Sen Gupta and Parekh (2009)[22] | Discusses various challenges in the higher education system of India |
| Ball and Barnes (2016)[1] | Customer psychology and needs are raised to customer delight if satisfied by companies |
| McNeilly and Barr (2006)[16] | Possibilities of customer delight are discussed |
| Schouten et al. (2007)[21] | A new, engaging experience of customers leads to customer delight |
| Madden et al. (2006)[15] | Online information and its impact on individuals, customers, and society |
| Bruno and Dąbrowski (2013)[2] | Content prudence is needed by students |
| Brodie et al. (2013) | Engagements and pleasurable experiences |
| Chitturi and Mahajan (2008)[4] | Happy engagement with companies results in happy families |
| Carlson et al. (2008) | Happy customers spread information about companies through voluntary engagement practices |

## 8.11 CONCLUSIONS

This study focuses on the nature, commonality, and degree of difficulties in the higher education system of India. Further, the opportunities in the advanced education system of India are explained. There is a need to change the cycle, approach, and way in which understudies must be locked in for productive confirmations. The computerized advertising technique—compelling coordinated advanced showcasing and correspondence procedures utilizing aggregate channel models—is expected to oversee advanced education frameworks and affirmation processes in this country.

## KEYWORDS

- **digitization**
- **sustainability**
- **transition in education**
- **advertising**
- **marketing**

## REFERENCES

1. Ball, J.; Barnes, D. C. Delight and the Grateful Customer: Beyond Joy and Surprise. *J. Serv. Theory Pract.* **2017,** *27* (1), 250–269.
2. Bruno, S.; Dąbrowski, D. *The Effect of Social Media Perception on Consumer Communication of Brands Working Paper Series A (Economics, Management, Statistics)*. 2013.
3. Chahal, N.; Dar, H. Higher Education Sector in India: Challenges of Sustainability. *Int. J. Manag. Res. Rev.* **2015,** *5* (3), 159–169.
4. Chitturi, R.; Raghunathan, R.; Mahajan, V. Delight by Design: The Role of Hedonic Versus Utilitarian Benefits. *J. Mark.* **2008,** *72* (3), 48–63.
5. Curran, K. Tips for Achieving High Positioning in the Results Pages of the Major Search Engines. *Inf. Technol. J.* **2004,** *3* (2), 202–205.
6. Dickey, M. R. The 22 Key Turning Points in the History of YouTube. In *Business Insider*, 2013; p 15.
7. Goldfarb, A.; Tucker, C. Digital Marketing. In *Handbook of the Economics of Marketing*; North-Holland, 2019; Vol. 1, pp 259–290.
8. Hiremath, S. S.; Albal, D. R. Current Scenario of Higher Education in India: Reflections on Some Critical Issues. *Int. Res. J. Soc. Sci. Humanit.* **2016,** *1* (1), 73–78.

9. Hudson, S., Roth, M. S.; Madden, T. J. *Customer Communications Management in the New Digital Era*; Center for Marketing Studies, Darla Moore School of Business, University of south Carolina, 2012; p 21.
10. Jonaki, B.; Prasenjit, P. Higher Education in India: Recent Issues and Trends. *Res. J. Educ. Sci.* **2016,** *2321,* 0508.
11. Kamal, Y. Study of Trend in Digital Marketing and Evolution of Digital Marketing Strategies. *Int. J. Eng. Sci.* **2016,** *6* (5), 5300–5302.
12. Kapur, D.; Mehta, P. B. Indian Higher Education Reform: From Half-baked Socialism to Half-baked Capitalism. *Center for International Development Working Paper* **2004,** *103,* 1–38.
13. Kingston, C. How to Use Twitter for Business and Marketing [Online]. socialmediaexaminer.com. http://www.socialmediaexaminer.com/how-to-use-twitter-for-business-and-marketing/ (Accepted 10. 4. 2016).
14. Lekha, H.; Thomas, B.. Indian Higher Education-Envisioning the Future. *Int. J. Curr. Eng. Sci. Res.* **2017**
15. Madden, A. D.; Ford, N. J.; Miller, D.; Levy, P. Children's Use of the Internet for Informationseeking: What Strategies do They Use and What Factors Affect their Performance, **2006**.
16. McNeilly, K. M.; Barr, T. F. I Love My Accountants–They're Wonderful: Understanding Customer Delight in the Professional Services Arena. *J. Ser. Mark.* **2006,** *20* (3), 152–159.
17. Merisavo, M. The Effects of Digital Marketing Communication on Customer Loyalty: An Integrative Model and Research Propositions, **2006**.
18. Nayar, A. Educating India. *Nature* **2011,** *472* (7341), 24.
19. Kumari, N.; Sharma, A. The Role of Higher Education in Economic Development. *Int. J. Commerce Manag.* **2017**.
20. Sanklecha, N. Current Scenario of Higher Education in India. *Int. J. Eng. Technol. Sci. Res.* **2017,** *4* (8), 571–574.
21. Schouten, J. W.; McAlexander, J. H.; Koenig, H. F. Transcendent Customer Experience and Brand Community. *J. Acad. Mark. Sci.* **2007,** *35,* 357–368.
22. Sen Gupta, A. K.; Parekh, V. Excellence in Higher Education in India: Way Forward. *J. Emerg. Knowl. Emerg. Mark.* **2010,** *1* (1), 14.
23. Singh, D. S. Impact of Digital Marketing on Indian Rural Banking. *SSRN*, 2016.
24. Singh, F. P. Higher Education System in India. *Int. J. Adv. Res. Sci. Eng.* **2016**
25. Wertime, K.; Fenwick, I. DigiMarketing. *ExecuGo Media*, 2008.
26. Wymbs, C. Digital Marketing: The Time for a New "Academic Major" has Arrived. *J. Mark. Educ.* **2011,** *33* (1), 93–106.

# CHAPTER 9

# Business Sustainability: Benefits and Challenges

DHRUV KISHORE BOLE

*State Institute of Hotel Management, Siddhpur, Gujarat, India*

## ABSTRACT

Industry-wide sustainability transformation is critical for achieving sustainable development goals (SDGs). A lack of understanding of the business value of sustainability, as well as implementation challenges and their causes, has led to disdain for sustainable business models among business owners and leaders, particularly those from small and medium-sized businesses. Previous research on the subject has been limited in its ability to provide comprehensive and elaborative information and insights and has fragmented information or is based on traditional research methods of analysis and observation, leaving business owners and leaders perplexed about what it means for them and as a result affecting sustainability initiatives. This chapter builds on previous studies by delving deeper into the business value of sustainability, its implementation challenges, causes, and potential solutions. The chapter would help business owners and leaders gain a more comprehensive understanding of the business value of sustainability, its implementation challenges, and identifying and leveraging available solutions to address implementation challenges, resulting in a more seamless transition to sustainable business models. According to the author, certain implementation challenges can be overcome by restructuring operations and shifting perspectives, whereas others may necessitate the assistance of business stakeholders. Implications are discussed.

Management for Sustainable Development: Integrating Social, Economic, and Environmental Goals.
Vishal Jain & Amit Mittal (Eds.)

## 9.1 INTRODUCTION

To address growing environmental, economic, and social issues, the United Nations established 17 sustainable development goals (SDGs) and urged member countries to contribute to their achievement.[62] Nations have recognized that mitigating business's environmental, economic, and social impacts through sustainable business practices can help resolve those issues and promote sustainable development. They created the SDG action plan as a result to promote business sustainability. Business owners and leaders responded by pledging to use sustainable business practices to reduce their environmental, economic, and social impact. Many business owners and leaders transitioned from unsustainable to sustainable business models by incorporating sustainable policies, procedures, and practices into their business functions, while many others transitioned to more sustainable business models by restructuring their current models.

However, many business owners and leaders have yet to embrace business sustainability. Their disdain for sustainable business models stems from two factors: a lack of understanding of sustainable business practices and their benefits, as well as the challenges associated with their implementation.[4] Many business owners, particularly those in micro and small businesses, believe that making the transition to sustainability is expensive. Such misconceptions have prevented business owners and leaders from weighing the costs and benefits of implementing sustainable business models and thus from investing in them. In contrast, sustainable business practices help organizations reduce operational costs over time and increase their bottom line. It also helps to preserve the environment and promote the welfare of individuals and communities, assisting organizations in meeting their social and environmental obligations.[44]

The challenges associated with implementing sustainable business models have also discouraged business owners and leaders from investing in them. Worse, these challenges have slowed the efforts of those seeking to improve the sustainability of their organizations.[46] However, the challenges have been accompanied by new opportunities that have provided potential solutions to the challenges. Before delving into the challenges that business owners and leaders face in their pursuit of sustainability, as well as the opportunities that it presents, it is critical to consider the benefits that sustainability-based management provides to organizations.

## 9.2 BUSINESS SUSTAINABILITY: BENEFITS

### *9.2.1 POSITIVE STAKEHOLDER RELATIONSHIPS*

Positive stakeholder relationships are critical to long-term profit and business success. Employees, investors, government agencies, local communities, consumers, and supply chain partners are the primary stakeholder groups that can influence an organization's success. These stakeholders have varying expectations and businesses must meet those expectations to build stronger stakeholder relationships. Sustainability-driven management provides an excellent framework for meeting stakeholder expectations which could help strengthen business-stakeholder relationships.[44] The Stakeholder Engagement Action Plan, a critical component of the business sustainability framework, assists sustainability managers in identifying which stakeholders to engage, understanding their expectations, and identifying the critical interventions required to meet those expectations. It also allows sustainability managers to collect stakeholder feedback and use it to improve stakeholder engagement in the future.[57] This type of strategic approach assists organizations in successfully engaging stakeholders and increasing opportunities to strengthen stakeholder relationships.

Different stakeholders have different interests, but their business expectations are becoming more common.[2] They are increasingly expecting businesses to contribute to economic and social development in addition to combating climate change. Because sustainability-focused businesses address pressing environmental, economic, and social issues, they meet stakeholder expectations for environmental, economic, and social development. Such ethical and responsible behavior guided by a business sustainability framework, fosters stakeholder's trust and belief in the organization, laying the groundwork for positive stakeholder relationships.[15]

### *9.2.2 OPPORTUNITIES TO IMPROVE CUSTOMER ACQUISITION AND RETENTION*

Sustainable business models give business owners and leaders more opportunities for customer acquisition and retention, resulting in increased growth and expansion as well as a competitive advantage.[10] Sustainable businesses are becoming more popular among consumers and will be in high demand in the future. This is because consumers are more aware than ever before of economic, social, and environmental issues and they prefer a more sustainable way of life, purchasing more sustainable goods and services as a result. By developing a sustainable brand, businesses would have more opportunities to gain consumer trust and build stronger business–consumer relationships.

According to studies, the demand for environmentally friendly products has risen significantly in recent years, particularly in the food, apparel, cosmetics, and pharmaceutical segments. Consumer purchasing habits are also shifting toward environmentally friendly products, although they are more expensive.[41,51,59] As a result of shifting consumer priorities, businesses that prioritize sustainability have higher consumer acceptance. High levels of consumer acceptance present opportunities for businesses to improve customer acquisition and retention, potentially leading to growth and a competitive advantage.

### 9.2.3 REDUCED OPERATIONAL COSTS

Businesses that incorporate sustainability into their core business processes benefit from lower operational costs.[12] Sustainable businesses use raw materials, energy, water, and other resources more efficiently as a result of their reduce, reuse, and recycle strategy, resulting in lower operating expenses. Sustainable business models, for example, reduce fresh water consumption and thus water costs by recycling wastewater for irrigation and landscaping. Similarly, by using energy-saving lighting, solar panels, and green office equipment, they save energy. According to the author, businesses that consistently improve their operational sustainability benefit from increased operational efficiency and cost savings.

Sustainability-based management, in addition to encouraging efficient resource use, increases employee productivity, which helps reduce human resource costs. Employees who work for environmentally conscious companies feel more connected because they can connect organizational values to their personal values. This increases their sense of belonging, which leads to greater job satisfaction and productivity. Embracing sustainability-based management has been shown to improve job satisfaction and reduce employee turnover.[48] Increased job satisfaction as a result of a stronger sense of belonging will lead to lower attrition and new hire costs, lowering human resource costs.[20]

Businesses that place a high priority on sustainability also get more attention from job seekers. According to a new global survey conducted by IBM Institute for Business Value, the vast majority of job seekers, prefer to work for environmentally responsible companies due to their concern for environmental and social issues.[23] Job seekers believe that a sustainable business is more likely to care for them. Numerous studies show that millennials and Gen Z prefer eco-friendly businesses over competitors. In the coming years, sustainable businesses will continue to attract a new generation of workers, particularly millennials and Gen Z. As a result of these emerging trends, sustainable businesses would benefit from increased employee engagement and loyalty, as well as increased visibility to job seekers.

### 9.2.4 MITIGATE SUPPLY CHAIN RISKS

A business sustainability framework can help companies mitigate the environmental, social, and governance (ESG) risks associated with their suppliers and other supply chain partners. These ESG risks are among the most common sources of supply chain risk. It not only causes procurement disruption but also exposes businesses to the risk of misrepresenting supplier's ESG efforts (greenwashing), both of which can have serious operational and financial consequences.[61] Furthermore, the presence of such risks may deter investors from making business investments because it puts their investment and its returns at risk.

Risk mapping, an important component of sustainability-based management, assists supply chain and sustainability managers in mitigating suppliers' ESG risks by collaborating with them. It gives them the ability to conduct comprehensive ESG risk assessments on all of their suppliers, identifying ESG risks and validating risk mitigation strategies. It also enables them to identify unknown risks faced by their suppliers and develop mitigation strategies to address those risks. Additionally, the risk mapping framework assists sustainability managers in developing their own strategies for mitigating ESG risks associated with suppliers or other supply chain partners. A company, for example, may be exposed to a social risk if one of its suppliers requires its employees to work outside of normal working hours without overtime pay to meet production volume. In this case, supply chain managers can either collaborate with suppliers to develop social risk reduction strategies, or they can diversify their own vendor portfolio to address the risk. Supply chain managers can diversify their supplier portfolios by bringing on second-tier suppliers from various regions with low ESG profiles, to meet supply shortages, as mentioned in the preceding scenario.

Another advantage of risk mapping is that it assists supply chain managers in evaluating the ESG risks of potential suppliers during the onboarding process. Screening suppliers for ESG risks can assist in bringing in suppliers with low ESG risk profiles, potentially lowering supply chain risks.[47] Risk mapping-based supply chain practices can help sustainability and supply chain managers in anticipating ESG risks and developing strategies to mitigate their effects. Without it, however, companies may fail to implement effective ESG controls, resulting in increased supply chain costs and the risk of reputational harm.

### *9.2.5 INCREASED INVESTMENT OPPORTUNITIES*

In addition to the previously mentioned benefits, sustainable business models increase the opportunities for business owners and leaders to seek investments. Sustainable business models are more appealing to private and public investors, such as banks and other lending institutions, due to their long-term viability. This is due to increased consumer acceptance, increased market relevance, increased government recognition, improved risk identification and mitigation capabilities, and lower operating costs.[11]

In addition to their long-term viability, improved transparency of sustainable business models also draws investors. Businesses that prioritize sustainability are extremely transparent in their operations. Sustainable businesses, for instance, make their environmental, economic, and social efforts as well as the outcomes of those efforts public through ESG disclosure. The disclosure also allows for tracking and comparing business's performance on sustainability issues.[52] This level of transparency assists investors in forecasting business risks and opportunities, as well as the viability of their investments, allowing them to make well-informed and calculated investment decisions. Sustainable business models are gaining acceptance not only from private and public investors but also from national governments. Sustainable business models that fall under the priority sector of the government's green financing scheme receive subsidized business loans up to a certain limit for sustainability-related investments.[54]

Investors seek not only economic profit but also social good. They expect businesses to pave the way for positive environmental and socio-economic change. Because sustainable business models help to reduce a company's environmental, economic, and social impact, they meet investor's expectations of driving positive environmental and socioeconomic development.[6] Sustainable investing is gaining traction as investors become more aware of the importance of sustainability. Companies that embrace sustainability will continue to attract investors' interest, while those that do not will lose.

Aside from the benefits, business sustainability presents its own set of challenges. These impediments deter business owners and leaders from pursuing sustainable business models. The following section of the book chapter discusses the challenges that business owners and leaders face when incorporating sustainability as well as possible solutions to those problems.

## 9.3 BUSINESS SUSTAINABILITY: CHALLENGES

### *9.3.1 LACK OF EMPLOYEE ENGAGEMENT IN SUSTAINABILITY INITIATIVES*

Getting employees to align with the company's sustainability goals is a common challenge for business owners and leaders.[34] Business cannot achieve sustainability unless employees at all levels personally participate in the company's sustainability efforts. Although business owners and leaders strive to engage employees and anticipate increased employee participation in the organization's sustainability program, many employees remain uninterested in the company's sustainability efforts. Their lack of interest in the company's sustainability initiatives can be attributed to a number of factors.

One of the most important factors contributing to employee disengagement is the absence of a sustainability-focused employee engagement policy.[33] This results in lower motivation over time, which in turn affects employee's sustainability-related work behaviors. To address this issue, senior management must develop and implement a framework that engages employees. This includes inviting employee's participation in sustainability related decision making and educating them on organizational sustainability initiatives while also recognizing and rewarding their contributions. The author emphasizes that reward is a double-edged sword and that senior management must use them wisely. This is because employees are observed to be at their best until their efforts are recognized and rewarded. It has also been discovered that, despite the presence of an internal sustainability recognition and reward program, employees do not participate in the business's sustainability program. This is because employees lack sustainability values, which cause them to differ from those of the organization. Notably, instilling sustainability values in people who do not have them is incredibly challenging.[40] Furthermore, correcting employee's work behaviors and inclining them toward sustainable work behaviors incurs significant costs in the form of training, counseling, and other similar activities. To address this issue, business owners and executives must integrate sustainable hiring and recruitment practices into their daily operations. Such measures will allow for the hiring of sustainability-focused employees rather than investing in activities to instill sustainable work behaviors in employees. The author emphasizes that hiring employees who care about sustainability will not guarantee employee's engagement in sustainability programs. Senior management must develop and implement a sustainable culture throughout their organizations. This includes enthusiastically communicating sustainability targets, accomplishments, and future goals to employees.[32] Employees should also be made aware of national sustainability regulations and the consequences of failing to follow them. Employees must also be informed about how their careless and negligent sustainability behavior can stymie the company's progress toward meeting its sustainability goals.

A lack of competitive compensation also contributes to low employee engagement and participation. It is critical to remember that, in addition to environmental protection, business sustainability entails minimizing business's negative effects on individuals and society. Organizations must pay competitive wages and salaries to motivate employees to engage in sustainable work behaviors rather than simply meeting the legal minimum wage.[30] Employees will feel more valued as a result of such approaches and their participation in the organization's sustainability program will increase, assisting the organization in meeting its sustainability goals.[32]

### *9.3.2 LOW DEMAND FOR SUSTAINABLE PRODUCTS*

Business owners and leaders attempting to implement sustainable models see low demand for sustainable products as a significant challenge. Consumers are increasingly purchasing environmentally friendly products and services, but this trend has yet to become mainstream, as many consumers remain hesitant to do so. This is due to two factors: the high cost of sustainable products, as well as their inferior performance in comparison to conventional products. According to a recent study by ASDA, higher prices deter consumers from purchasing sustainable products or switching to safer alternatives, particularly in the fast-moving consumer goods segment, which includes milk, bread, and other everyday items. This establishes that consumers want to promote sustainability, but not at the expense of purchasing expensive sustainable products. People with more purchasing power are switching to sustainable products, but those with less purchasing power are finding the transition difficult due to the high cost.[63] Some of the factors that contribute to the high cost of environmentally friendly products include low demand, raw material scarcity, decentralized operations, and high raw material and labor costs.

Because sustainable products are not yet in high demand, businesses only produce a limited number of them. Limited production of sustainable products results in high production costs, causing manufacturers to charge higher prices for such products than for mass-produced equivalents to maintain profit margins.[25] Similarly, shortages of certain sustainable raw materials in the region force manufacturers to import them, resulting in higher sourcing costs and, ultimately, higher production costs.[16] In addition, importing sustainable raw materials which are already in short supply would also increase the procurement cost. Electric vehicles (EVs) and solar panels, for example, require significant amounts of lithium and tellurium, both of these metals are scarce and getting scarcer. It is estimated that the world could face lithium shortages in the next 5 years.[58]

To address this issue, supply chain managers must recognize existing and potential bottlenecks in their supply chain for acquiring sustainable raw materials and resources, as well as foresee solutions to ease constraints. This includes evaluating raw material costs, negotiating competitive prices, and entering into long-term contracts with local, national, and international supply chain partners to meet procurement needs. This will ensure a consistent supply of sustainable raw materials and resources at competitive prices without disrupting production.

The high price of environmentally friendly products is also due to the high cost of raw materials. Many sustainable and organic raw materials are more expensive to grow and produce. Organic cotton, for example, is more expensive to produce because it is grown without the use of chemicals or pesticides. Higher raw material costs raise production costs, causing the final product's price to rise. Another factor that contributes to high costs is the decentralization of business operations. Decentralized manufacturers have more manufacturing or processing facilities and longer supply chains, resulting in higher operating costs. Such an additional cost burden raises the product's price.[8] Higher payroll cost also contributes to the high price of sustainable products. Sustainable businesses compensate their employees in accordance with labor laws to maintain social sustainability. Businesses that adhere to minimum wage laws have higher payroll costs, which ultimately result in higher production costs and product prices.[30]

Low demand for environmentally friendly products is also a result of their subpar performance. Consumers perceive many sustainable products as inferior to conventional products due to inferior performance, resulting in a negative consumer perception and a lack of demand for such products. Personal care and cleaning products, for example, are perceived by consumers to be less effective and aesthetically pleasing than standard products.[17]

Given the scarcity and inefficiency of certain existing sustainable materials, a larger-scale collaborative effort involving all sectors of every industry is required to identify and develop materials that are more environmentally and ecologically friendly as well as financially viable. Business owners and leaders must collaborate with their supply chain partners to identify or develop sustainable raw materials and resources that are less expensive, more efficient, readily available, and easier to produce. They must also stay current on new developments in sustainable raw materials and evaluate them to identify those that fit into their business case. The role of the national government in promoting research and development activities would also be critical. This type of strategic approach can assist in lowering production costs and, eventually, allowing products to be priced competitively with traditional products, resulting in increased product demand.

### *9.3.3 GREENWASHING THREAT*

Greenwashing is gradually becoming one of the most serious challenges impeding business leaders from investing in sustainable operations.[29] Many businesses intentionally engage in greenwashing, falsely marketing their products as environmentally friendly to capitalize on consumer demand for environmentally friendly products. False product sustainability has not only misled consumers but has also harmed environmentally conscious businesses. It has eroded consumer trust in sustainable products, diverting them away from sustainable behaviors. According to an OnBuy study, one of the most common reasons consumers are hesitant to purchase sustainable products is a lack of trust in product sustainability claims.[64] It has also had a negative impact on the demand for sustainable products, causing sustainability to no longer make sense as a business case, making business owners less interested in producing sustainable products or investing in sustainable business models. Businesses that intentionally greenwash must understand how their actions not only undermine the credibility of genuine environmentally friendly businesses but also cause consumers to avoid sustainable products, impeding the achievement of sustainability goals. Given the significance of sustainability and the willingness of consumers and other businesses to promote it, such businesses must view sustainability as a collaborative effort and embrace sustainable business models. They must recognize that they cannot ignore their social responsibilities to maximize profits.[9]

The risk of unintentional greenwashing has also deterred business owners and leaders, particularly small and medium-sized enterprises, from adopting sustainable business models. Most often, sustainable businesses, particularly small and medium-sized enterprises, become entangled in unintentional greenwashing, which typically occurs as a result of challenges associated with ESG disclosure. Financial implications in ESG reporting, a lack of skill sets, difficulty quantifying, and uncertainty in reporting standards are some of the challenges with ESG disclosure that have contributed to unintentional greenwashing.[13] Accurate ESG disclosure necessitates the use of cutting-edge technologies, improved process controls, and data streams that aid in the collection, analysis, and verification of ESG-related data. Many supply chain participants, for example, particularly small-scale raw material suppliers, may be technologically incapable of providing accurate ESG performance, putting the client at risk of unintentional greenwashing. Moreover, many supply chain partners are unable to adopt advanced technological solutions due to financial constraints. This is also true in client businesses.[45] In addition to data accuracy, the relevance and completeness of ESG-related data are critical in supporting sustainability claims. The publication of relevant and verified ESG data is dependent on employee's sustainability skills, which is another area where business owners and leaders face challenges. Quantifying the impact of a company's ESG efforts in ESG reporting is also a source of concern, given that some of the company's ESG impact is difficult to quantify.[36] ESG reporting introduces additional challenges for sustainability managers, such as uncertainty about which ESG standards and key performance indicator (KPIs) to use in ESG reporting. The three ESG reporting standards, such as the US Securities and Exchange Commission (SEC or Commission) in the United States, the International Sustainability Standards Board (ISSB) in the United Kingdom, and the Corporate Sustainability Reporting Directive (CSRD) in the European Union, are still in the works and will not be available until 2023–2025. While these standards may have different requirements, similarities and differences, they will require organizations to disclose certain mandatory ESG information, which is where the next challenge lies. Once these standards are released, both domestic and international businesses will be required to disclose their ESG performance in accordance with the adopted ESG standards of the country in which they operate. However, in the early years of the standard's rollout, businesses may face a shortage of standard-specific consultancy or advisory services to assist them with standard-specific ESG disclosure compliance. Scarcity may increase the likelihood of unintentional greenwashing via inaccurate disclosure. In the absence of stronger data management, businesses may unintentionally engage in greenwashing through inaccurate ESG disclosure. Investors, consumers, and regulatory agencies seek ESG disclosures to validate a company's sustainability claims and inaccurate ESG disclosures would lead to those stakeholders being misled.[53]

Because many factors contribute to this challenge, overcoming it requires a multifaceted approach. National governments, for example, must create a framework to encourage business owners and leaders to invest in sustainable business models, promote research and development activities to identify and develop more sustainable solutions, create national sustainability reporting standards, and build sustainability expertise through education and training. Such strategic efforts would help small and medium-sized businesses overcome the challenges of greenwashing.

### *9.3.4 LACK OF SUSTAINABLE LENDING*

The lack of sustainable lending poses a significant challenge to sustainable business investment. Many international banks have increased their disbursement of sustainable loans in recent years. However, the current sustainable lending rate represents only a small proportion of the global credit market.[60] The challenges associated with the sustainable lending process have made it difficult for banks and other lending institutions to extend sustainable financing. This has discouraged sustainability-minded business owners and leaders from investing in sustainable business models.

The exclusion of certain sectors from the green financing scheme is one of the major barriers to obtaining sustainable financing. Many countries have developed green financing schemes to promote business sustainability, but certain critical sectors have been left out. Countries are focusing more on EVs and renewable energy, but organic farming, waste recycling, and waste management have been left out of the green financing landscape. This has made it difficult for entrepreneurs in these sectors to obtain sustainable financing and the benefits that come with it. National governments must reconsider their green financing policies to ensure that all priority industries are covered and funds are allocated in the scheme for each priority sector. This will not only balance lending across all critical sectors but will also assist banks in closing financing gaps. The problem is exacerbated further by the government's credit allocation framework. Many national governments do not clearly communicate their support for the green transition.[42] To address this, national credit agencies must set green financing targets for banks in both urban and rural areas. They must investigate why green financing targets are not being met and seek explanations from banks for their failure to meet those targets. Such measures will hold banks accountable for their sustainable financing activities, with sustainable financing taking precedence.[31]

Another barrier to sustainable business investment is a lack of incentives for sustainable business models. In addition to easy access to sustainable financing, entrepreneurs and business owners expect the national government to incentivize sustainable business models through low lending interest rates, investment tax credits, emission reduction credits, and energy-efficiency subsidies. However, in many countries, these hopes have yet to be fulfilled.[50] Savings from incentivization could help entrepreneurs raise capital for future sustainability-related investments, reducing their reliance on outside funding.

A lack of ESG reporting standards and methods is another challenge that banks and other lending institutions face in sustainable lending. As a result of a lack of standards and reporting methods, banks are unable to assess and compare a business's sustainability targets and performance, which is an important criterion in sustainable lending. This is because many countries have yet to establish ESG reporting standards or mandate ESG performance disclosure. Global ESG reporting standards are currently in the works and will be available in a few years. Many private firms offer ESG reporting services based on their own methodologies, but at exorbitant prices that many small and medium-sized businesses cannot afford. As a result, many organizations make their own decisions about what data to report and whether to report at all. This results in significant disparity and irregularity in the ESG data of various businesses. In the absence of standard data on an organization's sustainability efforts, banks struggle to understand their ESG profiles and assess creditworthiness, making lending decisions difficult.[27,49] It is worth noting that ESG disclosure is an important criterion for banks when making sustainable lending decisions. To address this issue, banks must identify credible ESG reporting firms on a national and global scale, the credibility of whose ESG reports can be relied on. Banks can use third-party ESG performance standards, develop their own standards, or a combination of the two to assess their organization's sustainability efforts. When self-assessing, banks can conduct interviews or use online questionnaires to gather information about the organization's ESG efforts and determine its ESG performance. Banks must also establish a centralized database of ESG performance for both listed and unlisted companies. These strategies would not only help banks assess an organization's ESG performance, ESG risks, and ultimately, creditworthiness, but they would also alleviate bank concerns about greenwashing.[22] A company seeking investment for upgrades can claim to be green, but the veracity of its claim cannot be verified in the absence of standard reporting practices.

Another impediment to banks providing sustainable financing is business viability. Many businesses, particularly small and medium-scale enterprises (SMEs), are regarded as uninvestable by lending institutions due to the profits they generate. Banks prefer to finance large private corporations and government enterprises over private medium and small-scale enterprises because such projects are more financially viable for them.[14,43] It is imperative to note that small and medium-sized businesses supply large corporations and their role in achieving sustainable development is critical. National sustainable goals would be difficult to achieve unless small and medium-scale businesses reduce their environmental, economic, and social impacts by adopting sustainable business models. Banks must revise their SME lending model and devise strategies to address common SME lending challenges. This could include identifying current pain points in their SME lending process and collaborating with a national credit agency to resurrect SME lending to alleviate those pain points.[22] This could also include providing business loan insurance to SME clients or referring SME clients who have been denied loans to authorized P2P lenders.[5] Such strategic efforts would help banks leverage existing SME financing opportunities, resulting in improved access to green financing for SMEs.

The bank's inability to identify green projects is also a barrier to accessing sustainable financing. Entrepreneurs frequently complain that lending institutions perceive their sustainable business models to be the same as traditional business models. Employee's lack of knowledge about sustainability, particularly in rural areas, contributes to the problem. Banks must take a multifaceted approach to address this. They must educate their employees about sustainability and industry-specific sustainable lending while also reducing red tape in their lending processes. They must establish a dedicated department to oversee sustainable financing activities and assist entrepreneurs as needed during the process. This would not only help to prioritize and accelerate sustainable financing, but it would also help banks meet their sustainable financing targets.[22,26,65] Employees interact with entrepreneurs from a variety of industries during the financing process, so a thorough understanding of business sustainability and the green financing process would be beneficial. It must be kept in mind that sustainability is a broad and diverse topic and that in-depth knowledge is required to cover all of its facets.[3,18] Accenture, a globally recognized consulting firm, proposed a strategy for sustainable lending that can assist banks and other financial institutions in developing a sustainable lending strategy[22] (Figure 9.1). The framework can help banks accelerate sustainable financing by addressing issues such as a lack of ESG reporting standards, business creditworthiness and bank's inability to identify green projects.

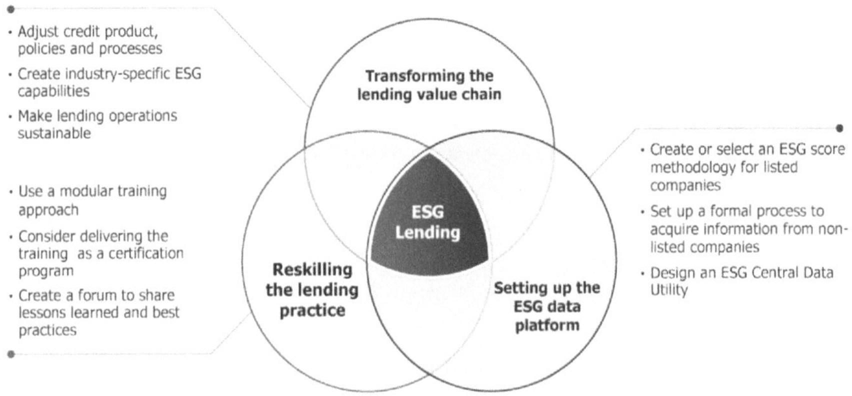


**FIGURE 9.1** Accenture's sustainable lending strategy for banks..[22] Reproduced with permission from ©2023Accenture.

*Source*: Reproduced with permission from Ref. [22]. Copyright © 2023 Accenture

Sustainable finance is gaining traction and banks are gradually adapting. Banks serve as a bridge between policymakers and environmentally conscious entrepreneurs and they must take the lead in capitalizing on the opportunities presented by sustainable financing. They must identify grey areas in sustainable lending and develop strategies to capitalize on opportunities to structure their sustainable lending operations to accelerate sustainable financing. They should see lending to SMEs as an opportunity to make a significant contribution to economic, social, and environmental protection while also protecting their loans. It is critical to note that their sustainable lending portfolio can have a direct impact on the sustainability of their business operations.

### *9.3.5 SHORTAGE OF ESG CONSULTANTS*

The scarcity of specialized ESG consultants, combined with the high cost of hiring such consultants, makes adopting sustainable business models challenging. Business owners and leaders, especially those in small and medium-sized businesses, are frequently perplexed about where to begin with sustainability initiatives, what elements and process improvements to prioritize, what ESG standards to adhere to, and what KPIs to use to track progress. Many of them are also unfamiliar with national sustainability regulations, as well as how to properly document ESG efforts and their outcomes. Business owners and leaders with little to no experience in business sustainability frequently seek the help of ESG consultants to guide them through the sustainability transition. ESG consultants are in short supply in the global sustainability consulting market, limiting their ability to meet the needs of organizations.[28] Expanding the pool of ESG professionals could aid in addressing this issue and the role of the national government would be critical in this regard. Developing ESG Specialization courses, incorporating them into higher education frameworks and establishing a national sustainability organization to facilitate sustainability training to businesses at the local and regional levels would all help to build a pool of ESG professionals over time.

Hiring an ESG consultant is frequently expensive, making it difficult for small businesses to afford them. The fee is based on the industry in which the company operates the scope of the advisory, the consultant's expertise, experience, and market value. Given that, mandatory ESG disclosure will soon become the new norm, demand for ESG consulting services is expected to skyrocket in the coming years, driving up ESG consultant fees even further. Business owners and leaders may want to consider hiring experienced sustainability professionals as an alternative to ESG consulting services. However, hiring an experienced sustainability manager to manage business sustainability operations as opposed to utilizing ESG consulting services may not be economically viable over the long term. It may eliminate advisory and consulting fees, but it will increase payroll expenses. Wage expectations may rise as more companies seek to hire sustainability managers, resulting in an increase in payroll costs that many businesses with razor-thin profit margins may be unwilling to accept. Even, if they do, it will have an impact on operating costs and, ultimately, product costs.[56] To reduce the high cost of ESG consultancy services, business leaders can form a cross-functional sustainability team from their existing workforce with knowledge of key ESG topics. They must designate a team leader to lead the team and oversee sustainability implementation and have an ESG training firm train the team on sustainability implementation. To get the most out of ESG training, businesses must take advantage of available opportunities to equip employees with ESG methodology knowledge. This includes educating team members about ESG through the sponsorship of webinars, e-learning courses, seminars, and industry events. Businesses could also form partnerships with academic institutions to provide ESG specialization courses to their employees at a reduced cost. This would help to develop ESG talent within the organization and, in turn, reduce reliance on ESG consultancy services.[7] While ESG reporting may appear to be costly at first, it will appear to be insignificant in the long run. Lower operating costs from more efficient resource use, such as raw materials, energy, and water, would offset the initial costs of ESG reporting.

### *9.3.6 SUSTAINABILITY NOT FITTING THE BUSINESS CASE*

Many business owners and leaders are hesitant to adopt a sustainable business model because they believe it is incompatible with their business case.[37] Business leaders frequently base their investment decisions on return capabilities and because sustainability-related investments have higher investment and implementation costs business leaders do not see the value in them. The author proposes that by simply shifting perspectives from "making a business case for sustainability" to "making the sustainability case of business," business owners and leaders will be able to see sustainability-related investments as a value-driven activity.[19] According to the author, business leaders should assess the severity of their operation's environmental, economic, and social impacts and forecast how these impacts will manifest in the future. In addition, they must consider how future consumer demand for sustainable businesses, as well as their products and services, will increase and how business compliance with national sustainability regulations will become the new standard. This will help them understand the internal and external risks that the company will face in the coming years, as well as its chances of survival in changing markets. With such market-oriented strategic evaluation, business leaders would be able to see the value in sustainability.

Many business owners and leaders assume that transitioning to, or developing, a sustainable business model is costly and has a slower payback. Business owners and leaders must recognize that the majority of investments in sustainability are focused on equipment and technological solutions and are one-time rather than recurring investments. Investing in sustainability pays off in the long run because it allows businesses to significantly reduce their costs through resource efficiency, resulting in cost savings. In addition, building a sustainable business can assist in gaining more consumer acceptance and differentiating themselves in the market, which can lead to increased revenue earning potential and business growth.[24] The author also suggests that business leaders consider extending their payback period. Allowing for a longer payback period can help business leaders in prioritizing investments in sustainability. Business owners and leaders must acknowledge that sustainable business models are a win-win situation in which companies can maintain operational profitability while also fulfilling their environmental and social responsibilities.

### *9.3.7 POLITICAL INSTABILITY*

Political instability is a challenge for business owners and leaders transitioning to sustainability, particularly in developing and poor countries. It can result in changes in governments, policymakers, and legislative bodies, which can lead to the creation of unfavorable business laws, which can have a negative impact on business and, ultimately, profits. For instance, increased trade restrictions, higher import and export tariffs, higher tax rates, and business compliance with new regulations, as well as delays in governmental approvals, may have a negative effect on business operations. Political unrest may also result from political instability, which may increase the likelihood of strikes and riots, resulting in employee absences, lower productivity, and higher operating costs.

To address the challenge posed by political instability, business owners and leaders must take a multifaceted approach. Purchasing political risk insurance is one method of mitigating political risk that business owners and leaders can consider. By purchasing political risk insurance, they can protect their businesses from losses caused by political risk events such as riots, protests, and civil war. It also safeguards businesses against financial losses caused by unanticipated currency value changes and labor laws, currency inconvertibility, asset confiscation, terrorist acts, and contract repudiation.[1] However, higher political risk necessitates a higher premium, potentially increasing operational costs. When considering political risk insurance, the author recommends that business owners and leaders become familiar with the policy's terms, conditions, and exclusions.

Influencing local politics through lobbying is another strategy used by multinational corporations to mitigate risks associated with political instability. This strategy entails hiring a lobbyist to persuade the government to create business-friendly policies. Lobbyists know which government officials share the same viewpoints as business, present a case that piques policymaker's interest, and eventually persuade the government to pass laws or implement policies that benefit the industry. Business owners and leaders can form their own coalition, hire lobbyists, or contract with a lobbying firm, or they can join an existing coalition.[21] However, lobbying services are expensive and out of reach for many business owners, particularly those with razor-thin profit margins. This presents another challenge for medium and small-scale business owners.

Business owners and leaders should also consider borrowing capital from local financial institutions, preferably government banks, and insuring it with business loan insurance. Business loan insurance reimburses the lending bank if the insured fails to repay the loan due to losses caused by political risks, pandemic-related closures, or permanent disability (Covered Risks). Leasing assets such as land, buildings, and equipment rather than making a personal capital investment in purchasing them is another viable option for business owners and leaders. This would safeguard business owner's personal capital investment.[55] It is critical to note that while leasing saves capital and lowers risk by lowering the business owner's personal capital investment, it raises operating costs. When deciding whether to buy or lease an asset, business owners and leaders must consider the asset's net cost, maintenance, resale value, and future relevance. The role of political leaders is critical to the country's political stability. Political leaders, according to the author, should engage and collaborate to bring stability to the country's political system. They must make sustainability a national priority and create a framework to support sustainable development. They must also be cautious about proposing and enacting business laws and policies that do not support business and make operations difficult because such government actions not only negatively impact business but also harm the loan portfolios of government banks. The author proposes that the national governments create a centralized database of sustainable business projects that includes information on sustainable business models, investors, and advisory firms. A centralized data repository can promote knowledge sharing, assisting new sustainability-focused business owners and entrepreneurs in developing or transitioning to sustainable business models. It can help to control data redundancy and inconsistency for sustainable development and harmonize records of sustainable organizations and agencies which will help in ensuring sustainable development in the country.[39]

Some of the sustainability challenges, according to business leaders, are difficult to overcome and are impeding their progress toward a greener, more sustainable, and socially responsible business world.[38] The challenges associated with business sustainability, in particular, have made incorporating business sustainability extremely difficult. Some businesses may face a few challenges, while others may face many. Business's inability to implement sustainability-based management as a result of challenges has harmed not only their competitiveness, brand value, and long-term survival but also their ability to meet their environmental, economic, and social responsibilities and thus SDGs. In the coming years, businesses that embrace sustainability-based management will undoubtedly benefit from increased customer engagement, improved brand image, and investor and regulatory agency recognition. The author emphasizes that each company is unique and that sustainable business practices can be integrated based on the company's nature, scale, and goals. The author recommends that business owners and leaders seize every opportunity to incorporate sustainability into their operations. They should not sacrifice business sustainability for profit nor should they regard it as a formality.

## 9.4 CONCLUSION

Adoption of business sustainability across industries is critical to meeting the SDGs. As previously stated, a lack of understanding of sustainable business practices and their benefits, as well as the challenges associated with their implementation, has prevented business owners and leaders from implementing them.[4] Prior studies conducted on the subject has their own limitations. Their ability to provide comprehensive and elaborative information and insights into the importance of sustainability for businesses, implementation challenges, causes of such challenges, and potential solutions were limited. Many prior studies did not address some of the implementation challenges discussed in this chapter, such as the scarcity of ESG consultants and political uncertainty, among other things. Moreover, the majority of the studies were based on traditional research methods of analysis and observation, leaving business owners and leaders perplexed about what it means for them, especially small and medium-sized entrepreneurs, making comprehension difficult and, as a result, affecting sustainability initiatives.[35] Furthermore, there is a patchwork of comprehensive information available on the subject, further complicating comprehension. This chapter builds on previous studies by highlighting the significance of adopting sustainable business models, as well as implementation challenges, causes, and potential solutions. The chapter adds to the literature on the subject by providing comprehensive and descriptive information and insights. Although the author claims that this chapter is insufficient to ensure impact, it is organized in such a way that comprehension of the subject is more likely, encouraging the implementation of sustainability initiatives. This chapter may be useful as a starting point for business owners, executives, sustainability managers, and strategists. In this chapter, the author used a straightforward, comprehensive, and elaborative approach to define the business value of implementing sustainability, as well as implementation challenges and potential solutions, to encourage the adoption of business sustainability. The benefits of having sustainable business models are highlighted first in this chapter, such as opportunities to improve customer acquisition and retention, lower operational costs, and attract investments. Second, the most common challenges for implementing sustainable business models, as well as their causes, are outlined. Third, solutions to the implementation challenges are proposed. Finally, the importance of incorporating sustainability into core business functions to meet environmental, economic, and social responsibilities is emphasized. The author also suggests that certain implementation challenges can be overcome by restructuring operations and shifting perspectives, whereas others may necessitate the assistance of business stakeholders such as governmental agencies, financial institutions, vendors, and consumers. The implications and practical contributions of the chapter will be useful to business owners and leaders who want to integrate sustainability into core business functions and improve sustainability performance.

Taken collectively, the author believes that the chapter's structure increases the likelihood that business owners and leaders would be able to comprehend the significance of adopting sustainable business models and understand why and how they must adopt sustainable business models. It would also aid in a broader understanding of challenges, as well as in identifying and leveraging available solutions to address challenges that may arise during the implementation of sustainability, resulting in a more seamless transition to sustainable business models. The industry-wide sustainability transformation required to meet the SDGs will be impossible unless businesses of all sizes adopt sustainability initiatives. After all, achieving SDGs necessitates a collaborative effort. The chapter is limited to academic publications that directly refer to the importance of business sustainability and the implementation challenges that may influence business sustainability adoption. In addition, the topic would be an interesting avenue for future research. Future research that focuses on evaluating the benefits of business sustainability as well as identifying new potential implementation challenges and their potential solutions, including case studies, may add value to the business sustainability context.

## KEYWORDS

- **sustainability**
- **business sustainability**
- **business sustainability challenges**
- **business sustainability benefits**
- **sustainable business models**
- **sustainable business practices**
- **sustainability-based management**
- **business sustainability framework**
- **sustainable business development**

## REFERENCES


1. Ali, T.; Butt, A.; Arslan, A.; Tarba, S. Y.; Sniazhana, A. S.; Kontkanen, M. International Projects and Political Risk Management by Multinational Enterprises: Insights from Multiple Emerging Markets. *Int. Market. Rev.* **2021,** *38* (6): 1113–1142. doi:10.1108/IMR-03-2020-0060.
2. Allredge, K.; Jacobs, F.; Teichner, W. *Great Expectations: Navigating Challenging Stakeholder Expectations of Brands* [Online], Dec 9, 2021. https://www.mckinsey.com/industries/consumer-packaged-goods/our-insights/great-expectations-navigating-challenging-stakeholder-expectations-of-brands (accessed Nov 14, 2022).
3. Aplanet. Facing up to ESG: Key Challenges for Sustainable Finance. *Aplanet* [Online], Aug 3, 2022. https://aplanet.org/resources/facing-up-to-esg-key-challenges-for-sustainable-finance/ (accessed Nov 3, 2022).
4. Apoga, R. R.; Petrovska, K. Barriers to Sustainable Digital Transformation in Micro-, Small-, and Medium-Sized Enterprises. *Sustainability* **2022,** *14* (20). doi:10.3390/su142013558.
5. Bahllio, J.; Gerhard, F.; Harlalka, A.; Havas, A.; Kremer, A. How Banks can Reimagine Lending to Small and Medium-Size Enterprises. *McKinsey* [Online], May 24, 2022. https://www.mckinsey.com/capabilities/risk-and-resilience/our-insights/how-banks-can-reimagine-lending-to-small-and-medium-size-enterprises (accessed Oct 18, 2022).
6. Bergstrom, S. How ESG Principles Help Companies Attract New Investors. *Industry Today* [Online], Aug 31, 2021. https://industrytoday.com/how-esg-principles-help-companies-attract-new-investors/ (accessed Nov 1, 2022).
7. Brachio, A. ESG Talent is Critical for Advancing Sustainability Strategy. *World Economic Forum* [Online], Jun 9, 2022. https://www.weforum.org/agenda/2022/06/esg-talent-is-critical-for-advancing-sustainability-strategies/ (accessed Nov 11, 2022).
8. Calhoun, S. *The Future of Manufacturing: Local, Decentralized Manufacturing* [Online], Apr 13, 2022. doi:10.1142/S021962201750002X (accessed Nov 17, 2022).

9. Chladek, N. *Why You Need Sustainability in Your Business Strategy*; Harvard Business School [Online], Nov 6, 2019. https://online.hbs.edu/blog/post/business-sustainability-strategies (accessed Oct 30, 2022).
10. Dalvi, M. G.; Rambabu, P.; Murthy, N. N.; Singh, A.; Gosavi, N. Business Sustainability—A Study of Most Sustainable Corporations. *Environ. Manag. Sustainable Dev. (Macrothink Inst.)* **2019,** *8* (2). doi:10.5296/emsd.v8i2.14790.
11. Eccles, R. G.; Klimenko, S. The Investor Revolution. *Harv. Bus. Rev. Magaz.* **2019,** May–June, 106–116. https://hbr.org/2019/05/the-investor-revolution (accessed Oct 25, 2022).
12. Ekins, P.; Zenghelis, D. The Costs and Benefits of Environmental Sustainability. *Sustain. Sci.* **2021** (Springer), 949–965. doi:10.1007/s11625-021-00910-5.
13. Farbstein, E.; Schmidt, A. Unintentional Greenwashing: What it is & how to Prevent it. *Normative* [Online], Jul 14, 2022. https://normative.io/insight/unintentional-greenwashing/(accessed Oct 26, 2022).
14. Fisher, P. *What are the Challenges of Green Finance*? The London Institute of Banking and Finance [Online], Oct 10, 2019. https://www.libf.ac.uk/news-and-insights/news/detail/2019/10/10/what-are-the-challenges-of-green-finance (accessed Nov 1, 2022).
15. Fobbe, L.; Hilletofth, P. The Role of Stakeholder Interaction in Sustainable Business Models. A Systematic Literature Review. *J. Cleaner Prod.* **2021,** *327* (10). doi.org/10.1016/j.jclepro.2021.129510.
16. Fredershausen, A. C.; Hannon, E.; Helmcke, S.; Nauclér, T. It's not Easy Buying Green: How to Win at Sustainable Sourcing. *McKinsey Sustainability* [Online], Feb 25, 2022. https://www.mckinsey.com/capabilities/sustainability/our-insights/its-not-easy-buying-green-how-to-win-at-sustainable-sourcing (accessed Nov 4, 2022).
17. Ganesan, B.; Unnithan, A. B. *Overcoming the Perceived Performance Inferiority of Sustainable Product: An Abstract*; Springer, 2020. doi:10.1007/978-3-030-42545-6_217.
18. Ghuman, J.; Phua, B. Sustainable Finance: What you Need to Know About its Challenges and Opportunities. *Go Beyond Partners* [Online], n.d.. https://www.gobeyondpartners.com/our-thinking/sustainable-finance-what-you-need-to-know-about-its-challenges-and-opportunities/ (accessed Oct 28, 2022).
19. Godelnik, R. 2021. Forget About the Business Case for Sustainability. *Medium* [Online], May 25, https://medium.com/age-of-awareness/forget-about-the-business-case-for-sustainability-c3d8c1d65ddf (accessed Nov 1, 2022).
20. Heimerl, P.; Haid, M.; Perkmann, U.; Rabensteiner, M. Job Satisfaction as a Driver for Sustainable Development in the Hospitality Industry? *Evid. Alp. Reg.* **2020,** *12* (17). doi: 10.3390/su12176754.
21. Iftinchi, V.; Hurduzeu, G. How Multinational Corporations use Lobbying and Advocacy to Mitigate Political Risks. *Oradea J. Bus. Econ.* **2018,** *3* (Special Issue), 18–26. doi: 10.47535/1991ojbe040.
22. Innig, C.; Jais, N.; Amodio, G. Retooling the Bank for Sustainable Lending. *Accenture* [Online], Oct 22, 2021. https://www.accenture.com/us-en/insights/banking/sustainable-lending (accessed Nov 19, 2022).
23. Institute for Business Value. *Sustainability at a Turning Point*; Institute for Business Value, 2021.
24. Jacobo-Hernandez, C. A.; Jaimes-Valdez, M. A.; Jiménez, S. O. Benefits, Challenges and Opportunities of Corporate Sustainability. *Management (Sciendo)* **2021,** *25* (1). doi:10.2478/manment-2019-0059.

25. Johansson, A.; Gustavsson, L.; Pejryd, L. Sustainable Operations Management Through Development of Unit Cost Performance Measurement. *Procedia Manuf. (Elsevier)* **2020,** *43,* 344–351. doi:10.1016/j.promfg.2020.02.171.
26. Khan, K. I.; Mata, M. N.; Martins, J. M.; Nasir, A.; Dantas, R. M.; Correia, A. B.; Saghir, M. U. Impediments of Green Finance Adoption System: Linking Economy and Environment. *Emerg. Sci. J.* **2022,** *6* (2). doi:10.28991/ESJ-2022-06-02-02.
27. Kumar, S. The Great ESG Reporting Divide. *The Outlook* [Online], May 27, 2022. https://www.outlookindia.com/business/the-great-esg-reporting-divide-news-198843 (accessed Nov 3, 2022).
28. Lacone, A.; Lee, S. ESG Consultant Shortage Looms as Corporate Reporting Race Begins. *Bloomberg Tax* [Online]. Jun 28, 2022. https://news.bloombergtax.com/financial-accounting/esg-consultant-shortage-looms-as-corporate-reporting-race-begins (accessed Oct 24, 2022).
29. Loh, L.; Yock, Y. The New Sustainability Challenge for Directors: Perils and Prospects in Greenwashing. *Independent Director's Databank* [Online], Feb 22, 2022. https://www.independentdirectorsdatabank.in/img/newsletter/2022/621e00fda7a47.pdf (accessed Oct 3, 2022).
30. Mair, S.; Druckman, A.; Jackson, T. Higher Wages for Sustainable Development? Employment and Carbon Effects of Paying a Living Wage in Global Apparel Supply Chains. *Ecol. Econ. (Elsevier)* **2019,** *159,* 11–23. doi:10.1016/j.ecolecon.2019.01.007.
31. Manjushree, S.; Giridhar, K. V. Problems and Prospects of Priority Sector Lending. *Shanlax Int. J. Commerce* **2018,** *6,* (2).
32. Martins, J. M.; Aftab, H.; Mata, M. N.; Majeed, M. U.; Aslam, S.; Correia, A. B.; Mata, P. N. Assessing the Impact of Green Hiring on Sustainable Performance: Mediating Role of Green Performance Management and Compensation. *Sustainability* **2021,** *18* (11). doi:10.3390/ijerph18115654.
33. Mboga, J.; Troiani, K. An Empirical Study: Employee Engagement and Linkage to Organization. *Int. J. Bus. Appl. Sci.* **2018,** *7* (2), 42–56.
34. McInerney, S. J.; Niewiarowski, P. H. Biomimicry Training to Promote Employee Engagement in Sustainability. *Biomimetics* **2022,** *7* (2). doi:10.3390/biomimetics7020071.
35. McManners, P. J. Increasing the Impact of Sustainability Research-A New Methodology. *J. Sustainability Res.* 2019. doi:doi.org/10.20900/jsr20190008.
36. Mehrotra, N.; Ahluwalia, D. S. Opinion: As ESG Risks and Performance Disclosures go Mainstream, Complex Challenges Continue to Plague the System. *Business Insider India* [Online], Jun 15, 2022. https://www.businessinsider.in/sustainability/article/opinion-as-esg-risks-and-performance-disclosures-go-mainstream-complex-challenges-continue-to-plague-the-system/articleshow/92229097.cms (accessed Oct 11, 2022).
37. Menestrel, M. L.; Rode, J.; Heinz, N.; Cornelissen, G. Encouraging Sustainability: Why the Business Case Isn't Enough. *INSEAD Knowledge* [Online], Jun 21, 2021. https://knowledge.insead.edu/responsibility/encouraging-sustainability-why-business-case-isnt-enough (accessed Oct 29, 2022).
38. Milanese, S.; Eikelenboom, M.; Stella, C.; Decadri, S. Overcoming the Challanges to Sustainability. *Arthur Little* [Online], 2022 (accessed Oct 30, 2022).
39. Mohammed, A.; Saleh, B. M. Centralized Database: A Prerequisite for Security and Sustainable Development in Nigeria. *Int. J. Innovative Res. Comput. Sci. Technol.* **2017,** *5* (1). doi:10.21276/ijircst.2017.5.1.7.
40. Negro, P. A.; Vargas, A. *Driving Organisational Culture Change for Sustainability*; Malmo University (Malmo University), 2019, p 59.

41. Nielsen. Global Sustainable Shoppers Report. *Nielsen* [Online], 2018. https://www.nielsen.com/wp-content/uploads/sites/3/2019/04/global-sustainable-shoppers-report-2018.pdf (accessed Nov 15, 2022).
42. Nikolaou, N. *The Transition to a Green Global Economy: The Case of Green Finance and Green Bonds*; Piraeus University, 2018. https://dione.lib.unipi.gr/xmlui/bitstream/handle/unipi/11332/Nikolaou_TMS1604.pdf?sequence=1&isAllowed=y.
43. Noh, H. J. *Financial Strategy to Accelerate Green Growth*; Asian Development Bank Institute, 2018. https://www.adb.org/sites/default/files/publication/452656/adbi-wp866.pdf
44. Nosratabadi, S.; Mosavi, A.; Shamshirband, S.; Zavadskas, E. K.; Rakotonirainy, A.; Chau, K. W. Sustainable Business Models: A Review. *Sustainability (MDPI)* **2019,** *11* (6). doi:10.1186/s41180-017-0016-5.
45. OECD. *Financing SMEs for Sustainability: Drivers, Constraints and Policies*; Organisation for Economic Co-operation and Development, 2022. doi:10.9790/487X-16511925.
46. Ogrean, C.; Herciu, M. Business Models Addressing Sustainability Challenges—Towards a New Research Agenda. *Sustainability (MDPI)* **2020,** *12* (9) (accessed Oct 13, 2022).
47. Olivier, J. Managing Risk Through Sustainable Supply Chains. *Deloitte* [Online], Sep 6, 2020. https://www.deloitte.com/global/en/services/risk-advisory/blogs/managing-risk-through-sustainable-supply-chains.html (accessed Oct 11, 2020).
48. Olupinyo, G. *Benefits of Sustainability: Improved Employee Attraction, Engagement and Retention* [Online], Jun 23, 2020. https://greenbusinessbureau.com/blog/how-sustainability-benefits-companies-by-increasing-employee-attraction-and-retention/ (accessed Oct 15, 2022).
49. Philipova, E. Growth and Challenges in Sustainable Finance. *Refinitiv* [Online]. Mar 10, 2022. https://www.refinitiv.com/perspectives/future-of-investing-trading/growth-and-challenges-in-sustainable-finance/ (accessed Nov 15, 2022).
50. Ponzi, D. *The Business of Greening: Policy Measures for Green Business Development in Asia;* Asian Development Bank, 2019. https://www.adb.org/sites/default/files/publication/482506/sdwp-059-policy-measures-green-business-asia.pdf.
51. Porter Novelli. *How to Build Deeper Bonds, Amplify Your Message & Expand Your Consumer Base*; Porter Novelli, 2018. https://www.porternovelli.com/findings/2018-porter-novelli-cone-purpose-study-how-to-build-deeper-bonds-amplify-your-message-expand-your-consumer-base/.
52. Pucker, K. P. Overselling Sustainability Reporting. *Harv. Bus. Rev. Mag.* **2021,** May–June. https://hbr.org/2021/05/overselling-sustainability-reporting.
53. Shannon, M.; Shulman, J.; Harnick, P. *Gearing up for the ESG Reporting Challenge*; KPMG, 2022. https://home.kpmg/xx/en/home/insights/2022/05/gearing-up-for-the-esg-reporting-challenge.html (accessed Nov 7, 2022).
54. Start Up India. Sustainable Finance Scheme. *Start Up India* [Online], n.d.. https://www.startupindia.gov.in/content/sih/en/government-schemes/sustainable-finance-scheme.html (accessed Nov 18, 2022).
55. Stowe, L. *5 Strategies for Mitigating Political Risk* [Online]. Sep 14, 2022. https://fiscalnote.com/blog/strategies-mitigating-political-risk (accessed Nov 11, 2022).
56. Sweeney, J. R. *The Cost and Benefits of Measuring Sustainability*; Georgia College Knowledge Box [Online], May, 2020. https://kb.gcsu.edu/cgi/viewcontent.cgi?article=1000&context=fac-staff.
57. Taylor, A.; Bancilhon, C.; Oger, C.; Morris, J. *Five-Step Approach to Stakeholder Engagement*; BSR [Online], 2019. https://www.bsr.org/en/reports/stakeholder-engagement-five-step-approach-toolkit (accessed Oct 20, 2022).

58. Than, K. Critical Minerals Scarcity Could Threaten Renewable Energy Future. *Stanford Earth Matters Magazine* [Online], Jan 17, 2018. https://earth.stanford.edu/news/critical-minerals-scarcity-could-threaten-renewable-energy-future.
59. The Economist. An Eco-wakening-Measuring Global Awareness, Engagement and Action for Nature. *The Economist* [Online], 2021. https://impact.economist.com/perspectives/sites/default/files/an_ecowakening_measuring_awareness_engagement_and_action_for_nature_final_may_18_2021.pdf (accessed Nov 11, 2022).
60. The World Bank. *What You Need to Know About Green Loans*; The World Bank [Online], Oct 4. 2021. https://www.worldbank.org/en/news/feature/2021/10/04/what-you-need-to-know-about-green-loans (accessed Nov 10, 2022).
61. Toscano, A.; Balzarotti, M.; Re, I. Sustainability Practices and Greenwashing Risk in the Italian Poultry Sector: A Grounded Theory Study. *Sustainability* **2022,** *14* (21). doi:10.3390/su142114088.
62. United Nations. *The 17 Goals. United Nations* [Online], n.d.. https://sdgs.un.org/goals (accessed Oct 28, 2022).
63. White, K.; Hardisty, D. J.; Habib, R. The Elusive Green Consumer. *Harv. Bus. Rev. Mag* [Online], July–August, 2019. https://hbr.org/2019/07/the-elusive-green-consumer.
64. Wright, G. 83% of Shoppers Mislead by Green & Sustainable Advertising. *Retail Gazette* [Online]. Jan 29, 2020. https://www.retailgazette.co.uk/blog/2020/01/83-of-shoppers-mislead-by-green-sustainable-advertising/#:~:text=Online%20retailer%20OnBuy%20conducted%20a,clean%E2%80%9D%20and%20%E2%80%9Cgreen.%E2%80%9D (accessed Nov 1, 2022).
65. Zhang, X.; Wang, Z.; Zhong, X.; Yang, S.; Siddik, A. B. Do Green Banking Activities Improve the Bank's Environmental Performance? The Mediating Effect of Green Financing. *Sustainability* **2022**, *14* (2), 989. doi:10.3390/su14020989.

# CHAPTER 10

# Does Fintech Foster Sustainable Finance? Evidence from Retail Banking in India

PARMINDER VARMA and SHIVINDER KAUR

*Chitkara Business School, Chitkara University, Punjab, India*

## ABSTRACT

Financial institutions play a major role in regional growth and development. With financial technology (FinTech) innovations disrupting the sector, incumbent banks are forced to adapt to the new environment. This disruption has the potential to foster sustainable banking practices, as new technologies may help promote efficiency, transparency, and financial inclusion. The impacts can be especially relevant for India, as it is a leader in consumer adoption of FinTech.

The aim of the present study is to assess how the disruption caused by FinTech and smart banks impacts the sustainability of retail banks in India. This is achieved by considering firm-level panel data covering the period from 2012 to 2018. Overall, the findings from panel regression analysis support the view that FinTech and smart branches influence sustainability. Investment in FinTech is found to be associated with superior long-term viability of retail banks in India, with the governance channel playing the main role in this effect. Meanwhile, investment in smart branches is associated with lower sustainability, and some evidence has been obtained on the potential environmental effects of mismanaging the use of smart branches. Thus, the findings indicate that FinTech may promote sustainability as long as environmental concerns over the digital transition are addressed.

Management for Sustainable Development: Integrating Social, Economic, and Environmental Goals.
Vishal Jain & Amit Mittal (Eds.)

## 10.1 INTRODUCTION

Financial institutions have a distinctive role in global, national, and regional economies. Banks are able to decrease information asymmetry between borrowers and savers, which allows for providing financial services to individuals and enabling corporate investment.[1] Companies' efforts to be sustainable have come under closer scrutiny from stakeholders in the wake of the recent COVID-19 epidemic, which has sped up their worldwide use of digital technology.[2] The relevance of these processes is exceptionally high in the banking industry, where financial technologies (FinTech) have disrupted traditional banking.[3] FinTech forces incumbent financial institutions to adapt to the shifting environment by investing in new technologies and digital distribution channels.[4] In addition to the direct effects on established banks, FinTech has indirect socioeconomic impacts, such as enhancing financial inclusion,[5] which makes the topic particularly relevant for emerging markets, such as India. This study focuses on how the disruption caused by FinTech and smart banks affects the sustainability of retail banks in India.

### *10.1.1 RELATION TO UN SDGs*

Given the importance of banks to regional growth, it stands to reason that sustainable banking practices would aid in the realization of the United Nations (UN) Sustainable Development Goals (SDGs).[5,6] Technologies such as mobile payments, blockchain, and AI could help reduce poverty, ensure food security, grant more women access to financial services, promote inclusive economic growth, improve infrastructure resilience, and reduce illicit financial flows, all of which correspond to SDGs 1, 2, 5, 8, 9, and 16, respectively.[7–11] Green FinTech start-ups may contribute to alleviating the impact of climate change[12] and enhancing environmental protection.[13,14] Thus, it is precious to consider the impacts of FinTech on sustainable banking.

### *10.1.2 FINTECH TRENDS: EMERGING MARKETS AND INDIA*

The adoption of FinTech and digital banking was rapid in the Asia-Pacific emerging markets,[15] and between 2017 and 2021, the market penetration of FinTech in this region attained levels that were comparable to those of developed markets (Figure 10.1).

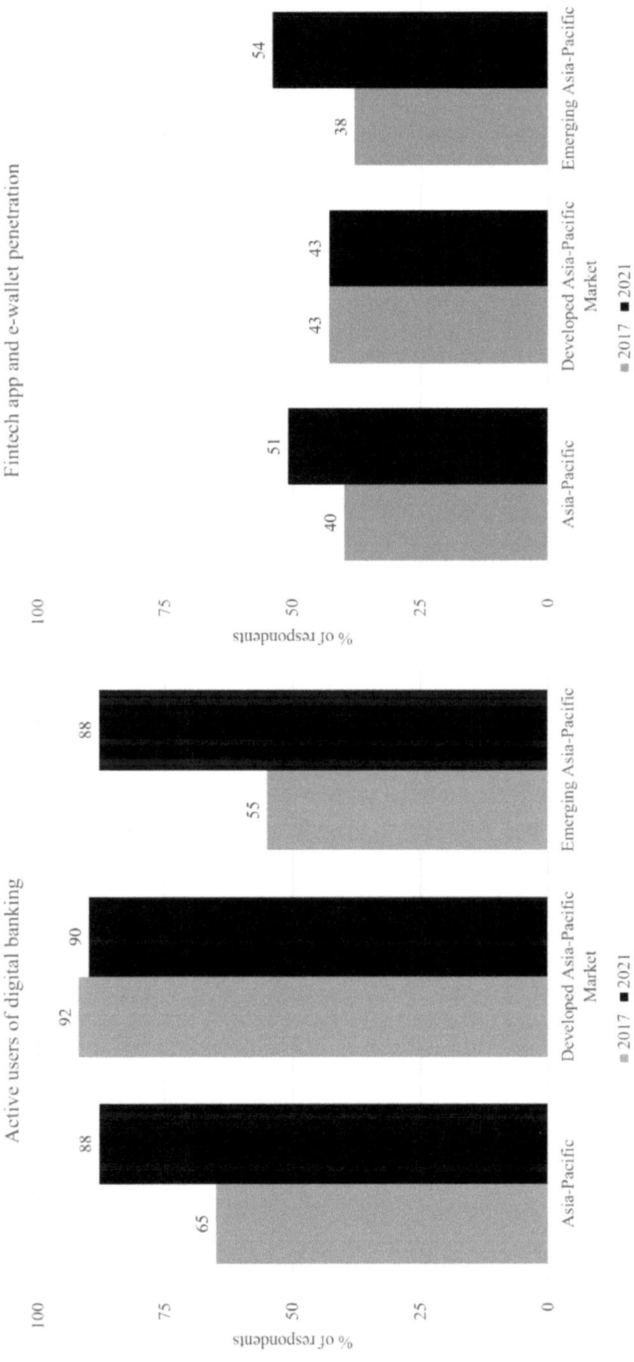


**FIGURE 10.1** FinTech adoption in Asia-Pacific markets.

*Source*: McKinsey Asia-Pacific PFS survey 2021

The data provided by McKinsey's report[15] show that, in the emerging Asia-Pacific markets, the relative number of digital banking users has increased from 55% in 2017 to 88% in 2021, and the shift toward digital distribution channels may have been accelerated following the coronavirus outbreak.[16] India is a significant market for FinTech growth as the country has a vast population. Indeed, India is regarded as the key ASEAN (Association of Southeast Asian Nations) market for FinTech prospects over the next decade.[17] India, along with China, is a leader in consumer adoption of FinTech, with an adoption rate of 87%,[18] highlighting that India provides a valuable context for investigating the effects of FinTech on banking sustainability.

### *10.1.3 IMPORTANCE OF SUSTAINABLE BANKING IN INDIA*

When it comes to funding the creation of new and valuable products, banks play a crucial role. As such, progress toward regional SDGs would be aided by India's stable and sustainable financial industry.[6] Banks' sustainability efforts could influence sustainable development through changes in waste management, energy consumption, and financial inclusion.[1] Considering the degree of income inequality in India, sustainable banking and easier access to financing could be particularly relevant for the country.[5] An indirect effect of improving the social and governance sustainability pillars is that it could help alleviate customers' concerns over digital banking in India about identity theft and misuse of private information.[19,20] Pradhan et al.[21] published research that connected India's sustainable economic growth and investments in information and communication technology infrastructure with financial inclusion. Nenavath[14] argued that green FinTech might reduce emissions and improve environmental safety in India.

### *10.1.4 RESEARCH PROBLEM*

The research aims to investigate the long-term viability of banks and the impact of FinTech on them. The research question to be explored is the following: "What is the effect of FinTech disruption and smart banking on the sustainability of retail banks in India?" The study's findings could have direct implications for achieving the UN SDGs and provide valuable insights for bank managers and policymakers to make informed decisions.

### *10.1.5 STRUCTURE*

The subsequent sections of the chapter are arranged in the following manner: Section 10.2 presents an outline of both FinTech and smart banking innovations, alongside the factors that determine sustainability; Section 10.3 describes the research methodology used in the study; Section 10.4 presents the result analysis and findings; Section 10.5 discusses the findings and their implications for the industry; Section 10.6 elaborates on the limitations of the study and presents several recommendations for future research; and Section 10.7 serves as the conclusion of this study.

## 10.2 LITERATURE REVIEW

### *10.2.1 FINTECH AND SMART BANKS*

FinTech may be grouped into several domains in terms of business models, namely: payment, capital markets, crowdfunding, wealth management, lending, and insurance services.[1] Innovative solutions, such as cell phone-enabled payment, facilitate access to financial services for unserved individuals.[11] New electronic forms of payment that rely on "mobile money"—which is among the fastest-growing FinTech solutions—improve financial inclusion[3] and allow smartphone users to quickly receive and spend cash transfers.[11] This can be particularly impactful in regions with poor coverage by traditional bank branches. Users are not only able to transfer and receive mobile money to and from other individuals through peer-to-peer (P2P) transfers, but they can also receive salary and government payments.[22] A prominent FinTech solution is blockchain, which is based on storing information in a collective database. Blockchain protocols can ensure that P2P exchanges are secure,[4] and smart contracts may help make financial transfers more transparent and efficient.[11]

The rising popularity of artificial intelligence (AI) solutions has led to the emergence of smart banks that rely on AI to provide financial services. These banks can use machine learning to analyze massive datasets, automate decision-making processes, and improve pricing for financial products.[23] Traditional banks may struggle to match these competitive advantages.[3] Notably, FinTech firms can stay in close contact more easily with the end users of their services. This helps them better understand local communities' preferences and adapt by offering unique, custom solutions.[1] Furthermore, the higher flexibility and responsiveness offered by FinTech could translate into significant socioeconomic impacts at the regional level.[4]

### 10.2.2 SUSTAINABILITY: DETERMINANTS AND RELATIONSHIP WITH FINTECH

Factors influencing sustainability can be grouped into firm-level and external determinants. The link between firm characteristics and sustainability performance can be explored within the context of legitimacy theory.[24] The core principle of this notion is that companies must demonstrate the social and ecological justification of their activities; otherwise, they may face the loss of public support.[25] This implies that better-performing banks would have more incentives to publish sustainability reports and follow best practices. Furthermore, larger banks could be under closer scrutiny and therefore face more significant pressure to follow sustainability practices to gain legitimacy.[26] The slack resource hypothesis is another critical theoretical perspective because it suggests that banks with greater size and profitability have more resources to allocate toward sustainability efforts.[27] In addition, economies of scale could lead to larger banks having lower relative costs of following sustainability practices.[28] The agency theory, which posits that there are inherent agency costs whenever control and ownership are separated, offers another perspective.[29] According to this view, disclosure of sustainability practices could be driven by high agency costs. This may link leverage to sustainability reporting, as companies could use voluntary disclosure to provide additional assurance to creditors.[30] The role of external determinants can be described within the framework of institutional theory, which implies that cultural, institutional, and political factors may incentivize banks to disclose sustainability practices.[31]

Disruptive technology such as FinTech and smart branches may affect sustainability in the banking sector through environmental, social, and governance channels. The environmental impact of new technology is unclear. On the one hand, digital channels increase efficiency, which should reduce resource waste,[3] but on the other, digital technologies have a considerable carbon footprint due to the increasing amount of infrastructure and data centers required to support digital operations.[32–34] Regarding social impacts, FinTech has been argued to improve the socioeconomic environment by increasing financial inclusion.[5,6] As for the governance component of sustainability, FinTech could increase transparency and accountability by improving information production and facilitating monitoring.[35] FinTech may affect banks' financial reporting quality through the information channel as its innovations provide more efficient access to information, which increases the total quantity and quality of information available to stakeholders. FinTech may also reduce information friction,[35] which would facilitate external auditing and allow for easier manipulation detection, which would, in turn, deter managers from misusing corporate resources. Managers would face higher costs for earnings management since FinTech would increase the probability of being detected.[29] As a result, agency costs should decrease, reducing resource waste, improving efficiency, and potentially freeing up additional resources for other sustainability activities.

Within developing economies, there is a scarcity of research on how sustainable banks are and how they relate to the use of financial technology.[36–39] Numerous recent studies have investigated the determinants that affect the scores of environmental, social, and corporate governance (ESG). These studies have looked at broad antecedents, including business size and performance[36, 39] and the effect of Islamic finance development.[38] However, as Vergara and Agudo[9] analyzed the relationship between FinTech and sustainability via a literature study and case studies, their results may not be generalizable to the whole Indian industry. In contrast, this study aims to provide insight into how ESG, and therefore bank sustainability, is influenced by the FinTech disruption. FinTech consumer adoption in India is among the highest in the world; therefore, it may be valuable to understand how the shift toward mobile banking and smart branches contributes to bank sustainability in the country.

## 10.3 RESEARCH METHOD

By utilizing quantitative regression techniques and analyzing secondary data, this research aims to address the research questions presented. The study echoes previous work on sustainability in selecting a suitable model specification and proxy variables.[36–39]

### *10.3.1 SAMPLE AND DATA*

This study employs a census survey design where the whole population is explored. The sample includes observations of Indian banks over the 2012–2018 periods, for which all the required data are available. By selecting this time frame, we can exclude the confounding effects of macroeconomic shocks like the global financial crisis and the COVID-19 epidemic. The data on bank-level financial variables were collected using the Bureau van Dijk service.[40] The data on FinTech-related variables were collected manually from publicly available sources, as described below, and the data on ESG rating were collected using the Refinitiv/Thomson Reuters service.[41] As a result of the scarcity of quality ESG data for Indian banks, the final sample only contains information for 10 institutions operating between 2012 and 2018. However, given that the included banks account for nearly 60% of the market, this was deemed adequate to guarantee external validity in the context of the Indian banking sector.

### 10.3.2 MODEL

The study follows similar research on sustainability determinants. The model employed by El Khoury et al.[39] and Crespi and Migliavacca[42] is adapted to include FinTech investment and additional controls. The legitimacy theory establishes a connection between firm-level characteristics and long-term viability and serves as the model's theoretical backbone.

The estimated model can be written in general as[39,42]:

$$\text{Sustainability}_{\text{it}} = \alpha_{\text{i}} + \beta_1 \text{ FinTech} + \gamma_1 \text{ Controls}_{\text{it}} + \varepsilon_{\text{it}} \qquad (10.1)$$

In eq 10.1, $\text{Sustainability}_{it}$ is the measure of the sustainability performance of a firm $i$ at time $t$; FinTech measures investment in financial technology; Control is a vector of control variables.

### 10.3.3 VARIABLES

Table 10.1 contains the description of employed variables.

Sustainability performance is measured using several ratings reported by Refinitiv.[43] An organization's environmental, social, and governance (ESG) score is determined using data provided by the organization itself. Over 400 ESG measures at the firm level are used to calculate the estimated ESG score, which is broken down into 10 categories: resource use, emissions, human rights, workforce, innovation, product responsibility, shareholders, management, community, and corporate social responsibility (CSR) strategy.[43] Scores on the environmental, governance, and social pillars are weighted averages of relative assessments based on reported information about the environment, government, and society. In order to calculate the ESG combined score, we take the ESG score and deduct the ESG controversies score. The ESG controversies score is a worldwide media monitoring system that tracks coverage of unfavorable events and controversies related to environmental, social, and governance issues. ESG ratings are used in

**TABLE 10.1** Definitions of the Variables.

| Variable | Description | Source |
|---|---|---|
| **Dependent** | | |
| ESG score | Environmental, social, and governance (ESG) score | [41] |
| Environmental pillar score | Evaluation using a weighted average relative to provided environmental information | [40] |
| Governance pillar score | Calculated using a weighted average relative rating based on disclosed governance data | [40] |
| Social pillar score | Average relative score weighted by social data given | [41 |
| ESG combined score | ESG score with ESG controversies overlay | [40] |
| ESG controversies score | Global media coverage of unfavorable occurrences and disputes in the areas of environment, society, and government | [41] |
| **Independent** | | |
| FT | FinTech: Volume of mobile banking transactions | [44] |
| SB | Smart branches: The use of a dummy variable counting as 1 if the bank has an AI-based automated assistant and 0 otherwise | News coverage on the Indian banks presenting or introducing related AI technologies |
| DC | Digital currencies: A dummy variable where 1 would indicate that the bank does indeed support digital currencies like Bitcoin, while 0 would indicate that it did not. | News coverage on the Indian banks adopting or supporting digital currencies |
| **Controls** | | |
| Size | Total bank assets expressed as a natural logarithm | [40] |
| Market power | Bank's total assets relative to the sum of total assets of all banks for that year | The data used in the author's calculations are from Ref. [40] |
| Leverage | The ratio of liabilities to total assets | [40] |
| Tier 1 ratio | Tier 1 capital to risk-weighted assets ratio | [40] |

**TABLE 10.1** *(Continued)*

| Variable | Description | Source |
|---|---|---|
| ROA | Net earnings divided by average total assets | [40] |
| NIM | The difference between investment returns and interest expenses divided by average earning assets | [40] |
| Efficiency (VRS) | DEA-based efficiency assuming variable returns to scale | The data used in the author's calculations are from Ref. [40] |
| Efficiency (DRS) | DEA-based efficiency assuming decreasing returns to scale | The data used in the author's calculations are from Ref. [40] |
| Trend | Years since 2012 | |

response to earlier research on business sustainability.[36–40] Several proxies for sustainability performance are included to enhance the study's validity and explore the robustness of the findings concerning the choice of the sustainability measure. In addition, considering ESG constituents separately should allow for identifying the channels through which FinTech and smart branch investment contribute to sustainability regarding retail banks in India. As discussed in Section 10.2.2, the link between disruptive technology and sustainability could be exhibited through all three ESG pillars. As such, it is essential for the set of sustainability proxies to be able to capture these effects. Since sustainability is used as the dependent variable, the study's design allows for clearly differentiating between the impacts of FinTech and smart branches on each of the ESG pillars.

The primary dependent variables are *FT* and *SB*. The number of mobile banking transactions is the metric used to describe *FT*, which stands for investment in financial technology. The information is obtained from the website of India's Central Bank.[44] *SB* measures investment in smart branches. It is a dummy variable that gets set to 1 if the bank has an AI-powered virtual assistant in place and 0 otherwise. In addition, the variable *DC* is used for robustness analysis. *DC* measures investment in digital currencies. It is a dummy variable set to 1 if the bank generally supports digital currencies, including Bitcoin, and 0 otherwise. The data on *SB* are taken from news coverage of the Indian banks presenting or introducing related AI technologies. The data on *DC* are obtained from news coverage of the Indian banks adopting or supporting digital currencies. The *FT proxy* is based on the central premise that the number of mobile banking transactions is representative of the level of investment in FinTech. The main assumption behind *SB* and *DC* proxies is that significant investment in either technology would accompany a press release in the media. *SB* and *DC* share the drawback of being binary variables. This prevents the model from differentiating between varying levels of investment in these technologies. Another issue with the examination of *DC* investment in India is that India's Reserve Bank banned cryptocurrency use in 2018. Another shortcoming shared by all three indicators is that they are contemporaneous with the observed sustainability. Significant investments in new technology would likely affect the banks' value and sustainability.

Following similar literature,[39,42] several firm-level control variables are introduced. A bank's size is quantified by taking the natural logarithm of its total assets. There is also market power, which compares a bank's total assets to the sum of all banks' total assets in a given year. The level of leverage is determined by comparing debt to total assets. The Tier 1 capital ratio, defined as Tier 1 capital divided by total risk-weighted assets, is an alternative hazard measurement. Return on assets (ROA) is a measure of profitability calculated by dividing net profits by average total assets. Net interest margin (NIM) is an alternative metric; it is calculated by subtracting investment returns from interest expenses and dividing the result by average earning assets. The study uses data envelopment analysis (DEA) to estimate bank efficiency, which aligns with previous studies of the Indian banking industry.[45] The efficiency benchmark is predicated on variable returns to scale (VRS). Another evaluation strategy considers the possibility of diminishing returns to scaling (DRS). Capital and labor are inputs for the DEA, measured as fixed assets plus deposits and the number of employees, respectively. The output is the total revenue calculated by adding the net interest revenue and the noninterest income. Previous research on financial sustainability serves as the primary reference for deciding on control variables at the business level. This study does not control for country-level factors. Since the study focuses on retail banking in India, exogenous factors are assumed to be common to all sample banks. The inclusion of a trend should help control for unobserved, time-varying determinants that may lead to spurious regression.

### *10.3.4 ESTIMATION*

Using Stata, we estimate the model in eq 10.1 employing panel regression. Since panel regression analysis adjusts for unobserved time-invariant individual effects and boosts the effective number of available degrees of freedom,[46] panel data analysis may allow for greater research validity than a standard cross-sectional study. Using the panel regression specification, it is possible to account for time-varying individual effects that were previously unknown. The cross-sectional effects are assumed to be associated with independent variables in the fixed effects estimator. The random effects estimator takes it as given that the random variables representing individual effects are independent of the regressors. Breusch–Pagan Lagrange Multiplier test[46] establishes if the random effects model improves upon a detailed pooling estimate. The Wald test is its corresponding fixed-effects test. The random effects estimator is the more effective method, as long as it is consistent. Its consistency is determined by performing the Hausman specification test.

Since model estimation is based on the assumptions of homoscedasticity and no serial correlation, the standard errors are modified using the heteroscedasticity and serial correlation-robust (HAC) standard errors.[46]

Similar studies on sustainability used lagged independent variables to avoid potential endogeneity between simultaneously observed variables. However, recent research[47,48] suggests that lagged explanatory variables may still be associated with endogeneity. This study employs both approaches. The baseline specification uses contemporary observations, and a robustness check is performed where the model is reestimated using lagged covariates.

## 10.4 RESULTS

### *10.4.1 DESCRIPTIVE ANALYSIS AND OBSERVED DYNAMICS*

Table 10.2 provides summary statistics for the dataset used in the analysis.

**TABLE 10.2** Summary Statistics.

| Variable | Mean | Median | Min | Max | Std. dev. | N |
|---|---|---|---|---|---|---|
| ESG score | 43.958 | 42.050 | 20.900 | 71.110 | 12.702 | 59 |
| Environmental pillar score | 42.921 | 41.190 | 10.260 | 80.580 | 16.505 | 59 |
| Governance pillar score | 38.750 | 40.490 | 0.470 | 81.450 | 23.815 | 59 |
| Social pillar score | 52.866 | 55.760 | 27.850 | 76.490 | 11.371 | 59 |
| ESG combined score | 41.645 | 37.560 | 20.900 | 69.360 | 12.983 | 59 |
| ESG controversies score | 61.731 | 62.670 | 13.240 | 100.000 | 28.366 | 59 |
| FT | 15.279 | 15.994 | 0.693 | 20.444 | 3.931 | 57 |
| SB | 0.153 | 0 | 0 | 1 | 0.363 | 59 |
| DC | 0.102 | 0 | 0 | 1 | 0.305 | 59 |
| Size | 25.049 | 25.244 | 23.144 | 26.998 | 0.900 | 59 |
| Market share | 0.064 | 0.049 | 0.008 | 0.275 | 0.061 | 59 |
| Leverage | 91.454 | 91.660 | 84.170 | 94.920 | 2.813 | 59 |
| Tier 1 capital ratio | 11.603 | 11.220 | 7.240 | 18.000 | 2.386 | 59 |
| ROA | 1.045 | 1.310 | -0.980 | 2.290 | 0.809 | 59 |
| NIM | 3.177 | 3.140 | 1.880 | 5.070 | 0.956 | 59 |
| Efficiency | 0.713 | 0.972 | 0.139 | 1.000 | 0.354 | 59 |
| Efficiency (DRS) | 0.808 | 1.000 | 0.139 | 1.000 | 0.312 | 59 |

The mean ESG score across the sample is 43.96, which reflects an overall mediocre sustainability performance by the sample Indian banks. The sample ESG score ranges from 20.90 to 71.11, suggesting considerable variability in scores across banks and years. The sample distribution of ESG scores and ESG score components is shown in Figure 10.2.

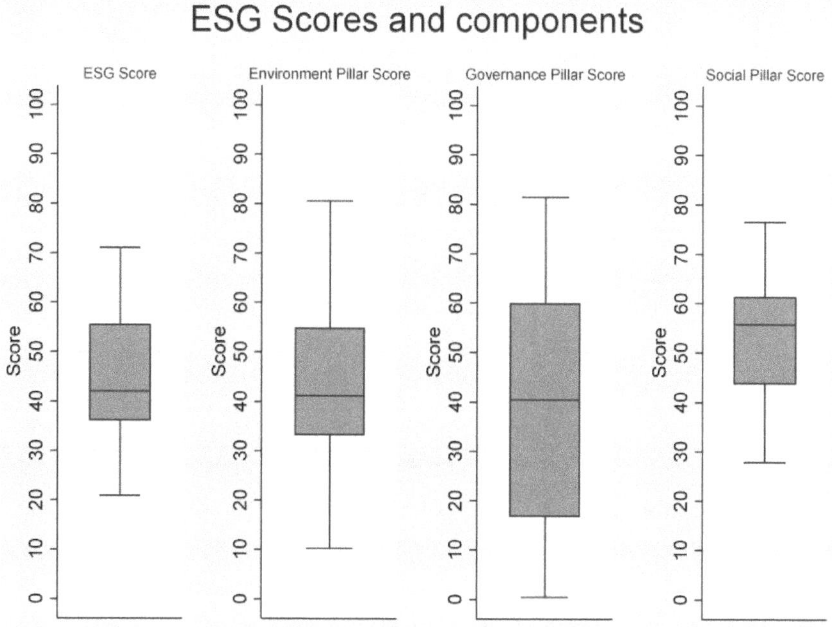


**FIGURE 10.2** Distribution of ESG scores and components.

The environmental pillar score has a comparable average of 42.92 while having a noticeably higher variance. Similarly, the governance pillar score is an estimated sample mean of 38.75 with an even larger range and standard deviation values. Given that certain companies in the sample perform extremely badly on measures of management, shareholders, and CSR strategy, it is noteworthy that the lowest governance score is close to zero. In comparison, the sample Indian banks' mean social pillar score is much higher at 52.89, indicating a more significant commitment to best practices in areas such as workforce, community engagement, human rights, and product accountability.

Overall, the sample exhibits substantial variability in the ESG score and its components, which should help identify the effect of specific firm-level factors such as FinTech investment on sustainability. Heterogeneity in ESG scores across sample banks is further illustrated in Figure 10.3.

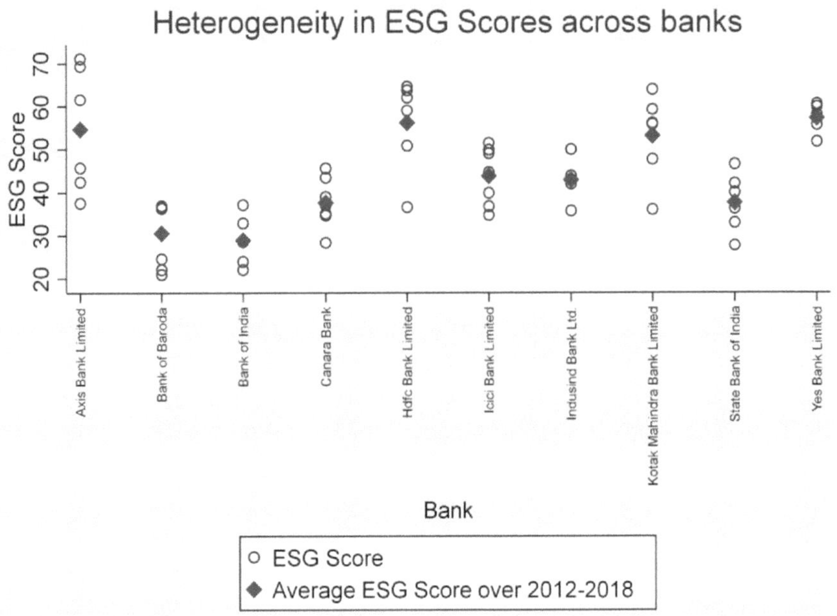


**FIGURE 10.3** Heterogeneity in ESG scores across banks.

The key observation that can be made from Figure 10.3 is that both within-group and between-group variations contribute to the overall variation in sustainability performance among the sample Indian banks. Specifically, for certain financial institutions, like Axis Bank, the diversity within the group is much bigger than the variation across financial institutions like Bank of Baroda, Bank of India, ICICI Bank, and IndusInd Bank. The main implication is that firm-level factors are arguably more influential on bank sustainability in the country than environmental factors. This supports using panel regression techniques to account for unobserved firm-specific variables of sustainability performance.

The mean ESG combined score is 41.65, slightly lower than the baseline ESG score (Table 10.2). It follows that overlaying sustainability performance with the controversies score lowers observed ESG levels, suggesting noticeable exposure of the sample Indian banks to adverse events in the media. The sample ESG controversies score ranges from 13.24 to 100, which indicates that some banks are associated with a substantial number of controversies, such as anticompetitive behavior, intellectual property infringements, high executive compensation, customer privacy concerns, and wage disputes. Given that the median controversies score in the sample is 62.67, it suggests that the average bank in the sample is significantly vulnerable to negative events reported in the media. Although the effect of combining the controversies score with the overall ESG score is discernible but relatively minor, this study will examine the factors that affect the unadjusted ESG score, and the controversies score separately. This should allow for distinguishing between sustainability issues directly observed in company reports and problems implied through media reports while still including media controversies in the account.

Regarding FinTech variables, firms that invest in smart branches or digital currencies constitute 15.3 and 10.2% of the sample, respectively (Table 10.2). The log-transformed mobile banking volume (*FT*) shows considerable variation. The distribution is skewed to the left, suggesting that a few banks in the sample appear to be investing little to no resources in FinTech. The heavy left tail of the distribution may lead to biased regression estimates due to the influence exerted by extreme outliers. As such, the analysis includes a robustness check where banks with uncharacteristically lower values of *FT* are removed from the sample. Similarly, an average market share of approximately 5–6% is considerably lower than the sample maximum of 27.5%. This is due to the sample including the market leader, the State Bank of India, which controls around a quarter of the whole market. It is possible that, due to the unique market position of the State Bank of India, it may be less representative of how FinTech affects sustainability in Indian banks. A robustness check is performed to address this by estimating the baseline model with the State Bank of India excluded from the sample.

One shortcoming of the provided statistics is that they fail to capture sustainability performance and FinTech investment dynamics. Figure 10.4 shows how the average ESG score across the sample varies from 2012 to 2018.

Two main observations can be made. Firstly, there appears to be no specific pattern of how cross-sectional variability in ESG scores changes over time. ESG scores varied less significantly in 2012 and 2016, while exhibiting a more comprehensive range of approximately 35 points for the rest of the sample period. This may be caused by changes in both firm-level and macroeconomic factors. Secondly, the overall trend is for the ESG score to increase over time for the sample Indian banks. Indeed, the average score across all firms increased each year except for 2016.

A significant implication of the observed improvement in ESG scores over time is that there may exist industry- or national-level factors that drive banks to improve their sustainability performance. As such, there is a risk of observing a spurious relationship between sustainability performance and FinTech investment. Figure 10.5 illustrates how FinTech investment, measured by mobile banking volume, varied over the sample period.

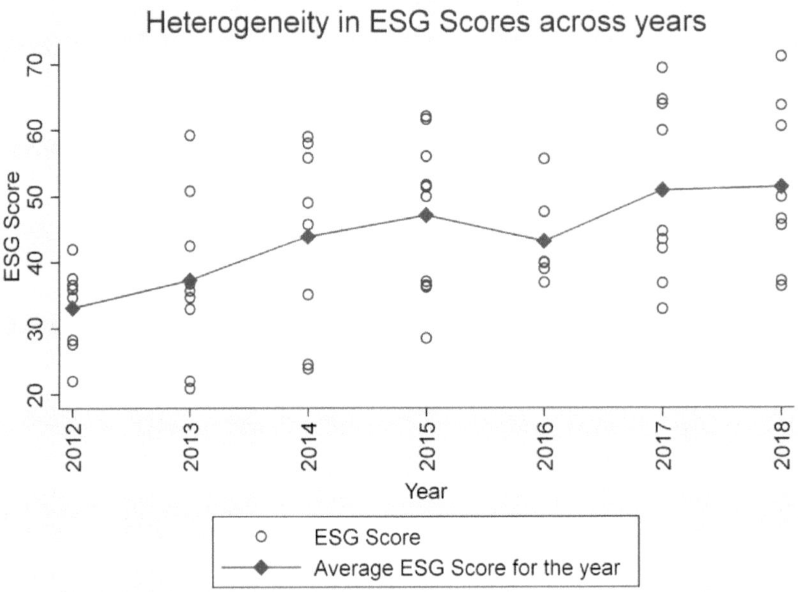


**FIGURE 10.4** Heterogeneity in ESG scores across years.

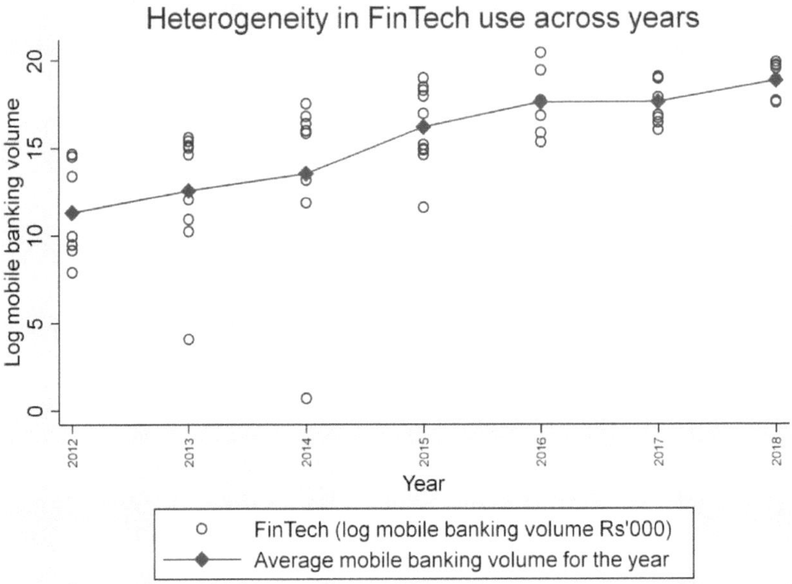


**FIGURE 10.5** Heterogeneity in FinTech use across years.

In line with expectations regarding incumbent banks' response to FinTech disruption, the sample Indian banks steadily increased their investment in FinTech from 2012 to 2018. Two outlier observations with deficient FinTech investment levels are observed for 2013 and 2014. As discussed above, a robustness check is performed where these outliers are excluded from the analysis. Overall, the key implication of rising FinTech investment for this analysis is that there is a risk of observing a spurious relationship between *FT* and ESG scores. A trend variable is introduced into the model to address this, which linearly increases with time. This should help ensure that if a significant relationship between FinTech and ESG scores was observed, it would not be due to a common positive trend.

To provide a general overview of the linkages between variables and to explore possible multicollinearity, Pearson's linear correlation coefficients are estimated for each pair of variables (Table 10.3).

Regarding ESG-based variables, the baseline ESG score positively correlates with the governance and social pillars and the combined ESG score. However, there is no statistically significant association between the ESG score and either the environmental pillar or the ESG controversies score. This indicates that social and governance factors may play a significant role in determining the sustainability performance of the sample banks. One possible explanation is that service companies, such as financial institutions, have a relatively small environmental impact due to the nature of the firms' operations. The ESG score, the overall ESG score, the governance pillar score, and the social pillar score positively correlate with FT. This suggests that the main channels through which FinTech investment may influence banks' sustainability are governance and social impact. There are no multicollinearity problems when estimating a linear model since the correlations between other factors are modest to low.

It is possible that sustainability performance varies nonlinearly with FinTech investment levels. Figure 10.6 illustrates this relationship.

There are two outlier observations with shallow FinTech values. As discussed above, a robustness check will be performed where the model is estimated, with these observations excluded from the sample. The rest of the observations follow a linear pattern for the baseline ESG score. Higher FinTech values are consistently associated with higher levels of ESG scores.

Similarly, more sustainable banks tend to invest in other disruptive technologies, such as digital currencies and smart branches (Figure 10.7).

The regression analysis below aims to evaluate whether the observed associations are partly due to firm-level characteristics. For instance, larger,

**TABLE 10.3** Correlation Table.

| Variable | (1) | (2) | (3) | (4) | (5) | (6) | (7) | (8) | (9) | (10) | (11) |
|---|---|---|---|---|---|---|---|---|---|---|---|
| (1) ESG score | 1.000 | | | | | | | | | | |
| (2) Environmental pillar score | 0.173 | 1.000 | | | | | | | | | |
| (3) Governance pillar score | 0.791* | –0.007 | 1.000 | | | | | | | | |
| (4) Social pillar score | 0.716* | 0.137 | 0.252* | 1.000 | | | | | | | |
| (5) ESG combined score | 0.920* | 0.153 | 0.710* | 0.685* | 1.000 | | | | | | |
| (6) ESG controversies score | 0.071 | –0.026 | 0.089 | 0.050 | 0.396* | 1.000 | | | | | |
| (7) FT | 0.626* | 0.243 | 0.527* | 0.603* | 0.507* | –0.192 | 1.000 | | | | |
| (8) Size | –0.216 | 0.008 | –0.306* | 0.058 | –0.304* | –0.328* | 0.372* | 1.000 | | | |
| (9) Leverage | –0.562* | 0.062 | –0.664* | –0.186 | –0.502* | –0.066 | –0.187 | 0.467* | 1.000 | | |
| (10) ROA | 0.378* | 0.048 | 0.536* | –0.068 | 0.386* | 0.273* | –0.103 | –0.483* | –0.738* | 1.000 | |
| (11) Efficiency | 0.570* | 0.119 | 0.638* | 0.136 | 0.500* | 0.060 | 0.326* | –0.047 | –0.662* | 0.668* | 1.000 |

*$p < 0.05$; all ESG scores are log-transformed.

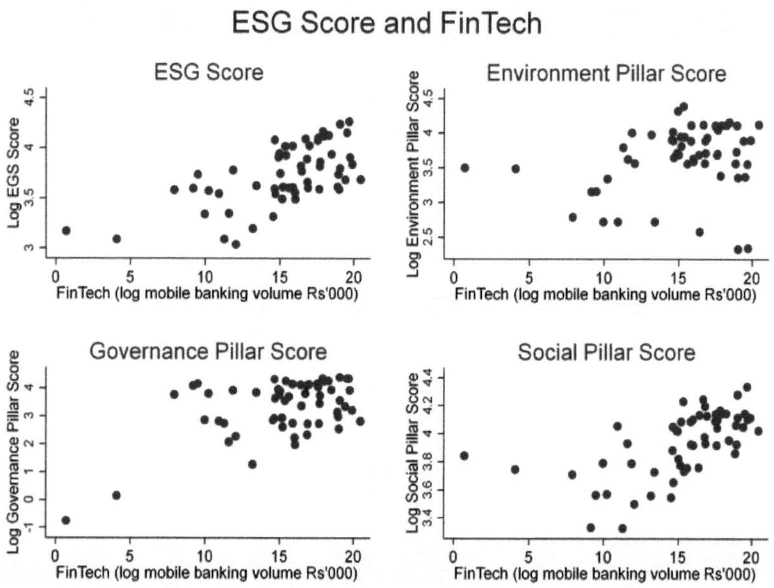


**FIGURE 10.6** Relationship between ESG score and FinTech.

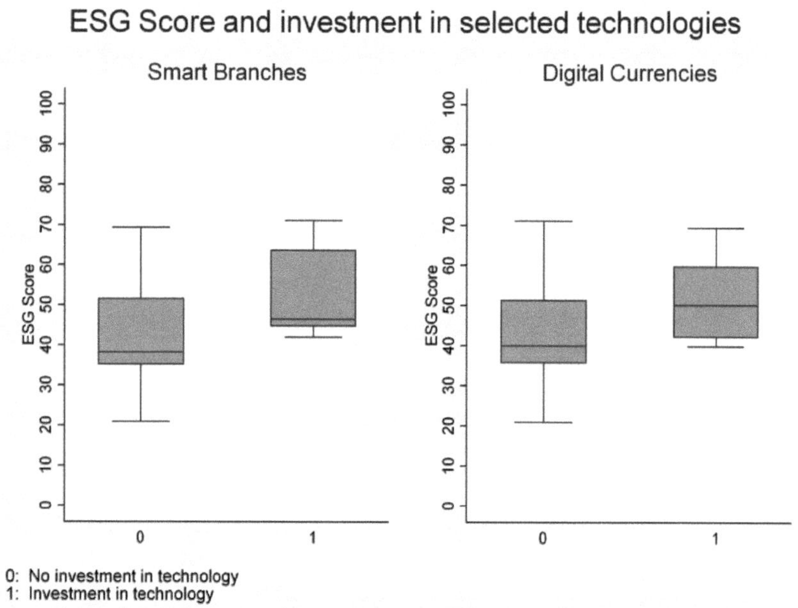


**FIGURE 10.7** ESG score and investment in selected technologies.

more efficient, or more profitable banks may have more resources to invest in FinTech while also adhering to sustainability practices more diligently due to increased scrutiny from shareholders and the public.

### 10.4.2 REGRESSION ANALYSIS

This section contains the main results of the study. Firstly, the model's validity is discussed using the key specifications and diagnostic tests. Secondly, the results from the baseline model are presented. This includes the estimated effects of investments in FinTech (FT), smart branches (SB), and digital currencies (DC) on the ESG score and its components. Finally, a comprehensive robustness analysis is performed. This analysis also investigates whether the primary results are affected by variations in the proxies used for firm-level factors and the inclusion of outliers.

#### 10.4.2.1 MODEL SPECIFICATION AND DIAGNOSTICS

The process of choosing an appropriate model specification follows the procedure outlined in Section 10.3. The applicability of a fixed effects model is considered first. This is done by carrying out the Wald test for firm-level and year-fixed effects. Considering the findings from Section 10.4.1 on the common trend between FinTech and ESG scores, the Wald test for year effects is estimated with and without a trend term. A random-effects Breusch–Pagan test is then conducted. Estimator selection is made via the Hausman specification test. Standard errors are made more robust to account for heteroscedasticity and serial correlation. The variances are concentrated within individual businesses. In addition, a post-estimation diagnostic test for groupwise heteroscedasticity is performed to explore whether a more efficient estimator could replace robust standard errors.

The output from specification tests is summarized in Table 10.4.

These are the outcomes. Both fixed and random effects estimators provide an enhancement over a straightforward pooled OLS estimator. This is reflected in both the Wald test and the Breusch–Pagan test statistics being significant at the 0.01 level. While year effects seem to further enhance the model, including a trend term makes the Wald statistic insignificant. As such, period-fixed effects can be excluded as long as a separate trend term is employed. This is preferable in this analysis as the sample size is relatively small. Introducing a single variable to account for unobserved time-varying effects would assume fewer degrees of freedom than year effects for the 2012–2018 period. Considering the findings from the descriptive analysis in Section 10.4.1 on a common trend between FinTech and the ESG score, including a trend term also has the advantage of explicitly controlling for a potential spurious relationship between these variables.

**TABLE 10.4** Specification and Diagnostic Tests.

| Test | Statistic |
|---|---|
| Wald test for firm-level effects | 5.61*** |
| Wald test for year effects | 0.24 |
| Wald test for year effects (trend excluded) | 2.68** |
| Breusch and Pagan Lagrange multiplier test for random effects | 21.01*** |
| Hausman specification test | 4.86 |
| Modified Wald test for groupwise heteroscedasticity | 1219.37*** |

*$p < 0.10$, **$p < 0.05$, ***$p < 0.01$.

The random effects estimator is consistent if the Hausman test result does not indicate significance at conventional levels. As the estimator is more effective than fixed effects, using random effects should improve the analysis's internal validity, which is crucial for smaller samples. It is appropriate to utilize robust clustered standard errors since the heteroscedasticity test findings show that the assumption of groupwise homoscedastic residuals is broken.

#### *10.4.2.2 MAIN RESULTS*

The study's key findings are organized according to a proxy for bank investments in disruptive technologies, such as FinTech (FT) and smart branches (SB). According to the dependent variables (1) ESG score, (2) environmental pillar score, (3) social pillar score, (4) governance pillar score, and (5) controversies score, five models are estimated. This allows for distinguishing between FinTech's effects on overall sustainability and specific components of sustainability performance. All models are estimated using random effects and robust standard errors clustered at the firm level, as detailed in Section 10.4.2.1.

#### *10.4.2.2.1 FinTech*

Table 10.5 presents the outcomes of the impact of FinTech, measured by mobile transaction volume, on sustainability performance.

**TABLE 10.5** Regression Output: Main Results (FinTech).

| | (1) | (2) | (3) | (4) | (5) |
|---|---|---|---|---|---|
| | **Coef./SE** | **Coef./SE** | **Coef./SE** | **Coef./SE** | **Coef./SE** |
| Size | −0.140*** | −0.145 | −0.013 | −0.503*** | −0.099 |
| | (0.042) | (0.155) | (0.048) | (0.148) | (0.136) |
| Leverage | 0.004 | 0.073 | −0.000 | −0.043 | 0.062 |
| | (0.014) | (0.055) | (0.006) | (0.049) | (0.059) |
| ROA | 0.022 | 0.108 | 0.099 | −0.072 | 0.462*** |
| | (0.046) | (0.177) | (0.073) | (0.141) | (0.161) |
| Efficiency | 0.303** | −0.002 | −0.061 | 0.968*** | −0.268 |
| | (0.142) | (0.550) | (0.184) | (0.360) | (0.335) |
| FT | 0.024** | 0.083 | 0.009 | 0.175*** | −0.017 |
| | (0.010) | (0.052) | (0.016) | (0.061) | (0.038) |
| Trend | 0.065*** | −0.068 | 0.088*** | −0.110 | 0.073 |
| | (0.013) | (0.080) | (0.020) | (0.073) | (0.073) |
| Constant | 6.047*** | −0.495 | 3.745*** | 17.014*** | 0.517 |
| | (0.836) | (3.495) | (1.294) | (4.348) | (4.078) |
| *N* | 57 | 57 | 57 | 57 | 57 |
| Wald chi-sq | 489.13*** | 13.91** | 839.74*** | 123.98*** | 9.97 |
| Adjusted R-sq | 0.766 | 0.151 | 0.605 | 0.758 | 0.195 |

*$p < 0.10$, **$p < 0.05$, ***$p < 0.01$.

ESG score, environmental pillar score, social pillar score, governance pillar score, and controversies score are dependent variables.

All models are estimated using random effects and robust standard errors, and clustering is performed at the firm level for all estimates.

The model's goodness-of-fit is influenced by the dependent variable in multiple ways. The model accounts for 75% of the variation in the dependent variable for both the ESG score and the governance pillar score. The social pillar score, where the adjusted R-squared is 0.605, likewise has a significant amount of variation explained by the model. The goodness-of-fit is noticeably poorer for the environmental pillar score and the controversies score models, which show an adjusted R-square of 0.151 and 0.195, respectively.

Furthermore, the Wald chi-square test findings for the combined significance of the covariates point to the absence of any real explanatory power for the controversies score for the analyzed firm-level factors. Media exposure to negative events may be driven mainly by managerial characteristics not adequately reflected in financial metrics such as firm size or leverage. Nevertheless, the results may provide valuable information on the link between controversies and FinTech investment, as they suggest that disruptive technologies enhance sustainability through selected channels.

FinTech investment, as measured by mobile transaction volume, appears to improve sustainability. Firstly, FinTech is found to affect the overall ESG score positively. The coefficient estimate of 0.024 is statistically significant at a 0.05 level. The coefficient may be understood as follows, given that both variables were log-transformed. For every 10% increase in mobile banking transactions, the ESG score is anticipated to rise by 0.24%. While the effect is relatively small, its cumulative effect on sustainability can be substantial, assuming that consumers will continue to shift toward mobile banking.

Second, Model 4 reveals that FinTech has a positive impact on the governance pillar of the ESG score, which provides valuable information. The calculated coefficient of 0.175 is statistically significant at the 0.01 level, and the effect is much stronger compared to the effect of FinTech on the overall score. Indeed, for every 10% increase in mobile banking volume, it is expected for the governance pillar score to improve by 1.75%. It appears that FinTech investment indirectly enhances sustainability through management, shareholders, and CSR strategy channels.

Finally, FinTech has a slight impact on the environmental and social pillar scores as well as the controversies score. The finding regarding the environmental pillar score aligns with the preliminary analysis conducted in Section 10.4.1. It is likely that financial institutions do not have a significant environmental footprint in the first place. Consequently, FinTech investment is unlikely to influence banks' environmental emissions, usage of materials, or employment of eco-friendly solutions and processes. The result of the social pillar score indicates that FinTech investment has no association with workforce and human rights practices, as well as banks' commitment to respecting business ethics and being good citizens.

Regarding control variables, smaller and more efficient banks score higher concerning sustainability performance. At the same time, neither profitability nor leverage seems to have explanatory power regarding the ESG score. Similar findings are obtained for Model 4. As was to be predicted, the trend term positively impacts the total ESG score, which represents industry-level or national factors that motivate Indian banks to adopt more sustainable practices.

It may be concluded that sustainable performance is improved by FinTech investment, and it appears that the main channel through which FinTech influences sustainability is governance. The sample banks with greater mobile banking volume, an indicator of FinTech investment, also had considerably better ESG governance pillar scores and overall ESG scores. At the same time, neither the environmental nor the social pillars are found to be impacted by FinTech investment. Overall, the results provide evidence of FinTech disruption enhancing the sustainability of retail banks in India.

#### *10.4.2.2.2 Smart Branches*

The findings on the influence of investment in smart branches on sustainability performance are summarized in Table 10.6.

**TABLE 10.6** Regression Output: Main Results (Smart Branches).

| | (1) | (2) | (3) | (4) | (5) |
|---|---|---|---|---|---|
| | Coef./SE | Coef./SE | Coef./SE | Coef./SE | Coef./SE |
| Size | −0.132*** | 0.019 | −0.016 | −0.404*** | −0.160 |
| | (0.036) | (0.089) | (0.048) | (0.119) | (0.106) |
| Leverage | 0.004 | 0.048* | 0.001 | −0.079 | 0.074 |
| | (0.012) | (0.026) | (0.009) | (0.061) | (0.057) |
| ROA | 0.016 | 0.075 | 0.078 | −0.230 | 0.487*** |
| | (0.047) | (0.144) | (0.067) | (0.261) | (0.149) |
| Efficiency | 0.414*** | 0.427 | 0.023 | 1.468** | −0.386 |
| | (0.149) | (0.350) | (0.186) | (0.681) | (0.338) |
| SB | −0.076* | −0.910*** | −0.068 | 0.015 | 0.429** |
| | (0.041) | (0.260) | (0.056) | (0.327) | (0.176) |
| Trend | 0.104*** | 0.123*** | 0.104*** | 0.096* | 0.013 |
| | (0.010) | (0.034) | (0.012) | (0.050) | (0.054) |
| Constant | 5.987*** | −1.943 | 3.719*** | 19.425*** | 0.865 |
| | (0.867) | (2.478) | (1.271) | (6.647) | (4.458) |
| *N* | 59 | 59 | 59 | 59 | 59 |
| Wald Chi-sq | 167.86*** | 49.55*** | 184.08*** | 135.27*** | 13.58** |
| Adjusted R-sq | 0.690 | 0.408 | 0.585 | 0.541 | 0.220 |

*$p < 0.10$, **$p < 0.05$, ***$p < 0.01$.

ESG score, social pillar score, governance pillar score, environmental pillar score, and controversies pillar score are dependent variables.

All models are estimated using random effects and robust standard errors, and clustering is performed at the firm level for all estimates.

Generally, the model's goodness-of-fit is moderate—the adjusted R-squared ranges from 0.22 for the controversies score model to 0.69 for the ESG score model. The share of variance in ESG pillars explained by the model ranges from 40.8 to 58.5%. Consistent with the findings provided in Section 10.4.2.2.1, the environmental pillar score and the controversies score have the worst goodness-of-fit. Likely, environmental impacts and exposure to negative publicity are not adequately captured by financial items and ratios. Nevertheless, the findings provide crucial information on the determinants of sustainability performance in the context of smart branches.

Overall, smart branches seem to have an adverse effect on sustainability. The *SB* variable is found to influence the overall ESG score negatively. The estimated coefficient is −0.076 and is significant at the 0.10 level. Thus, investing in smart branches is expected to reduce the ESG score. This appears to be counterintuitive, since, on paper, smart branches should improve efficiency, reduce resource waste, and enhance accessibility for consumers. However, the results from Model 2 provide more insight into why a negative effect may be observed. The corresponding *SB* coefficient is −0.910 and is significant at the 0.01 level. In other words, investing in smart bank branches significantly reduces the environmental pillar score. Considering that Models 4 and 5 show no effect of smart branches on the governance and social pillar scores, it can be argued that the environmental score is the key channel through which smart branches adversely influence banks' sustainability. A possible explanation is that digital activities are associated with a significant carbon footprint. Banks investing in smart branches likely have more data to be stored and processed, leading to higher usage of data centers and infrastructure, which produces more emissions and e-waste. From this perspective, shifting from traditional branches toward digital "smart" branches could be detrimental to the industry's sustainability in the long term if banks are not careful about how they organize and manage data storage and processing.

The governance and social pillar scores do not seem to be affected by the presence of smart branches. As for the governance pillar score, it is feasible that modern branches are run by the same management teams responsible for managing older ones. The findings on the social pillar score show that investing in smart branches does not noticeably influence the workforce or human rights practices. Interestingly, the *SB* variable affects the ESG controversies score, and there is a significant positive coefficient at the 0.05 level. Investing in smart branches is associated with higher exposure to negative media events. As for the control variables, the findings are similar to the model discussed in Section 10.4.2.2.1. Larger and less efficient banks tend to score lower concerning sustainability performance.

Overall, investment in smart branches is found to have a negative effect on sustainability performance. The key channel through which smart branches influence sustainability is the environmental impact. Banks that have put money into "smart branches" get far worse scores on the ESG environmental pillar and on the overall ESG scale. Meanwhile, neither the governance nor the social pillars are found to be impacted by smart branches' investment. The findings support the view that FinTech disruption negatively affects the sustainability of retail banks in India.

The results from estimating the baseline model align with the perspective that FinTech and smart branches influence sustainability in the financial industry. However, the estimated effects depend on the indicators of sustainability and investment in disruptive technology. On the one hand, FinTech investment represented by mobile banking volume appears to enhance sustainability. Banks that have invested in FinTech score higher in the governance pillar score and the overall ESG score, and banks with FinTech investments tend to have better ESG and governance pillar scores. The opposite is true concerning sustainability performance, as evaluated by the ESG score and the environmental pillar score, which drop when money is allocated to smart branches. The opposite is true concerning sustainability performance, as evaluated by the ESG score and the environmental pillar score, which drop when money is allocated to smart branches.

### *10.4.2.3 ROBUSTNESS ANALYSIS*

While the findings presented in Section 10.4.2.2 provide evidence for FinTech and smart branches impacting sustainability performance, several factors may raise concerns about the validity of the findings. Firstly, the choice of proxy variables for firm-level characteristics may affect the estimated coefficients. To address this, a variety of sensitivity checks are performed. Section 10.4.2.3.1 presents the output from the model, which uses investment in digital currencies as a proxy for FinTech. While regulators in India banned the use of cryptocurrency in 2018, it may be valuable to explore the channels through which digital currency investment could affect sustainability. Section 10.4.2.3.2 considers alternative proxies for firm-level factors: firm size, leverage, profitability, and efficiency. Section 10.4.2.3.3 discusses the potential impact of outliers and endogeneity. All models are estimated with FT as the main FinTech variable.

#### *10.4.2.3.1 Investment in Digital Currencies as a Proxy for FinTech Investment*

The results of the effect of investing in digital currencies on sustainability performance are provided in Table 10.7.

**TABLE 10.7** Regression Output: Main Results (Digital Currencies).

| | (1) | (2) | (3) | (4) | (5) |
|---|---|---|---|---|---|
| | **Coef./SE** | **Coef./SE** | **Coef./SE** | **Coef./SE** | **Coef./SE** |
| Size | −0.157*** | −0.073 | −0.039 | −0.420*** | −0.218** |
| | (0.041) | (0.117) | (0.052) | (0.144) | (0.101) |
| Leverage | 0.007 | 0.059 | 0.011 | −0.083 | 0.094 |
| | (0.015) | (0.037) | (0.011) | (0.066) | (0.060) |
| ROA | 0.021 | 0.110 | 0.089 | −0.231 | 0.383** |
| | (0.044) | (0.171) | (0.071) | (0.238) | (0.153) |
| Efficiency | 0.357** | 0.295 | 0.025 | 1.457** | −0.086 |
| | (0.149) | (0.462) | (0.173) | (0.608) | (0.328) |
| DC | −0.076 | −0.176 | 0.048 | −0.374** | 0.296 |
| | (0.065) | (0.139) | (0.032) | (0.167) | (0.310) |
| Trend | 0.102*** | 0.048 | 0.098*** | 0.114*** | 0.043 |
| | (0.009) | (0.046) | (0.012) | (0.035) | (0.038) |
| Constant | 6.392*** | −0.353 | 3.385** | 20.190*** | 0.337 |
| | (1.155) | (3.050) | (1.457) | (7.346) | (4.985) |
| *N* | 59 | 59 | 59 | 59 | 59 |
| Wald chi-sq | 348.73*** | 45.25*** | 119.64*** | 74.62*** | 19.79*** |
| Adjusted R-sq | 0.683 | 0.114 | 0.583 | 0.549 | 0.247 |

*$p < 0.10$, **$p < 0.05$, ***$p < 0.01$.

ESG score, social pillar score, governance pillar score, environmental pillar score, and controversies pillar score are dependent variables.

All models are estimated using random effects and robust standard errors, and clustering is performed at the firm level for all estimates.

The coefficient corresponding to the DC variable is not statistically significant for all models but one. Investments in virtual currency do not have any impact on the ESG score and its environmental and social pillars. However, at the 0.05 level of significance, the coefficient for the governance score is negative. One possible explanation is that managing investments in digital currencies provides more opportunities for managers to waste company resources and act in self-interest due to the cryptocurrency market's volatility. This result illustrates that the impact of FinTech on sustainability may depend on the technology used.

#### *10.4.2.3.2 Alternative Proxy Variables for Firm-Level Characteristics*

Four alternative models are considered. Model 1 replaces firm size with market share. Market share might provide a more relevant perspective on the firm's resource access. Model 2 replaces the leverage variable with the Tier 1 capital ratio, which is a significant measure of a bank's risk-taking within the basel framework. It may be a more appropriate measure of risk than leverage. Model 3 replaces ROA with NIM. NIM is a profitability measure specifically suited for the financial industry, and therefore, could have more explanatory power in the context of this study. Finally, Model 4 replaces efficiency estimated using the assumption of variable returns to scale with efficiency estimated based on diminishing returns to scale, which provides a more conservative estimate of efficiency.

Table 10.8 displays the obtained data.

The ESG score is the dependent variable.

Results from the ESG questionnaire will serve as the dependent variable.

The FT coefficient is found to be statistically significant in all models at the 0.05 level, and the consistent coefficient value across different specifications indicates the robustness of the results to the selection of proxy variables for firm-level financial measures.

#### *10.4.2.3.3 Alternative Specifications and Subsample Analysis*

This section considers four alternative models. Model 1 excludes the State Bank of India from the sample, as discussed in Section 10.4.1. Model 2 excludes banks with shallow FinTech levels, as noted in Section 10.4.1. Model 3 includes all FinTech-related variables simultaneously, namely *FT, DC,* and *SB.* To control for potential endogeneity between reported ESG scores and financial variables in the same year, Model 4 includes a lag of 1 year for all firm-level variables.

**TABLE 10.8** Regression Output: Robustness (Alternative Proxy Variables).

| | (1) | (2) | (3) | (4) |
|---|---|---|---|---|
| | **Coef./SE** | **Coef./SE** | **Coef./SE** | **Coef./SE** |
| Market share | −1.872*** | | | |
| | (0.596) | | | |
| Leverage | 0.002 | | 0.009 | −0.013 |
| | (0.011) | | (0.014) | (0.016) |
| ROA | 0.004 | 0.024 | | 0.043 |
| | (0.049) | (0.045) | | (0.047) |
| Efficiency | 0.395*** | 0.312** | 0.288** | |
| | (0.138) | (0.149) | (0.138) | |
| FT | 0.025** | 0.024*** | 0.023** | 0.026*** |
| | (0.010) | (0.009) | (0.009) | (0.008) |
| Trend | 0.049*** | 0.066*** | 0.063*** | 0.064*** |
| | (0.015) | (0.013) | (0.016) | (0.011) |
| Size | | −0.139*** | −0.135*** | −0.123*** |
| | | (0.036) | (0.040) | (0.036) |
| Tier 1 capital ratio | | −0.005 | | |
| | | (0.011) | | |
| NIM | | | 0.057 | |
| | | | (0.048) | |
| Efficiency (DRS) | | | | 0.056 |
| | | | | (0.055) |
| Constant | 2.825*** | 6.405*** | 5.344*** | 7.269*** |
| | (1.040) | (0.897) | (1.172) | (1.442) |
| *N* | 57 | 57 | 57 | 57 |
| Wald chi-sq | 283.92*** | 879.47*** | 110.17*** | 699.75*** |
| Adjusted R-sq | 0.778 | 0.770 | 0.793 | 0.712 |

$^{*}p < 0.10$, $^{**}p < 0.05$, $^{***}p < 0.01$.

Table 10.9 presents the relevant results.

**TABLE 10.9** Regression Output: Robustness (Alternative Specifications and Subsample Analysis).

| | (1) | (2) | (3) | (4) |
|---|---|---|---|---|
| | **Coef./SE** | **Coef./SE** | **Coef./SE** | **Coef./SE** |
| Size | $-0.139^{**}$ | $-0.154^{***}$ | $-0.133^{***}$ | |
| | (0.055) | (0.040) | (0.040) | |
| Leverage | 0.008 | 0.002 | 0.000 | |
| | (0.014) | (0.012) | (0.015) | |
| ROA | 0.020 | 0.019 | 0.035 | |
| | (0.048) | (0.052) | (0.054) | |
| Efficiency | $0.321^{**}$ | $0.307^{**}$ | $0.314^{**}$ | |
| | (0.150) | (0.142) | (0.153) | |
| FT | $0.025^{**}$ | $0.041^{***}$ | $0.025^{**}$ | |
| | (0.011) | (0.011) | (0.010) | |
| Trend | $0.064^{***}$ | $0.047^{***}$ | $0.066^{***}$ | $0.064^{***}$ |
| | (0.016) | (0.014) | (0.018) | (0.014) |
| SB | | | 0.003 | |
| | | | (0.061) | |
| DC | | | −0.051 | |
| | | | (0.074) | |
| L1.Size | | | | $-0.153^{***}$ |
| | | | | (0.045) |
| L1.Leverage | | | | 0.007 |
| | | | | (0.013) |
| L1.ROA | | | | 0.034 |
| | | | | (0.089) |
| L1.Efficiency | | | | $0.320^{*}$ |
| | | | | (0.171) |
| L1.FinTech | | | | $0.027^{***}$ |
| | | | | (0.009) |
| Constant | $5.651^{***}$ | $6.374^{***}$ | $6.157^{***}$ | $5.909^{***}$ |
| | (0.867) | (0.901) | (1.006) | (1.537) |
| *N* | 51 | 55 | 57 | 44 |
| Wald chi-sq | $5659.000^{***}$ | $1226.85^{***}$ | $897.39^{***}$ | $211.73^{***}$ |
| Adjusted R-sq | 0.761 | 0.748 | 0.782 | 0.772 |

$^{*}p < 0.10$, $^{**}p < 0.05$, $^{***}p < 0.01$.

"ESG score" is the dependent variable.

Firm-level clustering of resilient standard errors is used in the estimation of all models with random effects.

Variables lagged by 1 year are denoted as "L1."

Model 1 excludes the State Bank of India from the sample; Model 2 excludes banks with exceptionally low FinTech levels (log mobile banking volume <5); Model 3 includes all FinTech-related variables simultaneously; Model 4 lags all firm-level variables by 1 year.

Across all four alternative models, the impact of FinTech is statistically significant at the 0.05 level. Moreover, the coefficient value is similar across all specifications. As such, it can be argued that the findings are robust when outliers are omitted, possible endogeneity is controlled for, and all FinTech-related variables are included simultaneously.

Overall, the analysis supports the perspective that FinTech and smart branches influence the sustainability of retail banks in India.

## 10.5 DISCUSSION AND IMPLICATIONS

### *10.5.1 KEY CHANNELS FOR FINTECH TO INFLUENCE SUSTAINABILITY IN INDIA*

The findings of this analysis suggest that disruptive technology influences banking sustainability in India through two key channels: governance and environment.

#### *10.5.1.1 GOVERNANCE CHANNEL*

The results indicate that FinTech investment improves sustainability performance mainly through the governance channel. The key channel through which FinTech can improve sustainability is management. FinTech may help enhance banks' commitment to following best practices. Digital technology increases the transparency of reporting, and consequently, the scrutiny faced by banks. In response, banks could choose to adapt and spend more resources on sustainability to attain legitimacy, as suggested by the legitimacy theory. The current research by Gao et al.[35] supports this line of reasoning by demonstrating that FinTech facilitates enhanced information creation and external monitoring, hence decreasing opportunistic management behavior. Innovative solutions allow for more efficient access to information, which can facilitate better external monitoring, thereby deterring managers from engaging in opportunistic behavior and ultimately reducing agency costs. Another governance channel through which FinTech could contribute to sustainability is the CSR strategy channel. FinTech may provide banks with more detailed information on individuals' preferences and needs. As a result, banks could integrate economic and social dimensions of sustainability into their day-to-day decision-making processes more successfully.

#### *10.5.1.2 ENVIRONMENTAL CHANNEL*

The second significant result of the study is the observation that investment in smart branches appears to reduce sustainability performance. This mainly occurs through the environmental channel. The result is in line with recent studies showing that digital transformation incurs significant environmental costs.[32–34] For example, a single search query emits approximately 1.45 g of $CO_2$, which, over a year, amounts to approximately 26 kg of $CO_2$ per person, assuming 50 queries a day.[34] Internet services account for close to 7% of global electricity consumption, and the corresponding global greenhouse gas emissions exceed those of international air traffic.[34] While digital technology may also save energy due to efficiency gains, recent trends in cloud usage, AI, and cryptocurrency mining increase energy demand.[32,33] It has been suggested that only 6% of the data generated is being used.[34] Since smart branches heavily rely on data collection, storage, and analysis, it may be possible that the observed reduction in the ESG environmental pillar score reflects the environmental impacts of the potentially inefficient use of energy in managing data.

### *10.5.2 IMPLICATIONS AND PRACTICAL RECOMMENDATIONS*

This study's findings have direct implications for bank managers. Traditional banks in India need to boost their embrace of new technology to guarantee their long-term viability in light of the recent finding that FinTech investment improves banking sustainability. This fits the theory that traditional banks can only survive by acquiring or partnering with innovative FinTech firms. Adopting FinTech solutions could help achieve the CSR goals of financial institutions, which tie in with the UN SDGs and long-term national development in India. According to the findings of this research, banks may improve their governance by making use of the increased transparency provided by cutting-edge technology. This will allow for more precise monitoring, which in turn should reduce resource waste. However, the findings on the environmental impacts of smart branches raise concerns over inefficient data collection and storage processes. Policymakers in India are recommended to accelerate the adoption of renewable energy for ICT industries. Furthermore, policymakers should implement initiatives that would encourage extending the lifespan of servers, reusing heat waste from server farms, and deleting cloud-stored information that is no longer needed.

## 10.6 LIMITATIONS AND FUTURE RESEARCH

Several caveats exist with this research. The study's narrow geographic scope limits its applicability outside the Indian setting. Moreover, only major banks are represented in the sample due to poor data availability. While various proxies for disruptive technology have been employed, the findings have been observed to be sensitive to the choice of the proxy. The study does not cover the latest post-coronavirus data, thus offering no information on how the accelerated digital transformation may have influenced the link between technology and sustainability in the sector. These gaps might be filled by research that examines the role of exogenous shocks (like the COVID-19 epidemic) in hastening the transition to digital banking, the disparity between the effects on sustainability in developing and wealthy countries, and the consequences of financial inclusion.

## 10.7 CONCLUSION

The financial sector's contribution to regional growth and development is significant. It has been argued that FinTech can facilitate the achievement of UN SDGs, but there is little evidence of such effects in the existing literature. This research aimed to determine how the competition from FinTech and smart banks has affected the long-term viability of India's retail banking industry. The results showed that FinTech and smart branches influence sustainability in the financial industry. However, it was found that the estimated effects depend on the indicators of sustainability and investment in disruptive technology.

First, it was determined that financial technology investment improved long-term viability. A better governance pillar score and environmental, social, and governance (ESG) score were seen for banks that had made FinTech investments. Management is most likely to be FinTech's conduit for enhancing sustainability via governance. FinTech has the potential to enhance banks' commitment to sustainable practices. Indeed, digital technology increases transparency, and therefore, the scrutiny faced by institutions. Banks may adopt by spending more sustainability resources to maintain public legitimacy.

Furthermore, FinTech may discourage opportunistic managerial behavior since digital technology allows for better information production and external monitoring. It is also possible that FinTech provides banks with more information on customers' preferences, which helps integrate economic and social dimensions of sustainability into banks' decision-making. Second, both the ESG score and the environmental pillar score suggest that investing in smart branches negatively affects sustainability performance. Overall, the results support the idea that the digital transformation has a significant impact on the natural environment. Although smart branches could help save energy through efficiency gains, mismanaged use of cloud platforms and AI could instead increase energy demand.

Banks are encouraged to capitalize on new technology to enhance governance through higher transparency and more effective monitoring, which should reduce the waste of resources. However, it is also recommended to use available FinTech resources efficiently, as mismanaging data storage and processing smart branches could inflate energy consumption and costs, and consequently, the environmental impact of new technology. Therefore, policymakers are recommended to develop initiatives that encourage the adoption of renewable energy for ICT industries. Finally, it is suggested that conventional banks in India boost their use of modern technology to guarantee the sector's long-term viability. The link between FinTech and sustainability suggests that new technologies may facilitate the attainment of CSR goals by banks and regional UN SDGs in general.

## KEYWORDS

- **FinTech**
- **innovation**
- **financial services industry**
- **smart branches**
- **sustainability**
- **sustainable development**
- **panel regression analysis**
- **financial inclusion**

## REFERENCES


1. Varga, D. Fintech: Supporting Sustainable Development by Disrupting Finance. *Budapest Manag. Rev.* **2018,** *8* (11), 231–249.
2. Merello, P.; Barberá, A.; De la Poza, E. Is the Sustainability Profile of FinTech Companies a Key Driver of Their Value? *Technol. Forecast. Soc. Change* **2022,** *174,* 121290. https://doi.org/10.1016/j.techfore.2021.121290
3. Arslanian, H.; Fischer, F. Fintech and the Future of the Financial Ecosystem. In *The Future of Finance*; Arslanian, H., Fischer, F., Eds.; Palgrave Macmillan: London, 2019; pp 201–216.
4. Agarwal, S.; Zhang, J. Fintech, Lending and Payment Innovation: A Review. *Asia-Pac. J. Financ. Studies* **2020,** *49* (3), 353–367.
5. Arner, W.; Buckley, R. P.; Zetzsche, D. A.; Veidt, R. Sustainability, FinTech and Financial Inclusion. *Eur. Bus. Organ. Law Rev.* **2020,** *21* (1), 7–35.
6. Ubeda, F.; Forcadell, F. J.; Aracil, E.; Mendez, A. How Sustainable Banking Fosters the SDG 10 in Weak Institutional Environments. *J. Bus. Res.* **2022,** 146, 277–287.
7. Chikalipah, S. The Pyrrhic Victory of FinTech and its Implications for Achieving the Sustainable Development Goals: Evidence from Fieldwork in Rural Zambia. *World J. Sci. Technol. Sustain. Dev.* 2020. https://doi.org/10.1108/WJSTSD-06-2020-0058
8. Franco-Riquelme, J. N.; Rubalcaba, L. Innovation and SDGs Through Social Media Analysis: Messages from FinTech Firms. *J. Open Innov.: Technol. Mark. Complex.* **2021,** *7* (3), 165–181.
9. Vergara, C. C.; Agudo, F. L. Fintech and Sustainability: Do They Affect Each Other? *Sustainability* **2021,** *13* (13), 7012. https://doi.org/10.3390/su13137012
10. Farahani, M. S.; Esfahani, A.; Moghaddam, M. N. F.; Ramezani, A. The Impact of Fintech and Artificial Intelligence on COVID 19 and Sustainable Development Goals. *Int. J. Innov. Manag. Econ. Soc. Sci.* **2022,** *2* (3), 14–31.
11. Hoang, T. G.; Nguyen, G. N. T.; Le, D. A. Developments in Financial Technologies for Achieving the Sustainable Development Goals (SDGs): FinTech and SDGs. In *Disruptive Technologies and Eco-Innovation for Sustainable Development*; Akkucuk, U., Ed.; IGI Global: Hershey, 2022; pp 1–19.
12. Puschmann, T.; Hoffmann, C. H.; Khmarskyi, V. How Green FinTech can Alleviate the Impact of Climate Change—the Case of Switzerland. *Sustainability* **2020,** *12* (24), 10691. https://doi.org/10.3390/su122410691
13. Nassiry, D. The Role of Fintech in Unlocking Green Finance: Policy Insights for Developing Countries. *ADBI Working Paper No.* 883, 2018. https://www.econstor.eu/handle/10419/190304
14. Nenavath, S. Impact of Fintech and Green Finance on Environmental Quality Protection in India: By Applying the Semi-Parametric Difference-in-differences (SDID). *Renew. Energy* **2022,** *193,* 913–919.
15. McKinsey Emerging Markets Leap Forward in Digital Banking Innovation and Adoption. www.mckinsey.com [Online], 2021. https://www.mckinsey.com/industries/financial-services/our-insights/emerging-markets-leap-forward-in-digital-banking-innovation-and-adoption (accessed Sep 15, 2022).
16. Abdul-Rahim, R.; Bohari, S. A.; Aman, A.; Awang, Z. Benefit–Risk Perceptions of FinTech Adoption for Sustainability from Bank Consumers' Perspective: The Moderating Role of Fear of COVID-19. *Sustainability* **2022,** *14* (14), 8357. https://doi.org/10.3390/su14148357

17. BBVA June 2017 ASEAN FinTech Trends. www.bbvaresearch.com [Online], 2017. https://www.bbvaresearch.com/wp-content/uploads/2017/07/June-2017-ASEAN-Fintech-Trends1.pdf (accessed Sep 15, 2022).
18. EY EY Global FinTech Adoption Index. www.ey.com [Online], 2019. https://www.ey.com/en_gl/banking-capital-markets/what-is-next-for-asia-in-fintech-adoption (accessed Sep 15, 2022).
19. Shukla, U. N. Restoring Digitisation for Sustainable Banking Business in India. *Int. J. Bus. Forecast. Market. Intell.* **2019,** *5* (3), 304–320.
20. Chen, W. K.; Nalluri, V.; Lin, M. L.; Lin, C. T. Identifying Decisive Socio-Political Sustainability Barriers in the Supply Chain of Banking Sector in India: Causality Analysis using ISM and MICMAC. *Mathematics* **2021,** *9* (3), 240–253.
21. Pradhan, R. P.; Arvin, M. B.; Nair, M. S.; Hall, J. H.; Bennett, S. E. Sustainable Economic Development in India: The Dynamics between Financial Inclusion, ICT Development, and Economic Growth. *Technol. Forecast. Soc. Change* **2021,** *169,* 120758. https://doi.org/10.1016/j.techfore.2021.120758
22. Jagtiani, J.; Lemieux, C. Do Fintech Lenders Penetrate Areas that are Underserved by Traditional Banks? *J. Econ. Bus.* **2018,** *100,* 43–54.
23. Jaksic, M.; Marinc, M. Relationship Banking and Information Technology: The Role of Artificial Intelligence and FinTech. *Risk Manag.* **2019,** *21,* 1–18.
24. Deegan, C. M. Legitimacy Theory. *Account. Audit. Account. J.* **2019,** *32* (8), 2307–2329.
25. Gamerschlag, R.; Möller, K.; Verbeeten, F. Determinants of Voluntary CSR Disclosure: Empirical Evidence from Germany. *Rev. Manag. Sci.* **2011,** *5* (2/3), 233–262.
26. Hahn, R.; Kühnen, M. Determinants of Sustainability Reporting: A Review of Results, Trends, Theory, and Opportunities in an Expanding Field of Research. *J. Clean. Prod.* **2013,** *59,* 5–21.
27. Margolis, J. D.; Elfenbein, H. A.; Walsh, J. P. Does it Pay to be Good? A Meta-Analysis and Redirection of Research on the Relationship between Corporate Social and Financial Performance. *Ann Arbor* **2007,** *1001* (48109–1234), 1–68.
28. Ho, J. L.-C.; Taylor, M. E. An Empirical Analysis of Triple Bottom-Line Reporting and its Determinants: Evidence from the United States and Japan. *J. Int. Financ. Manag. Account.* **2007,** *18* (2), 123–150.
29. Jensen, M. C.; Meckling, W. H. Theory of the Firm: Managerial Behavior, Agency Costs and Ownership Structure. *J. Financ. Econ.* **1976,** *3* (4), 305–360.
30. Ho, V. H. Disclosure Overload? Lessons for Risk Disclosure and ESG Reform from the Regulation SK Concept Release. *Villanova Law Review* **2020,** *65* (1), 67–157.
31. Baldini, M.; Dal Maso, L.; Liberatore, G.; Mazzi, F.; Terzani, S. Role of Country-and Firm-level Determinants in Environmental, Social, and Governance Disclosure. *J. Bus. Ethics* **2018,** *150* (1), 79–98.
32. Geneva Environment Network Data, Digital Technology, and the Environment. www. genevaenvironmentnetwork.org [Online], 2021. https://www.genevaenvironmentnetwork.org/resources/updates/data-digital-technology-and-the-environment/ (accessed Sep 15, 2022).
33. Babinet, G. The Environmental Impact and Potential of Digital Technology. *Institut Montaigne* [Online], 2021. https://www.institutmontaigne.org/en/analysis/environmental-impact-and-potential-digital-technology (accessed Sep 15, 2022).
34. UN. The Growing Footprint of Digitalisation. *Foresight Brief* no. 27 [Online], 2021. https://wedocs.unep.org/bitstream/handle/20.500.11822/37439/FB027.pdf (accessed Sep 15, 2022).

35. Gao, H.; Wen, H.; Fang, J. How FinTech Improves Financial Reporting Quality? Evidence from Earnings Management", *SSRN Working Paper* [Online], 2022. https://dx.doi.org/10.2139/ssrn.4164645 (accessed Sep 15, 2022).
36. Drempetic, S.; Klein, C.; Zwergel, B. The Influence of Firm Size on the ESG Score: Corporate Sustainability Ratings Under Review. *J. Bus. Ethics* **2020,** *167* (2), 333–360.
37. Mejia-Escobar, J. C.; González-Ruiz, J. D.; Duque-Grisales, E. Sustainable Financial Products in the Latin America Banking Industry: Current Status and Insights. *Sustainability* **2020,** *12* (14), 5648. https://doi.org/10.3390/su12145648
38. Paltrinieri, A.; Dreassi, A.; Migliavacca, M.; Piserà, S. Islamic Finance Development and Banking ESG Scores: Evidence From a Cross-Country Analysis. *Res. Int. Bus. Finance* **2020,** *51,* 101100. https://doi.org/10.1016/j.ribaf.2019.101100
39. El Khoury, R.; Nasrallah, N.; Alareeni, B. The Determinants of ESG in the Banking Sector of MENA Region: A Trend or Necessity? *Compet. Rev. Int. Bus. J.* **2021**. https://doi.org/10.1108/CR-09-2021-0118
40. Bureau Van Dijk Orbis Database. www.bvdinfo.com [Online], 2022. https://www.bvdinfo.com (accessed Sep 15, 2022).
41. Refinitiv Refinitiv Data Services. www.refinitiv.com [Online], 2022. https://www.refinitiv.com (accessed Sep 15, 2022).
42. Crespi, F.; Migliavacca, M. The Determinants of ESG Rating in the Financial Industry: The Same Old Story or a Different Tale? *Sustainability* **2020,** *12* (16), 6398. https://doi.org/10.3390/su12166398
43. Refinitiv ESG Scores. www.refinitiv.com [Online], 2022. https://www.refinitiv.com/en/sustainable-finance/esg-scores (accessed Sep 15, 2022).
44. Reserve Bank of India Bankwise Volumes In NEFT/RTGS/MOBILE Transactions. rbi.org.in [Online], 2022. https://rbi.org.in/scripts/NEFTView.aspx (accessed Sep 15, 2022).
45. Sengupta, A.; De, S. Measuring Efficiency of Indian Banks using Window DEA analysis. In *Assessing Performance of Banks in India Fifty Years after Nationalization*; Sengupta, A., De, S., Eds.; Springer, Singapore, 2020; pp 101–111.
46. Greene, W. H. *Econometric Analysis*; Prentice Hall, Upper Saddle River, 2012.
47. Leszczensky, L.; Wolbring, T. How to Deal with Reverse Causality using Panel Data? Recommendations for Researchers based on a Simulation Study. *Sociol. Methods Res.* **2022,** *51* (2), 837–865.
48. Bellemare, M. F.; Masaki, T.; Pepinsky, T. B. Lagged Explanatory Variables and the Estimation of Causal Effect. *J. Polit.* **2017,** *79* (3), 949–963.

## CHAPTER 11

# Developing Sustainable Smart Cities

RAMANDEEP SAINI[1], BHAWYA BANSAL[1], and STANLEY OLIVER[2]

[1]*Chandigarh Business School of Administration, Landran, India*

[2]*Management Learning and Management Practice, Doctoral College, United Kingdom*

**ABSTRACT**

Sustainable development can be accomplished only when we ensure that all humans, women, men, and children, can enjoy dignity and human rights to expand their possibilities, secure their health, find decent jobs, and contribute to their economic growth. Today's twenty-first century is about how to leap further with Information and Communication Technology (ICT) enabling a radically new era of smart cities backed by smart devices. A smart city[1] is defined as an environment-friendly and lively city, which encourages sustainability and a good quality of life and is complementary to protechnological advancements. A smart city represents a holistically advanced community with its branches spreading into technology, security, sustainability, interconnectedness, and comfort.[2]

Smart cities are defined as the arena of integration of technology with the needs of the people and the environment at large. These cities become "smarter" when they continuously monitor residents and infrastructure with the help of tech-enabled sensor devices and ensure improved delivery and quality of services. This noticeably requires significant reliance on automation, internet connectivity, and the Internet of Things (IoT). But looking at the magnitude of carbon emissions associated with technological usage, the sustainability of smart cities emerges as a crucial issue. This chapter has therefore been written based on a problem statement in mind, and the research objectives have been framed after analyzing the research gap. The findings and recommendations for all stakeholders to work in integration for

Management for Sustainable Development: Integrating Social, Economic, and Environmental Goals.
Vishal Jain & Amit Mittal (Eds.)

the development of sustainable smart cities have been given under different headings.

## 11.1 INTRODUCTION

Sustainable smart cities are exposed to organizational, climate, and technological risks, making their management difficult and easy for manipulation.[3] It is rightly said that smart citizens are required for smart cities, and they need to understand the optimum solutions for usage of resources. In the absence of the easily available literature creating awareness about smart cities, the current chapter holds significance as it focuses on the problem statement, i.e., understanding the dynamics of sustainable smart cities. The readers will get a deep insight into the concept of sustainable smart cities after reading this chapter. To undertake this research, the following objectives were framed:

1. To understand the relationship between sustainability and smart cities along with understanding the role of big data and technology
2. To identify the advantages, disadvantages, and challenges of developing a sustainable smart city
3. To identify innovative practices being adopted for sustainable smart cities while emphasizing their uneven scope
4. To examine the level of awareness among people about achieving sustainable development
5. To give recommendations for the development of smart cities which are sustainable

To achieve these objectives, the data was collected from secondary resources like journals, reports, websites, etc., and the results have been presented in the following sections.

### *11.1.1 CHAPTER ORGANIZATION*

After the introductory Section 1, which mentions research methodology, the findings of the data analyzed from secondary sources have been presented in different sections. Sections 2 and 3 deal with the findings of Objective 1 while explaining the relationship between sustainability and smart cities and the role of big data and technology.

Sections 4, 5, and 6 are associated with Objective 2, where the advantages, disadvantages, and challenges of developing a sustainable smart city are explained. Sections 7 and 8 deal with Objective 3, where the innovative practice of sustainable smart cities has been explained along with the discussion on their scope around the world. Section 9 relates to Objective 4, where the findings of a survey undertaken to examine the level of awareness among people about achieving sustainable development have been discussed. Section 10 addresses Objective 5, where the recommendations have been given by the researchers for the future.

## 11.2 SMART CITIES AND SUSTAINABILITY

A smart city, also called an ecocity or a sustainable city, is an urban development operating on the Information and Communication Technology and the Internet of Things to collect real-time data for providing information which is useful for effectively managing natural resources and assets. The process includes real-time data collection from mechanical devices and citizens that is synthesized and analyzed in order to monitor, regulate, and manage energy consumption, transport systems, traffic, power grids, waste treatment plants, water supply networks, etc. Smart cities are hence optimized and managed across a city's boundaries and with the exchange of information between citizens, governments, physical objects, and other stakeholders.[4]

The smart city concept can be divided into three verticals: (a) technology (hardware and software know-how); (b) population (education, creation, and diversity); and (c) institutions (politics and governance). Thus, investing in the technology, the population, and the institutions all together can make the concept of sustainable development, smart cities, and quality of life possible. Smart cities promote the responsible management of natural resources, thereby allowing institutions to provide innovative and improved services for citizens.[5]

### *11.2.1 TECHNOLOGY-ORIENTED*

The ultimate objective of sustainable smart cities is to enhance the quality of life of the people. This category particularly highlights the importance of Information and Communication Technology to optimize and integrate the performance of operations in the city and the efficient use of resources. The prime focus is on implementing technological innovations with hard capital, i.e., the city infrastructure.

### 11.2.2 SUSTAINABILITY-ORIENTED

Here, the soft capital, such as human beings and societal arrangements, and the hard capital, such as the city infrastructure and other material resources, synergize through ICT and IoT to enhance the city's environmental quality and ensure a rich quality of life.

The dictionary meaning of sustainability is the ability or likeability to be maintained at a certain level. In the study of environmental science, sustainability means protecting and managing Earth's natural resources, flora and fauna, climate, ecosystems, and atmosphere so that both the current generation and future generations can meet their needs easily. Sustainability means meeting our requirements in such a manner that we do not compromise the chance of future generations to satisfy their requirements. Sustainability is not just environmental; it also encircles economic and social resources, where the role of smart cities becomes evident for providing the quality of life it promises.

When studying smart cities, the meaning of sustainable urban development must be understood clearly to understand the meaning of sustainability.[6] Sustainability is an approach of voluntary interventions in which investment direction, resource exploitation, institutional change, and technological development occur in sync with current and future needs.[7] The concept of a sustainable city became known in the 1990s as a concept[8] establishing a relationship between economic, social, and environmental sustainability aspects.[9]

Sustainability is a strategic goal for smart cities, where the best actions are taken to preserve and improve the ecological balance of such cities. A smart, sustainable city uses ICT and other technologies to improve its people's quality of life and the coherence of urban operations and services in order to ensure that the needs of current and future generations concerning all aspects—social, cultural, environmental, and economic—are fulfilled.

### 11.2.3 GEOGRAPHICAL SAFETY AND SUSTAINABLE SMART CITIES

Though smart cities will offer the best standard of living facilities empowered by unbeatable technological advancements, it is not possible to imagine a high-end city without being insured about the geographical safety of the city. Geographical safety is ensured when environmental safety and ecological balance go hand-in-hand with technological upgrades. Infrastructural developments alone cannot make sustainable smart cities because environmental safety and net-zero carbon emissions are the actual essence of a sustainable smart city. Smart cities, while promising increased efficiency and improved quality of life, can lead to an increase in energy consumption and the production of e-waste. The deployment of sensors and other electronic devices for monitoring and control purposes results in a higher demand for energy, which can have damaging effects on the environment if not properly managed. The production of the materials and technologies used in smart cities can also have harmful effects on the environment as they may require the extraction of raw materials and the emission of greenhouse gases. Additionally, the development of smart cities often requires significant infrastructure changes, such as the construction of new buildings and transportation systems, which can result in the destruction of ecosystems and wildlife habitats. The high density of radiation and sensors can also prove harmful to the quality of food grains and vegetables, thus directly and/or indirectly impacting the health of people.

Heavy reliance on technology and artificial intelligence is not what makes smart cities truly smart; instead, it is their agility and vision, which makes them smart. The preparedness and foresight to combat natural or manmade disasters, the agility for quick response and recovery, and the ability to minimize the damages are what truly make a city smart. We have seen many natural disasters recently, like Nepal, Uttarakhand floods and earthquakes in Turkey and Syria, causing massive destruction just because of infrastructural weaknesses. The Chennai floods of 2015 were linked to poor urban planning and inadequate drainage infrastructure, including the destruction of wetlands and other natural water catchment areas for development projects. Hence, to avoid such calamities, it is important that geographical safety in infrastructural development is also paid attention to while planning for smart cities.

### *11.2.4 CONSTITUENTS OF SUSTAINABLE SMART CITIES*

Sustainable smart city measures across various countries have recently shown a significant impact on the lives of people and brought noticeable changes to our society.[10] Smart cities are imperative to the sustainable future of the rapidly increasing urban population. Various studies point out that by 2050, a significant percentage, i.e., 66%[11] of the world's population will be residing in cities, which means an addition to the urban population and greater pressure on city resources.

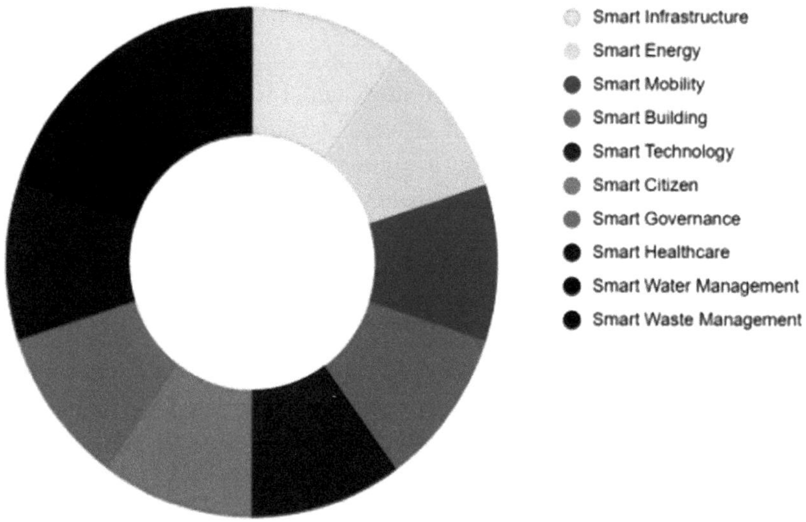


**FIGURE. 11.1** The components of a smart city.

The components of a smart city include smart energy, smart infrastructure, smart technology, smart mobility, smart buildings, etc. and above all smart citizens. Also, a smart city aims to be "smarter" by becoming more sustainable, equitable, efficient, and liveable.[12] To be able to be defined as a smart city, the city must foremost ensure clean, unpolluted, and breathable air, which can be achieved by minimizing carbon emissions and achieving carbon neutrality, which means having net-zero carbon emissions where the carbon emissions are offset by carbon reduction elsewhere. Fossil fuel-free and clean energy sources such as solar and wind power, also called green energy, will be the leading energy sources in a sustainable smart city. The focus will also remain on preserving the biodiversity of the place.

Innovative solutions should be applied for the advancement of energy conservation systems such as (i) the construction of suitable infrastructure for energy conservation systems and (ii) the adoption of new strategies, which will help in energy trading in distributed energy systems.[13] With Industry 4.0 driving the existence of smart cities, it will also initiate the advent of clean technology. The governance model is also expected to shift to a wholly electronic model with minimum or no physical visits to government offices. The e-governance model also helps in improving people's participation and the creation of smart citizens for the nation. The founding stones of smart cities are ICT and IoT, which will help create an environment of total connectivity between people and devices at all times. Total connectivity and IoT will be ensured with the help of community WiFi and quick wireless transfer of data. This data will be readily available to government agencies enabling them to take quick action in case of any contingency, thereby establishing enhanced public safety in smart cities. This connectivity will also ensure sustainable green transport like advanced public transportation and others like electric vehicles, carpooling, and bike-sharing.

According to the UN Environment Program (UNEP) 2021 Global Status Report[14] for Buildings and Construction, 36 percent of global final energy consumption is in the construction sector, and the issue will be resolved in smart cities with the help of green construction technology and green buildings. Green buildings prove to be environmentally responsible and resource-efficient throughout their lives. Workspaces can be transformed into smart work centers and co-working spaces to help reduce corporate energy consumption.

With technology playing a front-end role in smart cities, the onus of sustainability will be on the people. The governments can align with the UN Sustainable Development Goals and ensure effective resource allocation and provide real-time energy consumption data, but it is the people who have to adopt a sustainable lifestyle of waste reduction and energy management to make the idea of smart cities a success.

A sustainable smart city should achieve the following goals to become reliable, adaptable, accessible, scalable, and resilient:

- Improve the quality of life of its citizens;
- Ensure employment opportunities and economic growth;
- Provide citizens access to community and social services;
- Ensure efficient infrastructures like green public transportation, drainage, smart water supply, faster telecommunication, and other utilities; and
- Agility toward environmental issues and climate change.[15]

## 11.3 ROLE OF TECHNOLOGY AND BIG DATA

### *11.3.1 BIG DATA*

The author of Ref. [16] has been investigating the potential of ICT with their study based on it, named 'Big Data and the 2030 Agenda for Sustainable Development.' There is a consensus that suggests the massive potential of big data technology for the creation of sustainability and smart cities. These technologies are significant for the effective execution of smart cities, with their major highlight being real-time data sharing with the public. This data is shared through public dashboards and sent to individuals via personal messages. Big data helps synergize urbanization and sustainability and imagine a smart city in a data-analytic fashion to enhance and apply information-driven, calculated, and data-based long-term decisions about all urban operations.

### 11.3.2 INTERNET OF THINGS AND BLOCKCHAIN ACCOUNTING

Smart cities alone are the solution to effectively address the problem of the exponential growth of population and urbanization. The advent of IoT is the foundation of smart cities that further support city operations without human interaction. The idea of a smart city is evolving rapidly, but it is not yet mainstreamed throughout the globe due to many dividing factors such as governance, technology, and economics.[17] However, with strong intentions and strategies, the idea of a sustainable smart city can be executed.

The Internet of Things means physical objects, which have inbuilt sensors, processing abilities, software-enabled, and related technologies that automatically connect and exchange data with other electronic devices and internet-enabled systems over the internet or other communication networks. The IoT technology has enabled the datafication of cities forming the roots of data-driven smart cities. Data-driven operations are a significant subsystem in the creation and management of urbanism in both smart cities[18] and sustainable smart cities.[19]

Blockchain was invented and turned out to be Bitcoin's underlying infrastructure and ultimately the first-ever decentralized cryptocurrency, but now its application has progressed to cryptocurrencies and financial assets and is being increasingly used in creating cities of the future[20]

Distributed Ledger Technology (DLT), better known as the blockchain, is a technique to store any information in a secure manner such that the data can be trusted. Transactions are recorded in a permanent cryptographic signature called a hash. Trust is provided by the system using various techniques such as consensus, distributed ledger, smart contract, and cryptography. We can understand blockchain as a form of digital ledger that is distributed and replicated across various computers/servers of a blockchain network. A blockchain network is a consortium of multiple entities onboarded into the ecosystem of that specific blockchain system to solve a specific business problem. These entities stake their contribution to the blockchain network to enable the distributed characteristic of the blockchain system.

The various implementations of the blockchain system ensure that the distributed ledger can only be updated when a piece of information goes through a well-defined step to validate and verify the information before the ledger gets updated. This is ensured using techniques like Smart Contracts—a highly deterministic program that gets executed distributedly ensuring that a specific input will always result in a specific output.

Consensus—ensures that the outputs of different smart contracts are consistent with each other as they have computed the output result independently and distributedly. It's vital to ensure that the blockchain network is in sync to update the transaction log to the ledger based on the outcome of the distributed execution of smart contracts.

Digital Signatures—every server which executes a smart contract signs the result of its computation using its own digital identity. This digital signature is helpful to ensure that different servers have executed the smart contracts and helps to achieve nonrepudiation. The distributed ledger is maintained across different servers in a blockchain network. Any updates to the ledger need to have consensus across different nodes of the network based on the result of smart contract execution. The blockchain network generates a "block" which is a cryptographic representation of a set of transactions. A block consists of various transactions grouped by their hash to generate a cumulative hash of the entire block along with a reference to the previously generated block. In case anyone tries to tamper with the ledger of a node in the blockchain by changing any transaction information of a block, it would result in an entirely different hash for the block, which would not match with the information present on other nodes of the blockchain, and the system can just ignore this change and trust the information provided by the majority of nodes. Hence, trust is ensured by the design of the ecosystem.

IoT and blockchain technology have enabled multiple real-time data collection devices, which are ubiquitously used in smart cities. The immutability and transparency of blockchain scope out the need for human intervention and the elimination of any human errors taking place due to erroneous or tampered data.[21]

Blockchain enables trust over the data collected by various IoT sensors using the basic techniques of smart contracts, consensus, and distributed ledgers. It enables the communication and exchange of resources between two parties in a peer-to-peer network. These resources can be intangible, like digital documents, intellectual copyrights, or copyrights, or tangible, like lands and houses, cars, or physical money.[22] By and large, a blockchain network enables the efficient tracking of anything that has value by mitigating any security threats and reducing the monitoring cost involved.[23]

Sensor-based smart traffic meters are being used for tracking mobility and traffic management and detecting any type of infrastructure malfunction. This information can be uploaded to a blockchain ecosystem to leverage the immutability of a blockchain transaction record, and it helps to establish trust in the gathered information by design. Another exciting use case of IoT and blockchain is smart electric meters. IoT sensors can record details about internal heating and cooling and details about the amount of electricity being generated by the solar panels. This information can be recorded on blockchain by which the whole ecosystem of smart electric meters could leverage the basic features of blockchain to establish trust in the shared data by IoT sensors. Based on this trusted information, the ecosystem can reward the producer of electricity based on their contribution to the grid. Consumers can decide to directly buy from producers as well, in case they need to, and blockchain can be used to settle the payments. Producers can also act as consumers, therefore, known as 'prosumers' in the ecosystem. The grid can decide how much a producer needs to pay for their consumption based on their produced output of electricity and that trusted information can be fetched reliably from the blockchain network.

Blockchain helps by eliminating any duplicate efforts, hence easing data governance by streamlining business processes. It also automates e-device management ensuring foolproof data synchronization between Internet of Things devices.[24]

Blockchain technologies have numerous other potentially viable applications like security trading and settlement,[25] banking and insurance,[26] assets and finance management,[27] and several others, which can be leveraged in smart cities.

### *11.3.3 GEOSPATIAL TECHNOLOGY*

This is a basket of tools that help with geographic mapping. These tools include the following:

- WiFi – WiFi connectivity around the city is the foundation of a smart city. It enables linking all electronic devices from smartphones, CCTVs, and other devices to wireless sensors. In a smart city, the signals from these WiFi-enabled devices like smartphones and wearables are being used to determine a person's location, delivery location, etc.

- Bluetooth – Bluetooth is used in many devices like smartphones and smartwatches. These are based on a short-range wireless technology standard that is used for exchanging data between devices over short distances. They also have transmitters that send their location-emitting signals at regular intervals.
- Global Positioning System (GPS) – It is United States of America-owned radio navigation based on satellite. This system allows positioning, navigation, and timing services.
- Ultrawideband (UWB) – It is a short-range, wireless communication protocol that operates with the help of radio waves. With continuous radar imaging, it can find an object and its location and also communicate with it.

Geospatial technology helps to improve services like transportation. It is also helpful for playing an important role in reporting real-time data on any mishaps or accidents.

## 11.4 ADVANTAGES OF SUSTAINABLE SMART CITIES

- Effective decision-making based on data: Smart cities are built on information provided through the data collected around the city with the help of multiple sensors. The process of decision-making is carried out effectively when the updated data and facts are available in real-time.
- Creation of safer communities: Smart cities create a safe environment around the city with the help of CCTVs, automated accident detection, and IoT-led crowd management. Smart street lighting further helps in reducing crime and improving driving conditions.
- Improved urban transportation: Transportation systems are connected with modern technology for designing a smart transportation network that is clean and efficient. Traffic management offices can access real-time reporting and information for mishaps or accident issues and traffic congestion on important streets and then take quick action or coordinate with other agencies.
- Evolution of the Internet of Things: It is the building block of smart cities, enabling smart devices to interact with each other and provide live insights into incidents around the cities. This evolution toward intelligent devices and technology is being driven by smart cities. Blockchain is the upcoming disruptive revolution for secured connections and will

potentially bring many positive changes in the manner of our working and living in the upcoming centuries (Bhushan et al.).[28]

- Implementation of new business opportunities: With the advent of a new era of cities, many businesses such as IT solutions, internet service providers, data analysts, smart infrastructure developers, green real estate and construction companies, solar energy companies, and project management firms will see a sharp rise.
- Reduction of both economic and natural input costs: Gordon Moore's law establishes that every two years, computing power doubles and the relative cost reduces. Smart cities are set to prove it true for the existing and future disruptive technologies. Studies propose that the successful application of smart cities will help in designing a better use of public resources and enhanced quality of life, which will further help in keeping the operational cost of these administrative services low.[29]
- Safer communication: A smart city will be powered by technological advancements in the ICT sector, and collaborations with the private sector will go a long way toward benefiting society. Some examples of such technology are shooting detectors, license plate recognition, and fast emergency services. UNDESA stated that the ability to obtain and maintain citizen and city data by city officials would enable them to predict trends in urbanization and also promote a justified division of wealth between the rural and urban sectors.[30]
- Efficient public services: To manage the limited amount of natural resources, smart cities will have technologies that will provide insights to slow down the exhaustion of natural resources and decrease the wastage of soil, water, electricity, etc. with the help of real-time data connections. Big data and other emerging technologies allow autonomous city control and management of the well-being of its citizens. This can help lower eventualities like outbreaks of deadly diseases and the quick evacuation of citizens during natural disasters.[31,32]
- Cashless economy and governance: The advances in blockchain technology have led to the birth of a large number of distributed and decentralized systems. The major advantage of this technology is that it eliminates the need for a third party that acts as a mediator in systems or transactions, which require trust and accountability. The transactions involving money fundamentally involve a third-party, which is authorized to mediate the trade of goods or services based on the trustworthy governments and central banks and organizations. Blockchain, on the other hand, paves the way for a novel economic

system where any valuable items are exchanged without the use of money or any third-party approval. With the ever-growing sense of decentralized systems and to keep up with unpredictable international affairs, it is sensible to consider and build an alternative economic system that can function without any third-party acceptance. We can also see this being adopted by national governments to streamline internet transactions.[33]

- Reduced environmental footprint: A sustainable smart city will be built on the concept of green real estate and green buildings. It will have energy-efficient buildings, which help in enhancing the air quality and usage of renewable sources of energy, thus reducing the pressure on nonrenewable resources. Smart sensors will help regulate the use of energy, thus helping reduce the ecological impact on the environment.
- More digital equity: A sustainable smart city also needs to ensure that all people have access to high-speed internet service at all times at affordable prices. There is no discrimination in urban and rural areas. If people have access to public WiFi in local areas and the city, they will enjoy equal opportunities and a better standard of living.

## 11.5 DISADVANTAGES OF SUSTAINABLE SMART CITIES

- Significant capital investment in technology is required: Implementation of smart technology for building smart cities comes at high costs. Consumer expenditure on smart city initiative investment globally in 2022 is expected to rise to $158 billion.[34]
- There is a dependence on technology service companies: With the implementation costs expected to be so high, the only way to effectively design a sustainable smart city is a public–private partnership with the private company pooling its private funds for designing the future cities.
- Real estate becomes more expensive: Real estate in smart cities is embedded with sensor-based and IoT technologies, which will increase the complexity of designing the buildings. Though these buildings will be sustainable, with the addition of initial costs, the prices are also expected to rise.
- Larger technological gaps open up between smart cities and other cities: There are eminent chances that the rural and urban areas are discriminated against based on the investment and implementation of

technology in smart cities. A bias can be expected for geopolitically and strategically important cities around the world.

- Considerable increase in electronic waste: Smart cities will be hubs of industrial, IT, and commercial activities, and with heavy reliance on electronic gadgets, e-waste is expected to rise. Newer technologies and complex connectivity needs will lead to the massive dumping of old technologies and related hardware.
- Limited privacy: The government can access security cameras and intelligent systems operating in all public places. Maintaining their anonymity can become challenging for the citizens. Facial recognition and access to an individual's medical health records and browsing history will dramatically change the concept of a citizen's privacy or their personal space.
- Social control: The chances of data being manipulated or tampered for the benefit of the party that tracks and centralizes the data gathered with security cameras will rise. It can be misused by a political party, a MNC, the nation's government, or other concerned authorities. They will hold the unquestionable power to control a citizen's data and can even delete or create the identity of an individual.
- Demands 24x7 connection and power supply: Smart cities rely on continuous connectivity throughout the day to yield their benefits. The reliance on connection and power supply will increase manifold even in the household sector. If not managed effectively, it could wipe out all the benefits of a smart city.
- Difficulty in the precommerce stage: Even though large investors are available and pooling in funds, the smart city-level technologies are still in their infant precommercial stages. The technology, skills, and financial capacity to create such cities are still lacking. It will cause stiff competition and require a large upscaling of human capital skills.
- Pretraining is required: Policies should intentionally be imposed to improve educational awareness among people about smart cities by encouraging and adopting the usage of ICT tools and digital and technology skills.[35] A pretraining is required to prepare the citizens for the tech-dominated lives ahead because if people do not know how to befriend technology, then they will never reap its benefits. Without any proper training, citizens will find tech-enabled lives irrelevant and will find it difficult to adopt them. Also, since the citizens of smart cities will depend on machines, smart electronics, and fast networks, they might lose their creativity and decision-making and

could become incapable of performing normal human tasks. Training with regards to keeping cognitive skills sharp must also be given from time to time.

## 11.6 CHALLENGES FOR DEVELOPING SUSTAINABLE SMART CITIES

Even though there are numerous noticeable advantages of smart cities, nevertheless, there are also a handful of hurdles that slow down the process of this urban technological revamping. There is still much unknown about the challenges in building sustainable smart cities.[36]

- Infrastructure Development: Smart city projects thrive on IoT sensors that capture various data from electricity usage and air quality to river pollutants and hence require innovative infrastructure supported by agile hardware. The sensors that are installed in smart cities require high-level skills to be built and are also expensive. The setup is complex and costly. Most governments of developed countries are already finding it tough with other basic infrastructural challenges such as proper water pipes and sanitation, the internet, electricity generation, power supply, etc. In such situations, the funding for new infrastructure projects is skeptical, and approval processes can take numerous years.
- Infrastructure Agility and Scalability: The smart element in smart cities is expected to continuously change and evolve, and the technology that is deployed is expected to cope with the agility and scalability needs that arrive in the future of smart cities. Unscalable infrastructure will become redundant as smart cities continue to evolve. For instance, as the city's population rises, the use of buses, ride-sharing, and transportation infrastructure will also soar. This will also lead to a spike in the use of data to manage all the increasing demands. With the inability to scale up with the rising users, the full benefits of a connected, smart city cannot come true.
- Privacy Concerns: Personal data being collected in such high volumes by IoT smart sensors can undermine privacy and citizens' knowledge about the use of data. Losing digital independence is a heavy cost to ask for against a better quality of life. Educational initiatives on how smart cities can be used to enhance citizen awareness are needed. Governments and companies can gain the trust of people on this only by ensuring transparency.

- Security and Hackers: A major drawback of the sensor and IoT-enabled smart cities is the threat of security. These devices will deal with transmitting huge chunks of data in real-time. IoT devices have security loopholes as not all of them are cyber-resilient. Hackers and criminals, if they get access to a city's data, can use it for illegal intent or even hack the entire system of the city, causing a threat to all its citizens. The present Internet of Things (IoT) system suffers from many bugs and privacy risks, and blockchain shines as a viable solution to overcome these existing issues.[37] When such a huge number of devices are woven together by the same connections, the chances of security compromises rise. For achieving the vision of a robust smart city, the three prerequisites are—seamless security, authentication, and protection of data privacy and agility against attacks. These prerequisites are provided by blockchain technology, a distributed ledger technology that maintains an immutable database of all network transactions.[38]
- Hence, governments and IT professionals must take due notice while preparing smart city infrastructure.
- Disruption in the labor market: Smart cities will see the rise of automation and the increasing use of robots to replace manual work. Old jobs will be replaced with new jobs in the 21st century. People will have to be convinced to support the change and retrain with new skills. If the authorities of the city are not able to make this transition smoothly and with the full participation of their people, the cities will face a soaring number of cases of frictional unemployment and other social challenges.
- Education for Engagement: People, in general, are resistant to change, especially when the matter at hand is their life activities. Smart cities are designed to transform the standard of living and life conditions of the people. A healthy step toward building smart cities will be proving their benefits to the citizens and increasing their engagement in matters around the city because a smart city requires smart citizens. It can be done using old-style town hall meeting methods or via modern e-mail campaigns. Ensuring engagement from each fragment of society will help deliver the best intentions for smart cities.
- Social Inclusion: Smart solutions can help people to connect virtually and increase social cohesion. The darker side of this matter is the drawback of smart city benefits not being enjoyed by all groups of people in our society. There are three major causes of this, and by

failing to address these concerns, we could potentially nullify our best intentions.

First, certain age groups, especially the elderly, lack 'digital savviness' or have no access to modern connections and digital devices. There is an increasing elderly population that does not use mobile devices or apps. The second is the increased risk of health issues due to emerging technologies. Many studies suggest that advanced technologies are a leading cause of cancer. All people have to help the government in solving these issues. Hence, businesses and citizens are advised to help solve these problems.

- Lack of experienced professionals: Another imperative problem for smart cities is the shortage of skilled IT professionals. The idea of a smart city can only become a reality when it can lure and retain high-tech and creative talent. For planning, implementing, executing, and maintaining a smart city, tech experts are required. The government should devise ways to attract professionals and hire them before they start with their projects or are hired by private firms. These people are valuable for the management and continuous upgradation of the economic infrastructure through innovation. As the old traditional jobs are bound to disappear, talent is required to act as the catalyst in the process of creating new businesses and new jobs with continuous improvement.
- Inconsistent network connectivity: For smartly managing a city, several sensors, cameras, and actuators are installed throughout the city. These sensors generate a large volume of data and transmit it in real-time. This transmitted data should be analyzed and processed almost instantaneously in real-time for efficient management of city operations. This requires high-speed internet connectivity. Currently, most 4G networks are available, which are not efficient in dealing with large volumes of data and high-speed data transfer. Installation of a safe and fast network spectrum is hence essential to designing a well-operating smart city.
- Insufficient funds: Several reports and studies reveal that the cost associated with implementing a smart city strategy is the biggest roadblock. A smart city requires applying smart and innovative infrastructure for implementing digital technologies including a plethora of smart devices, which have to be installed for data collection across the cities along with high-speed connectivity devices. In addition, governments need to employ city planners and smart tech experts.

Further, the installed hardware requires frequent audits for maintenance. All of this adds up to the operation expenditure for a smart city.

## 11.7 INNOVATIVE PRACTICES AND RECENT ADVANCEMENTS AROUND THE WORLD

Today, our society has entered an enlightened decade and plans to change the world by moving closer to the SDG targets of 2030 through the revamping of the cities and their infrastructure.[39] The world is adapting to technological advancements to reach the goal of net-zero emissions. Designing a sustainable smart city needs more than a commitment. It requires continuous sustainable innovations, creativity, and expertise. Smart building technologies are driving the construction industry's commitment toward better and greener buildings. A number of studies determine the sustainability and smartness of cities based on a six-dimensional framework encompassing a city's mobility, ecology and environment, citizens, quality of living, governance model, and the whole economy.[40] Additionally,[41] there is a six-layered measurement system to classify a city as a sustainable smart city. These layers are the instrumentation layer, the city layer, the green city layer, the open integration layer, the innovation layer, and the application layer.

Low-energy smart heating, which automatically adjusts the heating in the buildings and helps in saving energy, is largely used in many smart cities like Barcelona and Brisbane. Berlin is promoting green startups that push the limits for the existing cities to transform into better and smarter cities. It is also encouraging local efforts like zero-waste dining in restaurants and packaging-free supermarkets. The Smart City Innovation Lab of Munich, Germany, allows creative technologists and local governments to work in collaboration and come up with smarter solutions for a smarter country, designing more walking and cycling installations, with a place for children and grown-ups to enjoy out-of-door conditioning, (As per a C40 study, investing in a transition to mass transportation and constructing corridors for encouraging cycling and walking can reduce carbon emigrations in metropolises by five to fifteen percent.)[42]

Freetown launched a three-year action plan—the 'Transform Freetown' plan—aiming to develop the city to fight back against its social challenges in the economy and environmental vulnerabilities. One of its initiatives is the #FreetownTheTreeTown campaign. As of data recorded in 2020, the megacity has planted around 245 k seedlings and grown 15 distinct species of trees across colorful spots. Using an advanced machine learning assessment of tree cover, a locally developed operation called Treetracker would be used to track the growth of the trees.[43]

Copenhagen, Denmark, the world's current smartest city, aims to become the first carbon-neutral city of the world by 2025.[44] Smart meters are installed and connected to the wireless data from phones and devices, sensors from sewers, and garbage cans for citizens to measure their real-time energy consumption and decrease traffic and carbon emissions. Sensors are enabling public facilities to automate lighting, heating, and cooling facilities based on the occupancy of the building.

Singapore is on the way to become a leader in Asia for intelligent and sustainable building solutions with its 80–80–80 initiative, which focuses on greening 80% of Singapore's buildings, 80% of super low-energy new building development, and achieving 80% improvement in energy efficiency by green buildings by 2030.[45] Stockholm, which bagged the World Smart City Award in 2019, is innovating smart, sustainable solutions in collaboration with academia and private enterprises.[44] Zurich, Switzerland, is among the best five smart cities on Earth, which ensures people's smart participation and encourages the citizens to take initiative and provide creative ideas.[46] The automobile sector is already diving into automated and self-driving cars, which is a breakthrough in the industry. Electric vehicles are the latest innovation, and it is important to set up proper infrastructure for them in the form of recharge plugins and battery-swapping centers. Norway is leading the EV penetration, where, in 2020, 75% of the total cars were electric. It aims to reach 100% EV penetration by 2025.[47] It is also working on the testing of electric buses and designing green energy systems and circular waste management. It has also committed to construction sites working with zero-emission systems and retrofitting smart sensors in existing buildings.

Under a program named Healthy Chicago 2.0, reducing health inequality is the main focus of developing community engagement, detecting the root causes of sickness, improving overall health, and leveraging data for optimal exploration.[48]

Smart grids running on blockchain technology, where the consumers can generate their solar electricity and sell it back to the grid, are being increasingly adopted in many countries such as Australia. Co-working centers and smart work centers with intelligent lighting are being adopted worldwide, and companies are encouraging their employees to become more sustainable and adopt cleaner ways of working.

Sensors are being used to measure the air quality, temperature, and humidity of the surroundings and publish this data for the citizens in real-time. It helps in easy accounting and trend analysis of the consumption of resources and measuring the effect of our actions on the environment.

In New York, regulations like the Climate Mobilization Act enact carbon emission caps on buildings. In this way, they help in materializing New York's commitment to sustainability.[49] Sydney, Australia, from July 2020 initiated using 100 percent renewable electric power to meet its demands. In this way, the city has reduced its carbon emissions by 18,000 metric tons per year.[50] With the help of sensors, the city keeps its people connected and informed about the environment's conditions. Provided with real-time information, even the citizens of San Francisco are changing the way they live. Paris has launched Vélib bike-sharing and reinventing Paris smart city projects to power its infrastructure for the carbon neutrality game. It uses sensor technology-enabled devices to detect infrastructure malfunctions, gauge energy consumption, and motivate citizens to decrease waste. Paris is the "sharing city" of the future. Paris's 'La Ville du quart d'heure' (the quarter-hour megacity) action aligns with providing easy access to workplaces, convenience stores, seminaries, conventions, and artistic conditioning. The conception for this environmental metamorphosis is grounded on four strong pillars—videlicet propinquity, diversity, viscosity, and ubiquity.[51]

In 2013, in Seoul, South Korea, the government launched an initiative for businesses to use to reduce waste and underutilized capacity, reduce the costs of the municipality, and boost new environment-friendly business opportunities.[52]

Devices are being designed for detecting malfunctions in the infrastructure. Governments have started to educate people about the coming changes through the medium of published open data, training programs, and innovation competitions for citizens. Cascais, Portugal, has achieved reduced operating costs by over 40 percent and boosted energy savings by over 20 percent with the help of integrating real-time business and data of the present road conditions. This system not only optimizes routes for the disposal and collection of waste but also helps in identifying the times for scrap collection.[53]

The Japanese police force, for the Tokyo Olympics, used artificial intelligence (AI) systems capable of predicting the criminal's next move and determining whether the same person has committed multiple crimes by comparing real-time data of each offense. The 'deep learning algorithm' of this AI teaches the computer systems in real-time based on a continuous collection of data. Further, the police also plan to introduce this AI to access social media websites to highlight danger-prone areas in the country or shady people who may be on the run after committing any crime.[54]

## 11.8 UNEVEN SCOPE AROUND THE GLOBE

The scope of sustainable smart cities is very uneven around the globe. Smart cities require continuous, huge funding, modern infrastructure, advanced technologies, human capital expertise, and high-speed connectivity. With countries undergoing and recovering from war-like situations, imagining smart cities becoming a reality is difficult.

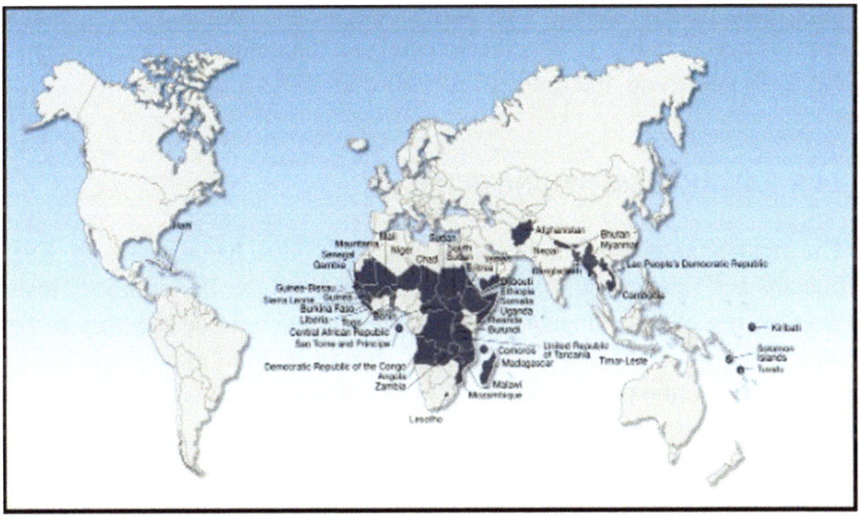


**FIGURE 11.2** Map of the least developed countries

*Source:* UNCTAD. https://unctad.org/topic/least-developed-countries/list

The above map shows the least developed 46 countries in the world. It includes 33 African countries, 9 Asian countries, 1 from the Caribbean, and 3 Pacific countries. The per capita income of these countries varies drastically from the leading smart cities of the world. As per a World Bank report,[55] the extremely poor people of the world reside in 5 countries, i.e., India, the Democratic Republic of Congo, Nigeria, Bangladesh, and Ethiopia. 85 percent (629 million) of the world's poor people are from South Asia and sub-Saharan Africa. These countries belong to the above two regions and are, interestingly, also the countries with the most population in the world.

In a highly contrasting world, to think of a unanimous future of smart cities is impossible. These countries need to rise to the level of developed countries before they transcend to become the cities of the future. It is also highly likely that the advent of smart cities will deepen the divide between the countries around the world. In a globally connected world, no country can be called a smart city when all the countries are dependent on each other in one way or another.

Also, smart cities focus on the elite class of society, which has access to electricity, the internet, and other related facilities. It further deepens the social divide in society and gives birth to social concerns.

Several studies suggest that high-speed connectivity can cause serious problems to humans like cancer and brain damage. In light of this fact, the improvement in the standard of living of people and their happiness in smart cities is questionable. Unless these social and humanitarian aspects of smart cities are addressed, the future of global smart cities is uncertain.

## 11.9 AWARENESS AMONG PEOPLE

The next generation will be born in a radically changing world where humans and robots would coexist in a house. With the world already losing time to stop climate change, the next generation could be the ones to face the consequences of their predecessors. It will be even more important for them to know and practice the Sustainable Development Goals given by the United Nations.

These goals comprehensively focus on the needs of the current and, more importantly, the next generation. A sustainable smart city should also focus on including all these SDGs in its city plan. SDGs could become a part of the academic curriculum of educational courses as well. To raise students' awareness of sustainability problems and build a platform for some real and constructive communication led by student leaders, they can be engaged in personalized activities.[56] The efforts being made by higher education institutions to sensitize graduates toward sustainability are promising but far from achieving the goals laid out by the United Nations by 2030.[57]

Sustainable development has four dimensions—environment, society, culture, and economy—which are woven together and do not exist separately. The school of thought of sustainability is for planning a future where these societal, environmental, and economic aspects are well-balanced in the direction of providing a better quality of life. It is often thought of as a long-term goal that is yet to be achieved (i.e., a sustainable lifestyle), while in reality, sustainable development means a synergy of many processes and pathways to create it (e.g., a sustainable lifestyle encompasses sustainable agriculture, sustainable forestry, sustainable food production and consumption, improved governance, research and technology, better education and hands-on training, etc.).

**FIGURE 11.3** Sustainable Development Goals

*Image Courtesy*: United Nations. https://www.un.org/sustainabledevelopment/

A standing issue in the way of sustainability is the intergenerational sustainability dilemma (ISD). It represents a school of thought where the current generation opts to just increase its gains without considering the needs of future generations, hence compromising intergenerational sustainability (IS). A major alarming feature of ISD is its unidirectional or irreversible nature as the actions of the current generation affect future generations. The survival of humans on Earth is dependent on whether or not we can solve the current intergenerational dilemmas and protect our natural resources. This can be done by initiating communication, having talks with the young generation, and maintaining cooperation across the views and ideas of the different generations.

In the autumn of 1997, in Paris, a meeting of the General Conference of the United Nations Educational, Scientific, and Cultural Organization (UNESCO) passed the Declaration on the Responsibilities of the Present Generations toward Future Generations. The declaration stated that the present generations are responsible for ensuring that the needs, interests, and rights of current and all future generations are completely protected. It is in a manner to care for your children and their children. It stressed that we need to make serious efforts to ensure that future as well as present generations validate their basic rights and their freedom of choice for economic, political, and social issues and can preserve humankind's cultural and religious diversity. It was also recognized that the Earth that is bequeathed by present generations to future generations should not be irreversibly damaged by uncontrolled human activities. It is to be acknowledged that each generation just inherits the Earth temporarily and is hence justifiably responsible for taking care of its usage of natural resources in a reasonable manner and ensuring that the right to a good and healthy life of the future generations is not prejudiced by irreversible modifications of our natural ecosystems, and other technological and scientific advancements in all fields do not ever harm any form of life on the planet Earth.

The current population in the world is the one who will sow the seeds of sustainability in the minds of the coming generations. By fulfilling our responsibilities today, we can build a generation that is more agile, responsive, and climate-conscious. A smart city must be sustainable to survive in the long term.

Being an aware generation ourselves, we can build a smart next generation in the following ways:

1. One of the ways by which we can make our future generations more aware is to educate them. Share their knowledge of environmental values and help them to adopt ecofriendly practices. The idea of reusing items, recycling, conserving resources, and showing compassion for the land and wildlife must be taught.
2. They must be made aware of the benefits of donations and charity and their impact on society by involving them.
3. Parents must encourage their children to participate in activities like beach cleanups or environment-friendly clubs or to participate in activities for saving trees, water, and soil.
4. Avoid red meat or meat in general or eat it as little as possible.
5. Support environmentally friendly companies and products by using your consumer power.

6. Use your voting rights wisely to choose representatives who understand and act in a manner that takes care of our natural world and protects our planet. Build the capacity to act together on sustainability.
7. Engage people by delivering insights that spark action amongst people by sharing blogs, videos, articles, and photos.
8. Ensure your family does not use plastic bags or single-use plastic bottles. Support the sustainable management of our natural resources.

According to a recent study,[58] a large population of Generation Z (those born since 1997) shoppers consciously choose and prefer to buy sustainable brands, and they do not mind spending 10 percent more on ecofriendly sustainable products. This report also states that Generation Z along with Millennials (those born between 1981 and 1996) make their purchase decisions based on many principles and values (personal, environmental, and social).

Many innovative technologies such as Next Generation Environmental Technologies (NGETs) focus on redesigning manufacturing processes and products at the molecular level to eliminate the use of hazardous materials. These are derived from "green chemistry." Even though green chemistry could have numerous benefits, both environmentally and economically, the development of NGETs is still in incubation. Substantial work is required to encourage NGETs to use and create new ones.

Countries like Spain are leading the education sector in preparing the next generation for smart cities by teaching robotics and IoT in primary education.[59] Smart education is the answer for smart citizens in a smart city. Combining digital technologies with education prepares children, who are the future human capital of a nation. By learning AI, IoT, and robotics, school children can reflect on their thinking and build their thinking about what robots and AI are by spotting examples in their surroundings. It develops children's intuition about the working of technology and sparks curiosity in them. This curiosity can grow into creativity and build the right skill set for the human capital of smart cities.

We cannot completely rely on the next generation for the development of smart cities. Professionals and tech experts of all ages are shaping the smart cities out there as we read of them. The role of the youth of today is to research, adapt, and accept the changes that are happening in the world. The youth must upskill themselves with the skills of the future to become prepared for future jobs.

The job requirements of smart cities are very different; about 47% of today's jobs[60] would be automated with the advent of smart city technology. The top five skills needed in the future are as follows:

1. Programing and software development
2. Artificial intelligence and machine learning
3. Data analytics and visualization
4. Cloud computing
5. Development operations

### 11.9.1 SURVEY

A survey was carried out by the authors to find out the level of awareness among people about the need for sustainability. Gauging the level of awareness among the people can be a constructive step to analyze and design how the citizens are to be prepared for the upcoming needs such as sustainable smart cities.

The sample for the survey was 765, which included school students in grades 11 and 12 and all adults above 18 years of age. The respondents were selected randomly from the Tricity—Mohali, Chandigarh, and Panchkula. The responses were collected through an online method, and respondents showed good participation. The questions were designed by the authors and approved by experts working in the domain of sustainability.

### 11.9.2 DATA ANALYSIS AND INTERPRETATION

The results of the survey were found to be more skewed toward the youth understanding the need for sustainability and enhancing it through their daily practices. The results highlighted that people are aware of the impacts of their habits on the environment. 83% do not know the required per capita carbon footprint to achieve the global warming level of 1.5 degrees as per the Paris Agreement 2015,[61] and 77% do not know the actual per capita carbon footprint of their country, but 97% have planted a tree once in their lives. This shows the low level of awareness among the respondents. Further, it has been found that 42.6% of people still throw away their old gadgets or let them sit in some corner of their homes. 3% of the respondents generally throw plastic bags anywhere, and 71% segregate dry waste and wet waste in their homes. The fashion industry also impacts sustainability as it consumes a lot of resources and later causes lots of dumping. 60% intend to purchase an EV instead of a fuel car for themselves, and 58% stay fit by exercising and running outdoors. Interestingly, 80% of the respondents look for energy stars while purchasing electric appliances, and 65% say that sustainable packaging affects their buying behavior. A positive correlation between the efforts of the governments and their impact on people's habits can be established by the fact that 88% have never thrown nonbiodegradable items in the river or any other water body, and 57% throw used plastic bags or other plastic items in the dustbin.

## 11.10 CONCLUSIONS AND RECOMMENDATIONS

There are a lot of our daily habits that affect the climate at large. Having more than 65 emails in your inbox, eating nonvegetarian food, or going to the gym to stay fit increases your per capita carbon footprint. The total of all the greenhouse gases, inclusive of carbon dioxide and methane, that are, directly or indirectly, generated by human actions is known as a carbon footprint. It can be elaborated as the total greenhouse gas emissions generated by an individual, organization, event, place, or service expressed as carbon dioxide equivalent ($CO_2e$). The greenhouse gases such as methane and carbon dioxide are emitted at the time of the burning of fossil fuels, consumption and production of food, manufacture of goods and materials, burning of wood, construction of roads, transportation, buildings, pollution, etc. As per World Bank 2021 data,[62] the highest per capita $CO_2$ emission in metric tons was topped by Saudi Arabia and the United States with 17.6 metric tons each, followed by Canada and Australia at 15.7 and 14.9. South Korea stands in the fifth position with 13.3 metric tons of emissions. China has a per capita emission of 6.7 metric tons. Simple habits like the car you own, your shopping bag, and even how you talk can impact your carbon footprint. A text message conversation creates a lower carbon footprint compared to a call.

Smart cities are not just about technological advancements but also about climate action advancements. The healthier the air we breathe, the longer our healthy lifespans will be in technology-driven smart cities. This is also the reason why smart cities today are focusing equally on modern infrastructure and green and sustainable infrastructure.

The fundamental goal of a sustainable and smart city is to offer a framework for meeting the needs of both present and coming generations of citizens.[63] When we talk about smart cities, we talk not only about metal buildings and high-speed connectivity, but we also talk about a greener, safer, and more sustainable city from which even the coming generations can benefit. A smart city is sustainable when it focuses equally on technology and humans. It focuses on providing the infrastructure along with an improved standard of living. Not only this, a smart city takes into consideration the changing business environment as after the outbreak of COVID-19, organizations have undergone major changes.[64] Here, the motive of governance is to improve technological advancement and quality of life but not at the cost of the environmental impact of urbanism.

This chapter has presented and discussed various aspects related to the development of smart cities, which are also sustainable. It has been strongly recommended to build such cities with collaboration and cooperation between key stakeholders in the government and the private sector while ensuring geographical safety. All these stakeholders must view this as a long-term sustainable infrastructure project while also keeping in mind today's need for short-term developments to cope with the increasingly digital, connected, and smart world. The potential of smart cities can only be maximized through the trust of citizens synergized with the businesses and governments that prioritize their safety, efficiency, and sustainability. Instead of focusing just on a tech solution, developers and tech companies need to also consider how this solution will impact the lives of people and other living beings that come into contact with it.

The authors believe and recommend that a "smart" city can only be developed when government, technology, and the people at large stand together to enrich the quality of life for everyone and everything involved. The purpose of technology is to bring all walks of people together rather than categorizing them based on their geographical location, income and status, education levels, etc.

## KEYWORDS

- **sustainability**
- **smart cities**
- **big data**
- **geospatial technology**
- **innovative practices**
- **internet of things**
- **blockchain**
- **accounting**
- **developments**

## REFERENCES


1. Llacuna, M.; Llinàs, C.; Meléndez, F. Lessons in Urban Monitoring Taken from Sustainable and Livable Cities to Better Address the Smart Cities initiative. *Technol. Forecast. Soc. Change* **2015,** *90,* 611–622.
2. Lazaro, G. C.; Roscia, M. Definition Methodology for the Smart Cities Model. *Energy* **2012,** *47* (1), 326–332.
3. Fahim, U.; Siddra, Q.; Muhammad, J.; Fadi, A.; Samad, M. E. Risk Management in Sustainable Smart Cities Governance: A TOE Framework. *Technol. Forecast. Soc. Change* **2021,** *167.*
4. Razmjoo, A.; Østergaard, P. A.; Denaï, M.; Nezhad, M. N.; Mirjalili, S. Effective Policies to Overcome Barriers in the Development of Smart Cities. *Energy Res. Soc. Sci.* **2021,** *79.*
5. Nam, T.; Pardo, T. A. In *Conceptualizing a Smart city with Dimensions of Technology, People, and Institutions*, Proceedings of the 12th Annual International Digital Government Research Conference: Digital Government Innovation in Challenging Times, ACM, 2011, pp 282–291.
6. Dizdaroglu, D.; Yigitcanlar, Integrating Urban Ecosystem Sustainability Assessment into Policy-Making: Insights from the Gold Coast City. *J. Environ. Plan. Manag.* **2016,** *59* (11), 1982–2006.
7. *Report of the World Commission on Environment and Development: Our Common Future,* WCED (World Commission on Environment and Development): United Nations, 1987.
8. Roy, M. Planning for Sustainable Urbanization in Fast-Growing Cities: Mitigation and Adaptation Issues Addressed in Dhaka, Bangladesh. *Habitat Int.* **2009,** *33* (3), 276–286.
9. Ahvenniemi, H.; Huovila, A.; Pinto-Seppä, I.; Airaksinen, M. What are the Differences between Sustainable and Smart Cities? *Cities* **2017,** *60,* 234–245.
10. Shorfuzzaman, M.; Hossain, M. S.; Alhamid, M.F. Towards the Sustainable Development of Smart Cities Through Mass Video Surveillance: A Response to the COVID-19 Pandemic. *Sustain. Cities Soc.* **2021,** *64.*
11. Urbanet. *The World Urban Population | Infographics* Available online at: https://www.urbanet.info/world-urban-population/#:~:text=According%20to%20projections%2C%20the%20urban,billion%20(66%25)%20by%202050, (accessed October 28, 2022).
12. NRDC. *What Are Smarter Cities?* Available online at: https://www.nrdc.org/, 2012.
13. Kim, H. M.; Han, S. S.; Seoul. *Cities* **2012,** *29,* 142–154.
14. UNEP, 2021 Global Status Report for Buildings and Construction [Online]. Oct 19, 2019. https://www.unep.org/resources/report/2021-global-status-report-buildings-and-construction, (accessed Oct 12, 2022).
15. Dhingra, M.; Chattopadhyay, S. Advancing Smartness of Traditional Settlements-Case Analysis of Indian and Arab old cities. *Int. J. Sustain. Built Environ.* **2016,** *5* (2), 549–563.
16. Maaroof, A. UNESCAP, Big Data and the 2030 Agenda for Sustainable Development [Online], https://www.unescap.org/sites/default/files/1_Big%20Data%202030%20Agenda_stock-taking%20report_25.01.16.pdf
17. Silva, B. N.; Khan, M.; Han, K. Towards Sustainable Smart Cities: A Review of Trends, Architectures, Components, and Open Challenges in Smart Cities. 2018.
18. Kitchin, R. Data-driven Networked Urbanism. *SSRN* 2015.
19. Bibri, S. E.; Krogstie, J. Smart Sustainable Cities of the Future: An Extensive Interdisciplinary Literature Review. *Sustain. Cities Soc.* **2017,** *31,* 183–212.

20. Yuan, Y.; et al. Blockchain and Cryptocurrencies: Model, Techniques, and Applications. *IEEE Trans Syst, Man, Cybern: Syst.* **2018.**
21. Bhushan, B.; Sinha, P.; MartinSagayam, K.; Andrew J. Computers & Electrical Engineering, Untangling Blockchain Technology: A Survey on the State of the Art, Security Threats, Privacy Services, Applications, and Future Research Directions. *Sci. Direct* **2021.**
22. Ali, M. S.; et al. Applications of Blockchains in the Internet of Things: A Comprehensive Survey. *IEEE Commun. Surv. Tutor.* **2019.**
23. Bhushan, B.; et al. Blockchain for Smart Cities: A Review of Architectures, Integration Trends, and Future Research Direction. *Sustain. Cities Soc.* **2020.**
24. Huang, K.; et al. Building Redactable Consortium Blockchain for Industrial Internet-of-Things. *IEEE Trans. Ind. Inf.* **2021.**
25. Morkunas, V. J.; et al. How Blockchain Technologies Impact Your Business Model. *Bus. Horiz.* **2019**
26. Ikeda, K.; et al. Applications of Blockchain in the Financial Sector and a Peer-to-Peer Global Barter Web. *Adv. Comput. Blockchain Technol: Platf. Tools Use Cases* **2018.**
27. Fu, Y.; et al. Big Production Enterprise Supply Chain Endogenous Risk Management based on Blockchain. *IEEE Access* **2019.**
28. Malik, A.; Gautam, S.; Abidin, S.; Bhushan, B. Blockchain Technology-Future Of IoT: Including Structure, Limitations And Various Possible Attacks. *IEEE* **2019.**
29. Zanella, A.; Bui, N.; Castellani, A.; Vangelista, L.; Zorzi, M. Internet of things for smart cities. *IEEE Int. Things J.* **2014,** *1* (1), 22–32.
30. United Nations. *Department of Economic and Social Affairs (UNDESA), Population Division, World Urbanization Prospects: The 2014 Revision* [Online], CD-ROM Edition 2014.
31. Aoun, C. *The Smart City Cornerstone: Urban efficiency* [Onlin] 2013.
32. Vanolo, A. Smart Mentality: The Smart City as a Disciplinary Strategy. *Urban Stud.* **2014,** *51* (5)
33. Ikeda, K.; Hamid, N. Applications of Blockchain in the Financial Sector and a Peer-to-Peer Global Barter Web [Online]. 2018.
34. Statista, Technology spending on smart city initiatives worldwide from 2018 to 2023 [Online]. https://www.statista.com/statistics/884092/worldwide-spending-smart-city-initiatives/(accessed October 20, 2022).
35. Hollands, R. G. Will the Real Smart City Please Stand up? Intelligent, Progressive or Entrepreneurial? *City* **2008,** *12* (3).
36. Khan, H. H.; Malik, M. N.; Zafar, R.; Goni, F. A.; Chofreh, A. G.; Klemeš, J. J.; Alotaibi, Y. Challenges for Sustainable Smart City Development: A Conceptual Framework. *Sustain. Dev.* **2020,** *28* (5), 1507–1518.
37. Saxena, S.; Bhushan, B.; Abdul Ahad, M. Blockchain-Based Solutions to Secure IoT: Background, Integration Trends and a Way Forward. *J. Netw. Comput. Appl. Sci. Direct.* **2021.**
38. Bhushan, B.; Sahoo, C.; Sinha, P.; Khamparia, A. Unification of Blockchain and Internet of Things (BIoT): requirements, working model, challenges and future directions. In *Wireless Networks, SpringerLink*; 2020.
39. Kolesnichenko, O.; Mazelis, L.; Sotnik, A.; Yakovleva, D.; Amelkin, S.; Grigorevsky, I.; Kolesnichenko, Y. Sociological Modeling of Smart City with the Implementation of UN Sustainable Development Goals. *Sustain. Sci.* **2021,** *16,* 581–599.

40. Giffinger, R.; Fertner, C.; Kramar, H.; Meijers, E. *Smart Cities: Ranking of European Medium-Sized Cities*; Centre of Regional Science (SRF), Vienna University of Technology: Vienna, Austria, 2007; pp 1–12.
41. Zygiaris, S. Smart City Reference Model: Assisting Planners to Conceptualize the Building of Smart City Innovation Ecosystems. *J. Knowl. Econ.* **2013,** *4* (2).
42. Focused Acceleration: A Strategic Approach to Climate Action in Cities to 2030. In *C40 Cities;* 2020.
43. Freetown City Council. Transform Freetown: An overview | 2019-2022, (2019); World Bank, An Obstacle or Opportunity? Building Urban Resilience in Freetown. (2019); UNEP, Transforming Sierra Leone's capital [Online]. 2020
44. Nikel, D. Copenhagen Aims to Be World's First Carbon Neutral Capital By 2025 [Online]. Forbes, Aug 22, 2019. https://www.forbes.com/sites/davidnikel/2019/08/22/copenhagen-aims-to-be-worlds-first-carbon-neutral-capital-by-2025/?sh=19b6e3957fb, (accessed Oct 29, 2022).
45. Singapore Building and Construction Authority [Online]. https://www1.bca.gov.sg/buildsg/sustainability/green-building-masterplans, (accessed Oct 28, 2022).
46. European Commission. Stockholm wins World Smart City Awards for European Project [Online]. https://cordis.europa.eu/article/id/411609-stockholm-wins-world-smart-city-awards-for-european-project/fr, (accessed Oct 18, 2022).
47. Hamza, M. These Are the Top 20 Sustainable Smart Cities in the World [Online]. https://www.disruptive-technologies.com/blog/the-top-20-sustainable-smart-cities-in-the-world, (accessed Oct 4, 2022).
48. Chicago Government. *Healthy Chicago 2025* [Online], 2020. https://www.chicago.gov/city/en/depts/cdph/provdrs/healthy_communities/svcs/healthy-chicago-2025.html (accessed Sep 4, 2022).
49. IEA. Trends and Developments in Electric Vehicle Markets [Online]. https://www.iea.org/reports/global-ev-outlook-2021/trends-and-developments-in-electric-vehicle-markets, (accessed Sep 18, 2022).
50. Australian Government. Australia's Long-Term Emissions Reduction Plan [Online]. https://www.industry.gov.au/sites/default/files/October%202021/document/australias-long-term-emissions-reduction-plan.pdf, (accessed Sep 25, 2022).
51. O'Sullivan, F.; Bliss, L. The 15-Minute City—No Cars Required—Is Urban Planning's New Utopia [Online], Nov 12, 2020. https://www.bloomberg.com/news/features/2020-11-12/paris-s-15-minute-city-could-be-coming-to-an-urban-area-near-you?leadSource=uverify%20wall, (accessed August 25, 2022).
52. Solve Urban Problems through Sharing Seoul Share Hub presentation of Sharing City Seoul, Seoul Share Hub., 2015.
53. Deloitte Insights. Urban future with a purpose by Miguel Eiras Antunes, Jean Gil Barroca, Daniela Guerreiro Oliveira.
54. Interesting Engineering: Japan Set to Launch AI System to Predict Crime; Engineering 360: Japan to Launch AI System to Predict Crime; Kyodo News: Kanagawa police eye AI-assisted predictive policing before Olympic 2018.
55. World Bank. Half of the World's Poor Live in Just 5 Countries [Online]. https://www.worldbank.org/en/topic/poverty#:~:text=Of%20the%20world's%20736%20million,Congo%2C%20Ethiopia%2C%20and%20Bangladesh., (accessed July 22, 2022).
56. Roy, S. G.; De Souza, S. P.; McGreavy, B.; Druschke, C. G.; Hart, D. D.; Gardner, K. Evaluating Core Competencies and Learning Outcomes for Training the Next Generation of Sustainability Researcher. *Sustain. Sci.* **2020,** *15,* 619–631.

57. O'Riordan, T.; Jacobs, G.; Ramanathan, J.; Bina, O., Investigating the Future Role of Higher Education in Creating Sustainability Transitions. *Environ. Sci. Policy Sustain. Dev.* **2020,** *62* (4), 4–15.
58. Petro, G. Gen Z is Emerging as the Sustainability Generation [Online]. https://www.forbes.com/sites/gregpetro/2021/04/30/gen-z-is-emerging-as-the-sustainability-generation/?sh=1fc6f8b78699, (accessed July 24, 2022).
59. Vaquero, M. G.; Saiz-Alvarez, J. M. Smart Cities in Spain—Policy, Sustainability, and the National Plan: New Political Measures, Agents, and Sustainability. In *Economic Modeling, Analysis, and Policy for Sustainability*; Goswami, A., Mishra, A., Eds.; IGI Global 2016; pp 266–283.
60. Deloitte. Smart Cities How Rapid Advances in Technology are Reshaping our Economy and Society [Online]. Available:https://www2.deloitte.com/content/dam/Deloitte/tr/Documents/public-sector/deloitte-nl-ps-smart-cities-report.pdf, (accessed July 31, 2022).
61. United Nations. The Paris Agreement [Online]. https://unfccc.int/process-and-meetings/the-paris-agreement/the-paris-agreement, (accessed July 17, 2022).
62. World Bank [Online]. https://www.worldbank.org/en/home, (accessed July 17, 2022).
63. Kumar, S.; Attri, K.; Kumar, V. Impact of Emerging Technologies in the Development of Smart and Sustainable Cities. *SSRN* **2022**.
64. Saini, R.; Khan, H.; Oliver, S. The Dynamics of the Remote Leadership: A COVID-19 Context. In *Responsible Leadership for Sustainability in Uncertain Times. Responsible Leadership and Sustainable Management*; Sharma, T., Sinha Ray, R., Mitra, N., Eds.; Springer: Singapore, 2022.

CHAPTER 12

# Prospect of Marigold Cultivation in Purulia District of West Bengal: A Way Forward Toward Socio-Economic Sustainability

PRIYANKA MAJUMDER[1], ASUTOSH GOSWAMI[1],
SHISHIR KUMAR MUNSHI[2], and SUHEL SEN[3]

[1]*Department of Earth Sciences and Remote Sensing, JIS University, Agarpara, West Bengal, India*

[2]*Bangladesh Academy for Rural Development, Cumilla, Bangladesh*

[3]*Department of Geography, Lovely Professional University, Phagwara, Punjab, India*

## ABSTRACT

Purulia district of West Bengal is arranged on the eastern edge of Chhota Nagpur level, where precipitation is considered a restricting variable for the fruitful development of farming. The region is not viewed as reasonable for the development of a long-span assortment of rice. So, the current paper intends to recognize the advantage in cost proportion of marigold production.

The paper gauges the benefit of cost proportion, ranch business pay, returns over factor cost, and family work pay of marigold production based on the standard cost or expenses of those parameters. For the positioning of expected requirements in the fruitful production of marigold, Garrett's positioning procedure has been utilized. The outcome shows that the assessed benefit cost proportion is viewed as higher for the large ranches (1:1.99) trailed by the medium (1:1.95), small (1:1.87), and marginal land possessions

Management for Sustainable Development: Integrating Social, Economic, and Environmental Goals.
Vishal Jain & Amit Mittal (Eds.)

(1:1.1.76). However, the gross assessed cost of development is recognized as higher for the large homesteads. The concentrate likewise demonstrates the possible imperatives for fruitful marigold development in the expressed region among which a deficient stock of compost and establishing materials, greater expense of water systems, and expanding climatic fluctuations will show up as the critical limitations. The current paper recognizes the financial suitability of marigold production in the review region.

## 12.1 INTRODUCTION

Farming plays an essential role in the development of the Indian economy.[1] This area ought to be enhanced by the cultivation-based framework for the quick monetary turn of events and business age in the country. The general expanding utilization of farming products upholds creation to satisfy the rising need.[2] In horticulture, India has a long tradition, which has expected a positive business status.[3] The assessed region under horticultural development in India is around 34000 hectares of which the significant states are viewed as Karnataka, Tamil Nadu, West Bengal, Andhra Pradesh, and Maharashtra. The Public Commission on Farming, considering horticulture as a critical base of the economy, has suggested 5 lakh hectares of region under gardening by 2000 A.D. to improve harvesting.[4] The interest for blossoms shows a rising pattern with the changing situation of the moderate economy, way of life, and social upsides of individuals of the nation coming about into a yearly development pace of the gardening industry of around 15%.[4]

The rising pattern of horticulture practice over the customary field crops is the consequence of better yields per unit region of the past. Not just that, gardening is considered a work-producing area in the country, which can uphold a family comprising 5 to 6 individuals. Gardening practice is done predominantly in urban communities. In India, the region under horticulture was recognized as 278,000 hectares during 2015–2016. Tamil Nadu is the main state concerning flower production with an area of 8383 hectares. Marigold, fundamentally a local of America, is considered a significant and famous blossom of India, which has a place with the group of *Asleraceae* and positions third in number after roses and chrysanthemums in India.[5] It is generally developed as a boundary plant in gardens. It is likewise viewed as a serious harvest, which is developed by the ranchers chiefly on a limited scope.[5] Gardening has turned into a major business as blossoms of different types have an enormous interest in improvement and as wellsprings of rejuvenating oil of which marigolds are thought to be perhaps the most beautiful plant.[6] The versatile limit of marigold is high under various kinds of soil conditions.[7] Marigold can be developed round the year, and it acquires notoriety among the groundskeepers and vendors due to its simple development procedure and wide flexibility.[8] Be that as it may, rich sandy soil is viewed as great for the effective development of marigold. Furthermore, the clinical worth of the leaves and blossoms of marigolds is viewed as exceptionally high. The medicinal oils of marigolds have significance in the fragrance business. The homestead-level development of marigold is viewed as entirely beneficial in Bangladesh because of its greater popularity compared with its cutthroat yields like potato, lentil, and mustard (Haque et al., 2012).[2] In Indian farming, horticulture is a significant part as customarily a critical populace is vegetable-preferring, or many are rigorously vegan. The radiation potential and agroclimatic circumstances in India are entirely appropriate for consistently developing assortments of products of the floriculture. Along with floriculture, vegetables are also the main defensive food providing all the supplements and rough filaments. The insights show that the region under horticulture development in the country has expanded from 2593 thousand hectares in 1991–1992 to 4495 thousand hectares in 2010–2011. The significance of floriculture in India's developing economy is all around recognized with the rising homegrown interest and ascend in per capita pay, the rising product potential, and the true capacity for giving economic security and vocation open doors to the provincial individuals. Notwithstanding, the vegetables face enormous vulnerabilities in creation, stockpiling, and promotion on large counts. At different phases of postcollect exercises, a huge amount of vegetables get spoiled. The people in the district of Purulia have a tendency to practice some nontraditional cash crops and floriculture. The ongoing research focuses on the financial matters of marigold development and postcollect misfortune has also been assessed. The westernmost district (Purulia) in West Bengal is a sloping district with inadequate population dispersion confronted with massive difficulties because of climate, low per capita pay, an unfortunate framework, standard barricades, and an unfortunate market setup. Bagmundi area is the most elevated part of the district with incredible potential for different green harvests, vegetables, and natural products including floriculture. The significant vegetables and organic products delivered by the area are found to be potatoes, pineapple, cabbage, etc. Late reports of unfortunate showcasing offices for marigold cultivators that lead to broadly fluctuating costs of production and bringing about ranchers' fomentation legitimize an intensive report and strategy definition. With this view, an effort has been made in this paper to analyze the financial aspects of marigold development and postreap misfortunes in the Purulia district of West Bengal. Farming plays a fundamental role in India's economy. This area gives unrefined substance to agro-based businesses. The main job of agribusiness in the economy of India is to create overflows for products to acquire unfamiliar trade. The horticultural areas have generally supported good development to guarantee economic security for the quick development of the populace. However, the primary difficulties confronted the ranchers' low returns on rural landscapes because of the significant expense of production. Food and agribusiness are critical to the accomplishment of the 2030 plan for maintainable advancement going from objectively finishing destitution and appetite to tending to environmental change and, furthermore, supporting normal assets. Hence, a suitable and supportable floricultural area can possibly address not just location appetite and lack of healthy sustenance but a few other challenges including destitution; water and energy use; environmental change; and impractical creation and utilization. Farming is the premise and precondition for supportable advancement. It provides essential and significant materials for worldwide supportable advancement. India, the second most crowded country with 1.3 billion occupants, is supposed to outperform China in the next seven years. As rising wages get to the next level of access to nourishment for increasingly more people, the current pattern of slow territorial development in food production because of changing temperatures and precipitation designs, along with expanded climate changeability, will introduce difficulties in fulfilling the food needs economically. Likewise, there is restricted scope for extension of yield and pastureland, proceeding with rivalry for useful assets, and developing water shortage. This incredible test cannot be perceived without maintainability. A down-to-earth cultivation is one that, for a really long time, overhauls natural quality and the resource base on which cultivation depends; obliges fundamental human food and fiber needs; is monetarily reasonable; and updates the personal satisfaction of farmers and society with everything taken into account.[10] Viable agriculture is subject to biotic and, moreover, abiotic stresses.[11] Plants are up against different biotic nerves and opposing environmental conditions. Biotic weights in plants are achieved by bugs, parasites, and microorganisms, which have been known since old-fashioned times. Creatures, organisms, nematodes, and diseases are the microorganisms in a general sense at risk for plant contamination.[12] Drought, cold, and severe aridity are integrated under abiotic stress, which causes expansive mishaps all over the planet.[13] The abiotic stress, for instance, drought, directly impacts plant-trouble interchanges by changing plant physiology and protects responses.[14] Dry season pressure is uncommonly hurtful during the conceptual stage, unequivocally during sprouting, yet even delicate dry seasons in different stages can in the same manner brief enormous setbacks. To ease disasters as a result of the dry season, new drought-permissive high-yielding rice groupings ought to be made as farmers face an issue in picking between a high-yielding combination and a drought-liberal one with a yield push factor.[15] A couple of vermin might change the plant's response to abiotic stress factors.[16] Rice is the staple food of the world. Around 900 million in the world rely on rice as producers or buyers, and the overall interest for rice will augment to 536–551 million tons in 2030.[17] The situation with rice production in India is clearly associated with food security and doable improvements. Rice is exposed to various biotic and, moreover, abiotic stresses, which present risks to the rice production and food security. The gathering of strong opposition is an essential variety of farmers, which can direct the terrible effects of climate change on rice.[18,19] The status of rice production in India is straightforwardly connected with food security and feasible improvement. The reception of assortment with solid resistance is a principal variation proportion of ranchers, which can moderate the hurtful impacts of environmental change on rice. Besides, the growth of rice requires the long-term stability of geoenvironmental factors, particularly in the amount of rainfall received. Expanded ranch efficiency of rice ranchers can be achieved by further developing rice assortments with better return, better quality and market worth, and resistance to biotic and abiotic stresses (dry spells, floods, outrageous temperatures, and bugs and sicknesses). Changing to assortments that are impervious to environmental stress is among the most commonly used transformation measures for onranch and nonranch job variation methodologies.[20] Purulia region of West Bengal is arranged on the eastern edge of the Chhota Nagpur plateau, where precipitation is considered a restricting component for the effective development of farming. The region is not viewed as reasonable for the development of long-length crop assortments due to geonatural limits. So the current study expects to recognize the advantage cost proportion of marigold development. According to the rules of the India Meteorological Department, this region cannot be assigned as dry spell-inclined. The coarse-grained soil of the region is characterized by a low dampness holding limit. The top soil becomes extremely dry not long after a spell of heavy showers, which moves as surface runoff following the inclination of the area. In the event in which a significant part of this measure of surface runoff is captured, the issue of water shortage can be limited to an impressive degree. This locale is described by a higher temperature, sufficient splendid sun sparkle hours, and an impressive measure of normal yearly precipitation (1100 mm to 1500 mm), which can uphold countless cash crops and plant items. Moreover, the undulations in topography will advance the surface runoff component. Various examinations have proactively been made for the monetary investigation of rice,[21,22] maize,[23,24] potato,[25] cucumber,[26] cabbage,[27] soybean,[28] garlic,[29,30] ginger,[31] cotton,[32] onion,[33] pineapple,[34] sorghum,[35] sunflower,[36] tomato,[37] wheat,[38] and so forth in the various regions of the world. This multitude of studies has just thought about the financial viewpoints for the development of these harvests. The current review will feature both the financial and ecological viewpoints for the development of marigold in the review region to distinguish the monetary, social, and natural manageability. The study will likewise appraise the advantage cost proportion, ranch business pay, return over factor cost, and family work pay of marigold production based on the standard cost or expenses of information items. Besides, the problems of marigold production have also been identified, assessed, and ranked with the help of Garrett's ranking method, and finally, we have computed the SWOT matrix for the justification of possible potentialities and upcoming limitations for its proper growth. Since capital and human labor are the two essential components in farming, an emphasis has also been made on identifying the role of labor and capital in marigold production with their level of significance and percentage of variation in output.

## 12.2 METHODOLOGY

The study depends on both essential and optional perceptions. The information on the assessed expenses for the different parameters has been gathered from the five blocks of the Purulia district of West Bengal. A multistage examination strategy has been utilized for the choice of two villages from each of the five blocks. These five blocks are predominantly Jhalda, Kashipur, Santuri, Para, and Bundwan, which have been chosen from the various pieces of the locale with different geoenvironmental statuses. The current study depends on the example of 100 ranchers with 10 ranchers chosen randomly from each block. The greater part of the farming fields in the western part of the region is viewed as negligible and small because of some geoclimatic obstacles. The ranchers of these blocks are sorted into four kinds, in particular marginal, small, medium, and large, where the spans of land property are under 1 hectare, 1 to 2 hectares, 2 to 4 hectares, or more than 4 hectares, respectively. The information on factors like the expense

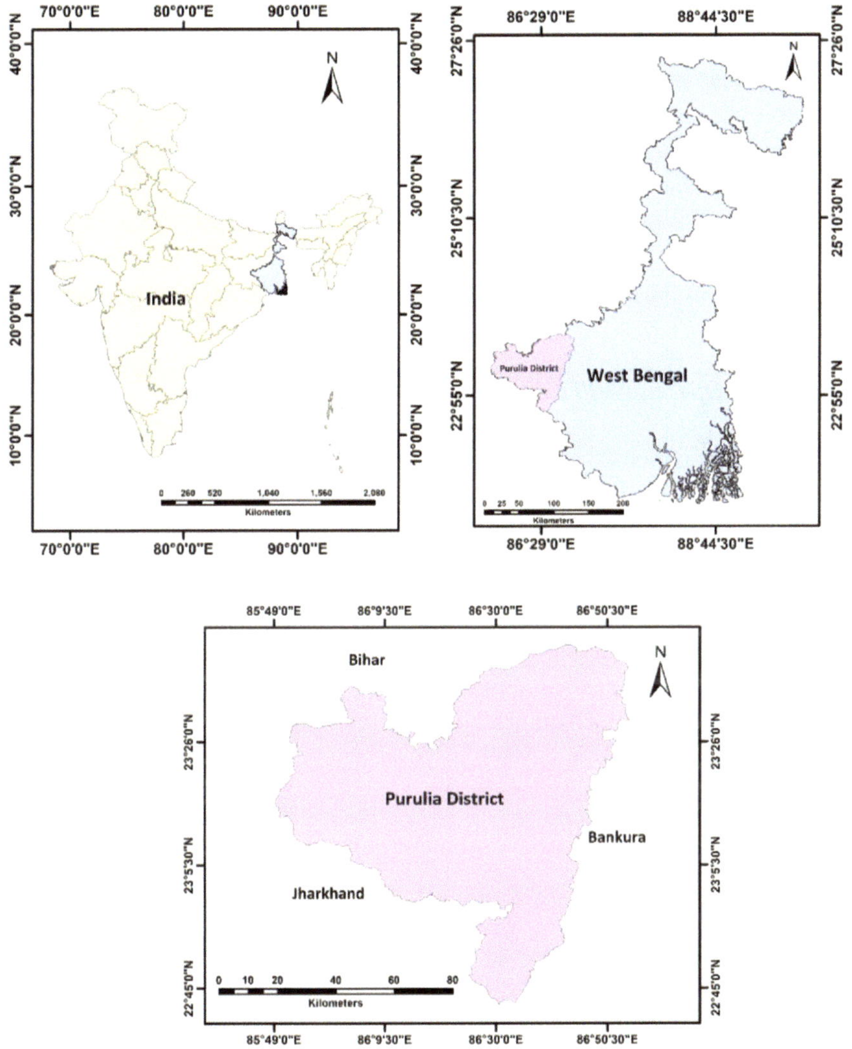


**FIGURE 12.1** Location map of the study area.

of establishing materials, transportation, composts and fertilizers, water systems, workers, pesticides, and so forth (factor expenses) and a few fixed costs like land income, the rental worth of possessed land, deterioration on fixed capital, and convergence on fixed capital has been accumulated from both the essential and optional overviews. For the assessment of the cost and advantage/return of various information on marigold cultivation in various ranch sizes, the basic normal has been worked out. For the positioning of possible requirements in the fruitful cultivation of marigold, Garrett's positioning method has been utilized. As indicated by this technique, the respondents/ranchers have been approached to dole out rank to all of the possible restricting variables, and the results of such rankings have been changed over into percentile positions by utilizing the Garret coefficient. The concentrate likewise features the strengths, weaknesses, opportunities, and threats (SWOT) for the marigold production in the district. The roles of workers and capital have been assessed through the Cobb Douglas creation assessment strategy.

### 12.2.1 COST-BENEFIT ANALYSIS

Cost A1: The expenses which the ranchers really incur including both money and kind consumption. It incorporates the following:

i. Wage for the recruited human workers
ii. Charges for bullock work
iii. Charges of apparatuses
iv. Cost of establishing materials
v. Cost of composts and manures
vi. Cost of plant assurance synthetic compounds or cost brought about for weed control
vii. Charges for the water system
viii. Cost of transportation
ix. Land income
x. Depreciation on fixed capital
xi. Interest on working capital

Cost $A_2$: Cost $A_1$ + the payable rent for leased-in land.

Cost $B_1$: Cost $A_2$ + interest incurred on fixed capital

Cost $B_2$: Cost $B_1$ + rental value of owned land + rental value of leased-in land

Cost $C_1$: Cost $B_1$ + imputed value of family labor

Cost $C_2$: Cost $B_2$ + imputed value of family labor

Cost $C_3$: Cost $C_2$ + 10% of cost $C_2$ (managerial cost)

Returns over variable cost (RVC) = Gross income – Cost $A_1$

Farm business income (FBI) = Gross income – Cost $A_2$

Family labor income (FLI) = Gross income – Cost $B_2$

### 12.2.2 POSITIONING OF IMPERATIVES

For the positioning of expected limitations in the effective cultivation of marigold in the Purulia district of West Bengal, Garrett's positioning procedure has been utilized. As per this strategy, the respondents/ranchers have been approached to assign rank to all of the expected restricting elements, and the results of such rankings have been changed over into percentile positions by utilizing the accompanying equation (eq. 12.1):

$$\text{Percentile position: } 100(\text{Rank}_{in} - 0.5)/N_j \quad (12.1)$$

where

$\text{Rank}_{in}$ = Rank allotted to the *i*th variable by the *n*th respondents
$N_j$ = Number of elements positioned by the *j*th respondents.

Every percentile position is changed over completely to Garrett's score esteem from the Garrett's positioning table.[26] The score upsides of the relative multitude of positions are then added to demonstrate the significance of the elements.

### 12.2.3 SWOT ANALYSIS

The current research depends solely on the essential overview where in excess of 100 households have been investigated. The study utilizes SWOT examination to provide recognizable proof of different issues and prospects of marigold cultivation in the said blocks of the district.

A SWOT examination procedure has been utilized to determine the best choices to foster the marigold production in the study area by mitigating the impact of future threats. The accompanying advances associated with this study are as follows:

i. Development of a lattice of exterior and interior elements.
ii. SWOT lattice examination.
iii. Development of a quantitative strategy programing matrix (QSPM).
iv. Priority is characterized by attractiveness scores.

Notwithstanding, the outer variable assessment grid (EFE or external factor evaluation framework) process utilizes five stages:

Stage 1: The initial step is to make an outer rundown, distinguish proof of elements, and separate openings into two gatherings.

Stage 2: Each component is assigned a weight. Each weight should have a worth somewhere in the range of 0 and 1 (or, on the other hand, in the event in which the scale is 10–100, a 10–100 range scale is utilized). 0 implies that the component is not significant, while 1 or 100 shows that the element is generally persuasive. Be that as it may, the absolute value of all loads is thought to be 1 or 100.

Stage 3: Each component is appraised from 1 to 4. The rating shows how powerful it is. The ongoing system answers this component. A rating shows regardless of whether a component is a huge threat (level = 1), a gentle threat (level = 2), a gentle opportunity (rank = 3), or a significant potentiality (rank = 4). On the off chance that a rating size of 1–4 is utilized, the qualities ought to be 4 or 3, and a shortcoming should be scored at 1 or 2.

Stage 4: In this step, weight is duplicated by the rating.

The internal factor evaluation (IFE) framework is an essential administration device used to assess qualities and shortcomings in practical business regions. IFE, along with the EFE grid, is a technique improvement device that can be utilized to assess the consequences of the organization's exercises compared to the organization's interior assets and shortcomings. An IFE grid can be made utilizing the accompanying 3 stages:

Stage 1: The initial step is to recognize the strengths and shortcomings.

Stage 2: The IFE grid is allotted loads in the range of 0.00 to 1.00 for each component, which shows the relative significance of each factor. 0 implies that it is not significant, while 1 implies that the variable is vital.

Stage 3: Practitioners normally use appraisals on the accompanying scale from 1 to 4. The rating demonstrates whether the variable addresses a significant shortcoming (grade = 1) or a minor shortcoming (grade = 2).

### *12.2.3.1 BASIC STANDARDS OF QUANTITATIVE STRATEGIC PLANNING MATRIX (QSPM)*

The grid (QSPM) is broadly used to assess their outside and inward conditions deliberately. It cautiously assesses the various advantages and disadvantages, makes choices, plays out the examination, and afterward selects an explicit strategy. The QSPM approach attempts to pick, unbiasedly, the best business methodology. The left segment of QSPM comprises exterior and interior factor components. The left section of the QSPM is acquired straightforwardly from the SWOT table. The top line comprises conceivable elective methodologies obtained from the SWOT investigation. The QSPM attractiveness score (AS) shows that every recorded element is significant or alluring to any elective methodology. The allure of the variables is addressed by the numbers 1 to 4 (1 = not appealing, 2 = to some degree alluring, 3 = sensible alluring, and 4 = exceptionally alluring). The sum of the total attractiveness score (STAS) is determined by adding the general engaging quality rating to every section of the QSPM procedure.

### *12.2.4 COBB–DOUGLAS PRODUCTION CAPABILITY*

For focusing on the data yield relationship of creating different harvests, Cobb–Douglas production ability has been fitted by using the given equation (eq. 12.2):

$$\text{Log } Y = \log a + b1 \log XL + b2 \log Xc \tag{12.2}$$

where Y = yield, XL = work, Xc = capital, b1 and b2 = versatility coefficients, and a = steady term.

To take a gander at the impact of different data resources (particularly workers and capital) on gross and net returns, the potential gains of the coefficient of confirmation are not entirely set in stone for every predominant size. Cobb–Douglas creation capability is comprehensively used in monetary perspectives, and its effectiveness is focused on across various regions. In this hypothesis, the development of the capacity application, arrangement crashing, and project risk assessment associated with a range of improvement projects are researched. Existing investigations on improvement time-cost compromise rarely explore the start of the crashing cost, which is described as required to contract the endeavor to the best range. In the ongoing composition, crashing cost capacity is either acknowledged as missing a ton of legitimization or comes from an improvised backslide examination of legitimate data from a couple of certified adventures. Cobb–Douglas creation capacity, which describes the piece of work and stuff expected considering the creation rate, gives a really important piece of exhibiting the cost abilities in the improvement of time-cost compromise issues during the scheduled crashing process.

## 12.3 RESULTS

### *12.3.1 PER SECTION OF LAND-ASSESSED VARIABLE EXPENSE OF MARIGOLD DEVELOPMENT*

The generally assessed variable expense for the marigold production in a section of landholding in the review region is recognized as Rs. 33,155.00, which differs from Rs. 32,500.00 in the peripheral land property to Rs. 33,550.00 in the enormous ranch sizes. Per section of land-assessed costs on different information for marigold production are introduced in subtleties in Table 12.1, which shows that the general expense of establishing materials for marigolds is assessed as Rs. 8800.00; however, it differs from negligible to huge homestead sizes. The typical assessed cost of establishing material for the minimal land property is Rs. 8300.00, which increments at the pace of Rs. 8800.00 and Rs. 9000.00 for the small and medium landholdings. However, for the enormous ranch measures, the standard expense of establishing material is viewed as Rs. 8850.00 (Table 12.1). As marigold production is a work-intensive endeavor, among every one of the assessed expenses of information things, the charge of work is recognized to be higher. The generally assessed compensation of work with the incorporation of charges of machinery is recognized as Rs. 11025.00, which ranges between Rs. 10,850.00 and Rs. 11,200.00 for the medium and large land possessions, respectively. The assessed general pay of recruited workers is determined as Rs. 6300.00; however, it differs from minor (Rs. 6000.00) to huge ranch sizes (Rs. 6600.00). Dissimilar to the pay of recruited workers, the compensation of family workers is viewed as declining with the increase in ranch size. The pay of family work for the minor ranch sizes is assessed as Rs. 2900.00, which declines at the pace of Rs. 2800.00, Rs. 2500.00, and Rs. 2400.00 for the small, medium, and large land estimates, respectively (Table 12.1). Since Purulia town is the principal market of the multitude of delivered merchandise, accordingly, the expense of transportation increases at the rate of Rs. 9.00 per km with the expanding distance from the Purulia town. The general expense of transportation is determined as Rs. 2500.00, and this rate is viewed as indistinguishable, independent of the ranch sizes. As expressed before, however, the study area gets a normal 1100–1500 mm of precipitation every year, except that the dryness of the locale is viewed as a hard reality. During rainstorm season, PET is without a doubt lower than the aggregate sum of precipitation coming about into an overabundance water measure of 500 to 800 mm, which moves as surface overflow. So, giving water systems to the standing yields is difficult for the review region. The general expense of the water system for marigold production in the region is viewed as Rs. 1392.5, which changes from Rs. 1450.00 for the small ranch sizes to Rs. 1350.00 for the large landholdings.

### *12.3.1.1 ASSESSMENT OF FIXED COSTS*

The expenses of depreciation on fixed capital, interest on fixed capital, land income, and rental worth of claimed land are fundamentally remembered for the class of fixed cost, among which the rental worth of the possessed land, which is known for Rs. 3200.00, is viewed as higher than the other fixed expenses of the classification. The generally assessed average fixed cost is determined as Rs. 3662.5, which ranges from Rs. 3800.00 for the minimal land possessions to Rs. 3550.00 for the large ranch sizes (Table 12.1).

**TABLE 12.1** Estimated Cost for Per Acre Cultivation of Marigold across the Different Farm Sizes in the Purulia District of West Bengal.

| Types of costs | Particulars | Farm size | | | | |
|---|---|---|---|---|---|---|
| | | Marginal | Small | Medium | Large | Overall |
| Variable costs | Planting material | 8300 | 8800 | 9000 | 8850 | 8737.5 |
| | Manure and fertilizer | 6000 | 6300 | 6500 | 6600 | 6350 |
| | Plant protection | 1500 | 1400 | 1320 | 1250 | 1367.5 |
| | Irrigation | 1400 | 1450 | 1370 | 1350 | 1392.5 |
| | Transportation | 2500 | 2500 | 2500 | 2500 | 2500 |
| | Hired | 6000 | 6200 | 6400 | 6600 | 6300 |
| | Family | 2900 | 2800 | 2500 | 2400 | 2650 |
| | Machinery | 2100 | 2050 | 1950 | 2000 | 2025 |
| | Interest on working capital | 1500 | 1700 | 1500 | 1750 | 1612.5 |
| | **Total variable cost** | **32,200** | **33,200** | **33,040** | **33,300** | **32,935** |
| Fixed costs | Depreciation on fixed capital | 180 | 180 | 165 | 145 | 167.5 |
| | Interest on fixed capital | 390 | 290 | 205 | 175 | 265 |
| | Land revenue | 30 | 30 | 30 | 30 | 30 |
| | Rental value | 3200 | 3200 | 3200 | 3200 | 3200 |
| | **Total fixed cost** | **3800** | **3700** | **3600** | **3550** | **3662.5** |

#### 12.3.1.2 ESTIMATION OF ABSOLUTE EXPENSE

The per section of land cost of different information things is worked out, and the subtleties are introduced in Table 12.2, which shows that the assessed all-out cost of marigold production is determined as Rs. 36,597.5, which is viewed as higher for the small ranch sizes (Rs. 36,900.00), trailed by the large, medium, and peripheral ranch sizes with the assessed complete expenses of Rs. 36,850.00, Rs. 36,640.00, and Rs. 36,000.00, respectively.

#### 12.3.1.3 ASSESSMENT OF DIFFERENT EXPENSES

Cost A1/A2 (with the rejection of pay of family work from the classification of variable expenses and consideration of deterioration on fixed capital and land income from the classification of fixed costs), otherwise called the functional expense of a ranch, is assessed as Rs. 30,482.5, which changes from Rs. 29,510.00 for the marginal ranch sizes to Rs. 31,075.00 for the large ranch sizes. Cost B1 with the incorporation of interest on fixed capital to the expense A2 amounts to Rs. 29,900.00 for the negligible ranch sizes, which increments at the pace of Rs. 30,900.00, Rs. 30,940.00, and Rs. 31,250.00 for the small, medium, and large landholdings, respectively. Cost B2, which incorporates the rental worth of possessed land to the expense B1, is assessed to be higher for the large ranch sizes (Rs. 34,450.00) and declines with the decrease of the ranch sizes. Costs C1 and C2, the expansion of the credited worth of family work to the costs B1 and B2, respectively, are viewed as Rs. 33,397.5 and Rs. 36,597.5, respectively. Both of these expenses (C1 and C2) are higher for the small farm sizes. However, the distinctions of expenses (C1 and C2) for the small and medium estimated land possessions are minimal, yet significant contrasts are noted between the expenses of minor and small ranch sizes. Cost C3 with the consideration of administrative expenses for cost C2 is assessed as Rs. 40,262.25 on a normal basis, which changes from at least Rs. 39,600.00 for the peripheral land possessions to a limit of Rs. 40,590.00 for the small ranch sizes (Table 12.2).

#### 12.3.1.4 INVESTIGATION OF INFORMATION YIELD RELATIONSHIPS

In the current study, an endeavor has likewise been made to distinguish the connection between the gross return and the assessed different expenses, for example, from A1 to C3, known as the information yield relationship.

The proportion of gross pay to cost A1 is viewed as higher for the large ranch sizes (1:2.62) followed by the medium (1:2.58), small (1:2.48), and large (1:2.39) land possessions. Comparative outcomes are obtained for the proportion of gross pay to cost B1 and the proportion of gross pay to cost B2. In both the cases, large landholdings represent the most elevated proportion.

**TABLE 12.2** Estimation of Various Costs in Marigold Cultivation across the Different Farm Sizes.

| Types of costs | Farm sizes | | | | |
|---|---|---|---|---|---|
| | Marginal | Small | Medium | Large | Overall |
| $A_1$ | 29,510 | 30,610 | 30,735 | 31,075 | 30,482.5 |
| $A_2$ | 29,510 | 30,610 | 30,735 | 31,075 | 30,482.5 |
| $B_1$ | 29,900 | 30,900 | 30,940 | 31,250 | 30,747.5 |
| $B_2$ | 33,100 | 34,100 | 34,140 | 34,450 | 33,947.5 |
| $C_1$ | 32,800 | 33,700 | 33,440 | 33,650 | 33,397.5 |
| $C_2$ | 36,000 | 36,900 | 36,640 | 36,850 | 36,597.5 |
| $C_3$ | 39,600 | 40,590 | 40,304 | 40,555 | 40,262.25 |

The general proportion of gross revisitation of cost C1 is identified as 1:2.28, which changes from at least 1:2.15 on account of minimal land sizes to a limit of 1:2.42 for the large land possessions. In particular, the general proportion of gross pay to the expense C3, otherwise called the advantage cost proportion, is assessed as 1:1.91, which ranges between 1:2.01 for the large ranch sizes and 1:1.97 for the medium measured land sizes (Table 12.3).

**TABLE 12.3** Input–Output Relationship of the Different Items of Marigold Cultivation across Various Farm Sizes.

| Basis | Farm size | | | | |
|---|---|---|---|---|---|
| | Marginal | Small | Medium | Large | Overall |
| On cost '$A_1$' basis | 2.385632 | 2.479582 | 2.576867 | 2.619469 | 2.517017961 |
| On cost '$B_1$' basis | 2.354515 | 2.456311 | 2.559793 | 2.6048 | 2.495324823 |
| On cost '$B_2$' basis | 2.126888 | 2.225806 | 2.311059 | 2.35942 | 2.252146474 |
| On cost '$C_1$' basis | 2.146341 | 2.252226 | 2.368421 | 2.419019 | 2.297327644 |
| On cost '$C_2$' basis | 1.955556 | 2.056911 | 2.161572 | 2.208955 | 2.096454676 |
| On cost '$C_3$' basis | 1.777778 | 1.869919 | 1.965066 | 2.007151 | 1.905631205 |

### 12.3.1.5 MONETARY RETURNS OF MARIGOLD PRODUCTION

The efficiency of marigold production per section of landholding is assessed as 34.88 quintals; however, it changes with the varieties of ranch sizes. It is observed to be higher on account of large ranch sizes (37 quintals/section of land) trailed by the medium, small, and minor land possessions with an assessed efficiency of 36 quintals/section of land, 34.5 quintals/section of land, and 32 quintals/section of land, respectively. The standard cost per quintal of marigold production is accounted to be Rs. 2200.00. The monetary returns of marigold production based on the complicated connection between net return and gross expense (C3) have been worked out and introduced in Table 12.4. As far as the pay measure is concerned, the following table (Table 12.4) shows that the gross return of marigold production per section of land is viewed as a limit of Rs. 81,400.00 for the large ranch sizes followed by the medium, small, and marginal land properties with the gross returns of Rs. 79,200.00, Rs. 75,900.00, and Rs. 70,400, respectively. The most reduced gross return of the marginal land property is the aftereffect of the least efficiency measure of 32 quintals/section of land. Essentially, the gross expenses, net returns, and advantage cost proportion of marigold production in the different ranch sizes have been worked out and introduced in a similar table, which likewise shows a comparative pattern like gross return as this is viewed as higher for the large ranch sizes and declines with the decrease of ranch sizes. The distinctions between gross returns and gross expenses are distinguished as Rs. 30,470.00, Rs. 35,310.00, Rs. 38,503.00, and Rs. 40,565.00 for the marginal, small, medium, and large land properties, respectively. From the continuous conversation, it is obvious that the advantage cost proportion of marigold harvesting is viewed as a limit of 1:1.99 for the large ranch sizes and declines with the downfall of land size to turn into at least 1:1.76 for the marginal ranch sizes. The current paper is likewise extremely significant as it has assessed the family work pay, ranch business pay, and returns over factor expenses of a homestead business. Returns over factor cost of marigold production in the region with the avoidance of cost A1 from the gross pay are viewed as a limit of Rs. 50,325.00 for the large ranches followed by the medium, small, and minimal land properties with the return measures of Rs. 48,465.00, Rs. 45,290.00, and Rs. 40,890.00, respectively. The by and large assessed family work pay for the marigold production is determined as Rs. 42777.5, which goes from a limit of Rs. 46,950.00 for the large land to at least Rs. 37,300.00 for the minimal land possessions (Table 12.4).

**TABLE 12.4** Benefit Cost Analysis of Per Acre Marigold Cultivation in the Purulia District of West Bengal.

| Bases | Farm size | | | | |
|---|---|---|---|---|---|
| | **Marginal** | **Small** | **Medium** | **Large** | **Overall** |
| Average yield (quintal/acre) | 32 | 34.5 | 36 | 37 | 34.875 |
| Price (Rs./quintal) | 2200 | 2200 | 2200 | 2200 | 2200 |
| Gross returns (Rs./acre) | 70,400 | 75,900 | 79,200 | 81,400 | 76,725 |
| Gross costs (Rs./acre) | 39,930 | 40,590 | 40,697 | 40,835 | 40,513 |
| Net returns (Rs./acre) | 30,470 | 35,310 | 38,503 | 40,565 | 36,212 |
| BC ratio | 1.763085 | 1.869919 | 1.946089 | 1.993388 | 1.893836546 |
| Gross income | 70,400 | 75,900 | 79,200 | 81,400 | 76,725 |
| Returns over variable cost (RVC) = Gross income – Cost $A_1$ | 40,890 | 45,290 | 48,465 | 50,325 | 46,242.5 |
| Farm business income (FBI) = Gross income – Cost $A_2$ | 40,890 | 45,290 | 48,465 | 50,325 | 46,242.5 |
| Family labor income (FLI) = Gross income – Cost $B_2$ | 37,300 | 41,800 | 45,060 | 46,950 | 42,777.5 |

### *12.3.2 RANKING OF FACTORIAL LIMITATIONS IN MARIGOLD PRODUCTION*

The production of marigold in the review region should not be liberated from its limits. A complete number of ten requirements with their all-out scores have been worked out and introduced in the following table (Table 12.5). Insufficient stock of composts, establishing materials, greater expense of the water system, and expanding climatic variables are a portion of the elements recorded as expected requirements, and these limitations have been positioned utilizing Garrett's positioning strategy. A larger percentage of the ranchers have communicated the absence of information on marigold production as rank 1 among the rundown of the requirements with an absolute score of 5461, followed by the lacking stock of seeds (rank 2), the deficient stock of manures (rank 3), and cost changes on the lookout (rank 4) with Garrett's all-out scores of 5447, 5427, and 5332, respectively. As per the respondents, expanding climatic fluctuations, the absence of recruited workers during the peak production phase, higher pay of employed workers, and the absence of legislative help will likewise show up as significant restricting elements for the fruitful presentation of marigold in the region

(Table 12.6). The observations of 7 individuals and their consolidated viewpoints have been recorded and presented in Table 12.7, which indicates that the factors like inadequate knowledge and insufficient supply of farming manures are some of the very limiting constraint factors for the marigold production in the study area.

**TABLE 12.5** List of Major Potential Constraints for Marigold Cultivation in the Purulia District of West Bengal.

| F | Factors |
|---|---|
| F1 | Higher wage of hired labor |
| F2 | Inadequate supply of planting materials |
| F3 | Lack of hired laborers during the peak time of cultivation |
| F4 | Increasing climatic variability |
| F5 | Higher cost of irrigation |
| F6 | Inadequate supply of plant protection chemicals including weed control |
| F7 | Lack of governmental support |
| F8 | Price fluctuations in the market |
| F9 | Lack of proper knowledge for cultivation |
| F10 | Inadequate supply of fertilizes and manures |

**TABLE 12.6** Ranking of Potential Constraints in Marigold Cultivation of the Purulia District of West Bengal.

| **Factors** | **Rank** | | | | | | | | | | | | |
|---|---|---|---|---|---|---|---|---|---|---|---|---|---|
| | **1** | **2** | **3** | **4** | **5** | **6** | **7** | **8** | **9** | **10** | **Total** | **Total score/100** | **Rank** |
| F1 | 1148 | 280 | 441 | 627 | 416 | 1363 | 168 | 180 | 261 | 162 | 5046 | 50.46 | 7 |
| F2 | 2296 | 280 | 693 | 285 | 520 | 329 | 420 | 216 | 174 | 234 | 5447 | 54.47 | 2 |
| F3 | 574 | 840 | 504 | 570 | 1404 | 470 | 168 | 324 | 232 | 90 | 5176 | 51.76 | 6 |
| F4 | 1148 | 770 | 567 | 684 | 520 | 329 | 252 | 720 | 116 | 126 | 5232 | 52.32 | 5 |
| F5 | 574 | 770 | 252 | 855 | 520 | 329 | 336 | 360 | 696 | 72 | 4764 | 47.64 | 9 |
| F6 | 328 | 980 | 756 | 399 | 676 | 329 | 252 | 144 | 261 | 432 | 4557 | 45.57 | 10 |
| F7 | 820 | 350 | 441 | 798 | 312 | 658 | 1050 | 288 | 116 | 126 | 4959 | 49.59 | 8 |
| F8 | 656 | 980 | 1638 | 114 | 624 | 517 | 294 | 144 | 203 | 162 | 5332 | 53.32 | 4 |
| F9 | 984 | 1680 | 630 | 342 | 208 | 517 | 504 | 216 | 290 | 90 | 5461 | 54.61 | 1 |
| F10 | 738 | 1190 | 441 | 1539 | 624 | 188 | 252 | 108 | 203 | 144 | 5427 | 54.27 | 3 |

**TABLE 12.7** Factor Ranking by the Individuals.

| Consolidated | | | | | | | | | | 1 | Participant 1 | | | | | | 1 | | | |
|---|---|---|---|---|---|---|---|---|---|---|---|---|---|---|---|---|---|---|---|---|
| 1 | 2 | 3 | 4 | 5 | 6 | 7 | 8 | 9 | 10 | | 1 | 2 | 3 | 4 | 5 | 6 | 7 | 8 | 9 | 10 |
| | 1 | 3 | 2 | 1 | 0 | 0 | 0 | 0 | 0 | 1 | **1** | 1 | 3 | 2 | 1 | 0 | 0 | 0 | 0 | 0 |
| 1 | | 3 | 3 | 1 | 0 | 0 | 0 | 0 | 0 | 2 | 1 | **1** | 3 | 3 | 1 | 0 | 0 | 0 | 0 | 0 |
| 0.33 | 0.33 | | 1 | 0.33 | 0 | 0 | 0 | 0 | 0 | 3 | 1/3 | 1/3 | **1** | 1 | 1/3 | 0 | 0 | 0 | 0 | 0 |
| 0.5 | 0.33 | 1 | | 0.33 | 0 | 0 | 0 | 0 | 0 | 4 | 1/2 | 1/3 | 1 | **1** | 1/3 | 0 | 0 | 0 | 0 | 0 |
| 1 | 1 | 3 | 3 | | 0 | 0 | 0 | 0 | 0 | 5 | 1 | 1 | 3 | 3 | **1** | 0 | 0 | 0 | 0 | 0 |
| 0 | 0 | 0 | 0 | 0 | | 0 | 0 | 0 | 0 | 6 | 0 | 0 | 0 | 0 | 0 | **1** | 0 | 0 | 0 | 0 |
| 0 | 0 | 0 | 0 | 0 | 0 | | 0 | 0 | 0 | 7 | 0 | 0 | 0 | 0 | 0 | 0 | **1** | 0 | 0 | 0 |
| 0 | 0 | 0 | 0 | 0 | 0 | 0 | | 0 | 0 | 8 | 0 | 0 | 0 | 0 | 0 | 0 | 0 | **1** | 0 | 0 |
| 0 | 0 | 0 | 0 | 0 | 0 | 0 | 0 | | 0 | 9 | 0 | 0 | 0 | 0 | 0 | 0 | 0 | 0 | **1** | 0 |
| 0 | 0 | 0 | 0 | 0 | 0 | 0 | 0 | 0 | | 10 | 0 | 0 | 0 | 0 | 0 | 0 | 0 | 0 | 0 | **1** |
| **Participant 2** | | | | | | **1** | | | | **3** | **Participant 3** | | | | | | **1** | | | |
| 1 | 2 | 3 | 4 | 5 | 6 | 7 | 8 | 9 | 10 | | 1 | 2 | 3 | 4 | 5 | 6 | 7 | 8 | 9 | 10 |
| **1** | 1 | 1 | 1 | 1 | 0 | 0 | 0 | 0 | 0 | 1 | **1** | 1 | 1 | 1 | 1 | 0 | 0 | 0 | 0 | 0 |
| 1 | **1** | 1 | 1 | 1 | 0 | 0 | 0 | 0 | 0 | 2 | 1 | **1** | 1 | 1 | 1 | 0 | 0 | 0 | 0 | 0 |
| 1 | 1 | **1** | 1 | 1 | 0 | 0 | 0 | 0 | 0 | 3 | 1 | 1 | **1** | 1 | 1 | 0 | 0 | 0 | 0 | 0 |
| 1 | 1 | 1 | **1** | 1 | 0 | 0 | 0 | 0 | 0 | 4 | 1 | 1 | 1 | **1** | 1 | 0 | 0 | 0 | 0 | 0 |
| 1 | 1 | 1 | 1 | **1** | 0 | 0 | 0 | 0 | 0 | 5 | 1 | 1 | 1 | 1 | **1** | 0 | 0 | 0 | 0 | 0 |
| 0 | 0 | 0 | 0 | 0 | **1** | 0 | 0 | 0 | 0 | 6 | 0 | 0 | 0 | 0 | 0 | **1** | 0 | 0 | 0 | 0 |
| 0 | 0 | 0 | 0 | 0 | 0 | **1** | 0 | 0 | 0 | 7 | 0 | 0 | 0 | 0 | 0 | 0 | **1** | 0 | 0 | 0 |
| 0 | 0 | 0 | 0 | 0 | 0 | 0 | **1** | 0 | 0 | 8 | 0 | 0 | 0 | 0 | 0 | 0 | 0 | **1** | 0 | 0 |
| 0 | 0 | 0 | 0 | 0 | 0 | 0 | 0 | **1** | 0 | 9 | 0 | 0 | 0 | 0 | 0 | 0 | 0 | 0 | **1** | 0 |
| 0 | 0 | 0 | 0 | 0 | 0 | 0 | 0 | 0 | **1** | 10 | 0 | 0 | 0 | 0 | 0 | 0 | 0 | 0 | 0 | **1** |

**TABLE 12.7** *(Continued)*

| Participant 4 | | | | | | 1 | | | | 5 | Participant 5 | | | | | | 1 | | | |
|---|---|---|---|---|---|---|---|---|---|---|---|---|---|---|---|---|---|---|---|---|
| 1 | 2 | 3 | 4 | 5 | 6 | 7 | 8 | 9 | 10 | | 1 | 2 | 3 | 4 | 5 | 6 | 7 | 8 | 9 | 10 |
| **1** | 1 | 1 | 1 | 1 | 0 | 0 | 0 | 0 | 0 | 1 | **1** | 1 | 1 | 1 | 1 | 0 | 0 | 0 | 0 | 0 |
| 1 | **1** | 1 | 1 | 1 | 0 | 0 | 0 | 0 | 0 | 2 | 1 | **1** | 1 | 1 | 1 | 0 | 0 | 0 | 0 | 0 |
| 1 | 1 | **1** | 1 | 1 | 0 | 0 | 0 | 0 | 0 | 3 | 1 | 1 | **1** | 1 | 1 | 0 | 0 | 0 | 0 | 0 |
| 1 | 1 | 1 | **1** | 1 | 0 | 0 | 0 | 0 | 0 | 4 | 1 | 1 | 1 | **1** | 1 | 0 | 0 | 0 | 0 | 0 |
| 1 | 1 | 1 | 1 | **1** | 0 | 0 | 0 | 0 | 0 | 5 | 1 | 1 | 1 | 1 | **1** | 0 | 0 | 0 | 0 | 0 |
| 0 | 0 | 0 | 0 | 0 | **1** | 0 | 0 | 0 | 0 | 6 | 0 | 0 | 0 | 0 | 0 | **1** | 0 | 0 | 0 | 0 |
| 0 | 0 | 0 | 0 | 0 | 0 | **1** | 0 | 0 | 0 | 7 | 0 | 0 | 0 | 0 | 0 | 0 | **1** | 0 | 0 | 0 |
| 0 | 0 | 0 | 0 | 0 | 0 | 0 | **1** | 0 | 0 | 8 | 0 | 0 | 0 | 0 | 0 | 0 | 0 | **1** | 0 | 0 |
| 0 | 0 | 0 | 0 | 0 | 0 | 0 | 0 | **1** | 0 | 9 | 0 | 0 | 0 | 0 | 0 | 0 | 0 | 0 | **1** | 0 |
| 0 | 0 | 0 | 0 | 0 | 0 | 0 | 0 | 0 | **1** | 10 | 0 | 0 | 0 | 0 | 0 | 0 | 0 | 0 | 0 | **1** |
| **Participant 6** | | | | | | **1** | | | | 7 | **Participant 7** | | | | | | **1** | | | |
| 1 | 2 | 3 | 4 | 5 | 6 | 7 | 8 | 9 | 10 | | 1 | 2 | 3 | 4 | 5 | 6 | 7 | 8 | 9 | 10 |
| **1** | 1 | 1 | 1 | 1 | 0 | 0 | 0 | 0 | 0 | 1 | **1** | 1 | 1 | 1 | 1 | 0 | 0 | 0 | 0 | 0 |
| 1 | **1** | 1 | 1 | 1 | 0 | 0 | 0 | 0 | 0 | 2 | 1 | **1** | 1 | 1 | 1 | 0 | 0 | 0 | 0 | 0 |
| 1 | 1 | **1** | 1 | 1 | 0 | 0 | 0 | 0 | 0 | 3 | 1 | 1 | **1** | 1 | 1 | 0 | 0 | 0 | 0 | 0 |
| 1 | 1 | 1 | **1** | 1 | 0 | 0 | 0 | 0 | 0 | 4 | 1 | 1 | 1 | **1** | 1 | 0 | 0 | 0 | 0 | 0 |
| 1 | 1 | 1 | 1 | **1** | 0 | 0 | 0 | 0 | 0 | 5 | 1 | 1 | 1 | 1 | **1** | 0 | 0 | 0 | 0 | 0 |
| 0 | 0 | 0 | 0 | 0 | **1** | 0 | 0 | 0 | 0 | 6 | 0 | 0 | 0 | 0 | 0 | **1** | 0 | 0 | 0 | 0 |
| 0 | 0 | 0 | 0 | 0 | 0 | **1** | 0 | 0 | 0 | 7 | 0 | 0 | 0 | 0 | 0 | 0 | **1** | 0 | 0 | 0 |
| 0 | 0 | 0 | 0 | 0 | 0 | 0 | **1** | 0 | 0 | 8 | 0 | 0 | 0 | 0 | 0 | 0 | 0 | **1** | 0 | 0 |
| 0 | 0 | 0 | 0 | 0 | 0 | 0 | 0 | **1** | 0 | 9 | 0 | 0 | 0 | 0 | 0 | 0 | 0 | 0 | **1** | 0 |
| 0 | 0 | 0 | 0 | 0 | 0 | 0 | 0 | 0 | **1** | 10 | 0 | 0 | 0 | 0 | 0 | 0 | 0 | 0 | 0 | **1** |

### 12.3.3 SWOT ANALYSIS

In the present paper, the SWOT examination procedure has been utilized to explore the qualities, shortcomings, future prospects, and limitations of the cultivating framework in the Purulia district of West Bengal. The example size of 100 ranchers has been chosen by arbitrary inspection from the community development (CD) blocks of Jhalda, Kashipur, Santuri, Para, and Bundwan. Ommani (2011)[39] utilized SWOT examinations to investigate the different issues in agribusiness. The technique for SWOT examination utilized by Ommani (2011) has been used in the current paper to explore the different open doors and dangers in marigold production. For all the CD blocks, the component of market facilities is distinguished as the most significant strength with a weighted score of 0.32 (Table 12.8). For the studied CD blocks, satisfactory precipitation is also viewed as a significant strength for the successful innovations in floriculture. This region likewise gets an impressive amount of brilliant daylight and radiation. This component is likewise thought to be a significant strength for the region with a weighted score of 0.24 (Table 12.8). However, the district gets a significant amount of precipitation, yet dry spells are the intermittent peculiarities of the area. In this way, the dry season is considered a significant soft spot for a greater part of the CD blocks. For a larger part of the chosen CD blocks, the element of satisfactory precipitation is distinguished as having huge strength. Then again, over-reliance on precipitation, shortcoming of agro-based industry, and absence of water protection rehearsals are a portion of the shortcomings recognized for a larger part of the CD blocks (Table 12.8). Furthermore, the market framework, transportation, credit support, and so on in the district are additionally observed to be immature. Opportunities for cultivation of other cash crops, expanding support by the public authority for farming turn of events, presentation of new advances in horticulture, and so on are a portion of the significant open doors for the horticultural possibility of the CD blocks. The future possibility of farming in the region will without a doubt rely on the minimization of the dangers. Expanding climatic changeability and value vacillations of harvests in the business sector have been recognized as significant threats for the study area.

#### 12.3.3.1 QSPM APPROACH

The QSPM is intended for the evaluation of the internal and external conditions of a business framework.[39] The framework conducts inside-and-out

**TABLE 12.8** SWOT Analysis in Agriculture.

| **Strengths** | **Weight** | **Score** | **Weighted score** | |
|---|---|---|---|---|
| Sufficient amount of rainfall | 0.05 | 4 | 0.2 | |
| Sunshine hours and radiation for a long time | 0.06 | 4 | 0.24 | |
| Adequate amount of labor force | 0.04 | 3 | 0.12 | **Internal factor evaluation matrix (IFEM)** |
| Application of new technology in agriculture | 0.02 | 3 | 0.06 | |
| Largescale variety of natural resources | 0.03 | 3 | 0.09 | |
| Practicing agroecological techniques | 0.02 | 3 | 0.06 | |
| Continuous support from the government | 0.09 | 3 | 0.27 | |
| Connection with a number of development organizations | 0.07 | 3 | 0.21 | |
| Availability of market facilities | 0.08 | 4 | 0.32 | |
| **Total** | | | **1.57** | |
| **Weaknesses** | **Weight** | **Score** | **Weighted score** | |
| Less diversification of crops | 0.06 | 1 | 0.06 | |
| High dependency on rainfall | 0.07 | 1 | 0.07 | |
| Shortcomings and limitations of the agro-based industry | 0.05 | 2 | 0.1 | |
| Problem of disintegrated landholdings | 0.06 | 1 | 0.06 | **Total weighted score 2.28** |
| Lack of market infrastructure, storage, transportation, credit support facilities, etc. | 0.03 | 2 | 0.06 | |
| Dearth of research facilities in agriculture | 0.06 | 1 | 0.06 | |
| Lack of availability of water conservation practices | 0.05 | 2 | 0.1 | |
| Largescale surface runoff | 0.04 | 2 | 0.08 | |
| Occurrence of drought | 0.06 | 1 | 0.06 | |
| Less investment of the private sector in agriculture | 0.03 | 1 | 0.03 | |
| Presence and active role of middleman | 0.03 | 1 | 0.03 | |
| **Total** | | | **0.71** | |

**TABLE 12.8** *(Continued)*

| **Strengths** | **Weight** | **Score** | **Weighted score** | |
|---|---|---|---|---|
| Opportunities | Weight | Score | Weighted score | |
| Scope for horticulture and other cash crops | 0.07 | 3 | 0.21 | |
| Increasing agro-based industries | 0.04 | 3 | 0.12 | |
| Development and adoption of new technologies | 0.06 | 4 | 0.24 | |
| Largescale governmental support for agriculture | 0.06 | 4 | 0.24 | |
| Largescale diversification in agriculture | 0.07 | 4 | 0.28 | **External factor evaluation matrix (EFEM)** |
| Largescale scope of organic farming | 0.04 | 3 | 0.12 | |
| Prospects of development for the food-processing sector | 0.04 | 3 | 0.12 | |
| Opportunities for agroecological practices | 0.04 | 3 | 0.12 | |
| Growing demand in the market for alternative crops | 0.05 | 4 | 0.2 | |
| **Total** | | | **1.65** | |
| **Threats** | **Weight** | **Score** | **Weighted score** | |
| Presence of a high risk of crop production | 0.06 | 2 | 0.12 | |
| Fluctuation of the price of crops in the market | 0.09 | 1 | 0.09 | |
| Largescale climatic variability | 0.12 | 1 | 0.12 | |
| Some crops may have a lower price | 0.06 | 1 | 0.06 | |
| Degradation of land | 0.07 | 1 | 0.07 | **Total weighted score** |
| Size of the agricultural field | 0.05 | 2 | 0.1 | |
| Less interest of people in agriculture | 0.08 | 2 | 0.16 | |
| **Total** | | | **0.72** | |

exploration to distinguish and assess the other options. Based on that, a specific activity is chosen. For the study area, seven weakness–threat (WT) strategies have been listed (Table 12.9). For a larger part of the chosen CD blocks, expanding the coverage of harvests is viewed as the most appealing key element with a sum of total attractiveness scores (STASs) of 5.57 (Barjora), 5.22 (Santuri), 5.5 (Jhalda-I), 5.22 (Jaypur), and 5.4 (Purulia-I) (Table 12.10). The advancement of the agro-based industry is likewise viewed as a critical key element with STASs of 5.11, 5.07, 5.04, 5.07, and 5.01 for the CD blocks Barjora, Santuri, Jhalda-I, Jaypur, and Purulia-I, respectively (Table 12.9).

**TABLE 12.9** Weakness–Threat (WT) Strategies.

| | |
|---|---|
| WT 1 | Increasing the diversification of crops |
| WT 2 | Use of sustainable water resource management practices |
| WT 3 | Promotion of the agro-based industry |
| WT 4 | Encouragement of private sector investment in agriculture |
| WT 5 | Encouragement of research facilities in agriculture |
| WT 6 | Development of market infrastructure, storage, transportation, credit support, etc. |
| WT 7 | Water conservation in the fields to check surface runoff |

**TABLE 12.10** QSPM Approach.

| CD blocks | Observations | WT1 | WT2 | WT3 | WT4 | WT5 | WT6 | WT7 |
|---|---|---|---|---|---|---|---|---|
| Barjora | STAS | 5.57 | 5.22 | 5.11 | 5.15 | 5.27 | 4.66 | 5.22 |
| | PRIORITY | 1 | 3 | 5 | 4 | 2 | 6 | 3 |
| Santuri | STAS | 5.22 | 4.87 | 5.07 | 4.95 | 5.01 | 4.84 | 4.64 |
| | PRIORITY | 1 | 5 | 2 | 4 | 3 | 6 | 7 |
| Jhalda I | STAS | 5.5 | 5.1 | 5.04 | 5.15 | 5.27 | 4.66 | 5.22 |
| | PRIORITY | 1 | 5 | 6 | 4 | 2 | 7 | 3 |
| Jaypur | STAS | 5.22 | 4.87 | 5.07 | 4.95 | 5.01 | 4.84 | 4.64 |
| | PRIORITY | 1 | 5 | 2 | 4 | 3 | 6 | 7 |
| Purulia I | STAS | 5.4 | 4.88 | 5.01 | 4.96 | 5.01 | 4.84 | 4.64 |
| | PRIORITY | 1 | 4 | 2 | 3 | 2 | 5 | 6 |

### 12.3.4 COBB–DOUGLAS PRODUCTION ESTIMATION

The upsides of $R^2$ are determined for each ranch size in order to analyze the effect that various information assets, particularly labor and capital, have on gross and net returns. At a level of 5% for the 0–15 day stage, the assessed coefficient of labor for marigolds (0.242) is thought to be certain and crucial. The stage from 30–45 days has an assessed coefficient of capital of 2.798, which is extremely high at the 1% level (Table 12.11). The relapse condition can explain almost all of the variety results for marigolds. The study area is thought to have the potential to grow a variety of marigolds, which is considered a cash crop. Similar to the second-stage maturity level, where 80% of the variety results can be explained by the relapse condition, almost 100% of the third-stage results can be explained by the relapse condition. Table 12.11 shows that the coefficients of labor and capital for marigolds are 2.88 and –0.383, respectively, at stage four, which are found to be significant at the 5% and 1% levels, respectively. The relapse condition can make sense of 100% of the variety results in this situation (Table 12.11).

**TABLE 12.11** Cobb–Douglas Stage-Wise Production Estimation of Marigolds.

| Stage (days) | Statistics | Labor | Capital |
|---|---|---|---|
| 0–15 | R square | 1.000 | |
| | Coefficients | 0.242 | 2.685 |
| | t Stat | 11.109* | 2.575 |
| 15–30 | R square | 0.634 | |
| | Coefficients | 2.044 | –1.254 |
| | t Stat | 1.070 | –0.244 |
| 30–45 | R square | 1.000 | |
| | Coefficients | –0.40 | 2.798 |
| | t Stat | –0.556 | 82.366** |
| 45–60 | R square | 1.000 | |
| | Coefficients | 2.88 | –0.383 |
| | t Stat | 60.09* | –0.27 |
| 60–75 | R square | 0.989 | |
| | Coefficients | –0.27 | 4.936 |
| | t Stat | –3.622 | 9.267 |
| 75–90 | R square | 1.000 | |
| | Coefficients | 0.010 | 0.025 |
| | t Stat | 25.053* | 6.173 |

## 12.4 CONCLUSIONS

Finally, the study shows that the availability of the viable geoclimatic parameters in the study area will provide some flexibility in the production of marigold, which has proven to be sustainable. Though there is a largescale paradigm shift in the mindset of the ranchers to grow cash crops and floricultural products in the study area, it needs to be implemented at a largescale to visualize its impact on the economy and livelihood. According to the models of the India Meteorological Department, this district cannot be assigned as dry season-inclined.[40] The coarse-grained soil of the region is characterized by a low dampness holding limit. The top soil becomes extremely dry not long after a spell of torrential rain, which moves as surface runoff following the incline of the area. On the off chance that a significant piece of this measure of surface runoff is captured, the issue of water shortage can be limited to an impressive degree. This district is characterized by a higher temperature, sufficient brilliant sun sparkle hours, and an extensive measure of normal yearly precipitation (1100 mm to 1500 mm), which can uphold an enormous number of cash crops and plant items. Furthermore, the undulations in topography will advance the surface runoff component. Mishra (2012) [40] proposed ideal land-use arrangements in the space of undulating geology with unique reference to this region. The present study plans to distinguish the assessed benefit cost proportion of marigold production in the Purulia district of West Bengal, where the geoclimatic circumstances are not favorable for the development of a long-length assortment of rice. For this reason, quantities of things and their assessed standard expenses have been recorded, and factual methodology has been followed to determine the net return, input–yield relationship, and advantage cost proportion of marigold production. From the continuous review, it is uncovered that the variable expenses of information things are viewed as expanding with the addition of ranch sizes. However, for the large homestead estimates, this multitude of expenses is accounted for to decline. Among the rundown of assessed variable expenses of information, the compensation of workers with the consideration of machine work is higher trailed by the expense of establishing material. It is reasoned that the ranchers engaged with the enormous land possessions are enjoying more on marigold production with significant consumption on human work, establishing materials, excrements and manures, transportation, and so on. Yet, because of the higher assessed efficiency of marigold in the large ranch estimates, the net returns are determined to be higher for the enormous landholdings. It is apparent from the study that the complete variable and fixed costs are viewed as higher for the small land property followed by the large, medium, and peripheral ranch sizes. The expense examination from A1 to C3 shows that the assessed gross expense of marigold production in the region changes from at least Rs. 70,400.00 for the minor land property to a limit of Rs. 81,400.00, despite the most elevated net returns obtained by the large ranch sizes. The marigold production in the review region is viewed as exceptionally compelling and sustainable in the large ranch sizes as demonstrated by its higher advantage cost proportion of 1:1.99. Additionally, the large ranchers can decrease the expense of development by substituting the recruited human workers with machine work. The study is beneficial for the farming communities that have excessive dependence on rice cultivation for their livelihood security. The study area is not suitable for the cultivation of long-duration varieties of rice due to the low moisture retention capacity of the top soil. Moreover, the occurrence of frequent droughts makes this situation completely unfavorable for the growth of paddy, particularly during the nonrainy season. However, marigold production may be considered an alternative source of livelihood strategy in this drought-prone district of West Bengal. The less requirement of water and availability of laborers are some of the wonderful advantages in the study area to promote marigold cultivation. The present study will provide policymakers with adequate knowledge about the alternative livelihood strategies in the study area other than traditional subsistence farming.

## KEYWORDS

- **Chhota Nagpur**
- **marigold**
- **Purulia**
- **factor cost**
- **benefit cost**
- **ranch business**
- **marginal land**
- **financial suitability**

## REFERENCES

1. Baksh H.; Yadav J. N.; Yadav V. P. S.; Yadav H.; Deshwal A. K. Profitability and Production of Marigold Flowers in Faridabad District of Haryana. *Indian Res. J. Ext. Educ.* **2019,** *19,* 25–28.
2. Haque M. A.; Monayem Miah M. A.; Hossain S.; Alam M. Economics of Marigold Cultivation in Some Selected Areas of Bangladesh. Bangladesh. *J. Agric. Res.* **2012,** *37* (4), 711–720.
3. Verma L. K.; Nag N. K.; Solanki A.; Singh P. Economics Analysis of Marigold Flowers in Baghpat District of Uttar Pradesh. *SSRG Int. J. Agric. Env. Sci.* **2019,** *6* (4), 5–8.
4. Singh A. K.; Singh M. K.; Singh, R. R. The Economics of Marigolds Flowers in Eastern Uttar Pradesh. *J. Rural Agric. Res.* **2013,** *13* (2), 75–78.
5. Sai Y. K.; Banafar K. N. S.; Sahu T.; Chandravanshi V. Economic Analysis of Marigold in Surajpur District of Chhattisgarh. *J. Pharmacogn. Phytochem.* **2018,** *7* (2), 2018–2020.
6. Gawle S. K.; Chaturvedi M. K.; Yadav K. N. Analysis of Socio-Economic Profile of Marigold Grower in Adoption of Improved Marigold Production Technology. *J. Plant Dev. Sci.* **2012,** *4* (2), 225–230.
7. Deb R.; Uddin A. Entrepreneurship Through Marigold Cultivation: Evidence from Laxmibill Area of Tripura. *J. Entrep. Manag.* **2015,** *4* (3), 40–54.
8. Kolambkar R. A.; Suryawanshi R. R.; Deshmukh K. V. Economic Analysis of Production of Marigold in Western Maharashtra. *J. Agric. Res. Technol.* **2015,** *40* (2), 305–308.
9. Sen S. Temporal analysis of Vegetation Health of Murti River Basin: An Approach Through Geospatial Technique. *Int. J. Res. Eng. Sci.* **2021,** *9* (5), 49–56.
10. Hel S. V. D. Science for Change: A Survey on the Normative and Political Dimensions of Global Sustainability Research. *Glob. Environ. Change* **2018,** 52, 248–258.
11. Goswami, A. Assessment of Trends and Variability of Pre-Monsoon Rainfall for Some Selected Districts of Western Part of West Bengal. *Environ. Ecol.* **2018,** *36* (4), 1047–1052.
12. Shaffer R.; Deller S.; Marcouiller D. Rethinking Community Economic Development. *Econ. Dev. Q.* **2006,** *20* (1), 59–74.
13. Goswami, A. Identifying the Trend of Meteorological Drought in Purulia District of West Bengal, India. *Environ. Ecol.* **2019,** *37* (1B), 387–392.
14. Seherm H.; Coakley S. Plant Pathogens in a Changing World. *Australas. Plant Pathol.* **2003,** *32* (2), 157–165.
15. Yamano T.; Dar M. H.; Panda A.; Gupta I.; Malabayabas M. L.; Kelly E. Impact and Adoption of Risk-Reducing Drought-Tolerant rice in India. *3ie Impact Evaluation Report 72, New Delhi*, 2018.
16. Singh P.; Pandey P. C.; Petropoulos G. P.; Pavlides A.; Srivastava P. K.; Koutsias N.; Deng K. A. K.; Bao Y. Hyperspectral Remote Sensing in Precision Agriculture: Present Status, Challenges, and Future Trends [Online]; *Hyperspectral Remote Sensing* 2020, pp 121–146.
17. Ngala G. N. In *Constraints to Increased Quality Rice Production for Food, Market and Development with Special Reference to Tropical Africa*, African Crop Science Conference Proceedings; 2013, vol 11, pp 617–620.
18. Wu H.; Hubbard K. G.; Wilhite D. An Agricultural Drought Risk-Assessment Model for Corn and Soybeans. *Int. J. Climatol.* **2004,** *24* (6), 723–741.

19. Li, Q. L.; Ju, Z. H.; Huang, J. M.; Li, J. B.; Li, R. L.; Hou, M. H.; Wang, C. F.; Zhong, J. F. Two Novel SNPs in HSF1 Gene are Associated with Thermal Tolerance Traits in Chinese Holstein Cattle. *DNA Cell Biol.* **2011a,** *30,* 247–254.
20. Westengen O. T.; Brysting A. K. Crop Adaptation to Climate Change in the Semi-Arid Zone in Tanzania: The Role of Genetic Resources and Seed Systems. *Agric. Food Sec.* **2014,** *3* (3), 01–12.
21. Nirmala B.; Muthuraman P. Economic and Constraint Analysis of Rice Cultivation in Kaithal District of Haryana. *Indian Res. J. Ext. Educ.* **2009,** *9* (1), 47–49.
22. Odoemenem I. U.; Inuksuk J. A. Economic Analysis of Rice Production in Cross River State, Nigeria. *J. Dev. Agric. Econ.* **2011,** *3* (9), 469–474.
23. Koondhar M. A.; Chandio A. A.; Ge H.; Xu X.; Koondhar M. A. Economic Analysis of Hybrid Maize Cultivation in Distt; Naushahro Feroze, Sindh, Pakistan. *J. Pov. Invest. Dev.* **2015,** *18,* 56–62.
24. Srikanth B.; Kausadikar H. H.; Jondhale R. N.; Gandhi N Economic Analysis of Maize Production and Marketing in Khammam District, Telangana. *Asian J. Agric. Ext. Econ. Soc.* **2017,** *20* (4), 1–13.
25. Ghulghule J. N.; Asmatoddin M.; Thombre A. P.; Birajdar K. A. An Economic Analysis of Potato Cultivation in Latur District of Maharashtra. *Int. J. Com. Bus. Manag.* **2009,** *2* (1), 12–14.
26. Kumar P.; Chauhan R. S.; Grover R. K. An Economic Analysis of Cucumber (Cucumissativus L.) Cultivation in Eastern Zone of Haryana (India) Under Polyhouse and open Field Condition. *J. Appl. Nat. Sci.* **2017,** *9* (1), 402–405.
27. Koza A.; Sahu A. K.; Das S.; Patra N. K. Economics of Cabbage Cultivation and Post-harvest Losses in Phek District of Nagaland. *Econ. Aff.* **2018,** *63* (1), 229–235.
28. Agarwal P. K.; Singh O. P. An Economic Analysis of Soybean Cultivation in Hoshangabad District of Madhya Pradesh. *Indian J. Econ. Dev.* **2015,** *11* (4), 869–876.
29. Meena L. K.; Bairwa S. L.; Lakra K.; Pardhi R.; Raghuwanshi, N. K. An Economic Analysis of Garlic Production in Baran District of Rajasthan. *Econ. Aff.* **2013,** *58,* 559–562.
30. Honyal A. S.; Gunadal N. M.; Harshitha H. C. Cost and Return Structure of Marigold Production- An Economic Approach. *Int. J. Sci. Dev. Res.* **2022,** *7* (7), 350–354.
31. Kadam A. S.; Suryawanshi R. R.; Dhengale S. S.; Shinde H. R. Economic Analysis of Production of Ginger in Sangli District of Maharashtra. *Int. J. Chem. Stud.* **2019,** *7* (6), 1456–1460.
32. Hanks J.; Martin S. W. Economic Analysis of Cotton Conservation Tillage Practices in the Mississippi Delta. *J. Cotton Sci.* **2007,** *11,* 75–78.
33. Agarwal P. K.; Kumar M. An Economic Analysis of Onion Cultivation in Giridih District of Jharkhand. *Econ. Aff.* **2018,** *63* (3), 703–707.
34. Mathew S.; Wadkar S. S.; Kshirsagar P. J. Economic Analysis of Pineapple Production in Sindhudurg District of Maharashtra. *Int. Res. J. Agric. Econ. Stat.* **2017,** *8* (2), 351–356.
35. Grover D. K.; Kumar S. Sorghum (Fodder) Cultivation in Punjab—An Economic Analysis. *Agric. Econ. Res. Rev.* **2013,** *26* (1), 55–62.
36. Arya B.; Zechariah J. An Economic Analysis of Production and Marketing of Sunflower in Raigarh District of Chhattisgarh. *J. Pharmacogn. Phytochem.* **2018,** *7* (5), 1844–1846.
37. Agarwal P. K.; Banerjee A. Economic Analysis of Tomato Cultivation in Kandi Block of West Bengal, India. *Econ. Aff.* **2019,** *64* (3) 643–647.

38. Yadav H.; Singh S. K.; Singh G. P.; Singh K. K. An Economic Analysis of Wheat Cultivation in Etawah Districts of Uttar Pradesh, India. *Plant Arch.* **2014,** *14* (1), 393–399.
39. Ommani A. R. Strengths, Weaknesses, Opportunities and Threats (SWOT) Analysis for Farming System Businesses Management: Case of Wheat Farmers of Shadervan District, Shoushtar Township, Iran. *Afr. J. Bus. Manag.* **2011,** *5* (22), 9448–9454.
40. Mishra S. Drought and its Management in West Bengal. *Indian J. Landsc. Ecol. Stud.* **2012,** *35* (1), 20–28.

# CHAPTER 13

# Environmental Risk and Green Economy: A Way of Sustainable Development

PRASENJIT GHOSH

*Department of Economics, Jadavpur University*

## ABSTRACT

Environmental degradation has become a serious matter of concern for policymakers and environmental economists. It is considered a hindrance to the inflow of foreign investment as foreigners would not prefer to invest in an economy surrounded by greenhouse gases (GHGs), like carbon dioxide—an indicator of air quality deterioration. However, adequate investment, specifically foreign direct investment (FDI), is a prerequisite for economic growth and generating employment opportunities in any economy. Therefore, it is imperative to reduce the emission of various GHGs to attract FDI, and, in turn, economic growth will be amplified. The green economy—an economy with a risk-free environment—may solve the problem of GHGs emission. With the help of a green economy, a country would achieve a higher level of growth, more employment opportunities, and proper utilization of natural resources through FDI. As a consequence, a country would reach economic, environmental, and social sustainability, which is nothing but sustainable development, an intention of all nations.

## 13.1 INTRODUCTION

Development indicates growth, as well as amelioration, in the living standard of people and the right to access all socio-economic facilities freely and equally. This would be possible through equal and adequate distribution of

Management for Sustainable Development: Integrating Social, Economic, and Environmental Goals. Vishal Jain & Amit Mittal (Eds.)

all the benefits of development among people of the economy. But growth is nothing but an enhancement of the level of production, which, in turn, elevates the extraction and depletion of raw materials from the environment to produce goods and services according to the wants and desires of all members of society. To increase the level of production, various natural raw materials are used excessively, and, thereby, produce a substantial quantity of solid pollutants and greenhouse gases (GHGs). Consequently, productive activities deteriorate the quality of the environment at an intolerable level. Moderate levels of waste and GHG emissions are not matters of concern for policymakers and have no harmful impact on economic and productive activities. In this respect, the receptive capacity of the environment plays an important role by nullifying the negative effects of waste and various gaseous pollutants on the economy. This absorptive capacity of the environment performs properly up to a certain level of pollution but a larger quantity of pollutants may, much higher than *assimilative* capacity, have unpleasant effects on society.

It is worth mentioning that most countries are engrossed in the magnification of productive activities without considering the detrimental impacts on environmental quality. As growth has been a prerequisite for development, this process speedily deteriorates environmental quality. In this way, the process of growth is significantly superintending for environmental degradation and excessive diminution of resources, specifically non-renewable resources, creating uncertainty about the availability of natural deposits for future generations. This type of uncertainty and insecurity about the availability of resources for the future generation is not desirable for the appropriate process of development. To make the process of growth desirable, it is imperative to corroborate a balanced availability of necessary raw materials between people of current and future periods. This situation stipulates the achievement of sustainable development in the economy. But, by avoiding or neglecting the driving factors behind the decay of atmosphere quality, productive activities elevate the environmental risk in the economy.

Capital is a very important input for the production process. An adequate level of investment is essential, and a precondition, for implementing all productive activities properly. However, all investors prefer to invest in a risk-free zone with maximum return. For that reason, risk-free investment is always desirable but an investment with a risk factor is not desirable for investors. It is obvious that foreign investors are meagerly interested in investing in a country that is experiencing a risky environment. The reason is investment in countries with a risky environment may increase the expenditure of investors for unproductive activities and result in a lesser level of return. In this country, investors have to expend huge money on buying technology to reduce pollution levels. And, it would be a very tough task for them to face the stringent regulations of the concerned country. Furthermore, due to productive activities, the emission of detrimental gases is responsible for global warming and there are so many negative impacts of global warming on productive and economic activities. Managing and overcoming all these problems increase the expenditure level of the investors and result in a lower level of profit from the investment.[7]

This study has been structured into six sections. The introductory part has been included in Section 13.1. Section 13.2 conveys various consequences of environmental degradation. The desirable structure of any economy, that is, sustainable development, is described in Section 13.3. In this section, two dimensions of sustainability—weak and strong—have also been described, and in addition, sustainable development goals for sustainability have been categorized. Section 13.4 considers the assessment of the capacity of foreign direct investment (FDI) in the process of achieving sustainable development and the trend of FDI tendency in an economy with environmental risk. The green economy may be a way out of environmental risk, as is described in Section 13.5. The role of the green economy in achieving sustainable development is also depicted in the subsection of Section 13.5. The conclusion of the discussion has been displayed in Section 13.6.

## 13.2 ENVIRONMENTAL DEGRADATION AND ITS CONSEQUENCES

In earlier times, the process of development completely skipped the catastrophic sides of the environment. However, environmental degradation has become a major concern in present times. Due to huge industrial growth, the emission of various GHGs like carbon dioxide has been significantly responsible for global warming. Global warming considerably hampers the process of development by increasing the sea level, melting glaciers, intrusion of saltwater in the agricultural field, and destruction of cropland. Along with this, global warming is also a responsible factor behind drought and frequent storms. Thus, neglecting the damage to the environment and focusing only on productive activities may have a devastating impact on the present as well as future generations. In any economy, to meet the huge demand of the people, it is a requisite to carry out productive activities properly but production units are significantly responsible for emitting GHGs, which in turn elevates global warming. In this circumstance, some nonproductive activities, like deforestation, are very pertinent as the forest can absorb GHGs from the atmosphere and make the environment pollution-free. For that reason, deforestation is blameworthy for reducing the GHGs' absorbing capacity of the environment, which in turn amplifies the number of harmful gases in the environment. Emitted GHGs deteriorate human health by creating various diseases like cancer, chronic heart disease, and lung diseases. The most important thing is excessive use of exhaustible resources signals the unavailability of those resources in the future time and creates a situation of misbalance between present and future generations with respect to accessing innate materials for productive purposes. Under these circumstances, environmental mortification has been considered a matter of concern for environmentalists. As productive activities are not possible with zero pollution or emission, they can be reduced to a minimum level with maximum output and it leads to the new concept of sustainable development (SD). SD considers economic and productive activities, as well as associated external costs in the economy, and suggests the inclusion of external costs in production costs and prefers the use of environmentally friendly technology and production methods.[12]

## 13.3 SUSTAINABLE DEVELOPMENT

Keeping in view the importance of intergenerational equity, the phrase "sustainable development" is very important and compulsory for the overall development of all countries. This term was introduced by the Commission on Environment and Development, United Nations, through the Brundtland Report in 1987. This report, titled "Our Common Future," gave a relevant definition that may reduce the immoderate use of resources and also help to make a balanced development between current and future generations. According to Brundtland Report, "sustainable development" is a process of productive and economic activities that helps the people of the present generation to access natural resources according to their needs and that does not hamper the availability of that for the future generation. The process of sustainable development maintains a stock of resources in such a way the present and succeeding generations can access productive resources equally and adequately. Thus, sustainable development has been playing the role of representative for the people of future generations and assures them to fulfill the wants or desires of the future generation.

Naturally, each country desires to sustain its development status by achieving SD. But three goals are prerequisites to bring off SD—these are economic sustainability (ES), environmental sustainability (ENS), and social sustainability (SS). The combined effect of these three pillars leads to the situation of SD in any economy, that is,

$$SD = (ES \cap ENS \cap SS)$$

ES is the process that will meet the wants or desires of the people of the present generation by using natural resources efficiently and sustaining the production process properly for a long period of time. Limited natural resources in the environment have been significantly responsible for impeding the process of sustaining production process for a long period. To meet their own needs, people of the present generation are extracting natural resources excessively. As a consequence, productive activities are not only taking resources but also returning a considerable quantity of pollutants and waste to the environment. Under these circumstances, two problems arise—one is the reduction of natural resources in size and the other is environmental degradation if the returned pollutants and waste are not recycled into any usable product or converted into an environmentally friendly product, that is, the quantity of waste is above the absorptive capacity of the environment. It is imperative to carry out production activities without negatively impacting the environment, which leads to the situation of ENS. Comprehensible that ES is obvious for sustainable development and ENS is compulsory for the proper functioning of ES. Basically, ENS is the process of maintaining parity between its two main functions—to supply natural resources for economic and productive activities and assimilate all the wastes and emitted gases produced by various productive units. The parity between these two functions would be possible if people use resources properly and moderately and, as a result, it would be possible for the environment to lessen the negative ramifications of productive activities substantially. With ES and ENS, SS is very crucial for any economy. SS focuses on the socio-economic status of the people and, for that purpose, it is a prerequisite to amplify the employment generation, poverty reduction, enhance diversity, access to healthcare, and education, as well as improvement of living standards. SS is very crucial as it assures fulfilling all human activities properly.[5]

Modern technology has been considered a catalyst that will consummate all the required conditions of ES and ENS. Advanced techniques and production methods can reduce the emission of harmful gas and various pollutants without hampering normal productive activities and at the same time meliorate the living standard of people. The transfer of advanced technology from developed to developing countries would help the concerned countries to use the resources efficiently, which in turn reduces the excessive use of natural deposits. In this way, the advantages of technology create a situation of ES and ENS in the economy. Thus, the transfer or use of appropriate technology can amplify the process of sustainable development.[13]

### 13.3.1 WEAK AND STRONG SUSTAINABILITY

Achieving sustainability is very crucial for the proper development of any country. Furthermore, the identification of the sustainability of any economy is more important as it helps to understand the present development status of the country. In this respect, weak sustainability, as defined by David Pearce and Atkinson,[19] is very relevant to indicate sustainable development. This indicator shows that the total capital stock (K) is the aggregate of capital produced by man (KM) and capital (KN) taken from nature and it should be non-decreasing, that is,

$$\text{Total stock of capital (K)} = K_M + K_N$$

Total stock of capital (K) is not declining because the reduction of natural capital is replenished by sufficient enhancement of manmade capital.[11] It is considered that manmade capital can be applied in place of natural capital and this situation leads to weak sustainability of any country. This type of situation leads to sustainability and it is indicated by the Pearce–Atkinson Measure (PAM). This indicator is based on the degree of substitutability between manmade technology and natural capital.

Pearce and Atkinson[19] proposed an indicator of weak sustainability, based on perfect substitution between natural and manmade capital. Pearce and Atkinson Measure (PAM) is defined as:

$$\text{PAM} = (S/Y) - (\delta M/Y) - (\delta N/Y)$$

where Y is total output, S is total savings, $\delta M$ is depreciation rate of manmade capital, and $\delta N$ is depreciation rate of natural capital. If PAM > 0, then the economy is considered as sustainable development and it would be possible if per capita saving is larger than the aggregate of per capita manmade ($\delta M$) and natural ($\delta N$) capital of depreciation.

It has been assumed that there are two inputs—manmade capital (M) and natural capital (N), and the output is $Q$. Production function is $Q = f$ (M, N). Isoquant curve $Q^*$ is shown in Figure 13.1. Perfect substitutability between M and N and the positive value of PAM indicate the potentiality of achieving sustainability in any economy. The substitutability of M for N is the only way to achieve sustainable development. According to Pearce and

Atkinson, manmade capital offsets the reduction of natural capital, and then current and subsequent generations would access the resources properly. And, the intensity of substitution between M and N has been measured by the elasticity of substitution (σ).

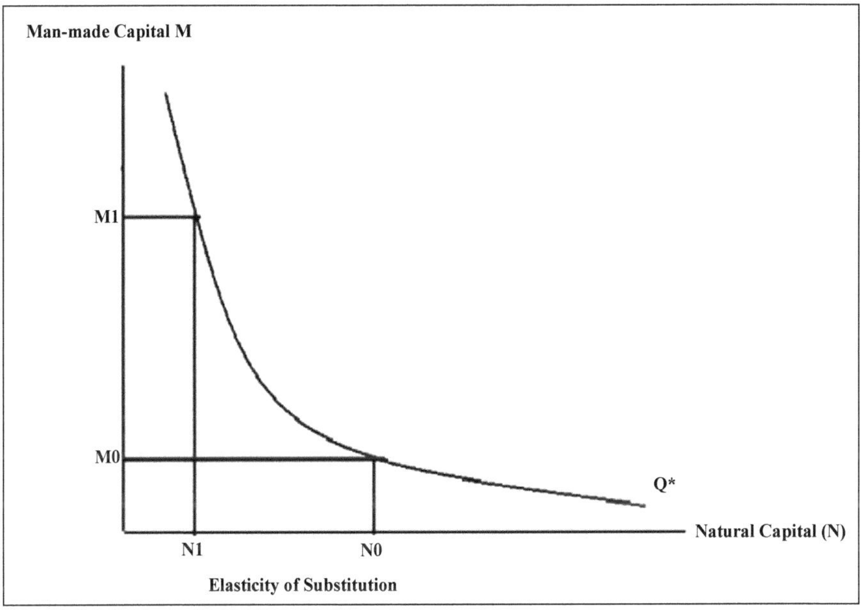


**FIGURE 13.1** Elasticity of substitution between manmade capital (M) and natural capital (N).

$$\text{Elasticity of substitution } (\sigma) = [d \ln(M/N)]/ [d \ln(MRTS)]$$
$$= [d \ln(M/N)]/ [d \ln(f_N/f_M)]$$

There are two extreme cases, $\sigma = 0$ and $\sigma = \infty$.

If $\sigma = 0$, then there is no chance of substitution between manmade capital and natural capital; and the isoquant curve becomes L-shaped. Obviously, manmade capital and natural capital complement each other in the process of production. But, in the economy, there exist some nonproducible resources, and present and future generations would access the resources if the abundance of the resources sustains for a long period. It would be possible by creating or innovating alternative technologies or production methods that will help to replenish the reduction of natural deposits in the economy. Then, zero substitutability between manmade capital and natural capital would not ensure continuous development in the economy.

On the other hand, if $\sigma = \infty$, then the addition of manmade capital and reduction of one-unit N would not lead to any change in the marginal product of either of them as there is perfect substitution between manmade capital and natural capital and MRTS becomes constant. And, isoquant curve between M and N will be a straight line.

$$\text{i.e., MRTS} = (dQ/dM)/(dQ/dN)$$

But it is not possible all the time. For that reason, the inclusion of perfect substitutability between natural and manmade capital is unrealistic and estimates of natural capital depreciation are not available. Thus, substitutability must be between zeros to infinity to achieve sustainable development.

### *13.3.2 SUSTAINABLE DEVELOPMENT GOALS AND SUSTAINABILITY*

To achieve sustainable development, it is imperative to achieve three objectives—ES, ENS, and SS. For that reason, 17 sustainable development goals (SDGs) were introduced by the United Nations Development Program (UNDP) in 2015 for establishing sustainability in any economy. SDGs emphasize economic and social development and it would be possible by acquiring sustainability in economic, environmental, and social fields. It is clear that for sustainable development, simultaneous strategy and policy are required for the said three fields.[26] For ES, in a poverty-free economy, all people can access food, experience good health and well-being of the people, access quality education, and society must be free from gender bias and provision of clean water and sanitation.

ENS would be possible if people get clean energy at an affordable rate, targeting the level of economic growth. Further, more people should use innovative technology for their productive purposes and it is needful to improve the infrastructure, and there should not be any type of inequality in society regarding consumption and production. SS is associated with reverberations of climate change and monitoring animals below water and life on land.

## 13.4 FDI AND SUSTAINABLE DEVELOPMENT IN INDIA

To achieve sustainable development, first of all, ES is mandatory. ES means meeting the needs and desires of the general people without creating any adverse impact on the environment. The establishment of economic and ENS requires the mobilization of adequate capital in the economy; as capital helps the country to reach the targeted level of production as well as reduce environmental degradation. In this regard, FDI and the inflow of modern technologies from one country to another country have been playing a crucial role to boost the activities of development. As a result, a country can build up infrastructure and modernize its economic and productive activities.

FDI is associated with enhancing the process of economic growth and it is an important driving force to revamp the quality of the environment. Investment has been playing a crucial role in amplifying economic and environmental efficiency as it will spread new industries that are associated with low emissions of GHG, that is, least chance of global warming. Actually, FDI helps the country to shift from a traditional economy to a green economy. Here, the traditional economy indicates a brown economy—an economy that focuses on economic growth without including the environmental degradation associated with productive activities. For that reason, it is desirable to attract FDI by introducing various relevant policies in the economy.[32]

FDI also helps domestic countries by providing advanced technology in the domestic countries, which in turn intensifies productivity. But FDI indicates a transition from domestic ownership to foreign ownership, and, as a result, domestic firms may face a loss and there is a negative impact on productivity. A country would thus prefer to allow the inflow of foreign investment if the net benefit is positive from FDI. In this circumstance, it is noteworthy that some small firms may exit the market if they face loss due to ownership transfer. Leaving few firms from the market may elevate the overall net benefit of the country due to FDI. The net benefit of the host country by FDI may increase productivity considerably. It would be possible if domestic personnel absorb all the foreign technologies in their production units through training and learning by doing. The increasing trend of net benefit will be sustained for a long period if all production units in the country immerse the modern technologies and production methods.[1]

Raza and Hussain[20] show an interdependence influx of FDI and economic and productive activities in a positive direction but a higher level of productivity may enhance environmental degradation. Using imported environmentally friendly technology may meliorate the quality of the atmosphere and, as a consequence, FDI leads to environment-friendly production. In this regard, FDI plays the role of a catalyst by invigorating the formation of human capital and the transfer of modern or environmentally friendly technology. Thus, FDI has appeared as a driving force behind economic growth or green growth in developing countries.

In this regard, the government needs various policies that will attract FDI in the specific key sectors-manufacturing, transport, and communication—of the economy. It is manifested that the development of the important sectors of an economy stipulates the overall improvement of that economy.

ENS indicates the process through which the accessibility of natural materials will remain almost unchanged. Substitution by manmade capital and human capital for natural capital ensures equal distribution of natural capital between current and future generations. Robert Goodland[9] mentioned three methods to maintain the same level of natural resources. Firstly, advanced technologies and modern production methods have the potentiality to replenish the dwindled natural capital. Secondly, for maintaining the same level of renewable resources, enhancement of the regeneration rate of resources compared to the extraction rate would be most appropriate. Thirdly, it is indispensable to use innate resources efficiently and appropriately for productive purposes. FDI may play a foremost role in implementing the above-mentioned methods and also play the role of catalyst to amplify ENS.

All countries are trying to get capital from a foreign source because FDI magnifies the process of sustainability and helps the country to grab all the benefits from sustainable development. For that reason, countries can frame their policies by considering the circumstances that will captivate the inflow of foreign capital. Most of the countries with favorable policies attract foreign investors and, as a consequence, that country would have advanced technology, upgraded human capital, and substitutes for exhaustible resources. All these benefits will help the concerned country to reduce unemployment and poverty. In addition, FDI also improves the environmental quality by setting abatement technology. In this regard, as FDI is socially desirable, the Indian government also attracts long-term FDI by creating a risk-free environment in various sectors like telecommunication, construction activities, and software and hardware of computers.[6]

Foreigners would be interested in investing in other countries if they would get more returns smoothly and without any hazards. Along with various productive and economic constraints, foreign investors also consider the consequences associated with the environmental risk to the economy before deciding on investment. The abatement cost for pollution reduction or improvement of environmental quality is significantly hampering the level of return from investment. For that reason, foreign firms or companies want a minimum level of pollution, emission, and waste in the economy for investment. A developing country, like India, has been experiencing huge levels of environmental hazards. As a consequence, foreigners are not interested in investing in the Indian economy. However, without an adequate level of FDI, the Indian economy would not achieve the expected level of growth. To get a sufficient level of FDI, it is important to reduce the environmental risks and various hazards associated with productive activities. Figure 13.2 shows the transition process from a traditional economy to a green economy and finally sustainable development in any economy.

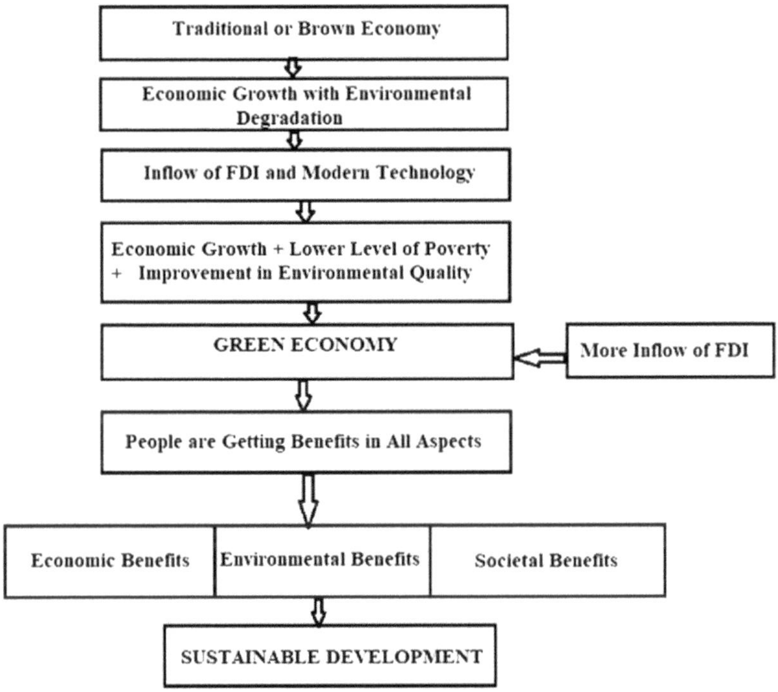


**FIGURE 13.2** Schematic diagram of transformation from brown economy to sustainable development (Author's own).

### *13.4.1 RELATIONSHIP BETWEEN ENVIRONMENTAL RISKS AND FDI MAGNITUDE*

An economy with environmental degradation indicates that environmental risks have been associated with various economic and productive activities. In this situation, productive activities are produced by several uncontrolled solid wastes and GHGs; those that are harming the activities of other sectors, that is, creating external costs. It also hampers human health by creating various diseases. In this regard, emissions of carbon dioxide, nitrogen oxide, and sulfur dioxide are notably deteriorating the condition of the environment. The emission of these gases is the determining factor of environmental risk.

Under the concerned matter of environmental degradation, the government has introduced various instruments to reduce the emanation of GHGs like the imposition of a pollution tax. But the imposition of a pollution tax retards the process of production or may generate an extra burden on producers or investors. Following this situation, foreign investors are least interested in investing in the economy experiencing environmental risk as they expect a heavy financial burden or lower level of profit and stringent regulation for controlling pollution may create various impediments in the way of productive activities and there exist some health issues due to pollution. And these circumstances do not entice foreign investors and the result is a lower magnitude of investment in the domestic countries.[3] On the other hand, inundation of FDI is the prerequisite condition for amplifying economic activities, that is, economic growth and employment opportunities. The capacity of FDI is pivotal to escalating positive growth rate and financial stability and is vital for economic reforms,[23] and FDI also helps the economy to deploy enriched human capital with skilled and advanced technology for sustainable development.[4] But to attract investors, a pollution and environment-risk-free economy are vital, which in turn enhances economic growth and employment level. As a consequence, higher levels of production and employment opportunities encourage all the productive units to install various advanced technologies to reduce emission levels and prevent the loss of raw materials.[8] Otherwise various economic and productive activities will hinder the potentiality of social and ENS, which are needed for sustainable development. The production of GHGs and various wastes are the main obstacles in the way of sustainable development of any economy.

To overcome the problems of poverty, unemployment, excessive extraction of natural resources, and the catastrophic side of environmental destruction, the green economy has been playing an important role. An adequate level of finance, modern technology, poverty reduction, and equity are the prerequisites for a green economy. In addition, low carbon economic management, technology, and abatement of climate change are also required. Implementation of the above policies and strategies requires a huge level of investment. In this case, FDI has been considered a catalyst to elevate the development process properly.[14] Figure 13.3 displays the trend of FDI tendency and emission of carbon dioxide in India and Figure 13.4 shows the movement of FDI and GDP growth in India. However, according to Figures 13.3 and 13.4, FDI does not play any considerable and desirable influencing role in the process of sustainable development as there is a negative correlation but not significant (−0.12) relationship between intensity of FDI and GDP growth in India.

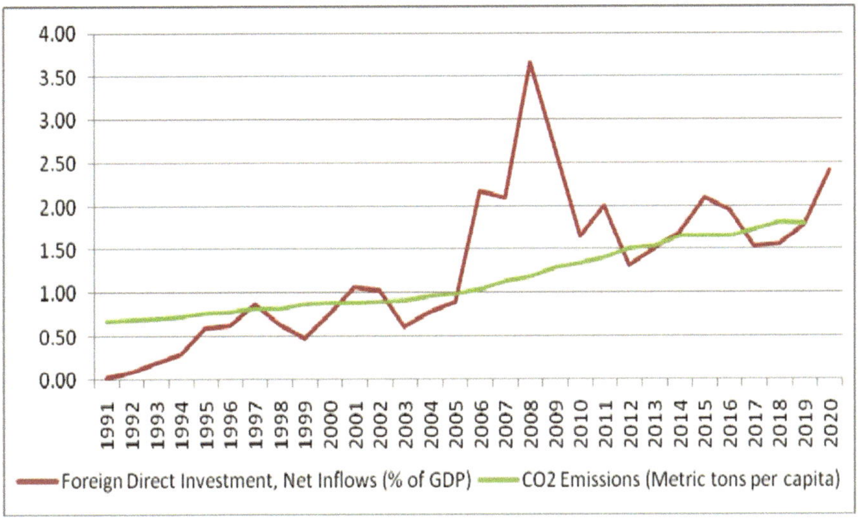


**FIGURE 13.3** Trend of Foreign Direct Investment and Emission of Carbon dioxide in India (Author's own)

*Data Source*: World Development Indicators (WDI), World Bank Report, https://databank.worldbank.org/source/world-development-indicators

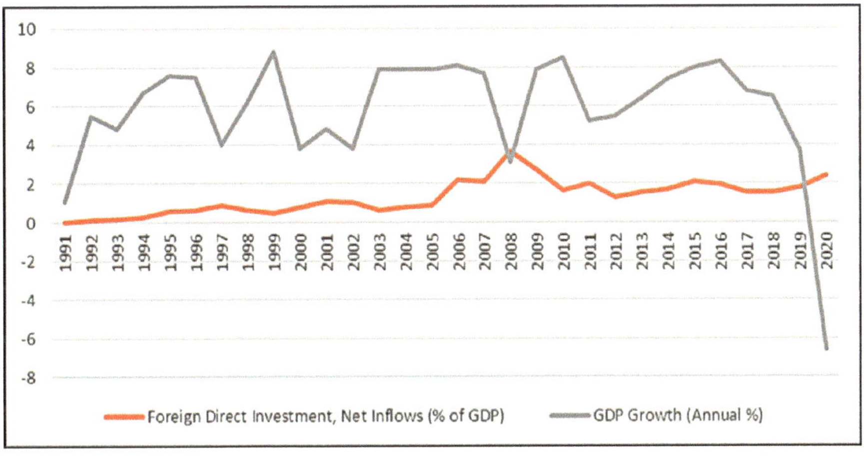


**FIGURE 13.4** Trend of GDP Growth and Foreign Direct investment in India (Author's own)

*Data Source*: World Development Indicators (WDI), World Bank Report, https://databank.worldbank.org/source/world-development-indicators

An economy will get complete benefit from FDI if it enhances GDP and reduces environmental degradation substantially. For that reason, the following relations have been considered below.

Actual GDP growth= GDP (FDI) – [EC (FDI) + EC (MTech)]

where, EC= external cost

MTech = Modern technology and environment friendly method of production

$$\text{Here, } dGDP/dFDI > 0$$

$$dEC/dFDI > 0$$

$$dEC/dMTech < 0;$$

$$\text{If } (dGDP/dFDI) < (dEC/dFDI + dEC/dMTech),$$

Then, actual GDP growth will be negative. Here, the combined effect of external cost due to FDI and modern technology is much higher than GDP growth due to FDI, because foreign investors do not consider the environmental degradation due to productive activities. It is associated with the brown economy.

$$\text{If } (dGDP/dFDI) > (dEC/dFDI + dEC/dMTech),$$

Then, actual GDP growth will be positive. In this case, the growth of GDP is higher than the combined growth rate of EC due to FDI and MTech. The enhancement of external cost (EC) due to FDI is offset by a reduction of external cost due to the use of modern technology and environmentally friendly methods of production. It is associated with a green economy.

The tendency of FDI has been considered a catalyst to reduce environmental degradation and improve the process of sustainable development. But FDI may be responsible for environmental decadence because, generally, foreign investors have preferred to invest in any country to grab all the profit and take ownership of the domestic firms by exploiting domestic innate resources. They would get a lower level of return if they invest in reducing the emission of GHG. For that reason, foreign investors, generally, do not want to apply environmentally friendly technology in the production units. They expended on basic and essential infrastructure as these factors extend the level of profit considerably.[18] Fahri Seker[22] also supports the association between the magnitude of FDI and environmental quality in a negative direction but not significantly. For improving environmental quality, it is essential to use FDI for environmentally friendly sectors and simultaneously keep monitoring the detrimental impacts of FDI on the environment.

## 13.5 GREEN ECONOMY—A WAY OUT

The influx of FDI may have some positive influence on economic growth as well as a negative impact on environmental quality. The positive impact is considered a benefit and the negative impact is a cost due to FDI.

Net Benefit = (Benefit – Cost) from FDI
If net benefit > 0, then FDI is accepted
If net benefit < 0, then FDI is rejected

FDI does not indicate positive net benefit always. There is a chance of loss due to the outpouring of FDI in terms of ENS. In case of negative benefits, the way out may be the green economy. It is an approach to reduce all the stumbling blocks in the way of sustainable development and helps the economy to run all productive activities properly and efficiently along with ENS. United Nations Environment Program (UNEP) has defined the concept of "green economy" and it conveys that a green economy is a strategy or an approach to reduce environmental risk and suggests how to use natural deposits to avoid scarcity and energy waste. According to UNEP,[28] green economies have been playing a crucial role by improving the well-being of the people and equality among all members of society and at the same time reducing environmental risks and scarcities of ecological resources.[29] In a green economy, it is imperative to reduce the emission of GHGs and solid wastes during various economic activities. As a green economy provides a pollution-free environment, it would have been possible to carry out economic and productive activities at a lesser cost with the least degradation of environmental quality.[3] The green economy is an economy that will reduce the devastating effects on the environment due to productive activities and suggests the government introduce various policies that should be associated with the reduction of GHG emissions, specifically carbon dioxide, and the production of various pollutants. This economy also amplifies the economic growth and employment level and reduces the level of poverty. It is clear that a green economy focuses on the improvement of the living standard and enhances equality among the people in every aspect of society may increase the well-being of the people, and at the same time reduce environmental degradation.[28]

People of the green economy have been experiencing better life due to higher levels of income and employment. These are possible by investing a huge level of capital as capital has been used for abating environmental degradation and it also leads to appropriate management of raw materials for economic growth. Adequate investment—public and private—and implementation of relevant policies are preconditions for the establishment of a green economy. It has the capacity to reduce poverty and unemployment in key sectors like agriculture and at the same time preserve natural resources. Not only has that green economy also suggested framing policies for improving environmental quality. The first and most important strategy of the green economy is the reduction of deforestation and expansion of reforestation in the economy. Forest is an important factor as it can absorb huge levels of GHG from the atmosphere and supply raw materials for productive sectors and food for animals. The livelihood of the rural poor people is also associated with the forest. A shift to a green economy requires strict and strong government policies regarding pollution control and mobilizing capital to invest in various sectors. Continuous monitoring of the performance of the green economy is very crucial to introducing or eliminating various government strategies. In this regard, the cooperation of various international institutions is obligatory to sustain the green economy for a long period of time and needs a huge level of investment to implement the various objectives of the green economy appropriately. Satisfactory levels of investment in terms of public, private, and FDI are crucial determining factors to implement a green economy and corresponding policies and strategies of the government needed to replenish the reduced stock of natural capital. Investment associated with a green economy is known as green investment and this type of investment elevates the economic and productive activities and also invests in advanced technology and modern production methods. As a consequence, necessary resources have been used efficiently and preserved properly; and it would be possible to provide necessary resources to the succeeding time period equally and adequately.[28]

The first priority of all countries is to achieve economic growth. The level of growth may be either traditional GDP or green GDP. Traditional GDP or Brown GDP is the expansion of production level without considering the external cost of the productive activities. It is clear that green GDP is more desirable compared to brown GDP as it considers the expansion of output as well as the quality of the environment. Thus, green GDP not only indicates economic progress but also includes costs associated with environmental degradation and also maintains SS. Traditional GDP was indicated by brown economic growth and green GDP focuses on the sustainable development of any economy. It is easily decidable that proper implementation of a green economy mainly conveys sustainable development. Here, green growth is an indicator of the economic progress of any economy without environmental degradation.[15]

In the present scenario, the green economy has been attracting the attention of researchers and scientists for development in a proper way. According to Al-Taai,[2] the proper way of development means sustainable development and it would be possible by implementing a green economy. A green economy ensures the reduction of poverty and unemployment and a higher level of living standard and an expected level of welfare and simultaneously maintains the desired level of environmental quality. In this circumstance, renewable and non-renewable resources have been used in such a way that will optimize the level of output, employment, and welfare of the economy. In addition, it also ensures the rights of the people in the present and future, that is, equal distribution of raw materials. In the way to achieve a green economy, the main hindrance is capital scarcity as an adequate level of investment enhances prosperity and the living standard of the people. The green economy enhances output levels by protecting the environment from pollution. The process of economic development and qualitative environment are two opposite things and they are influencing each other effectively. A green economy can negotiate between them and emphasize the expected level of development with proper environmental protection. This strategy is known as green economic development or sustainable development. A green economy is mainly associated with the environment, economy, and social equity. This type of development attracts foreign investment and the result is a higher level of employment.[27] Foreign aid has also been playing a crucial role in promoting economic development with sustainability and at the same time improving environmental quality.[30]

The main attention of the green economy is to create several alternatives or substitutes for natural capital or limited raw materials for production in every sector of the economy. Coordination between various sectors in a substitutable manner has been suggested by the green economy. It mainly focuses on the appropriate interaction between humans and the environment, and society would experience non-toxic and harmless waste and emissions. This type of ecological society will help to eliminate all types of discrepancies between the economy and politics.[17]

Matthew E. Kahn[15] in his article suggests promoting the eco-friendly project and setting up businesses that have no harmful impacts on the environment. It would be preferable to use renewable resources instead of exhaustible resources to produce goods and services to fulfill the demands of the people and the government should introduce various instruments like a carbon tax to reduce pollution levels. Alternatively, firms can reduce pollution levels by using a "cap and trade" policy at a minimum level of cost. In this regard, it is worth mentioning that the pollution-controlling process must be associated with the same or increasing level of output. Otherwise, there will be a chance of unemployment due to a lower level of output in the economy. Thus, it is indispensable to develop new technology or production methods that will accelerate the level of production as well as minimize the level of waste and GHG emissions. In addition, it is essential to protect human health from environmental degradation; and the use of green technology leads to well-planned use of resources and ensures the availability of resources for the future generation. In this way, the establishment of a green economy would confirm the sustainable development of the economy.

The process of growth in a green economy indicates green growth. Through this process, long-term investment increases ENS and at the same time reduces the poverty level. It mainly emphasizes increasing income levels and that will reduce poverty and inequality in the economy. A prerequisite for green growth is an investment that will help to produce various substitute products for exhaustible resources and also reduce the emission level of harmful gases. As a result, people will get more return from productive units and as a result higher levels of saving and then more capital formation. A higher level of capital can offset the decreased level of natural capital and this unchanged level of capital would maintain the same level of consumption or level of production. As a consequence, economic growth will be sustained for a long period of time.[24] In a green economy, greater importance has been given to natural capital. It enhances the social security and purchasing capacity of poor people by conserving the ecosystem and also provides environmental techniques for productive activities. It also improves the quality and availability of drinking water and provides proper sanitation facilities and which in turn enhances SS in the economy.[10]

In this regard, a green economy may play a crucial role in attracting FDI as well as improving environmental quality. The green economy is an economy associated with minimum emission of GHG, well-organized use of innate resources, specifically exhaustible resources, and economic and productive resources should be done in a socially desirable way. In the green economy, people can access all the benefits and facilities at the desired level which in turn improves the living standard in society. And it would be possible by creating employment opportunities and income for the people. An adequate level of investment has been playing a crucial role in enhancing growth level as well as income level. But part of the investment should be expended for environmental improvement and the remaining part for productive purposes.

Investment in an economy with a minimum level of environmental hazard would reconstruct the agriculture and industrial sectors and improve their economic condition. The financial condition of the people may improve by creating employment opportunities. And it would be possible to distribute natural resources among present and future generations and create a sustainable living standard for the people; these situations lead to a situation of ENS and SS.[29]

In a green economy, the process of development may increase speedily by using sustainable technology. Application of this technology in productive and economic activities produces a lesser quantity of waste and harmful emissions. As a result, the radical change of sustainable technology helps the economy to reduce environmental risk substantially. This technology is very much associated with ENS but reconstruction of the economy and society is a prerequisite to achieving sustainable development.[25]

### *13.5.1 GREEN ECONOMY AND SUSTAINABLE DEVELOPMENT*

The green economy indicates a process to accomplish sustainable development in the economic and environmental fields. It helps the economy to complete economic and productive activities appropriately and upgrade the living standard of the people without hampering the normal activities of future generations. A green economy always uses natural raw materials for growth in such a way that would not be responsible for any type of environmental risk. Actually, it makes a change in the method of production, consumption, and use of required resources; and suggests avoiding inefficient and obsolete methods, and pollution-creating technology. For long-term sustainable development, it is indispensable to incorporate sustainable management of resources and need proper control of the management system.[16]

Sustainable economic development is the combined result of three system-biological, economic, and social. In other words, it maximizes the output and maintains the quality and availability of raw materials properly. In this regard, valuation of environmental benefits is very important and with the help of cost-benefit analysis, it would be possible to accept the desirable productive unit. There are also three angles of sustainable development—economic, political, and epistemological dimensions. Sustainable development from an economic point of view indicates the preservation of natural deposits and maximization of human welfare before finishing the stock of resources. The political dimension of sustainable development considers the proper management of necessary resources through the political process. Thirdly, sustainable development can be achieved epistemologically. It indicates that scientific knowledge of resource management can be used to maintain the same level of availability of raw materials.[21]

## 13.6 CONCLUSION

Environmental degradation has become a serious matter of concern for policymakers and environmental economists. It has been considered a hindrance to the influx of FDI as foreigners would not prefer to invest in an economy surrounded by massive pollution and concomitantly the environmental risk becomes an impediment in the way of sustainable development. But without adequate investment, specifically FDI, the expected level of economic growth and employment opportunities would not be possible. Based on secondary data, FDI and GDP growth or economic growth have not shown any significant relationship in the Indian context. However, FDI would play an important role in the enhancement of economic growth at such a level that would offset the loss or external cost due to environmental degradation. In this situation, the green economy has been playing a pivotal role by amplifying economic growth as well as improving the atmosphere quality. A green economy has been associated with the improvement of atmosphere quality and at the same time reduces poverty and unemployment; leading to the country achieving sustainable development—an intention of all countries. A green economy would amplify the process of sustainable development and improve SS and ENS. Here, green economy and sustainable development complement each other and green economy is the new approach and strategy to abrogate all the negative outcomes of the environmental risk (like emission of carbon dioxide) and help the economy to achieve SD. Policymakers suggest introducing various advanced technologies and production methods to reduce the degradation quality and lead to a situation of a green economy and eventually sustainable development.

## KEYWORDS

- **environmental degradation**
- **sustainable development**
- **green economy**
- **FDI**
- **carbon dioxide**

## REFERENCES


1. Aitken, B. J.; Harrison, A. E. Do Domestic Firms Benefit from Direct Foreign Investment? Evidence from Venezuela. *Am. Econ. Rev.* **1999,** *89* (3), 605–618. doi:http://dx.doi.org/10.1257/ aer.89.3.605
2. Al-Taai, S. H. H. Green Economy and Sustainable Development. *Earth Environ. Sci.* **2021,** *779,* 1–12. doi:10.1088/1755-1315/779/1/012007
3. Arumova, E.; Belyaeva, E.; Bitarova, M.; Panaseykina, V. Green Economy as a Direction of Sustainable Development of Coastal Areas, Advances in Economics. *Bus. Manag. Res.* **2019,** *10,* 192–197.
4. Asongu, S.; Akpan, U. S.; Isihak, S. R. Determinants of Foreign Direct Investment in Fast-growing Economies: Evidence from the BRICS and MINT Countries, *Financ. Innov.* **2018,** *4* (26), 1–27. doi:https://doi.org/10.1186/s40854-018-0114-0
5. Basiago, A. D. Economic, Social, and Environmental Sustainability in Development Theory and Urban Planning Practice. *Environmentalist* **1999,** *19,* 145–161.
6. Bhushan, A.; Mittal, I. Role of Foreign Direct Investment in the Development of Indian Economy. *RMS J. Manag. IT,* **2015,** *7* (1 and 2), 132–137.
7. Ekins, P.; Zenghelis, D. The Costs and Benefts of Environmental Sustainability. *Sustain. Sci.* **2021,** *16,* 949–965.
8. Feng, H.; Liu, Z.; Wu, J.; Iqbal, W.; Ahmad, W.; Marie, M. Nexus between Government Spending's and Green Economic Performance: Role of Green Finance and Structure Effect. *Environ. Technol. Innov.* **2022,** *27,* 1–16.
9. Goodland, R. The Concept of Environmental Sustainability. *Annu. Rev. Ecol. Syst.* **1995,** *26,* 1–24.
10. Gostieva, N.; Kazarinova, E.; Samarina, E.; Balabanova, A. Green Economy as an Object of State Regulation of Sustainable Development, *EDP Sci.* **2020,** doi:https://doi.org/10.1051/e3sconf/202017404037
11. Gowdy, J. M.; McDaniel, C. N. The Physical Destruction of Nauru: An Example of Weak Sustainability. *Land Econ.* **1999,** *75* (2), 333–338.
12. Haque, M S. Environmental Discourse and Sustainable Development: Linkages and Limitations. *Ethics Environ.* **2000,** *5* (1), 3–21.
13. Hope, K. R. Promoting Sustainable Community Development in Developing Countries: The Role of Technology Transfer. *Commun. Dev. J.* **1996,** *31* (3), 193–200.
14. Kadekodi, G. K. Is a 'Green Economy' Possible? *Econ. Polit. Wkly.* **2013,** *48* (25), 44–49.
15. Kahn, M. E. The Green Economy. *Foreign Policy, No. 172* (May/June 2009), 34–38, 2009.
16. Kousar, S.; Bhutta, A. I.; Ullah, M. R.; Shabbir, A. Why is the Shift from Brown Economy to Green Economy Important in South Asian Economies? [Online] *A Panel Cointegration Analysis*. https://assets.researchsquare.com/files/rs-1486884/v1_covered.pdf?c=1650984984 doi: https://doi.org/10.21203/rs.3.rs-1486884/v1
17. Kumar, B.; Kumar, P. Green Economy: Policy Framework for Sustainable Development. *Curr. Sci.* **2011,** *100* (7), 961–962.
18. Milani, B. What Is Green Economics? *Race Poverty Environ.* **2006,** *13* (1), 42–44.
19. Moraji, A.; Ganessamurthy, K. Role of Foreign Direct Investment in Indian Economy. In *FDI-Astute Conduit for Trade Integration and Sustainable Development*; Uthayasuriyan, K., Ed., 2015; pp 145–148. https://www.researchgate.net/publication/339676220_Role_of_Foreign_Direct_Investment_in_Indian_Economy

20. Pearce, D. W.; Atkinson, G. D. Capital Theory and the Measurement of Sustainable Development: An Indicator of "Weak" Sustainability. *Ecol. Econ.* **1993,** *8* (2), 103–108. doi:10.1016/0921-8009(93)90039-9
21. Raza, S. S.; Hussain, A. The Nexus of Foreign Direct Investment, Economic Growth and Environment in Pakistan. *Pak. Dev. Review,* **2016,** *55* (2), 95–111.
22. Redclift, M. The Multiple Dimensions of Sustainable Development. *Geography* **1991,** *76* (1), 36–42.
23. Seker, F.; Ertugrul, H. M.; Cetin, M. The Impact of Foreign Direct Investment on Environmental Quality: A Bounds Testing and Causality Analysis for Turkey. *Renew. Sustain. Energy Rev.* **2015,** *52,* 347–356.
24. Shalini, S. The Role of Foreign Direct Investment (FDI) in India- An Overview. *Int. J. Res. Anal. Rev.* **2020,** *7* (1), 91–100.
25. Smulders, S.; Toman, M.; Withagen, C. Growth Theory and 'Green Growth'. *Oxf. Rev. Econ. Policy* **2014,** *30* (3), 423–446.
26. Soderholm, P. The Green Economy Transition: The Challenges of Technological Change for Sustainability. *Sustain. Earth* **2020,** *3* (6), 1–11. doi:https://doi.org/10.1186/s42055-020-00029-y
27. Swaminathan, M. S.; Kesavan, P. C. Achieving the Sustainable Development Goals. *Curr. Sci.* **2016,** *110* (2), 127–128.
28. Tsou, J. The Greening Economy. *Race Pov. Environ.* **2006,** *13* (1), 51–55.
29. UNEP. Towards a Green Economy: Pathways to Sustainable Development and Poverty Eradication—A Synthesis for Policy Makers [Online], 2011. https://sustainabledevelopment.un.org/content/documents/126GER_synthesis_en.pdf
30. Voumik, L. C.; Shah, F. H. A Green Economy in the Context of Sustainable Development and Poverty Eradication: What are the Implications for Bangladesh? *J. Econ. Sustain. Dev.* **2014,** *5* (3), 119–131.
31. Williams, M. Aid, Sustainable Development and the Environmental Crisis. *Int. J. Peace Stud.* **1998,** *3* (2), 19–33.
32. World Bank Report. World Bank Indicators [Online]. http://databank.worldbank.org/data/country/IND/556d8fa6/Popular_countries# On October 15.07.2022, 8.25 pm.
33. Yue, S.; Yang, Y.; Hu, Y. Does Foreign Direct Investment Affect Green Growth? Evidence from China's Experience. *Sustainability* **2016,** *8* (158), 1–14. doi:10.3390/su8020158

CHAPTER 14

# Centralized Mechanical Resource System for Resource Allocation to Multi-Location Projects

AJAY TRIPATHI[1], PANKAJ KUMAR SHRIVASTAVA[2], PUSHPENDRA SINGH[3], and ABHIJEET SINGH[4]

[1]*Mechanical Engineering Department, AKS University, Satna, Madhya Pradesh, India*

[2]*Mechanical Engineering Department, Government Engineering College, Bhojpur, Ara, Bihar, India*

[3]*Department of Electrical Engineering, Rajkiya Engineering College, Banda, Uttar Pradesh, India*

[4]*Department of Applied Science & Humanities (Electronics), Rajkiya Engineering College, Banda, Uttar Pradesh, India*

## ABSTRACT

Proper planning and scheduling of resources is the main key to manage any organization effectively. The scheduling and sequencing of the different tasks poses enormous challenges due to the presence of inherent uncertainties. These works' repetitiveness is determined by the activities they entail, the connections between those activities within a given unit, and the resources needed to complete the tasks. Allocating resources for recurring construction operations is a huge difficulty. A resource may not be required for the full period of the project; also the project operations may not necessarily demand a constant quantity of resources. Construction of repeating projects with same or comparable units makes the problem more tedious. Therefore, managing

Management for Sustainable Development: Integrating Social, Economic, and Environmental Goals.
Vishal Jain & Amit Mittal (Eds.)

resources is inevitable in the design and execution of a construction project. This paper is written focusing on a government organization Uttar Pradesh Public Works Department and conceptualizes a Centralized Mechanical Resource System (CMRS) which shall be responsible for allocating mechanical resources to work of individual units in a specific geographical location whenever demand is placed to CRMS with an objective to minimize the mechanical resources usage cost and maximize the resource utilization by imposing certain priority rules for allocation.

## 14.1 INTRODUCTION

Construction industries are always aspiring to enhance the quality of work and reduce the operational expenditure by becoming more efficient. The efficient execution of the task can help the organizations to improve their performance and cut down the operating cost. This is done in the construction industry by grouping various tasks into distinct departments according to their nature, which increases performance effectiveness. Based on the particular nature of the work they do, organizations specialize more and perform more efficiently by concentrating their efforts.

A construction organization is concerned with construction and maintenance of civil structures across different locations of a definite geographical area through different construction and maintenance units established at different locations. At unit level, different mechanical resources are allocated to individual units based on nature of work performed by that unit. The mechanical resources perform the work of the units they belong. This situation is analogous to Multi Project Management.[1]

An important aspect of project management is scheduling time accurately. This is a critical component of Project Planning as this will decide the deadline for the completion of a project.[2]

## 14.2 OVERVIEW OF PUBLIC WORKS DEPARTMENT OF UTTAR PRADESH

The Public Works Department (PWD) of the state of Uttar Pradesh is structured into divisions, which are often divided based on the geological regions and types of work the PWD performs. The PWD's individual divisions carry out tasks related to the construction and maintenance of roads, buildings, and bridges, among other things. The divisions are set up all over the state of Uttar Pradesh. Depending on the size, volume, and type of employment available in the district, a district may contain numerous divisions of the same or different character. The kind of job and volume of work that are projected to be handled by each division in the future determines the type and quantity of mechanical resources that are allotted to each division. Regardless of whether the division has work to do or not, in practise these mechanical resources are devoted in nature and can only be used by the same division. The majority of the time, a division is either overworked or underutilized due to a lower work load, which has the opposite effect on the installed capacity of the mechanical resources. The mechanical resources given to each division are of the same type and carry out various tasks in each division.

| **Divisions** | **Mechanical resources** |
|---|---|
| D1 | Truck, Tipper, Road Roller, Tractor, Air Compressor, Water Tanker |
| D2 | Tipper, Road Rollers, Paver Finisher, Hot Mix Plant, Loader |
| D3 | Truck, Road Rollers, Loader, Tractor, Water Tanker |
| D4 | Truck, Road Roller, Tractor, Water Tanker |

The above structure shows a general distribution of mechanical resources to each division in a district—D1, D2, D3, and D4—to carry out the work specific to that division. These divisions use the mechanical resources mentioned above as needed, according to their needs.

### *14.2.1 CHARACTERISTICS OF THE WORK LOAD OF THE DIVISIONS IN U.P.P.W.D.*

Since the work (Finance) which is allotted to different divisions comes through different schemes run by the state government, Central government, or from some international sources, the planning is generally done on year basis. Needlessly to say, the schemes change from time to time and thereby the work load also changes. Considering different divisions at the same time frame it is found that during the same time period some of the divisions are overloaded and some are running with very low work load or even virtually idle. Divisions in districts do invite open tenders on behalf of government from eligible contractors who are registered in the department to carry out the specified work. Tender documents contain particulars of work to be executed by the selected contractor. The documents also specify the role and support to be extended by the department to selected contractor in the execution of the work. The contractor performs the work in accordance with the specifications of the work. Department supplies some essential materials/tools/plants/machines etc. which are available in the department to contractor on charge/hire charge basis at a rate which is specified in the tender document. An amount equal to the charge of the same facility is deducted from the total bill of the contractor.

### *14.2.2 EXISTING MECHANICAL RESOURCE ALLOCATION SYSTEM*

The planning regarding the resource allocation to one particular division is generally done at the time of establishment of that division which continues over the years to come. Considering different divisions at the same time frame it is found that during the same time period some of the divisions are overloaded and some are running with very low work load or even virtually idle, despite the fact that the dedicated resources of underutilized divisions were not shifted to over utilized divisions to take care of extra work load due to lack in dynamism in resource shifting and various inherent characteristics. The above situation is a common phenomenon in the departments and prevails throughout. The decision regarding the closure/merger/shifting of such under load or idle divisions are of course taken by the competent authorities, but this decision takes considerable amount of time due to inherent characteristics of decision-making and implementation. When any work is performed by the contractor, the concerned division supplies some essential materials/tools/plants/machines etc. which are available in the division or even the concerned division arranges the same from other divisions of the department and provides to contractor on charge/hire charge basis at a rate which is specified in the tender document or in the approved departmental schedules. An amount equal to the charge of the same facility is deducted from the total bill of the contractor. Since a division has limited mechanical resources, it is common practice that contractors do arrange those m/cs on themselves if the same is not supplied by the department. It is in practice that the essential m/cs are provided by the concerned division only and it often happens that either the required m/c is allocated to some other work or is not available in that division. At the same time it is also found that the required m/c is functional and idle in other divisions of the same district but cannot be allocated to work of the division where it is required due to the fact that the concerned officer in charge of the mechanical resources in that division is responsible for the resources of the same division only and is not aware of the status of other divisions. This is a common phenomenon and prevails in the divisions throughout the year.

## ***14.2.3 SYSTEM CHARACTERISTICS***

### *14.2.3.1 DIVISION*

The organization of Public Works Department is structured in divisional frame work. A district may have one or more than one division based on the nature and quantum of work available in the district and area of the district. The geographical areas of operation of divisions are identified. A division is responsible for planning and execution of construction/maintenance of roads, bridges, or buildings falling under their jurisdiction. Division does the survey and inspection, prepares the estimates for the construction of these infrastructures, gets these estimates technically sanctioned from competent authorities of the department and then these estimates are sent for budget approval and allotment from state finance authorities. Once the budget is approved for the project from the authority, it is allocated to respective division for tendering process. Division floats the tender for the project and receives bids from eligible contractors and agencies. From among all the bidders, one which meets the requisite criteria of technical and financial parameters as laid down in tender document is selected to award the work. The work when allotted to a bidder has to be completed in stipulated time and within the sanctioned budget in accordance with the technical guidelines, specifications, work standards, and norms. Division provides in house facilities/materials/resources to bidders to carry out execution of the work. The cost of these resources is deducted from the bills of the contractors at a rate (hire charge/usage cost) which is mentioned in the tender document.

### *14.2.3.2 MECHANICAL RESOURCES*

A division owns different mechanical resources which carry out specific construction activities. These resources are road construction machineries, tools, and plants e.g. Truck, Tipper, Tractor, Static Road Roller, Vibratory Road Roller, Excavator, Loader, Transit Mixture, Scrapper, Asphalt Paver Finisher, Bitumen Sprayer, Air Compressor, Water Tanker, Asphalt Plant, Cement Concrete Plant, Water Bound Macadam Plant etc. These mechanical resources may be of different capacities and make. The complete detail e.g.

purchase price, make, age, capacity, location, status whether functional or under repair, hire charges rate, shifting charge rate, idle charge rate, over time rate, name of the owner (driver/helper) etc. are available. Each mechanical resource is identified by its unique identification number.

### *14.2.3.3 PROJECT*

A project consists of different activities performed by different mechanical resources. Projects are typically broken down into tasks and subtasks that demand for either renewable (workforce, machines, tools, etc.) or nonrenewable (raw materials, fuel, energy, etc.) resources. The same set of finite resources is frequently competed by the tasks and their subtasks. Tasks may also be subject to broader time limits brought on by organizational or technological limitations.[3] Start and end dates for specific projects are known. Every project is executed at specific location. A Project is executed by the selected bidder who provides required material and human resource to carry out all required activities in coordination with Project Manager who supervises the project and ensures that all activities are performed as per the laid down specifications, norms, and standards. A project is identified by its unique name and identification number. All mechanical resources are utilized to carry out different activities of project. Type of mechanical resource and their duration of work is known for projects. Project manager is responsible for placing a request to CMRS for allocation of mechanical resources.

### *14.2.3.4 CENTRALIZED MECHANICAL RESOURCE SYSTEM (CMRS)*

There is a single resource center which is solely responsible for resource allocation to different projects running under different divisions. This works as a Centralized Mechanical Resource Center (CMRS) and acts as a central server capable of two-way communication with resource owner. Resource owner is in charge of the individual mechanical resource and executes the operation of the mechanical resource he is associated with. Every Project Manager has to file a request to CMRS for allocation of required mechanical resources which are required for the execution of project activities. All requisite information related to mechanical resources are available with CMRS, e.g., Resource I.D. Number, Name of Resource, Capacity of Resource, Status of Resource whether functional, Idle or under repair, Resource Owner details, Location of Resource, Usage Cost of Resource, Idle Cost of Resource, Over

Time Cost of Resource, Out sourcing Cost of Resource, Shifting Cost of Resource etc. Resource Manager is in charge of the CMRS and is responsible for proper functioning of mechanical resource with a view to maximizing the resource utilization and minimizing the usage cost of resource in coordination with Project Manager and selected Contractor.

## 14.3 RESOURCE ALLOCATION

Contractors must raise the quantity of work done per unit time as the demand for shorter delivery dates grows by increasing the resources used by activities and scheduling more activities concurrently. Simultaneous optimization of all the problems is well known as multi-objective or multi-criteria optimization problem in Operation Research.[4]

Generally, the objective of the resource allocation problem is to maximize or minimize a function "*P*" of "*n*" variables under "*m*" constraints.

$$\text{Max/Min } P = P\,(X_1, X_2, X_3 \ldots X_n)$$

Under the following constraints:

$$f_1(X_1, X_2, X_3 \ldots X_n) \le 0$$

$$f_2(X_1, X_2, X_3 \ldots X_n) \le 0$$

$$f_3(X_1, X_2, X_3 \ldots X_n) \le 0$$

..........

$$f_m(X_1, X_2, X_3 \ldots X_n) \le 0$$

The interaction between project activities through explicit and implicit dependencies, which may be subject to some degree of uncertainty, leads to the complexity of resource allocation. The 1960s saw the development of project management resource allocation algorithms. The time-cost trade-off problem, the project duration problem, and the resource leveling problem were the three types of resource allocation challenges that were the focus of the early research. It is expected that a rigorous order in the collection of activities for all three problem categories outlines the completion-to-start precedence restrictions between activities. A multi-mode resource allocation dilemma known as the time-cost tradeoff problem appears when certain activity durations can be shortened at the expense of higher direct costs. The resource to be allocated is thus thought of as the project budget. The continuous mode assignment problem, which entails computing all combinations of project length and matching least-cost schedule, can be solved by using network flow techniques if the cost incurred for each activity is a convex function in the activity duration.[5] Projects have three interconnected goals: to stick to the budget, finish on schedule, and achieve client-satisfactory standards. Unexpected issues will inevitably develop as the project progresses because we live in uncertain world. These unforeseeable occurrences will jeopardize the project's schedule, money, and requirements. Now, the PM must choose how to compromise one project aim for another (e.g., to stay on schedule by assigning extra resources to the project may mean it will run over the predetermined budget.) Unless the established timetable and budget are excessively generous or the difficulty of fulfilling the standards has been significantly underestimated, the project is likely doomed to failure if the schedule, budget, and specs are strictly predetermined.[6] The efficient management of a construction project mostly hinges on effective resource planning and scheduling. The scheduling and sequencing of repetitive tasks while dealing with uncertainty and resource limitations is a problem that plagues the construction industry today.

These works' repetitiveness is determined by the activities they entail, the connections between those activities within a given unit, and the resources needed to complete the tasks. Allocating resources for recurring construction operations is a huge difficulty. A resource may not be required for the full period of the project; project operations may not necessarily demand a constant quantity of resources. Construction of repeating projects with same or comparable units makes the problem more urgent. Therefore, managing resources is a crucial role in the design and execution of a construction project. It is essential to note that for efficient resource usage, the workload and resource distribution must coincide. In reality, one of the major problems with multi-project management is resource allocation.[7] Making wise choices on the allocation of mechanical resources requires a real-time diagnosis of the current state of such resources. Effective resource allocation will result from a network of two-way communication between planning and execution. The management of mechanical resources in the execution of civil construction projects belonging to various divisions at the district level shall be the responsibility of the Centralized Mechanical Resource System.

### 14.3.1 MULTI-PROJECT RESOURCE ALLOCATION

Multi-Project Environment[8] can be characterized as –

A. Resource-unconstrained Multi-project scheduling—Most widely used CPM and PERT techniques deal with time aspect only and consider resources in abundance, i.e., resource availability is considered throughout the length of the project in adequate quantity. However in real world multi-project environment deals with resource scarcity and hence resource-constrained multi-project scheduling is essential.

Resource unconstrained multi-projects face many difficulties –

a) Optimal use of resources.
b) Control of resource wastage
c) Lavish use of resources leads to cost overruns and profit loss
d) Underutilization of resources
e) Lack of coordination, communication, and commitment

B. Resource-constrained Multi-project scheduling—The Resource Constrained Multi Project Scheduling Problem results from the fact that most multi-projects share similar resource pools whose capacities are insufficient to sustain all project operations simultaneously (RCMPSP).

Resource constrained projects face issues in

a) Prioritization of resources based on experience and critical path identification
b) Lack of coordination, communication, and collaboration
c) Unskilled labor
d) Outdated machinery
e) Unqualified supervision
f) Quality issues
g) Reworks
h) Awareness of using new technologies

## 14.4 MECHANICAL RESOURCES

An organization's tasks and resources might take on a variety of shapes. The resources could be equipment in a workshop, airport runways, workers at a construction site, processing power in a data center, and so on. The tasks could be activities in a production process, airport takeoffs and landings, phases of a construction project, computer programme executions, and so on. Each work may be assigned a certain priority level, the earliest time it could start, and a deadline. The goals can also be expressed in a variety of ways. One goal might be to do the last task as quickly as possible, and another might be to finish as few tasks as possible that are past their respective due dates.[9]

## 14.5 CENTRALIZED MECHANICAL RESOURCE SYSTEM

Resources play vital role in timely and economical completion of projects in construction industry. Resource allocation for multiple projects running at different geographical locations becomes critical from the organizational stake point of view since many trade-offs are to be taken care of, e.g., time and cost, cost and quality etc. Timely completion of projects with expected quality of work and keeping project cost under predetermined level are core objectives of construction organization. Ensuring required resources to be allocated at right time to specific jobs from in-house capacity or from outsourcing is pivotal to success of a project.

A centralized Mechanical Resource System is developed to cater the need of an organization involved in construction work of several projects running in parallel for the purpose of allocation of mechanical resources to different activities of different projects running at different geographical locations within a specific region with an aim to maximize resource utilization and minimize resource usage cost.

### *14.5.1 ASSUMPTIONS*

While developing a Centralized Mechanical Resource System the following assumptions are made related to mechanical resources, work etc.

1. Type, capacity, and quantity of mechanical resources under a district are known.
2. Place/situation of mechanical resource where it is kept in a district are known.
3. Distance of mechanical resource from work site is known.
4. A district can have many divisions based on size of the district or nature of work.
5. Mechanical resources can serve to any division based on the availability.
6. A district has many stores spread across the district where mechanical resources are kept and are sent to the site to perform the work and shifted after completion of work.
7. Mechanical resources which are required to work on site are sent from the nearest store to minimize the shifting cost and are sent back to nearest store after the work is completed.
8. Idle cost, shifting cost, and hire charge to use a mechanical resource are known.

9. Every mechanical resource is assumed to have operators and helpers/cleaners.
10. Whether mechanical resources are under repair, functional, working, idle, or unavailable, are known.
11. Mechanical resource may work under regular working hours, overtime hours or may be outsourced depending on need and availability.
12. Cost of regular working time is least; then cost of overtime and outsourcing is most expensive and these costs are known.
13. A mechanical resource is allocated first under regular working time then under overtime and if mechanical resources are not available or busy, outsourcing is done.
14. One day consists of 8 regular working hours and 16 overtime hours whereas outsourcing is unlimited.
15. A project may consist of many works and these works may require different mechanical resources.
16. A work can be completed under regular working time or under overtime of resources or a combination of both, but if a work requires a resource which is outsourced, it is outsourced completely.
17. Mechanical resources are not dedicated to any project; rather they can serve any work of every project depending on need and availability.
18. Every mechanical resource is identified by unique code associated with it.
19. If a work requires a mechanical resource which is not available in the district or is under repair, the resource is outsourced.

### 14.5.2 PROJECT AND WORKS

1. A project is a set of different works to be performed to finish a project.
2. Projects run across different locations in a district.
3. No. of projects to be completed by mechanical resources is known.
4. No. and type of works under every project are known.
5. No. and type of mechanical resources required to perform in a work are known.
6. Time required to complete a work by a mechanical resource is known.
7. Total time or no. of days required to complete a project is known.
8. EST (Earliest Start Time), LST (Latest Start Time), EFT (Earliest Finish Time), and LFT (Latest Finish Time) of all works of every project is known.

9. Sequence or process route to complete a project is known.
10. Priority rules regarding the resource allocation can be incorporated into the system.
11. Works once started shall not be left incomplete in between.
12. Regular work starts every day at 9.00 am and finishes at 5.00 pm, total 8 hours a day.

## 14.6 DEVELOPMENT OF CMRS DATABASE

To make the Centralized Mechanical Resource System able to allocate mechanical resources, all the required information is required to be input into the system. This information relates with different aspects of the organization. Since our study is limited to geographical limits of a district, we shall input that information pertaining to the district only.

### *14.6.1 DISTRICT-LEVEL DATABASE*

The information pertaining to a district does relate with different divisions that originate projects and demand for different mechanical resources from CMRS. This information relates with the name of the divisions, their identification code, and area of working. Procedure for developing district-level database is shown in Figure 14.1.

An output when all the information related to district is entered in CMRS is shown in Table 14.1

### *14.6.2 MECHANICAL RESOURCE DATABASE*

This database contains all the information regarding mechanical resources which are available at district level to shoulder the responsibilities of any division under the same district. This information relates with type of mechanical resources and their quantity, capacity, identification number of resources, their location and status whether a resource is working, free, under repair, or is unavailable at district. These resources do attract hire charges, i.e., rental/usage charges to be borne by the project they are working for. These hire charges are different for regular working hours and for overtime. The resources shall be allocated mostly under regular hire charges to avoid the additional cost burden on projects. Regular working time and over time

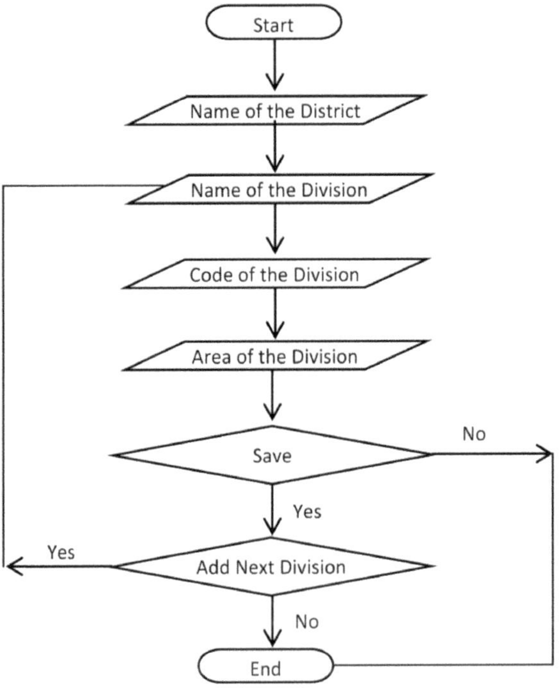


**FIGURE 14.1** Flow chart for the preparation of district-level database.

**TABLE 14.1** District-Level Database.

| Sr. no. | Name of the division | Division code | Area of working |
|---|---|---|---|
| 1 | Provincial Division | PRD | Meja, Korao |
| 2 | Construction Division No. 1 | CD1 | Sadar |
| 3 | Construction Division No. 2 | CD2 | Sorao |
| 4 | Construction Division No. 3 | CD3 | Phoolpur |
| 5 | Construction Division No. 4 | CD4 | Handia |
| 6 | P.M.G.S.Y. Division | PMG | Allahabad |
| 7 | National Highways Division No. 1 | NH1 | Allahabad |

duration is limited to 8 hours even if the work is completed before the end of 8 hours. If a mechanical resource is not available in the district, engaged in any work or is under repair, it may be outsourced from the market at a specific cost of outsourcing which is always greater than regular and overtime hire charges. If a resource is not functional at any project site and is kept idle, it attracts idle charges. Due care is to be given to make resources fully functional during their schedule working period. During the resource allocation process, resources are required to be shifted from one location to another. These shifting charges are also included in the database.

The procedure for developing a mechanical resource database is shown in Figure 14.2.

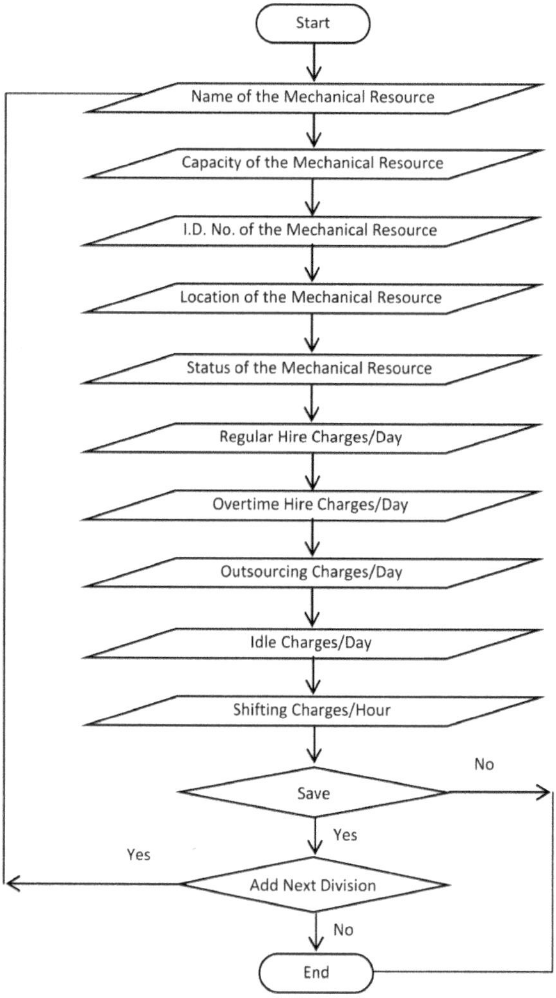


**FIGURE 14.2** Flowchart for the preparation of Mechanical Resource Database.

An output when all the information related to mechanical resources is entered in CMRS is shown in Table 14.2.

**TABLE 14.2** Mechanical Resource Database.

| Name of the M/c | Capacity of the M/c | Quantity of the M/c | Identification number of the M/c | Location | Status of the M/c | Regular Hire Charge/ day (8hrs) | Over time Hire Charge/ day (8 hrs) | Outsource Charge/ day (8 hrs) | Idle Charge/ Day | Shifting Charge/ Hr |
|---|---|---|---|---|---|---|---|---|---|---|
| Static Road Roller | 8-10 Ton | 8 | ALDMEDSPC0301 | Rampur | Working | 1600 | 2400 | 3200 | 1200 | 200 |
| | | | ALDMEDSPC0302 | Allahabad | Working | | | | | |
| | | | ALDPRDAGM3803 | Meja | Under Repair | | | | | |
| | | | ALDPRDAGM3804 | Khiri | Working | | | | | |
| | | | ALDCD3GRW3805 | Phulpur | free | | | | | |
| | | | ALDCD3ANG2906 | Jhunsi | free | | | | | |
| | | | ALDCD1JSP3807 | Allahabad | Working | | | | | |
| | | | ALDCD1JSP2508 | Handia | Working | | | | | |
| Tipper | 10 Ton | 4 | ALDMEDTAT3601 | Allahabad | Working | 2400 | 3600 | 4800 | 1600 | 300 |
| | | | ALDPRDTAT1202 | Meja | Working | | | | | |
| | | | ALDCD1TAT1201 | Allahabad | free | | | | | |
| | | | ALDPRDASL0802 | Phulpur | Under Repair | | | | | |
| Tractor | 6 Cum | 2 | ALDPRDJSP4801 | Allahabad | Working | 1600 | 2400 | 3200 | 1200 | 200 |
| | | | ALDCD1ESC1202 | Phulpur | free | | | | | |
| Excavator | 1 Cum | 2 | ALDMEDJCB0801 | Meja | Working | 6400 | 9600 | 12800 | 2500 | 800 |
| | | | ALDMEDJCB0602 | Handia | free | | | | | |
| Water Tanker | 2000 Ltr | 3 | ALDPRDESC1501 | Khiri | Working | 1600 | 2400 | 3200 | 1200 | 200 |
| | | | ALDPRDESC1502 | Rampur | Working | | | | | |
| | | | ALDPRDESC1503 | Allahabad | Under Repair | | | | | |

**TABLE 14.2** *(Continued)*

| Name of the M/c | Capacity of the M/c | Quantity of the M/c | Identification number of the M/c | Location | Status of the M/c | Regular Hire Charge/ day (8hrs) | Over time Hire Charge/ day (8 hrs) | Outsource Charge/ day (8 hrs) | Idle Charge/ Day | Shifting Charge/ Hr |
|---|---|---|---|---|---|---|---|---|---|---|
| Vibratory Road Roller | 8-10 Ton | 2 | ALDMEDL&T0601 | Allahabad | Working | 3200 | 4800 | 6400 | 2400 | 400 |
| | | | ALDMEDL&T0602 | Meja | free | | | | | |
| Paver | 50 TPH | 2 | ALDMEDAPL0601 | Allahabad | Working | 3200 | 4800 | 6400 | 2400 | 400 |
| | | | ALDMEDAPL0602 | Meja | free | | | | | |
| Bitumen Sprayer | 10 Ton | 2 | ALDMEDAPL0801 | Allahabad | Working | 2400 | 3600 | 4800 | 1600 | 300 |
| | | | ALDMEDAPL0602 | Meja | free | | | | | |
| Air Compressor | 500 psi | 2 | ALDMEDELG0801 | Allahabad | Working | 1600 | 2400 | 3200 | 1200 | 200 |
| | | | ALDMEDELG0602 | Meja | free | | | | | |
| Leveller | 1 Cum | - | - | - | Unavailable | - | - | 4800 | 1600 | - |

### *14.6.3 DEPARTMENTAL STORES DATABASE*

This database contains the information regarding all the departmental stores where mechanical resources are kept safely after their job is finished. Resources are transferred from these stores to project locations when any demand is placed by the division. The flowchart for the preparation of departmental store is shown in Figure 14.3.

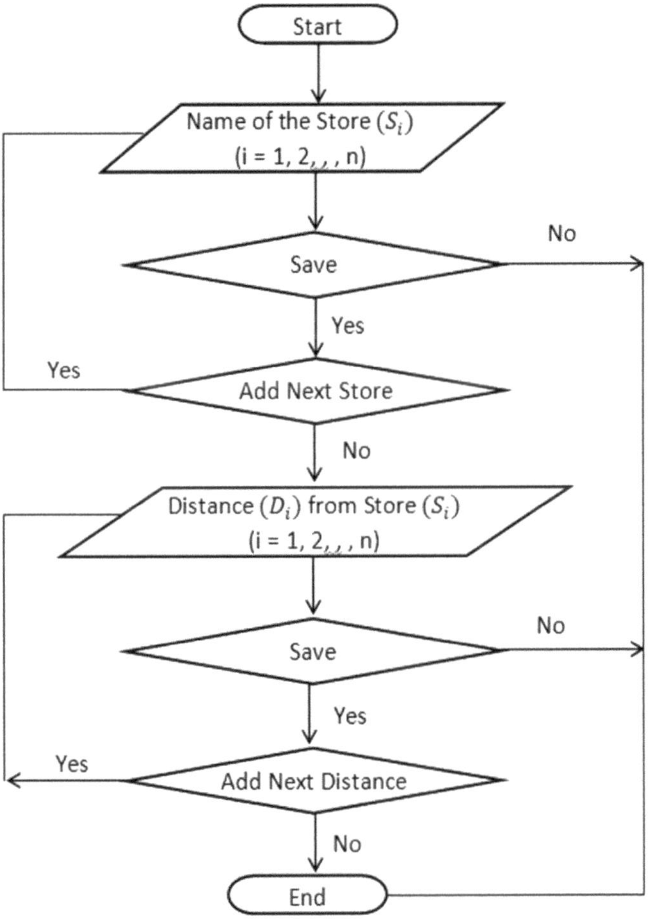


**FIGURE 14.3** Flowchart for the preparation of Departmental Store Database.

An output when all the information of departmental stores is entered in CMRS is shown in Table 14.3.

**TABLE 14.3** Departmental Store Database.

| Location | | Alopibag | Teliyarganj | Kutchahry | Jhunsi | Saidabad | Phoolpur | Phaphamau | Sorao | Lalgopalganj | Manauri | Naini | Meja | Korao | Karchhana |
|---|---|---|---|---|---|---|---|---|---|---|---|---|---|---|---|
| | | **1** | **2** | **3** | **4** | **5** | **6** | **7** | **8** | **9** | **10** | **11** | **12** | **13** | **14** |
| Alopibag | 1 | 0 | 6 | 4 | 7 | 32 | 36 | 14 | 29 | 40 | 32 | 8 | 54 | 74 | 34 |
| Teliyarganj | 2 | 6 | 0 | 5 | 13 | 38 | 42 | 8 | 23 | 34 | 31 | 14 | 60 | 80 | 40 |
| Kutchahry | 3 | 4 | 5 | 0 | 11 | 36 | 40 | 10 | 25 | 36 | 33 | 12 | 58 | 78 | 38 |
| Jhunsi | 4 | 7 | 13 | 11 | 0 | 25 | 29 | 21 | 36 | 47 | 39 | 15 | 61 | 81 | 41 |
| Saidabad | 5 | 32 | 38 | 36 | 25 | 0 | 30 | 46 | 55 | 72 | 64 | 40 | 86 | 106 | 66 |
| Phoolpur | 6 | 36 | 42 | 40 | 29 | 30 | 0 | 36 | 51 | 62 | 68 | 44 | 90 | 110 | 70 |
| Phaphamau | 7 | 14 | 8 | 10 | 21 | 46 | 36 | 0 | 15 | 26 | 39 | 22 | 68 | 88 | 48 |
| Sorao | 8 | 29 | 23 | 25 | 36 | 55 | 51 | 15 | 0 | 32 | 61 | 37 | 83 | 103 | 63 |
| Lalgopalganj | 9 | 40 | 34 | 36 | 47 | 72 | 62 | 26 | 32 | 0 | 65 | 48 | 94 | 114 | 74 |
| Manauri | 10 | 32 | 31 | 33 | 39 | 64 | 68 | 39 | 61 | 65 | 0 | 40 | 86 | 106 | 66 |
| Naini | 11 | 8 | 14 | 12 | 15 | 40 | 44 | 22 | 37 | 48 | 40 | 0 | 46 | 66 | 26 |
| Meja | 12 | 54 | 60 | 58 | 61 | 86 | 90 | 68 | 83 | 94 | 86 | 46 | 0 | 20 | 25 |
| Korao | 13 | 74 | 80 | 78 | 81 | 106 | 110 | 88 | 103 | 114 | 106 | 66 | 20 | 0 | 45 |
| Karchhana | 14 | 34 | 40 | 38 | 41 | 66 | 70 | 48 | 63 | 74 | 66 | 26 | 25 | 45 | 0 |

## 14.7 WORK ARRIVAL PROCESS

Any project which is considered for the allocation of mechanical resources must consist of following details (these details are to be provided by the client division):

- **Name of the Division:** This is the client division which requests to CMRS for the allocation of mechanical resources for the execution of different works of a project.
- **Name of the Project:** This is the name of the Project given by client division for which CMRS is expected to allocate mechanical resources.
- **Location of the Project:** This is the place where the project is to be executed.
- **Priority of the Project (Yes/No):** The priority for any project is to be decided by the client division based on the urgency of the project.
- **Project Duration:** This is the total number of days which are allocated for the completion of the project. It must be an integer value.
- **Date of Start of the Project:** This is the start date of the project from which the project shall start. This date is Earliest Start Date of first work of the project also.
- **Date of Completion of the Project:** This is the completion date of the project by which the project shall be finished. This date is Latest Finish Date of last work of the project also.
- **Type/Name and number of Works:** A project consists of several works which are linked to each other. There is a precedence relationship among all the works e.g. in the following mentioned project of annual repair of M.G. Road, the work of renewal cannot be started unless patch formation work is completed and patch formation can only be done when site cleaning is finished.
- **Work Duration:** This is the actual duration required to complete a work. Sum of duration of all the works in a project is always less than the project duration due to the fact that some time cushion is provided to complete a project to meet contingent situations, uncontrolled delays, obstructions in working, nonfavorable working conditions, or any other unforeseen situations.
- **Project Time Float:** This is the difference between project duration and sum of duration of all works in a project. This time float or cushion is made available to any project to accommodate delays and obstruction caused due to any reason while the project is running. This cushion is utilized judiciously so that the project is completed before

the end date. Time float is the excess time allotted to any project in addition to duration of different works of a project. This time float can be utilized among one or all the works of project as per the need that arises.

- **Quantity and type of mechanical resources required:** Quantity of mechanical resources required to complete different works of the project. This helps in allocating no. of required mechanical resources to different works.

With the help of the above-mentioned information, following is calculated:

Project Duration = Date of Completion of Project − Date of Start of Project

Total Time float = Project Duration − Sum of duration of all works

## 14.8 MATHEMATICAL FORMULATION

$P_i$ = No. of projects, let there be "m" projects running at different geographical locations ($i = 1, 2, \ldots, m$)

$DoSP_i$ = Date of start of project "*I*"

$DoCP_i$ = Date of completion of project "*i*"

$PDP_i$ = Duration of project "*i*" = Date of completion of project "*i*" – date of start of project "*i*" + 1 = $DoCP_i - DoSP_i + 1$

$W_{i0}$ = Null work, this work is an imaginary work added to any project for calculation purpose only. Null work does not consume any time and does not require any resource also.

$W_{ij}$ = No. of works, let there be "*n*" works including null work also in project "*m*" ($j = 0, 1, 2, \ldots, n$)

$D_{ij}$ = Duration of work "*j*" of project "*i*" in days

$TFP_i$ = Time float of project "*i*"

= Date of completion of project "*i*" – date of start of project "*i*" – sum of duration of all works "*j*" of project "*i*" + 1 = $DoCP_i - DoSP_i - \sum D_{ij} + 1$

$EFD\ W_{i0}$ = Earliest finish date of null work of project "*i*," this is the preceding date of Date of start of Project

= Date of Start of project "*i*" – 1

= $DoSP_i - 1$

$LFD\ W_{i0}$ = Latest Finish Date of Null Work of Project "*i*," this is the latest date after which the project can be started

= Date of Start of project "*i*" + Time float of project "*i*" – 1

= $DoSP_i + TFP_i - 1$

$ESD_{ij}$ = Earliest Start Date of work "j" of project "*i*"

= Earliest Finish Date of work "*j* – 1" of project "*i*" + 1

= $EFD_{ij-1} + 1$

$LSD_{ij}$ = Latest Start Date of work "*j*" of project "*i*"

= Latest Finish Date of work "*j* – 1" of project "*i*" +1

= $LFD_{ij-1} + 1$

$EFD_{ij}$ = Earliest Finish Date of work "*j*" of project "*i*"

= Earliest Start Date of work "*j*" of project "*i*" + Duration of work "*j*" of project "*i*" – 1

= $ESD_{ij} + D_{ij} - 1$

$LFD_{ij}$ = Latest Finish Date of work "*j*" of project "*i*"

= Latest Start Date of work "*j*" of project "*i*" + Duration of work "*j*" of project "*i*" – 1

= $LSD_{ij} + D_{ij} - 1$

With the help of above information and formulae, project summary sheet for all the projects is generated by the software. For instance 6 different projects which belong to different divisions in the district Allahabad are forwarded independently by the respective divisions to CMRS for allocating mechanical resources to respective projects. Upon arrival of projects to CMRS, the officer in charge of CMRS enters the details of the projects one by one into the system. The details when entered into the system do take the form as shown in Table 14.4.

It is evident from the observation of Project summary sheets that different works in turn complete a project. Works consume time for their completion and require different mechanical resources to execute them. A project may require several mechanical resources to execute different works of that project. Some resources may be required to first work; some may be needed for second and so on. If all the resources required by different works are allocated to a project in the beginning of the project, resources which are not required by first work shall remain idle till the time that work is started or keeping those resources unutilized which have finished their jobs

**TABLE 14.4** Project Information Database.

| Proect No. 1 | | | | | |
|---|---|---|---|---|---|
| Name of the Project | Annual Repair of M.G. Road | | | | |
| Location of the Project | M.G. Road, Phoolpur, Allahabad | | | | |
| Project I.D. No. | ALDCD3ARR011 | | | | |
| Division of the Project | C.D.-3, P.W.O., Allahabad | | | | |
| Project Priority | Yes | | | | |
| Date of Start of Project | 01/01/2020 | | | | |
| Date of Completion of Project | 11/03/2020 | | | | |
| Project Duration | 71 | | | | |
| Project Time Float | 15 | | | | |
| Particulars | | Work-0 | Work-1 | Work-2 | Work-3 |
| | | Null Work | Site Cleaning | Patch Format ion | Renewal |
| Earliest Start Date | | | 01/01/2020 | 06/01/2020 | 19/01/2020 |
| Latest Start Date | | | 16/01/2020 | 21/01/2020 | 03/02/2020 |
| Earliest Finish Date | | 31/12/2019 | 05/01/2020 | 18/01/2020 | 25/02/2020 |
| Latest Finish Date | | 15/01/2020 | 20/01/2020 | 02/02/2020 | 11/03/2020 |
| Duration | | 0 | 5 | 13 | 38 |
| Resource reqd. Qty. | Excavator | 0 | 1 | 0 | 0 |
| | Tractor | 0 | 1 | 0 | 0 |
| | Tipper | 0 | 0 | 1 | 1 |
| | Static Road Roller | 0 | 0 | 1 | 1 |
| | Vibratory Road Roller | 0 | 0 | 0 | 1 |
| | Bitumen Sprayer | 0 | 0 | 0 | 1 |
| | Air Compressor | 0 | 0 | 0 | 1 |
| | Asphalt Paver | 0 | 0 | 0 | 1 |
| | Laveler | 0 | 0 | 0 | 0 |
| | Water Tanker | 0 | 0 | 0 | 0 |

| Proect No. 2 | | | | | | | |
|---|---|---|---|---|---|---|---|
| Name of the Project | Construction of D.B. Road | | | | | | |
| Lo cation of the Project | D.B. Road, Meja, Allahabad | | | | | | |
| Project I.D. No. | ALDPRDCON002 | | | | | | |
| Division of the Project | P.O.,P.W.D., Allahabad | | | | | | |
| Project Priortiy | No | | | | | | |
| Date of Start of Project | 05/01/2020 | | | | | | |
| Date of Completion of Project | 25/03/2020 | | | | | | |
| Project Duration | 81 | | | | | | |
| Project Time Float | 19 | | | | | | |
| Particulars | | Work-0 | Work-1 | Work-2 | Work-3 | Work-4 | Work-5 |
| | | Null Work | Earth Work | Compaction of 45-90 mm size grit | Compaction of 45-63 mm size grit | Compaction of 25-50 mm size grit | P.C. Work |
| Earliest Start Date | | - | 05/01/2020 | 15/01/2020 | 30/01/2020 | 14 /02/2020 | 26/02/2020 |
| Latest Start Date | | - | 24/01/2020 | 03/02/2020 | 18/02/2 020 | 04 /03/2020 | 16/03/2020 |
| Earliest Finish Date | | 04/01/2020 | 14/01/2020 | 29/01/2020 | 13/02/2 020 | 25/02/2020 | 06 /03/2020 |
| Latest Finish Date | | 23/01/2020 | 02/02/2020 | 17/ 02/2020 | 03/03/2 020 | 15/03/2020 | 25/03/2020 |
| Duration | | 0 | 10 | 15 | 15 | 12 | 10 |
| Resource reqd. Qty. | Excavator | 0 | 1 | 0 | 0 | 0 | 0 |
| | Tractor | 0 | 1 | 0 | 0 | 0 | 0 |
| | Tipper | 0 | 0 | 2 | 2 | 2 | 3 |
| | Static Road Roller | 0 | 1 | 1 | 1 | 1 | 1 |
| | Vibratory Road Roller | 0 | 0 | 0 | 0 | 0 | 1 |
| | Bitumen Sprayer | 0 | 0 | 0 | 0 | 0 | 1 |
| | Air Compressor | 0 | 0 | 0 | 0 | 0 | 1 |
| | Asphalt Paver | 0 | 0 | 0 | 0 | 0 | 1 |
| | Laveler | 0 | 1 | 0 | 0 | 0 | 0 |
| | Water Tanker | 0 | 0 | 1 | 1 | 1 | 0 |

**TABLE 14.4** *(Continued)*

| Project No. 3 | | | | | |
|---|---|---|---|---|---|
| Name of the Project | Construction of R.R. Road | | | | |
| Location of the Project | R.R. Road, Sadar, Allahabad | | | | |
| Project I.D. No. | ALDCD1CON008 | | | | |
| Division of the Project | C.D. 1, P.W.D. Allahabad | | | | |
| Project Priority | Yes | | | | |
| Date of Start of Project | 05/01/2020 | | | | |
| Date of Completion of Project | 09/02/2020 | | | | |
| Project Duration | 36 | | | | |
| Project Time Float | 8 | | | | |
| Particulars | Work-0 | Work-1 | Work-2 | Work-3 | Work-4 |
| | Null Work | Compaction of 45-90 mm size grit | Compaction of 45-63 mm size grit | Compaction of 25-50 mm size grit | P.C. Work |
| Earliest Start Date | | 05/01/2020 | 13/01/2020 | 21/01/2020 | 27/01/2020 |
| Latest Start Date | | 13/01/2020 | 21/01/2020 | 29/01/2020 | 04/02/2020 |
| Earliest Finish Date | 04/01/2020 | 12/01/2020 | 20/01/2020 | 26/01/2020 | 01/02/2020 |
| Latest Finish Date | 12/01/2020 | 20/01/2020 | 28/01/2020 | 03/02/2020 | 09/02/2020 |
| Duration | 0 | 8 | 8 | 6 | 6 |
| Resource reqd. Qty. | | | | | |
| Excavator | 0 | 0 | 0 | 0 | 0 |
| Tra ctor | 0 | 0 | 0 | 0 | 0 |
| Tipper | 0 | 2 | 2 | 2 | 3 |
| Static Road Roller | 0 | 1 | 1 | 1 | 1 |
| Vibratory Road Roller | 0 | 0 | 0 | 0 | 1 |
| Bitumen Sprayer | 0 | 0 | 0 | 0 | 1 |
| Air Compressor | 0 | 0 | 0 | 0 | 1 |
| Asohalt Paver | 0 | 0 | 0 | 0 | 1 |
| Laveler | 0 | 0 | 0 | 0 | 0 |
| Water Tanker | 0 | 1 | 1 | 1 | 0 |

| Project No. 4 | | | | | | |
|---|---|---|---|---|---|---|
| Name of the Project | Annual Repair of B.B. Road | | | | | |
| Location of the Project | B.B. Road, Sadar, Allahabad | | | | | |
| Project I.D. No. | AIDCD1ARR001 | | | | | |
| Division of the Project | C.D.-1, P.W.D., Allahabad | | | | | |
| Project Priority | Yes | | | | | |
| Date of Start of Project | 01/01/2020 | | | | | |
| Date of Completion of Project | 18/05/2020 | | | | | |
| Project Duration | 139 | | | | | |
| Project Time Float | 14 | | | | | |
| Particulars | Work-0 | Work-1 | Work-2 | Work-3 | Work-4 | Work-5 |
| | Null Work | Site Cleaning | Surface Pre paration | Patch Formation | Renewal | Shoulder Making |
| Earliest Start Date | | 01/01/2020 | 16/01/2020 | 31/01/2020 | 01/03/2020 | 15/04/2020 |
| Latest Start Date | | 15/01/2020 | 30/01/2020 | 14/02/2020 | 15/03/2020 | 29/04/2020 |
| Earliest Finish Date | 31/12/2019 | 15/01/2020 | 30/01/2020 | 29/02/2020 | 14/04/2020 | 04/05/2020 |
| Latest Finish Date | 14/01/2020 | 29/01/2020 | 13/02/2020 | 14/03/2020 | 28/04/2020 | 18/05/2020 |
| Duration | 0 | 15 | 15 | 30 | 45 | 20 |
| Resource reqd. Qty. | | | | | | |
| Excavator | 0 | 1 | 0 | 0 | 0 | 1 |
| Tractor | 0 | 1 | 1 | 0 | 0 | 1 |
| Tipper | 0 | 0 | 0 | 1 | 4 | 0 |
| Static Road Roller | 0 | 0 | 0 | 1 | 2 | 1 |
| Vibratory Road Roller | 0 | 0 | 0 | 0 | 2 | 0 |
| Bitumen Spayer | 0 | 0 | 0 | 1 | 1 | 0 |
| Air Compressor | 0 | 0 | 1 | 0 | 1 | 0 |
| Asphalt Paver | 0 | 0 | 0 | 0 | 1 | 0 |
| Laveler | 0 | 0 | 1 | 0 | 0 | 1 |
| Water Tanker | 0 | 0 | 1 | 0 | 0 | 1 |

**TABLE 14.4** *(Continued)*

| Project No. 5 | | | | |
|---|---|---|---|---|
| Name of the Project | Annual Repair of J.M. Road | | | |
| Location of the Project | J.M. Road, Korao, Allahabad | | | |
| Project I.D. No. | ALDPRDARR091 | | | |
| Division of the Project | P.O., P.W.D., Allahabad | | | |
| Project Priority | No | | | |
| Date of Start of Project | 03/01/2020 | | | |
| Date of Completion of Project | 02/03/2020 | | | |
| Project Duration | 60 | | | |
| Project Time Float | 10 | | | |
| Particulars | Work-0 | Work-1 | Work-2 | Work-3 |
| | Null Work | Site Cleaning | Patch Formation | enewal |
| Earliest Start Date | | 03/01/2020 | 11/01/2020 | 21/01/2020 |
| Latest Start Date | | 13/01/2020 | 21/01/2020 | 31/01/2020 |
| Earliest Finish Date | 02/01/2020 | 10/01 /2020 | 20/01/2020 | 21 /02/2020 |
| La test Finish Date | 12/01/2020 | 20/01/2020 | 30/01/2020 | 02/03/2020 |
| Duration | 0 | 8 | 10 | 32 |
| Resource reqd. Qty. Excavator | 0 | 1 | 0 | 0 |
| Tractor | 0 | 1 | 0 | 0 |
| Tipper | 0 | 0 | 1 | 1 |
| Stati c Road Roller | 0 | 0 | 1 | 1 |
| Vibra tory Rca d Roller | 0 | 0 | 0 | 1 |
| Btiumen Sprayer | 0 | 0 | 0 | 1 |
| Air Compressor | 0 | 0 | 0 | 1 |
| Asphalt Pa ver | 0 | 0 | 0 | 1 |
| Laveler | 0 | 0 | 0 | 0 |
| Water Tanker | 0 | 0 | 0 | 0 |

| Project No. 6 | | | | | |
|---|---|---|---|---|---|
| Name of the Project | Construction of A B. Road | | | | |
| Location of the Project | AB. Road,Sadar, Allahabad | | | | |
| Project I.D. No. | ALDCD1CON013 | | | | |
| Division of the Project | C.D.-1, P.W.D., Allahabad | | | | |
| Project Priority | Yes | | | | |
| Date of Start of Project | 05/01/2020 | | | | |
| Date of Completion of Project | 07/02/2020 | | | | |
| Project Duration | 34 | | | | |
| Project Time Float | 4 | | | | |
| Particulars. | Work-0 | Work-1 | Work-2 | Work-3 | Work-4 |
| | Null Work | Compaction of 45-90 mm size girt | Compaction of 45-63 mm size grit | Compaction of 25-50 mm size grit | P.C. Work |
| Earliest Start Date | | 05/01/2020 | 13/01/2020 | 23/01/2020 | 29/01/2020 |
| Latest Start Date | | 09/01/2020 | 17/01/2020 | 27/01/2020 | 02/02/2020 |
| Ea rliest Finish Date | 04/01/2020 | 12/01/2020 | 22/01/2020 | 28/01/2020 | 03/02/2020 |
| Latest Finish Date | 08/01/2020 | 16/01/2020 | 26/01/2020 | 01/02/2020 | 07/02/2020 |
| Duration | 0 | 8 | 10 | 6 | 6 |
| Resource reqd. Qty. Excavator | 0 | 0 | 0 | 0 | 0 |
| Tractor | 0 | 0 | 0 | 0 | 0 |
| Tipper | 0 | 3 | 3 | 3 | 3 |
| Static Road Roller | 0 | 2 | 2 | 2 | 1 |
| Vibratory Road Roller | 0 | 0 | 0 | 0 | 1 |
| Bitumen Sprayer | 0 | 0 | 0 | 0 | 1 |
| Air Compressor | 0 | 0 | 0 | 0 | 1 |
| Aspha lt Paver | 0 | 0 | 0 | 0 | 1 |
| Laveler | 0 | 0 | 0 | 0 | 0 |
| Water Tanker | 0 | 1 | 1 | 1 | 0 |

in preceding works and are kept idle since the complete project has not yet finished even when that resource is not required in successive works of that project. This is undesirable from the resource utilization point of view and at the same time shall attract cost burden on the project also. In multi-project environment where an organization has to feed for demand of multiple projects at the same time, idleness of resources can have a devastating effect also. It is possible that some work of any other parallel project may demand a resource which is kept idle to other project locations. This situation shall ask for outsourcing of resources to demanding project costing heavy cost liability and at the same time if required resource is not made available; the project schedules may get hampered resulting in time overshoot of the project and other nonfavorable consequential situations. To avoid such an undesirable situation it is always recommended to allocate resources to any project initially for first work and as that work approaches to its end, next required resource shall be allocated to execute next work of that project. This way the capacity utilization of resources shall be maximum and unnecessary cost burdens and project delays may be avoided.

## 14.9 ALLOCATION OF MECHANICAL RESOURCES

Projects which are running at different geographical locations demand different mechanical resources from CMRS. Projects are solely dependent on CMRS for resource allocation. Resources are always limited in numbers and have to be allocated judiciously so as to fulfill the resource demands of projects under regular working hours, thereby avoiding impact of additional costs of resource overtime and resource outsourcing costs. Demand to CMRS from divisions comes well in advance to the project start date. CMRS allocates mechanical resources to different works of projects based on certain parameters. These parameters are "Priority Rules" for resource allocation. Priority rules may relate to different parameters of projects and works. There may be numerous priority rules based on the situation and need of the organization, but we have limited ourselves to most common of them.

### *14.9.1 PRIORITY RULES*

Mechanical resources are allocated to individual works of different projects based on certain priority rules. These rules may relate to the following parameters of work and projects:

a) **Project priority:** This parameter is defined by the concerned division as there are certain projects which are important and have to be finished as soon as possible due to various technical, social, weather etc. reasons. Some projects are funded by some external national/international agency or policy of the government and are time bound in nature whose fund has to be utilized in stipulated time period. There may be certain projects which are routine in nature and slight delay in their completion does not affect the system. So all the projects shall be categorized by the concerned divisions in either Yes or No category. Projects with priority "Yes" shall be chosen first for allocation of mechanical resources.
b) **Earliest Start Date:** This is the second priority rule. Works of different projects which have earliest ESD shall be chosen first for allocation of mechanical resources.
c) **Total Time float:** This is the third priority rule. Projects having minimum total time float shall be chosen first for allocation of mechanical resources.
d) **Duration required for work completion:** This is the fourth priority rule. Works with minimum completion time as compared to other works of different projects shall be chosen first for allocation of mechanical resources.

There may be other priority rules as may be defined and required which can be accommodated into the system. Once all the information related to mechanical resources, projects, stores, and priority rules are defined and entered into the system, we can now proceed with selection process of works of different projects for allocation of mechanical resources.

### *14.9.2 WORK SELECTION PROCESS FOR ALLOCATION OF MECHANICAL RESOURCES*

For the allocation of mechanical resources we shall select first work of all the projects and apply our priority rules to decide that which first work of different projects shall be first for allocation of mechanical resources as compared to other first work of different projects. An example of list of all corresponding first works related to individual projects requiring allocation of mechanical resources by CRMS is shown in Table 14.5.

The above table shows a comparative status of all the first works with complete details which are now ready for allocation of mechanical resources based on the priority rules.

**TABLE 14.5** List of First Work of all Projects for Allocation of Mechanical Resources.

| | Sr. No. of Project | 1 | 2 | 3 | 4 | 5 | 6 |
|---|---|---|---|---|---|---|---|
| | Name of Project | A.R. of M.G. Road | Cont. of D.B. Road | Cont. of R.R. Road | A.R. of B.B. Road | A.R. of J.M. Road | Cont. of A.B. Road |
| | Location of Project | M.G. Road, | D.B. Road, Meja | R.R. Road, Sadar | B.B. Road | J.M. Road, Korao | A.B. Road, Sadar |
| | Project I.D. No. | ALDCD3ARR011 | ALDPRDCON002 | ALDCD1CON008 | ALDCD1ARR001 | ALDPRDARR091 | ALDCD1CON013 |
| | Division of Project | C.D.-3 | P.D. | C.D.-1 | C.D.-1 | P.D. | C.D.-1 |
| | Project Priority | Yes | No | Yes | Yes | No | Yes |
| | Date of Start of Project | 01/01/2020 | 05/01/2020 | 05/01/2020 | 01/01/2020 | 03/01/2020 | 05/01/2020 |
| | Date of Completion of Project | 11/03/2020 | 25/03/2020 | 09/02/2020 | 18/05/2020 | 03/02/2020 | 07/02/2020 |
| | Project Duration | 71 | 81 | 36 | 139 | 60 | 34 |
| | Project Time Float | 15 | 19 | 8 | 14 | 10 | 4 |
| | Name of Work | Site Cleaning | Ea rth Work | 45-90 Grit | Site Cleaning | Site Clea ning | 45-90 Grit |
| | Sr. No. of Work | 1 | 1 | 1 | 1 | 1 | 1 |
| | Earliest Start Date | 01/01/2020 | 05/01/2020 | 05/01/2020 | 01/01/2020 | 03/01/2020 | 05/01/2020 |
| | Latest Start date | 16/01/2020 | 24/01/2020 | 13/01/2020 | 15/01/2020 | 13/01/2020 | 09/01/2020 |
| | Earliest Finish Date | 05/01/2020 | 14/01/2020 | 12/01/2020 | 15/01/2020 | 10/01/2020 | 12/01/2020 |
| | Latest Finish Date | 20/01/2020 | 02/02/2020 | 20/01/2020 | 29/01/2020 | 20/01/2020 | 16/01/2020 |
| | Duration | 5 | 10 | 8 | 15 | 8 | 8 |
| Resource reqd. & Qty. | Excavator | 1 | 1 | 0 | 1 | 1 | 0 |
| | Tractor | 1 | 1 | 0 | 1 | 1 | 0 |
| | Tipper | 0 | 0 | 2 | 0 | 0 | 3 |
| | Static Road Roller | 0 | 1 | 1 | 0 | 0 | 2 |
| | Vibratory Road Roller | 0 | 0 | 0 | 0 | 0 | 0 |
| | Bitumen Sprayer | 0 | 0 | 0 | 0 | 0 | 0 |
| | Air Compressor | 0 | 0 | 0 | 0 | 0 | 0 |
| | Asphalt Paver | 0 | 0 | 0 | 0 | 0 | 0 |
| | Laveler | 0 | 1 | 0 | 0 | 0 | 0 |
| | Water Tanker | 0 | 0 | 1 | 0 | 0 | 1 |

The first work of all the projects shall be evaluated based on hierarchy of priority rules, i.e., Project Priority "Yes"– Work ESD "Earliest" – Project time float "Minimum" – Work Duration "Minimum."

#### *14.9.2.1 STEP 1: LIST ALL THE FIRST WORK OF PROJECTS WITH PRIORITY "YES"*

This list shall be generated by the system including all the first works of projects with priority "Yes."

All the projects with priority "Yes" shall be allocated mechanical resources prior to projects with priority "No." If there are no projects with priority "Yes," the second priority criteria of earliest "ESD" shall be considered. If there is only one "Yes" priority project, it shall be allocated first.

An example of list of all works of different projects with priority "Yes" is shown in Table 14.6.

#### *14.9.2.2 STEP 2: LIST ALL THE FIRST WORKS OF PROJECTS WITH PRIORITY "YES" AND EARLIEST ESD*

This list shall be generated by the system including all the first works of projects with priority " Yes" and earliest ESD as shown in Table 14.7.

#### *14.9.2.3 STEP 3: LIST ALL THE WORKS WITH PRIORITY "YES," EARLIEST ESD AND MINIMUM PROJECT FLOAT TIME*

This list shall be generated by the system including all the first works of projects with priority "Yes," earliest ESD and minimum project float time as shown in Table 14.8.

#### *14.9.2.4 STEP 4: LIST ALL THE WORKS WITH PRIORITY "YES," EARLIEST ESD, MINIMUM PROJECT TIME FLOAT, AND MINIMUM DURATION*

This list shall be generated by the system including all the first works of projects with priority "Yes," earliest ESD, minimum project time float, and minimum duration as shown in Table 14.9.

**TABLE 14.6** List of first Work of all the Projects with "Yes" Priority.

| **Order of Resource Allocation** | **1** | **2** | **3** | **4** | **5** | **6** |
|---|---|---|---|---|---|---|
| Sr. No. of Project | 1 | 3 | 4 | 6 | 2 | 5 |
| Name of Project | A.R. of M.G. Road | Cont. of R.R. Road | A.R. of B.B. Road | Cont. of | Cont. of D.B. Road | A.R. of J.M. Road |
| Location of Project | M.G.Road, | R.R. Road, Sadar | B.B. Road, Sadar | A.B. Road, | D.B. Road, Meja | J.M. Road, Korao |
| Project I.D. No. | ALDCD3ARR011 | ALDCD1CON008 | ALDCD1ARR001 | ALDCD1CON013 | ALDPRDCON002 | ALDPRDARR091 |
| Division of Project | C.D.-3 | C.D.-1 | C.D.-1 | C.D.-1 | P.D. | P.D. |
| Project Priority | Yes | Yes | Yes | Yes | No | No |
| Date of Start of Project | 01/01/2020 | 05/01/2020 | 01/01/2020 | 05/01/2020 | 05/01/2020 | 03/01/2020 |
| Date of Completion of Project | 11/03/2020 | 09/02/2020 | 18/05/2020 | 07/02/2020 | 25/03/2020 | 03/02/2020 |
| Project Duration | 71 | 36 | 139 | 34 | 81 | 60 |
| Project Time Float | 15 | 8 | 14 | 4 | 19 | 10 |
| Name of Work | Site Cleaning | 45-90 Grit | Site Cleaning | 45-90 Grit | Ea rth Work | Site Clea ning |
| Sr. No. of Work | 1 | 1 | 1 | 1 | 1 | 1 |
| Earliest Start Date | 01/01/2020 | 05/01/2020 | 01/01/2020 | 05/01/2020 | 05/01/2020 | 03/01/2020 |
| Latest Start date | 16/01/2020 | 13/01/2020 | 15/01/2020 | 09/01/2020 | 24/01/2020 | 13/01/2020 |
| Earliest Finish Date | 05/01/2020 | 12/01/2020 | 15/01/2020 | 12/01/2020 | 14/01/2020 | 10/01/2020 |
| Latest Finish Date | 20/01/2020 | 20/01/2020 | 29/01/2020 | 16/01/2020 | 02/02/2020 | 20/01/2020 |
| Duration | 5 | 8 | 15 | 8 | 10 | 8 |

**TABLE 14.6** *(Continued)*

| | Order of Resource Allocation | 1 | 2 | 3 | 4 | 5 | 6 |
|---|---|---|---|---|---|---|---|
| Resource reqd. & Qty. | Excavator | 1 | 0 | 1 | 0 | 1 | 1 |
| | Tractor | 1 | 0 | 1 | 0 | 1 | 1 |
| | Tipper | 0 | 2 | 0 | 3 | 0 | 0 |
| | Static Road Roller | 0 | 1 | 0 | 2 | 1 | 0 |
| | Vibratory Road Roller | 0 | 0 | 0 | 0 | 0 | 0 |
| | Bitumen Sprayer | 0 | 0 | 0 | 0 | 0 | 0 |
| | Air Compressor | 0 | 0 | 0 | 0 | 0 | 0 |
| | Asphalt Paver | 0 | 0 | 0 | 0 | 0 | 0 |
| | Laveler | 0 | 0 | 0 | 0 | 1 | 0 |
| | Water Tanker | 0 | 1 | 0 | 1 | 0 | 0 |

**TABLE 14.7** List of first Work of all the Projects with "Yes" Priority and Earliest ESD.

| **Order of Resource Allocation** | **1** | **2** | **3** | **4** | **5** | **6** |
|---|---|---|---|---|---|---|
| Sr. No. of Project | 1 | 4 | 3 | 6 | 5 | 2 |
| Name of Project | A.R. of M.G. Road | A.R. of B.B. Road | Cont. of R.R. Road | Cont. of | A.R. of J.M. Road | Cont. of |
| Location of Project | M.G. Road, | B.B. Road, Sadar | R.R. Road, Sadar | A.B. Road, | J.M. Road, Korao | D.B. Road, Meja |
| Project I.D. No. | ALDCD3ARR011 | ALDCD1ARR001 | ALDCD1CON008 | ALDCD1CON013 | ALDPRDARR091 | ALDPRDCON002 |
| Division of Project | C.D.-3 | C.D.-1 | C.D.-1 | C.D.-1 | P.D. | P.D. |
| Project Priority | Yes | Yes | Yes | Yes | No | No |
| Date of Start of Project | 01/01/2020 | 01/01/2020 | 05/01/2020 | 05/01/2020 | 03/01/2020 | 05/01/2020 |
| Date of Completion of Project | 11/03/2020 | 18/05/2020 | 09/02/2020 | 07/02/2020 | 03/02/2020 | 25/03/2020 |
| Project Duration | 71 | 139 | 36 | 34 | 60 | 81 |
| Project Time Float | 15 | 14 | 8 | 4 | 10 | 19 |
| Name of Work | Site Cleaning | Site Cleaning | 45-90 Grit | 45-90 Grit | Site Cleaning | Earth Work |
| Sr. No. of Work | 1 | 1 | 1 | 1 | 1 | 1 |
| Earliest Start Date | 01/01/2020 | 01/01/2020 | 05/01/2020 | 05/01/2020 | 03/01/2020 | 05/01/2020 |
| Latest Start date | 16/01/2020 | 15/01/2020 | 13/01/2020 | 09/01/2020 | 13/01/2020 | 24/01/2020 |
| Earliest Finish Date | 05/01/2020 | 15/01/2020 | 12/01/2020 | 12/01/2020 | 10/01/2020 | 14/01/2020 |
| Latest Finish Date | 20/01/2020 | 29/01/2020 | 20/01/2020 | 16/01/2020 | 20/01/2020 | 02/02/2020 |
| Duration | 5 | 15 | 8 | 8 | 8 | 10 |

**TABLE 14.7** *(Continued)*

| | Order of Resource Allocation | 1 | 2 | 3 | 4 | 5 | 6 |
|---|---|---|---|---|---|---|---|
| Resource reqd. & Qty. | Excavator | 1 | 1 | 0 | 0 | 1 | 1 |
| | Tractor | 1 | 1 | 0 | 0 | 1 | 1 |
| | Tipper | 0 | 0 | 2 | 3 | 0 | 0 |
| | Static Road Roller | 0 | 0 | 1 | 2 | 0 | 1 |
| | Vibratory Road Roller | 0 | 0 | 0 | 0 | 0 | 0 |
| | Bitumen Sprayer | 0 | 0 | 0 | 0 | 0 | 0 |
| | Air Compressor | 0 | 0 | 0 | 0 | 0 | 0 |
| | Asphalt Paver | 0 | 0 | 0 | 0 | 0 | 0 |
| | Laveler | 0 | 0 | 0 | 0 | 0 | 1 |
| | Water Tanker | 0 | 0 | 1 | 1 | 0 | 0 |

**TABLE 14.8** List of First Works of all the Projects with "Yes" Priority, Earliest ESD, and Minimum Project Time Float.

| **Order of Resource Allocation** | **1** | **2** | **3** | **4** | **5** | **6** |
|---|---|---|---|---|---|---|
| Sr. No. of Project | 4 | 1 | 6 | 3 | 5 | 2 |
| Name of Project | A.R. of B.B. Road | A.R. of M.G. Road | Cont. of A.B. Road | Cont. of | A.R. of J.M. Road | Cont. of |
| Location of Project | B.B. Road, Sadar | M.G. Road, | A.B. Road, Sadar | R.R. Road, | J.M. Road, Korao | D.B. Road, Meja |
| Project I.D. No. | ALDCD1ARR001 | ALDCD3ARR011 | ALDCD1CON013 | ALDCD1CON008 | ALDPRDARR091 | ALDPRDCON002 |
| Division of Project | C.D.-1 | C.D.-3 | C.D.-1 | C.D.-1 | P.D. | P.D. |
| Project Priority | Yes | Yes | Yes | Yes | No | No |
| Date of Start of Project | 01/01/2020 | 01/01/2020 | 05/01/2020 | 05/01/2020 | 03/01/2020 | 05/01/2020 |
| Date of Completion of Project | 18/05/2020 | 11/03/2020 | 07/02/2020 | 09/02/2020 | 03/02/2020 | 25/03/2020 |
| Project Duration | 139 | 71 | 34 | 36 | 60 | 81 |
| Project Time Float | 14 | 15 | 4 | 8 | 10 | 19 |
| Name of Work | Site Cleaning | Site Cleaning | 45-90 Grit | 45-90 Grit | Site Cleaning | Earth Work |
| Sr. No. of Work | 1 | 1 | 1 | 1 | 1 | 1 |
| Earliest Start Date | 01/01/2020 | 01/01/2020 | 05/01/2020 | 05/01/2020 | 03/01/2020 | 05/01/2020 |
| Latest Start date | 15/01/2020 | 16/01/2020 | 09/01/2020 | 13/01/2020 | 13/01/2020 | 24/01/2020 |
| Earliest Finish Date | 15/01/2020 | 05/01/2020 | 12/01/2020 | 12/01/2020 | 10/01/2020 | 14/01/2020 |
| Latest Finish Date | 29/01/2020 | 20/01/2020 | 16/01/2020 | 20/01/2020 | 20/01/2020 | 02/02/2020 |
| Duration | 15 | 5 | 8 | 8 | 8 | 10 |

**TABLE 14.8** *(Continued)*

| **Order of Resource Allocation** | | **1** | **2** | **3** | **4** | **5** | **6** |
|---|---|---|---|---|---|---|---|
| Resource reqd. & Qty. | Excavator | 1 | 1 | 0 | 0 | 1 | 1 |
| | Tractor | 1 | 1 | 0 | 0 | 1 | 1 |
| | Tipper | 0 | 0 | 3 | 2 | 0 | 0 |
| | Static Road Roller | 0 | 0 | 2 | 1 | 0 | 1 |
| | Vibratory Road Roller | 0 | 0 | 0 | 0 | 0 | 0 |
| | Bitumen Sprayer | 0 | 0 | 0 | 0 | 0 | 0 |
| | Air Compressor | 0 | 0 | 0 | 0 | 0 | 0 |
| | Asphalt Paver | 0 | 0 | 0 | 0 | 0 | 0 |
| | Laveler | 0 | 0 | 0 | 0 | 0 | 1 |
| | Water Tanker | 0 | 0 | 1 | 1 | 0 | 0 |

**TABLE 14.9** List of first Work of all the Projects with "Yes" Priority, Earliest ESD, Minimum Project time Float, and Minimum Duration.

| **Order of Resource Allocation** | **1** | **2** | **3** | **4** | **5** | **6** |
|---|---|---|---|---|---|---|
| Sr. No. of Project | 4 | 1 | 6 | 3 | 5 | 2 |
| Name of Project | A.R. of B.B. Road | A.R. of M.G.Road | Cont. of A.B. Road | Cont. of | A.R. of J.M. Road | Cont. of |
| Location of Project | B.B. Road, Sadar | M.G.Road, | A.B. Road, Sadar | R.R. Road, | J.M. Road, Korao | D.B. Road, Meja |
| Project I.D. No. | ALDCD1ARR001 | ALDCD3ARR011 | ALDCD1CON013 | ALDCD1CON008 | ALDPRDARR091 | ALDPRDCON002 |
| Division of Project | C.D.-1 | C.D.-3 | C.D.-1 | C.D.-1 | P.D. | P.D. |
| Project Priority | Yes | Yes | Yes | Yes | No | No |
| Date of Start of Project | 01/01/2020 | 01/01/2020 | 05/01/2020 | 05/01/2020 | 03/01/2020 | 05/01/2020 |
| Date of Completion of Project | 18/05/2020 | 11/03/2020 | 07/02/2020 | 09/02/2020 | 03/02/2020 | 25/03/2020 |
| Project Duration | 139 | 71 | 34 | 36 | 60 | 81 |
| Project Time Float | 14 | 15 | 4 | 8 | 10 | 19 |
| Name of Work | Site Cleaning | Site Clea ning | 45-90 Grit | 45-90 Grit | Site Cleaning | Earth Work |
| Sr. No. of Work | 1 | 1 | 1 | 1 | 1 | 1 |
| Earliest Start Date | 01/01/2020 | 01/01/2020 | 05/01/2020 | 05/01/2020 | 03/01/2020 | 05/01/2020 |
| Latest Start date | 15/01/2020 | 16/01/2020 | 09/01/2020 | 13/01/2020 | 13/01/2020 | 24/01/2020 |
| Earliest Finish Date | 15/01/2020 | 05/01/2020 | 12/01/2020 | 12/01/2020 | 10/01/2020 | 14/01/2020 |
| Latest Finish Date | 29/01/2020 | 20/01/2020 | 16/01/2020 | 20/01/2020 | 20/01/2020 | 02/02/2020 |
| Duration | 15 | 5 | 8 | 8 | 8 | 10 |

**TABLE 14.9** *(Continued)*

| | **Order of Resource Allocation** | **1** | **2** | **3** | **4** | **5** | **6** |
|---|---|---|---|---|---|---|---|
| Resource reqd. & Qty. | Excavator | 1 | 1 | 0 | 0 | 1 | 1 |
| | Tractor | 1 | 1 | 0 | 0 | 1 | 1 |
| | Tipper | 0 | 0 | 3 | 2 | 0 | 0 |
| | Static Road Roller | 0 | 0 | 2 | 1 | 0 | 1 |
| | Vibratory Road Roller | 0 | 0 | 0 | 0 | 0 | 0 |
| | Bitumen Sprayer | 0 | 0 | 0 | 0 | 0 | 0 |
| | Air Compressor | 0 | 0 | 0 | 0 | 0 | 0 |
| | Asphalt Paver | 0 | 0 | 0 | 0 | 0 | 0 |
| | Laveler | 0 | 0 | 0 | 0 | 0 | 1 |
| | Water Tanker | 0 | 0 | 1 | 1 | 0 | 0 |

Now all the first works of available projects are placed in order of their priority rules from first to last. The above list is now ready for allocation of mechanical resources. From the above list it is clear that resource allocation work shall start from first work of project 4, then first work of project 1, and so on.

## 14.10 RESOURCE ALLOCATION PROCESS

The process of resource allocation involves selection of resources which are available in the district and are free to perform and shifting them to desired project location prior to commencement of work at project site. From the final resource allocation list first work of project on order no. 1 shall be chosen for resource allocation.

During the resource allocation process the following situations may arise:

- Resource required is free and numbers of resources required are same as numbers of free resources.
- Resource required is free and numbers of resources required are less than the numbers of free resources.
- Resource required is free and numbers of resources required are more than the numbers of free resources.
- Resource required will be free from a future date which is in between the earliest start date of work and latest start date of the work.
- Resource required will be from a future date which is beyond the latest start date of work.
- Resource required is not available.
- Response of the CMRS in the above situations is elaborated below:

1. **When Resource required is free and numbers of resources required are same as numbers of free resources:** Under this situation, all the free resources have to be allocated to project. Here, the distance between the project site and the location of resource shall not play any role in allocation since we are left with no choice of selecting a resource which is closest to project location, so all the free resources shall be allocated to the project.
2. **When Resource required is free and numbers of resources required are less than the numbers of free resources:** Under this situation, we can select a free resource which is closest to project location to minimize the resource shifting cost, so from among all the free resources, one which is closest to project location shall be allocated to the project.

3. **When Resource required is free and numbers of resources required are more than the numbers of free resources:** Under this situation, all the free resources have to be allocated to project since free resources are less than required resources. After all the free resources are allocated, the left required resources have to be outsourced to the project.
4. **When Resource required will be free from a future date which is in between the earliest start date and latest start date of the work:** As we are aware that every project is having some float of time to meet any contingent situation, delay, or obstruction caused in the execution of the project and due to some unforeseen situations. All the works in a project can utilize this time float since any delay within allotted float time range does not affect the project completion date. As long as availability date of required resource is in between earliest start date and latest start date of work of project, it is well within the project float time and required resources can be allocated to project from their next allocation date. An important aspect of utilization of project float time is whether to utilize complete float to only one work or apportion float to different works of the project. While utilizing the project float time to any work, we can use any criteria to decide the amount of float time to be utilized by any specific work. Since projects are always associated with uncertainties, we shall always have some cushion of time to meet any unavoidable situation in the future. It is always recommended to utilize project float time judiciously and to do this job we can put a condition for the allocation of resource when the next allocation date of resource is in between earliest and latest start date of work that allocate resource only when resource allocation date is slightly ahead say one or two days of earliest start date or we can put a condition of percentage of project float time.
5. **When Resource required will be from a future date which is beyond the latest start date of work:** This situation states that required resource will be available after the latest start date of work, i.e., even over the project float time. Since there is no more time cushion beyond project float is available in project, we are bound to outsource the required resource.
6. **When Resource required is not available:** A construction project demands for several mechanical resources, some of them are common and some are very specialized. Some resources are seldom used in projects for any specific activity. It is not possible for an organization

to own all types of resources and neither recommended also since construction machineries are very expensive and require trained man power to operate. Those specialized machines are beneficial to outsource even being costlier to outsource. Under the situation when a resource required is not available in the district, it shall be outsourced.

The step-by-step procedure for allocation of mechanical resources to works of different projects based on predecided priority parameters and decision-making is elaborated with the help of flowchart as shown in Figure 14.4.

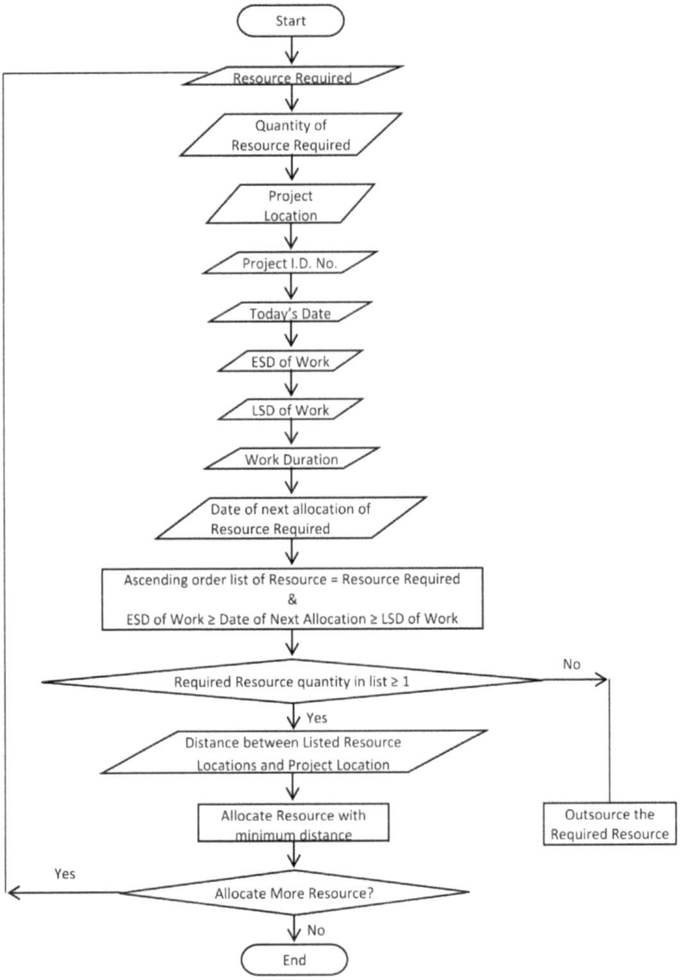


**FIGURE 14.4** Flowchart for resource allocation.

The response of CMRS for resource allocation with reference to the example is elaborated hereunder.

After the selection of first works of different projects, the final list was prepared by the system incorporating all the priority rules laid down by the system administrator. Now this list is ready for resource allocation. We shall choose the work of first project in order. This work requires one number of excavators and tractor each. We shall proceed with one number of resource allocations at a time only. In first go, excavator is chosen as resource required and number of resources required is equal to one. We need to enter certain information related to work and resource into the system which shall help the software to take decisions. Project location and its I.D. No. are required to allocate resource to specific project. Today's date is also required as when the current status of resources is displayed, the "next allocation date" of all the resources which are free shall be from today only in date format for information processing. Earliest start date and latest start date of work to which resources are to be allocated are required to allocate a resource whose next allocation date falls within the range of earliest and latest start date of work. When the current list of all the resources which is required is displayed, we need to check whether the resource required is available or not, whether resource which is available is in adequate quantity as required or not, whether resource which is available is free for allocation within the ESD and LSD range of work or not. An ascending order list of information containing the current status of all the excavators in the district fulfilling the mentioned criteria, i.e., ESD of Work $\geq$ Date of Next Allocation $\geq$ LSD of Work is displayed in Table 14.10.

The above list displays the current status and contains 2 nos. of required resources. We can see that one resource is working and shall be free from 16.05.2020 whereas next resource is free from today, i.e., it can be allocated to desired project location. So this resource shall be chosen for the allocation by the system. Once this resource is allocated, the next resource required by the same work is to be allocated. Again the same process of resource allocation shall be followed. This job of allocation shall continue till resource requirement of all the first works of different projects is completed. Here, we have an option to allocate all the resources required to complete different works of a project, but since works in project shall be completed one by one, the resources which are allocated and shifted to project location in advance shall have to wait for preceding works to finish and will result in loss of productivity. Again, there is a chance that a new project may arrive to CMRS for resource allocation from a specific date, and if we have shifted

**TABLE 14.10** Resource Allocation Sheet.

| Sr. No. | Resource I.D. No. | Status | Location | Assigned Project I.D. No. | Present Work Start Date | Present Work Completion Date | Next Allocation Date |
|---|---|---|---|---|---|---|---|
| 1 | ALDMEDJCB0801 | Working | Meja | ALDCD3ARR002 | 02.04.2020 | 15.05.2020 | 16.05.2020 |
| 2 | ALDMEDJCB0602 | free | Handia | - | - | - | Today |

the required free resources in advance to previous project location, we need to reallocate that resource to new project location and would bear the shifting cost leading to cost burden to the project.

## 14.11 CONCLUSION

The Centralized Mechanical Resource System incorporates all the essential information related to projects and resources; thus the system is capable of taking an effective decision for resource allocation aiming at effective resource utilization, minimizing usage cost, and enabling system engineers for effective planning, scheduling, and resource management. Different priority rules as required by the organization can be incorporated for logic building. CMRS is very helpful in resource allocation under multi-location/ multi-project environment.

## KEYWORDS

- **OR in government**
- **project management**
- **scheduling**
- **effective governance**
- **capacity**
- **utilization**
- **optimization**
- **resources**
- **priority**
- **operation**

## REFERENCES

1. Tripathi, A.; Shrivastava, P. K. Factors Influencing Capacity Utilization of Mechanical Resources in Construction Industries, *Int. J. Rec. Tech. Eng.* **2020,** *9* (2), 695–698.
2. Suri, P. K.; Bhushan, B.; Jolly, A. Time Estimation for Project Management Life Cycle: A Simulation Approach. *IJCSNS Int. J. Com. Sci. Net. Sec.* **2009,** *9* (5), 211–215.

3. Rieck, J.; Zimmermann, J.; Gather, T. Mixed-Integer Linear Programming for Resource Leveling Problems. *Eur. J. Opera. Res.* **2012,** *221,* 27–37.
4. Siripong, M.; Jennifer, R. M. Construction Resource Allocation using a genetic algorithm, *J. Ark. Acad. Sci.* **1995,** *49,* 99–103.
5. Christoph, S. *Resource Allocation in Project Management*, 3rd ed.; GOR Publications: USA, 2005.
6. Samuel, J. M.; Jack, R. M.; Scott, M. S.; Margaret, M. S. Project Management in Practice. *Inf. Proce. Manage.* **2009,** *45,* 397–400.
7. Payne, J. H. Management of Multiple Simultaneous Projects: A State-of-the-Art Review. *Int. J. Pro. Manage.* **1995,** *13,* 163–168.
8. Marimuthu, K.; Palaneeswaran, E.; Benny, R.; Ananthanarayanan, K. Resource Unconstrained and Constrained Project Scheduling Problems and Practices in a Multi Project Environment. *Adv. Manage. Civil Engg. Proj.* **2018,** *2018,* 1–13.
9. Pinedo, M. L. *Scheduling: Theory, Algorithms and Systems*, 3rd ed.; Springer: New York.

## CHAPTER 15

# Sustainability: Business Model and Trends in Emerging Markets

TRIPTI BARTHWAL[1] and AKANKSHA SRIVASTAVA[2]

[1]*Lal Bahadur Shastri Institute of Management & Development Studies, Lucknow, Uttar Pradesh, India*

[2]*Babu Banarasi Das University, Lucknow, Uttar Pradesh, India*

## ABSTRACT

The high rate of population growth coupled with an aspiration for an affluent lifestyle among a vast majority of people has led to the consumption of far more resources than ever. The triple bottom line approach forms the basis for sustainable business models (SBM) and considers the interests of various stakeholders along with that of the environment and society. They are the basis of competitive advantage because they help immerse sustainability into business value and processes and thus facilitate corporate innovation for sustainability. This chapter discusses the concept of sustainability and SBM. Next the features of SBM have been discussed along benefits of adopting it for a business. Challenges in implementing a SBM will follow. After that the sustainability trends specifically in context of India have been discussed. These include sustainability in Indian businesses, sustainability reporting, India's performance on sustainable development goals, customer's perception toward sustainable products and challenges.

## 15.1 INTRODUCTION

Most of the current advancements in the social and economic arena owe themselves to rapid developments in the fields of information communication

Management for Sustainable Development: Integrating Social, Economic, and Environmental Goals.
Vishal Jain & Amit Mittal (Eds.)

technology, medical sciences, energy, etc. From the time of advent of the Industrial Revolution, businesses have been leveraging on technological advancements to propel their growth. This has led to substantial changes in the means of production and consumption, especially in the last few years.

According to the Global Footprint Network (2014),[23] if the present rate of population and consumption growth continues, by 2030, we would be twice of the earth's resources. As a result, there is an increase in pressure on businesses to respond to sustainability concerns. However, the fact that the growth and development of the society or a Nation is highly dependent on the profits generated by these businesses and industries, cannot also be ignored. It is thus imperative to strike a balance or to reach a common ground where growth, development, and profit generation can co-exist with safeguarding the planet. Therefore, sustainable business practices are not only desirable but also essential.

## 15.2 SUSTAINABILITY

The term "sustainability" with reference to business, implies conducting business in a way that does not create an adverse influence on the environment, community, or society in general. It involves formulation of business strategies and plans keeping environmental and societal considerations in mind. Sustainability in no way implies that a firm should not focus on its profits or financial performance. It actually broadens the parameters of measuring corporate performance to include, apart from the financial dimension, the environmental and social dimensions. This is referred to as the triple bottom line.

Hart[8] proposed three types of sustainability goals:

i. Bringing down levels of pollution, by decreasing the levels of emissions and harmful discharges.
ii. Minimizing pollution and the serious negative effects on the environment emerging as a result of a used product being ending up as waste by making a new product from the "waste" product. This is known as product stewardship or 'cradle-to-cradle' approach.

A sustainable company is one which uses environment-friendly materials and processes, has a green supply chain, makes use of technology that generates no damaging emissions or waste and also successfully addresses the concerns of the stakeholders.

Business organizations have a pivotal role in making sustainable development successful or a failure. Thus, companies across the world are increasingly acknowledging that it is their prime responsibility to contribute in addressing sustainability concerns. It is thus becoming an inherent part of the business model of organizations and they are increasingly scouting for greener solutions.

## 15.3 SUSTAINABLE BUSINESS MODEL

A business model is the basis on which organizations conduct business and create, deliver, and capture value. It is important because it is a means by which organizations can innovate to gain competitive advantage and to increase performance. The following three elements of a business model, proposed by Richardson[21] form its core:

a. Value proposition
b. Value creation and delivery
3. Value capture.

Value proposition refers to a combination of value or benefits that a company pledges to deliver to its existing and future customers. Generally, businesses generate value by grabbing new business opportunities, exploring new markets and creating new avenues for revenue. Value creation is actually the foundation of any business model. When a business is able to convert its value creation into a business that is sustainable through a business model, it is known as value capture.

Jackson[18] described the features of a sustainable economy which include: minimizing consumption, of personal resources, prioritizing good of the society and environment over mere economic growth, a circular system where everything is reused and thus nothing is considered as waste, delivery of functionality instead of product, amplifying human creativity, a collaborative system. These features can serve as key pointers in developing a SBM but this would require a fundamental shift in the way a business is envisioned and run.

Bocken and his associates[2] proposed the following characteristics of the model of a sustainable business in 2014:

- Doing more with less, meaning thereby, maximizing material productivity and energy efficiency through ways like lean manufacturing, reducing the total number of products required by increasing the functionality of a product, etc.

- Doing away with waste by transforming waste into a useful input for production, through ways like circular economy, sharing assets, reuse, recycle, etc., thereby generating value from waste.
- Minimizing negative impact on the environment along with tackling the challenge of resource constraint emanating from the current production. This is done by substituting renewable with non-renewable resources with the help of solar and wind energy innovations.
- Doing away with physical products by providing such services that substitute for them, yet fulfil customer's needs.
- Ensuring good health and welfare of the stakeholders by making an effort that the firm generates maximum possible positive societal and environmental impact.
- Exploring ways to reduce consumption and production, such as doing away with unnecessary or over complex features and functions, to minimize the use of materials and energy, redesigning in order to lower the rate of product replacement.
- Keeping gains to the society and the environment, over and above monetary gains.
- Maximizing environmental and social gains by developing sustainable ideas that can be implemented on a large scale.

To achieve sustainability in business, few changes in the existing business model will not work. It will require a fundamental shift in the business model. Building a sustainable business requires an organization wide innovative mindset. Innovation has been a proven solution in redesigning products and services, organization survival, growth, and renewal. Companies aiming to transform their business model for sustainability need to bring changes in their proposition, creation, and capture of value. Thus, it can be said that business model innovation (BMI) not only brings together the ideas, but also furthers the concepts of "value" and "innovation". As mentioned by Amit and Zott (2012),[24] BMI does not imply transforming what a business does, but how it is done.

As rightly pointed out by Laukkanen and Patala (2014),[25] BMI is not merely about process and product innovation, but it involves an innovative mindset throughout the organizational system. It would generally start with process or product innovation which would facilitate BMI in the long run.

Sustainable BMI consists of an eight step sequential and repetitive process, which are as under:

- **Ideation:** Firstly, the objective of innovation in business model is clarified, and key stakeholders involved are identified and after that the value proposition and the initial idea of the concept are generated.
- **Designing the concept:** First draft of the key elements of the business model is put in writing.
- **Developing a prototype:** Some virtual prototypes are then developed and evaluated to improve and share the business model concept with others. Benchmarking is also done at this step.
- **Experimenting:** Through controlled experiments, main premises and variables of the concept are tested.
- **Detail design:** Then a thorough analysis is conducted to bring out the specific details of the components of the business model and the interrelationships among them.
- **Piloting:** The model is tested by running its initial version in a small part of the target market.
- **Launch:** After the pilot run, the business model is presented to all concerned departments in the organization and the target market.
- **Adaptation and diversification:** based on the basic plans, future projections and requirements, the business model is tweaked and if the magnitude of changes required in large then the complete process may be repeated.

The above features would bear outcomes only when sustainability is a part of strategic planning. For this, reward and incentives systems should be woven around sustainability goals, meaning thereby, individual and team rewards should be awarded keeping sustainability as a key parameter. This will make obvious the commitment of top management toward sustainability. Besides the above features, one aspect that should be given top priority is to deep root sustainability measurement within financial reporting. This can lead to better sustainability performance because then sustainability would be treated as the principal concern of the organization. Towards that end, many business heads are making sustainability a part of their corporate strategy. This is also imperative because, customers also tend to prefer sustainable products and companies. In fact, incorporating the concerns of all stakeholders along with consideration for environment, society, and profit, rather than giving weightage only to is considered as the core of SBMs.

## 15.4 THE RATIONALE FOR SUSTAINABLE BUSINESS MODEL

The following reasons clearly explain why companies are seeking sustainability in their business model.

- Sustainability has become the source of competitive advantage. Today's consumers are increasing becoming socially and ecologically responsible, and they expect businesses to act similarly. As awareness among consumers is rising, they are actively demanding and looking out for sustainable products, and this is forcing companies to change their products, systems, technologies, and most importantly, the business model. In a research by Nielsen (2015)[26] more than 66% of millennial respondents and more than half Baby Boomers were ready to shell out more for products from sustainable brands.
- Besides customers, even employees want to work for a company which has sustainability on its agenda. Research published in "Decade of Disruption: Future of the Sustainable Workplace in the Age of COVID-19 and Climate Change" confirmed this as close to two-thirds of respondents expressed their preference of working for a company with strong environmental policies. In the report "Advancing Sustainability: HR's Role by the Society for Human Resource Management", it was found that in companies that adopted sustainable practices, employee morale was 55% higher, 43% more efficiency was observed in business processes and an increase in employee loyalty by 38%.
- SBM improves operations and optimizes resource usage leading to higher workforce efficiency and cutting down of costs. Critics of sustainability initiatives point that these cut down a company's profit. The truth, however, is that these initiatives may appear expensive on the face value, but their long-term positive outcomes justify the investment.
- Sustainability initiatives act as an armor for a business. With growing concerns about sustainability, governments around the world, through regulations, are tightening the noose around companies, which do not adopt sustainable initiatives. Integrating sustainability into the business strategy will safeguard the firm and help it to abide by these regulations in a timely manner.
- It is a misconception that in a SBM costs are very high and thus profit dries up. The fact is that besides bringing down cost, sustainability can result in propelling profit level. This has been proved in a study

(2014) "Profits with Purpose: How Organizing for Sustainability Can Benefit the Bottom Line," by McKinsey in which 40 organizations were researched. It states that research by Deutsche Bank revealed that companies with high ratings in ESG factors displayed superior performance in the market in both mid- and long-range terms. Moreover, the cost of capital (in regard to both debt and equity) was found to be much lower in case of sustainable companies.

## 15.5 CHALLENGES

Adopting a SBM is definitely full of benefits, but it comes with its sets of challenges as well, some of which are as under:

- Sustainability initiatives come with a price tag attached to them. These initiatives do lead to higher profits in the long run, but they require a good amount of initial investment. For companies with deep pockets, this may not be an area of concern but for those with weak balance sheets or new companies, this is a major challenge.
- Incorporating sustainability into a company's strategy would mean departure from several past practices. For that the employees will have to be suitably trained, guided and supported. This will involve time, money, and even disturbance in the regular operations. The employee appraisal system will have to be updated to measure their performance along the ecological dimension, besides their regular objectives and targets. Employees may not welcome such changes and there can be resentment.
- The economic, environmental, and social value creation potential of SBMs is very difficult to comprehend because of the absence of clear criteria and a clear measurement system for it.
- Even if a system of measurement is developed, it would be challenging to make it comprehensive because the assessment would involve multiple stakeholders with different stakes and objectives. A bigger challenge is to determine industry-specific sustainability metrics and the necessary tools to measure them.
- A company moving toward sustainability would fail if its suppliers do not fall in line with its approach. It may not be easy to convince suppliers to accept and adopt the new philosophy, especially for mid-sized and small companies.

## 15.6 SUSTAINABILITY TRENDS IN EMERGING MARKETS: AN INDIAN PERSPECTIVE

An emerging market or an emerging economy is defined as a market that possesses few features of a developed market, but does not qualify to be called a developed market. Brazil, Russia, India and China, Saudi Arabia, Taiwan, Indonesia, Iran, Mexico, South Korea, and Turkey are considered the ten largest emerging economies. The following trends are specifically related to India but may apply to other emerging markets as well.

Emerging markets present a unique contradiction since the call for rapid growth and development poses perpetual threats to environmental health. Market leaders in emerging economies, the native culture, to a great extent, determine the sustainability agenda. Sustainability managers in emerging markets, in terms of resource allocation, generally do not go for gigantic sustainable plans. They take baby steps initially and gradually scale-up.

Although the concept of sustainability and a circular economy may have strongly surfaced on a global level in the late 1970s, but in India, it runs in our blood. For several decades, we have been repairing, recycling, reusing, refurbishing, etc. Yet, we have not been able to pay much attention to these practices while running businesses. The discussion has been divided into sub-sections: Sustainability in Indian businesses, customer attitude toward sustainable goods, India's performance on sustainable development goals, sustainability reporting and challenges.

- ***Sustainability in Indian businesses***

There has been considerable research on sustainability initiatives of the developed economies, but in comparison to them, studies on sustainability efforts in the emerging economies has been relatively less researched. As a result of this, it is generally assumed that either businesses in emerging economies lack the willingness or the financial ability to undertake sustainability initiatives. This assumption was challenged by Wyeth and Nulkar[22] who studied in detail the sustainability practices of companies within India and found out that businesses, especially large corporations and several SMEs are not only becoming increasingly responsive toward their role in safeguarding the environment, but are also imposing it on their supply chain. Among the sustainability measures, Indian companies put energy and carbon reduction on top priority and using renewable energy through solar panels and wind farms. Water reuse and recycling is also an important area of focus.

Like the rest of the world, the Indian corporate sector is concerned about sustainability issues like water shortage, resource depletion, rising energy costs, cost savings through resource reuse. They have started to adopt the concept of circular economy where resources move in a sequential manner so that the pollutants released into the air is minimized and waste is converted into reusable products. New business models based on circular economy and design thinking are emerging. From the customer's perspective, from food to fashion to lifestyle to electronic gadgets, sustainable brands will be valued high and thus they will be able to generate higher demand and sales.

Also, the Indian government, in the past few years, through its policies has made it imperative for business organizations to pursue sustainability goals. The Government of India under the Paris Climate Pact, has resolved to reduce, by 33–35%, the carbon intensity of its GDP by 2030 with reference to 2005 levels, and also to generate 40% of its energy through renewables by 2030. The Ministry of Corporate Affairs in 2011 issued National Voluntary Guidelines on Social, Environmental and Economic Responsibilities of Business. Three initiatives by the Government of India have raised the pressure on Indian companies not to overlook sustainability while doing business:

- The Ministry of Corporate Affairs in 2011 has made it mandatory for the 100 largest Indian companies to publicly disclose their sustainability initiatives under the National Voluntary Guidelines on Social, Environmental and Economic Responsibilities of Business.
- The Bureau of Energy Efficiency has launched an energy-efficiency cap and trade program and has made it compulsory for companies in the energy-intensive sectors to comply with it.
- As per the provisions of Section 135 of Indian Companies Act 2013, every private or public company or a subsidiary of a foreign company having a net worth of 5 billion Indian rupees or more, a turnover of 10 billion rupees or more, or a net profit of 50 million rupees or more during the preceding financial year company registered under Act should mandatorily allocate 2% of their profits toward CSR activities.

Businesses in India have started to adopt the model of a circular economy. This led to the setting up of new businesses which transform wet and dry waste into useful products. New products, services and business organizations based on new business models are emerging in different domains. A good example is that of Uber and Ola which are based on a sharing economy. Many Indian companies have incorporated sustainability measures proactively in their corporate and business affairs. Some of the notable sustainability practices of Indian companies are discussed below:

State Bank of India, the provider of the largest banking network in India, in order to encourage environmental protection and reduce the felling of trees, has rapidly increased ATMs and debit cards usage and introduced paperless banking and thus eliminated the need of withdrawal forms, deposit slips, and cheques.

In all the refineries, pipeline installations and major marketing installations/terminals of Indian Oil, adhere to ISO-14001 standards. Desulfurization of refinery fuel gas and low-sulfur fuel oil and has led to the reduction of harmful gaseous emissions. The R&D Centre of Indian Oil has developed eco-friendly biodegradable lube formulations.

With an objective to cut down on the discharge of effluents and raise productivity, Dabur uses biogas, energy efficient equipment and biofuels in boilers. Its R&D team has developed the water-efficient CIP system, which recycles the used water in fruit juice manufacturing and converts fruit waste into organic manure.

Under #CutTheCrap project, initiated by the Mahindra Group 11 facilities have gone zero waste certified by recycling, reusing, and composting waste. Through another initiative, "Rise for Good" they adopted eco-friendly technology and sustainable processes that reduced wastage. They have also made their offices plastic-free. Under the Haryali Program, the group focuses on planting trees, and since its inception, they have grown over 16.4 million trees across India. Tech Mahindra, through its Green Marshals Program, focuses on disseminating information on how daily activities can be carried out in a manner that protects the environment. The Group is also aims to transform the way India travels to a more sustainable mode by working on the manufacturing of electric vehicles (EVs). This is also in alignment with the Nation's vision of adoption of EVs in the commercial and personal segment by 2030.

Tata Group has a strong self-commitment toward sustainability, but in order to put its best foot forward in this regard, they are guided by global standards for sustainable business practices. The Tata Sustainability Group (TSG) is responsible for driving the circular economy concept at the Group level. It has collaborated with the Ellen MacArthur Foundation in bringing about a transformation to the circular economy. Tata Global Beverages' Tetley factory, since 2012, is "zero waste to landfill" factory which has recycled all its waste, including tissue, general waste, cardboard, metal and tea dust discard. By sourcing a segment of their electricity demand from a closely located solar farm, the factory has been able to cut down on its $CO_2$ emissions by 19%.

Since last several years, ITC has been successful in soil and moisture conservation, by achieving the distinction of water positive, carbon positive, solid waste recycling positive, using renewable energy. Its hotels have achieved the distinction of the greenest luxury hotel chain. It has set up its own specific targets for lowering down energy consumption, water usage and waste generation, etc. at the level of the business unit level. Aditya Birla Group has deeply worked on "<2 C Futures" and how businesses must make basic changes and tweak processes to strongly handle global warming.

The MNC Unilever's Indian subsidiary Hindustan Unilever's (HUL) sustainability efforts appear to be in the right direction. In comparison to 2008, its production processes consumed 54% less water in 2021; there is usage of 100% renewable grid electricity in its factories, offices, warehouses, and other facilities; safely disposed off more than 150,000 tons of post-consumer-use plastic waste; and is jointly operating with other parties to remove cutting of trees from its supply chain. More than 67% of the tea sourced for different brands of Unilever was acquired from green sources. Similarly, Kissan ketchup claims that in 2020, it has made a significant breakthrough with 93% of tomatoes sourced sustainability.

Some other initiatives which although are small but they point toward a step in the right direction are many companies like PepsiCo, MakeMyTrip, Livspace, and Dunzo made sustainable choices in Diwali (2022) gifts. PepsiCo India choose the NGO – Mitti Café, which provides livelihood for underprivileged people with disabilities – for hand crafted, sustainable gifts. MakeMyTrip gifted special sweet hampers, which were made of organic products with no chemical preservatives. Moreover, the packaging was also of recyclable plastic. Livspace Diwali gifts include home decoration items which are procured from local artisans; plants, snacks and sweets in aesthetically designed recyclable containers.

- ***Customer attitude towards sustainable goods***

The outbreak of COVID-19 has accelerated the preference toward sustainable goods because customers are now more concerned about their health than ever before and hence want to avoid chemical-based products in favor of organic and sustainable goods. For the purpose of market testing, brands like Diageo, Dettol, and WOW Skin Science launched sustainable packaging during the pandemic. Understanding the importance of being sustainable, in 2020, companies such as Coca-Cola, Marico, Nestle India, Future Consumer, HUL, PepsiCo, Parle Agro declared that by 2025, they will switch over to 100% recyclable packaging. This clearly signals that companies in India have become serious about their carbon footprints. In fact, it is a win–win situation because companies with genuine environmental concerns are generally tend to develop a more credible brand image thereby easily influencing consumers and thus have a more loyal client base. This is supported by Kantar Brand Z data, which depicts that brands with a weak purpose generate 70% growth only whereas, brands with strong purpose tend to grow by 175%. Not only this, they tend to have more committed and happy employees who develop a sense of pride for their company.

In a survey conducted by Bain and Company in June 2022, published in The Times of India, consumers in India are becoming increasingly concerned about sustainability to the extent that among the top-five key purchasing criteria at least 43% place sustainability and 60% of consumers are ready to pay more for sustainability. Gen Z and Millennials are leaders in this group of customers. Choosing a sustainable brand or product reflects an important part of the customer psyche. Customers feel satisfied when they do their bit toward environmental protection. If they cannot take up major initiatives, they want to do the least by purchasing green products. Also, this saves the customer from the guilt of buying a "wrong" product.

However, this customer readiness does not translate in purchase for multiple reasons. These include the fact that in the market share of packaged goods, sustainable products comprise only 5%. As a result, consumers fail to find suitable products to meet their need, face problems in identifying credible sustainable products, and do not understand how to validate their claims. In a research (Lan and Ching, 2012),[27] it was found that regular products made from traditional technologies or materials are perceived to be way better than their sustainable counterparts, referred to as the "sustainability liability. Professor Alexander Chernev and Blair,[4] from Kellogg School of Management, in his paper (2020) explained this when he studied the relationship between customer awareness that a product is sustainable and perceptions of that product's performance. He clarified that it is like a zero-sum game or compensatory reasoning where customers perceive that if a product is good on one attribute, it must have deficiencies in others. This would obviously send a cue to companies not to invest in the expensive technology of manufacturing sustainable products.

However, companies need not to be doubtful about their investments in sustainability because customer perception about the efficacy of sustainable products is changing for the better. One very obvious proof of this is the customer perception towards Tesla electric cars, which score high on both sustainability and performance. This is according to Chernev and Chernev[4], the halo effect in which one characteristic of an object overshadows its other characteristics. So, customers under the influence of this effect tend to focus on sustainable initiatives of the company and perceive that it must be producing high quality products.

Apart from scoring high on sustainability parameters, customers expect companies to be more transparent. Specifically, Gen Z is very particular and would not mind blacklisting a company which compromises or misleads on ethics and sustainability. They abhor greenwashing and lip service.

- ***India's performance on Sustainable Development Goals***

The sustainable development goals (SDGs) constitute a section of the United Nations 2030 Agenda for Sustainable Development and consist of 17 interrelated global goals to make the world more sustainable. They were created to be a benchmark to work toward a more sustainable and better future for all. The SDGs aim to safeguard the world, and bring about a marked improvement in the quality of lives and future of every individual around the world. They are a part of the United Nations Agenda for Sustainable Development (2030). The SDGs are as under:

1. Eliminating all forms of poverty
2. Wiping out hunger
3. Good health and well-being
4. Improvement in education
5. Gender equality and women's empowerment
6. Water and sanitation
7. Affordable and clean energy
8. Economic growth
9. Infrastructure and industrialization
10. Reduced Inequality
11. Sustainable cities and communities
12. Sustainable consumption and production
13. Climate action
14. Life below water
15. Biodiversity, forests, desertification
16. Peace, justice and strong institutions
17. Partnerships for the goals

In September 2015, 193 countries accepted these goals. These goals have to be implemented by 2030 and this it necessitates a massive endeavor apart from the side of the government, the corporates also. Talking about our country in particular, the government treating SDGs as a blueprint for formulating national policies and regulations. Businesses need to work in tandem with government initiatives.

Reporting of SDGs is a three-step process consisting of

a) developing priority SDG targets;
b) measuring and analysis; and,
c) reporting, integrating and implementing change.

In the SDG Report 2022, India ranked 121 among 163 nations with a score of 60.32. The total score measures the level of progress made in achieving all the 17 SDGs. The score indicates the level (percentage) of SDG achievement, thereby 100 representing achievement of all SDGs. If we analyze the score goal wise with respect to India, the following emerges:

Every Nation's actions create a good or bad effect on the other Nation's abilities to achieve the SDGs. This is known as the spillover index. It evaluates spillovers by a country along three dimensions: environmental and social impacts manifested in trade, economy and finance, and security). As far as our country is concerned, its score is 99.3. The higher the score the greater are the positive and lesser negative spillover effects.

In the climate summit at Glasgow, several countries resolved their allegiance toward the climate by setting net-zero goals and India made a commitment to go net-zero by 2070.

- ***Sustainability Reporting***

Indian companies have started to conduct valuation and reporting of natural and social capital among the various forms of capital they manage. Environmental, social, and governance (ESG) disclosures or sustainability reporting, describes the performance of businesses in bringing about an improvement in the area of sustainability. On the basis of fiscal 2021 data published by CRISIL in 2022, wherein ESG risk assessment across 53 sectors involving 586 Indian companies was conducted, and a very impressive trend is evident. In comparison to the last few years, ESG scores of most of the companies have improved mainly because of improved levels of disclosures and better performance across different dimensions.

The non-profit Climate Disclosure Project (CDP) has ranked India on the sixth number in the world based on the number of companies committed

**TABLE 15.1** SDG Achievement Status in India.

| SDGs | Current scenario | Future prospects |
|---|---|---|
| Goal 1: Eliminating all forms of poverty | Serious challenges exist | Score relatively improving, but not enough to achieve the goal |
| Goal 2: Wiping out hunger | Substantial challenges exist | Score constant or rising at less than half of the required rate |
| Goal 3: Health | Substantial challenges exist | Score relatively rising, but not enough to attain goal |
| Goal 4: Improvement in education | Substantial challenges exist | Score constant or rising at less than half of the required rate |
| Goal 5: Gender equality and women's empowerment | Substantial challenges exist | Score constant or rising at less than half of the required rate |
| Goal 6: Water and Sanitation | Substantial challenges exist | Score relatively improving, but not enough to achieve the goal |
| Goal 7: Energy | Serious challenges exist | Score relatively improving, but not enough to attain goal |
| Goal 8: Economic Growth | Serious challenges exist | Score relatively improving, but not enough to attain goal |
| Goal 9: Infrastructure, industrialization | Substantial challenges exist | Score relatively improving, but not enough to attain goal |
| Goal 10: Inequality | Substantial challenges exist | Data about trend not available |
| Goal 11: Cities | Substantial challenges exist | Score going down |
| Goal 12: Sustainable consumption and production | Goal fulfilled | Working towards maintaining SDG achievement |
| Goal 13: Climate Action | Goal fulfilled | Working towards maintaining SDG achievement |
| Goal 14: Oceans | Substantial challenges exist | Score stagnating or rising at less than half of the required rate |
| Goal 15: Biodiversity, forests, desertification | Substantial challenges exist | Score constant or rising at less than 50% of the required rate |
| Goal 16: Peace, justice and strong institutions | Substantial challenges exist | Score constant or rising at less than 50% of the required rate |
| Goal 17: Partnerships for the goals | Substantial challenges exist | Score constant or rising at less than 50% of the required rate |

*Source:* https://dashboards.sdgindex.org/profiles/india[10]

to achieving net-zero emissions because since 2019, there has been a 50% rise in the number of companies in this category. This will be further strengthened by SEBI's guidelines to enforce ESG disclosures for the top 1000 listed businesses in the form of an annual "business responsibility and sustainability report" (BRSR). This would presumably make a lot of difference primarily, because till now, the Indian businesses were only confining themselves to the simpler options like recycling water and other material or operational changes like using renewable energy instead of fossil fuel. But now, big Indian businesses will have to mandatorily publish their material ESG risks and opportunities, strategies to handle these risks and their financial implications.

The journey toward this end in fact has started. In 2011, a socially responsible company like Infosys, on its own set up a target to become carbon-neutral. In order to become carbon-neutral, it invested in 60 megawatts (MW) of solar energy and carbon reduction projects by replacing firewood cooking in villages by eco-friendly options. As reported by Business Today in 2011, the global alliance that helps firms set climate goals, known as Science Based Targets initiative (SBTi), declared that around 62 Indian companies have resolved to reduce emissions and set up a deadline for themselves to this end. These include HDFC which has a 2031–2032; and Reliance Industries, which set a deadline for 2035. Tata Consultancy Services (TCS) and the State Bank of India (SBI) aim to be carbon-neutral by 2030. The same deadline has been set up by the Indian Railways. Even in sectors like iron and steel, where reduction in harmful emissions is next to impossible, Indian companies are emerging as leaders with respect to sustainability initiatives.

A mere replacement of conventional sources of energy by renewable energy and working towards SBTi targets would not suffice. Companies should weave in sustainability at every stage of the product lifecycle—starting with creating the concept of the product, procurement of raw material, designing the product, and then finally getting it manufactured.

Not only as responsible corporate citizens should companies focus on sustainability but also because the stock market also seems to lap up companies which are serious about sustainability. This trend applies both to manufacturing and services sector. This is because institutional investors are placing high weightage on non-financial disclosures like ESG ratings for their investment decisions. Even 78% of global investors are giving more significance to ESG than they did 5 years back. A case in point is that of the tobacco business of ITC which received severe thrashing by ESG concerns in the last few years.

- ***Sustainable Bonds***

Several Indian firms are scouting the international sustainable bond markets for acquiring reasonably priced capital. There are two types of Sustainable or ESG (environmental social governance) bonds: Sustainability-linked bonds and the use of proceeds bonds.

The SLBs are meant to focus on boosting key performance indicators (KPIs) derived from 17 SDGs designed by the United Nations and sustainability performance targets (SPTs) of a company. However, it is not binding upon the company to prove that all the capital generated from SLB has directly led to the improvement of the KPIs because as long as the SPTs are being achieved, it can also be used for the company's other expenses.

The "use of proceeds" bonds are, however, different. Funds raised through them are required to be channelized toward green, social, or sustainability initiatives, such as green buildings, energy efficiency, and affordable housing. They are of four types:

- Green bonds: Used for financing sectors, such as renewable energy, green buildings, prevention and control of pollution.
- Social bonds: Used for raising funds for projects with positive social outcomes, such as employment generation, food security, basic infrastructure.
- Sustainability bonds: Used to finance projects which are a combination of green and social projects.
- Transition bonds: Used to raise funds for decarbonization of brown industries (industries with very high GHG emissions).

*(Source: "Green, Sustainability, and Social Bonds for COVID-19 Recovery," Asian Development Bank, February 2021. Accessed from: https://www.adb.org/sites/default/files/publication/678191/green-sustainability-social-bonds-covid-19-recovery.pdf)*

The Axis Bank in 2021 issued sustainability bonds, funds from which were used for diverse green and social projects. Sriram Transport Finance Company's bond was meant to generate funds to provide for MSMEs and low cost finance to small road transport operators from underprivileged sections of the society. This bond was issued for the first time in 2020 and then again in 2021. In 2021, UltraTech Cement, Adani Electricity, Mumbai and JSW Steel issued sustainability-linked bonds worth USD 1.7 billion. The financing cost for these bonds is connected with the accomplishment of targets set by the company. In case the company underperforms in these targets, financing becomes more expensive.

Comprehending the strong liking of international investors toward sustainability issues, companies in India, mostly in RE (renewable energy) project development have been excessively drawing upon the international green bonds market which also aids them in refinancing their existing high priced debt. Besides green bonds, Indian companies are also moving into the latest domains, such as social bonds, sustainability bonds, and SLBs.

In some sectors of the Indian economy, such as electricity, the movement toward sustainability has been made possible by mature technologies, like solar PV and onshore wind turbines. But in certain energy-intensive sectors, heavy road transport, aviation, shipping, iron and steel, cement, plastics, fertilizers, and aluminum, this transition does not seem to be in near sight. This is not so because of the absence of core technologies with the capability to reduce carbon levels in these sectors. In fact, such technologies, such as carbon capture, energy storage, and green hydrogen are very much available. What is required is to develop them further and implement them. Also, such sectors require complex transformations to reduce their emissions. Therefore, investors do not find these sectors very lucrative.

- ***Challenge***

The biggest challenge is the mammoth investment required for decarbonization because GHG emissions in the past 20 years have increased four times. CRISIL forecast is that an investment close to Rs. 22–25 lakh crore in the next 7 years will be required to reduce them and investments in hydrogen, CCUS, pump hydro, geothermal, and biomass-linked technologies will more than triple by 2030. Also. the use of IoT technology to monitor points of energy loss, resource and energy efficiency, and optimization of energy through fault diagnostics are coming up as the hottest areas for investment.

However, the silver lining is that renewables are turning up as the most economical source of energy and thus the ROI becomes quite impressive. Between 2020 and 2070, India will have to invest close to USD 10.1 trillion to reach net-zero targets. Also as projected by World Economic Forum estimate suggests that by 2070 USD 15 trillion economic opportunity will be created in India to reduce carbon footprints. This would range from solar power equipment, drip irrigation modules, EVs, conversion of waste into usable form, and many others.

On the flip side, if Indian companies are unsuccessful in bringing down their carbon emissions by 2025, they face the danger of losing $274 billion in exports every year as several MNCs gear to keep a check on the emissions of their supply chain. The choice is for Indian companies to make.

## 15.7 CONCLUSION

Sustainable growth requires focus, commitment and consistent efforts in the right direction. It never occurs by chance. It is growth that is continuous and has the capability to fulfil the requirements of the present population without curbing the capability of upcoming generations to fulfil their requirements. It is actually the new key to consistent and long-term success. Companies which will not tread the path of sustainability will see only short-term success.

Government of India's initiatives including the enactment of legislations like the Air and Water Acts and the Environment Protection Act, and the creation of the Nodal Ministry of Environment and Forests have struck the right chord in setting India's direction toward sustainable development. Enactments and laws can never ensure environmental protection. The willingness and commitment to the cause has to come from business houses which are considered most guilty of exploiting natural resources and degrading the environment.

Business corporations in India are continuously aiming to lower down emissions. Among top 10 Indian companies based on the market capitalization, eight have fixed net-zero targets for themselves between 2030 and 2050. But India still is lagging behind in the achievement of the SDGs. Though the efforts of the top companies are quite appreciable, yet if these are not adopted by a larger number of big and small companies, the road ahead would be very tough.

## KEYWORDS

- **sustainability**
- **sustainable business model**
- **sustainable development goals**
- **sustainability reporting**
- **sustainable bonds**

## REFERENCES


1. Adams, R.; Jeanrenaud, S.; Bessant, J.; Denyer, D.; Overy, P. Sustainability-Oriented Innovation: A Systematic Review. *Int. J. Manag. Rev.* **2015,** *18* (2), 180–205.
2. Bocken, N. M. P.; Short, S. W.; Rana, P.; Evans, S. A Literature and Practice Review to Develop Sustainable Business Model Archetypes. *J. Clean. Prod.* **2014,** *65,* 42–56.
3. Chen, Y.-S.; Lai, S.-B.; Wen, C.-T. The Influence of Green Innovation Performance on Corporate Advantage in Taiwan. *J. Bus. Ethics* **2006,** *67,* 331–339.
4. Chernev, A.; Blair, S. When Sustainability is not a Liability: The Halo Effect of Marketplace Morality. *J. Consum. Psychol.* **2021,** *31* (3), 551–569.
5. Chesbrough, H.; Rosenbloom, R. The Role of the Business Model in Capturing Value from Innovation: Evidence from Xerox Corporation's Technology Spin-off Companies. *For. Ind.* **2002,** *11,* 529e555.
6. Foo, M. Y. Green Purchasing Capabilities and Practices Towards Triple Bottom Line Performance: Moderating Effects of Institutional Pressure/. Foo Meow Yee. Ph.D. Thesis. University of Malaya: Kuala Lumpur, 2018.
7. Hart S. L. The Natural Resource-based View of the Firm. *Acad. Manag. Rev.* **1995,** *20* (4), 986–1014.
8. Hart, S. L. Beyond Greening: Strategies for a Sustainable World. *Harv. Bus. Rev.* **1997,** *75* (1), 66–76.
9. Hind, P.; Wilson, A.; Lenssen, G. Developing Leaders for Sustainable Business. *Corp. Gov.* **2009,** *9* (1), 7–20.
10. https://dashboards.sdgindex.org/profiles/india
11. https://timesofindia.indiatimes.com/business/india-business/60-in-india-willing-to-pay-a-premium-for-sustainability-products-reveals-survey/articleshow/92030126.cms
12. https://www.businesstoday.in/magazine/bt500-indias-most-valuable-companies/story/bt500-the-esg-imperative-for-indias-largest-firms-312406-2021-11-17.
13. https://www.crisil.com/en/home/newsroom/press-releases/2022/05/india-inc-improving-esg-disclosures-gradually.html
14. https://www.mckinsey.com/business-functions/sustainability/our-insights/profits-with-purpose-how-organizing-for-sustainability-can-benefit-the-bottom-line
15. https://www.nielsen.com/wp-content/uploads/sites/3/2019/04/Global20Sustainability20Report_October202015.pdf
16. https://www.shrm.org/resourcesandtools/tools-and-samples/toolkits/documents/11-0066_advsustainhr_fnl_full.pdf
17. https://www.unily.com/insights/guides/future-of-the-sustainable-workplace-in-the-age-of-covid-19-and-climate-change
18. Jackson, T. *Prosperity Without Growth: Economics for a Finite Planet*; Earthscan: London, 2009
19. Lin, Y. C.; Chang, C. C. A. Double Standard: The Role of Environmental Consciousness in Green Product Usage. *J. Mark.* **2012,** *76* (5), 125–134.
20. Ottosson S.; Moldavska M.; Ogorodnyk O.; Skogsrød T. In *What is and How to Develop Sustainable Innovation?* International Conference on Leadership, Innovation and Entrepreneurship (ICLIE), Dubai, April 20–22, 2016, 2016.
21. Richardson, J. The Business Model: An Integrative Framework for Strategy Execution. *Strateg. Change* **2008,** *17* (5–6), 133–144.
22. Wyeth, G. B.; Nulkar, G. Sustainability in Emerging Markets: Evidence from India. Sustain. *J. Record.* **2014,** *7* (2), 109–115.

## CHAPTER 16

# Sustainable Innovation is Empathy Turned into Action

C. V. SURESH BABU and D. RAJ SRIKAR

*Department of Information Technology, Department of Information Technology, Hindustan Institute of Technology and Science, Bay Range Campus, Padur, Chennai, India*

## ABSTRACT

Sustainable innovation refers to the development of new goods, services, and technologies that meet the requirements of the present without affecting the ability of future generations to do the same. It covers a wide range of fields, from energy to transportation to agriculture to architectural design, and it aims to provide solutions that address environmental and social problems while still promoting economic growth. In essence, sustainable innovation is the development of novel, ground-breaking approaches to improving resource utilization, decreasing waste and emissions, and implementing systems that are both robust and resilient to the test of time. By incorporating cutting-edge technology like renewable energy, as well as adopting sustainable practices like the circular economy and sustainable agriculture, sustainable innovation gives a means to build a better and more sustainable future for all people. In this chapter, we will discuss some crucial features of sustainable innovations, including their significance, prerequisites, and advantages. In addition to this, we will also analyze the outcomes of previous attempts to implement sustainable innovations, and we will come up with an alternative approach that is innovative while also being sustainable.

Management for Sustainable Development: Integrating Social, Economic, and Environmental Goals.
Vishal Jain & Amit Mittal (Eds.)

## 16.1 INTRODUCTION

Sustainable innovation refers to the introduction of new goods, services, or processes that are beneficial not just to the business but also to society as a whole.

Innovation is critical to the existence of a company, as well as its growth. Companies that are unable to innovate will inevitably lag behind their competitors, and, eventually, cease to exist as a separate entity. On the other hand, traditional types of innovation might result in profitable goods, services, and operations; nevertheless, they may also inflict injury to workers or deplete the environment's resources to an extreme extent. To incorporate sustainable innovation, organizations may make deliberate modifications to their goods, services, or operations, and as a result, it will provide long-term social and environmental benefits at the same time, generating maximum profits for the business. This chapter provides insights into the importance and various types of sustainable innovations and how they advance humankind.

The objective of sustainable innovation is "without sacrificing the demands of future generations, meeting the requirements of current generations," as stated in the definition of the term.[1] Concerns such as global warming and the protection of human rights have to be actively included in the innovation processes of companies. Companies that go above and beyond to achieve quick advantages are more likely to be the ones to engage in sustainable innovation. They look at things from a more distant perspective and invest in both people and technology with an eye toward the future.

Innovation and sustainability are, without a doubt, two of the most explored issues that are now available in the world. It was only a matter of time before innovation research expanded to incorporate sustainability, which led to the merger of the two ideas into the phrase "sustainable innovation.[2]

The difficulty in defining sustainability, in general, as well as sustainable development, is reflected in the lack of a clear definition for sustainable innovation. Sustainability-driven innovation, according to Arthur D. Little,[3] is "the development of new market spaces, goods and services, or processes motivated by social, environmental, or sustainability challenges." Like, in the context of innovation in general, there is a rising awareness that in addition to new ideas, the process of commercializing technology, commodities, and services and engaging in entrepreneurial endeavors are all essential components of sustainable innovation.[4]

Only sustainable businesses will be successful. People with talent gravitate toward sustainable businesses. Sustainable businesses attract a greater number of clients than their rivals that use less environmentally friendly business practices. According to the findings of a recent survey that was carried out by Deloitte, 49% of respondents from both the millennial (people born from 1981 to 1996) and Gen Z (people born between 1997 and 2012) generations claimed that their ethics had impacted the job choice that they had made.[5]

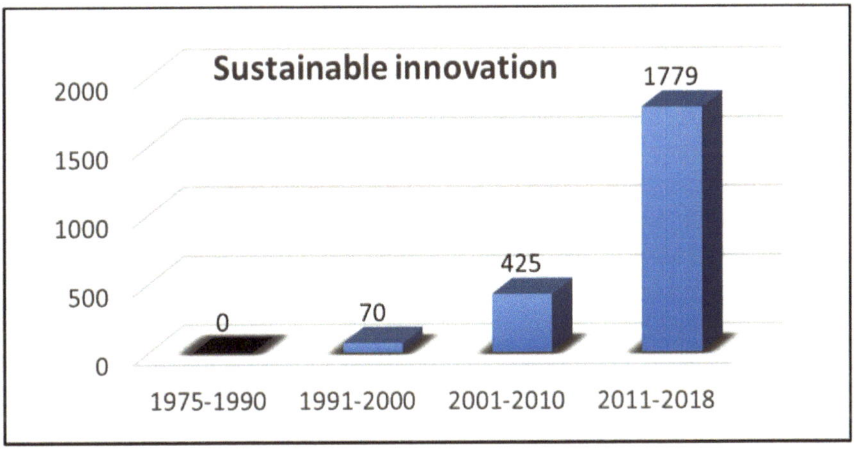


**FIGURE 16.1** How the number of papers published on the theme of "sustainable innovation" has changed throughout the years.

## 16.2 IMPORTANCE OF SUSTAINABLE INNOVATIONS

Sustainable businesses are more robust. This includes making it through difficult times, maintaining more consistent share prices, and increasing long-term income.

The principles of the innovation theory are often associated with the increase of economic activity and are linked to the modernization of novelties. The conceptual foundations for innovation mapping, on the other hand, come mostly from fields like management and economics.[6]

Valuable patents are produced by businesses that consider the requirements of their customers. To put it the other way, an emphasis on sustainability stimulates innovation of a larger quantity as well as better quality. Companies that are involved in sustainable innovation have a broader perspective and seek information from diverse points of view. They get information and solutions from other parties, including as representatives from a variety of sectors and stakeholders in the business.

To achieve the objectives of environmental sustainability, action will indeed be necessary on a variety of fronts, one of which is making the best of the potential offered by technological innovation by using it to its fullest. Even though important innovations can be disseminated through the public and commercial channels that already exist at the national level, these kinds of activities have not been sufficient to achieve the objectives of global sustainability, particularly in terms of meeting the requirements of the world's poorest, most susceptible, or marginalized people in the present day as well as in the future.

About 72% of consumers in the Gen Z age group are prepared to spend additional money on a service that was created in a sustainable manner. Additionally, 59% of consumers of all ages stated that it was essential that the foods they purchased were eaten in a sustainable manner, which is an increase from 50% in 2017 when the same question was asked.[7]

The concept of sustainable development proposes that progress may be achieved by bringing together goals that are both short term and long term in nature, as well as activities that are both local and global in scope and concerns, and both economic and environmental. Regardless of whether there is an environmental, economic, or social conflict between people and the environment, sustainable development aims to provide a solid theoretical foundation for decision-making. This is the goal of sustainable development.[8]

According to research,[2] the number of papers written on the topic of sustainable innovation has significantly increased during the past several years. A total of 70 papers were published in the first investigated era, which ran from 1975 to 1990. In the years 1991 to 2000, and notably in 1993, when three articles were published, the first instance of an article on this subject was discovered. The number of articles climbed six times during the next period to 425 articles. The interest in this subject surged after 2011, when there were four times as many publications as there had been in the prior year, totaling 1770. Using the same methodology to papers published on innovation and sustainability, we can observe that since 2008, there has been an eight-fold increase in the quantity of information available on sustainable innovation compared to the whole period before to that.

The concept of sustainable innovation has attracted considerable attention during the past ten years, in a manner akin to the original ideas of innovation and sustainability; the trend of the number of articles published between the years 2008 and 2018 is shown in Figure 16.2.

An analysis of the actual number of articles that have been written on the topic of sustainable innovation reveals that 269 articles were written before the year 2008, and 2005 articles were written between the years 2008 and 2018. This progression is also shown in the graph that can be seen in Figure 16.2, which shows that there were 52 papers published in 2008 and 392 articles published in 2018. The number of publications that have been published on sustainable innovation has typically risen over the course of time, which mirrors the development of the two fundamental principles. We can see that there was a minor rise in the number of things in 2009 when compared to 2008, and then there was a first surge in 2010, when the number of items approximately doubled. The increasing trend continued after 2010, exhibiting modest increases until 2014, with the exception of the same year, 2012, when there was a tiny decrease in the number of articles published. After 2010, the upward trend continued, showing small increases until 2014. When compared to 2014, there was a second increase in the number of articles published in 2015. More than 100 articles were published until 2018; the trend started in 2015 and significantly increased.

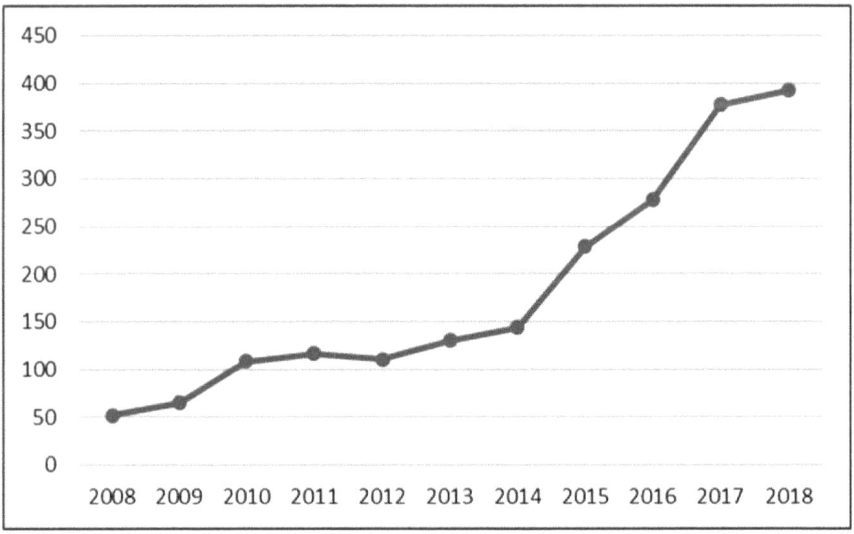


**FIGURE 16.2** The progression over time of the volume of papers published between 2008 and 2018 that covered the subject of "sustainable innovation."

The topic of sustainable innovation is becoming more and more important, as evidenced by the published articles' increasing number of citations. The progression of the citation count for articles on sustainable innovation is shown in Figure 16.3.

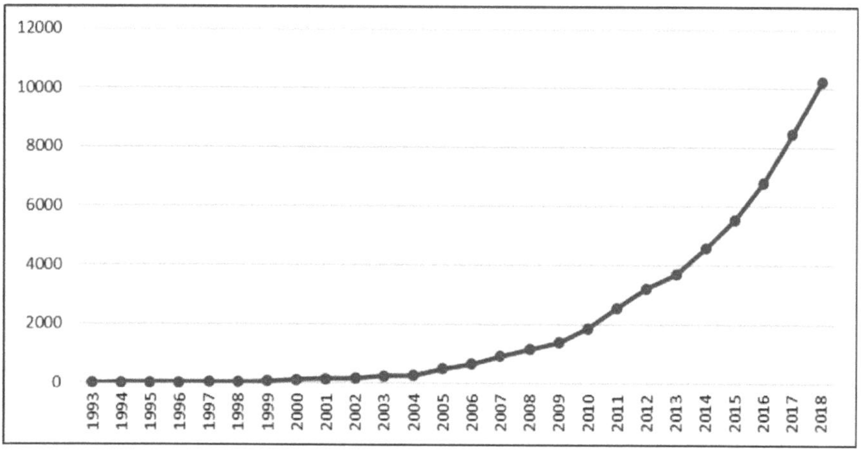


**FIGURE 16.3** The progression of the total number of references to publications on "sustainable innovation" between the years 1993 and 2018.

There has been a discernible increase in the total number of citations, but what is remarkable is how they have evolved throughout the years. There were a total of two citations registered in 1993; from that year, the number progressively increased until it reached 100 citations in the year 2000. Almost 1100 citations were recorded in 2008, and 10,236 citations were recorded in 2018. The number of citations increased with time. If we keep the same separation of the era into two sections, before and after 2008, then the number of citations in the previous 10 years has surpassed 16 times that of the period before 2008.[2]

It is clear that interest in the idea of sustainable innovation has grown over the past few years as evidenced by the yearly increase in the number of articles published on the subject. Figure 16.4 lists the top 20 journals based on the number of published papers from the perspective of the journal in which publications on this subject are published.

## 16.3 REQUIREMENTS OF SUSTAINABLE INNOVATIONS

Maintaining sustainability requires time, attention, and work. The first thing that has to be done is to focus on picking the low-hanging fruit that won't substantially change what needs to be done. For example, a car manufacturer may be able to lower the amount of electricity required for the manufacture and sale of cars. Second, companies need to consider how they may modify the ways they provide value to their customers. For instance, a firm that manufactures automobiles has to consider itself to be in the business of selling mobility. This opens the door to the possibility of manufacturing electric automobiles or even providing services for car sharing. In conclusion, the most sophisticated method is to work together. Collaboration is not only enjoyable but also results in the creation of specialized markets that are difficult for others to replicate.

| Nr.crt | Journal Name | Article no. |
|---|---|---|
| 1 | Sustainability | 58 |
| 2 | Journal of Cleaner Production | 56 |
| 3 | Business Strategy and the Environment | 12 |
| 4 | Managing Environmentally Sustainable Innovation Insights from The Construction Industry | 10 |
| 5 | Ecological Economics | 59 |
| 6 | International Journal of Technology Management | 40 |
| 7 | Futures | 39 |
| 8 | Technology Analysis Strategic Management | 39 |
| 9 | Research Policy | 37 |
| 10 | Journal of Business Ethics | 30 |

**FIGURE 16.4** The top 10 journals with the highest number of articles published on the subject of "sustainable innovation."

The capacity to think systemically is essential for innovative sustainability. Companies that engage in sustainable innovation don't simply focus on themselves when they make decisions. Instead, they adopt a more holistic perspective of the whole system of which they are a part, taking into consideration not just other companies but also the environment, the communities, and the other stakeholders. They have a keen awareness of the effects that their activities have on the operations of other organizations, as well as the reverse.

The architecture of an organization must be flexible enough to accommodate environmentally responsible ideas. Traditional innovations are usually achieved in a distinct R&D department or unit, whereas sustainable innovations are more likely to be successful when they have become deeply ingrained in the corporate culture of the organization.[9] In contrast to this, conventional innovations, which have a greater chance of becoming lucrative when they are already in operation, are implemented afterward. The pursuit of short-term profitability will, if the company does not inculcate the ethics of sustainable development, result in the suppression of innovative ideas that are focused on sustainable practices without allowing such ideas the time to mature. This will take place if the company does not establish a culture of sustainability from the very beginning.

In order to be sustainable, innovations need to be approached with a long-term and systemic perspective that takes into consideration the interdependencies and feedback loops between the many components of a system. A culture of creativity, resource efficiency, social equality, and stakeholder involvement are all significant needs for sustainable innovations. Cooperation and collaboration among stakeholders are other crucial prerequisites for sustainable innovations. If sustainable innovations can fulfill these objectives, they will be able to contribute to increased economic development, increased social equity, and increased environmental sustainability.

The following aspects are required for sustainable innovations:

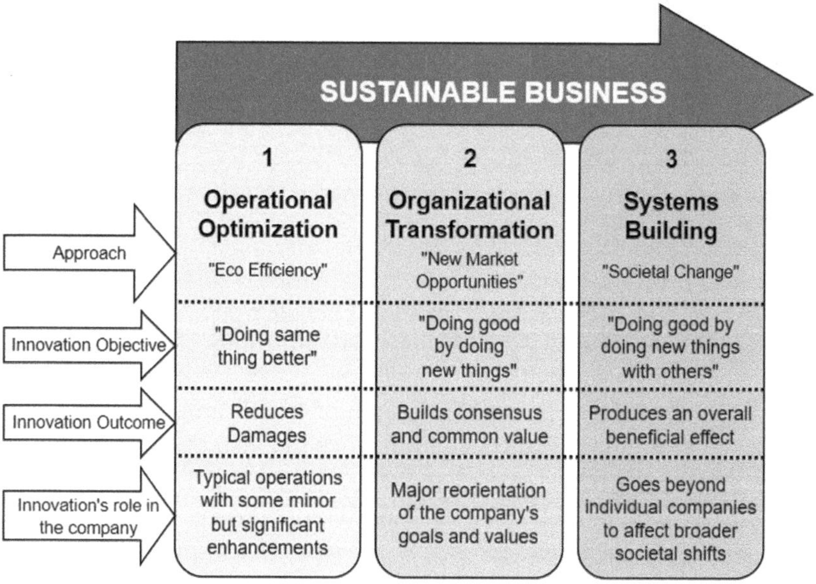


**FIGURE 16.5** Three categories of sustainable innovation available to businesses.

### 16.3.1 OPERATIONAL OPTIMIZATION

The process of ensuring that a company's operations are running as efficiently and effectively as they possibly may, is referred to as "optimization." In most cases, the objective is to reduce existing expenditures while simultaneously increasing operating capabilities.[12] Without fundamentally altering the business model of organizations, they can improve their procedures of operations. It's possible to come up with different approaches to "do the same things better" while simultaneously lowering the detrimental effects that these activities have on humans as well as the environment (e.g., lowering the amount of packaging used and making use of renewable energy). This may be done rather rapidly if, in addition to the established standards of quality or profitability, social and environmental concerns are also taken into consideration. This strategy is often referred to as "eco-efficiency," which stands for environmental effectiveness.

### *16.3.2 ORGANIZATIONAL TRANSFORMATION*

To bring about a more dramatic shift, businesses may come up with innovative new products and services which either fulfil the needs of humanity or make the ecosystem that we exist in better. At this point in the process, the focus shifts from "doing less harm" to "doing good by having accomplished new things," with the former taking precedence over the latter. These businesses are aware that practicing environmental responsibility has the potential to expand their consumer base.[12] The biofuel that is created from coffee waste is one example of sustainable innovation. Another example is the modular design of smartphones, which demonstrates how firms may use this form of sustainable innovation. The organizational transformation necessitates a fundamental shift in the viewpoint on the part of enterprises, away from improving existing standards and toward developing new standards.

### *16.3.3 SYSTEMS BUILDING*

Working with others to have positive effects on people and the environment is the most sophisticated type of sustainable innovation.[13] Organizations in this area are aware that they are a component of an environment and that it is impossible for a single organization to attain sustainability on its own. With others, they want to "do good by doing new things." Beyond the boundaries of the organization, these individuals who construct systems take into account not just partners from previously unconnected fields of business, but also marginalized players in their ideas.

Every company will have to figure out what form of sustainable innovation is most suited to meet its needs to be successful. It's possible that some companies may cycle through various types in order. Others could implement a wide array of cutting-edge methods. To wean itself off of fossil fuels, for example, an oil and gas company may invest in breakthroughs in renewable technologies while simultaneously seeking efficiency in minimizing carbon emissions. This would allow the company to discourage the usage of fossil fuels gradually. Both of these objectives would be met at the same time if this were implemented.

## 16.4 SCOPE OF SUSTAINABLE INNOVATIONS

Sustainable innovation is when a firm makes purposeful improvements to its goods, services, or operations to provide long-term advantages for the environment and society while still providing financial success for the company. This kind of innovation may be considered "green." Richard Adams, a researcher who looked at relevant, academic, and commercial studies, produced this definition after doing the study that led to it.[10]

The following describes how sustainable innovation applies to goods, services, and processes:

### *16.4.1 DEVELOPING NOVEL PRODUCTS AND SERVICES*

Businesses have the chance to manufacture and supply unique goods or services that may directly contribute to the accomplishment of sustainability if they take part in sustainable innovation and participate in sustainable innovation activities.

For instance, the double-decker buses in London are powered by an eco-friendly biofuel manufactured from coffee waste, thanks to the work of the British company Bio-bean, which is both a B Corporation and a start-up. Moreover, via a recycling process, Bio-bean transforms used coffee grounds into ecologically beneficial products like coffee pellets and coffee logs as a substitute for carbon-intensive fuels like imported coal briquettes and wood logs. As an alternative fuel source, these goods are usable.

Bio-bean brought in around $10 million (USD) in yearly revenue in the year 2020, thanks to its innovative repurposing of a material that was previously considered to be garbage. This helps to build a circular economy.

**FIGURE 16.6** Coffee pellets and coffee logs were used to find a new use for the waste.

### *16.4.2 CHANGING OPERATIONAL PROCESSES*

To innovate in a way that is sustainable requires more than simply coming up with new services or goods. Businesses are able to innovate in a way that is sustainable by changing the procedures through which they operate while continuing to provide the same products and services. Several different industries, such as manufacturing, marketing, design, and even human resources, are prone to undergoing shifts in operations from time to time.

For instance, the Dutch social venture Fairphone offers cellphones that were manufactured using components that are not harmful to the environment. In contrast to Bio-bean, which produced unique products (such as coffee waste-derived logs and pellets), Fairphone products do not have any creative technological characteristics.[14]

**FIGURE 16.7** Modular design of Fairphone significantly lowers the environmental impact.
*Image courtesy*: alphaCOMMERCE. https://alphacommerce.xyz/sustainability/product/fairphone-modular-phones-sustainable-electronics/

Fairphone offers an alternative by fundamentally altering the process of producing smartphones to make it fairer and more sustainable. They ethically mine their materials and provide their workers with decent working conditions and salaries. They also utilize recycled materials. Because the manufacturing of a smartphone is responsible for around 80% of its total emissions, Fairphone makes their devices last as long as possible.[15] Because of their modular design, they are easy to update and repair, and they produce far less electronic waste.

## 16.5 APPLICATIONS OF SUSTAINABLE INNOVATIONS

### *16.5.1 SOLAR GLASS*

The use of solar glass could cause a shift in the manner that residential and commercial buildings are constructed. Solar glass is a project in environmentally responsible engineering which has garnered a significant amount of attention over the course of several years.[16]

Researchers from the University of Michigan are now working on further developing it. As its name implies, the solar glass would be capable of collecting and retaining the energy from the sun. According to the findings of the research team, the United States has between 5 and 7 billion square meters of open window space. This amount of space is adequate to power an entire 40% of the country's energy consumption using solar glass.

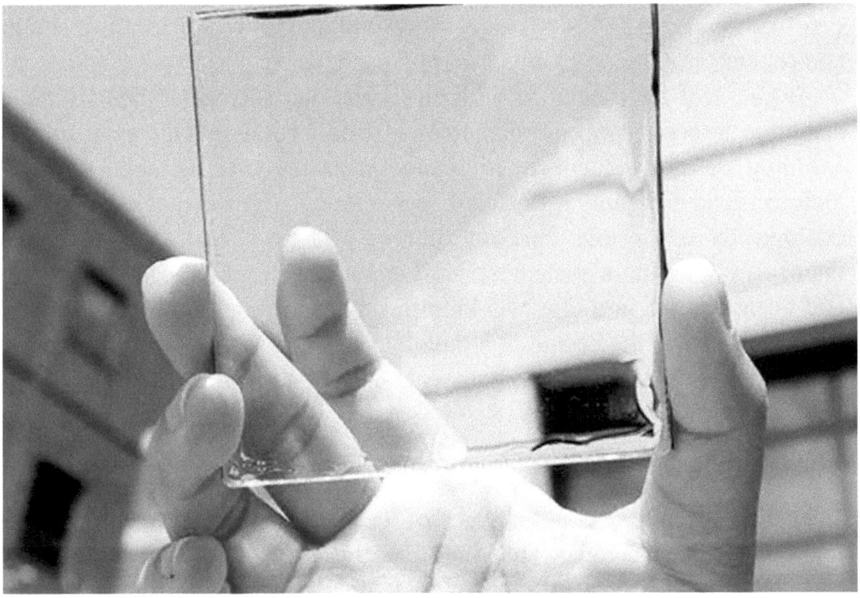

**FIGURE 16.8** Transparent solar glass.

*Image courtesy*: Solar Magazine. Richard Lunt / Michigan State University. https://solarmagazine.com/solar-panels/transparent-solar-panels/

To absorb invisible wavelengths of sunlight, the solar-harvesting device makes use of organic molecules that were invented by Lunt and his colleagues. They can "tune" these materials such that they absorb just the wavelengths of light in the ultraviolet and near-infrared ranges, which allows them to turn this energy into electricity.[17]

### *16.5.2 GREEN BUILDINGS*

Leadership in Energy and Environmental Design, more often referred to as LEED®, is an organization that offers a certification that is acknowledged on a global scale as a mark of excellence in environmentally responsible building techniques.[18] Buildings are responsible for roughly 30% of all greenhouse gas emissions and 35% of all garbage that is transferred to landfills, despite the fact that they account for as much as 70% of the water that is used in municipal water systems. LEED is able to assist practically all different types of buildings in lowering their carbon emissions, conserving resources, and lowering their operating costs because it places an emphasis on environmentally responsible business practices and uses a methodology that has been shown to be comprehensive. When it comes to achieving LEED certification, Canada has a steady place among the top-performing nations and regions around the globe.

Because of advancements in both technology as well as human understanding, the concept of environmentally friendly building is always changing. Building design and construction are increasingly being approached by architects and designers who have a deeper knowledge of what it means to be ecologically responsible. This concept covers a far broader variety of subjects than just improving a system's energy efficiency would suggest. Architects and designers are in a one-of-a-kind position to bring about true and positive change since the design of a building has such a huge effect, not just on economics but also on the environment and the people who live in it.[19]

### 16.5.3 SMOG FREE TOWER

Daan Roosegaarde is the innovator of the very first smog vacuum cleaner that has ever been created. The Smog Free Tower has a height of over 23 feet and is 7 m in diameter. It draws in contaminated air and purifies it through an ionization process before releasing it back into the atmosphere. When operating at full capacity, the tower is capable of purifying 30,000 $m^3$ of air per hour.

Because of Roosegaarde's architecture, it is even possible to wear rings that are crafted from the compressed smog particles that were gathered by the tower. When you purchase and wear a Smog Free Ring, you are helping to create an area of pure air that is more than 10,700 square feet (1000 square meters) in size. Since it was first conceived, the project has received a great deal of attention and has been recognized with several accolades. Mexico, South Korea, Poland, the Netherlands, and China are just some of the countries that have recently begun tower initiatives.[20,21]

### 16.5.4 EDIBLE CUTLERY

Bakey's is an Indian start-up company that manufactures edible cutlery and is situated in Hyderabad, in the state of Telangana. The edible cutlery may be purchased in basic, sweet, or savory tastes, depending on one's preference. They contain no artificial ingredients, are vegan-friendly, and, if left unconsumed, will decompose naturally. Narayana Peesapaty, a former researcher at ICRISAT, established Bakey's in 2010 as a sustainable alternative to throwaway utensils manufactured with plastic, wood, and bamboo, such as bamboo chopsticks. Plastic cutlery is not recyclable, and as a result, it contributes to significant volumes of garbage on an annual basis. Bakey's stood as a fantastic eco-friendly alternative to using plastic cutlery.[22]

**FIGURE 16.9** Smog free tower.

*Image courtesy*: TCD. https://www.thecooldown.com/green-tech/smog-free-tower-air-pollution-engagement-rings/

The special cutlery is crafted by combining rice flour, wheat flour, and jowar (also known as sorghum) flour. Narayana exclusively uses jowar because, in contrast to finger millet and other types of millets, which have a flavor that is overbearing, jowar has a flavor that is rather neutral and allows for a variety of flavors to be combined with it.

### *16.5.5 CLOUDFISHER*

The CloudFisher net in Morocco is the biggest fog-harvesting project that is currently operational anywhere in the world. Peter Trautwein, a volunteer engineer with the German Water Foundation, was the one who came up with the idea for the CloudFisher technology.[23] It is predicated on the concept that the web of a spider naturally captures dew droplets from the haze in the same way as the technology does. As a result of this, the net is responsible for supplying areas of Morocco with potable water which would otherwise be in need of relief from the effects of a drought.

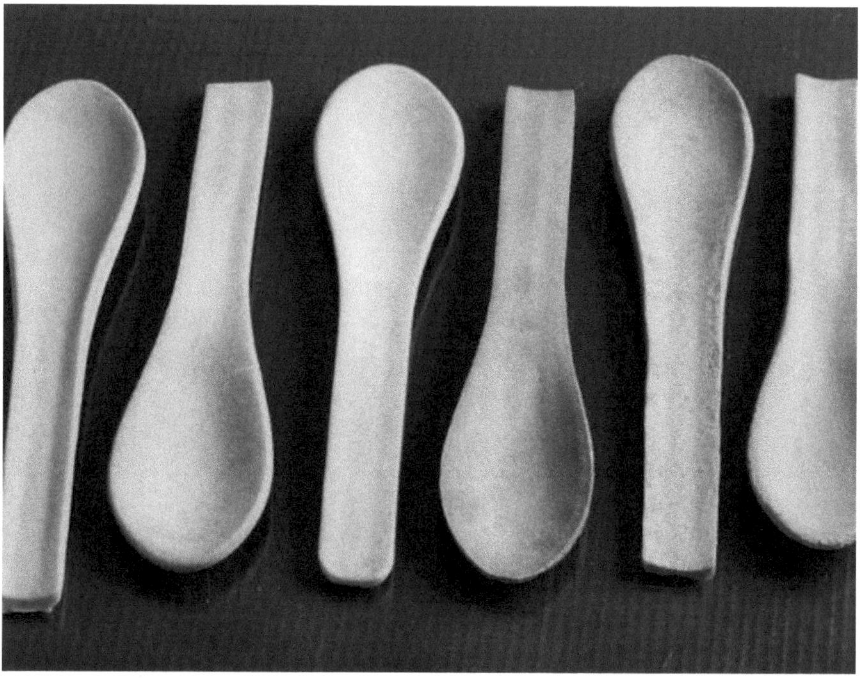

**FIGURE 16.10** Edible cutlery manufactured by Bakey's.

*Image courtesy*: TastingTable. https://www.tastingtable.com/691645/edible-cutlery-utensils-bakeys-india-food-packing-waste/

The body of the CloudFisher is composed of many minute triangles, each of which is encased inside a durable grid constructed out of plastic. Because of the way the wind often blows in these mountains, the fog is driven into the nets that are strung vertically on the cliff faces. The net is constructed to collect droplets of water inside its mesh, which then flow into a trough below and ultimately into a reservoir, which is where the drinkable water is kept.[24]

## 16.6 ADVANCEMENTS IN THE FUTURE

Our modern society is more intelligent and interconnected than ever before, and the non-renewable resource occupies a central role in this transformation. This is due to the fact that everyone strives to either minimize their use of the resource or maximize its utility. At this point in history, the key to achieving sustainable development is to have access to an increasing number of more sophisticated solutions.[25] It is essential to promote a more effective use of resources, a competitive economy, and an economy that is based on innovation and knowledge if a city is to experience development that is both intelligent and sustainable. It is essential that we use intelligent solutions in order to promote the sustainable expansion of cities in modern time.

**FIGURE 16.11** CloudFisher fog collector.

*Source*: Reprinted from designboom. Courtesy: aqualonis gmbh. https://www.designboom.com/technology/cloudfisher-fog-net-water-foundation-02-02-17/

Sustainable innovation is going to be very essential to the process of making the planet a more sustainable place. Sustainable innovation may contribute to the reduction of negative consequences and the promotion of sustainability in all aspects of society by fostering the creation of innovative solutions that solve environmental and social problems. To accomplish long-term sustainability objectives and build a better future for everyone, both businesses and governments together need to make sustainable innovation a top priority.

Based on the many aspects that were covered earlier on in this chapter, the development of Smart Cities may be one potential for an approach which would integrate various components of sustainable technological advancements. Smart cities are designed to be sustainable, efficient, and liveable. Sustainable innovations in smart cities have the potential to significantly improve the standard of living for citizens while simultaneously reducing the negative effect that urbanization has on the surrounding environment. Smart cities can make use of technology and data to reduce the amount of trash produced, improve resource management, reduce congestion and emissions, and make metropolitan environments more liveable.

Sustainable innovations in smart cities can include the implementation of smart grids for more efficient energy management, smart transportation systems to reduce emissions, and the use of sensors and the Internet of Things (IoT) devices to monitor and manage waste and water systems. In addition, smart cities may prioritize sustainable urban planning and design by including green spaces and supporting alternative means of transportation like as walking and cycling.

The issues that have surfaced in smart cities have sparked a desire for higher-quality services and prompted cities to start the journey of smartization. This process involves integrating technology into all aspects of the urban environment in an effort to enhance the quality of life for all city residents. The problems that have surfaced in smart cities have led to the desire for higher-quality services.[26]

The applications of sustainable innovations that we reviewed before may also be used to build innovative and efficient goods and services, and to change the operational processes within the city.

- Solar glass may be scaled up and installed in skyscrapers to replace regular glass for smart cities to make use of the sun's energy and convert it into electrical energy that can be used to power the entire infrastructure up.
- Smart cities can implement green buildings that follow environmentally friendly architecture, which reduces greenhouse gas emissions and recycle most of the garbage produced, thereby lowering the amount of hazardous garbage that eventually ends up in landfills.
- The production of greenhouse gases from transportation, which is one of the primary causes of climate change, is another area in which smart cities have the potential to improve.
- Air pollution is a major problem in urban areas since it is the primary contributor to photochemical smog, which blankets the whole city

and has a negative impact on citizens' quality of life. The reaction that creates it involves the mixing of air with the exhaust gases and pollutants that arise from human activity. The level of air pollution in the city can be brought under control by installing smog free towers throughout the city that act as sponges for the smog.

- Plastic is the single most important factor contributing to the contamination of land. The vast majority of waste that winds up in landfills is composed of plastic. It is possible to significantly cut down on the amount of waste plastic that is thrown away and ends up in landfills by switching to manufacturing processes that use biodegradable plastic or any other eco-friendly materials.
- When there is a lack of precipitation for an extended period, it might be difficult to provide enough water to all of the buildings within an entire metropolitan city because of the size of the area. CloudFisher and other forms of advanced water harvesting technologies may be utilized to develop solutions to the problems that arise in these kinds of circumstances.
- Smart grids have the potential to help in achieving a balance between the supply and demand of energy, hence, lowering the need for the production of electricity from fossil fuels.
- Intelligent transportation systems have the potential to cut down on traffic congestion as well as pollution, thereby enhancing air quality and lowering the carbon footprint of metropolitan cities.

Cities have the potential to improve the future for everyone by giving sustainable innovations top priority, which in turn will promote economic development, social equity, and environmental sustainability.

## 16.7 BENEFITS OF SUSTAINABLE INNOVATIONS

According to research by Flammer et al.,[27] businesses that are mindful of their stakeholders are more likely to generate patents, as well as inventions that have a greater potential for major effect. To phrase it the other way, maintaining a focus on sustainability encourages innovation that is not only more effective but also more widespread in scope. Sustainable innovation encourages a broader way of thinking in businesses, as well as the acquisition of information from a variety of sources. They get the information and solutions they need from other parties, such as stakeholders and representatives from different industries.

Also, businesses that care about sustainability are more adaptable than their rivals, which really is crucial in a world which is becoming more turbulent. According to the findings of research carried out by Bansal et al.,[28] businesses with a sustainability orientation were more likely to have less share price volatility, survive a crisis, and generate better long-term profits than those without such an orientation.

It is to the industrial industry's advantage to place more of an emphasis on sustainable practices and environmental friendliness. Even while focused developments might be beneficial to companies, looking at the "larger picture" is the best way to leverage the benefits of an environmental emphasis on the environment.

Even though they are closely connected, "becoming green" and sustainability are not the same thing. In spite of the fact that these names are regularly interchanged with one another, the color green is more commonly associated with a particular item or approach. Examples of this would include modifying a process so that it does not hurt the environment or creating a product that is comprised completely of materials that have been recycled.

The following are five essential strategies for embracing sustainability and going green to benefit businesses:[29]

### *16.7.1 REDUCE ENERGY-RELATED COSTS*

The prices that industries must pay for electricity and water are of the highest significance to them. These expenditures may be reduced if the focus is instead placed on making improvements. These kinds of changes usually result in savings on an annual basis rather than in more rapid reductions in costs in the near term.

Switching to lighting that is more energy-efficient and altering lighting settings in line with your production schedule are both great ways to bring down your long-term power bills. It will be to everyone's advantage to carry out routine checks on the apparatus. Leaks in air compressors, for instance, might cause unnecessary expenditures of money and energy. Changing the manner that the items are packed may result in reduced prices as well as the liberation of unused space within the facility. The use of machinery and equipment that are efficient with energy, such as those powered by solar and wind energy, would greatly cut monthly utility bills. Implementing cost-cutting measures such as recycling and going paperless may help bring down the overall price of supplies.

### *16.7.2 ATTRACT NEW CUSTOMERS AND INCREASE SALES*

Increasing an organization's marketability is one of the many benefits of implementing sustainable business practices. Because consumers are more concerned about environmental issues, the company's image will benefit from any changes made. The expansion of the consumer base as well as the increase in sales will be facilitated by bringing the organization's activities to the notice of the media. This is very important for companies who want to secure contracts from the government since sustainable green manufacturing criteria are regularly taken into consideration.

Customers are now able to rapidly (and publicly) support or criticize firms for their lack of green practices by using technology and social media. This may be done in either a positive or negative manner. Before this point, consumers did not have access to this capability.

### *16.7.3 TAX INCENTIVES*

Manufacturers who proactively embrace greater sustainable improvements are entitled for a broad range of government incentives and rebates, on both the federal as well as state levels. These credits and rebates may be found at both the state and federal levels. Any form of business may be qualified to get cash incentives, depending on the circumstances. In order to verify this information, one option is to investigate the statutes and policies of the state in which the potential headquarters of the firm are located.

### *16.7.4 BOOST WORKFORCE MORALE AND INNOVATIONS*

Cooperation from a number of different stakeholders is required for the advancement of sustainable practices. When employees collaborate on the design and implementation of projects that are environmentally friendly and sustainable, it helps to cultivate a culture that values collaboration and a commitment to ongoing improvement in the workplace. Productivity on the job may be boosted when workers feel motivated and have a sense of pride in their place of employment. It is possible that the ability of manufacturers to effectively communicate with their internal audiences about the importance of changes as well as the implications those changes are having on the organization and the ecosystem may have a positive influence on the corporate culture of the manufacturer.

### *16.7.5 SOCIETAL IMPACT*

The activities you take, in addition to increasing the profitability of your company, may also have the potential to bring about a change in present conditions, depending on the specifics of the situation. By making adjustments to your way of life, you may cut down on not just the amount of pollution you release into the environment, but also the amount of carbon that your lifestyle produces. Generational advantages are the benefits that will accrue to future generations as a result of cleaner air and water, a reduction in the number of landfills, and an increase in the utilization of renewable energy sources. These benefits are referred to as "generational benefits."

In most instances, a company's holistic strategy, which takes into account each stage of said manufacturing process in addition to logistics, is more closely linked to the concept of sustainability than any other aspect of the business. For example, you may decide to purchase environmentally friendly items that are constructed from recycled components. However, this would not be consistent with sustainable principles if the product in question was created outside of the country and then delivered to the country through practices that were harmful to the environment.

One among the most significant advantages of implementing sustainable innovations in smart cities is the reduction of environmental impact. Smart cities may reduce their impact on the environment by lowering their carbon footprint, conserving resources, reducing the amount of garbage they produce, and using technology to optimize resource management.

## 16.8 CONCLUSION

A company's capacity for innovation is critical to both its future growth and its continued survival. Businesses that are unable of innovating fall behind their rivals and, in the long term, are ultimately compelled to close their doors. Businesses need to actively incorporate environmental and human rights issues into their innovation processes. In this chapter, we took a look at the progression of the number of papers published on the subject of sustainable innovation throughout the course of the previous years.

According to the concept of sustainable development, success is achieved when local and global activities, worry about the economy and the environment, and short-term and long-term goals are all brought together. It is remarkable that the concept of sustainable innovation has received a considerable amount of attention over the course of the preceding ten years, in a manner that is comparable to how the underlying principles of innovation and sustainability did in the beginning. The ever-increasing number of citations to the previously published papers is evidence of how significant the topic of sustainable innovation is becoming.

The fundamental prerequisites for sustainable innovations, which were identified as system building, organizational transformation, and operational optimization, were examined in this chapter. Two methods for applying sustainability innovations were identified: creating new goods and services and altering operational procedures. A few examples are covered as part of this.

The five essential strategies for embracing sustainability and going green to benefit businesses have been defined which are attracting new customers and increasing sales, societal impact, boosting workforce morale and innovations, tax incentives, and reducing energy-related costs.

Gaining an understanding of the behavior of industrial organizations helps to propagate strategies that may boost business performance and provide them a real advantage over their competitors. In addition, the acknowledgement of the social benefits that come with the implementation of sustainable innovation techniques motivates the reduction of negative impacts on society and the environment.

In order for companies to embrace sustainability, they need to find out how to fulfil and even surpass the rising expectations of their customers, all while proving that sustainability can result in lucrative business. According to the findings of recent research, sustainable development methods are rapidly becoming the standard for both the needs of creative manufacturing organizations and the expectations of consumers. On the other hand, opinions on both sides of the market differ about how important it is to give some aspects of sustainability a higher priority than others. It is also possible to argue that innovations are intimately associated with education, more specifically with environmentally responsible business practices.[30]

Sustainable developments in smart cities have the potential to dramatically enhance the quality of life for citizens while simultaneously decreasing the effect that urbanization has on the environment. Smart cities are capable of maximizing the use of available resources, minimizing the amount of waste produced, and improving the general liveability of urban areas because of their use of technology and data. Cities have the capacity to build a brighter future for everyone by giving sustainable innovations first priority, which in turn promotes economic development, social equity, and environmental sustainability.

Sustainable innovation is an important step toward creating a more sustainable world. By combining economic, social, and environmental concerns, sustainable innovation can lead to new solutions that address the challenges facing society. Through the development and implementation of sustainable innovations, we can create a better future for all.

## KEYWORDS

- **CloudFisher**
- **edible cutlery**
- **green buildings**
- **smog free tower**
- **solar glass**
- **sustainable businesses**
- **sustainable innovations**

## REFERENCES


1. Commission, B. *Our Common Future: Report of the World Commission on Environment and Development*; Oxford University Press, 1987.
2. Maier, A.; Sorina, C.; Sucala, D.; Morar, D. Importance of Sustainable Innovation in the Current Economic Environment. **2019**.
3. Little, A. D. How Leading Companies are Using Sustainability-Driven Innovation to Win Tomorrow's Customers In *Little Innovation High Ground*; Arthur, D., Ed, 2005.
4. Dorin, M. Quality and Innovation as a Source of Sustainability in Construction. 2018.
5. Chapter 4: Driven to Act. In *A Call for Accountability and Action—The Deloitte Global 2021 Millennial and Gen Z Survey*; Deloitte, 2021; pp 29–34.
6. Smith, K. Innovation Process. In *The Oxford Handbook of Innovation*; Fagerberg, J.; Mowery, D. C.; Nelson, R. R., Eds.; Oxford University Press, Oxford, 2005; p 148.
7. 4 Sustainable Behaviours of Gen Z's Shopping Habits. GreenMatch [Online], February 26, 2021. https://www.greenmatch.co.uk/blog/2018/09/gen-zs-sustainable-shopping-habits
8. Olaru, M.; Schmid, J.; Sarbu, A.; Maier, D. In *A Study of the Impact of Investments in Economic Value of the Firm in International Competition*, BASIQ International Conference—New Trends in Sustainable Business and Consumption; Konstanz, Germany, 2016.
9. Bertels, S.; Papania, L.; Papania, D. Embedding Sustainability in Organizational Culture. In *A Systematic Review of the Body of Knowledge*; London, Canada, 2010.

10. Adams, R.; Jeanrenaud, S.; Bessant, J.; Overy, P.; Denyer, D.Innovating for Sustainability. A Systematic Review of the Body of Knowledge. *NBS*, 2012.
11. NBS. Executive Report: Innovating for Sustainability. *Network for Business Sustainability* [Online], 2012, London.
12. Lee, J. Y. What is Sustainable Innovation? *Network for Business Sustainability (NBS)* [Online], October 19, 2021.
13. Lambert, G.; Gray, B. Make 2+2 = 5: Collaborate for New Solutions. *Network for Business Sustainability (NBS)* [Online], July 24, 2018.
14. Bleekemolen, B. *Impact Report Vol. 1—Fairphone*; Fairphone, Amsterdam, 2018.
15. Wilson-Powell, G. *Is It Really Green?: Everyday Eco Dilemmas Answered*; Penguin Books, Australia, 2021.
16. Traverse, C. J.; Pandey, R.; Barr, M. C.; Lunt, R. R. Emergence of Highly Transparent Photovoltaics for Distributed Applications. *Nat. Ener.* **2017,** *2* (11), 849–860.
17. Lunt, R. Transparent Solar Technology Represents 'Wave of the Future'. *Msutoday* [Online], October 23, 2017.
18. The Global Standard in Green Building. *Canada Green Building Council* [Online] n.d. https://www.cagbc.org/our-work/certification/leed/
19. 6FamousArchitectsSharetheirTopSustainableDesignTips. *Terramai*[Online],n.d.https:// www.terramai.com/blog/6-famous-architects-share-their-top-sustainable-design-tips/
20. Roosegaarde, D. Smog Free Tower. *Studio Roosegaarde* [Online], n.d. https://www. studioroosegaarde.net/project/smog-free-tower
21. Roos, R. A. *The Smog Free Tower "Solution" of Daan Roosegaarde*, 2015.
22. Bakeys Foods Private Limited. *IndiaMart* [Online]. https://www.indiamart.com/bakeys-foods-limited/
23. Chen, J.; Willis, M. *Making Use of Mother Nature: Converting Fog into Drinkable Water Utilizing a Series of CloudFisher Nets*. Worcester Polytechnic Institute, 2017.
24. Jewell, C. Pioneering Fog-Harvesting Technology Helps Relieve Water Shortages in Arid Regions. *WIPO*, June 2018.
25. Batagan, L. Smart Cities and Sustainability Models. *Inform. Econ.* **2011,** *15,* 80–87.
26. Bifulco, F.; Tregua, M.; Amitrano, C. C.; D'Auria, A. ICT and Sustainability in Smart Cities Management. *Int. J. Public Sector Manag.* 2016.
27. Flammer, C.; Kacperczyk, A. The Impact of Stakeholder Orientation on Innovation: Evidence from a Natural Experiment, 2014.
28. Ortiz-de-Mandojana, N.; Bansal, T. The Long-Term Benefits of Organizational Resilience through Sustainable Business Practices. *Strateg. Manag. J.* 2015.
29. Lagas, B. Five Benefits of Embracing Sustainability and Green Manufacturing [Online], September 10, 2015.
30. Stverkova, H.; Czerna, K.; Pohludka, M. In *The Importance of Innovation in Terms of a Sustainable Entrepreneurship in Environment*, IOP Conference Series: Earth and Environmental Science; vol 900, November 1, 2021, p 7.

# CHAPTER 17

# Optimizing Sentiment Analysis Model for Sustainable Stock Forecasting Management

NEHA PUNETHA[1], GOONJAN JAIN[2], and RUBY RANI[3]

[1]*Department of Applied Mathematics, Delhi Technological University, Delhi, India*

[2]*Delhi Technological University, Delhi, India*

[3]*Department of Computer Science, University of Warwick*

## ABSTRACT

This chapter provides a description of how mathematical optimization tools can be applied to the method of analyzing the sentiment of news headlines in order to forecast stock market trends. In the twenty-first century, the rapid development of digital data acquisition has resulted in exponentially expanding data stored in databases, warehouses, and other data storage facilities. For this investigation, we devised an unsupervised MCDM-based model to anticipate future stock projections and assign suitable emotion tags to news headlines. We use a method called Combinative Distance-based Assessment (CODAS) to combine all of the scores derived from the evaluations and ratings provided in the suggested modal. After that, we determined the general feeling of each review by playing a game called Rock Paper Scissors. We employed four datasets, all of which yielded outstanding results, to assess the model's generalizability. We were able to obtain more precision than with more traditional approaches. When doing research and making investment decisions based on several web-based news sources, we use a method that combines MCDM and a game model.

Management for Sustainable Development: Integrating Social, Economic, and Environmental Goals. Vishal Jain & Amit Mittal (Eds.)

## 17.1 INTRODUCTION

The Indian stock market is the heart and soul of the country's fast-growing economy. Companies across the country relied heavily on the sale of stock to raise finances. Our stock market's performance is highly correlated with the expansion of our economy. The stock market is one of the most unpredictable marketplaces because of the powerful influence of human emotions. As a matter of fact, traders' emotions are just one of many factors that affect the stock market's direction. Investing in the stock market is vital to the financial sector since a high stock market value is a modern indicator of a healthy economy. Due to the unpredictability of the stock market, any individual investor has equal potential for profit or loss. If the occurrence can be predicted, investors stand a better chance of making a profit or minimizing losses.

Due to widespread ignorance and underinvestment, stock market forecasting techniques are critical in attracting new investors and retaining existing ones. Therefore, there is a strong connection between economic uncertainty and media attention. Every time new information is released, the public's impression of a corporation or its business strategy shifts. These days, traders and investors have constant access to up-to-date news attributable to the internet's delight, and the news constantly shapes their feelings and influences their investment decisions. When making investment decisions, the news has always been a vital source. Investors and groups of investors are finding it increasingly difficult to sift through the vast amount of available news for the most relevant stories as the number of news sources and stories themselves continues to grow exponentially. To get the most out of the investment strategy, it is critical to make an informed decision on when to invest. This limitation forces the use of computing, which collects and analyzes news stories from various news sources, extracts the most important ones, and uses those results to predict whether a stock's price will go up or down in real-time. Consider news stories about a corporation as the primary source of information and attempt to identify the news as positive or negative. If the news sentiment is optimistic, the stock price is more likely to increase, but the price is more likely to decrease if it is pessimistic.

### *17.1.1 WHY IT'S IMPORTANT TO STUDY STOCK MARKET FORECASTING*

Companies can raise capital and trade openly on stock exchanges. In a safe, controlled atmosphere, ownership and capital are exchanged. Investors assess a company's performance before purchasing its stock to prevent buying risky stocks. People are inspired to invest in stock markets. Obtaining capital enables firms to grow and create jobs for the economy. Economic development, wealth creation, and trade all depend on this investment. Stock markets allow people to invest money in a company in return for a share of the company's future profits (knowing that the risk of losses exists too). Investors and dealers may buy and sell stocks swiftly due to the high liquidity of the world's most important stock exchanges. Some stocks continue to pay dividends every month even though the value of the investment has dropped. The money is yours to do with as you like. The right to participate in corporate governance voting is also available. Spreading your risk over several asset classes, industry sectors, and geographical areas may be accomplished by diversifying your stock portfolio. The likelihood of favorable returns on your portfolio will rise as a result.

### 17.1.2 THE EFFECT OF SENTIMENTS ON THE STOCK MARKET

Stock sentiment analysis, which employs text mining, natural language processing, and computational approaches to extract sentiments from a text automatically, is another approach to knowing the stock trend forecast.[1] Its goal is to identify a text's polarity at the phrase or class level, determining whether it represents a positive, negative, or neutral viewpoint.[2] Reliable social media, tweets from official Twitter accounts, and financial news articles are critical textual sources employed in stock market prediction. During the pandemic, the need for medicines rises; therefore, the stock trend of Pharma companies will increase, as illustrated in Figure 17.1. Figure 17.2 depicts the same trend in the BSE SENSEX. These are two examples of a stock trend where human sentiments affect the stock trend.

Figure 17.3 shows the steps to predict stock based on the sentiment feedback of the customer. If the social media, comments, or news headlines are positive, then the client's belief in that company or organization will increase, which will motivate clients to buy the stocks and their purchases will increase. Similarly, if the social media comments are negative, customers' interest in that organization will decrease, and purchasing will drop down.

### 17.1.3 SOCIAL MEDIA'S IMPACT ON THE STOCK MARKET

- The field of sentiment analysis investigates computerized methods of gleaning emotional overtones from the text.[3] The proliferation of user-generated content moderation services made available to the general public is directly attributable to the surge in the popularity of social media.[4]

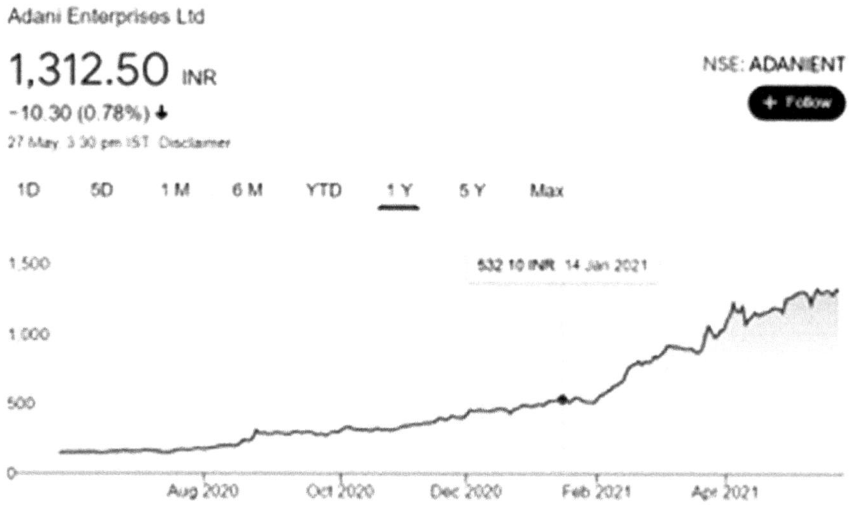


**FIGURE 17.1** The Pharma company dashboard during lockdown in April 2021.

**FIGURE 17.2** The BSE SENSEX dip at the time of the declaration of nationwide lockdown.

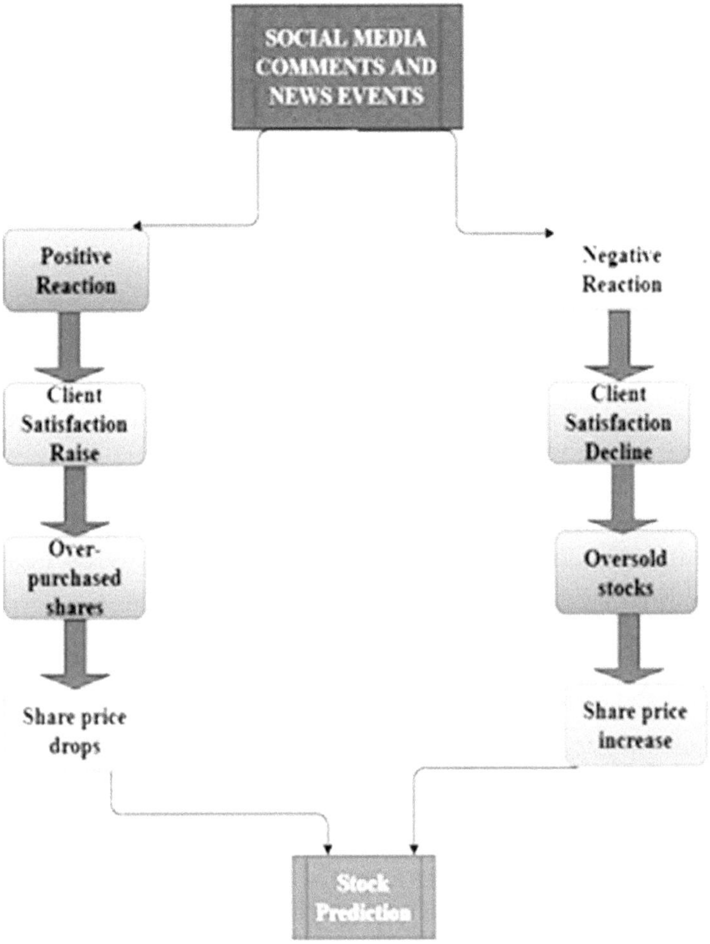


**FIGURE 17.3** The effect of social media on stock.

- Computational linguistics and social network analysis have significantly benefited from widespread communication and the ready availability of opinions from representatives worldwide simultaneously. Like everyone else, traders in the stock market are increasingly relying on social media as a reliable source of information.[5]
- It's evident that in today's world, everyone forms opinions regarding the society in which they participate. They express favorable and unfavorable opinions on various topics, including people, things, and events.[6] Feelings can be used to describe certain kinds of thoughts and emotions.[7]

- When news hits the market, individuals begin discussing it and expressing positive or negative views through their thoughts. Sentiment analysis professionals can use this information to foresee how the market or a company's stock will perform.[8]

Stock sentiment analysis, which employs text mining, natural language processing, and computational approaches to extract sentiments from a text automatically, is another approach to knowing the stock trend forecast. It aims to determine whether a given text is positive, negative, or neutral at the phrase or class level (Ming et al. 2014). Before the internet, people used to seek professional advice and read newspapers to keep track of the businesses they wanted to invest in. These activities are now carried out over the internet. There are two types of stock-related data available online: numerical data in the form of historical prices and textual information in the form of news items available on news media blogs or websites. Text analysis in the form of sentiment analysis was required, which automatically deduced the substance of the news item, i.e., whether it was positive, negative, or neutral. This research sheds light on how examining news item headings and categorizing news emotions can anticipate stock market trends. We designed a text classification algorithm to anticipate the market response to news reports. Assuming that news items affect the stock market, this attempt is to study the association between stock market patterns and headlines. To solve today's complex challenges, we need to compile information from various sources, some of which may be more reliable than others. The literature proposes various statistical and nonstatistical decision-making strategies when modeling intricate business or technical processes. In recent years, several strategies have seen a surge in popularity and widespread use; among these is the multiple-criterion decision-making (MCDM) approach. Statistical methods (i.e., probability theory) are helpful in modeling processes using partial or faulty data, which is common in real-world problems due to the absence of precise data.

### *17.1.4 CONTRIBUTION*

1. In this study, we proposed an optimization technique-based approach for sentiment analysis of news headlines.
2. We utilized CODAS and a zero-sum game model to perform this task.
3. We implemented the proposed approach on four datasets to demonstrate the rationality and availability of the proposed approach.

4. The evaluated results are superior to the existing conventional approaches.

## 17.2 RELATED WORK

An improved Levenberg–Marquardt (LM) training algorithm for stock prices was published by Billah et al.[9] Balahur proposes an approach based on the structure, length, and specific language of tweets to analyze sentiment in Twitter data. They demonstrate that using generalized features enhances sentiment categorization outcomes dramatically. Vu et al.[10] improved the named-entity identification approach for noise reduction on the Twitter dataset. Martin[11] used a neural network with Twitter sentiment analysis for stock market move prediction. Liu et al.[12] present a framework for multitask learning that enables concurrent learning across numerous related tasks. Khedr and Yaseen's[7] goal is to build an effective model to anticipate stock market future trends with a low error ratio and increase prediction accuracy.

Chen utilized CNN [13] to analyze the Chinese stock market. The Recurrent Convolutional Neural Network model was proposed by Vargas, Lima, and Evsuko.[6] It forecasts intraday fluctuations in the S&P 500 index. Kim et al.[14] combine the LSTM model with many GARCH-type models. Maqsood et al.[15] require the use of many websites for social media to create an analysis of feelings for a specific occurrence. The NBA model is used by Liu and Wang[10] to index sector-level data. Stock vectors are best shown by the work of Pang et al.[11] High-dimensional historical data for several stocks and an index or stock index make up the input.

Lim et al.[16] used news headlines from the business press mined for sentiment analysis. Recurrent neural network (RNN) and text categorization were both tested for their ability to predict the mood of a business news headline. Hossain et al.[17] use the clustering method to analyze the word distribution on the front page of a prominent daily English newspaper published in Bangladesh. Zhang et al.[18] showed that a lightweight regression model includes a term's statistical distribution across the polarity range. The study by Wu et al.[19] looked at news stories from the Knowledge Management Winner newspaper. Li et al.[20] proposed a topic modeling framework for sentiment analysis. Punetha et al.[21] introduced the Bayesian game mathematical model for sentiment classification. Costola et al.[22] used machine learning techniques. Swathi et al.[23] introduced a TLBO LSTM model for stock sentiment analysis. Cruz et al.[24] conducted the stock sentiment analysis on COVID-19 data. The author[25] forecasted the short-term stock predictions for sentiment analysis using supervised models.

Although supervised learning algorithms are good at spotting the subjectivity problem and can access many topics, these systems still need human labor, language proficiency, and labeled data.[26] Unlike supervised learning, unsupervised learning systems require little human effort, although their ability to do so has not yet been fully demonstrated. The shortcomings of lexicon-based methods include their disregard for the complexity and range of human emotions and their reliance on techniques for additional emotional categories, features, and granularities.[27]

## 17.3 PRELIMINARIES

### *17.3.1 MCDM*

MCDA, "Multicriteria Decision Analysis," is a valuable tool that can help us make many difficult decisions. It best solves problems where you must choose between two or more options. It has everything that makes a good tool for making decisions: It helps us focus on what is important, is easy to use, and is logical and consistent. In operations research, multiple-criteria decision-making (MCDM) has developed as a subfield focused on creating computer and mathematical instruments to aid in the subjective assessment of performance criteria by decision-makers.[28] Using MCDA, groups can discuss how to solve problems in a way that considers the values of all participants to be most significant when used for group decision-making. It allows for more sophisticated discussions on the tradeoffs between the available choices. It makes it easier for people to think through, rethink, question, adapt, choose, ponder again, test, and settle on a plan of action. The study of MCDM has recently flourished at the crossroads of management, science, and operations research. Multiattribute Decision-Making (or MADM) and Multiobjective Decision-Making (or MODM) are two types of MCDM (multicriteria decision-making).[29]

In most cases, MADM uses discrete decision variables and a small set of potential solutions. The goal of MODM is to determine, given a set of constraints, the optimal option among infinite possibilities. Unlike in MADM, where each criterion is tied to a single, continuous property, in MODM, the link between criterion and objective is more direct. In recent years, however, the terms MADM and MCDM have been used interchangeably to refer to the same category of issues. The following text will also refer to multiattribute decision-making problems as MCDM. MCDM's inherent qualities ultimately endear it to researchers and practitioners.[30] Belton and Stewart describe some of these characteristics as follows: (1) "MCDM aims to account for numerous contradictory criteria explicitly;" (2) It helps organize the management challenge; (3) It gives a model that may act as a debate focal point; and (4) It provides a process that leads to reasonable, defensible, and explicable judgments. There are five components to MCDA problems.

1. An individual or group of decision-makers with opinions.
2. Decision possibilities
3. Evaluation criteria (interests)
4. Outcomes or repercussions connected with the conjunction of alternative and interest

Different modeling strategies have been proposed in DM applications and theories. Models for assisting with decision-making have been provided, and several methods for helping with alternative formulation have been discussed, all of which take into account the complexity of the process.[31] People participating in the DM process, intended goals, information that is accessible, time, and other factors all affect the choice of a problem-solving strategy and a model. The ability of many criteria techniques to address issues marked by several competing interests is their most significant asset. Characters can tackle problems that cannot be solved by using standard optimization models using these strategies. More people use MCDM techniques and methodologies to evaluate alternatives and conduct comparative analyses.[32]

### *17.3.2 COMBINATIVE DISTANCE-BASED ASSESSMENT (CODAS) METHOD*

This method evaluates the appropriateness of options using two factors. The essential and fundamental metric concerns the alternatives' Euclidean separation from the anti-ideal. A secondary measurement system is taxicab distance.[33] The alternative with the most significant distances from the anti-ideal solution is preferred. In this procedure, the taxicab distance is used as a backup measurement if two alternatives are not comparable based on Euclidean distance.[32] Although the CODAS prefers the $L_1$-norm in different spaces, it might also consider two other types of spaces. Consider the case where we have criteria and choices.[34]

### 17.3.3 GAME THEORY

Theoretically, the game theory may analyze several participants' cooperative and antagonistic social interactions. Game theory is commonly viewed as a practical application of the study of technique, or at the very minimum, the optimized feature of competitive and autonomous individuals operating within a coordinated approach. The pioneers of contemporary game theory might be the economist Oskar Morgenstern and mathematician John von Neumann, both of whom worked in the 1940s.[35] Famous mathematician John Nash is often cited as making the first substantial advancement after von Neumann and Morgenstern's initial work. The game, which simulates a fictitious interaction between rational actors, is a crucial idea in game theory. According to game theory, a player's reward is inextricably linked to the opponent's strategic decision.

Participants' names, preferences, and prospective game strategies are all made public, as well as the results of those decisions. For the given model, there can be additional requirements or presumptions.[36] Game theory has many applications beyond international economics, including neuroscience, developmental theory, military, governance, and entrepreneurship. It is a relatively young and developing academic discipline despite its many successes. Once a Nash equilibrium is attained, no player can maximize their payoff by modifying their decisions unilaterally. This may also be understood as "no regrets" in the sense that, after a choice has been made, the player will not regret the consequences of that choice. In the majority of cases, the Nash equilibrium is attained gradually. However, once the Nash equilibrium is reached, it cannot be changed. After understanding how to calculate the Nash equilibrium, we analyze how a unilateral move will affect the situation. Is it coherent in any way? Because of this, the Nash equilibrium is said to have "no regrets." Usually, there may be more than one equilibrium in a game.

Most of the time, however, this happens in games with more complicated possibilities than two options for two players. Repeated simultaneous games achieve one of these equilibria after much trial and error. It is most common for two businesses to consider several possibilities over time until they reach equilibrium when setting pricing for highly replaceable goods like plane tickets or soft drinks.

### 17.3.4 ZERO-SUM GAME

It is a mathematical representation in game theory and economics of a situation in which one party gains an advantage and suffers an equal loss. Put another way, the net improvement in the game's outcome is zero. The total will be zero if all the participants' gains and losses are tallied together. Put another way, the total profits and losses of the parties involved in an interaction can be less than zero or greater than zero. Linear programing duality, or Nash equilibrium, is commonly used to solve zero-sum games, although the minimax theorem is also helpful in these situations. Nonzero-sum games like the Prisoner's Dilemma are nothing new.

#### *17.3.4.1 ROCK PAPER SCISSOR GAME*

We can turn to the classic game of Rock, Paper, and Scissors to demonstrate the fundamental premise of adaptive artificial intelligence technology. To forecast future behavior, the system analyzes a person's decision-making methods to detect patterns in their behavior. Rock-paper-scissors is a hand game typically played between two people in which they each make one of three shapes with their spread palms. Three different poses feature an outstretched hand. The "rock" wins against the "scissors," the "scissors" triumph over the "paper," and the "paper" wins against the "rock"; if both players throw the "rock," the game ends in a draw. Figure 17.4 is the matrix of the zero-sum game.[37]

| | **Rock** | **Paper** | **Scissors** |
|---|---|---|---|
| **Rock** | 0,0 | -1,1 | 1, -1 |
| **Paper** | 1, -1 | 0,0 | -1,1 |
| **Scissors** | -1,1 | 1, -1 | 0,0 |

**FIGURE 17.4** Matrix of the zero-sum game.

## 17.4 PROPOSED METHODOLOGY

This section explains the proposed methodology for sentiment analysis of news headlines illustrated in Figure 17.5. The proposed methodology consists of specific steps explained below. First, the news headlines were collected, and then the written text was preprocessed to clean up the data. After that, we evaluate the context and emotion score and then feed this numerical data into the CODAS algorithm, which in the end gives us the assessment score; then, for sentiment tagging, we apply the zero-sum game. Then, at the end, we give the sentiment tag of each written text. Below are the steps explained in detail.

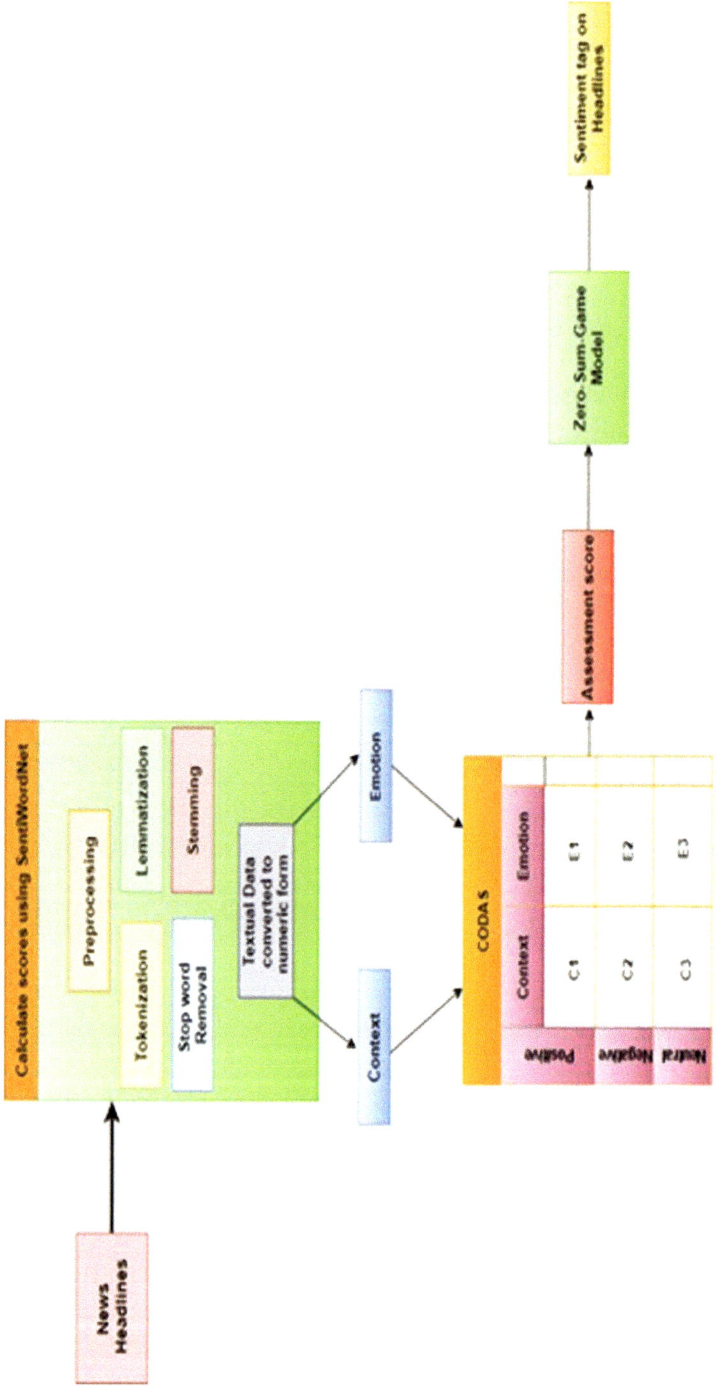


**FIGURE 17.5** The pipeline of the proposed model.

- **Step 1. News Sources:** The initial step is collecting news. This study gathered information via press releases and traditional financial news sources issued by the respective companies. In this stage, we scraped web news from Indian companies such as Infosys and Wipro over ten years and saved the information in a database. The subsequent step involved natural language processing in extracting emotion from unstructured news articles. Stop words were eliminated. The remaining practical terms were subsequently employed to analyze the feelings. We assessed the performance to classify sentiments.
- **Step 2. Textual Preprocessing:** It is common practice to carry out data cleaning as a preprocessing component to ensure that the data is free of errors and outliers. Text preprocessing is the initial step in the NLP algorithm development procedure.
- **Step 3. Tokenization:** Splitting the sentence into words.
- **Step 4. Stop word removal:** In the texts, stop words are the most often used terms (a, an, etc.). These terms do not aid in distinguishing between two texts; hence, they do not carry any meaningful significance.
- **Step 5. Stemming:** It transforms a word into its basic form.
- **Step 6. Lemmatization:** Lemmatization is a part of speech that must be determined to determine a word's lemma. This assists in converting the term to its correct root form. More computational linguistic resources, such as part-of-speech taggers, are required to accomplish this.
- **Step 7. Analyzing the SentiWordNet context score of recent headlines:** This stage utilizes SentiWordNet[38] to evaluate the relevance of textual remarks based on their context. It lists words whose positive or negative polarity can filter. From the reviews, we pull out the POS-tagged content words. To determine comment context scores, we parse Sentiscores for each word's positive and negative polarity values. We compare the positive, negative, and neutral ratings of SentiWordNet for each textual tactic.[39]
- **Step 8. Calculate assessment score evaluation:** In recent years, numerous real-world problems have benefited from multicriteria decision-making. Researchers have also proposed and refined many approaches and strategies over the years. To deal with these kinds of complex decision-making scenarios, we suggest a new CODAS technique.[34] The proposed method employs two types of distances—Euclidean and Taxicab—to evaluate the options in light of several criteria. The negative-ideal-solution distances are used here. The

option with longer distances is preferable as a result. But in this procedure, the Euclidean distance is utilized as the primary measure, while the Taxi distance is the secondary metric. Several established MCDM methods have been compared to the results obtained using the CODAS method. Results from this study suggest that the proposed approach is practical for solving MCDM-related issues.[40] The following algorithm is used for the context scores.

**Algorithm 1:** Assessment score evaluation

**Step 1:** *Construct a decision matrix (X).*

$$(X) = [c_{ij}]_{n\times m} = \begin{bmatrix} c_{11} & c_{12} & \cdots & c_{1m} \\ c_{21} & c_{22} & \cdots & c_{2m} \\ \vdots & \vdots & \vdots & \vdots \\ c_{n1} & c_{n2} & \cdots & c_{nm} \end{bmatrix} \quad \forall (i, j \in Natural\ No.)$$

*where* $c_{ij}$ $(c_{ij} \geq 0)$

**Step 2:** *Calculate the normalized decision matrix.*

$$n_{ij} = \begin{cases} \dfrac{x_{ij}}{\max\limits_i x_{ij}} \ if\ j \in N_b \\ \dfrac{\min\limits_i x_{ij}}{x_{ij}} \ if\ j \in N_c \end{cases}$$

*where* $N_b$ *and* $N_c$ *denote benefit and cost criteria, respectively*

**Step 3:** *Calculate the weighted normalized decision matrix* $S_{ij} = w_\tau n_{ij}$, *where* $w_\tau (0 < w_\tau < 1)$ *denotes the weight of* $j^{th}$ *criteria* $\sum_{\tau=1}^{m} w_\tau = 1$.

**Step 4:** *Evaluate* $(Ins_j)$.

$$\left.\begin{array}{l} Ins = [Ins_j]_{1\times m} \\ Ins_j = \min\limits_i s_{ij} \end{array}\right\}$$

**Step 5:** *Evaluate Euclidean* $(\kappa_i)$ *and Taxicab distance* $(\xi_i)$ *from the* $(Ins_j)$.

$$\left.\begin{array}{l} \kappa_i = \sqrt{\sum\limits_{j=1}^{m} (s_{ij} - Ins_j)^2} \\ \xi_i = \sum\limits_{j=1}^{m} |s_{ij} - Ins_j| \end{array}\right\}$$

**Step 6:** *Evaluate* $(R_a)$.

$$R_a = [\hbar_{ik}]_{n \times n}$$

**Step 7:** *Calculate each alternative's assessment score* $(H_i)$.

$$\hbar_{ik} = (\kappa_i - \kappa_k) + (\psi(\kappa_i - \kappa_k) \times (\xi_i - \xi_k)) \text{ where } \psi(x) = \begin{cases} 1 & \text{if } |x| \geq \tau \\ 0 & \text{if } |x| < \tau \end{cases}$$

$$H_i = \sum_{k=1}^{n} \hbar_{ik}$$

**Step 8:** *Place the alternative in the highest to lowest evaluation scores.*

**Step 9. Play the rock paper scissor game between headlines:** Now we apply the rock-paper-scissor game model for sentiment tagging. The sentiment analysis task is completed by applying algorithm 3 and categorizing rock, paper, and scissor tactics as positive, negative, and neutral. Then we give sentiment tagging to each review and complete the sentiment analysis task.[41]

**Algorithm 3:** *Zero-Sum-Game-Modal*

*"Input R1*
*Input R2*

*If (R1=Positive) then*
    *If (R2=Positive) print Draw*
    *If (R2=Negative) print Lost*
    *If (R2=Neutral) print Win*
*If (R1= Negative) then*
    *If (R2=Positive) print Win*
    *If (R2=Negative) print Draw*
    *If (R2=Neutral) print Lost*
*If (R1= Neutral) then*
    *If (R2=Positive) print Lost*
    *If (R2=Negative) print Win*
    *If (R2=Neutral) print Draw*
*Report the error and exit*
*Draw: display cancel output*
*Succeed: announce victory and exit.*
*exit: the program exits*

### 17.4.1 PERFORMANCE EVALUATION AND DISCUSSION

In this part, we use five assessment metrics derived from the confusion measure presented in Figure 17.6 to assess the effectiveness of the proposed approach. We implemented our proposed approach on the four dataset types listed below, and its comparisons with other approaches were shown in different sections.

#### 17.4.1.1 DATASET COLLECTION

For comparison of the proposed model, we collected four datasets. The data statics of the collected dataset are mentioned in Table 17.1.

**TABLE 17.1** Data Statistics of the Collected Dataset.

| Sr. no. | Dataset | Positive class | Negative class |
|---|---|---|---|
| 1 | SemEval 2017 Task 5 | 450 | 550 |
| 2 | S&P CNX NIFTY | 655 | 345 |
| 3 | Financial Dataset (stock tweets and Twitter messages) | 600 | 400 |
| 4 | WIPRO and INFOSYS news dataset | 549 | 451 |

### 17.4.2 EVALUATION METRICS

The efficiency of a given categorization technique on experimental data where the actual values have been determined can be represented in a confusion matrix table. We will utilize these 4 cells to showcase our experimental dataset (having 1000 observations, for instance). The evaluation criteria in the matrix's cells are shown in Figure 17.6. Let us take each of these into account.[42]

1. **Accuracy:** Accuracy refers to how close a measurement comes to the actual value being measured. In other words, it tells us how well our classification model can anticipate the classes specified in the problem statement.
2. **F1-score:** The F1-score is employed in binary classification analysis to assess the validity of a test. It computes a score based on the test's precision p and recall r.
3. **Precision:** The precision metric is used to get around what accuracy cannot do. The precision shows how many of the positive predictions

were correct. It can be calculated as the True Positive or the number of predictions that turned out to be true.

4. **Recall:** The percentage of successes in making favorable forecasts relative to the number of successes.
5. **Matthews Correlation Coefficient (MCC):** The MCC is used to assess the accuracy of binary classifications. Brian Matthews developed the MCC in 1975 as an instrument for model evaluation. Similar to the chisquare statistic for a 2 × 2 tabular form, it evaluates the gaps between observed and expected data.[43] An alternate metric resistant to the problem of uneven sample sizes is provided by estimating the Pearson product–moment correlation coefficient between measured and projected values using a contingency matrix.[44] When determining its value, the coefficient takes into account all four of the outcomes that are potentially possible. The only way to earn high scores on this reliable metric is to have correct predictions in these four categories[45] as that is the only method.

| | | ACTUAL | |
|---|---|---|---|
| | | Negative | Positive |
| PREDICTION | Negative | TRUE NEGATIVE | False Negative |
| | Positive | False Positive | TRUE POSITIVE |

**FIGURE 17.6** Representation of the confusion matrix.

### *17.4.3 EVALUATION ON DATASET 1*

Using two datasets (SemEval 2017 Task 5 and Yahoo Finance), Atzeni et al.[46] proposed a granular method for sentiment analysis. The results of the different methods' tests on the two datasets are shown in Table 17.1. Compared to the current model, the proposed model performs very well.

**TABLE 17.2** Comparison of Different Approaches to the SemEval 2017 Task.

| Approaches | SemEval 2017 | Yahoo finance |
|---|---|---|
| N-gram | 0.718 | 0.634 |
| N-gram + BN synsets | 0.787 | 0.627 |
| N-gram + BN synsets + semantic frames | 0.799 | 0.655 |
| Proposed Model | 0.789 | 0.681 |

### 17.4.4 EVALUATION ON DATASET 2

The authors of a study that was released by Yadav et al.[47] monitored the S&P CNX NIFTY Index futures traded on the NSE futures market between 01/01/2009 and 31/10/2009. The NIFTY 50 is an index that is used in the stock market to monitor the performance of fifty Indian companies that are involved in a diverse array of industries. Figure 17.7 is a depiction of the performance that was given.

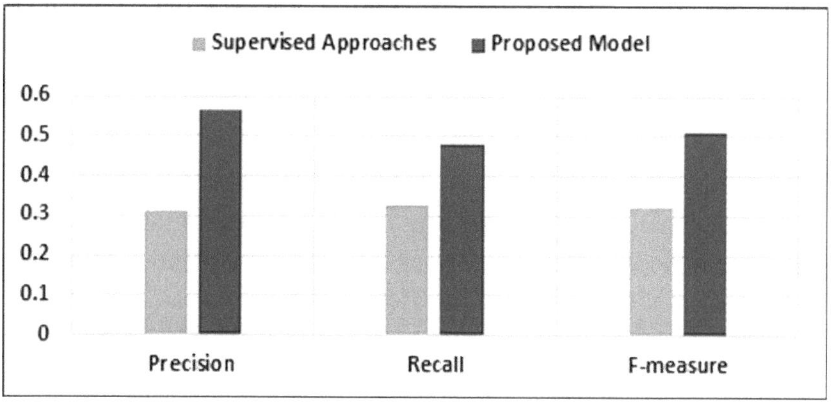


**FIGURE 17.7** Comparison of the proposed approach and supervised approaches.

Measures of precision, recall, and accuracy used to assess the effectiveness of the proposed and supervised models are depicted in Figure 17.7. Results near the cutting edge are preserved in the suggested paradigm.

### 17.4.5 EVALUATION ON DATASET 3

Dridi et al.[48] employed stock tweets, Twitter messages, and news statements and headlines from SemEval-2017 Task 5 to create two financial datasets.

They advocated using multiple feature sets, including the lexical and semantic features and combinations thereof, illustrated in Figure 17.8. The various evaluation metrics' performance is superior to the existing approaches shown in Figure 17.8.

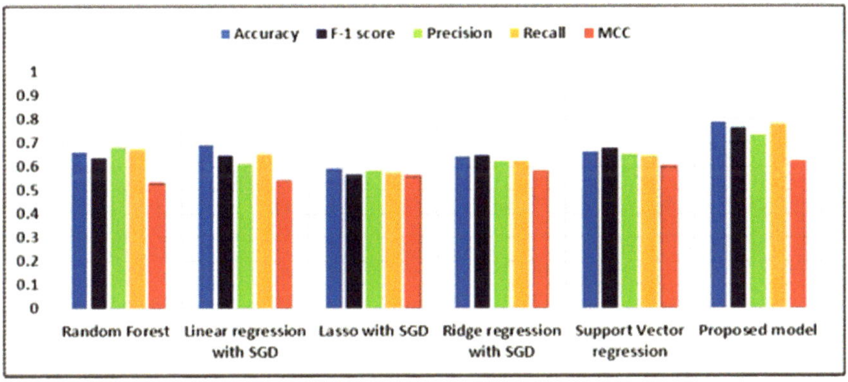


**FIGURE 17.8** Comparison of supervised approaches with a proposed model.

### *17.4.6 EVALUATION ON DATASET 4*

We have identified the various sentiment categories as positive, negative, and neutral. The well-known Naïve Bayes, Knn, and SVM classifiers classify a stock news headline in the appropriate category. The result is compared with the human annotations, and the accuracy is computed with *equation 1.*

$$Accuracy = \frac{sum(abs(EXP_{output} - ACT_{output})}{2} \qquad (17.1)$$

We applied the above-proposed model to the WIPRO and INFOSYS news datasets. We compared the results with the existing approaches[3] in Tables 17.2 and 17.3 in Figure 17.5. The SVM achieves the best results of any known method, but the proposed model's performance outperforms any existing methods.

The achieved accuracy of the proposed model is 87% in the INFOSYS dataset and 76.71% in the WIPRO dataset. To see the overall performance, we calculate all the models' average performance, which is visually depicted in Figure 17.9.

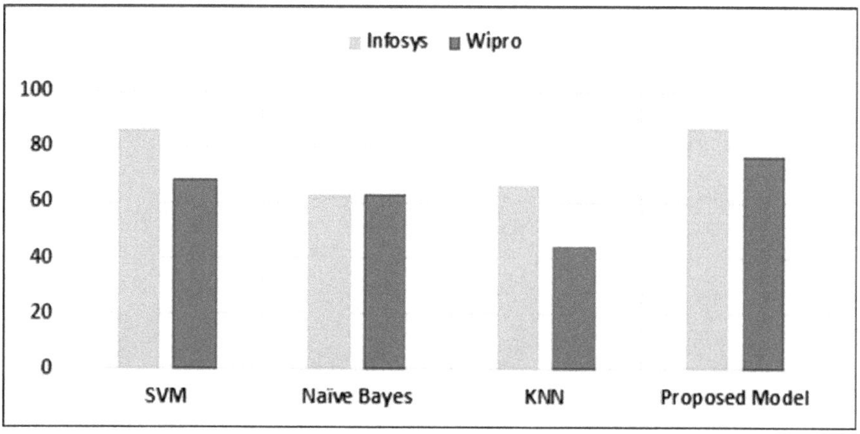


**FIGURE 17.9** The average performance of models in terms of accuracy.

## 17.5 DISCUSSION

To conclude at last, we observed that there are various ways and methods to predict the stock market using different approaches, but in this era of the internet, where we are at the peak of knowledge and have different resources as well as technology, there is a need to use intelligent ways to optimize our results to gain more efficient results. Some of the ways are as follows:

i. Future studies should focus on predicting stock market movements by combining structured data (previous inventory prices) and textual data from a wide variety of sources, including financial and social media. In addition, the text mining approach needs to enhance the selection of functions, display features, and reduction procedures to get better outcomes in the bond market forecasts.
ii. To create more accurate stock market predictions in the future, we will need to convert from full-text sentiment analysis to event-based sentiment analysis because the algorithms for choosing key sentences, extracting events, and recognizing event sentiments are grossly inadequate.
iii. MCDM is a subfield of optimization theory in mathematics. Mathematical optimization is an area of practical application in mathematics with various applications. "Optimization" comes from the same root as "optimal," which means "the best." When you "optimize" something, you "make it the best it can be." Mathematical models influence the proposed model to predict the best outcome.[49]

iv. **Limitations of the proposed model:** The CODAS approach evaluates a multicriteria system of variables to maximize and minimize values. This approach permits easy comparison and verification of the final measurement result. In cases of data fluctuation, CODAS's drawbacks may be less stable than those of the SAW and TOPSIS methods. The outcome may be susceptible to tiny data variations, and the resulting rankings may vary from those produced by other approaches. We present a new CODAS technique to address these complex decision-making scenarios.

v. Similarly, game theory has many limitations and benefits, as follows. Its final scores do not always reflect the actual situation; the result might not be logical. The study's main drawback is that it depends on the weights of the MCDM. The proposed model fails if the alternatives and criteria are less than 2. Another drawback is that for tagging, we used zero-sum games. The fundamental flaw of game theory is that it, along with most economic models, assumes that humans are reasonable, self-interested, and convenience agents. After all, we are social creatures, which means we cooperate even if it costs us.

Numerous underexplored problems arising from competing interests are illuminated by game theory. For instance, the phenomena of bargaining and coalition building are explained and described. At least in the case of two-player zero-sum games, game theory gives a scientific, quantitative method for participants to use to discover an optimal strategy. Assuming that everyone is aware of their own and everyone else's payoffs is unrealistic. Mixed-tactics games are notoriously difficult to solve, and they get even more so when the payoff matrix grows large. Not all questions of competitiveness can be answered by applying game theory.

## 17.6 CONCLUSIONS

This article suggests a method of optimization for predicting sentiment about stock prices. First, relevant real-time news headlines and press releases from various business news sources were filtered to predict the mood toward corporations. The proposed model used the MCDM CODAS method for evaluating the assessment score of all the parameters of the written text, and then the final sentiment tag was given with the help of the zero-sum game theory. While the accuracy of the suggested model is adequate, it can be enhanced by adding more sophisticated machine-learning techniques or data mining techniques.

The future scope of this paper is open. To determine how one firm's sentiment impacts the others' sentiment over time, we can scrutinize the sentiment of alternative brands. To determine whether they impact the state of the market as a whole, we can also investigate additional factors like social and legal challenges. With the help of this suggested model, financial modeling projects like portfolio management, risk assessment, and strategic planning could be undertaken. Future studies may expand the analysis, and a new model might be included. Comparing stock market forecasts with sentiment analysis technologies also includes alternative models. Establishing a platform that includes potential future changes to the current model can help achieve this.

## KEYWORDS


- **stock market**
- **sentiment analysis**
- **CODAS model**
- **news**
- **MCDM**
- **game theory**
- **sustainable**
- **zero-sum game**


## REFERENCES


1. Agarwal, B.; Mittal, N.; Bansal, P.; Garg, S. Sentiment Analysis Using Common-Sense and Context Information. *Comput. Intell. Neurosci.* **2015,** *2015*. doi: 10.1155/2015/715730.
2. Li, M.; Jin, L.; Wang, J. A New MCDM Method Combining QFD with TOPSIS for Knowledge Management System Selection from the User's Perspective in Intuitionistic Fuzzy Environment. *Appl. Soft Comput.* **2014,** *21,* 28–37. doi: 10.1016/j.asoc.2014.03.008.
3. Joshi, K.; Bharathi, H. N.; Rao, J. Stock Trend Prediction Using News Sentiment Analysis. *Int. J. Comput. Scie. Inform. Technol.* **2016,** *8* (3), 67–76. doi: 10.5121/IJCSIT.2016.8306.
4. Li, M.; Chen, L.; Zhao, J.; Li, Q. Sentiment Analysis of Chinese Stock Reviews Based on BERT Model. *Appl. Intel.* **2021,** *51* (7), 5016–5024. doi: 10.1007/S10489-020-02101-8/tables/5.
5. Gite, S.; Khatavkar, H.; Kotecha, K.; Srivastava, S.; Maheshwari, P.; Pandey, N. Explainable Stock Prices Prediction from Financial News Articles Using Sentiment Analysis. *PeerJ Comput. Sci.* **2021,** *7,* 1–21. doi: 10.7717/peerj-cs.340/supp-1.

6. Vargas, M. R.; de Lima, B. S. L. P.; Evsukoff, A. G. In *Deep Learning For Stock Market Prediction From Financial News Articles*, 2017 IEEE International Conference on Computational Intelligence and Virtual Environments for Measurement Systems and Applications (CIVEMSA), Annecy, France, 2017; pp 60–65 [Online]. https://ieeexplore.ieee.org/abstract/document/7995302/
7. Khedr, A. E.; Salama, S. E.; Yaseen, N. Predicting Stock Market Behavior Using Data Mining Technique and News Sentiment Analysis. *Int. J. Intel. Syst. Appl.* **2017,** *9* (7), 22–30. doi: 10.5815/Ijisa.2017.07.03.
8. de Oliveira Carosia, A. E.; Coelho, G. P.; da Silva, A. E. A. Investment Strategies Applied to the Brazilian Stock Market: A Methodology Based on Sentiment Analysis with Deep Learning. *Expert Syst. Appl.* **2021,** *184,* 115470. doi: 10.1016/J.Eswa.2021.115470.
9. Auciello, O. In *IEEE Xplore Full-Text 李玲琪 自聚焦 写波导*, Proceedings of the 2011 IEEE International Conference On Robotics And Biomimetics; 2011. https://ieeexplore.ieee.org/stamp/stamp.jsp?arnumber=4405051&casa_token=gefetzjuyooaaaaa:2_hb4aucknivv9sjogzkpkv8gb_dwiutu0a4gfmycc44liemkz7opjktfzmc8tamzxw5nfb93iru%0ahttps://ieeexplore.ieee.org/stamp/stamp.jsp?tp=&arnumber=9511469%0ahttps://ieeexplore-ie (accessed Aug 4, 2022).
10. Zaman, M.; Botti, L.; Thanh, T. V. Weight of Criteria in Hotel Selection: An Empirical Illustration Based on Tripadvisor Criteria. *Eur. J. Tour. Res.* **2016,** *13,* 132–138. doi: 10.54055/ejtr.v13i.236.
11. Martín-Valdivia, M. T.; Martínez-Cámara, E.; Perea-Ortega, J. M.; Ureña-López, L. A. Sentiment Polarity Detection in Spanish Reviews Combining Supervised and Unsupervised Approaches. *Expert Syst. Appl.* **2013,** *40* (10), 3934–3942. doi: 10.1016/j.eswa.2012.12.084.
12. Liu, P.; Qiu, X.; Xuanjing, H. In *Recurrent Neural Network for Text Classification with Multi-Task Learning*, IJCAI International Joint Conference on Artificial Intelligence, vol. January 2016, 2016; pp 2873–2879.
13. Chen, S.; He, H. In *Stock Prediction Using Convolutional Neural Network*, IOP Conference Series: Materials Science and Engineering, vol 435 (1), Oct. 2018; p 012026. doi: 10.1088/1757-899x/435/1/012026.
14. Kim, H. Y.; Won, C. H. Forecasting the Volatility of Stock Price Index: A Hybrid Model Integrating LSTM with Multiple GARCH-Type Models. *Expert Syst. Appl.* **2018,** *103,* 25–37. doi: 10.1016/j.eswa.2018.03.002.
15. Nazir, F.; Ghazanfar, M. A.; Maqsood, M.; Aadil, F.; Rho, S.; Mehmood, I. Social Media Signal Detection Using Tweets Volume, Hashtag, and Sentiment Analysis. *Multimed. Tools Appl.* **2019,** *78* (3), 3553–3586. doi: 10.1007/s11042-018-6437-z/figures/14.
16. Lim, S. L. O.; Lim, H. M.; Tan, E. K.; Tan, T. P. Examining Machine Learning Techniques in Business News Headline Sentiment Analysis. *Lect. Notes Electr. Eng.* **2020,** *603,* 363–372. doi: 10.1007/978-981-15-0058-9_35/cover.
17. Hossain, A.; Karimuzzaman, M.; Hossain, M. M.; Rahman, A. Text Mining and Sentiment Analysis of Newspaper Headlines. *Information* **2021,** *12,* 414. doi: 10.3390/info12100414.
18. Zhang, H.; et al. Leveraging Statistical Information in Fine-Grained Financial Sentiment Analysis. *World Wide Web* **2022,** *25* (2), 513–531. doi: 10.1007/s11280-021-00993-1/tables/5.
19. Wu, T.; et al. Video Sentiment Analysis with Bimodal Information-Augmented Multi-Head Attention. *Knowl.-Based Syst.* **2022,** *235,* 107676. doi: 10.1016/j.knosys.2021.107676.

20. Li, J.; Li, G.; Liu, M.; Zhu, X.; Wei, L. A Novel Text-Based Framework for Forecasting Agricultural Futures Using Massive Online News Headlines. *Int. J. Forecast.* **2022,** *38* (1), 35–50. doi: 10.1016/j.ijforecast.2020.02.002.
21. Punetha, N.; Jain, G. Bayesian Game Model Based Unsupervised Sentiment Analysis of Product Reviews. *Expert Syst. Appl.* **2023,** *214,* 119128. doi: 10.1016/j.eswa.2022. 119128.
22. Costola, M.; Hinz, O.; Nofer, M.; Pelizzon, L. Machine Learning Sentiment Analysis, COVID-19 News and Stock Market Reactions. *Res. Int. Bus. Finance* **2023,** *64,* 101881. doi: 10.1016/j.ribaf.2023.101881.
23. Swathi, T.; Kasiviswanath, N.; Rao, A. A. An Optimal Deep Learning-based LSTM for Stock Price Prediction Using Twitter Sentiment Analysis. *Appl. Intell.* **2022,** 1–14. doi: 10.1007/s10489-022-03175-2/figures/10.
24. Valle-Cruz, D.; Fernandez-Cortez, V.; López-Chau, A.; Sandoval-Almazán, R. Does Twitter Affect Stock Market Decisions? Financial Sentiment Analysis during Pandemics: A Comparative Study of the H1N1 and the COVID-19 Periods. *Cogn. Comput.* **2022,** *14* (1), 372–387. doi: 10.1007/s12559-021-09819-8/tables/17.
25. Qiu, Y.; Song, Z.; Chen, Z. Short-Term Stock Trends Prediction Based on Sentiment Analysis and Machine Learning. *Soft Comput.* **2022,** *26* (5), 2209–2224. doi: 10.1007/s00500-021-06602-7/figures/8.
26. Ghadikolaei, A. S.; Esbouei, S. K.; Antuchevičienė, J. Applying Fuzzy MCDM for Financial Performance Evaluation of Iranian Companies. *Technol. Econ. Dev. Econ.* **2014,** *20* (2), 274–291. doi: 10.3846/20294913.2014.913274.
27. Jing, N.; Wu, Z.; Wang, H. A Hybrid Model Integrating Deep Learning with Investor Sentiment Analysis for Stock Price Prediction. *Expert Syst. Appl.* **2021,** *178*. doi: 10.1016/j.eswa.2021.115019.
28. Rotter, P. Relevance Feedback Based on n-Tuplewise Comparison and the ELECTRE Methodology and an Application in Content-based Image Retrieval. *Multimed. Tools Appl.* **2014,** *72* (1), 667–685. doi: 10.1007/s11042-013-1384-1/figures/13.
29. Akhavan, P.; Barak, S.; Maghsoudlou, H.; Antuchevičienė, J. FQSPM-SWOT for strategic alliance planning and partner selection; case study in a holding car manufacturer company. *Technol. Econ. Dev. Econ.* **2015,** *21* (2), 165–185. doi: 10.3846/20294913.2014.965240.
30. Qin, Y.; Qi, Q.; Shi, P.; Scott, P. J.; Jiang, X. A Multi-Criterion Three-Way Decision-Making Method under Linguistic Interval-Valued Intuitionistic Fuzzy Environment. *J. Ambient Intell. Humaniz. Comput.* **2022,** 1–15. doi: 10.1007/S12652-022-04102-6/tables/12.
31. Vyas, V.; Uma, V.; Ravi, K. Aspect-based Approach to Measure Performance of Financial Services Using Voice of Customer. *J. King Saud Univ.-Comput. Inf. Sci.* **2020.** doi: 10.1016/j.jksuci.2019.12.009.
32. Yuan, X.; Wu, W. The WASPAS and AHP Optimization Methods Applied on Vibro-Diagnostic Models for Rotational Machines. *Eng. Comput. 1,* 3. doi: 10.1007/s00366-021-01377-9.
33. Prasad, R. V, Rajesh, R.; Thirumalaikumarasamy, D. Selection of Coating Material for Magnesium Alloy Using Fuzzy AHP-TOPSIS. **2046.** doi: 10.1007/s12046-019-1261-3s.
34. Goswami, S. S.; Jena, S.; Kumar Behera, D. In *Implementation of CODAS MCDM Method for the Selection of Suitable Cutting Fluid*, Implementation of CODAS MCDM Method for the Selection of Suitable Cutting Fluid; 2021. doi: 10.1109/sasm51857.2021.9841150.
35. Rabinovich, Z.; Naroditskiy, V.; Gerding, E. H.; Jennings, N. R. Computing Pure Bayesian-Nash Equilibria in Games with Finite Actions and Continuous Types. *Artif. Intell.* **2013,** *195,* 106–139. doi: 10.1016/j.artint.2012.09.007.

36. Haurie, A.; Krawczyk, J. B.; Zaccour, G.; *Games and Dynamic Games:* 2012.
37. Madani, K.; Lund, J. R. California's Sacramento–San Joaquin Delta Conflict: From Cooperation to Chicken. *J. Water Resour. Plann. Manag.* **2012,** *138* (2), 90–99. doi: 10.1061/(asce)wr.1943-5452.0000164.
38. Esuli, A.; Sebastiani, F. In *SENTIWORDNET: A Publicly Available Lexical Resource for Opinion Mining*, Proceedings of the 5th International Conference on Language Resources and Evaluation, LREC; vol. 2006, 2006; pp 417–422 [Online]. http://nmis.isti.cnr.it/sebastiani/publications/2007tr02.pdf (accessed Sep 23, 2021).
39. Vashishtha, S.; Susan, S. Highlighting Keyphrases Using Senti-Scoring and Fuzzy Entropy for Unsupervised Sentiment Analysis. *Expert Syst. Appl.* **2021,** *169*. 10.1016/j.eswa.2020.114323.
40. Annette, J. R.; Banu, A. Ranking Cloud Render Farm Services for a Multi Criteria Recommender System. **2046,** doi: 10.1007/s12046-018-0981-0s.
41. Jain, N.; Mittal, S. Bayesian Nash Equilibrium Based Gaming Model for Eco-Safe Driving. *J. King Saud Univ.-Comput. Inform. Sci.* **2021.** doi: 10.1016/j.jksuci.2021.07.004.
42. Fiok, K.; Karwowski, W.; Gutierrez, E.; Wilamowski, M. Analysis of Sentiment in Tweets Addressed to a Single Domain-Specific Twitter Account: Comparison of Model Performance and Explainability of Predictions. *Expert Syst. Appl.* **2021,** *186*. doi: 10.1016/j.eswa.2021.115771.
43. Kaden, M.; Hermann, W.; Villmann, T. In *Optimization of General Statistical Accuracy Measures for Classification Based on Learning Vector Quantization*, 22nd European Symposium on Artificial Neural Networks, Computational Intelligence and Machine Learning, ESANN 2014—Proceedings 2014; pp 47–52. https://citeseerx.ist.psu.edu/viewdoc/download?doi=10.1.1.431.5465&rep=rep1&type=pdf (accessed Jan 30, 2022).
44. Powers, D. M. W.; Evaluation: From Precision, Recall and F-Measure to ROC, Informedness, Markedness and Correlation [Online], Oct 2020. http://arxiv.org/abs/2010.16061 (accessed Jan 30, 2022).
45. Chicco, D. Ten Quick Tips for Machine Learning in Computational Biology. *Biodata Mining* **2017,** *10* (1). doi: 10.1186/s13040-017-0155-3.
46. Atzeni, M.; Dridi, A.; Reforgiato Recupero, D. Fine-Grained Sentiment Analysis on Financial Microblogs and News Headlines. *Commun. Comput. Inform. Sci.* **2017,** *769*, 124–128. doi: 10.1007/978-3-319-69146-6_11.
47. Yadav, R.; Kumar, A. V.; Kumar, A. News-Based Supervised Sentiment Analysis for Prediction of Futures Buying Behaviour. *IIMB Manag. Rev.* **2019,** *31* (2), 157–166. doi: 10.1016/j.iimb.2019.03.006.
48. Dridi, A.; Atzeni, M.; Reforgiato Recupero, D. Finenews: Fine-Grained Semantic Sentiment Analysis on Financial Microblogs and News. *Int. J. Mach. Learn. Cyber.* **2019,** *10* (3), 2199–2207. doi: 10.1007/s13042-018-0805-x.
49. Sohrabi, M. K.; Azgomi, H. Evolutionary Game Theory Approach to Materialized View Selection in Data Warehouses. *Knowl-Based Syst.* **2019,** *163,* 558–571. doi: 10.1016/j.knosys.2018.09.012.

# Index

## G



## H



## I



## L



## M

## T



## U



## V



## W



## Z